English Legal System
Essential Cases and Materials

**NOT TO BE
TAKEN AWAY**

English Legal System
Essential Cases and Materials

Second Edition

Catherine Elliott

PEARSON
Longman

Harlow, England • London • New York • Boston • San Francisco • Toronto
Sydney • Tokyo • Singapore • Hong Kong • Seoul • Taipei • New Delhi
Cape Town • Madrid • Mexico City • Amsterdam • Munich • Paris • Milan

Pearson Education Limited

Edinburgh Gate
Harlow
Essex CM20 2JE
England

and Associated Companies throughout the world

Visit us on the World Wide Web at:
www.pearsoned.co.uk

_____

First published 2006
Second edition published 2009

© Pearson Education Limited 2006, 2009

ISBN: 978-1-4082-2512-7

British Library Cataloguing-in-Publication Data
A catalogue record for this book is available from the British Library.

Library of Congress Cataloging-in-Publication Data
Elliott, Catherine, 1966–
    English legal system : essential cases and materials / Catherine Elliott. — 2nd ed.
        p. cm.
    Rev. ed. of: English legal system sourcebook, 2006.
    Includes bibliographical references and index.
    ISBN 978-1-4082-2512-7 (pbk.)
    1. Law—Great Britain.   2. Justice, Administration of—Great Britain.   3. Courts—
Great Britain.   I. Elliott, Catherine, 1966– English legal system sourcebook.   II. Title.
    KD658.E43 2009
    349.42—dc22

                                                                    2009009543

10   9   8   7   6   5   4   3   2   1
13   12   11   10   09

Typeset in 9/12.5 pt Stone Serif by 35
Printed and bound in Great Britain by Ashford Colour Press Ltd, Gosport, Hants

The publisher's policy is to use paper manufactured from sustainable forests.

Brief contents

Part 4 DISPUTE RESOLUTION

Contents

11 The legal professions   129

12 The jury system   157

Part 3 HUMAN RIGHTS

 **mylaw**chamber

Visit the *English Legal System, Essential Cases and Materials, 2nd edition* mylawchamber site at **www.mylawchamber.co.uk/elliottquinnelscases** to access valuable learning material.

FOR STUDENTS
Do you want to give yourself a head start come exam time?

Companion website support
- Use the updates to major changes in the law to make sure you are ahead of the game by knowing the latest developments.
- Use the online glossary to revise key terms you will need to know.
- Use the live weblinks to help you read more widely around the subject, and really impress your lecturers.

Preface

The aim of this book is to introduce students to primary source materials to help develop their interest and understanding of the English legal system. I wanted to portray the legal system as a living, dynamic subject which is continually evolving. My priority has been to select samples of publications which students will enjoy reading, to create a desire in them to go away and read more. In selecting materials, my focus has been on choosing, where possible, documents which are recent, very topical and which raise controversial issues that students may already have heard about through the news. These priorities mean that the lengths of the chapters vary considerably, as some subjects give rise to a lot of recent, controversial, primary source material, while other subjects may only require a single, concise extract. Because I want students to read and enjoy the whole book, I preferred to keep some chapters short and to the point.

There are a lot of useful documents that are freely available on the internet. There is, therefore, little benefit in simply replicating lengthy extracts from these documents. Instead, this book confronts the problem of 'information overload'. Students have difficulty in finding their way to relevant primary source material on the internet. When they do manage to find this material, they often feel intimidated by the size of the publications and unable to appreciate quickly the core issues contained in them. Therefore, what this book offers is a quick introduction to the type of documents that throw light on this subject and which are frequently available free on the internet. Having been introduced to a sample of this material, the student will then feel confident to tackle the full publication, and relevant references to websites are provided after each extract when they can be found on the internet.

The result, I hope, is an exciting new book which will help enrich the study of this subject. The book can be used alongside the textbook *English Legal System* by myself and Frances Quinn, but it can also be read independently because each extract is preceded by a clear introduction explaining its significance and context.

Catherine Elliott
London, 2009

Acknowledgements

We are grateful to the following for permission to reproduce copyright material:

Illustration and Photo

Illustration on page 5 (main court room of the Supreme Court) from www.feildenandmawson.com/supreme-court, Copyright Feilden+Mawson LLP; Photo on page 5 (the new Supreme Court in Parliament Square) by Adrian Pingstone, June 2004.

Tables

Table on pages 111–12 from Department for Constitutional Affairs, www.dca.gov.uk/judicial/ethmin.htm; Table on pages 112–13 from Department for Constitutional Affairs, www.dca.gov.uk/judicial/womjudfr.htm, Crown Copyright material is reproduced with permission under the terms of the Click-Use Licence.

Text

Extract on pages 4–6 from Paragraphs 2–7, www.dca.gov.uk/consult/supremecourt/index.htm#ch1; Extract on pages 6–7 from Paragraphs 2–3, www.parliament.uk/documents/upload/JudicialSCR071103pdf; Extract on pages 7–8 from Statement in its entirety, www.justis.com/pdf2/lrpdf/WLR/19661/19661155.PDF, Crown Copyright material is reproduced with permission under the terms of the Click-Use Licence; Extract on pages 8–9 from *The Law Reports (&) Weekly Law Reports*, Paragraphs 1, 18, 19, 20, 33 and 38, [2001] QB 955, The Incorporated Council of Law Reporting for England and Wales; Extract on pages 10–12 from Paragraphs 1, 17–21, (2005) 2 AC 580 (2005) 3 WLR 29, The Incorporated Council of Law Reporting for England and Wales; Extract on pages 12–14 from Paragraphs 1, 23–26, 39–45, The Incorporated Council of Law Reporting for England and Wales; Extract on pages 15–19 from 2000 WL 1274054, Lord Justice Ward, para 1, 16, 9.3, 10, 7.7 and last page of Lord Justice Brooke's speech, Extracts from 'The Law Reports' and the 'Weekly Law Reports' reproduced by permission of The Incorporated Council of Law Reporting for England and Wales, Megarry House, 119 Chancery Lane, London WC2A 1PP, www.lawreports.co.uk; Extract on pages 21–3 from Paragraphs 122–138, 141–144 from 'The Governance of Britain' (2007), published by the Ministry of Justice, www.official-documents.gov.uk/document/cm71/7170/7170.pdf; Extract on pages 24–7 from Paragraphs 181–194 from the House of Lords' judicial business website www.parliament.the-stationery-office.co.uk/pa/ld200506/ldjudgmt/jd051013/jack-1.htm; Extract on pages 28–9 from Paragraphs 6–11 from the report 'Post-Legislative Scrutiny – The Government's Approach' (Command Paper 7320), published by the Ministry of Justice, www.official-documents.gov.uk/document/cm73/7320/7320.pdf, Crown Copyright material is reproduced with permission under the terms of the Click-Use Licence; Extract on pages 31–2 from Whole judgment of Lord Parker CJ (1961) 1 QB 394, The Incorporated Council of Law Reporting for England and Wales; Extract on pages 32–3 from Whole judgment of Lord Parker CJ (1964) 2 QB 7 (1964) 2 WLR 542, The Incorporated Council of Law Reporting for England and Wales; Extract on pages 33–4 from Introduction and whole judgment of Lord Parker CJ (1960) 1 WLR 830, Extracts from 'The Law Reports' and the 'Weekly Law Reports' reproduced by permission of The Incorporated Council of Law Reporting for England and Wales, Megarry House, 119 Chancery Lane, London WC2A 1PP; Extract on pages 35–8 from Paragraphs 1, 8–10, 14–15, 19, 21, www.publications.parliament.uk/pa/ld200203/ldjudgmt/jd030313/quinta-1.htm; Extract on pages 38–9 from Paragraphs

32, 33 and 43, www.publications.parliament.uk/pa/ld200405/ldjudgmt/jd050428/quint-1.htm, Crown Copyright material is reproduced with permission under the terms of the Click-Use Licence; Extract on pages 40–1 from Pages 623 and 634, [1993] AC 593, The Incorporated Council of Law Reporting for England and Wales; Extract on pages 41–2 from Paragraphs 114–118 (2004) 1 AC 816 (2003) 3 WLR 568, Extracts from 'The Law Reports' and the 'Weekly Law Reports' reproduced by permission of The Incorporated Council of Law Reporting for England and Wales, Megarry House, 119 Chancery Lane, London WC2A 1PP; Extract on pages 43–5 from Paragraphs 1, 7–9, 21, www.publications.parliament. uk/pa/ld200304/ldjudgmt/jd041014/gen4-1.htm; Extract on pages 45–51 from Paragraphs 4–7, 25–36, 38–50, www.publications.parliament.uk/pa/ld200304/ldjudgmt/jd040621/gha-1.htm; Extract on page 53 from Section 2(2), www.opsi.gov.uk/acts/acts1972/19720068.htm; Extract on pages 53–4 from Office of Public Sector Information, www.opsi.gov.uk/stat.htm; Extract on pages 55–6 from Section 1, www.opsi.gov.uk/acts/acts2006a; Extract on pages 56–8 from Paragraphs 1–6, 18–24, 26–28, 37–41, www.opsi.gov.uk/acts/acts2006a, Crown Copyright material is reproduced with permission under the terms of the Click-Use Licence; Extract on pages 60–3 from Facts and procedure paras 1–3, Law paras 1–15 (1974) 1 WLR 1107, Extracts from 'The Law Reports' and the 'Weekly Law Reports' reproduced by permission of The Incorporated Council of Law Reporting for England and Wales, Megarry House, 119 Chancery Lane, London WC2A 1PP; Extract on pages 73–4 from LexisNexis Professional on-line database, Reproducing [1835–42] All ER Rep 151, Reproduced by permission of Reed Elsevier (UK) Limited, trading as LexisNexis.; Extract on page 76 from Volume [1975] 1 Weekly Law Reports page 482, The Incorporated Council of Law Reporting for England and Wales; Extract on pages 76–7 from (1950) 2 KB 86, The Incorporated Council of Law Reporting for England and Wales; Extract on pages 78–9 from (1947) KB 130, Extracts from 'The Law Reports' and the 'Weekly Law Reports' reproduced by permission of The Incorporated Council of Law Reporting for England and Wales, Megarry House, 119 Chancery Lane, London WC2A 1PP; Extract on pages 82–4 from Paragraphs 143–146 and 157–166, Ministry of Justice website, www.justice.gov.uk/docs/constitutional-renewal-white-paper.pdf; Extract on pages 86–7 from Paragraphs 0.1–0.5, Department for Constitutional Affairs, www.dca.gov.uk/majrep/lawcom/halliday.htm#summary, Author, John Halliday; Extract on pages 91–2 from Executive summary, www.dca.gov.uk/consult/inquiries/index.htm#part1, Crown Copyright material is reproduced with permission under the terms of the Click-Use Licence; Extract on pages 92–3 from Amnesty International website; Extract on pages 87–91 from Paragraphs 2.7.1–2.7.7 and 2.8.1–2.8.16, Department for Constitutional Affairs, www.dca.gov.uk/pubs/reports/lawcomm_vision.htm; Extract on pages 124–7 from Department for Constitutional Affairs, www.dca.gov.uk/judicial/diversity/bb_judge.pdf; Extract on pages 127–8 from Department for Constitutional Affairs, www.dca.gov.uk/consult/courtdress/orcreport.pdf; Extract on pages 114–15 from Paras 2.64–2.67, www.cja.gov.uk/files/cja_annual_review_2005.pdf; Extract on pages 115–16 from Department for Constitutional Affairs www.dca.gov.uk/judicial/appointments/let-sir-colin-campbell.pdf; Extract on pages 116–18 from www.cja.gov.uk; Extract on pages 118–21 from Paragraphs 2.63–2.67, Department for Constitutional Affairs www. dca.gov.uk/judicial/ja-arep2004/partone.htm; Extract on pages 121–24 from Paragraphs 113–116, 118–130, 132, 133, www.justice.gov.uk/docs/con-stitutional-renewal-white-paper.pdf, Crown Copyright material is reproduced with permission under the terms of the Click-Use Licence; Extract on pages 98–103 from Pages 125, 127, 128, 129, 132–136, [2000] 1 AC 119, Extracts from 'The Law Reports' and the 'Weekly Law Reports' reproduced by permission of The Incorporated Council of Law Reporting for England and Wales, Megarry House, 119 Chancery Lane, London WC2A 1PP ; Extract on pages 103–10 from Paragraphs 1, 12–14, 16–18, 172–194, House of Lords Select Committee on the Constitution, www.parliament.the-stationery-office.co.uk/pa/ld200607/ldselect/ldconst/151/151.pdf, Crown Copyright material is reproduced with permission under the terms of the Click-Use Licence; Extract 11. from www.sra.org.uk/securedown-load/file/276, © The Law Society; Extract on pages 130–2, www.sra.org.uk/securedownload/file/276, Solicitors Regulation Authority website, © The Law Society; Extract on pages 133–5 from First two paragraphs of Chairman's Foreword and paragraphs 19–23 and 36–42, www.barcouncil.org.uk/news/TheEntrytotheBarWorkingPartyFinalReport/, By kind permission of The General Council of the Bar.;

Extract on pages 136–9 from Pages 12–14, www.olscc.gov.uk/docs/miners_special_report.pdf; Extract on pages 144–8 from Sections 1–3, 27–29, 71, 72, 112–116, www.opsi.gov.uk/acts/acts2007/ukpga_20070029_en_1; Extract on pages 152–4 from Sections 4 and 5, www.opsi.gov.uk/acts/acts2006/pdf/ukpga_20060029_en.pdf; Extract on pages 155–6 from Paragraphs 27–38, www.opsi.gov.uk/acts/acts2006/en/ukpgaen_20060029_en.pdf; Extract on pages 139–44 from Paras 1, 2, 5–12, 14–24, 32–34, www.legal-services-review.org.uk/content/report/foreword.htm, Author, Sir David Clementi; Extract on pages 149–52 from Paragraphs 7–25, www.opsi.gov.uk/acts/acts2007/en/ukpgaen_20070029_en.pdf; Extract on page 178 from Office of Public Sector Information, www.opsi.gov.uk/acts.htm; Extract on pages 161–5 from Report no. 05/04, authors: Roger Matthews, Lynn Hancock and Daniel Briggs (2004), www.homeoffice.gov.uk/rds/pdfs2/r227.pdf; Extract on pages 172–7 from Paragraphs 173–184, 190–197 and recommendations Section 43, Author: Sir Robin Auld www.criminal-courts-review.org.uk/; Extract on pages 158–61 from Paragraphs 1–5, 8, 23–27, www.publications.parliament.uk/pa/ld200607/ldjudgmt/jd071017/abdro-1.htm; Extract on pages 165–71 from Department for Constitutional Affairs, Paragraphs: Introduction, 1, 2, 3 and 6 www.dca.gov.uk/criminal/procrules_fin/contents/pd_protocol/pd_protocol.htm, Crown Copyright material is reproduced with permission under the terms of the Click-Use Licence; Extract on pages 179–82 'Judicial perspectives on the conduct of serious fraud trials' from Criminal Law Review 2007 p751 obtained from the Westlaw on-line database, Page 752, 754, 755, 757–760, Author: Robert Julian, published by Sweet & Maxwell Limited; Extract on pages 184–8 from Westlaw on-line database, Paragraphs 1–3, 24, 29, 30, 48–59, 62, Employment Appeal Tribunal, Reproduced by permission of Reed Elsevier (UK) Limited, trading as LexisNexis.; Extract on pages 188–90 from Pages 49–55, Department for Constitutional Affairs www.dca.gov.uk/magist/support/response.pdf; Extract on pages 192–3 from Ministry of Justice, www.justice.gov.uk/about/about.htm, Crown Copyright material is reproduced with permission under the terms of the Click-Use Licence; Extract on pages 193–4 from Pages 1 and 2, Times Online, 28 April 2005, www.timesonline.co.uk/article/0,,19809–1589127,00.html, Authors: Philippe Naughton and Simon Freeman; Extract on pages 194–8 from Paragraphs 70–98, Ministry of Justice, www.justice.gov.uk/docs/constitutional-renewal-white-paper.pdf; Extract on pages 202–7 from Office of Public Sector Information www.opsi.gov.uk/acts/acts1998/80042-b.htm; Extract on pages 208–11 from House of Lords, www.publications.parliament.uk/pa/ld200405/ldjudgmt/jd041216/a&oth-6.htm; Extract on pages 211–14 from www.number-10.gov.uk/output/Page8041.asp; Extract on pages 214–17 from Paragraphs 1, 3, 37–43, www.publications.parliament.uk/pa/ld200607/ldjudgmt/jd071031/home-1.htm; Extract on pages 225–8 from Summary at pages ii–v, www.homeoffice.gov.uk/rds/pdfs2/rdsolr1003.pdf, Author: Paul Quinton, Crown Copyright material is reproduced with permission under the terms of the Click-Use Licence; Extract on pages 230–33 from Pages 7–8, www.lag.org.uk/shared_asp_files/GFSR.asp?NodeID=92476 Legal Action April 2008 p. 7. Author: Jon Robins, This article appeared in April 2008 'Legal Action' p. 7. 'Legal Action' is the journal of Legal Action Group.; Extract on pages 238–9 from www.legalservices.gov.uk; Extract on pages 254–7 from Paragraphs 1.1–1.4 and 2.1–2.22, https://consult.legalservices.gov.uk/inovem/consult.ti/bestvaluetendering/listdocuments; Extract on pages 247–54 'Does mode of delivery make a difference to criminal case outcomes and clients' satisfaction? The public defence solicitor experiment' from Pages 121, 122, 125, 126, 127, 128, 129, 131, 132, Westlaw on-line database, Originally published in the Criminal Law Review in 2004 at p. 120, Authors: Cyrus Tata, Tamara Goriely, Paul McCrone, Peter Duff, Martin Knapp, Alistair Henry, Becki Lancaster and Afrom Sherr, published by Sweet & Maxwell Limited; Extract on pages 258–61 from Foreword and Executive summary, https://consult.legalservices.gov.uk/inovem/gf2.ti/f/59106/1978245.1/pdf/-/BVT_consultation_response_no_cover_16070; Extract on page 269 from www.polfed.org/we_stand_D93FA810488D48608FDD6B7826A70F20.asp, The Police Federation of England and Wales; Extract on pages 263–5 from Paragraphs 3.11–3.30, www.homeoffice.gov.uk/documents/PACE-cover/cons-2007-pace-review?view=Binary; Extract on pages 266–9 from Paragraphs 3.1–3.7; 4.1–4.6; 8.1–8.5; 10.1–10.4, www. homeoffice.gov.uk/documents/PACE-cover/PACE-ResponseSummary?view=Binary; Extract on pages 290–3 from Independent Police Complaints Commission www.ipcc.gov.uk/stopandsearchfullreport.pdf; Extract on pages 270–82 from Paragraphs

46.1–46.34 and Recommendations 1–70, www.archive.official-documents.co.uk/document/cm42/4262/4262.htm; Extract on pages 283–90 from Foreword (pages i and ii) and Executive summary (pages vii to xv), www.homeoffice.gov.uk/rds/pdfs05/hors294.pdf, Authors: Janet Foster, Tim Newburn and Anna Souhami; Extract on page 310 from Department for Constitutional Affairs www.dca.gov.uk/consult/courts/broadcasting-cp28-04.htm, Author: Lord Chancellor, Lord Falconer of Thoroton, Crown Copyright material is reproduced with permission under the terms of the Click-Use Licence; Extract on pages 301–6 from Paragraphs 29–54, ICLR [2005] 1 WLR 2532, Extracts from 'The Law Reports' and the 'Weekly Law Reports' reproduced by permission of The Incorporated Council of Law Reporting for England and Wales, Megarry House, 119 Chancery Lane, London WC2A 1PP; Extract on pages 306–9 from Home Office website, www.homeoffice.gov.uk/documents/victims-code-of-practice?view=Binary; Extract on pages 295–300 from Paragraphs 5.1–6.6, Crown Prosecution Service www.cps.gov.uk; Extract on pages 321–9 from www.homeoffice.gov.uk/rds/pdfs/hors170.pdf Authors: Carol Hedderman and Loraine Gelsthorpe; Extract on pages 312–18 from Foreword and paragraphs 22–48, www.justice.gov.uk/docs/securing-future.pdf, Author: Lord Carter; Extract on pages 318–21 from Paragraphs 1.1–1.4 and 9.1–9.18, www.justice.gov.uk/docs/sentencing-guidelines-evolutionary-approach.pdf, Author: Lord Gage; Extract on pages 331–3 from Pages 61–63, www.homeoffice.gov.uk/rds/pdfs2/hors242.pdf, Author: Tim Newburn; Extract on pages 333–8 from Pages 5–10, www.youth-justice-board.gov.uk, Authors: Aidan Wilcox and Carolyn Hoyle; Extract on pages 339–40 from Sections 1 and 9, www.opsi.gov.uk/acts/acts2008/ukpga_20080004_en_1; Extract on pages 342–6 from Paragraphs 1–9 and 21–23, Department for Constitutional Affairs, www.dca.gov.uk/civil/final/overview.htm, Author: Lord Woolf; Extract on pages 346–8 from Executive summary and paragraphs 2.1–2.7, Department for Constitutional Affairs www.dca.gov.uk/civil/reform/ffreform.htm#part1; Extract on pages 350–2 from Paragraphs 1–7, Department for Constitutional Affairs, www.dca.gov.uk; Extract on pages 352–5 from Paragraphs 1 and 2, Better Regulation Commission www.brc.gov.uk/publications/liticompensation.asp, Crown Copyright material is reproduced with permission under the terms of the Click-Use Licence; Extract on pages 349–50 from Are high costs failing those looking for justice?, *The Times* 13 November 2008 (Rose, N.); Extract on pages 360–1 from Foreword at p. 1 and paragraph 1.14, Department for Constitutional Affairs, www.dca.gov.uk; Extract on pages 361–5 from www.opsi.gov.uk/acts/acts2007/en/ukpgaen_20070015_en_1; Extract on pages 357–60 from Paragraphs 1.1–1.4 and 1.15–1.25, www.tribunals-review.org.uk/leggatthtm/leg-01.htm, Author: Sir Andrew Leggatt; Extract on pages 367–9 from Paragraphs 1–9, 15, 16, 18–32, 34–48, 50–59 and 67, Department for Constitutional Affairs www.dca.gov.uk/consult/supremecourt/index.htm; Extract on pages 393–8 from www.opsi.gov.uk/acts/acts2005/50004–d.htm#23; Extract on pages 405–9 from www.ccrc. gov.uk/CCRC_Uploads/420165_CCRC_AR_V9lo.pdf; Extract on pages 379–93 from Department for Constitutional Affairs www.dca.gov.uk/consult/qcfuture/qcresp.htm; Extract on pages 398–405 from www.opsi.gov.uk/acts/en2005/2005en04.htm; Extract on pages 411–14 from Civil Justice Council, www.adr.civiljusticecouncil.gov.uk/Category.go?category_id=7, Authors: Margaret Doyle, Katrina Ritters and Steve Brooker; Extract on pages 414–16 from Pages 3–6, Department for Constitutional Affairs www.dca.gov.uk/civil/adr/adrmon05.pdf; Extract on pages 416–19 from Civil Justice Council, www.adr.civiljusticecouncil.gov.uk/Category.go;jsessionid=caah16_jPJVyfA?category_id=7, Author: Hazel Genn, Crown Copyright material is reproduced with permission under the terms of the Click-Use Licence.

The Financial Times

Extract on pages 229–30 from De Menezes jury rejects police account, *Financial Times*, 13 December 2008 (Murphy, M.).

In some instances we have been unable to trace the owners of copyright material, and we would appreciate any information that would enable us to do so.

Table of cases

Table of statutes

Table of statutory instruments

Table of treaties

Table of secondary legislation of the European Communities

Regulations

Reg. 1612/68 *61*

Directives

Dir. 64/221 *61, 62*
  art. 3 *61, 63*
    (1) *62, 63*
Dir. 2000/78/EC *184*

PART 1

SOURCES OF LAW

1

Case law

Introduction

This chapter looks at:

- the consultation paper on the establishment of a Supreme Court;

- the response of the Law Lords to the planned abolition of the House of Lords in its judicial capacity;

- the 1966 Practice Statement setting out the House of Lords' approach to the rules of judicial precedent;

- the Court of Appeal's approach to judicial precedent;

- the impact of Privy Council cases following recent developments in criminal law; and

- how judges decide cases in practice by reference to the case of **Re A (Children)** [2001], where the Court of Appeal had to grapple with the moral dilemma of whether doctors should operate to separate conjoined twins, knowing that the operation would cause the weaker twin to die.

A new Supreme Court

The Constitutional Reform Act 2005 contains provisions for the abolition of the highest court in the land, the House of Lords and its replacement with a new Supreme Court. The new court is expected to start working in 2009. The government's plans on this subject were outlined in a Consultation Paper. A Consultation Paper is a document that the government publishes to alert interested parties that changes to the law are being considered. The publication provides an opportunity for those who wish to do so, to put forward the reasons why they oppose or support these changes and also to put forward any alternative changes they would like to be made.

In the Consultation Paper on the Supreme Court, the government discussed why it considered it necessary to abolish the House of Lords and replace it with a new Supreme Court.

Constitutional Reform: A Supreme Court for the UK (2003), Consultation Paper

Why change?

The functions of the highest courts in the land are presently divided between two bodies. The Appellate Committee of the House of Lords receives appeals from the courts in England and Wales and Northern Ireland, and in civil cases from Scotland. The Judicial Committee of the Privy Council, in addition to its overseas and ecclesiastical jurisdiction, considers questions as to whether the devolved administrations, the Scottish Parliament, the National Assembly for Wales and the Northern Ireland Assembly are acting within their legal powers. Both sets of functions raise questions about whether there is any longer sufficient transparency of independence from the executive and the legislature to give people the assurance to which they are entitled about the independence of the judiciary. The considerable growth of judicial review in recent years has inevitably brought the judges more into the political eye. It is essential that our systems do all that they can to minimise the danger that judges' decisions could be perceived to be politically motivated. The Human Rights Act 1998, itself the product of a changing climate of opinion, has made people more sensitive to the issues and more aware of the anomaly of the position whereby the highest court of appeal is situated within one of the chambers of Parliament.

It is not always understood that the decisions of the 'House of Lords' are in practice decisions of the Appellate Committee and that non-judicial members of the House never take part in the judgments. Nor is the extent to which the Law Lords themselves have decided to refrain from getting involved in political issues in relation to legislation on which they might later have to adjudicate always appreciated. The fact that the Lord Chancellor, as the Head of the Judiciary, was entitled to sit in the Appellate and Judicial Committees and did so as Chairman, added to the perception that their independence might be compromised by the arrangements. The Human Rights Act, specifically in relation to Article 6 of the European Convention on Human Rights, now requires a stricter view to be taken not only of anything which might undermine the independence or impartiality of a judicial tribunal, but even of anything which might appear to do so. So the fact that the Law Lords are a Committee of the House of Lords can raise issues about the appearance of independence from the legislature. Looking at it from the other way round, the requirement for the

The new Supreme Court in Parliament Square – independent and geographically opposite the Houses of Parliament.

(Source: Adrian Pingstone)

The main court room of the Supreme Court.

(Source: www.feildenandmawson.com/supreme-court/)

appearance of impartiality and independence also increasingly limits the ability of the Law Lords to contribute to the work of the House of Lords, thus reducing the value to both them and the House of their membership.

The position of the Appellate Committee as part of the House of Lords has inevitably limited the resources that can be made available to it. Space within the Palace of Westminster is at a premium, especially at the House of Lords end of the building. Although the facilities for hearings in Committee rooms 1 and 2 are good, the Law Lords' administration works in cramped conditions: one Law Lord does not even have a room. The position in the Palace cannot be improved without asking other peers to give up their desks. A separately constituted Supreme Court suitably accommodated could ensure that these issues were properly addressed.

In proposing that the time has come to change these arrangements, no criticism is intended of the way in which the members of either Committee have discharged their functions. Nor have there been any accusations of actual bias in either the appointments to either body or their judgments arising from their membership of the legislature. The arrangements have served us well in the past. Nonetheless, the Government has come to the conclusion that the present position is no longer sustainable. The time has come for the UK's highest court to move out from under the shadow of the legislature.

The Lord Chancellor has had an important role in preserving judicial independence. The Secretary of State for Constitutional Affairs will have a continuing responsibility for this vital safeguard. He will, both within Government and publicly, be responsible for defending judicial independence from any attack. As noted in the consultation paper *Constitutional Reform: A New Way of Appointing Judges*, consideration should be given to whether that responsibility should be embodied in statute setting up the proposed new Judicial Appointments Commission.

The Government believes that the establishment of a separate Supreme Court will be an important part of a package of measures which will redraw the relationship between the Judiciary, the Government, and Parliament to preserve and increase our judges' independence.

The consultation paper is available at:
www.dca.gov.uk/consult/supremecourt/index.htm

Judicial response to Supreme Court reform

The House of Lords submitted its response to the consultation process. While the majority of the Law Lords agreed with the establishment of a new Supreme Court, a significant minority was opposed to this reform.

The Law Lords' Response to the Government's Consultation Paper on Constitutional reform: A Supreme Court for the United Kingdom

A number of serving Law Lords believe that, on pragmatic grounds, the proposed change is unnecessary and will be harmful. The present arrangements work well. They believe that the Law Lords' presence in the House is of benefit to the Law Lords, to the House, and to others including the litigants. Appeals are heard in a unique, suitably prestigious, setting for this country's court of final appeal. The 'House of Lords' as a judicial body is recognised by that name throughout the common law world. Overall, it is believed, it has a fine record and reputation. The Law Lords who do not support the proposed change consider these real advantages need not be, and should not be, put in jeopardy. They consider that the cost of the change would be wholly out of proportion to any benefit. Other serving Law Lords regard the functional separation of the judiciary at all levels from the legislature and the executive as a cardinal feature of a modern, liberal, democratic state governed by the rule of law. They consider it important, as a matter of constitutional principle, that this functional separation should be reflected in the major institutions of the state, of which the final court of appeal is certainly one.

. . . [W]e are at one in regarding it as essential that a new Supreme Court of the United Kingdom, if established, should be properly accommodated and resourced, and equipped with the facilities it will need to discharge its public duties to the best possible effect. The Consultation Paper eschews any detailed consideration of this fundamental aspect. While some preliminary thought has, we appreciate, been given to the accommodation which a Supreme Court will require, no business plan has to our knowledge been prepared and no estimate of cost made. The building in which the Court is housed must reflect the importance of the rule of law in a modern democracy; and it must afford the judges (plus their librarians, secretaries, judicial assistants, law reporters, press officer, IT staff, doorkeepers and security staff) the resources and facilities they need.

 The Law Lords' response to the Supreme Court consultation paper is available at: **www.parliament.uk/documents/upload/JudicialSCR071103.pdf**

The House of Lords and judicial precedent

In 1966 the House of Lords issued a Practice Statement. This announced that the House was no longer bound by its own previous decisions and explained when it would choose to exercise this discretion not to follow its previous decisions.

Practice Statement (Judicial Precedent)
House of Lords, July 26, 1966

Lord Gardiner LC

Their Lordships regard the use of precedent as an indispensable foundation upon which to decide what is the law and its application to individual cases. It provides at least some degree of certainty upon which individuals can rely in the conduct of their affairs, as well as a basis for orderly development of legal rules.

Their Lordships nevertheless recognise that too rigid adherence to precedent may lead to injustice in a particular case and also unduly restrict the proper development of the law. They propose, therefore, to modify their present practice and, while treating former decisions of this House as normally binding, to depart from a previous decision when it appears right to do so.

In this connection they will bear in mind the danger of disturbing retrospectively the basis on which contracts, settlements of property and fiscal arrangements have been entered into and also the especial need for certainty as to the criminal law.

This announcement is not intended to affect the use of precedent elsewhere than in this House.

The Court of Appeal and judicial precedent

The Civil Division of the Court of Appeal is usually bound by its own previous decisions, but there are a number of exceptions to this, which were extended by the Court of Appeal in **R v Brent London Borough Council Housing Benefit Review Board, *ex parte* Khadim** (2001). The arguments for the appellant were put forward by the barrister, Mr Cox.

R (Kadhim) v Brent London Borough Council Housing Benefit Review Board (2001), Court of Appeal

Buxton LJ

History and nature of the case

1 This appeal raises a short but not altogether straightforward issue as to the proper construction of regulations 3 and 7(1)(a) of the Housing Benefit (General) Regulations 1987. Regulation 7(1)(a) addresses one of the cases in which a person otherwise eligible is not permitted to claim housing benefit under the Social Security Act 1992: where (for the moment putting the matter colloquially) the claimant lives with and pays rent to one of his relations.
. . .

Unless the present case can be treated as an exception to the general rule of precedent, we are bound to follow the same approach as did this court in **Goonery**'s case.

Per incuriam?

18 The only escape from the ratio of a previous decision of the Court of Appeal has for long been thought to be provided by the three categories of case set out in the judgment in **Young v Bristol Aeroplane Co Ltd** [1944] KB 718. Of those, the only one even potentially applicable to the present case is that the court is not bound by a previous decision reached per incuriam. That rule is, however, to be understood in narrow terms. As Sir Raymond Evershed MR put it in **Morelle Ltd v Wakeling** [1955] 2QB 379, 406:

> . . . as a general rule the only cases in which decisions should be held to have been given per incuriam are those of decisions given in ignorance or forgetfulness of some inconsistent statutory provision or of some authority binding on the court concerned: so that in such cases some part of the decision or some step in the reasoning on which it is based is found, on that account, to be demonstrably wrong.

19 This statement suffices to exclude this case from the jurisprudence of **Young v Bristol Aeroplane Co Ltd** [1944] KB 718. The complaint in the present case is not that the court in the **Thamesdown BC v Goonery** case overlooked the Regulations; or failed to apply any

authority in relation to them that bound it; but simply that it made an unwarranted assumption about the meaning of the Regulations. Mr Cox rightly disclaimed any reliance on the *per incuriam* rule.

Assumption without argument

20 Mr Cox relied, instead, on a slender line of authority for a proposition, applicable in all courts, that a ratio or part thereof is not binding if it was assumed to be correct without the benefit of argument to that effect. This proposition is accepted as correct by *Cross & Harris, Precedent in English Law*, at p 164, but its authority and its precise terms need careful analysis.

. . .

The rule as to issues assumed without argument

33 We therefore conclude, not without some hesitation, that there is a principle stated in general terms that a subsequent court is not bound by a proposition of law assumed by an earlier court that was not the subject of argument before or consideration by that court. Since there is no direct Court of Appeal authority to that general effect we should indicate why we think the principle to be justified.

. . .

The ambit of the rule, and the present case

38 Like all exceptions to, and modifications of, the strict rule of precedent, this rule must only be applied in the most obvious of cases, and limited with great care. The basis of it is that the proposition in question must have been assumed, and not have been the subject of decision. That condition will almost always only be fulfilled when the point has not been expressly raised before the court and there has been no argument upon it: as Russell LJ went to some lengths in **National Enterprises Ltd** *v* **Racal Communications Ltd** to demonstrate had occurred in the previous case **Davies Middleton & Davies Ltd** *v* **Cardiff Corpn** 62 LGR 134. And there may of course be cases, perhaps many cases, where a point has not been the subject of argument, but scrutiny of the judgment indicates that the court's acceptance of the point went beyond mere assumption. Very little is likely to be required to draw that latter conclusion: because a later court will start from the position, encouraged by judicial comity, that its predecessor did indeed address all the matters essential for its decision.

Judicial precedent and the Privy Council

Under the rules of judicial precedent, the House of Lords binds all the lower courts in the United Kingdom. The Privy Council predominantly hears appeals from the Channel Islands and some former Commonwealth countries. Its decisions are merely persuasive for lower courts in the United Kingdom, but they are not binding. In the criminal law context, the Court of Appeal has recently been reluctant to respect these well-established rules of precedent. There is a partial defence of provocation to murder which reduces an offender's liability from murder to manslaughter. This defence is available where a defendant has been put into a sudden and temporary rage due to provocation. There is a requirement in the legislation that the defence should only be available if a reasonable person in the same position as the defendant would have reacted in the same way. The problem is that in practice a reasonable person might never react by killing another person, however seriously

→

they are provoked. The defence would therefore almost never succeed if this test was strictly applied. Instead, the House of Lords in the case of **R v Smith (Morgan)** (2001) took the view that, in applying this test, a reasonable person could be given all the characteristics of the actual defendant. So if the defendant was a schizophrenic suffering from severe depression, the court could ask whether a reasonable person suffering from schizophrenia and depression would have reacted in this way to the provocation. The Privy Council, however, disagreed in a later case, **Attorney-General for Jersey v Holley** (2005), and stated that this was a misinterpretation of the legislation. The Court of Appeal technically under the rules of precedent should be bound by the House of Lords' judgment of **Smith (Morgan)** but in its recent case of **R v James and Karimi** (2006) the Court of Appeal has applied the Privy Council judgment of **Holley**.

Attorney-General for Jersey *v* Holley (2005), Privy Council

Lord Nicholls of Birkenhead

1 This appeal from the Court of Appeal of Jersey calls for examination of the law relating to provocation as a defence or, more precisely, as a partial defence to a charge of murder. Jersey law on this subject is the same as English law. In July 2000 the House of Lords considered the ingredients of this defence in the **Morgan Smith** case (**R v Smith (Morgan)** [2001] 1 AC 146). The decision of the House in that case is in direct conflict with the decision of their Lordships' board in **Luc Thiet Thuan v The Queen** [1997] AC 131. And the reasoning of the majority in the **Morgan Smith** case is not easy to reconcile with the reasoning of the House of Lords in **R v Camplin** [1978] AC 705 or **R v Morhall** [1996] AC 90. This appeal, being heard by an enlarged board of nine members, is concerned to resolve this conflict and clarify definitively the present state of English law, and hence Jersey law, on this important subject.

. . .

The legal issue

The two views

17 Against this background their Lordships turn to consider the point where the substantial difference in judicial views has emerged. Exceptional excitability or pugnacity is one thing. But what if the defendant is suffering from serious mental abnormality, as in the **Morgan Smith** case where the defendant suffered from severe clinical depression? Is he, for the purposes of the defence of provocation, to be judged by the standard of a person having ordinary powers of self-control?

18 The view of the minority in the case of **Morgan Smith** is that he is. The standard is a constant, objective standard in all cases. The jury should assess the gravity of the provocation to the defendant. In that respect, as when considering the subjective ingredient of provocation (did the defendant lose his self-control?), the jury must take the defendant as they find him, 'warts and all', as Lord Millett observed. But having assessed the gravity of the provocation to the defendant, the standard of self-control by which his conduct is to be evaluated for the purpose of the defence of provocation is the external standard of a person having and exercising ordinary powers of self-control. That is the standard the jury should apply when considering whether or not the provocation should be regarded as sufficient to bring about the defendant's response to it: see Lord Millett, at p 211.

19 This view accords with the approach applied by their Lordships' board in **Luc Thiet Thuan** *v* **The Queen** [1997] AC 131, an appeal from Hong Kong. On a trial for murder the defendant relied on the defences of diminished responsibility and provocation. Medical evidence showed the defendant suffered from brain damage and was prone to respond to minor provocation by losing his self-control and acting explosively. The trial judge directed the jury that this medical evidence was not relevant on the defence of provocation. The jury rejected both defences. The correctness of the judge's direction on provocation was the issue on the appeal. The board, Lord Steyn dissenting, upheld the judge's direction. Lord Goff of Chieveley noted that mental infirmity of the defendant, if itself the subject of taunts by the deceased, may be taken into account as going to the gravity of the provocation. He continued, at p 146:

> But this is a far cry from the defendant's submission that the mental infirmity of a defendant impairing his power of self-control should as such be attributed to the reasonable man for the purposes of the objective test.

20 The majority view expressed in the **Morgan Smith** case [2001] 1 AC 146 rejects this approach. According to this view, the standard of self-control required by the common law and by the statute is not the constant standard of a person having and exercising ordinary self-control. The required standard is more flexible. The jury should apply the standard of control to be expected of the particular individual. The jury must ask themselves whether the defendant 'exercised the degree of self-control *to be expected of someone in his situation*' (emphasis added): see Lord Slynn of Hadley, at p 155. Lord Hoffmann expressed the view, at p 163, that the effect of the change in the law made by section 3 of the Homicide Act 1957 was that in future the jury 'were to determine not merely whether the behaviour of the accused complied with some legal standard but could determine for themselves what the standard in the particular case should be.'

Lord Hoffmann continued, at p 173:

> The law expects people to exercise control over their emotions. A tendency to violent rages or childish tantrums is a defect in character rather than an excuse. The jury must think that the circumstances were such as to make the loss of self-control sufficiently *excusable* to reduce the gravity of the offence from murder to manslaughter. This is entirely a question for the jury. In deciding what should count as a sufficient excuse, they have to apply what they consider to be appropriate standards of behaviour; on the one hand making allowance for human nature and the power of the emotions but, on the other hand, not allowing someone to rely upon his own violent disposition.

21 Lord Clyde, at p 179, expressed the expected standard of self-control in these terms:

> the standard of reasonableness in this context should refer to a person exercising the ordinary power of self-control over his passions *which someone in his position is able to exercise* and is expected by society to exercise. By position I mean to include all the characteristics which the particular individual possesses and which may in the circumstances bear on his power of control other than those influences which have been self-induced. (Emphasis added.)

22 This majority view, if their Lordships may respectfully say so, is one model which could be adopted in framing a law relating to provocation. But their Lordships consider there is one compelling, overriding reason why this view cannot be regarded as an accurate statement

of English law. It is this. The law of homicide is a highly sensitive and highly controversial area of the criminal law. In 1957 Parliament altered the common law relating to provocation and declared what the law on this subject should thenceforth be. In these circumstances it is not open to judges now to change ('develop') the common law and thereby depart from the law as declared by Parliament. However much the contrary is asserted, the majority view does represent a departure from the law as declared in section 3 of the Homicide Act 1957. It involves a significant relaxation of the uniform, objective standard adopted by Parliament. Under the statute the sufficiency of the provocation ('whether the provocation was enough to make a reasonable man do as [the defendant] did') is to be judged by one standard, not a standard which varies from defendant to defendant. Whether the provocative act or words and the defendant's response met the 'ordinary person' standard prescribed by the statute is the question the jury must consider, not the altogether looser question of whether, having regard to all the circumstances, the jury consider the loss of self-control was sufficiently excusable. The statute does not leave each jury free to set whatever standard they consider appropriate in the circumstances by which to judge whether the defendant's conduct is 'excusable'.

23 On this short ground their Lordships, respectfully but firmly, consider the majority view expressed in the **Morgan Smith** case is erroneous.

R *v* James and Karimi (2006), Court of Appeal

Lord Phillips CJ

1 These two appeals have been heard together because each turns on the true interpretation of section 3 of the Homicide Act 1957 ('section 3'). The court has sat five strong because they raise a novel and important question of the law relating to precedent. Should this court accept that the decision of the Privy Council in **Attorney-General for Jersey *v* Holley** [2005] UKPC 23; [2005] 2 AC 580 has effectively overruled the decision of the House of Lords in **R *v* Smith (Morgan)** [2001] 1 AC 146?

23 The procedure adopted and the comments of members of the Board in **Attorney-General for Jersey *v* Holley** [2005] AC 580 suggest that a decision must have been taken by those responsible for the constitution of the Board in **Holley's case** to depart from the position stated in the above passages and to use the appeal as a vehicle for reconsidering the decision of the House of Lords in **R *v* Smith (Morgan)** [2007] 1 AC 146, not just as representing the law of Jersey but as representing the law of England. A decision was taken that the Board hearing the appeal to the Privy Council should consist of nine of the twelve Lords of Appeal in Ordinary. Those sitting were Lord Bingham of Cornhill, the senior Law Lord, Lord Nicholls of Birkenhead, Lord Hoffmann, Lord Hope of Craighead, Lord Scott of Foscote, Lord Rodger of Earlsferry, Lord Walker of Gestingthorpe, Baroness Hale of Richmond and Lord Carswell. Counsel for the defendant is reported [2005] 2 AC 580, 585 as submitting that 'the Privy Council should not determine whether a decision of the House of Lords is wrongly decided'. It seems to us that a decision had already been taken that this was precisely what the Board should do.

24 In the event the Board divided six/three. The majority concluded that **Morgan Smith** had been wrongly decided and that the majority in **Luc Thiet Thuan *v* The Queen** [1997]

AC 131 had accurately stated the law. The dissentients were Lord Bingham, Lord Hoffmann and Lord Carswell. Lord Nicholls began the advice of the majority as follows [2005] 2 AC 580, para 1:

> 1. This appeal from the Court of Appeal of Jersey calls for examination of the law relating to provocation as a defence or, more precisely, as a partial defence to a charge of murder. Jersey law on this subject is the same as English law. In July 2000 the House of Lords considered the ingredients of this defence in the **Morgan Smith** case (**R v Smith (Morgan)** [2001] 1 AC 146). The decision of the House in that case is in direct conflict with the decision of their Lordships' board in **Luc Thiet Thuan v The Queen** [1997] AC 131. And the reasoning of the majority in the **Morgan Smith** case is not easy to reconcile with the reasoning of the House of Lords in **R v Camplin** [1978] AC 705 or **R v Morhall** [1996] AC 90. This appeal, being heard by an enlarged board of nine members, is concerned to resolve this conflict and clarify definitively the present state of English law, and hence Jersey law, on this important subject.

25 At the end of their dissenting opinion, Lord Bingham and Lord Hoffmann added the following comment at para 68:

> We must however accept that the effect of the majority decision is as stated in paragraph 1 of the majority judgment.

26 It seems to us that this can only mean that they accepted that the decision of the majority clarified definitively the present state of English law. Lord Carswell, who gave an individual dissenting opinion, stated at para 69, that he fully agreed with the reasons given and the conclusions reached in the dissenting opinion of Lord Bingham and Lord Hoffmann. Our understanding is that Lord Carswell's agreement extended to Lord Bingham and Lord Hoffmann's acceptance that the decision of the majority clarified definitively the present state of English law.

. . .

Practical considerations

39 Thus far the nine Lords of Appeal in Ordinary, who set out in **Holley's case** to 'clarify definitively' this difficult area of English criminal law, appear to have succeeded. The decision of the majority has been taken to be the law on three occasions by this court and, as we understand the position, is being followed in directions to juries in England and Wales. If these appeals, or any other raising the same issue, reach the House of Lords, the result would seem to be a foregone conclusion. Half of the Law Lords were party to the majority decision in **Holley**. Three more in that case accepted that the majority decision represented a definitive statement of English law on the issue in question. The choice of those to sit on the appeal might raise some nice questions, but we cannot conceive that, whatever the precise composition of the Committee, it would do other than rule that the majority decision in **Holley** represented the law of England. In effect, in the long term at least, **Holley** has overruled **Morgan Smith**.

40 If we accept what Professor Ashworth describes as 'the purist strain of argument' and allow these appeals, our decision, until reversed by the House of Lords as it surely will be, will have to be followed by judges directing juries in trials around the country. Sir Allan was right to refer to this as reducing the law to a game of ping-pong. We do not wish to produce such a result. If we are not to do so, however, two questions must be faced: (i) how do we justify disregarding very well established rules of precedent? and (ii) what principles do we put in place of those that we are disregarding? The two questions are obviously interrelated.

41 As to the first question, it is not this court, but the Lords of Appeal in Ordinary who have altered the established approach to precedent. There are possible constitutional issues in postulating that a Board of the Privy Council, however numerous or distinguished, is in a position on an appeal from Jersey to displace and replace a decision of the Appellate Committee on an issue of English law. Our principles in relation to precedent are, however, common law principles. Putting on one side the position of the European Court of Justice, the Lords of Appeal in Ordinary have never hitherto accepted that any other tribunal could overrule a decision of the Appellate Committee. Uniquely a majority of the Law Lords have on this occasion decided that they could do so and have done so in their capacity as members of the Judicial Committee of the Privy Council. We do not consider that it is for this court to rule that it was beyond their powers to alter the common law rules of precedent in this way.

42 The rule that this court must always follow a decision of the House of Lords and, indeed, one of its own decisions rather than a decision of the Privy Council is one that was established at a time when no tribunal other than the House of Lords itself could rule that a previous decision of the House of Lords was no longer good law. Once one postulates that there are circumstances in which a decision of the Judicial Committee of the Privy Council can take precedence over a decision of the House of Lords, it seems to us that this court must be bound in those circumstances to prefer the decision of the Privy Council to the prior decision of the House of Lords. That, so it seems to us, is the position that has been reached in the case of these appeals.

43 What are the exceptional features in this case which justify our preferring the decision in **Holley** to that in **Morgan Smith**? We identify the following:

(i) All nine of the Lords of Appeal in Ordinary sitting in **Holley** agreed in the course of their judgments that the result reached by the majority clarified definitively English law on the issue in question.

(ii) The majority in **Holley** constituted half the Appellate Committee of the House of Lords. We do not know whether there would have been agreement that the result was definitive had the members of the Board divided five/four.

(iii) In the circumstances, the result of any appeal on the issue to the House of Lords is a foregone conclusion.

44 We doubt whether this court will often, if ever again, be presented with the circumstances that we have described above. It is those circumstances which we consider justify the course that we have decided to take, and our decision should not be taken as a licence to decline to follow a decision of the House of Lords in any other circumstances.

45 For the reasons that we have given, we approach the individual appeals on the premise that the relevant principle of law is to be found in the majority decision of the Privy Council in **Attorney-General for Jersey v Holley** [2005] 2 AC 580 and not the majority decision of the House of Lords in **R v Smith (Morgan)** [2001] 1 AC 146. We turn now to the individual appeals.

How do judges really decide cases?

Sometimes when the judges hear a case they can point to an earlier court case or a piece of legislation which clearly provides the legal answer to the litigation. However, sometimes there is no clear precedent and the judges have more difficulty in determining how the case should be decided. One such case is that of **Re A (Children)** [2001]. The case concerned the legality of an operation to separate conjoined twins, Jodie and Mary. They each had their own vital organs, arms and legs. The weaker twin, Mary, had a poorly developed brain, an abnormal heart and virtually no lung tissue. She had only survived birth because a common artery enabled her sister to circulate oxygenated blood for both of them. An operation to separate the twins required the cutting of that common artery. Mary would die within minutes because her lungs and heart were not sufficient to pump blood through her body. The doctors believed that Jodie had between a 94 and 99% chance of surviving the separation, would have only limited disabilities and would be able to lead a relatively normal life. If the doctors waited until Mary died naturally and then carried out an emergency separation operation, Jodie would only have a 36% chance of survival. If no operation was performed, they were both likely to die within three to six months because Jodie's heart would eventually fail.

The question to be determined by the Court of Appeal was whether the operation could lawfully be carried out and, in particular, whether the doctors would be committing the offence of murder against Mary, who would be killed by the operation. The Court of Appeal concluded that the operation could be lawfully carried out.

Re A (Children) [2001], Court of Appeal

Ward LJ

I Introduction to the case of the Siamese twins

In the past decade an increasing number of cases have come before the courts where the decision whether or not to permit or to refuse medical treatment can be a matter of life and death for the patient. I have been involved in a number of them. They are always anxious decisions to make but they are invariably eventually made with the conviction that there is only one right answer and that the court has given it.

In this case the right answer is not at all as easy to find. I freely confess to having found it truly difficult to decide – difficult because of the scale of the tragedy for the parents and the twins, difficult for the seemingly irreconcilable conflicts of moral and ethical values and difficult because the search for settled legal principle has been especially arduous and conducted under real pressure of time.

The problems we have faced have gripped the public interest and the case has received intense coverage in the media. Everyone seems to have a view of the proper outcome. I am very well aware of the inevitability that our answer will be applauded by some but that as many will be offended by it. Many will vociferously assert their own moral, ethical or religious values. Some will agree with Justice Scalia who said in the Supreme Court of the United States of America in **Cruzan v Director, Missouri Department of Health** (1990) 110 S. Ct. 2841, 2859:

The point at which life becomes 'worthless', and the point at which the means necessary to preserve it become 'extraordinary' or 'inappropriate', are neither set forth in the constitution nor known to the nine Justices of this Court any better than they are known to nine people picked at random from the Kansas City telephone directory. . . .

It is, however, important to stress the obvious. This court is a court of law, not of morals, and our task has been to find, and our duty is then to apply the relevant principles of law to the situation before us – a situation which is quite unique . . .

Exceptionally we allowed the Archbishop of Westminster and the Pro-Life Alliance to make written submissions to us. We are grateful for them. We are also very grateful for the very considerable research undertaken by the Bar and by the solicitors and for the powerful submissions counsel have advanced which have swayed me one way and another and left me at the conclusion of the argument in need of time, unfortunately not enough time, to read, to reflect, to decide and then to write . . .

II The facts in more detail

16 The Grounds of Appeal

The parents have appealed on the grounds that the learned judge erred in holding that the operation was (i) in Mary's best interest, (ii) that it was in Jodie's best interest, and (iii) that in any event it would be legal. The appeal has accordingly ranged quite widely over many aspects of the interaction between the relevant principles of medical law, family law, criminal law and fundamental human rights . . .

IV Family law

. . .

9.3 The weight to be given to these parents' wishes

. . .

In their natural repugnance at the idea of killing Mary they fail to recognise their conflicting duty to save Jodie and they seem to exculpate themselves from, or at least fail fully to face up to the consequence of the failure to separate the twins, namely death for Jodie. In my judgment, parents who are placed on the horns of such a terrible dilemma simply have to choose the lesser of their inevitable loss. If a family at the gates of a concentration camp were told they might free one of their children but if no choice were made both would die, compassionate parents with equal love for their twins would elect to save the stronger and see the weak one destined for death pass through the gates.

This is a terribly cruel decision to force upon the parents. It is a choice no loving parent would ever want to make. It gives me no satisfaction to have disagreed with their views of what is right for their family and to have expressed myself in terms they will feel are harshly and unfairly critical of them. I am sorry about that. It may be no great comfort to them to know that in fact my heart bleeds for them. But if, as the law says I must, it is I who must now make the decision, then whatever the parents' grief, I must strike a balance between the twins and do what is best for them.

10 How is the balance to be struck?

The analytical problem is to determine what may, and what may not, be placed in each scale and what weight is then to be given to each of the factors in the scales.

(i) The universality of the right to life demands that the right to life be treated as equal. The intrinsic value of their human life is equal. So the right of each goes into the scales and the scales remain in balance.

(ii) The question which the court has to answer is whether or not the proposed treatment, the operation to separate, is in the best interests of the twins. That enables me to consider and place in the scales of each twin the worthwhileness of the treatment. That is a quite different exercise from the proscribed (because it offends the sanctity of life principle) consideration of the worth of one life compared with the other. When considering the worthwhileness of the treatment, it is legitimate to have regard to the actual condition of each twin and hence the actual balance sheet of advantage and disadvantage which flows from the performance or the non-performance of the proposed treatment. Here it is legitimate, as John Keown demonstrates, and as the cases show, to bear in mind the actual quality of life each child enjoys and may be able to enjoy. In summary, the operation will give Jodie the prospects of a normal expectation of relatively normal life. The operation will shorten Mary's life but she remains doomed for death. Mary has a full claim to the dignity of independence which is her human entitlement. In the words of the Rabbinical scholars involved in the 1977 case in Philadelphia (see George J Annas (1987) 17 Hastings Center Report 27), Mary is 'designated for death' because her capacity to live her life is fatally compromised. The prospect of a full life for Jodie is counterbalanced by an acceleration of certain death for Mary. That balance is heavily in Jodie's favour.

(iii) I repeat that the balancing exercise I have just conducted is not a balancing of the Quality of Life in the sense that I value the potential of one human life above another. I have already indicated that the value of each life in the eyes of God and in the eyes of law is equal. Remember Lord Mustill's observation in **Airedale NHS Trust** v **Bland** [1993] AC 789.

(iv) In this unique case it is, in my judgment, impossible not to put in the scales of each child the manner in which they are individually able to exercise their right to life. Mary may have a right to life, but she has little right to be alive. She is alive because and only because, to put it bluntly, but nonetheless accurately, she sucks the lifeblood of Jodie and she sucks the lifeblood out of Jodie. She will survive only so long as Jodie survives. Jodie will not survive long because constitutionally she will not be able to cope. Mary's parasitic living will be the cause of Jodie's ceasing to live. If Jodie could speak, she would surely protest, 'Stop it, Mary, you're killing me'. Mary would have no answer to that. Into my scales of fairness and justice between the children goes the fact that nobody but the doctors can help Jodie. Mary is beyond help.

Hence I am in no doubt at all that the scales come down heavily in Jodie's favour. The best interests of the twins is to give the chance of life to the child whose actual bodily condition is capable of accepting the chance to her advantage even if that has to be at the cost of the sacrifice of the life which is so unnaturally supported. I am wholly satisfied that the least detrimental choice, balancing the interests of Mary against Jodie and Jodie against Mary, is to permit the operation to be performed.

V Criminal law

. . .

7.7 Offending the sanctity of life principle
. . . [One] reason why the right of choice should be given to the doctors is that the proposed operation would not in any event offend the sanctity of life principle. That principle may

be expressed in different ways but they all amount to the same thing. Some might say that it demands that each life is to be protected from *unjust attack*. Some might say as the joint statement by the Anglican and Roman Catholic bishops did in the aftermath of the **Airdale NHS Trust *v* Bland** judgment [1993] AC 789 that because human life is a gift from God to be preserved and cherished, the deliberate taking of human life is prohibited except in self-defence or the legitimate defence of others. The Archbishop defines it in terms that human life is sacred, that is inviolable, so that one should never aim to cause an *innocent* person's death by act or omission. I have added the emphases. The reality here – harsh as it is to state it, and unnatural as it is that it should be happening – is that Mary is killing Jodie. That is the effect of the incontrovertible medical evidence and it is common ground in the case. Mary uses Jodie's heart and lungs to receive and use Jodie's oxygenated blood. This will cause Jodie's heart to fail and cause Jodie's death as surely as a slow drip of poison. How can it be just that Jodie should be required to tolerate that state of affairs? One does not need to label Mary with the American terminology which would paint her to be 'an unjust aggressor', which I feel is wholly inappropriate language for the sad and helpless position in which Mary finds herself. I have no difficulty in agreeing that this unique happening cannot be said to be unlawful. But it does not have to be unlawful. The six year boy indiscriminately shooting all and sundry in the school playground is not acting unlawfully for he is too young for his acts to be so classified. But is he 'innocent' within the moral meaning of that word as used by the Archbishop? I am not qualified to answer that moral question because, despite an assertion or was it an aspersion? by a member of the Bar in a letter to *The Times* that we, the judges, are proclaiming some moral superiority in this case, I for my part would defer any opinion as to a child's innocence to the Archbishop for that is his territory. If I had to hazard a guess, I would venture the tentative view that the child is not morally innocent. What I am, however, competent to say is that *in law* killing that six year old boy in self-defence of others would be fully justified and the killing would not be unlawful. I can see no difference in essence between that resort to legitimate self-defence and the doctors coming to Jodie's defence and removing the threat of fatal harm to her presented by Mary's draining her life-blood. The availability of such a plea of quasi self-defence, modified to meet the quite exceptional circumstances nature has inflicted on the twins, makes intervention by the doctors lawful.

. . .

Robert Walker LJ

I will summarise my conclusions as to the applicable principles as simply as I can.

(i) The feelings of the twins' parents are entitled to great respect, especially so far as they are based on religious convictions. But as the matter has been referred to the court the court cannot escape the responsibility of deciding the matter to the best of its judgment as to the twins' best interests.

(ii) The judge erred in law in equating the proposed surgical operation with the discontinuance of medical treatment (as by disconnecting a heart-lung machine). Therefore the Court of Appeal must form its own view.

(iii) Mary has a right to life, under the common law of England (based as it is on Judeo-Christian foundations) and under the European Convention on Human Rights. It would be unlawful to kill Mary intentionally, that is to undertake an operation with the primary purpose of killing her.

(iv) But Jodie also has a right to life.

(v) Every human being's right to life carries with it, as an intrinsic part of it, rights of bodily integrity and autonomy – the right to have one's own body whole and intact and (on reaching an age of understanding) to take decisions about one's own body.

(vi) By a rare and tragic mischance, Mary and Jodie have both been deprived of the bodily integrity and autonomy which is their natural right. There is a strong presumption that an operation to separate them would be in the best interests of each of them.

(vii) In this case the purpose of the operation would be to separate the twins and so give Jodie a reasonably good prospect of a long and reasonably normal life. Mary's death would not be the purpose of the operation, although it would be its inevitable consequence. The operation would give her, even in death, bodily integrity as a human being. She would die, not because she was intentionally killed, but because her own body cannot sustain her life.

(viii) Continued life, whether long or short, would hold nothing for Mary except possible pain and discomfort, if indeed she can feel anything at all.

(ix) The proposed operation would therefore be in the best interests of each of the twins. The decision does not require the court to value one life above another.

(x) The proposed operation would not be unlawful. It would involve the positive act of invasive surgery and Mary's death would be foreseen as an inevitable consequence of an operation which is intended, and is necessary, to save Jodie's life. But Mary's death would not be the purpose or intention of the surgery, and she would die because tragically her body, on its own, is not and never has been viable.

I would therefore dismiss this appeal.

2

Statute law

Introduction

This chapter looks at:

- government plans to modernise Parliament;
- the role of the House of Lords in the light of litigation challenging the legality of the Hunting Act 2004 outlawing certain forms of hunting; and
- moves to improve post-legislative scrutiny.

182 Yet these considerations notwithstanding, the Attorney-General accepts, as he has throughout this litigation, that the courts are properly seised of this challenge to the 1949 Act, and that the attack upon its validity is in no way foreclosed either by the endorsement upon it of the Speaker's certificate of compliance with the 1911 Act, or by the long passage of time since its enactment, or by its subsequent invocation by both main political parties to enact other legislation too. Your Lordships must, therefore, cast aside any initial inhibitions about entering upon this unusual challenge. There is no need here for judicial reticence. Rather your Lordships must examine the challenge for all the world as if the 1949 Act had only recently received the Royal Assent.

183 The effect of the 1949 Act, as several of your Lordships have already made clear, was to amend the terms of the 1911 Act itself. Its sole purpose, indeed, was to weaken the conditions controlling the use of the 1911 Act. This it did by reducing from three sessions to two, and from two years to one, the period by which the House of Lords was thereafter able to delay the enactment of legislation promoted by the House of Commons. The side note to section 2(1) of the 1911 Act, as enacted, described its original purpose as the 'Restriction of the powers of the House of Lords as to Bills . . .'. The 1949 Act restricted those powers still further. That is the long and the short of it.

184 Was that something which the House of Commons was entitled to achieve by use of the 1911 Act itself? Was it, in other words, open to the House of Commons to use the 1911 Act (itself of course enacted with the consent of the House of Lords) to overcome the subsequent refusal by the House of Lords in 1949 to consent to the proposed further restriction of their powers? That is the core question raised in these proceedings. A related question too arises: what, if any, limitations are there upon the use of the 1911 Act to effect constitutional change?

185 The appellants' objection to the use of the 1911 Act to force through the 1949 Act is an obvious one. Put simply it is this. Here were the two main constituent elements of Parliament, the House of Commons and the House of Lords (the third, the Monarch, playing only a formal role in the legislative process) agreeing in 1911 to the specific conditions under which the House of Commons would thereafter be able to enact its legislative programme without the consent of the House of Lords. How could it then be right, thirty-eight years later, for the House of Commons, without the Lords' consent, to use the 1911 Act procedure to alter those very conditions, making it easier still for future House of Lords' objections to be overridden? The 1911 Act must be regarded as a 'concordat' or 'new constitutional settlement' (two of the terms coined by the Court of Appeal below), a consensual arrangement which could not then be changed at the instance of one party only. And not merely is the point an obvious one; so too are its attractions. To do as the House of Commons did in 1949 must strike many as quite simply unfair, akin to reneging on a deal.

186 How, then, do the appellants give juridical expression to this central objection to the 1949 Act? It is their main submission in these proceedings that powers conferred on a body by an enabling Act may not be enlarged or modified by that body unless there are express words authorising such enlargement or modification. True it is, they must acknowledge, section 2(1) of the 1911 Act refers on its face to 'any Public Bill'. But, submits Sir Sydney Kentridge QC, that is not enough: express words were needed to permit the House of Commons to extend its powers still further. Sometimes (if rarely) legislation contains a

Henry VIII clause, a power conferred on a delegate body to amend the enabling Act itself. But no such clause is to be found in the 1911 Act and without it that Act could not be amended save with the consent of both Houses of Parliament. The 1911 Act settled the conditions under which in future the House of Commons would be able to override the House of Lords' rejection of its Bills. Those conditions having been agreed, they could not thereafter be altered save with the further consent of the House of Lords.

187 Persuasive though I confess to having initially found this argument, I have finally reached the view that it must fail. Its central plank, the suggested analogy with delegated powers, I now think to be unsustainable. The 1911 Act was not like a statute by which Parliament as the sovereign legislative body confers, say, regulation-making powers upon a Minister, powers plainly then incapable of enlargement without a Henry VIII clause. The 1911 Act in truth conferred no further legislative powers upon the House of Commons. Rather it redefined the sovereign parliament's legislative process by providing in certain circumstances for main legislation without the need for the House of Lords' consent. Nor was the situation brought about by this re-definition of the legislative process analogous to the establishment of colonial legislatures by an imperial Parliament the source of much of the case law put before us. An imperial Parliament conferring powers on a colonial legislature cannot realistically be equated to the House of Lords, under threat in 1911 that enough new Liberal peers would be created to secure the future enactment of the government's Bills, agreeing instead to a weakening of its powers of veto. The Commonwealth cases were in truth addressed to a very different political reality. The appellants' main argument must fail.

188 There was, however, as I understood it, a second string to the appellants' bow, Sir Sydney's argument that in any event, even if his principal argument as to the need for express words fails, Parliament cannot have intended the expression 'any Public Bill' to be understood to encompass even proposed amendments to the 1911 Act itself so that the expression must be understood as to that extent qualified.

189 In support of this argument the appellants point to certain extreme possibilities open to the House of Commons if the Attorney-General's arguments be right. Provided only that the 1911 Act procedure was used to achieve it, the House of Commons could have forced through in two years (and, if the 1949 Act is valid, can now force through in one) wholesale amendments to the conditions governing that Act's further use. For example, the Act could be amended to allow all future Bills to be treated just like money Bills and forced through within one month: see section 1 of the 1911 Act. Or, indeed, notwithstanding that 'a Bill containing any provision to extend the maximum duration of Parliament beyond five years' is on its face excluded from the scope of section 2, that exclusion itself could be removed by amendment and the Act's procedure then be used afresh to extend Parliament's life.

190 Whilst, therefore, literally construed, the 1911 Act would have permitted its use to amend the very conditions to which that use had been made subject, the court could and should instead construe the phrase 'any Public Bill' restrictively so as to guard against such politically unreasonable consequences.

191 It appears to have been this argument which found most favour with the Court of Appeal. But it was not, of course, accepted in full: the Court of Appeal was not prepared to construe the expression 'any Public Bill' in the 1911 Act sufficiently restrictively to preclude any dilution whatever of the conditions governing the Act's future use. Rather the court held that modest amendments could be forced through but not fundamental ones. Concluding, however, that the 1949 Act had effected only a modest amendment to the 1911 Act, the appellants' case still failed.

192 It is this argument, of course, which raises the related question mentioned in para 184 above: what, if any, limitations are there upon the use to which the 1911 Act can be put to effect constitutional change? The ultimate logic of the Attorney-General's argument is that there are no such limitations. Sir Sydney, for his part, however, must contend that the 1911 Act procedure is certainly not available to abolish the House of Lords: for that would be to destroy the constitutional settlement embodied in the 1911 Act no less completely than any amendment, however fundamental, to the specified conditions governing its use.

193 It is not difficult to understand why the Court of Appeal reached the conclusion it did as to the kind of changes achievable by use of the 1911 Act. And it is easy to understand too why each side rejects that conclusion: Sir Sydney because his argument needs to succeed in full measure; the Attorney-General because the Court of Appeal's judgment now casts real doubt over what use can be made of the 1911 Act to effect significant constitutional change in future.

194 In common, I think, with all your Lordships, I would reject the Court of Appeal's approach as unwarranted in law and unworkable in practice. But in common too, I think, with the majority of your Lordships I am not prepared to give such a ruling as would sanction in advance the use of the 1911 Act for all purposes, for example to abolish the House of Lords (rather than, say, alter its constitution or method of selection) or to prolong the life of Parliament, two of the extreme ends to which theoretically this procedure could be put. Although, as I have said, the strict logic of the respondent's position suggests that the express bar on the House of Commons alone extending the life of Parliament could be overcome by a two-stage use of the 1911 Act procedure, the Attorney-General acknowledged in argument that the contrary view might have to be preferred. Let us hope that these issues will never be put to the test. But if they are, they will certainly deserve fuller argument than time has allowed on the present appeal.

195 One thing, however, remains certain. There is no proper basis on which a qualification to the wide words 'any Public Bill' could be implied into section 2 of the 1911 Act to bar its use to achieve the particular amendments effected by the 1949 Act. It is unnecessary to resort to Hansard to conclude that both Houses of Parliament must inevitably have recognised in 1911 the real possibility that that Act's procedure would thereafter be used to amend itself. I too, therefore, would dismiss this appeal.

The judgment **R (Jackson and Others)** v **Attorney-General** (2005) is available on Parliament's website at:

www.parliament.the-stationery-office.co.uk/pa/ld200506/ldjudgmt/ jd051013/jack-1.htm

Post-legislative scrutiny

In 2006 the Law Commission published a paper recommending that a formal process of post-legislative scrutiny should be introduced which would check how the legislation that has been enacted by Parliament is working in practice. This recommendation has been accepted by the Government in its report 'Post-legislative Scrutiny – The Government's Approach' (2008). The process of post-legislative scrutiny would normally be carried out on selected statutes by committees of the House of Commons.

Post-Legislative Scrutiny – The Government's Approach

The government's overall approach to post-legislative scrutiny

6 The Commission noted that 'No-one . . . has registered an objection to the proposition that there should be more post-legislative scrutiny', but also identified some important factors which need to be taken into account in any system which is established. The need for flexibility – avoiding a 'one-size-fits-all' approach – was noted, and the Commission concluded there was no 'merit in proposing blanket scrutiny of all measures'.

7 The Government agrees with this overall approach. There are clear benefits in selective post-legislative scrutiny of Acts. Such scrutiny will help to improve the legislation itself, not only after it has been reviewed – if this leads to amendment – but also when it is being first formulated since the knowledge that it will be subject to some form of review after enactment should help to focus preparatory work more clearly. It will also allow lessons to be learned, both where problems are identified but also where things have gone well.

8 At the same time, it is important that any system must be proportionate to need. Any system must therefore:

- concentrate on appropriate Acts, not waste resources attempting detailed reviews of *every* Act;
- avoid re-running what are basically policy debates already conducted during passage of the Act;
- reflect the specific circumstances of each Act (eg associated secondary legislation or surrounding policy environment);
- be complementary to the scrutiny which can already take place, in particular through existing Commons select committee activity.

9 The Government therefore considers that the basis for a new process for post-legislative scrutiny should be for the Commons committees themselves, on the basis of a Memorandum on appropriate Acts submitted by the relevant Government department, and published as a Command paper, to decide whether to conduct further post-legislative scrutiny of the Act in question. In some cases (though not ordinarily if the Commons Committee has decided to conduct a review) it might be appropriate for a different parliamentary body – whether Lords or Commons or Joint – to conduct further scrutiny. In this way, all Acts would receive a measure of post-legislative scrutiny within Government and would be specifically considered for scrutiny within Parliament. Some, on a considered and targeted basis, would then go on to receive more in-depth scrutiny. This would reflect the approach proposed earlier by the Lords Constitution Committee.

10 The Commission's proposed model seeks to combine in a complementary fashion internal departmental scrutiny with parliamentary scrutiny, with the central power of initiative for parliamentary scrutiny itself balanced between the Commons departmental committees and other elements within Parliament. The Government broadly endorses this approach but considers that greater clarity is necessary in the way the prime role of the Commons committees should be recognised. Much of the activity of Commons committees, even if not overtly labelled in that way, in practice involves examination of the effectiveness of existing primary legislation. It would be undesirable for that work to be subject to duplication or conflicting work from other committees.

11 The Government considers that its proposal will be a valuable and proportionate approach towards achieving the objective of better post-legislative scrutiny. This approach is set out in more detail in the Government's response to the individual Law Commission recommendations, as appended. In practice, given the lengths of time involved in the passage of new legislation and the lead times involved for the preparation of the Memoranda envisaged in these proposals, the operation of the proposed system and its effectiveness will have to be kept under continuous review. If the kind of Memorandum for parliamentary scrutiny which is proposed involves a disproportionate workload in their production, or if they do not prove to be the kind of document which Parliament finds helpful, then it would be appropriate to consider alternative approaches.

The report 'Post-Legislative Scrutiny – The Government's Approach' (Command Paper 7320) is available at:
www.official-documents.gov.uk/document/cm73/7320/7320.pdf

3

Statutory interpretation

Introduction

This chapter looks at:

- cases illustrating the different rules of statutory interpretation: the literal rule, the golden rule and the mischief rule;

- the purposive approach to statutory interpretation and the limits to this approach;

- when the courts will make direct reference to *Hansard* (the official record of parliamentary proceedings); and

- the impact of the Human Rights Act 1998 on statutory interpretation.

patrol, or other similar duty in relation to the prohibited place, and, if any person acts in contravention of, or fails to comply with, this provision, he shall be guilty of a misdemeanour.' In the present case the defendant had obtained access to – it matters not how – and was on the Air Force station on May 11, 1963, and there and then, it was found, he obstructed a member of Her Majesty's Royal Air Force.

The sole point here, and a point ably argued by the defendant, is that if he was on the station he could not be in the vicinity of the station, and it is only an offence under this section to obstruct a member of Her Majesty's Forces while he is in the vicinity of the station. The defendant has referred to the natural meaning of 'vicinity', which I take to be, quite generally, the state of being near in space, and he says that it is inapt to and does not cover being in fact on the station as in the present case.

I am quite satisfied that this is a case where no violence is done to the language by reading the words 'in the vicinity of' as meaning 'in or in the vicinity of'. Here is a section in an Act of Parliament designed to prevent interference with members of Her Majesty's forces, among others, who are engaged on guard, sentry, patrol or other similar duty in relation to a prohibited place such as this station. It would be extraordinary, I venture to think it would be absurd, if an indictable offence was thereby created when the obstruction took place outside the precincts of the station, albeit in the vicinity, and no offence at all was created if the obstruction occurred on the station itself. It is to be observed that if the defendant is right, the only offence committed by him in obstructing such a member of the Air Force would be an offence contrary to section 193 of the Air Force Act, 1955, which creates a summary offence, the maximum sentence for which is three months, whereas section 3 of the Official Secrets Act, 1920, is, as one would expect, dealing with an offence which can be tried on indictment and for which, under section 8, the maximum sentence of imprisonment is one of two years. There may be, of course, many contexts in which 'vicinity' must be confined to its literal meaning of 'being near in space' but under this section, I am quite clear that the context demands that the words should be construed in the way I have said. I would dismiss this appeal.

The mischief rule

The mischief rule for interpreting statutes was laid down in **Heydon's case** in the 16th century and requires judges to consider three factors:

1 what the law was before the statute was passed;
2 what problem (or mischief) the statute was trying to remedy;
3 what remedy Parliament was trying to provide.

Below is an example of the mischief rule being applied by the courts.

Smith *v* Hughes (1960), High Court

Police officers preferred two informations against Marie Theresa Smith and four informations against Christine Tolan alleging that on various dates, they, being common prostitutes, did solicit in a street for the purpose of prostitution contrary to section 1(1) of the Street Offences Act, 1959.

The magistrate found the following facts in relation to the first information against Smith. The defendant was a common prostitute who lived at No. 39 Curzon Street, London, . . . , and used the premises for the purposes of prostitution. On November 4, 1959, between 8.50 p.m. and 9.05 p.m. the defendant solicited men passing in the street, for the purposes of prostitution, from a first-floor balcony of No. 39 Curzon Street (the balcony being some 8–10 feet above street level). The defendant's method of soliciting the men was (i) to attract their attention to her by tapping on the balcony railing with some metal object and by hissing at them as they passed in the street beneath her and (ii) having so attracted their attention, to talk with them and invite them to come inside the premises with such words as 'Would you like to come up here a little while?' at the same time as she indicated the correct door of the premises.

It was contended on behalf of the defendant, inter alia, that the balcony was not 'in a street' within the meaning of section 1(1) of the Street Offences Act, 1959, and that accordingly no offence had been committed.

Lord Parker CJ

These are six appeals by way of case stated by one of the stipendiary magistrates sitting at Bow Street, before whom informations were preferred by police officers against the defendants, in each case that she 'being a common prostitute, did solicit in a street for the purpose of prostitution, contrary to section 1(1) of the Street Offences Act, 1959'. The magistrate in each case found that the defendant was a common prostitute, that she had solicited and that the solicitation was in a street, and in each case fined the defendant.

The facts, to all intents and purposes, raise the same point in each case; there are minute differences. The defendants in each case were not themselves physically in the street but were in a house adjoining the street. In one case the defendant was on a balcony and she attracted the attention of men in the street by tapping and calling down to them. In other cases the defendants were in ground-floor windows, either closed or half open, and in another case in a first-floor window.

The sole question here is whether in those circumstances each defendant was soliciting in a street or public place. The words of section 1(1) of the Act of 1959 are in this form: 'It shall be an offence for a common prostitute to loiter or solicit in a street or public place for the purpose of prostitution.' Observe that it does not say there specifically that the person who is doing the soliciting must be in the street. Equally, it does not say that it is enough if the person who receives the solicitation or to whom it is addressed is in the street. For my part, I approach the matter by considering what is the mischief aimed at by this Act. Everybody knows that this was an Act intended to clean up the streets, to enable people to walk along the streets without being molested or solicited by common prostitutes. Viewed in that way, it can matter little whether the prostitute is soliciting while in the street or is standing in a doorway or on a balcony, or at a window, or whether the window is shut or open or half open; in each case her solicitation is projected to and addressed to somebody walking in the street. For my part, I am content to base my decision on that ground and that ground alone. I think the magistrate came to a correct conclusion in each case, and that these appeals should be dismissed.

The purposive approach

Historically, the preferred approach to statutory interpretation was to look for a statutes' literal meaning. However, over the last three decades, the courts have accepted that the literal approach can be unsatisfactory. Instead, the judges have been increasingly influenced by the European approach to statutory interpretation which focuses on giving effect to the purpose of the legislation. In **Regina v Secretary of State for Health ex parte Quintavalle (on behalf of Pro-Life Alliance)** (2003) the House of Lords expressly used a purposive approach to statutory interpretation in order to interpret the Human Fertilisation and Embryology Act 1990. This Act had been passed in response to medical developments in fertility treatment. In July 1978 the first child was born using *in vitro* fertilisation techniques (where the egg is fertilised outside the mother's womb). This prompted considerable ethical and scientific debate as to the social, ethical and legal implications of these scientific developments. In 1982 a Committee of Inquiry was established under the chairmanship of Dame Mary Warnock and in the light of its report the 1990 Act was passed. This Act aimed to regulate and outlaw certain practices involving the use of human embryos. However, at the time that the Act was passed embryos could only be created by a process of fertilisation with sperm. After the Act was passed a new scientific process was developed known as cell nuclear replacement (CNR). Under this process an embryo can be created without fertilising an egg but by removing the nucleus from one egg and replacing it with another nucleus. This process was used in the cloning process to create the famous Dolly the sheep.

In the **Quintavalle** case of 2003, the appellant, acting on behalf of the pressure group Pro-Life, argued before the House of Lords that because CNR was a new process it was not covered by the 1990 Act and therefore the Human Fertilisation and Embryology Authority did not have the authority under the Act to licence research involving CNR. It pointed out that in s. 1 of the Act an embryo regulated by the Act is defined as 'a live human embryo where fertilisation is complete' and that CNR does not involve a process of fertilisation. This argument was rejected by the House of Lords which applied a purposive approach to interpreting the 1990 Act.

R v Secretary of State for Health *ex parte* Quintavalle (on behalf of Pro-Life Alliance) (2003), House of Lords

Lord Bingham

My Lords,

1 The issues in this appeal are whether live human embryos created by cell nuclear replacement (CNR) fall outside the regulatory scope of the Human Fertilisation and Embryology Act 1990 and whether licensing the creation of such embryos is prohibited by section 3(3)(d) of that Act.

. . .

The approach to interpretation

8 The basic task of the court is to ascertain and give effect to the true meaning of what Parliament has said in the enactment to be construed. But that is not to say that attention

should be confined and a literal interpretation given to the particular provisions which give rise to difficulty. Such an approach not only encourages immense prolixity in drafting, since the draftsman will feel obliged to provide expressly for every contingency which may possibly arise. It may also (under the banner of loyalty to the will of Parliament) lead to the frustration of that will, because undue concentration on the minutiae of the enactment may lead the court to neglect the purpose which Parliament intended to achieve when it enacted the statute. Every statute other than a pure consolidating statute is, after all, enacted to make some change, or address some problem, or remove some blemish, or effect some improvement in the national life. The court's task, within the permissible bounds of interpretation, is to give effect to Parliament's purpose. So the controversial provisions should be read in the context of the statute as a whole, and the statute as a whole should be read in the historical context of the situation which led to its enactment.

9 There is, I think, no inconsistency between the rule that statutory language retains the meaning it had when Parliament used it and the rule that a statute is always speaking. If Parliament, however long ago, passed an Act applicable to dogs, it could not properly be interpreted to apply to cats; but it could properly be held to apply to animals which were not regarded as dogs when the Act was passed but are so regarded now.

10 . . . More pertinent is the guidance given by the late Lord Wilberforce in his dissenting opinion in **Royal College of Nursing of the United Kingdom v Department of Health and Social Security** [1981] AC 800. The case concerned the Abortion Act 1967 and the issue which divided the House was whether nurses could lawfully take part in a termination procedure not known when the Act was passed. At p 822 Lord Wilberforce said:

> In interpreting an Act of Parliament it is proper, and indeed necessary, to have regard to the state of affairs existing, and known by Parliament to be existing, at the time. It is a fair presumption that Parliament's policy or intention is directed to that state of affairs. Leaving aside cases of omission by inadvertence, this being not such a case, when a new state of affairs, or a fresh set of facts bearing on policy, comes into existence, the courts have to consider whether they fall within the Parliamentary intention. They may be held to do so, if they fall within the same genus of facts as those to which the expressed policy has been formulated. They may also be held to do so if there can be detected a clear purpose in the legislation which can only be fulfilled if the extension is made. How liberally these principles may be applied must depend upon the nature of the enactment, and the strictness or otherwise of the words in which it has been expressed. The courts should be less willing to extend expressed mean-ings if it is clear that the Act in question was designed to be restrictive or circumscribed in its operation rather than liberal or permissive. They will be much less willing to do so where the subject matter is different in kind or dimension from that for which the legislation was passed. In any event there is one course which the courts cannot take, under the law of this country; they cannot fill gaps; they cannot by asking the question 'What would Parliament have done in this current case – not being one in contemplation – if the facts had been before it?' attempt themselves to supply the answer, if the answer is not to be found in the terms of the Act itself.

Both parties relied on this passage, which may now be treated as authoritative.

Section 1(1)(a)

14 It is against this background that one comes to interpret section 1(1)(a). At first reading [the Pro-Life] construction has an obvious attraction: the Act is dealing with live human embryos 'where fertilisation is complete', and the definition is a composite one including

the last four words. But the Act is only directed to the creation of embryos *in vitro*, outside the human body (section 1(2)). Can Parliament have been intending to distinguish between live human embryos produced by fertilisation of a female egg and live human embryos produced without such fertilisation? The answer must certainly be negative, since Parliament was unaware that the latter alternative was physically possible. This suggests that the four words were not intended to form an integral part of the definition of embryo but were directed to the time at which it should be treated as such . . . The crucial point . . . is that this was an Act passed for the protection of live human embryos created outside the human body. The essential thrust of section 1(1)(a) was directed to such embryos, not to the manner of their creation, which Parliament (entirely understandably on the then current state of scientific knowledge) took for granted.

15 Bearing in mind the constitutional imperative that the courts stick to their interpretative role and do not assume the mantle of legislators, however, I would not leave the matter there but would seek to apply the guidance of Lord Wilberforce quoted above in paragraph 10:

(1) Does the creation of live human embryos by CNR fall within the same genus of facts as those to which the expressed policy of Parliament has been formulated? In my opinion, it plainly does. An embryo created by *in vitro* fertilisation and one created by CNR are very similar organisms. The difference between them as organisms is that the CNR embryo, if allowed to develop, will grow into a clone of the donor of the replacement nucleus which the embryo produced by fertilisation will not. But this is a difference which plainly points towards the need for regulation, not against it.

(2) Is the operation of the 1990 Act to be regarded as liberal and permissive in its operation or restrictive and circumscribed? This is not an entirely simple question. The Act intended to permit certain activities but to circumscribe the freedom to pursue them which had previously been enjoyed. Loyalty to the evident purpose of the Act would require regulation of activities not distinguishable in any significant respect from those regulated by the Act, unless the wording or policy of the Act shows that they should be prohibited.

(3) Is the embryo created by CNR different in kind or dimension from that for which the Act was passed? Plainly not: as already pointed out, the organisms in question are, as organisms, very similar.

While it is impermissible to ask what Parliament would have done if the facts had been before it, there is one important question which may permissibly be asked: it is whether Parliament, faced with the taxing task of enacting a legislative solution to the difficult religious, moral and scientific issues mentioned above, could rationally have intended to leave live human embryos created by CNR outside the scope of regulation had it known of them as a scientific possibility. There is only one possible answer to this question and it is negative. . . .

19 For these reasons I would dismiss the appeal with costs.

Lord Steyn

Purposive interpretation

21 . . . The pendulum has swung towards purposive methods of construction. This change was not initiated by the teleological approach of European Community jurisprudence, and the influence of European legal culture generally, but it has been accelerated by European ideas: see, however, a classic early statement of the purposive approach by Lord Blackburn in **River Wear Commissioners** *v* **Adamson** (1877) 2 App Cas 743, 763. In any event, nowadays the shift towards purposive interpretation is not in doubt. The qualification is that the degree of liberality permitted is influenced by the context, e.g. social welfare legislation and tax statutes may have to be approached somewhat differently. For these slightly different reasons I agree with the conclusion of the Court of Appeal that section 1(1) of the 1990 Act must be construed in a purposive way.

The House of Lords' judgment of **Regina** *v* **Secretary of State for Health** *ex parte* **Quintavalle (on behalf of Pro-Life Alliance)** (2003) is available on Parliament's website at:
www.publications.parliament.uk/pa/ld200203/ldjudgmt/jd030313/ quinta-1.htm

The limits of the purposive approach

In a more recent case involving the interpretation of the Human Fertilisation and Embryology Act 1990 the House of Lords refused to take a purposive approach to interpreting the statute. In **Quintavalle** *v* **Human Fertilisation and Embryology Authority** (2005) the case concerned an application to the Human Fertilisation and Embryology Authority (HFEA) for permission to carry out tests on an embryo to determine whether, if the embryo grew to be a child, that child would be able to provide human blood or tissue that would enable its brother to survive a rare genetic disorder. Schedule 2 provides:

(1) A licence under this paragraph may authorise any of the following in the course of providing treatment services—

. . .

(d) practices designed to secure that embryos are in a suitable condition to be placed in a woman or to determine whether embryos are suitable for that purpose.

The critical question was whether tissue testing is a practice designed to determine whether an embryo is 'suitable' for placing in a woman which is permissible under Schedule 2 of the Act. In interpreting the word 'suitable' the House of Lords refused in this context to apply a purposive interpretation but concluded that HFEA did have the power to issue the licence.

Quintavalle *v* Human Fertilisation and Embryology Authority (2005), House of Lords

Lord Hoffmann

32 Lord Wilberforce's remarks [in **Royal College of Nursing of the United Kingdom** *v* **Department of Health and Social Security** (1981)] provided valuable assistance to the House in **R (Quintavalle)** *v* **Secretary of State for Health** [2003] 2 AC 687. . . . The House followed Lord Wilberforce's guidance in holding that there was a 'clear purpose in the legislation' which could 'only be fulfilled if the extension [was] made'.

33 But, like all guidance on construction, Lord Wilberforce's remarks are more appropriate to some cases than others. This is not a case in which one starts with the presumption that Parliament's intention was directed to the state of affairs existing at the time of the Act. It obviously intended to regulate research and treatment which were not possible at the time. Nor is it a case, like the first **Quintavalle** case, in which the statutory language needs to be extended beyond the 'expressed meaning'. The word 'suitable' is an empty vessel which is filled with meaning by context and background. Nor is it helpful in this case to ask whether some new state of affairs falls within 'the same genus' as those to which the expressed policy has been formulated. That would beg the question because the dispute is precisely over what the genus is. If 'suitability' has the meaning for which the authority contends, then plainly PGD and HLA typing fall within it. If not, then not. Finally, Lord Wilberforce's recommendation of caution in the construction of statutes concerning controversial subjects 'involving moral and social judgments on which opinions strongly differ' would be very much to the point if everything which the Act did not forbid was permitted. It has much less force when the question is whether or not the authority has power to authorise it.

Lord Brown

43 The ethical questions raised by such a process are, it need hardly be stated, profound. Should genetic testing be used to enable a choice to be made between a number of healthy embryos, a choice based on the selection of certain preferred genetic characteristics? Is it acceptable to follow a procedure resulting in the birth of a child designed to secure the health of a sibling and necessarily therefore intended to donate tissue (including perhaps bone marrow) to that sibling? Is this straying into the field of 'designer babies' or, as the celebrated geneticist, Lord Winston, has put it, 'treating the offspring to be born as a commodity?' These are just some of the questions prompted by this litigation. But troubling though such questions are, the arguments are certainly not all one way, as may be demonstrated by the facts of this very case.

 The House of Lords' judgment **Quintavalle v Human Fertilisation and Embryology Authority** (2005) is available on Parliament's website at: **www.publications.parliament.uk/pa/ld200405/ldjudgmt/jd050428/quint-1.htm**

Reference to *Hansard*

While Parliament passes legislation, the courts have to interpret the legislation when applying it to particular cases. Sometimes the courts can have difficulty in determining what Parliament intended provisions of the legislation to mean. In the past the courts refused to look at Parliamentary debates published in *Hansard* in order to determine this intention. The House of Lords changed this position in the important case of **Pepper v Hart** [1993], ruling that in limited circumstances the courts could refer to *Hansard*. The case concerned the interpretation of the Finance Act 1976 in order to calculate how much tax some teachers were required to pay.

Pepper v Hart [1993], House of Lords

Lord Browne-Wilkinson

The case was originally argued before your Lordships without reference to any Parliamentary proceedings. After the conclusion of the first hearing, it came to your Lordships' attention that an examination of the proceedings in Parliament in 1976 which lead to the enactment of sections 61 and 63 might give a clear indication which of the two rival contentions represented the intention of Parliament in using the statutory words. Your Lordships then invited the parties to consider whether they wished to present further argument on the question whether it was appropriate for the House (under Practice Statement (Judicial Precedent) (1966)) to depart from previous authority of this House which forbids reference to such material in construing statutory provisions and, if so, what guidance such material provided in deciding the present appeal. The taxpayers indicated that they wished to present further argument on these points. The case was listed for rehearing before a committee of seven members not all of whom sat on the original committee . . .

My Lords, I have come to the conclusion that, as a matter of law, there are sound reasons for making a limited modification to the existing rule (subject to strict safeguards) unless there are constitutional or practical reasons which outweigh them. In my judgment, subject to the questions of the privileges of the House of Commons, reference to Parliamentary material should be permitted as an aid to the construction of legislation which is ambiguous or obscure or the literal meaning of which leads to an absurdity. Even in such cases references in court to Parliamentary material should only be permitted where such material clearly discloses the mischief aimed at or the legislative intention lying behind the ambiguous or obscure words. In the case of statements made in Parliament, as at present advised I cannot foresee that any statement other than the statement of the Minister or other promoter of the Bill is likely to meet these criteria. I accept Mr Lester's submissions, but my main reason for reaching this conclusion is based on principle. Statute law consists of the words that Parliament has enacted. It is for the courts to construe those words and it is the court's duty in so doing to give effect to the intention of Parliament in using those words. It is an inescapable fact that, despite all the care taken in passing legislation, some statutory provisions when applied to the circumstances under consideration in any specific case are found to be ambiguous. One of the reasons for such ambiguity is that the members of the legislature in enacting the statutory provision may have been told what result those words are intended to achieve. Faced with a given set of words which are capable of conveying that meaning it is not surprising if the words are accepted as having that meaning. Parliament never intends to enact an ambiguity. Contrast with that the position of the courts. The courts are faced simply with a set of words which are in fact capable of bearing two meanings. The courts are ignorant of the underlying Parliamentary purpose. Unless some thing in other parts of the legislation discloses such purpose, the courts are forced to adopt one of the two possible meanings using highly technical rules of construction. In many, I suspect most, cases references to Parliamentary materials will not throw any light on the matter. But in a few cases it may emerge that the very question was considered by Parliament in passing the legislation. Why in such a case should the courts blind themselves to a clear indication of what Parliament intended in using those words? The court cannot attach a meaning to words which they cannot bear, but if the words are capable of bearing more than one meaning why should not Parliament's true intention be enforced rather than thwarted?

Restrictions on referring to *Hansard*

In **Wilson** v **Secretary of State for Trade and Industry** [2004] the House of Lords imposed restrictions on when the courts could refer to *Hansard*. Only statements made by a Minister or other promoter of legislation could be looked at by the court, other statements recorded in *Hansard* had to be ignored. In that case a lawyer, Mr Sumption, was appointed to put forward the concerns that Parliament had if *Hansard* was too readily relied upon, as this could actually serve to subvert the will of Parliament as expressed in the legislation passed.

Wilson *v* First County Trust Ltd (No. 2) (2004), House of Lords

Lord Hope

114 The concern which [Mr Sumption] expressed was directed to the use of *Hansard* in this case for the purpose of seeking to discover from debates in Parliament the reasons which Parliament had for making the enactment. He said that this was quite different from seeking to discover what words mean. It was one thing to refer to *Hansard* to ensure that legislation was not misconstrued in favour of the executive. That use could be said to be in support of the principle of Parliamentary sovereignty. It was another to refer to it in order to form a view as to whether Parliament had given sufficient reasons for doing what it did and, if not, whether the legislation was incompatible with Convention rights. To use *Hansard* in this way was to use it for a purpose which was adverse to the intention of Parliament.

115 Mr Sumption put forward two objections to this use of *Hansard* on grounds of principle. The first was that it involved examining the nature and quality of Parliament's reasoning in a case where there was no doubt about what Parliament had enacted. Where it was used for the purpose explained in **Pepper** v **Hart** there was a threshold that had to be satisfied – the test of ambiguity. Here there was no such threshold, as the suggestion was that *Hansard* could be resorted to however clear were the provisions set out in the enactment. The second was that its object was not to give effect to the will of Parliament but to measure the sufficiency of reasons given for the legislation against standards derived from the Convention. He said that this was contrary to Article 9 of the Bill of Rights. It was not for the courts to consider whether speeches made during debates in Parliament had put forward Convention-compliant reasons for supporting it.

116 I think that there is much force in these criticisms of the approach which the Court of Appeal took to this issue. But it would be going too far to say, as Mr Sumption did, that there are no circumstances where use may be made of *Hansard* where the purpose of doing so is to answer the question whether legislation is compatible with Convention rights. The boundaries between the respective powers and functions of the courts and of Parliament must, of course, be respected. It is no part of the court's function to determine whether sufficient reasons were given by Parliament for passing the enactment. On the other hand, it has to perform the tasks which have been given to it by Parliament. Among those tasks is that to which section 4(1) refers. It has the task of determining, if the issue is raised, whether a provision of primary legislation is compatible with a Convention right. It does not follow from recognition that there is an area of judgment within which the judiciary will defer to the elected body on democratic grounds that the court is absolutely disabled from forming its own view in these cases as to whether or not the legislation is compatible. That question is ultimately for the court not for Parliament, as Parliament itself has enacted. The harder that question is to answer, the more important it is that the court is equipped with the information that it needs to perform its task.

117 This, then, is the justification for resorting to *Hansard* in cases where the question at issue is not one of interpretation but whether the legislation is compatible. A cautious approach is needed, and particular care must be taken not to stray beyond the search for material that will simply inform the court into the forbidden territory of questioning the proceedings in Parliament. To suggest, as the Court of Appeal did [2002] QB 74, 94, para 36, that what was said in debate tends to confuse rather than illuminate would be to cross that boundary. It is for Parliament alone to decide what reasons, if any, need to be given for the legislation that it enacts. The quality or sufficiency of reasons given by the promoter of the legislation is a matter for Parliament to determine, not the court.

118 But proceedings in Parliament are replete with information from a whole variety of sources. It appears in a variety of forms also, all of which are made public. Ministers make statements, members ask questions or propose amendments based on information which they have obtained from their constituencies, answers are given to written questions, issues are explored by select committees by examining witnesses and explanatory notes are provided with Bills to assist members in their consideration of it. Resort to information of this kind may cast light on what Parliament's aim was when it passed the provision which is in question or it may not. If it does not this cannot, and must not, be a ground for criticism. But if it does, the court would be unduly inhibited if it were to be disabled from obtaining and using this information for the strictly limited purpose of considering whether legislation is compatible with Convention rights. This is an exercise which the European Court may wish to perform in order to determine, for example, whether the aim of the contested legislation was a legitimate one or whether an interference with the peaceful enjoyment of possession was justified . . . It is an exercise which the domestic court too may perform when it is carrying out the task under section 4(1) of the 1998 Act which has been entrusted to it by Parliament.

 The House of Lords' judgment **Wilson v Secretary of State for Trade and Industry** [2004] is available on Parliament's website at: **www.publications.parliament.uk/pa/ld200203/ldjudgmt/jd030710/will-1.htm**

Human Rights Act 1998 and statutory interpretation

The House of Lords has had to consider the impact of section 3 of the Human Rights Act 1998 when interpreting statutes. Section 3 provides that: 'So far as it is possible to do so, primary and subordinate legislation must be read and given effect in a way which is compatible with the Convention rights.' The case of **Attorney-General's Reference No. 4 of 2002; Sheldrake v DPP** (2004) involved two separate appeals which were considered together because they raised the same legal issue. They were concerned with whether the imposition of a legal burden on a defendant to prove that they had not committed an offence breached the presumption of innocence protected in Article 6 of the European Convention. The House of Lords concluded that the relevant legislation did not breach the European Convention and in reaching this conclusion it considered its role in interpreting statutes following the Human Rights Act 1998.

Attorney-General's Reference No. 4 of 2002; Sheldrake v DPP (2004), House of Lords

Lord Bingham

My Lords,

1 Sections 5(2) of the Road Traffic Act 1988 and 11(2) of the Terrorism Act 2000, conventionally interpreted, impose a legal or persuasive burden on a defendant in criminal proceedings to prove the matters respectively specified in those subsections if he is to be exonerated from liability on the grounds there provided. That means that he must, to be exonerated, establish those matters on the balance of probabilities. If he fails to discharge that burden he will be convicted. In this appeal by the Director of Public Prosecutions and this reference by the Attorney-General these reverse burdens ('reverse' because the burden is placed on the defendant and not, as ordinarily in criminal proceedings, on the prosecutor) are challenged as incompatible with the presumption of innocence guaranteed by Article 6(2) of the European Convention for the Protection of Human Rights and Fundamental Freedoms (1953) (Cmd 8969). Thus the first question for consideration in each case is whether the provision in question does, unjustifiably, infringe the presumption of innocence. If it does the further question arises whether the provision can and should be read down in accordance with the courts' interpretative obligation under section 3 of the Human Rights Act 1998 so as to impose an evidential and not a legal burden on the defendant. An evidential burden is not a burden of proof. It is a burden of raising, on the evidence in the case, an issue as to the matter in question fit for consideration by the tribunal of fact. If an issue is properly raised, it is for the prosecutor to prove, beyond reasonable doubt, that that ground of exoneration does not avail the defendant.

. . .

7 Until the coming into force of the Human Rights Act 1998, the issue now before the House could scarcely have arisen. The two statutory provisions which it is necessary to consider are not obscure or ambiguous. They afford the defendant (Mr Sheldrake) and

the acquitted person a ground of exoneration, but in each case the provision, interpreted in accordance with the canons of construction ordinarily applied in the courts, would (as already noted) be understood to impose on the defendant a legal burden to establish that ground of exoneration on the balance of probabilities. Until October 2000 the courts would have been bound to interpret the provisions conventionally. Even if minded to do so, they could not have struck down or amended the provisions as repugnant to any statutory or common law rule. Domestic law would have required effect to be given to them according to their accepted meaning. Thus the crucial question is whether the European Convention and the Strasbourg jurisprudence interpreting it have modified in any relevant respect our domestic regime and, if so, to what extent.

The Convention and the Strasbourg jurisprudence

8 Article 6 of the Convention provides, so far as relevant:

> 1. In the determination of his civil rights and obligations or of any criminal charge against him, everyone is entitled to a fair and public hearing within a reasonable time by an independent and impartial tribunal established by law . . .
> 2. Everyone charged with a criminal offence shall be presumed innocent until proved guilty according to law.

9 The right to a fair trial has long been recognised in England and Wales, although the conditions necessary to achieve fairness have evolved, in some ways quite radically, over the years, and continue to evolve. The presumption of innocence has also been recognised since at latest the early 19th century, although (as shown by the preceding account of our domestic law) the presumption has not been uniformly treated by Parliament as absolute and unqualified. There can be no doubt that the underlying rationale of the presumption in domestic law and in the Convention is an essentially simple one: that it is repugnant to ordinary notions of fairness for a prosecutor to accuse a defendant of crime and for the defendant to be then required to disprove the accusation on pain of conviction and punishment if he fails to do so. The closer a legislative provision approaches to that situation, the more objectionable it is likely to be. To ascertain the scope of the presumption under the Convention, domestic courts must have regard to the Strasbourg case law. It has there been repeatedly recognised that the presumption of innocence is one of the elements of the fair criminal trial required by Article 6(1): see, for example, **Bernard** v **France** (2000) 30 EHRR 808, para 37.

. . .

21 From this body of authority certain principles may be derived. The overriding concern is that a trial should be fair, and the presumption of innocence is a fundamental right directed to that end. The Convention does not outlaw presumptions of fact or law but requires that these should be kept within reasonable limits and should not be arbitrary. It is open to states to define the constituent elements of a criminal offence, excluding the requirement of mens rea. But the substance and effect of any presumption adverse to a defendant must be examined, and must be reasonable. Relevant to any judgment on reasonableness or proportionality will be the opportunity given to the defendant to rebut the presumption, maintenance of the rights of the defence, flexibility in application of the presumption, retention by the court of a power to assess the evidence, the importance of what is at stake and the difficulty which a prosecutor may face in the absence of a presumption. Security concerns do not absolve member states from their duty to observe basic

standards of fairness. The justifiability of any infringement of the presumption of innocence cannot be resolved by any rule of thumb, but on examination of all the facts and circumstances of the particular provision as applied in the particular case.

. . .

The House of Lord's judgment **Attorney-General's Reference No. 4 of 2002;**
Sheldrake v DPP (2004) is available on Parliament's website at:
www.publications.parliament.uk/pa/ld200304/ldjudgmt/jd041014/gen4-1.htm

Statutory interpretation and the Human Rights Act: further analysis

The case of **Ghaidan v Godin-Mendoza** (2004) was concerned with the interpretation of the Rent Act 1977 following the Human Rights Act 1998. The Rent Act 1977 creates protected tenancies which give tenants very favourable rights, including in practice low rents. Under the legislation the protected tenancy passes on the death of the protected tenant to the surviving spouse living in the house or the person living with the protected tenant 'as his or her wife or husband'. Before the Human Rights Act 1998 was passed this was interpreted by the House of Lords as not including homosexual relationships. In the **Ghaidan** appeal, it was successfully argued that the 1977 Act had to be interpreted, following the Human Rights Act 1998, in a way that did not discriminate against homosexuals.

Ghaidan v Godin-Mendoza (2004), House of Lords

Lord Nicholls of Birkenhead

4 I must first set out the relevant statutory provisions and then explain how the Human Rights Act 1998 comes to be relevant in this case. Paragraphs 2 and 3 of Schedule 1 to the Rent Act 1977 provide:

2(1) The surviving spouse (if any) of the original tenant, if residing in the dwelling-house immediately before the death of the original tenant, shall after the death be the statutory tenant if and so long as he or she occupies the dwelling-house as his or her residence.

(2) For the purposes of this paragraph, a person who was living with the original tenant as his or her wife or husband shall be treated as the spouse of the original tenant.

3(1) Where paragraph 2 above does not apply, but a person who was a member of the original tenant's family was residing with him in the dwelling-house at the time of and for the period of 2 years immediately before his death then, after his death, that person or if there is more than one such person such one of them as may be decided by agreement, or in default of agreement by the county court, shall be entitled to an assured tenancy of the dwelling-house by succession.

5 On an ordinary reading of this language paragraph 2(2) draws a distinction between the position of a heterosexual couple living together in a house as husband and wife and a homosexual couple living together in a house. The survivor of a heterosexual couple may become a statutory tenant by succession, the survivor of a homosexual couple cannot. That was decided in **Fitzpatrick**'s case. The survivor of a homosexual couple may, in competition with other members of the original tenant's 'family', become entitled to an assured tenancy under paragraph 3. But even if he does, as in the present case, this is less advantageous. Notably, so far as the present case is concerned, the rent payable under an assured tenancy is the contractual or market rent, which may be more than the fair rent payable under a statutory tenancy, and an assured tenant may be evicted for non-payment of rent without the court needing to be satisfied, as is essential in the case of a statutory tenancy, that it is reasonable to make a possession order. In these and some other respects the succession rights granted by the statute to the survivor of a homosexual couple in respect of the house where he or she is living are less favourable than the succession rights granted to the survivor of a heterosexual couple.

6 Mr Godin-Mendoza's claim is that this difference in treatment infringes Article 14 of the European Convention on Human Rights read in conjunction with Article 8. Article 8 does not require the state to provide security of tenure for members of a deceased tenant's family. Article 8 does not in terms give a right to be provided with a home: **Chapman** v **United Kingdom** (2001) 33 EHRR 18, 427, para 99. It does not 'guarantee the right to have one's housing problem solved by the authorities': **Marzari** v **Italy** (1999) 28 EHRR CD 175, 179. But if the state makes legislative provision it must not be discriminatory. The provision must not draw a distinction on grounds such as sex or sexual orientation without good reason. Unless justified, a distinction founded on such grounds infringes the Convention right embodied in Article 14, as read with Article 8. Mr Godin-Mendoza submits that the distinction drawn by paragraph 2 of Schedule 1 to the Rent Act 1977 is drawn on the grounds of sexual orientation and that this difference in treatment lacks justification.

7 That is the first step in Mr Godin-Mendoza's claim. That step would not, of itself, improve Mr Godin-Mendoza's status in his flat. The second step in his claim is to pray in aid the court's duty under section 3 of the Human Rights Act 1998 to read and give effect to legislation in a way which is compliant with the Convention rights. Here, it is said, section 3 requires the court to read paragraph 2 so that it embraces couples living together in a close and stable homosexual relationship as much as couples living together in a close and stable heterosexual relationship. So read, paragraph 2 covers Mr Godin-Mendoza's position. Hence he is entitled to a declaration that on the death of Mr Wallwyn-James he succeeded to a statutory tenancy.

. . .

Section 3 of the Human Rights Act 1998

25 I turn next to the question whether section 3 of the Human Rights Act 1998 requires the court to depart from the interpretation of paragraph 2 enunciated in **Fitzpatrick's** case.

26 Section 3 is a key section in the Human Rights Act 1998. It is one of the primary means by which Convention rights are brought into the law of this country. Parliament has decreed that all legislation, existing and future, shall be interpreted in a particular way. All legislation must be read and given effect to in a way which is compatible with the Convention rights 'so far as it is possible to do so'. This is the intention of Parliament, expressed in section 3, and the courts must give effect to this intention.

27 Unfortunately, in making this provision for the interpretation of legislation, section 3 itself is not free from ambiguity. Section 3 is open to more than one interpretation. The

difficulty lies in the word 'possible'. Section 3(1), read in conjunction with section 3(2) and section 4, makes one matter clear: Parliament expressly envisaged that not all legislation would be capable of being made Convention-compliant by application of section 3. Sometimes it would be possible, sometimes not. What is not clear is the test to be applied in separating the sheep from the goats. What is the standard, or the criterion, by which 'possibility' is to be judged? A comprehensive answer to this question is proving elusive. The courts, including your Lordships' House, are still cautiously feeling their way forward as experience in the application of section 3 gradually accumulates.

28 One tenable interpretation of the word 'possible' would be that section 3 is confined to requiring courts to resolve ambiguities. Where the words under consideration fairly admit of more than one meaning the Convention-compliant meaning is to prevail. Words should be given the meaning which best accords with the Convention rights.

29 This interpretation of section 3 would give the section a comparatively narrow scope. This is not the view which has prevailed. It is now generally accepted that the application of section 3 does not depend upon the presence of ambiguity in the legislation being interpreted. Even if, construed according to the ordinary principles of interpretation, the meaning of the legislation admits of no doubt, section 3 may nonetheless require the legislation to be given a different meaning. The decision of your Lordships' House in **R v A (Complainant's Sexual History)** [2002] 1 AC 45 is an instance of this. The House read words into section 41 of the Youth Justice and Criminal Evidence Act 1999 so as to make that section compliant with an accused's right to a fair trial under Article 6. The House did so even though the statutory language was not ambiguous.

30 From this it follows that the interpretative obligation decreed by section 3 is of an unusual and far-reaching character. Section 3 may require a court to depart from the unambiguous meaning the legislation would otherwise bear. In the ordinary course the interpretation of legislation involves seeking the intention reasonably to be attributed to Parliament in using the language in question. Section 3 may require the court to depart from this legislative intention, that is, depart from the intention of the Parliament which enacted the legislation. The question of difficulty is how far, and in what circumstances, section 3 requires a court to depart from the intention of the enacting Parliament. The answer to this question depends upon the intention reasonably to be attributed to Parliament in enacting section 3.

31 On this the first point to be considered is how far, when enacting section 3, Parliament intended that the actual language of a statute, as distinct from the concept expressed in that language, should be determinative. Since section 3 relates to the 'interpretation' of legislation, it is natural to focus attention initially on the language used in the legislative provision being considered. But once it is accepted that section 3 may require legislation to bear a meaning which departs from the unambiguous meaning the legislation would otherwise bear, it becomes impossible to suppose Parliament intended that the operation of section 3 should depend critically upon the particular form of words adopted by the parliamentary draftsman in the statutory provision under consideration. That would make the application of section 3 something of a semantic lottery. If the draftsman chose to express the concept being enacted in one form of words, section 3 would be available to achieve Convention-compliance. If he chose a different form of words, section 3 would be impotent.

32 From this the conclusion which seems inescapable is that the mere fact the language under consideration is inconsistent with a Convention-compliant meaning does not of itself make a Convention-compliant interpretation under section 3 impossible. Section 3 enables language to be interpreted restrictively or expansively. But section 3 goes further than this. It is also apt to require a court to read in words which change the meaning of the enacted legislation, so as to make it Convention-compliant. In other words, the intention of Parliament in enacting section 3 was that, to an extent bounded only by what is 'possible', a court can modify the meaning, and hence the effect, of primary and secondary legislation.

33 Parliament, however, cannot have intended that in the discharge of this extended interpretative function the courts should adopt a meaning inconsistent with a fundamental feature of legislation. That would be to cross the constitutional boundary section 3 seeks to demarcate and preserve. Parliament has retained the right to enact legislation in terms which are not Convention-compliant. The meaning imported by application of section 3 must be compatible with the underlying thrust of the legislation being construed. Words implied must, in the phrase of my noble and learned friend Lord Rodger of Earlsferry, 'go with the grain of the legislation'. Nor can Parliament have intended that section 3 should require courts to make decisions for which they are not equipped. There may be several ways of making a provision Convention-compliant, and the choice may involve issues calling for legislative deliberation.

34 Both these features were present in **S (Children) (Care Order: Implementation of Care Plan) Re** [2002] 2 AC 291. There the proposed 'starring system' was inconsistent in an important respect with the scheme of the Children Act 1989, and the proposed system had far-reaching practical ramifications for local authorities. Again, in **R (Anderson) v Secretary of State for the Home Department** [2003] 1 AC 837 section 29 of the Crime (Sentences) Act 1997 could not be read in a Convention-compliant way without giving the section a meaning inconsistent with an important feature expressed clearly in the legislation. In **Bellinger v Bellinger** [2003] 2 AC 467 recognition of Mrs Bellinger as female for the purposes of section 11(c) of the Matrimonial Causes Act 1973 would have had exceedingly wide ramifications, raising issues ill-suited for determination by the courts or court procedures.

35 In some cases difficult problems may arise. No difficulty arises in the present case. Paragraph 2 of Schedule 1 to the Rent Act 1977 is unambiguous. But the social policy underlying the 1988 extension of security of tenure under paragraph 2 to the survivor of couples living together as husband and wife is equally applicable to the survivor of homosexual couples living together in a close and stable relationship. In this circumstance I see no reason to doubt that application of section 3 to paragraph 2 has the effect that paragraph 2 should be read and given effect to as though the survivor of such a homosexual couple were the surviving spouse of the original tenant. Reading paragraph 2 in this way would have the result that cohabiting heterosexual couples and cohabiting heterosexual couples would be treated alike for the purposes of succession as a statutory tenant. This would eliminate the discriminatory effect of paragraph 2 and would do so consistently with the social policy underlying paragraph 2. The precise form of words read in for this purpose is of no significance. It is their substantive effect which matters.

36 For these reasons I agree with the decision of the Court of Appeal. I would dismiss this appeal.

Lord Steyn

My Lords,

38 I confine my remarks to the question whether it is possible under section 3(1) of the Human Rights Act 1998 to read and give effect to paragraph 2(2) of Schedule 1 to the Rent Act 1977 in a way which is compatible with the European Convention on Human Rights. In my view the interpretation adopted by the Court of Appeal under section 3(1) was a classic illustration of the permissible use of this provision. But it became clear during oral argument, and from a subsequent study of the case law and academic discussion on the correct interpretation of section 3(1), that the role of that provision in the remedial scheme of the 1998 Act is not always correctly understood. I would therefore wish to examine the position in a general way.

39 I attach an appendix to this opinion which lists cases where a breach of an ECHR right was found established, and the courts proceeded to consider whether to exercise their interpretative power under section 3 or to make a declaration of incompatibility under section 4. For the first and second lists (A and B) I am indebted to the Constitutional Law Division of the Department of Constitutional Affairs but law report references and other information have been added. The third list (C) has been prepared by Laura Johnson, my judicial assistant, under my direction. It will be noted that in 10 cases the courts used their interpretative power under section 3 and in 15 cases the courts made declarations of incompatibility under section 4. In five cases in the second group the declarations of incompatibility were subsequently reversed on appeal: in four of those cases it was held that no breach was established and in the fifth case (**Hooper**) the exact basis for overturning the declaration of incompatibility may be a matter of debate. Given that under the 1998 Act the use of the interpretative power under section 3 is the principal remedial measure, and that the making of a declaration of incompatibility is a measure of last resort, these statistics by themselves raise a question about the proper implementation of the 1998 Act. A study of the case law reinforces the need to pose the question whether the law has taken a wrong turning.

40 My impression is that two factors are contributing to a misunderstanding of the remedial scheme of the 1998 Act. First, there is the constant refrain that a judicial reading down, or reading in, under section 3 would flout the will of Parliament as expressed in the statute under examination. This question cannot sensibly be considered without giving full weight to the countervailing will of Parliament as expressed in the 1998 Act.

41 The second factor may be an excessive concentration on linguistic features of the particular statute. Nowhere in our legal system is a literalistic approach more inappropriate than when considering whether a breach of a Convention right may be removed by interpretation under section 3. Section 3 requires a broad approach concentrating, amongst other things, in a purposive way on the importance of the fundamental right involved.

42 In enacting the 1998 Act Parliament legislated 'to bring rights home' from the European Court of Human Rights to be determined in the courts of the United Kingdom. That is what the White Paper said: see Rights Brought Home: The Human Rights Bill (1997) (cm 3782), para 2.7. That is what Parliament was told. The mischief to be addressed was the fact that Convention rights as set out in the ECHR, which Britain ratified in 1951, could not be vindicated in our courts. Critical to this purpose was the enactment of effective remedial provisions.

43 The provisions adopted read as follows:

3. Interpretation of legislation

(1) So far as it is possible to do so, primary legislation and subordinate legislation must be read and given effect in a way which is compatible with the Convention rights.

(2) This section—
(a) applies to primary legislation and subordinate legislation whenever enacted;
(b) does not affect the validity, continuing operation or enforcement of any incompatible primary legislation; and
(c) does not affect the validity, continuing operation or enforcement of any incompatible subordinate legislation if (disregarding any possibility of revocation) primary legislation prevents removal of the incompatibility.

4. Declaration of incompatibility

(1) Subsection (2) applies in any proceedings in which a court determines whether a provision of primary legislation is compatible with a Convention right.

(2) If the court is satisfied that the provision is incompatible with a Convention right, it may make a declaration of that incompatibility.

(3)–(6).

If Parliament disagrees with an interpretation by the courts under section 3(1), it is free to override it by amending the legislation and expressly reinstating the incompatibility.

44 It is necessary to state what section 3(1), and in particular the word 'possible', does not mean. First, section 3(1) applies even if there is no ambiguity in the language in the sense of it being capable of bearing two *possible* meanings. The word 'possible' in section 3(1) is used in a different and much stronger sense. Secondly, section 3(1) imposes a stronger and more radical obligation than to adopt a purposive interpretation in the light of the ECHR. Thirdly, the draftsman of the Act had before him the model of the New Zealand Bill of Rights Act which imposes a requirement that the interpretation to be adopted must be reasonable. Parliament specifically rejected the legislative model of requiring a reasonable interpretation.

45 Instead the draftsman had resort to the analogy of the obligation under the EEC Treaty on national courts, as far as possible, to interpret national legislation in the light of the wording and purpose of directives. In **Marleasing SA *v* La Comercial Internacional de Alimentación SA** (Case C-106/89) [1990] ECR I-4135, 4159 the European Court of Justice defined this obligation as follows:

It follows that, in applying national law, whether the provisions in questions were adopted before or after the directive, the national court called upon to interpret it is required to do so, as far as possible, in light of the wording and the purpose of the directive in order to achieve the result pursued by the latter and thereby comply with the third paragraph of Article 189 of the Treaty.

Given the undoubted strength of this interpretative obligation under EEC law, this is a significant signpost to the meaning of section 3(1) in the 1998 Act.

46 Parliament had before it the mischief and objective sought to be addressed, viz the need 'to bring rights home'. The linch-pin of the legislative scheme to achieve this purpose was section 3(1). Rights could only be effectively brought home if section 3(1) was the prime remedial measure, and section 4 a measure of last resort. How the system modelled on the

4

Delegated legislation

Introduction

This chapter looks at:

- a case study on delegated legislation; and
- the impact of the Legislative and Regulatory Reform Act 2006 on the power to make delegated legislation.

EEC interpretative obligation would work was graphically illustrated for Parliament during the progress of the Bill through both Houses. The Lord Chancellor observed that 'in 99% of the cases that will arise, there will be no need for judicial declarations of incompatibility' and the Home Secretary said 'We expect that, in almost all cases, the courts will be able to interpret the legislation compatibly with the Convention': *Hansard* (HL Debates,) 5 February 1998, col 840 (3rd reading) and *Hansard* (HC Debates,) 16 February 1998, col 778 (2nd reading). It was envisaged that the duty of the court would be to strive to find (if possible) a meaning which would best accord with Convention rights. This is the remedial scheme which Parliament adopted.

. . .

49 A study of the case law listed in the Appendix to this judgment reveals that there has sometimes been a tendency to approach the interpretative task under section 3(1) in too literal and technical a way. In practice there has been too much emphasis on linguistic features. If the core remedial purpose of section 3(1) is not to be undermined a broader approach is required. That is, of course, not to gainsay the obvious proposition that inherent in the use of the word 'possible' in section 3(1) is the idea that there is a Rubicon which courts may not cross. If it is not possible, within the meaning of section 3, to read or give effect to legislation in a way which is compatible with Convention rights, the only alternative is to exercise, where appropriate, the power to make a declaration of incompatibility. Usually, such cases should not be too difficult to identify. An obvious example is **R (Anderson) *v* Secretary of State for the Home Department** [2003] 1 AC 837. The House held that the Home Secretary was not competent under Article 6 of the ECHR to decide on the tariff to be served by mandatory life sentence prisoners. The House found a section 3(1) interpretation not 'possible' and made a declaration under section 4. Interpretation could not provide a substitute scheme. **Bellinger** is another obvious example. As Lord Rodger of Earlsferry observed '. . . in relation to the validity of marriage, Parliament regards gender as fixed and immutable': [2003] 2 WLR 1174, 1195, para 83. Section 3(1) of the 1998 Act could not be used.

50 Having had the opportunity to reconsider the matter in some depth, I am not disposed to try to formulate precise rules about where section 3 may not be used. Like the proverbial elephant such a case ought generally to be easily identifiable. What is necessary, however, is to emphasise that interpretation under section 3(1) is the prime remedial remedy and that resort to section 4 must always be an exceptional course. In practical effect there is a strong rebuttable presumption in favour of an interpretation consistent with Convention rights. Perhaps the opinions delivered in the House today will serve to ensure a balanced approach along such lines.

The House of Lords' judgment of **Ghaidan *v* Godin-Mendoza** (2004) is available on parliament's website at:
www.publications.parliament.uk/pa/ld200304/ldjudgmt/jd040621/gha-1.htm

Case study of delegated legislation

A considerable amount of delegated legislation is made as a result of section 2(2) of the European Communities Act 1972. This section provides that provisions in European legislation can be introduced into domestic law through delegated legislation. One example of such legislation is the Asylum Seekers (Reception Conditions) Regulations 2005.

European Communities Act 1972

2. . . . (2) Subject to Schedule 2 to this Act, at any time after its passing Her Majesty may by Order in Council, and any designated Minister or department may by regulations, make provision—

(a) for the purpose of implementing any Community obligation of the United Kingdom, or enabling any such obligation to be implemented, or of enabling any rights enjoyed or to be enjoyed by the United Kingdom under or by virtue of the Treaties to be exercised; or

(b) for the purpose of dealing with matters arising out of or related to any such obligation or rights or the coming into force, or the operation from time to time, of subsection (1) above;

 The European Communities Act 1972 is published at:
www.opsi.gov.uk/acts/acts1972/19720068.htm

Statutory Instrument 2005 No. 7

IMMIGRATION
The Asylum Seekers (Reception Conditions) Regulations 2005

Made	*10th January 2005*
Laid before Parliament	*14th January 2005*
Coming into force	*5th February 2005*

The Secretary of State, being a Minister designated for the purposes of section 2(2) of the European Communities Act 1972 in relation to measures relating to immigration, asylum, refugees and displaced persons, in exercise of the powers conferred upon him by that section, hereby makes the following Regulations:

Citation and commencement

1.—(1) These Regulations may be cited as the Asylum Seekers (Reception Conditions) Regulations 2005 and shall come into force on 5th February 2005.

(2) These Regulations shall only apply to a person whose claim for asylum is recorded on or after 5th February 2005.

→

Interpretation

2.—(1) In these Regulations—

(a) 'the 1999 Act' means the Immigration and Asylum Act 1999;

(b) 'asylum seeker' means a person who is at least 18 years old who has made a claim for asylum which has been recorded by the Secretary of State but not yet determined;

. . .

(2) For the purposes of these Regulations—

(a) a claim is determined on the date on which the Secretary of State notifies the asylum seeker of his decision on his claim or, if the asylum seeker appeals against the Secretary of State's decision, the date on which that appeal is disposed of; and

(b) an appeal is disposed of when it is no longer pending for the purposes of the Immigration Acts.

Families

3.—(1) When the Secretary of State is providing or arranging for the provision of accommodation for an asylum seeker and his family members under section 95 or 98 of the 1999 Act, he shall have regard to family unity and ensure, in so far as it is reasonably practicable to do so, that family members are accommodated together.

(2) Paragraph (1) shall only apply to those family members who confirm to the Secretary of State that they agree to being accommodated together.

. . .

Des Browne
Minister of State

Home Office
10th January 2005

 Statutory instruments are available on the website of the Office of Public Sector Information at:
www.opsi.gov.uk/stat.htm

Power to make delegated legislation

Parliament has passed the Legislative and Regulatory Reform Act 2006 which gives the executive very wide powers to make delegated legislation. The official aim of the Act is to make it simpler and faster to amend existing legislation. It allows ministers to issue statutory instruments to amend legislation or implement recommendations of the Law Commission. The Act risks amounting to a significant shift in power from a democratically elected parliament to the executive.

Legislative and Regulatory Reform Act 2006

PART 1

ORDER-MAKING POWERS

Powers

1 Power to remove or reduce burdens

(1) A Minister of the Crown may by order under this section make any provision which he considers would serve the purpose in subsection (2).

(2) That purpose is removing or reducing any burden, or the overall burdens, resulting directly or indirectly for any person from any legislation.

(3) In this section 'burden' means any of the following—
    (a) a financial cost;
    (b) an administrative inconvenience;
    (c) an obstacle to efficiency, productivity or profitability; or
    (d) a sanction, criminal or otherwise, which affects the carrying on of any lawful activity.

(4) Provision may not be made under subsection (1) in relation to any burden which affects only a Minister of the Crown or government department, unless it affects the Minister or department in the exercise of a regulatory function.

(5) For the purposes of subsection (2), a financial cost or administrative inconvenience may result from the form of any legislation (for example, where the legislation is hard to understand).

(6) In this section 'legislation' means any of the following or a provision of any of the following—
    (a) a public general Act or local Act (whether passed before or after the commencement of this section), or
    (b) any Order in Council, order, rules, regulations, scheme, warrant, byelaw or other subordinate instrument made at any time under an Act referred to in paragraph (a), but does not include any instrument which is, or is made under, Northern Ireland legislation.

(7) Subject to this Part, the provision that may be made under subsection (1) includes—
    (a) provision abolishing, conferring or transferring, or providing for the delegation of, functions of any description,

→

(b) provision creating or abolishing a body or office,
and provision made by amending or repealing any enactment.

(8) An order under this section may contain such consequential, supplementary, incidental or transitional provision (including provision made by amending or repealing any enactment or other provision) as the Minister making it considers appropriate.

(9) An order under this section may bind the Crown.

(10) An order under this section must be made in accordance with this Part.

Explanatory Notes

INTRODUCTION

1 These explanatory notes relate to the Legislative and Regulatory Reform Act 2006. They have been prepared by the Cabinet Office in order to assist the reader in understanding the Act. They do not form part of the Act and have not been endorsed by Parliament.

2 The notes need to be read in conjunction with the Act. They are not, and are not meant to be, a comprehensive description of the Act. So where a section or part of a section does not seem to require any explanation or comment, none is given.

SUMMARY AND BACKGROUND

3 Part 1 of the Act provides powers for a Minister of the Crown to make orders. The powers replace the power in the Regulatory Reform Act 2001 ('the 2001 Act') to make Regulatory Reform Orders ('RROs'). Part 1 sets out what the powers are, the conditions and restrictions which apply to them, and the procedure which must be followed in exercising them.

4 The impetus for this Part comes from the Government's review of the first four years of the operation of the 2001 Act, and from the findings of the Better Regulation Task Force contained in its report *Less is More: Reducing Burdens, Improving Outcomes*, published in March 2005.

5 Part 1 contains two order-making powers which are subject to a number of substantive and procedural protections which are outlined below.

6 It is important to note that in addition to these protections, at second reading in the House of Commons the then Parliamentary Secretary in the Cabinet Office, Mr Jim Murphy MP, gave 'a clear undertaking (. . .) that orders will not be used to implement highly controversial reforms' (*Hansard*, 9 Feb. 2006: Column 1058–1059).

. . .

COMMENTARY ON SECTIONS

PART 1: ORDER-MAKING POWERS

Powers

Section 1: power to remove or reduce burdens

18 Section 1 confers power on a Minister of the Crown to make any provision by order which he considers would serve the purpose of removing or reducing any burden, or removing or reducing the overall burdens, to which any person is subject as a direct or indirect result of

any legislation. Legislation is defined in subsection (6). The power is a broad one, and it is intended to be so. In the first place, it may be noted that the Minister may make 'any' provision which would serve the purpose stated, subject only to the restrictions set out in the Act.

19 Subsection (3) defines a 'burden' as:

- a financial cost;
- an administrative inconvenience;
- an obstacle to efficiency, productivity or profitability; or
- a sanction, criminal or otherwise, which affects the carrying on of any lawful activity.

20 *A financial cost*: this limb of the definition covers any financial costs, including administrative costs and policy or 'compliance' costs resulting from understanding and complying with legislation . . .

21 *An administrative inconvenience*: this limb of the definition covers administrative inconvenience even where it does not result in a financial cost. For example, a requirement on an individual to fill in a form may not result in financial cost, but could be inconvenient for that person.

22 *An obstacle to efficiency, productivity or profitability*: in some cases legislation may not impose a cost on a person but may prevent them from being as efficient, productive or profitable as they would otherwise be.

23 *'Obstacle to efficiency'* could cover, for example, obstacles to the economically or administratively efficient exercise of a person's or body's existing statutory functions. This could include provisions in legislation which prevent a regulator from carrying out its functions of inspection or enforcement in a risk-based way, thus requiring the regulator to expend administrative effort and cost on low risk activities or operators, and preventing it targeting its resources at the high risk . . .

24 *'Obstacle to productivity'*: a tenancy restriction preventing farmers diversifying into non-agricultural activities to improve the viability of their business, might be an example of a bar on productivity. So an order could remove or reduce a restriction resulting from legislation that farmers may only use certain land for agricultural purposes.
. . .

26 *'Obstacle to profitability'*: this limb of the definition could cover the *opportunity costs* of complying with legislation, for example, where compliance with the legislation means the loss of a financial benefit that could otherwise have been obtained. Restrictions on selling alcohol, or on Sunday trading might in principle be examples of obstacles to profitability. So for example an order could remove or reduce restrictions on the sale of methylated spirits on a Sunday. There are no actual costs imposed upon a business when it is prohibited from trading such spirits on a Sunday, only a loss of profit as a result of the ban.

27 *A sanction which affects the carrying on of any lawful activity*: this limb of the definition covers sanctions, criminal or otherwise, which affect the carrying on of a lawful activity. This could include a criminal sanction which affects the carrying on of an activity which is itself lawful, such as supplying financial services. It could not include sanctions for activities which are themselves unlawful, such as dealing in class A drugs, or people trafficking. So an order could remove or reduce criminal sanctions which relate to the carrying on of a particular lawful activity, but not sanctions relating to offences under the general criminal law. It is therefore possible by order to reduce the sanction for a particular criminal offence where it is no longer considered to be targeted or appropriate, for example by replacing the sanction of a term of imprisonment with a fine.

28 The reference in subsection (2) to 'removing or reducing the overall burdens' is intended to allow for one statutory regime to be replaced by another which is less burdensome overall for a person. This means that existing burdens can be increased, or a new burden could be imposed, where this is for the purpose of reducing the overall burdens resulting from legislation to which a person is subject.

. . .

37 'Legislation' is defined in subsection (6) and includes local as well as public general Acts, and subordinate legislation as well as primary legislation. Local Acts cover limited areas or particular bodies or institutions, such as particular charities or port authorities: their chapter numbers are small roman numerals. The definition of 'legislation' does not include any instrument which is Northern Ireland legislation within the meaning of section 24 of the 1978 Act (such as Acts of the Parliament of Northern Ireland, or Orders in Council made under section 1(3) of the Northern Ireland (Temporary Provisions) Act 1972).

38 Subsection (7) provides that the provision that can be made by order under this section includes provision which:

- abolishes, confers or transfers, or provides for the delegation of, functions of any description (which would include functions of legislating);
- creates or abolishes a body or office;
- amends or repeals any enactment.

39 An order under this section could transfer regulatory functions from one regulator to another where this was, for example, for the purpose of reducing burdens upon those being regulated by reducing the number of separate inspections or requirements to provide information to which they were subject.

40 Subsection (8) confers power for an order made under this section to make such *consequential, supplementary, incidental or transitional provision* as the Minister considers appropriate, including provision amending or repealing any enactment or other provision. Although 'enactment' does not include an enactment comprised in, or an instrument made under, an Act of the Scottish Parliament (as a result of Schedule 1 to the 1978 Act), subsection (8) enables the amendment or repeal of *other provision* for consequential, supplementary, incidental or transitional purposes, and this extends to the amendment or repeal of Acts of the Scottish Parliament and instruments made under them. Whilst an order under this section cannot remove or reduce burdens arising from Northern Ireland legislation, provision can be made under this subsection amending or repealing Northern Ireland legislation for consequential, supplementary, incidental or transitional purposes.

41 The effect of this power (and the equivalent power in section 2(7)), taken with the restrictions in sections 9 and 10, is that the only type of provision an order can make amending or repealing legislation which would be within the legislative competence of the Scottish Parliament, or which is Northern Ireland legislation, is provision which is consequential, supplementary, incidental or transitional.

 The Legislative and Regulatory Reform Act 2006 and accompanying Explanatory Notes are available on the website of the Office for Public Sector Information at: **www.opsi.gov.uk/acts/acts2006a**

5

European law

Introduction

This chapter looks at:

- the decision of the European Court of Justice that directives should have direct effect;
- the attempt to establish a European Constitution; and
- the most recent efforts to modernise the European Union through the Reform Treaty.

Direct effect

Directives are an important source of law. Their impact on national law has been strengthened by the European Court of Justice recognising that they can create rights for individuals (and not just governments), known as direct effect. The first case to recognise that directives have direct effect was the case of **Van Duyn v Home Office** (1974).

Van Duyn v Home Office (1974), European Court of Justice

I. Facts and procedure

1 The Church of Scientology is a body established in the United States of America, which functions in the United Kingdom through a college at East Grinstead, Sussex. The British Government regards the activities of the Church of Scientology as contrary to public policy. On July 25, 1968, the Minister of Health stated in the House of Commons that the government was satisfied that scientology was socially harmful. The statement included the following remarks:

> Scientology is a pseudo-philosophical cult . . . The government are satisfied having reviewed all the available evidence that scientology is socially harmful. It alienates members of families from each other and attributes squalid and disgraceful motives to all who oppose it; its authoritarian principles and practice are a potential menace to the personality and well being of those so deluded as to become its followers; above all its methods can be a serious danger to the health of those who submit to them. There is evidence that children are now being indoctrinated. There is no power under existing law to prohibit the practice of scientology; but the government have concluded that it is so objectionable that it would be right to take all steps within their power to curb its growth . . . Foreign nationals come here to study scientology and to work at the so-called 'college' in East Grinstead. The government can prevent this under existing law . . . and have decided to do so. The following steps are being taken with immediate effect . . . (e) Work permits and employment vouchers will not be issued to foreign nationals . . . for work at a scientology establishment.

No legal restrictions are placed upon the practice of scientology in the United Kingdom nor upon British nationals (with certain immaterial exceptions) wishing to become members of or take employment with the Church of Scientology.

2 Miss Van Duyn is a Dutch national. By a letter dated May 4, 1973, she was offered employment as a secretary with the Church of Scientology at its college at East Grinstead. With the intention of taking up that offer she arrived at Gatwick Airport on May 9, 1973, where she was interviewed by an immigration officer and refused leave to enter the United Kingdom. It emerged in the course of the interview that she had worked in a scientology establishment in Amsterdam for six months, that she had taken a course in the subject of scientology, that she was a practising scientologist and that she was intending to work at a scientology establishment in the United Kingdom. The ground of refusal of leave to enter which is stated in the document entitled 'Refusal of leave to enter' handed by the immigration officer to Miss Van Duyn reads:

> You have asked for leave to enter the United Kingdom in order to take employment with the Church of Scientology but the Secretary of State considers it undesirable to give anyone leave to enter the United Kingdom on the business of or in the employment of that organisation . . .

The power to refuse entry into the United Kingdom is vested in immigration officers by virtue of section 4(1) of the Immigration Act 1971. Leave to enter was refused by the immigration officer acting in accordance with the policy of the government and with rule 65 of the relevant Immigration Rules for Control of Entry which Rules have legislative force. Rule 65 reads:

> Any passenger except the wife or child under 18 of a person settled in the United Kingdom may be refused leave to enter on the ground that his exclusion is conducive to the public good, where—(a) the Secretary of State has personally so directed, or (b) from information available to the immigration officer it seems right to refuse leave to enter on that ground – if, for example, in the light of the passenger's character, conduct or associations it is undesirable to give him leave to enter.

3 Relying on the community rules on freedom of movement of workers and especially on Article 48 of the EEC Treaty, Regulation 1612/68 and Article 3 of Directive 64/221, Miss Van Duyn claims that the refusal of leave to enter was unlawful and seeks a declaration from the High Court that she is entitled to stay in the United Kingdom for the purpose of employment and to be given leave to enter the United Kingdom.

Before deciding further, the High Court has stayed the proceedings and requested the Court of Justice, pursuant to Article 177 of the EEC Treaty, to give a preliminary ruling on the following questions. 1. Whether Article 48 of the Treaty establishing the European Economic Community is directly applicable so as to confer on individuals rights enforceable by them in the court of a member state. 2. Whether Directive 64/221 adopted on February 25, 1964, in accordance with the Treaty establishing the European Economic Community is directly applicable so as to confer on individuals rights enforceable by them in the courts of a member state. 3. Whether upon the proper interpretation of Article 48 of the Treaty establishing the European Economic Community and Article 3 of Directive 64/221/EEC a member state in the performance of its duty to base a measure taken on grounds of public policy exclusively on the personal conduct of the individual concerned is entitled to take into account as matters of personal conduct (a) the fact that the individual is or has been associated with some body or organisation the activities of which the member state considers contrary to the public good but which are not unlawful in that state, (b) the fact that the individual intends to take employment in the member state with such a body or organisation, it being the case that no restrictions are placed upon nationals of the member state who wish to take similar employment with such a body or organisation.

. . .

Law

1 By order of Pennycuick V-C, of March 1, 1974, lodged at the court on June 13, the Chancery Division of the High Court of Justice of England, referred to the court, under Article 177 of the EEC Treaty, three questions relating to the interpretation of certain provisions of community law concerning freedom of movement for workers.

2 These questions arise out of an action brought against the Home Office by a woman of Dutch nationality who was refused leave to enter the United Kingdom to take up employment as a secretary with the 'Church of Scientology'.

3 Leave to enter was refused in accordance with the policy of the Government of the United Kingdom in relation to the said organisation, the activities of which it considers to be socially harmful.

First question

4 By the first question, the court is asked to say whether Article 48 of the EEC Treaty is directly applicable so as to confer on individuals rights enforceable by them in the courts of a member state.

5 It is provided, in Article 48(1) and (2), that freedom of movement for workers shall be secured by the end of the transitional period and that such freedom shall entail: 'the abolition of any discrimination based on nationality between workers of member states as regards employment, remuneration and other conditions of work and employment'.

6 These provisions impose on member states a precise obligation which does not require the adoption of any further measure on the part either of the community institutions or of the member states and which leaves them, in relation to its implementation, no discretionary power.

7 Paragraph 3, which defines the rights implied by the principle of freedom of movement for workers, subjects them to limitations justified on grounds of public policy, public security or public health. The application of these limitations is, however, subject to judicial control, so that a member state's right to invoke the limitations does not prevent the provisions of Article 48, which enshrine the principle of freedom of movement for workers, from conferring on individuals rights which are enforceable by them and which the national courts must protect.

8 The reply to the first question must therefore be in the affirmative.

Second question

9 The second question asks the court to say whether Council Directive 64/221 of February 25, 1964, on the co-ordination of special measures concerning the movement and residence of foreign nationals which are justified on grounds of public policy, public security or public health is directly applicable so as to confer on individuals rights enforceable by them in the courts of a member state.

10 It emerges from the order making the reference that the only provision of the Directive which is relevant is that contained in Article 3(1) which provides:

> Measures taken on grounds of public policy or public security shall be based exclusively on the personal conduct of the individual concerned.

11 The United Kingdom observes that, since Article 189 of the Treaty distinguishes between the effects ascribed to regulations, directives and decisions, it must therefore be presumed that the Council, in issuing a directive rather than making a regulation, must have intended that the directive should have an effect other than that of a regulation and accordingly that the former should not be directly applicable.

12 If, however, by virtue of the provisions of Article 189 regulations are directly applicable and, consequently, may by their very nature have direct effects, it does not follow from this that other categories of acts mentioned in that Article can never have similar effects. It would be incompatible with the binding effect attributed to a directive by Article 189 to exclude, in principle, the possibility that the obligation which it imposes may be invoked by those concerned. In particular, where the community authorities have, by directive, imposed on member states the obligation to pursue a particular course of conduct, the useful effect of such an act would be weakened if individuals were prevented from relying on it before their national courts and if the latter were prevented from taking it into consideration as an element of community law. Article 177, which empowers national courts to refer to the court questions concerning the validity and interpretation of all acts of the community institutions, without distinction, implies furthermore that these acts may be invoked by individuals in the national courts. It is necessary to examine, in every case, whether the nature, general scheme and wording of the provision in question are capable of having direct effects on the relations between member states and individuals.

13 By providing that measures taken on grounds of public policy shall be based exclusively on the personal conduct of the individual concerned, Article 3(1) of Directive 64/221 is intended to limit the discretionary power which national laws generally confer on the authorities responsible for the entry and expulsion of foreign nationals. First, the provision lays down an obligation which is not subject to any exception or condition and which, by its very nature, does not require the intervention of any act on the part either of the institutions of the community or of member states. Secondly, because member states are thereby obliged, in implementing a clause which derogates from one of the fundamental principles of the Treaty in favour of individuals, not to take account of factors extraneous to personal conduct, legal certainty for the persons concerned requires that they should be able to rely on this obligation even though it has been laid down in a legislative act which has no automatic direct effect in its entirety.

14 If the meaning and exact scope of the provision raise questions of interpretation, these questions can be resolved by the courts, taking into account also the procedure under Article 177 of the Treaty.

15 Accordingly, in reply to the second question, Article 3(1) of Council Directive 64/221 of February 25, 1964, confers on individuals rights which are enforceable by them in the courts of a member state and which the national courts must protect.

European Constitution

In 2004 the European Union drafted a new European Constitution which would have modernised its governing institutions and decision-making processes. In order to come into force, it needed to be ratified by all member states. France and the Netherlands, dramatically rejected the Constitution in national referendums so the European Constitution was never brought into force. An American organisation, the Congressional Research Service, considered what the impact of the European Constitution would have been if it had been ratified.

The European Union's Constitution

Kristin Archick

Toward a European Constitution

The Convention on the Future of Europe. The Convention began work in March 2002 in Brussels, Belgium. EU member states appointed former French President Valéry Giscard d'Estaing to serve as chairman, and charged the 105-member Convention with addressing several key tasks, including examining and better defining the distribution of power between the EU's institutions and the member states; encouraging the development of the EU as a coherent foreign policy actor; and strengthening the Union's democratic legitimacy. In October 2002, the Convention decided to develop a draft constitutional treaty – commonly referred to as a 'constitution' – to merge and reorganise the EU's four existing treaties into a single document and lay out new proposals for institutional reform. In July 2003, the Convention finalised a 240-page 'Draft Treaty establishing a Constitution for Europe' and concluded its work. The draft was divided into four parts: Part One set out the definition and objectives of the Union and outlined its competences and institutional framework; Part Two enshrined the EU Charter of Fundamental Rights, completed in 2000, into EU law; Part Three addressed the policies and functioning of the Union, detailing how the EU would reach and implement its decisions; Part Four spelled out 'general and final provisions' dealing with procedures for the text's ratification and possible future revisions.

The Intergovernmental Conference. In October 2003, EU leaders convened an Intergovernmental Conference (IGC) to work out the definitive text of the new constitutional treaty to codify any alterations of the EU's structures and functions. The Convention on the Future of Europe's draft treaty from July 2003 served as the basis for discussions at the IGC. By December 2003, consensus had reportedly been reached on most issues proposed by the Convention, but EU leaders were unable to conclude the treaty primarily because of a dispute over the proposed voting rule changes. Spain and Poland feared that the simplified voting rules proposed by the Convention would give larger member states an advantage; the current weighted voting system tends to favour smaller and medium-sized states. The change in government following Spain's March 2004 election, however, helped break the deadlock because the new Spanish government dropped its predecessors' outright opposition to altering the voting rules, which forced Poland to be more flexible also. EU leaders succeeded in finalising the constitution in June 2004; they signed it on October 29, 2004, and set November 2006 as the target date for the constitution's entrance into force.

The ratification crisis

In order to come into effect, the EU's constitutional treaty must be ratified by all 25 member states through either parliamentary approval or public referenda. Twelve states have completed ratification, but the constitution's future has been thrown into doubt following its rejection by French and Dutch voters in separate referenda in May and June 2005. In both countries, some arguments against the constitution reflected concerns that it would enshrine liberal economic trends that could undermine French or Dutch social protections. In addition, many French and Dutch voters viewed a 'no' vote as a way to express dissatisfaction with their unpopular national governments, the EU bureaucracy, and Turkey's prospective EU membership. Other reasons for rejecting the constitution differed. In France, some feared that the constitution – by paving the way for further EU enlargement – would erode French influence in the EU, while Dutch voters complained that the EU's big countries were already too strong and that certain provisions of the constitution would increase their power even more.

Following the French and Dutch 'no' votes, it became unclear whether other EU members would proceed with their ratification plans. Proponents of moving forward hoped that if most members approved the constitution, this would help force a second vote in those states that rejected it. However, on June 6, 2005, UK Foreign Secretary Jack Straw announced that there was 'no point' in continuing to plan for a UK poll, and effectively postponed the UK's referendum indefinitely. At their June 16–17, 2005 summit, EU leaders reaffirmed their commitment to the constitution but announced that decisions about the timing of ratification were for each member state to determine. They acknowledged that the initial ratification dead-line of November 2006 was no longer tenable and did not set a new target date. Experts say this decision effectively puts the constitution on hold until at least mid-2007. Nevertheless, some members are continuing with ratification; on July 10, 2005, voters in Luxembourg approved the constitution.

EU officials are quick to emphasise that the EU can continue to operate without the constitution and could enlarge further under the rules set out in the Nice Treaty of 2000. Some commentators speculate that certain elements of the EU constitution could be implemented by agreement among EU leaders or by amending the existing EU treaties. Others suggest that parts of the constitutional treaty might be renegotiated, although this would likely be extremely difficult given that the existing draft is already replete with compromises among member states and because opposition to the treaty comes from disparate directions. The EU may be facing a period of stagnation, at least in the short term, as members grapple with internal reforms and the EU's future shape and identity. Many experts believe that big decisions, such as agreement on the EU's next seven-year budget, may be more difficult. Given that considerable opposition to the constitution is tied to concerns about EU enlargement, some predict that the 'no' votes could also impede efforts toward further expansion, especially to Turkey and possibly the Balkans.

Key provisions in the EU's Constitution

The text of the EU's constitutional treaty is 341 pages. Major changes to the EU's governing institutions, decision-making processes, and policies include:

- *A new president of the European Council.* The constitution abolishes the rotating six-month presidency in favour of an individual – elected by member states for a term of two and one-half years, renewable once – to ensure policy continuity and raise the EU's profile on the world stage.
- *A new EU foreign minister.* This new post is also intended to boost the EU's international visibility, and combine into one position the current responsibilities of the Council's High Representative for the EU's Common Foreign and Security Policy (CFSP) and the External Relations Commissioner, who coordinates the European Commission's diplomatic activities and manages the EU's development programs. The EU foreign minister will be an agent of the Council of Ministers (representing the member states), as well as a vice-president of the Commission.
- *A revamped European Commission.* In the first Commission appointed under the constitution, each member will retain one commissioner. After this term (in 2014), to help decrease gridlock, the number of commissioners will be reduced to correspond to two-thirds of the number of member states. Small states had initially opposed slimming down the Commission, fearing that it would decrease their influence. However, the European Council may alter the number of commissioners, thus leaving the door open to a larger Commission in the future.
- *Increased parliamentary powers.* The constitution extends the European Parliament's right of 'co-decision' with the Council of Ministers to many additional policy areas, including

agriculture and home affairs issues. It caps the Parliament at 750 and includes other provisions to encourage closer ties between EU bodies and national parliaments.

● *Simplified voting procedures*. The constitution simplifies the EU's current system of qualified majority voting (QMV), a complex weighted voting formula. Beginning in 2009, decisions made by QMV will pass if supported by 55% of member states (comprising at least 15 of them) representing at least 65% of the EU's population. A blocking minority must consist of at least four countries. The use of QMV is also expanded to policy areas previously subject to unanimity, including asylum and immigration. Member states will retain national vetoes, however, in sensitive areas such as taxation and most aspects of foreign policy.

● *A new exit clause*. The text sets out for the first time in EU law procedures for a member state to voluntarily withdraw from the Union. It also retains EU provisions that allow certain rights of a member state to be suspended if it is deemed to have breached core EU values.

● *A new solidarity clause*. This provision affirms that the EU 'shall act jointly in a spirit of solidarity' if any member is the victim of a terrorist attack or other natural or man-made disaster; it calls on member states to offer assistance, including military resources, to the victimised member.

● *Steps toward building a common defense policy*. The text asserts that the Union shall seek 'the progressive framing of a common Union defense policy', which 'will lead to a common defense'. It establishes a 'mutual assistance clause' permitting a member state that is the victim of armed aggression to ask for military assistance from the other members. Member states may also engage in 'structured cooperation,' which would allow a smaller group of members – especially those with higher-end defense capabilities – to cooperate more closely on military issues. And the text calls for a 'European Armaments, Research, and Military Capabilities Agency' to coordinate defense technology research, encourage harmonisation of arms procurement procedures, and ensure interoperability of defense equipment throughout the EU.

Almost all of the changes in the constitution represent compromises between member states who favour greater EU integration and those who prefer to keep the Union on an intergovernmental footing in which member states can better guard their national sovereignty. Also evident in many of the provisions are compromises between big and small states. Critics contend, however, that the constitution does little to simplify the EU. They point out that some changes would not take effect until 2009 or 2014 and that the creation essentially of two EU presidents could generate rivalry and confusion. In addition, skeptics assert that many of the most difficult issues that are often the source of gridlock – such as foreign policy and taxation – will remain subject to national vetoes.

Implications for the United States

Many experts assert that passage of the EU constitution would have positive implications for the US–EU relationship because certain provisions – such as the new president and foreign minister positions – are designed to promote an EU able to 'speak with one voice' on foreign policy issues. Such an EU would be a more credible partner for the United States in tackling common challenges such as terrorism and Middle East instability. Supporters of this view also note that efforts to encourage a common EU defense policy and the proposal for 'structured cooperation' in the constitution seek to improve European defense capabilities. A more militarily-capable Europe, they argue, could shoulder a greater degree of the security burden with the United States. Conversely, some contend that a failure to ratify the constitution could inhibit EU efforts to be a more effective US partner because EU attention would likely remain focused on internal reforms rather than on external challenges. The difficulties with ratifying the constitution have also sparked renewed discussion of a 'core Europe,' in which a vanguard of EU member states would drive further integration. If such a 'core Europe' developed that did not include the UK or other economically liberal or pro-Atlanticist states, some say that this could increase US–EU tensions. Some US analysts also worry that voter rejection of the constitution could stymie the opening of accession talks with Turkey, which the United States strongly supports. Other US experts who worry that a larger and potentially more united and more confident EU may seek to rival the United States are more sanguine about the potential demise of the EU constitution. They contend that a more unified EU would likely lessen Washington's leverage on individual members and could complicate US efforts to rally support for its initiatives in institutions such as the United Nations or NATO. These skeptics remain concerned that parts of the constitution that promote greater EU defense coordination could lead to the eventual development of EU military structures that would duplicate those of NATO, be financially costly, and weaken the transatlantic link.

US–EU trade relations are unlikely to be significantly affected by the constitution, which does not alter the roles of the European Commission or Council of Ministers in formulating or approving the EU's common external trade policy. Although EU rules allow the Council to approve or reject trade agreements negotiated by the Commission with QMV, in practice, the Council tends to employ consensus and will probably continue to do so regardless of the changes in EU voting procedures.

The Reform Treaty – brief overview

Following a two-year period of reflection after the rejection of the European Constitution by many European citizens, a Reform Treaty was agreed in 2007. It adopts the most important of the planned reforms of the failed Constitution in a pragmatic and minimalist format, rather than the more grandiose presentation of the Constitution (which would have got rid of all the previous EU treaties and replaced them with a single Constitution). The treaty leaves all the existing European treaties in place and simply makes key amendments.

The treaty was expected to come into force in the summer of 2009, but its future was thrown into doubt when it was itself rejected in an Irish referendum in 2008, though European leaders have decided to try and push ahead with the ratification process and Ireland will have a second chance to approve the treaty.

The Reform Treaty

The Treaty at a glance

On December 13, 2007, EU leaders signed the Treaty of Lisbon, thus bringing to an end several years of negotiation about institutional issues.

The Treaty of Lisbon amends the current EU and EC treaties, without replacing them. It will provide the Union with the legal framework and tools necessary to meet future challenges and to respond to citizens' demands.

1 A more democratic and transparent Europe, with a strengthened role for the European Parliament and national parliaments, more opportunities for citizens to have their voices heard and a clearer sense of who does what at European and national level.

- A strengthened role for the European Parliament: the European Parliament, directly elected by EU citizens, will see important new powers emerge over the EU legislation, the EU budget and international agreements. In particular, the increase of co-decision procedure in policy-making will ensure the European Parliament is placed on an equal footing with the Council, representing Member States, for the vast bulk of EU legislation.
- A greater involvement of national parliaments: national parliaments will have greater opportunities to be involved in the work of the EU, in particular thanks to a new mechanism to monitor that the Union only acts where results can be better attained at EU level (subsidiarity). Together with the strengthened role for the European Parliament, it will enhance democracy and increase legitimacy in the functioning of the Union.
- A stronger voice for citizens: thanks to the Citizens' Initiative, one million citizens from a number of Member States will have the possibility to call on the Commission to bring forward new policy proposals.
- Who does what: the relationship between the Member States and the European Union will become clearer with the categorisation of competences.
- Withdrawal from the Union: the Treaty of Lisbon explicitly recognises for the first time the possibility for a Member State to withdraw from the Union.

2 A more efficient Europe, with simplified working methods and voting rules, streamlined and modern institutions for a EU of 27 members and an improved ability to act in areas of major priority for today's Union.

- Effective and efficient decision-making: qualified majority voting in the Council will be extended to new policy areas to make decision-making faster and more efficient. From 2014 on, the calculation of qualified majority will be based on the double majority of Member States and people, thus representing the dual legitimacy of the Union. A double majority will be achieved when a decision is taken by 55% of the Member States representing at least 65% of the Union's population.
- A more stable and streamlined institutional framework: the Treaty of Lisbon creates the function of President of the European Council elected for two and a half years, introduces a direct link between the election of the Commission President and the results of the European elections, provides for new arrangements for the future composition of the European Parliament and for a smaller Commission, and includes clearer rules on enhanced cooperation and financial provisions.
- Improving the life of Europeans: the Treaty of Lisbon improves the EU's ability to act in several policy areas of major priority for today's Union and its citizens. This is the case in particular for the policy areas of freedom, security and justice, such as combating terrorism or tackling crime. It also concerns to some extent other areas including energy policy, public health, civil protection, climate change, services of general interest, research, space, territorial cohesion, commercial policy, humanitarian aid, sport, tourism and administrative cooperation.

3 A Europe of rights and values, freedom, solidarity and security, promoting the Union's values, introducing the Charter of Fundamental Rights into European primary law, providing for new solidarity mechanisms and ensuring better protection of European citizens.

- Democratic values: the Treaty of Lisbon details and reinforces the values and objectives on which the Union is built. These values aim to serve as a reference point for European citizens and to demonstrate what Europe has to offer its partners worldwide.
- Citizens' rights and Charter of Fundamental Rights: the Treaty of Lisbon preserves existing rights while introducing new ones. In particular, it guarantees the freedoms and principles set out in the Charter of Fundamental Rights and gives its provisions a binding legal force. It concerns civil, political, economic and social rights.
- Freedom of European citizens: the Treaty of Lisbon preserves and reinforces the 'four freedoms' and the political, economic and social freedom of European citizens.
- Solidarity between Member States: the Treaty of Lisbon provides that the Union and its Member States act jointly in a spirit of solidarity if a Member State is the subject of a terrorist attack or the victim of a natural or man-made disaster. Solidarity in the area of energy is also emphasised.
- Increased security for all: the Union will get an extended capacity to act on freedom, security and justice, which will bring direct benefits in terms of the Union's ability to fight crime and terrorism. New provisions on civil protection, humanitarian aid and public health also aim at boosting the Union's ability to respond to threats to the security of European citizens.

4 Europe as an actor on the global stage will be achieved by bringing together Europe's external policy tools, both when developing and deciding new policies. The Treaty of Lisbon will give Europe a clear voice in relations with its partners worldwide. It will harness Europe's economic, humanitarian, political and diplomatic strengths to promote European interests and values worldwide, while respecting the particular interests of the Member States in Foreign Affairs.

- A new High Representative for the Union in Foreign Affairs and Security Policy, also Vice-President of the Commission, will increase the impact, the coherence and the visibility of the EU's external action.
- A new European External Action Service will provide back up and support to the High Representative.
- A single legal personality for the Union will strengthen the Union's negotiating power, making it more effective on the world stage and a more visible partner for third countries and international organisations.
- Progress in European Security and Defence Policy will preserve special decision-making arrangements but also pave the way towards reinforced cooperation amongst a smaller group of Member States.

 This concise explanation of the Reform Treaty is available on the European Union's website at:
http://europa.eu/lisbon_treaty/glance/index_en.htm

The Impact of the Reform Treaty

Can you explain the new voting system in the Council of Ministers?

The standard system of voting in the Council of Ministers will be 'qualified majority voting' (QMV). It will be based on the principle of the double majority. Decisions in the Council of Ministers will need the support of 55% of Member States (currently 15 out of 27 EU countries) representing a minimum of 65% of the EU's population. To make it impossible for a very small number of the most populous Member States to prevent a decision from being adopted, a blocking minority must comprise at least four Member States; otherwise, the qualified majority will be deemed to have been reached even if the population criterion is not met.

The European Council agreed that the new system will take effect in 2014. In the first three years, until 2017, a Member State may request that an act be adopted in accordance with the qualified majority as defined in the current Treaty of Nice.

Will more decisions be taken by qualified majority voting?

Yes. The Treaty of Lisbon will extend qualified majority voting to new policy areas. It is very much in the European Union's interest to adopt a more streamlined approach to decision-making, including on issues such as fighting climate change, energy security and emergency humanitarian aid to hot-spots around the globe. Some of the other changes address issues like citizens' initiatives, diplomatic and consulate protection, and procedural matters. Unanimity will be retained in areas including tax, foreign policy, defence and social security.

What are the main institutional changes introduced by the Treaty?

From 2014 the number of the commissioners will be reduced in size in order to streamline the Commission. There will no longer be a commissioner from every country – but from two-thirds of the Member States. Commissioners will be selected on a system of equal rotation among the Member States to serve five-year terms. So there would be a national from each Member State in two Commissions out of three.

The European Parliament will have no more than 751 members. The delegate numbers for each country have been fixed to a maximum of 96 and a minimum of 6 for each Member State.

A new permanent post, the President of the European Council, is created. He or she will be appointed by the European Council for a two and a half years period. This will provide greater continuity and stability to the work of the European Council.

It creates a High Representative of the Union for Foreign Affairs and Security Policy. He or she will also become Vice-President of the Commission, and will chair the External Relations Council. This will strengthen coherence in external action and raise the EU's profile in the world, 'putting a face' on the Union.

How will the Charter of Fundamental Rights improve the rights of European citizens?

The Treaty of Lisbon makes a cross-reference to the Charter as a real catalogue of rights that the EU believes all citizens of the Union should enjoy *vis-à-vis* the Union's institutions and the Union's law binding guarantees. The six chapters of the Charter cover the following aspects: individual rights related to dignity; freedoms, equality, solidarity, rights linked to citizenship status and justice. These rights are drawn essentially from other international instruments, like the European Convention on Human Rights, giving them legal embodiment in the Union.

The institutions of the Union must respect the rights written into the Charter. The same obligations are incumbent upon the Member States when they implement the Union's legislation. The Court of Justice will ensure that the Charter is applied correctly. The incorporation of the Charter does not alter the Union's powers, but offers strengthened rights and greater freedom for citizens.

This is a sample of the questions and answers available on the European Union's official website to explain the impact of the Reform Treaty on European citizens. They are published on the European Union's official website at:
http://europa.eu/lisbon_treaty/faq/index_en.htm#1

6

Custom

Introduction

This chapter looks at:

- custom in contract law; and
- custom in international law.

Custom in contract law

Custom used to be an important source of law in the English legal system. It is significantly less important today, but it remains on occasion a source of law. For example, the terms of a contract may be unclear and the courts can look at the customs of an industry to determine what the parties intended the terms of the contract to be. In **Hutton v Warren** (1836) a tenant proved by pointing to a local custom, that on leaving the premises in accordance with the notice issued by the landlord, he had a right to an allowance for labour and seeds he had expended on the land.

Hutton *v* Warren (1836), Court of Exchequer

Parke B

On the first point we think that the plaintiff must be taken, in the absence of evidence to the contrary, to have held under the defendant on the same terms that be held under his father, so far as those terms were applicable to a tenancy from year to year. No evidence was given to the contrary on the trial and, indeed, this objection does not appear to have been there raised on the part of the plaintiff. The second question requires some consideration. The custom of the country as to cultivation and the term of quitting with respect to allowances for seed and labour, is clearly applicable to a tenancy from year to year and, therefore, if this custom was, by implication, imported into the lease, the plaintiff and defendant were bound by it after the lease expired. We are of opinion that this custom was, by implication, imported into the lease. It has long been settled that, in commercial transactions, extrinsic evidence of custom and usage is admissible to annex incidents to written contracts in matters with respect to which they are silent. The same rule has also been applied to contracts in other transactions of life, in which known usages have been established and prevailed. This has been done on the principle of presumption that, in such transactions, the parties did not mean to express in writing the whole of the contract by which they intended to be bound, but a contract with reference to those known usages. Whether such a relaxation of the strictness of the common law was wisely applied where formal instruments have been entered into, and particularly leases under seal, may well be doubted; but the contrary has been established by such authority, and the relations between landlord and tenant have been so long regulated on the supposition that all customary obligations not altered by the contract, are to remain in force, that it is too late to pursue a contrary course; and it would be productive of much inconvenience if this practice were now to be disturbed. The common law, indeed, does so little to prescribe the relative duties of landlord and tenant since it leaves the latter at liberty to pursue any course of management he pleases, provided he is not guilty of waste, that it is by no means surprising that the courts should have been favourably inclined to the introduction of those regulations in the mode of cultivation which custom and usage have established in each district to be the most beneficial to all parties. Accordingly, in **Wigglesworth *v* Dallison** afterwards affirmed in a writ of error, the tenant was allowed an away-going crop though there was a formal lease under seal. There the lease was entirely silent on the subject of such a right and Lord Mansfield said that the custom did not alter or contradict the lease but only superadded something to it.

Custom in international law

Custom is particularly important in the context of international law where fixed legal rules (in treaties, for example) are less developed. The International Committee of the Red Cross has undertaken a study to promote customary international humanitarian law. It issued a press release to draw attention to this work.

Customary Law Study Enhances Legal Protection of Persons Affected by Armed Conflict
Press release of the International Committee of the Red Cross, 17 March 2005

Following more than eight years of research, the International Committee of the Red Cross (ICRC) has made public a study of customary international humanitarian law applicable during armed conflict . . . By identifying 161 rules of customary international humanitarian law, the study enhances the legal protection of persons affected by armed conflict. 'This is especially the case in non-international armed conflict, for which treaty law is not particularly well developed', said Mr Kellenberger [the president of the ICRC]. 'Yet civil wars often result in the worst suffering. The study clearly shows that customary international humanitarian law applicable in non-international armed conflict goes beyond the rules of treaty law. For example, while treaty law covering internal armed conflict does not expressly prohibit attacks on civilian objects, customary international humanitarian law closes this gap. Importantly, all conflict parties – not just States but also rebel groups, for example – are bound by customary international humanitarian law applicable to internal armed conflict.'

In addition to treaty law such as the Geneva Conventions and their Additional Protocols, customary international humanitarian law is a major source of rules applicable in times of armed conflict. While treaty law is based on written conventions, customary international humanitarian law derives from the practice of States as expressed, for example, in military manuals, national legislation or official statements. A rule is considered binding customary international humanitarian law if it reflects the widespread, representative and uniform practice of States accepted as law.

In late 1995, the International Conference of the Red Cross and Red Crescent commissioned the ICRC to carry out the study. It was researched by ICRC legal staff and dozens of experts representing different regions and legal systems, including academics and specialists drawn from governments and international organisations. The experts reviewed State practice in 47 countries as well as international sources such as the United Nations, regional organisations and international courts and tribunals.

'The ICRC fully respected the academic freedom of the authors and editors of the study', said Mr Kellenberger. 'It considers the study an accurate reflection of the current state of customary international humanitarian law. The ICRC will make use of it in its work to protect and assist victims of armed conflict worldwide. I also expect scholars and governmental experts to use the study as a basis for discussions on current challenges to international humanitarian law.'

7 | Equity

Introduction

This chapter looks at:

- the continued application of equitable maxims by the courts; and

- the availability of equitable remedies to achieve justice in practice.

Equitable maxims

Equity remains an important source of law. It has developed maxims which have to be satisfied before equitable rules can be applied. One such maxim is that 'He who seeks equity must do equity'. This means that anyone who seeks equitable relief must be prepared to act fairly towards their opponent. In **Chappell v Times Newspapers Ltd** (1975) there was an industrial dispute between some newspaper publishers and their employees. The publishers threatened to treat their contracts of employment as terminated if the union did not agree to call off strike action. Six employees went to court to seek an injunction (an equitable remedy) to prevent the employers carrying out their threat. The injunction was refused.

Chappell v Times Newspapers Ltd (1975)

There is a general principle which lies enshrined in the maxim 'He who seeks equity must do equity.' That maxim, like the other maxims of equity, is not to be construed or enforced as if it were a section in an Act of Parliament; but it expresses in concise form one approach made by the court when the discretionary remedy of an injunction is sought. If the plaintiff asks for an injunction to restrain a breach of contract to which he is a party, and he is seeking to uphold that contract in all its parts, he is, in relation to that contract, ready to do equity. If on the other hand he seeks the injunction but in the same breath is constrained to say that he is ready and willing himself to commit grave breaches of the contract at the behest of a body or person (whether his union or not) engaged in an active campaign of organising the repeated commission of such breaches, then it seems to me that the plaintiff cannot very well contend that in relation to that contract he is ready to do equity. One may leave on one side any technicalities of law or equity and simply say, in the language of childhood, that he is trying to have it both ways: he is saying 'You must not break our contract but I remain free to do so.'

Delay defeats equities

Where a claimant takes an unreasonably long time to bring an action, equitable remedies will cease to be available. This principle is contained in the equitable maxim 'delay defeats equities' and is illustrated by the case of **Leaf v International Galleries** (1950). In that case the claimant had bought a painting of Salisbury Cathedral described (innocently) by the seller as a genuine Constable. Five years later the buyer discovered that it was not a genuine Constable and claimed the equitable remedy of rescission. The Court of Appeal refused to award this remedy because of the five-year delay from the date of the sale.

Leaf v International Galleries (1950)

Jenkins LJ

It is true that this was a representation of great importance, which went to the root of the contract and induced him to buy. Clearly if, before he had taken delivery of the picture, he had obtained other advice and come to the conclusion that the picture was not a Constable, it would have been open to him to rescind. It may be that if, having taken delivery of the picture on the faith of the representation and having taken it home, he had, within a reasonable time, taken other advice and satisfied himself that it was not a Constable, he might have been able to make good his claim to rescission notwithstanding the delivery. That point I propose to leave open. What in fact happened was that he took delivery of the picture, kept it for some five years, and took no steps to obtain any further evidence as to its authorship; and that, finally, when he was minded to sell the picture at the end of a matter of five years, the untruth of the representation was brought to light. In those circumstances, it seems to me to be quite out of the question that a court of equity should grant relief by way of rescission . . . [O]f course, it may be said that the plaintiff had no occasion to obtain any further evidence as to the authorship of the picture until he wanted to sell; but in my judgment contracts such as this cannot be kept open and subject to the possibility of rescission indefinitely. Assuming that completion is not fatal to his claim, I think that, at all events, it behoves the purchaser either to verify or, as the case may be, to disprove the representation within a reasonable time, or else stand or fall by it. If he is allowed to wait five, ten, or twenty years and then reopen the bargain, there can be no finality at all. I, for my part, do not think that equity will intervene in such a case, more especially as in the present case it cannot be said that, apart from rescission, the plaintiff would have been without remedy. The county court judge was of opinion, and it seems to me that he was clearly right, that the representation that the picture was a Constable amounted to a warranty. If it amounted to a warranty, and that was broken, as on the findings of the county court judge it was, then the plaintiff had a right at law in the shape of damages for breach of warranty. That remedy he did not choose to exercise, and, although he was invited at the hearing to amend his claim so as to include a claim for breach of warranty, he declined that opportunity. That being so, it seems to me that he has no justification at all for now coming to equity five years after the event and claiming rescission. Accordingly, it seems to me that this is not a case in which the equitable remedy of rescission, assuming it to be available in the absence of fraud in respect of a completed sale of chattels, should be allowed to the plaintiff. For these reasons, I agree that the appeal fails and should be dismissed.

Equity in practice

Equity plays an important role in achieving justice where there is a contract. Under the law of contract, everybody who wants to be part of a contract must bring something to the contract. For example, if I want to make a contract to buy a car, I must bring money to pay for it, which in this context is called consideration. Occasionally, a strict requirement of consideration under the common law can cause injustice, so equity has stepped in and developed a doctrine called promissory estoppel which gets round the requirement of consideration. Lord Denning developed this doctrine of promissory estoppel in the important case of **Central London Property Trust Limited** v **High Trees House Limited** [1947]. The case involved a block of flats owned by the plaintiffs. In September 1939, the plaintiff had leased the block to the defendants, who planned to rent out the individual flats, use the income to cover their payments on the lease, and make a profit on top. Unfortunately, their plans were rather spoiled by the fact that the Second World War had just broken out, and

→

many people left London, making it difficult to find tenants. As a result, a lot of the flats were left empty. The plaintiffs therefore agreed that the defendant could pay just half the ground rent stipulated in the lease. By 1945, the flats were full again, and the plaintiffs claimed the full ground rent for the last two quarters of 1945. The plaintiffs stated that the agreement was only ever intended to last until the war was over, or the flats fully let, whichever was the sooner. Both events had happened by the time payment for the last two quarters of 1945 was due, and so they believed that they were entitled to full payment for that period.

The court accepted this argument, holding that the full rent was payable for the two quarters in question, and from then on. Of more importance is the fact that Denning J went on to state that the plaintiff would not have been entitled to recover the rent for the period 1940–45, even though there was no consideration for the promise to accept the reduced rent, because of the equitable doctrine of promissory estoppel.

Central London Property Trust Limited v High Trees House Limited [1947]

Denning J

If I were to consider this matter without regard to recent developments in the law, there is no doubt that had the plaintiffs claimed it, they would have been entitled to recover ground rent at the rate of £2,500 a year from the beginning of the term, since the lease under which it was payable was a lease under seal which, according to the old common law, could not be varied by an agreement by parol (whether in writing or not), but only by deed. Equity, however stepped in, and said that if there has been a variation of a deed by a simple contract (which in the case of a lease required to be in writing would have to be evidenced by writing), the courts may give effect to it as is shown in **Berry v Berry** (1929). That equitable doctrine, however, could hardly apply in the present case because the variation here might be said to have been made without consideration. With regard to estoppel, the representation made in relation to reducing the rent, was not a representation of an existing fact. It was a representation, in effect, as to the future, namely, that payment of the rent would not be enforced at the full rate but only at the reduced rate. Such a representation would not give rise to an estoppel, because, as was said in **Jorden v Money** (1854), a representation as to the future must be embodied as a contract or be nothing.

But what is the position in view of developments in the law in recent years? The law has not been standing still since **Jorden v Money**. There has been a series of decisions over the last fifty years which, although they are said to be cases of estoppel are not really such. They are cases in which a promise was made which was intended to create legal relations and which, to the knowledge of the person making the promise, was going to be acted on by the person to whom it was made and which was in fact so acted on. In such cases the courts have said that the promise must be honoured. The cases to which I particularly desire to refer are: **Fenner v Blake** (1900), **In re Wickham** (1917), **Re William Porter & Co. Ltd** (1937) and **Buttery v Pickard** (1946). As I have said they are not cases of estoppel in the strict sense. They are really promises – promises intended to be binding, intended to be acted on, and in fact acted on. **Jorden v Money** (1854) can be distinguished, because there the promisor made it clear that she did not intend to be legally bound, whereas in the cases to which I refer the proper inference was that the promisor did intend to be bound. In each case the court held the promise to be binding on the party making it, even though under the old common law it might be difficult to find any consideration for it. The courts have not gone so far as to give a cause of action in damages for the breach of such a promise, but they have refused to allow the party making it to act inconsistently with it. It is in that sense, and that sense only, that such a promise gives rise to an estoppel. The decisions are a natural result of the fusion of law and equity: for the cases of **Hughes *v* Metropolitan Ry. Co.** (1877), **Birmingham and District Land Co. *v* London & North Western Ry. Co.** (1887) and **Salisbury (Marquess) *v* Gilmore** (1942), afford a sufficient basis for saying that a party would not be allowed in equity to go back on such a promise. In my opinion, the time has now come for the validity of such a promise to be recognised. The logical consequence, no doubt is that a promise to accept a smaller sum in discharge of a larger sum, if acted upon, is binding notwithstanding the absence of consideration: and if the fusion of law and equity leads to this result, so much the better. That aspect was not considered in **Foakes *v* Beer** (1884). At this time of day however, when law and equity have been joined together for over seventy years, principles must be reconsidered in the light of their combined effect. It is to be noticed that in the Sixth Interim Report of the Law Revision Committee, pars. 35, 40, it is recommended that such a promise as that to which I have referred, should be enforceable in law even though no consideration for it has been given by the promisee. It seems to me that, to the extent I have mentioned that result has now been achieved by the decisions of the courts.

8

Treaties

Introduction

This chapter looks at:

- the Treaty on European Union signed in 2002; and
- government plans to put on a statutory footing the procedures followed for the ratification of a Treaty.

The Treaty on European Union

An important treaty is the Treaty on European Union which was signed in 2002. Below are the first two articles of this treaty.

The Treaty on European Union

Article 1

By this Treaty, the HIGH CONTRACTING PARTIES establish among themselves a EUROPEAN UNION, hereinafter called 'the Union'. This Treaty marks a new stage in the process of creating an ever closer union among the peoples of Europe, in which decisions are taken as openly as possible and as closely as possible to the citizen. The Union shall be founded on the European Communities, supplemented by the policies and forms of cooperation established by this Treaty. Its task shall be to organise, in a manner demonstrating consistency and solidarity, relations between the Member States and between their peoples.

Article 2

The Union shall set itself the following objectives:

- to promote economic and social progress and a high level of employment and to achieve balanced and sustainable development, in particular through the creation of an area without internal frontiers, through the strengthening of economic and social cohesion and through the establishment of economic and monetary union, ultimately including a single currency in accordance with the provisions of this Treaty,
- to assert its identity on the international scene, in particular through the implementation of a common foreign and security policy including the progressive framing of a common defence policy, which might lead to a common defence, in accordance with the provisions of Article 17,
- to strengthen the protection of the rights and interests of the nationals of its Member States through the introduction of a citizenship of the Union,
- to maintain and develop the Union as an area of freedom, security and justice, in which the free movement of persons is assured in conjunction with appropriate measures with respect to external border controls, asylum, immigration and the prevention and combating of crime,
- to maintain in full the *acquis communautaire* and build on it with a view to considering to what extent the policies and forms of cooperation introduced by this Treaty may need to be revised with the aim of ensuring the effectiveness of the mechanisms and the institutions of the Community.

The objectives of the Union shall be achieved as provided in this Treaty and in accordance with the conditions and the timetable set out therein while respecting the principle of subsidiarity as defined in Article 5 of the Treaty establishing the European Community.

The full Treaty on European Union can be found on the Europa website at:
**http://europa.eu.int/eur-lex/pri/en/oj/dat/2002/c_325/
c_32520021224en00010184.pdf**

Ratification of treaties

In 2008 the Ministry of Justice published a White Paper, 'The Governance of Britain – Constitutional Renewal,' along with a draft Constitutional Renewal Bill. It is looking at ways to improve the current constitution, including putting on a statutory footing the procedures followed for the ratification of a treaty.

The Governance of Britain – Constitutional Renewal (2008)

Treaties

Background: 'The Governance of Britain' Green Paper

143 Every year the UK becomes party to many international treaties. These result in binding obligations for the UK under international law across a wide range of domestic and foreign policy issues. Treaties which come into force after governments have expressed their consent to be bound through a formal act such as ratification are subject to the Ponsonby Rule'. This rule requires the treaty to be laid before both Houses of Parliament as a Command Paper for a minimum period of 21 sitting days prior to ratification.

144 *The Governance of Britain* Green Paper set out the Government's belief that Parliament should have the right to scrutinise treaties prior to their ratification.

145 In the Green Paper the Government went on to propose that the procedure for allowing Parliament to scrutinise treaties should be formalised and committed to consulting on an appropriate means for putting the Ponsonby Rule on a statutory footing.

146 The Government published the consultation document *War Powers and Treaties: Limiting Executive Powers* on 25 October 2007. The document explained the current procedures for ratifying treaties and set out options for putting the existing arrangements for parliamentary scrutiny of treaties onto a statutory footing.

. . .

The way forward

157 The Government has given all of the responses to the consultation careful consideration and proposes that the present arrangements for parliamentary scrutiny of treaties should be placed on a statutory footing. The minimum 21 sitting-day period during which treaties must be laid before Parliament should remain unchanged, but should be made mandatory in the draft Constitutional Renewal Bill, subject to a procedure to accommodate exceptional circumstances.

158 A vote against the ratification of a treaty in either House of Parliament should be given legal effect. In the event of a vote by the House of Commons against ratification of a treaty, the Government could not proceed to ratify it. If the Government later wished to re-present the same treaty to Parliament for ratification, it would have to lay an explanatory statement before both Houses and re-start the 21 sitting-day laying period from the beginning, in which a further debate and vote could be triggered. Another negative vote would again block ratification. In other words, the House of Commons would have the last word. In the event of a vote by the House of Lords against ratification of a treaty, the Government could not proceed to ratify it, unless it first laid an explanatory statement before both Houses explaining why the treaty should be ratified notwithstanding the views of the Lords. The Government believes that this approach would respect the primacy of the House of Commons, while recognising the importance of the role of the Lords in treaty scrutiny.

159 The legislation should make provision for alternative procedures for consulting and informing Parliament so as to provide flexibility when needed in exceptional circumstances. The consultation document (paragraphs 148–155) sets out examples where the Government has informed and consulted Parliament on a treaty using various alternative procedures, in circumstances where it was not possible to publish and lay the treaty for 21 sitting days prior to ratification. These examples show that such cases are very rare, but that they still can and do occur; for example, a treaty may need to be ratified during a Parliamentary recess, in circumstances where delay would be detrimental to the national interest. Other cases of urgency may occur, very rarely, when Parliament is sitting. In such cases, the Government would inform and consult Parliament by the most expeditious and practical means available (see paragraphs 148–155 of the consultation document for examples of such alternative procedures which have been used in the past. These examples include making an oral announcement to Parliament, laying a written statement, and consulting Opposition leaders during a recess).

160 In such exceptional cases, the Government proposes that the legislation would require it to lay a statement before Parliament at the earliest opportunity to explain why the treaty requires ratification without completing the normal period of Parliamentary scrutiny, and the steps taken or to be taken to consult Parliament by an alternative more rapid means. This would ensure that Parliament is able to call Government to account for any treaty where it has invoked this alternative procedure. This requirement to lay a written statement would not preclude Government from informing and consulting Parliament by any additional procedural means practically available.

161 The draft Constitutional Renewal Bill should exclude treaties covered by section 12 of the European Parliamentary Elections Act 2002 and Clause 5 of the EU (Amendment) Bill 2007 from the proposed arrangements, since these treaties will already be subject to specific arrangements. Section 12 of the European Parliament Elections Act 2002 provides that no treaty which provides for any increase in the powers of the European Parliament is to be ratified unless it has been approved by an Act of Parliament. Clause 5 of the EU (Amendment) Bill 2007 provides that any future treaty amending the founding EU treaties in accordance with Article 48(2) to (5) of the Treaty on European Union may not be ratified unless approved by an Act of Parliament.

162 The Bill should also exclude treaties relating to taxation, in view of the specific provision for Parliamentary scrutiny which is already provided under other legislation, namely the Inheritance Tax Act 1984, the Income and Corporation Taxes Act 1988 and the Finance Act 2006. This category of treaties is an established exception to the Ponsonby Rule. The relevant Acts of Parliament provide that an Order in Council to implement the treaty is subject to an affirmative resolution of the House of Commons, and a copy of the treaty is attached to the draft Order.

163 All Government Departments and Agencies are continuing to analyse and reflect on the range of treaties which have been or might be concluded on all aspects of domestic and foreign policy, to determine whether there are any other categories which should be excluded from the requirements of the Bill, for example because there are already other specific arrangements for parliamentary scrutiny. If the Government has any additional category to propose when the Bill is introduced, it will be proposed in the form of an additional clause on the face of the Bill.

164 Useful suggestions were made during the consultation on the setting up of parliamentary committees to scrutinise treaties prior to ratification. The Government would welcome any institutional change which would enhance the capacity of Parliament to contribute to the scrutiny of treaties within the statutory framework proposed. It is for the Houses themselves to decide upon such arrangements, as well as such other procedural matters as the means by which Parliament may trigger a debate or request an extension of the laying period. Accordingly, such matters should not be put on a statutory footing, as it properly remains within the competence of each House to regulate its internal procedures.

165 The Government awaits with interest any proposals that may emerge from the Houses of Parliament for such enhancements, and will be pleased to engage in a dialogue with the committees concerned to ensure that any new arrangements work in the most constructive and expeditious manner possible. The Government does not consider that a formal mechanism for the scrutiny of treaties prior to signature is practical or workable, given the diverse circumstances and timeframes in which treaty negotiations are conducted.

166 Clauses to reflect these proposals can be found in the draft Constitutional Renewal Bill (CM 7342-2).

The government White Paper 'Governance of Britain – Constitutional Renewal' (2008) is available on the website of the Ministry of Justice at:
www.justice.gov.uk/docs/constitutional-renewal-white-paper.pdf

9 Law reform

Introduction

This chapter looks at:

- the work of the Law Commission;
- a protocol aimed at improving the working relations between the Law Commission and government departments so that more reports produced by the Law Commission result in legislation;
- efforts made by the government through the passing of the Inquiries Act 2005 to improve the efficiency of public inquiries; and
- controversy surrounding the passing of the Inquiries Act 2005.

The Law Commission

The Law Commission is an increasingly important and influential reform body funded by the government. In 2003, the government set up a wide ranging review of the Commission, which was chaired by John Halliday.

Quinquennial Review of the Law Commission (March 2003)

John Halliday

Executive summary

Overview

0.1 The Law Commission's contribution to improvements in the law is held in high esteem by the wide variety of its stakeholders who were consulted during this review. The review has found no grounds for disturbing the present functions of the Commission, or for proposing fundamental changes in its methods of working. The thrust of this report is that the recent developments made by both the Commission and Government to strengthen working processes should be taken further over the coming years. The aim of such developments should be to maximise the public benefits to be derived from law reform: the delivery of public benefit should become a 'golden thread' running through all processes, from project selection, through project management, recommendations, implementation, and final evaluation of outcomes.

0.2 The public is the ultimate customer for the product, or benefits, of law reform. Government is, and should continue to be, the primary customer for the product of the Law Commission's work, since Government is responsible for decisions and action on its proposals. The Commission should also continue to take into account, the additional interests of the judiciary in its work, and make sure that its working links with the judiciary, and the Judicial Studies Board, are as systematic and productive as they need to be.

0.3 The Lord Chancellor and his Department should continue to be responsible and accountable for managing the interests of Government as a whole in the work of both the Law Commission and its cost-effectiveness. Efforts made in recent years to strengthen the working relationship between Government and the Commission are welcome, but the review finds scope for further development. In particular, both the Commission and Government must learn to appreciate that close and effective communication throughout the law reform process does not pose a threat to the independence of the Commission.

0.4 The review did not look in detail at individual projects. It is important, however, that the Commission's work on codifying criminal law should take account of the Government's latest thinking on how this should be achieved and by whom. The implications of the Government's decisions must be assessed and carried through into the Law Commission's programme.

0.5 The Law Commission has many strengths, especially the high quality of its output. These need to be sustained during any future improvement programme. Scope for improvement lies predominantly in the timeliness and impact of the Commission's work, rather than its quality. Performance will be at its best when:

- the projects selected are those most likely to result in public benefits through successful law reform;
- Government commits itself in advance to act on successful outcomes from those projects;
- projects are managed to the highest standards, with regular reviews to ensure timeliness and to reappraise likely outcomes;
- links between the Commission and all its stakeholders are as strong as they can be;
- the Commission's internal systems, and the systems for managing the relationship between Government and the Commission, are efficient and effective; and
- the Commission and its 'sponsors' in the Lord Chancellor's Department have the necessary vision, commitment, skills and resources.

 The full report of the quinquennial review of the Law Commission is available at: **www.dca.gov.uk/majrep/lawcom/halliday.htm**

Protocol between the government and the Law Commission

Following John Halliday's quinquennial review of the Law Commission, the government and the Law Commission agreed on a protocol which lays down guidance on how they should work together to facilitate the passing of legislation implementing Law Commission recommendations. This protocol is called 'Working Together to Deliver the Benefits of Clear, Simple and Modern Law' (2006).

Working Together to Deliver the Benefits of Clear, Simple and Modern Law (2006)

2.7 Responding to Law Commission Reports

2.7.1 Once the Law Commission has produced a report, it is important that Government considers and responds to it as soon as practicable. If there is delay in reaching conclusions on a report, or in implementing recommendations that have been accepted, there is a risk that the proposals will become out of date. This in turn can create more work for departments, in terms of further analysis and drafting, if and when the matter is eventually taken forward.

Response procedure

2.7.2 The Government department with lead responsibility for the subject matter of a Law Commission report is responsible for ensuring, in consultation with other interested departments, that the Government reaches a timely decision whether to accept, modify or reject each recommendation in the report. It should then provide a written response to the Commission, itemising these decisions.

2.7.3 The Ministerial Committee on the Law Commission has agreed that departments should aim to respond to a Commission report within six months of its publication. Where this is not possible, the department should provide a detailed interim response within the same time-frame, indicating so far as possible which recommendations it is minded to accept, modify or reject, together with a timetable for further consideration and decision. In any event, departments are required to give a definitive decision on whether they intend to implement a report, within two and a half years of its publication. Interim and final responses should be sent to the Chief Executive of the Law Commission and copied to the Ministerial Committee secretariat.

2.7.4 If, when considering a report, officials are minded to advise ministers either to reject it or substantially modify any of its significant recommendations, the department should first give the Law Commission the opportunity to discuss and comment on officials' reasons before they finalise their advice for ministers.

2.7.5 Once conclusions have been reached, it is usual for the lead department to announce the outcome, probably to Parliament by way of written Ministerial Statement in the Commons and Parliamentary Answer in the Lords. The department should give the Commission reasonable notice of the content and timing of the announcement.

2.7.6 The secretariat to the Ministerial Committee on the Law Commission is responsible for monitoring progress on responding and implementing Commission reports. When a report is published the secretariat will write to the appropriate department reminding it of the requirement to respond within six months. A further reminder letter will be sent after 5 months. The secretariat also seeks brief updates from departments on all outstanding reports each January and July to inform the Ministerial Committee of progress in implementing Commission recommendations.

2.7.7 Within two and a half years of a report being published, departments must provide a final response, by taking one of the following three actions: 1. provide a final decision on the report, 2. confirm that it is under active consideration – and give a firm date by which a decision will be reached or 3. explicitly state that no further work on the report is planned. In the latter event, the secretariat will treat the Commission's report as 'not implemented' and remove it from the system for monitoring outstanding reports. This process becomes increasingly artificial and burdensome with the passage of time, as it becomes increasingly more likely that the recommendations and any draft Bill would require substantial reconsideration, and that those who worked on the report at the Commission would no longer be available to assist. Departments should send their final response to the Chief Executive of the Law Commission and copied to the Ministerial Committee secretariat.

. . .

2.8 Legislating Law Commission recommendations

Introduction

2.8.1 This section discusses the issue of finding Parliamentary time to pass the legislation necessary to give effect to Law Commission recommendations. Most of the Commission's proposals for law reform do require legislation. The Commission's work will be wasted or lose much of its value if Parliamentary time cannot be found, or if legislation is so delayed that the recommendations are overtaken by other changes to the law or in society.

2.8.2 Once the Commission has reported, it is the responsibility of the relevant department to decide whether to accept all or some of its recommendations, accept them with modifications or reject them. And, if it is required, it is the responsibility of the department to secure the necessary legislation. In most cases, it will be necessary for the department to get policy clearance from the relevant Cabinet Committee and bid for a place in the Government's legislative programme, although some smaller bills may be suitable for handing out to a private member or peer.

2.8.3 Over the last two decades there has been an increasing problem in getting Law Commission recommendations implemented. The pressure on parliamentary time, and the inevitable focus that brings on legislating the Government's immediate priorities has meant that Commission proposals have either had to wait longer than desirable to be implemented or have not been implemented at all. The Commission's proposals may in some cases be either uncontroversial or technical (or both) and as such may be suitable for streamlined special Parliamentary procedures. Departments should consider, when putting together their bids for the legislative programme, bidding for time for outstanding Law Commission bills and whether they can use the available streamlined procedures in appropriate cases.

Regulatory Reform Orders

2.8.4 Some Law Commission proposals will be suitable for implementation by Regulatory Reform Order (RRO) under the Regulatory Reform Act 2001 (RRA). This should be preferred to primary legislation wherever appropriate.

2.8.5 The RRA provides wide powers to amend and re-enact legislation. The main requirements are that the reform includes measures to reduce burdens imposed by Statute, and that the sponsoring minister is satisfied that it meets various tests. There is also a requirement for the minister to consult before laying an RRO before Parliament. Further guidance on RROs can be found at: www.cabinet-office.gov.uk/regulation/act/index.htm

2.8.6 It is possible that when departments and the Law Commission are considering a possible law reform project, it will be apparent that the likely outcome of the project will fall within the scope of the RRA. Departments and the Commission should be alive to this possibility. It is more likely that it will not be until the Commission is beginning to formulate its policy and recommendations that the means of implementing its proposals can sensibly be considered. The Commission will always consider whether its proposals could be implemented by RRO and will seek the views of the lead department as soon as the possibility of using the RRO procedure becomes apparent. It may also seek advice from the Cabinet Office on whether the kinds of reform that might be proposed are of a similar nature to those Parliament has already accepted as being within the scope of the RRA. The department should give an indication of whether ministers are likely to consider that the proposals are suitable for an RRO in terms of being uncontroversial and passing the statutory tests.

2.8.7 If the possibility of using an RRO emerges before the Law Commission consults on the options for reform, the Commission's consultation paper should refer to this possibility.

2.8.8 Where the Law Commission believes its proposals can be implemented by RRO, and in the light of discussions with the department concludes this is the appropriate legislative mechanism, it will prepare a draft Order to include in its report.

2.8.9 Once the possibility of an RRO has been identified, and in particular when the Law Commission is drafting an Order to be included in its report, the department should consider the timing of the statutory ministerial consultation. Where the department is likely to accept most or all of the Commission's recommendations, it may be appropriate to draft and publish the ministerial consultation in parallel with the Commission's report. This will help reduce the time needed between publication of the report and laying the RRO. Also, because the Commission always consults widely on its proposals, it may be possible to keep the ministerial consultation document relatively short, concentrating on the suitability of the proposals for implementation by RRO, and cross-referring to the Commission's consultation on the policy.

Primary legislation

2.8.10 Many Law Commission proposals will still require primary legislation. For example, it will not be possible to use an RRO to implement reforms that deal solely with common law or recently amended statutes. Departments will need to bid for a bill as part of the normal process for planning the legislative programme.

2.8.11 The Chair of the Cabinet Committee on the Legislative Programme (LP) normally seeks bids from Cabinet colleagues for places in the Government's main legislative programme for forthcoming Parliamentary sessions at least one year in advance. Bids for 'handout' bills (short uncontroversial measures which can be offered for use by private members) are also sought around six months before the start of each session. To inform these bidding rounds, a list of all outstanding Law Commission bills will be circulated to departments. Departments should ensure that ministers consider the bills for which they have lead responsibility alongside their other legislative priorities.

2.8.12 Departments other than those with lead responsibility are also invited to consider whether any outstanding Law Commission proposals could be included within the scope of bills for which they intend to bid. As Commission proposals tend to be relatively uncontroversial, their inclusion in a wider bill will often not add much in terms of additional debate or other workload and handling issues.

2.8.13 In bidding for a slot for a Law Commission bill, departments will be able to stress the benefits of the proposed reforms identified through the impact assessment process . . . They can also point to the advantages that many Law Commission bills enjoy in terms of the two main constraints on space in the legislative programme.

- Drafting resources. Law Commission reports that require implementation by primary legislation include a bill drafted by Parliamentary Counsel seconded to the Commission. This greatly reduces the call on the time of Parliamentary Counsel in Whitehall, and the work a department needs to do to get the bill ready for introduction to Parliament. Conversely, the longer the delay between publication of the Commission's report and implementation by the department the greater the effort required by the department to ensure the draft bill remains current and comprehensive.
- Time on the floor of each House. In the Commons, under Standing Order 59, bills that mainly implement Law Commission proposals are automatically referred to Second Reading Committee. In the Lords, the committee stage of technical and non-controversial bills may be taken off the floor of the House in Grand Committee or a public bill committee.

2.8.14 The pro-forma used by LP Committee has been amended to allow departments to indicate whether a bill implements Law Commission proposals. This will ensure that the Parliamentary business managers, when planning the Parliamentary programme, are aware of the scope for taking advantage of these accelerated procedures.

2.8.15 Departments should also consider whether a bill should be offered for pre-legislative scrutiny. The availability of a draft bill in a Law Commission report will often enable earlier submission. Pre-legislative scrutiny does not guarantee a place in the legislative programme, although in some cases these bills may experience a smoother Parliamentary passage. Further guidance on pre-legislative scrutiny can be found in Chapter 17 of the Cabinet Office's *Guide to Legislative Procedures*.

2.8.16 Finally, departments should consider whether a bill is suitable to start its Parliamentary passage in the Lords. This will often be the case with Law Commission bills which tend not to have a high political profile. This is also helpful to business managers in planning the legislative programme.

The report 'Working Together to Deliver the Benefits of Clear, Simple and Modern Law' (2006) is available on the internet at: **www.dca.gov.uk/pubs/reports/lawcomm_vision.htm**

Inquiries Act 2005

One process that can lead to legal reform is the establishment of an inquiry when a particular problem or incident is causing public disquiet. The government became concerned that some of these inquiries were expensive and inefficient and undertook a consultation process to look at the inquiry system.

Effective Inquiries (2004)

Executive summary

There has been a long standing practice in the UK of setting up formal and open inquiries, where necessary, to look into matters that have caused public concern. Ministers are not under any statutory duty to set up such inquiries, but have found them to be a useful method of dealing with matters that have warranted formal, independent investigation. The types of inquiry discussed here are not conducted by Government or by any permanent organisations, but by independent, temporary bodies set up for the purpose. These bodies may or may not have statutory powers, for example to require the production of evidence or the attendance of witnesses. Inquiries are funded through public money, and are usually asked to report their conclusions to Ministers, but during their lifetimes they are independent from Government and Parliament . . .

In general, inquiries of this type have helped to restore public confidence through a thorough investigation of the facts and timely and effective recommendations to prevent recurrence of the matters causing concern. Many inquiries have helped to bring about valuable and welcomed improvements in public services. (Examples are discussed in response to question 20 from the Public Administration Select Committee, in the main body of the paper.) However, there have been cases where inquiries have been marred by arguments about procedure, or have taken much longer or cost more than expected. The Government believes that there is a strong case for considering what steps could be taken to make inquiry procedures faster and more effective, and to contain cost escalation.

As part of this work, there is a need to consider whether current legislation provides a suitable basis for appropriate and effective inquiries.

The consultation paper 'Effective Inquiries' can be found on the internet at: **www.dca.gov.uk/consult/inquiries/index.htm**

Controversy surrounding the Inquiries Act 2005

Following this consultation process the Inquiries Act 2005 was passed. However, Amnesty International has been heavily critical of this legislation, suggesting that inquiries established under the Act will not be sufficiently independent of the government.

Amnesty International Urges Judiciary Not to Partake in Inquiry Sham
Press release, 20 April 2005

Amnesty International calls on all judges, whether in the United Kingdom (UK) or in other jurisdictions, to decline appointments as chairs or panel members to any inquiry established under the recently enacted Inquiries Act 2005, including an inquiry into allegations of state collusion in the murder of Patrick Finucane. The organisation is also urging the Act's repeal.

Amnesty International supports the call of Geraldine Finucane, Patrick Finucane's widow, to all senior judges in England, Wales and Scotland not to serve on an inquiry into her husband's case held under the new legislation.

'By proposing to hold an inquiry into the Finucane case under the Inquiries Act 2005, the UK government is trying to eliminate independent scrutiny of the actions of its agents. Any judge sitting on such an inquiry would be presiding over a sham', Amnesty International said.

Patrick Finucane, an outspoken human rights lawyer, was shot dead in his home in Belfast, Northern Ireland, on 12 February 1989 by Loyalist paramilitaries. In the aftermath of his killing, *prima facie* evidence of criminal conduct by police and military intelligence agents, acting in collusion with Loyalist paramilitaries in his murder, emerged. In addition, allegations have emerged of a subsequent cover-up by different government agencies and authorities.

In April 2004, an independent report, commissioned by the UK and Irish governments, concluded that 'only a public inquiry will suffice' in Patrick Finucane's case.

Instead, in the face of strong criticism and opposition, the UK executive railroaded the Inquiries Bill through Parliament and managed to have it passed as legislation as the Inquiries Act 2005 on 7 April 2005, the last possible day before Parliament was dissolved. Any inquiry, held under the new Act, would be controlled by the executive which, under it, is empowered to block public scrutiny of state actions. It will affect not only Patrick Finucane's case, but also other major incidents which would warrant public scrutiny of the actions of the state, such as failures of public services, deaths in prisons, rail disasters and army deaths in disputed circumstances.

'The Inquiries Act 2005 undermines the rule of law, the separation of powers and human rights protection. It cannot be the foundation for an effective, independent, impartial or thorough judicial inquiry in serious allegations of human rights violations. Nor would it provide for public scrutiny of all the relevant evidence', Amnesty International said.

'The Inquiries Act 2005 deals a fatal blow to any possibility of public scrutiny of and accountability for state abuses. Any inquiry under this legislation would automatically fall far short of the requirements in international human rights law and standards for effective remedies for victims of human rights violations and their families. One of the first tasks of the new UK Parliament should be to immediately repeal the Act.'

Once again, Amnesty International calls on the UK authorities to immediately establish a truly independent judicial inquiry into collusion by state agents with Loyalist paramilitaries in Patrick Finucane's murder; into reports that his killing was the result of state policy; and into allegations that different government authorities played a part in the subsequent cover-up of collusion in his murder.

Background

In May 2002, the UK and Irish governments appointed Justice Peter Cory, formerly a judge in the Canadian Supreme Court, to investigate a number of killings in which official collusion was alleged, including the killing of Patrick Finucane. In April 2004, the UK authorities published Justice Cory's reports but refused at that time to announce a public inquiry into Patrick Finucane's case.

Instead of announcing a public judicial inquiry under the Tribunals of Inquiry (Evidence) Act 1921, the government eventually announced that it would introduce new legislation under which an inquiry into the Finucane case would be established. There was no consultation prior to the publication of the Bill. The new Inquiries Act 2005 repeals the Tribunals of Inquiry (Evidence) Act 1921.

Under the new Act:

- the inquiry and its terms of reference would be decided by the executive; no independent parliamentary scrutiny of these decisions would be allowed;
- each member of an inquiry panel, including the chair of the inquiry, would be appointed by the executive and the executive would have the discretion to dismiss any member of the inquiry;
- the executive can impose restrictions on public access to the inquiry, including on whether the inquiry, or any individual hearings, would be held in public or private;
- the executive can also impose restrictions on disclosure or publication of any evidence or documents given, produced or provided to an inquiry;
- the final report of the inquiry would be published at the executive's discretion and crucial evidence could be omitted at the executive's discretion, 'in the public interest'.

Lord Saville of Newdigate, the chair of the Bloody Sunday Tribunal of Inquiry, pointed out that the Inquiries Act 2005 'makes a very serious inroad into the independence of any inquiry; and is likely to damage or destroy public confidence in the inquiry and its findings'. Lord Saville also said: 'As a Judge, I must tell you that I would not be prepared to be appointed as a member of an inquiry that was subject to a provision of this kind.'

Judge Peter Cory, with specific reference to the possibility of an inquiry into the Finucane case held under the Inquiries Act 2005, stated: 'It seems to me that the proposed new Act would make a meaningful inquiry impossible.'

PEOPLE WORKING IN THE LEGAL SYSTEM

10

Judges

Introduction

This chapter looks at:

- the independence of the judiciary;
- the tensions in the relationship between the judges and the executive;
- statistics analysing the background of the judges;
- criticism of the judicial appointment process;
- further plans to reform the judicial appointment process;
- government efforts to increase judicial diversity; and
- small steps taken to modernise and simplify the clothes that judges wear in court.

Independence of the judiciary

Judges must both be independent and be seen to be independent. This issue arose in the extradition proceedings that were brought against the former dictator of Chile, Senator Pinochet. When the case had originally reached the House of Lords, Lord Hoffmann had sat on the bench. However, he was subsequently revealed to have been involved with Amnesty International, which had an interest in the case. A further appeal was therefore allowed to the House of Lords in the light of this irregularity in the proceedings.

R v Bow Street Metropolitan Stipendiary Magistrate and Others, *ex parte* Pinochet Ugarte (No. 2) (1999)
House of Lords

Lord Browne-Wilkinson

My Lords,

Introduction

This petition has been brought by Senator Pinochet to set aside an order made by your Lordships on 25 November 1998. It is said that the links between one of the members of the Appellate Committee who heard the appeal, Lord Hoffmann, and Amnesty International ('AI') were such as to give the appearance that he might have been biased against Senator Pinochet. On 17 December 1998 your Lordships set aside the order of 25 November 1998 for reasons to be given later. These are the reasons that led me to that conclusion.

. . .

The link between Lord Hoffmann and AI

It appears that neither Senator Pinochet nor (save to a very limited extent) his legal advisers were aware of any connection between Lord Hoffmann and AI until after the judgment was given on 25 November. Two members of the legal team recalled that they had heard rumours that Lord Hoffmann's wife was connected with AI in some way. During the 'Newsnight' programme on television on 25 November, an allegation to that effect was made by a speaker in Chile. On that limited information the representations made on Senator Pinochet's behalf to the Home Secretary on 30 November drew attention to Lady Hoffmann's position and contained a detailed consideration of the relevant law of bias. It then read:

> It is submitted therefore that the Secretary of State should not have any regard to the decision of Lord Hoffmann. The authorities make it plain that this is the appropriate approach to a decision that is affected by bias. Since the bias was in the House of Lords, the Secretary of State represents the senator's only domestic protection. Absent domestic protection the senator will have to invoke the jurisdiction of the European Court of Human Rights.

After the representations had been made to the Home Office, Senator Pinochet's legal advisers received a letter dated 1 December 1998 from the solicitors acting for AI written in response to a request for information as to Lord Hoffmann's links. The letter of 1 December, so far as relevant, reads as follows:

Further to our letter of 27 November, we are informed by our clients, Amnesty International, that Lady Hoffmann has been working at their international secretariat since 1977. She has always been employed in administrative positions, primarily in their department dealing with press and publications. She moved to her present position of programme assistant to the director of the media and audio visual programme when this position was established in 1994. Lady Hoffmann provides administrative support to the programme, including some receptionist duties. She has not been consulted or otherwise involved in any substantive discussions or decisions by Amnesty International, including in relation to the Pinochet case.

On 7 December a man anonymously telephoned Senator Pinochet's solicitors alleging that Lord Hoffmann was a director of the Amnesty International Charitable Trust. That allegation was repeated in a newspaper report on 8 December. Senator Pinochet's solicitors informed the Home Secretary of these allegations. On 8 December they received a letter from the solicitors acting for AI dated 7 December which reads, so far as relevant, as follows:

On further consideration, our client, Amnesty International have instructed us that after contacting Lord Hoffmann over the weekend both he and they believe that the following information about his connection with Amnesty International's charitable work should be provided to you. Lord Hoffmann is a director and chairperson of Amnesty International Charity Ltd ('AICL'), a registered charity incorporated on 7 April 1986 to undertake those aspects of the work of Amnesty International Ltd ('AIL') which are charitable under UK law. AICL files reports with Companies House and the Charity Commissioners as required by UK law. AICL funds a proportion of the charitable activities undertaken independently by AIL AIL's board is composed of Amnesty International's Secretary General and two Deputy Secretaries General. Since 1990 Lord Hoffmann and Peter Duffy QC have been the two directors of AICL. They are neither employed nor remunerated by either AICL or AIL. They have not been consulted and have not had any other role in Amnesty International's interventions in the case of Pinochet. Lord Hoffmann is not a member of Amnesty International. In addition, in 1997 Lord Hoffmann helped in the organisation of a fund raising appeal for a new building for Amnesty International UK. He helped organise this appeal together with other senior legal figures, including the Lord Chief Justice, Lord Bingham. In February your firm contributed £1,000 to this appeal. You should also note that in 1982 Lord Hoffmann, when practising at the Bar, appeared in the Chancery Division for Amnesty International UK.

Further information relating to AICL and its relationship with Lord Hoffmann and AI is given below. Mr Alun Jones for the CPS does not contend that either Senator Pinochet or his legal advisers had any knowledge of Lord Hoffmann's position as a director of AICL until receipt of that letter.

Senator Pinochet's solicitors informed the Home Secretary of the contents of the letter dated 7 December. The Home Secretary signed the authority to proceed on 9 December 1998. He also gave reasons for his decision, attaching no weight to the allegations of bias or apparent bias made by Senator Pinochet.

On 10 December 1998, Senator Pinochet lodged the present petition asking that the order of 25 November 1998 should either be set aside completely or the opinion of Lord Hoffmann should be declared to be of no effect. The sole ground relied upon was that Lord Hoffmann's links with AI were such as to give the appearance of possible bias. It is important to stress that Senator Pinochet makes no allegation of *actual bias* against Lord Hoffmann; his claim is based on the requirement that justice should be seen to be done as well as actually being done. There is no allegation that any other member of the committee has fallen short in the performance of his judicial duties.

. . .

Conclusions

. . .

2 Apparent bias

As I have said, Senator Pinochet does not allege that Lord Hoffmann was in fact biased. The contention is that there was a real danger or reasonable apprehension or suspicion that Lord Hoffmann might have been biased, that is to say, it is alleged that there is an appearance of bias not actual bias.

The fundamental principle is that a man may not be a judge in his own cause. This principle, as developed by the courts, has two very similar but not identical implications. First it may be applied literally: if a judge is in fact a party to the litigation or has a financial or proprietary interest in its outcome then he is indeed sitting as a judge in his own cause. In that case, the mere fact that he is a party to the action or has a financial or proprietary interest in its outcome is sufficient to cause his automatic disqualification. The second application of the principle is where a judge is not a party to the suit and does not have a financial interest in its outcome, but in some other way his conduct or behaviour may give rise to a suspicion that he is not impartial, for example because of his friendship with a party. This second type of case is not strictly speaking an application of the principle that a man must not be judge in his own cause, since the judge will not normally be himself benefiting, but providing a benefit for another by failing to be impartial.

In my judgment, this case falls within the first category of case, viz. where the judge is disqualified because he is a judge in his own cause. In such a case, once it is shown that the judge is himself a party to the cause, or has a relevant interest in its subject matter, he is disqualified without any investigation into whether there was a likelihood or suspicion of bias. The mere fact of his interest is sufficient to disqualify him unless he has made sufficient disclosure: see *Shetreet, Judges on Trial* (1976), p 303; De Smith, Woolf and Jowell, *Judicial Review of Administrative Action*, 5th edn (1995), p 525. I will call this 'automatic disqualification'.

In **Dimes v Proprietors of Grand Junction Canal** (1852) 3 HLCas 759, the then Lord Chancellor, Lord Cottenham, owned a substantial shareholding in the defendant canal which was an incorporated body. In the action the Lord Chancellor sat on appeal from the Vice-Chancellor, whose judgment in favour of the company he affirmed. There was an appeal to your Lordships' House on the grounds that the Lord Chancellor was disqualified. Their Lordships consulted the judges who advised, at p 786, that Lord Cottenham was disqualified from sitting as a judge in the cause because he had an interest in the suit. This advice was unanimously accepted by their Lordships. There was no inquiry by the court as to whether a reasonable man would consider Lord Cottenham to be biased and no inquiry as to the circumstances which led to Lord Cottenham sitting. Lord Campbell said, at p 793:

> No one can suppose that Lord Cottenham could be, in the remotest degree, influenced by the interest he had in this concern; but, my Lords, it is of the last importance that the maxim that no man is to be a judge in his own cause should be held sacred. And that is not to be confined to a cause *in which he is a party*, but applies to a cause in which he has an interest. (Emphasis added.)

On occasion, this proposition is elided so as to omit all references to the disqualification of a judge who is a party to the suit: see, for example, **Reg. v Rand** (1866) LR 1 QB 230; **Reg. v Gough** [1993] AC 646, 661. This does not mean that a judge who is a party to a suit is not disqualified just because the suit does not involve a financial interest. The authorities cited in the **Dimes** case show how the principle developed. The starting-point was the case in which a judge was indeed purporting to decide a case in which he was a party. This was held to be absolutely prohibited. That absolute prohibition was then extended to cases where, although not nominally a party, the judge had an interest in the outcome.

The importance of this point in the present case is this. Neither AI, nor AICL, have any financial interest in the outcome of this litigation. We are here confronted, as was Lord Hoffmann, with a novel situation where the outcome of the litigation did not lead to financial benefit to anyone. The interest of AI in the litigation was not financial; it was its interest in achieving the trial and possible conviction of Senator Pinochet for crimes against humanity.

By seeking to intervene in this appeal and being allowed so to intervene, in practice AI became a party to the appeal. Therefore if, in the circumstances, it is right to treat Lord Hoffmann as being the alter ego of AI and therefore a judge in his own cause, then he must have been automatically disqualified on the grounds that he was a party to the appeal. Alternatively, even if it be not right to say that Lord Hoffmann was a party to the appeal as such, the question then arises whether, in non-financial litigation, anything other than a financial or proprietary interest in the outcome is sufficient automatically to disqualify a man from sitting as judge in the cause.

Are the facts such as to require Lord Hoffmann to be treated as being himself a party to this appeal? The facts are striking and unusual. One of the parties to the appeal is an unincorporated association, AI. One of the constituent parts of that unincorporated association is AICL AICL was established, for tax purposes, to carry out part of the functions of AI those parts which were charitable which had previously been carried on either by AI itself or by AIL. Lord Hoffmann is a director and chairman of AICL, which is wholly controlled by AI, since its members (who ultimately control it) are all the members of the international executive committee of AI. A large part of the work of AI is, as a matter of strict law, carried on by AICL which instructs AIL to do the work on its behalf. In reality, AI, AICL and AIL are a close-knit group carrying on the work of AI.

However, close as these links are, I do not think it would be right to identify Lord Hoffmann personally as being a party to the appeal. He is closely linked to AI but he is not in fact AI. Although this is an area in which legal technicality is particularly to be avoided, it cannot be ignored that Lord Hoffmann took no part in running AI. Lord Hoffmann, AICL and the executive committee of AI are in law separate people. Then is this a case in which it can be said that Lord Hoffmann had an 'interest' which must lead to his automatic disqualification? Hitherto only pecuniary and proprietary interests have led to automatic disqualification. But, as I have indicated, this litigation is most unusual. It is not civil litigation but criminal litigation. Most unusually, by allowing AI to intervene, there is a party to a criminal cause or matter who is neither prosecutor nor accused. That party, AI, shares with the government of Spain and the CPS, not a financial interest but an interest to establish that there is no immunity for ex-heads of state in relation to crimes against humanity. The interest of these parties is to procure Senator Pinochet's extradition and trial a non-pecuniary interest. So far as AICL is concerned, clause 3(c) of its memorandum provides that one of its objects is 'to procure the abolition of torture, extra-judicial execution and disappearance'. AI has, amongst other objects, the same objects. Although AICL, as a charity, cannot campaign to change the law, it is concerned by other means to procure the abolition of these crimes against humanity. In my opinion, therefore, AICL plainly had a non-pecuniary interest, to establish that Senator Pinochet was not immune.

That being the case, the question is whether in the very unusual circumstances of this case a non-pecuniary interest to achieve a particular result is sufficient to give rise to automatic disqualification and, if so, whether the fact that AICL had such an interest necessarily leads to the conclusion that Lord Hoffmann, as a director of AICL, was automatically disqualified from sitting on the appeal? My Lords, in my judgment, although the cases have all dealt with automatic disqualification on the grounds of pecuniary interest, there is no good reason in principle for so limiting automatic disqualification. The rationale of the whole rule is that a man cannot be a judge in his own cause. In civil litigation the matters in issue will normally have an economic impact; therefore a judge is automatically disqualified if he stands to make a financial gain as a consequence of his own decision of the case. But if, as in the present case, the matter at issue does not relate to money or economic advantage but is concerned with the promotion of the cause, the rationale disqualifying a judge applies just as much if the judge's decision will lead to the promotion of a cause in which the judge is involved together with one of the parties. Thus in my opinion if Lord Hoffmann had been a member of AI he would have been automatically disqualified because of his non-pecuniary interest in establishing that Senator Pinochet was not entitled to immunity. Indeed, so much I understood to have been conceded by Mr Duffy.

Can it make any difference that, instead of being a direct member of AI, Lord Hoffmann is a director of AICL, that is of a company which is wholly controlled by AI and is carrying on much of its work? Surely not. The substance of the matter is that AI, AIL and AICL are all various parts of an entity or movement working in different fields towards the same goals. If the absolute impartiality of the judiciary is to be maintained, there must be a rule which automatically disqualifies a judge who is involved, whether personally or as a director of a company, in promoting the same causes in the same organisation as is a party to the suit. There is no room for fine distinctions if Lord Hewart CJ's famous dictum is to be observed: it is 'of fundamental importance that justice should not only be done, but should manifestly and undoubtedly be seen to be done': see **Rex v Sussex Justices,** *ex parte* **McCarthy** [1924] 1 KB 256, 259.

Since, in my judgment, the relationship between AI, AICL and Lord Hoffmann leads to the automatic disqualification of Lord Hoffmann to sit on the hearing of the appeal, it is unnecessary to consider the other factors which were relied on by Miss Montgomery, viz. the position of Lady Hoffmann as an employee of AI and the fact that Lord Hoffmann was involved in the recent appeal for funds for Amnesty. Those factors might have been relevant if Senator Pinochet had been required to show a real danger or reasonable suspicion of bias. But since the disqualification is automatic and does not depend in any way on an implication of bias, it is unnecessary to consider these factors. I do, however, wish to make it clear (if I have not already done so) that my decision is not that Lord Hoffmann has been guilty of bias of any kind: he was disqualified as a matter of law automatically by reason of his directorship of AICL, a company controlled by a party, AI.

For the same reason, it is unnecessary to determine whether the test of apparent bias laid down in **Reg. v Gough** [1993] AC 646 ('is there in the view of the court a real danger that the judge was biased?') needs to be reviewed in the light of subsequent decisions. Decisions in Canada, Australia and New Zealand have either refused to apply the test in **Reg. v Gough**, or modified it so as to make the relevant test the question whether the events in question give rise to a reasonable apprehension or suspicion on the part of a fairminded and informed member of the public that the judge was not impartial: see, for example, the High Court of Australia in **Webb v The Queen**, 181 CLR 41. It has also been suggested that the test in **Reg. v Gough** in some way impinges on the requirement of Lord Hewart CJ's dictum that justice should appear to be done: see **Reg. v Inner West London Coroner,** *ex parte* **Dallaglio** [1994] 4 All ER 139, 152a–b. Since such a review is unnecessary for the determination of the present case, I prefer to express no view on it.

It is important not to overstate what is being decided. It was suggested in argument that a decision setting aside the order of 25 November 1998 would lead to a position where judges would be unable to sit on cases involving charities in whose work they are involved. It is suggested that, because of such involvement, a judge would be disqualified. That is not correct. The facts of this present case are exceptional. The critical elements are (1) that AI was a party to the appeal; (2) that AI was joined in order to argue for a particular result; (3) the judge was a director of a charity closely allied to AI and sharing, in this respect, AI's objects. Only in cases where a judge is taking an active role as trustee or director of a charity which is closely allied to and acting with a party to the litigation should a judge normally be concerned either to recuse himself or disclose the position to the parties. However, there may well be other exceptional cases in which the judge would be well advised to disclose a possible interest.

Finally on this aspect of the case, we were asked to state in giving judgment what had been said and done within the Appellate Committee in relation to Amnesty International during the hearing leading to the order of 25 November. As is apparent from what I have said, such matters are irrelevant to what we have to decide: in the absence of any disclosure to the parties of Lord Hoffmann's involvement with AI, such involvement either did or did not in law disqualify him regardless of what happened within the Appellate Committee. We therefore did not investigate those matters and make no findings as to them.

The judgment of the House of Lords **R** v **Bow Street Metropolitan Stipendiary Magistrate and Others,** *ex parte* **Pinochet Ugarte (No. 2)** (1998) is available on the internet at:

www.publications.parliament.uk/pa/ld199899/ldjudgmt/jd990115/pino01.htm

Judges and the executive

The three branches of the British government are the executive, the legislature and the judiciary. It is essential that these three powers maintain constructive relations in order to support the rule of law and the democratic constitution. In recent years, tensions have been visible between the executive and the judiciary, in particular, and the House of Lords Select Committee on the Constitution has issued a report trying to remind the executive of the importance of respecting the independence of the judiciary.

Relations between the Executive, the Judiciary and Parliament (2007)
House of Lords Select Committee on the Constitution

CHAPTER 1 INTRODUCTION AND BACKGROUND

Introduction

1 Constructive relationships between the three arms of government – the executive, the legislature and the judiciary – are essential to the effective maintenance of the constitution and the rule of law. In recent years, the character of these relationships has changed significantly, both because of changes in governance and because of wider societal change. . . .

The Constitutional Reform Act 2005 and the Concordat

12 In previous reports we have expressed our dismay about circumstances in which the Government have announced policy or introduced a bill without apparently being sufficiently aware of the impact of the initiative upon the fundamentals of the constitution. A prime example of confusion about whether an initiative is a simple 'machinery of government' change or a major constitutional reform was the announcement in June 2003 – in the midst of a Cabinet reshuffle – that the office of Lord Chancellor was to be abolished and that a Supreme Court of the United Kingdom was to be established. That announcement took place without any apparent understanding of the legal status of the Lord Chancellor and without consultation with the judiciary (or anyone else outside government).

13 Soon after that announcement, Lord Woolf (then Lord Chief Justice) and Lord Falconer (then Lord Chancellor) started negotiations over the key principles and principal arrangements that should govern the new situation in which the Lord Chief Justice rather than the Lord Chancellor would be head of the judiciary. The outcome of those talks was set out in January 2004 in an agreement known as 'the Concordat' (formally entitled 'The Lord Chancellor's Judiciary-Related Functions: Proposals'). Many aspects of the Concordat were put on a statutory footing by the CRA, but it is clear to us that the Concordat continues to be of great constitutional importance.

14 Lord Falconer agreed with this: 'it seems to me to be a document of constitutional significance because, although much of it was then enacted in the Constitutional Reform Act, it sets out the basic principles on which the judges and the executive will relate to each other in the future. I have never known any piece of legislation to be utterly comprehensive; there are bound to be issues that come up in the future where it is the principle that matters rather than precise detailed legislation and I believe the Concordat will be important for that'. Similarly, the current Lord Chief Justice, Lord Phillips, told us: 'I would like to think it has an entrenched quality about it. It has certainly been treated as if it were a constitutional document laying down the division of functions, now largely of course overtaken by the Act but not exclusively, and where the Act does not cover something one needs to go back to the Concordat'. . . .

16 The terms of the CRA itself differed in several respects from the announcement of 3 June 2003 and the Constitutional Reform Bill as introduced to the House of Lords in 2004. Part 1 of the CRA is about the rule of law, a provision to which we return shortly. Part 2 sets out the main duties and powers of the reformed office of Lord Chancellor, the new role of the Lord Chief Justice of England and Wales as head of the judiciary, and other provisions relating to judicial leadership. Part 3 concerns the new Supreme Court of the United Kingdom. Part 4 deals with judicial appointments and discipline. Clearly the Concordat and the CRA taken together have made important changes to the relationships between the judiciary, the executive and Parliament.

17 As well as redefining formal powers and duties, the CRA and the Concordat were intended to change the attitudes and perceptions relating to these leadership roles. Lord

Falconer told us that 'having a leader of the judges drawn from the judiciary rather than a politician drives a sense of ownership and momentum. It gives the judiciary confidence that the pressure for change, if it comes from the head of the judiciary, comes from the profession and not from the politicians. Judges have always sought to improve the core processes'. The Lord Chief Justice said that under the changes brought about by the Concordat and the CRA he and the Lord Chancellor 'become partners in the administration of justice, but as a matter of constitutional principle the Lord Chief Justice is now the senior partner'.

18 In her paper for us, Professor Kate Malleson (Professor of Law at Queen Mary, University of London) forecast that 'the idea of a partnership as expressed in the Concordat may well provide a basis for the future relationship, but it would be unrealistic to expect it to be a partnership without tensions. The consequence of a more active judiciary with greater autonomy will inevitably be a more dynamic relationship between the branches of government in which the judiciary have a more structured and active role in defending themselves from criticism and ensuring that the proper resources and support for the courts are in place' (Appendix 3). That comment, written in November 2006, has proved to be prescient. The creation of the new Ministry of Justice has thrown up issues of profound disagreement between the Government and the judiciary. By May 2007, the judiciary were expressing frustration that 'in the event there has been no real change in attitude at all. The Lord Chancellor and his staff in the DCA continued to act as if he retained primary responsibility for the administration of justice and had sole responsibility for deciding what resources should be allocated to this and how they should be deployed'.

Table 1 The **Craig Sweeney** case: sequence of events

Monday, 12 June 2006	Craig Sweeney sentenced to life imprisonment for abducting and sexually assaulting a three-year-old girl; eligible for parole in 5 years and 108 days.
	Home Secretary John Reid attacks sentence as 'unduly lenient' and asks the Attorney-General to examine the case as the tariff 'does not reflect the seriousness of the crime'.
	The Attorney-General's spokesman states that 'the Attorney will make a decision purely on the merits of the case and not in response to political or public pressure'. He adds that 'calling for the file in no way implies that there will be a reference by the Attorney – still less does it imply any criticism of the sentencing judge'. It is also widely reported that the Attorney-General feels that John Reid's comments are 'not terribly helpful'.
	The Chief Crown Prosecutor for South Wales explains the sentencing guidelines in the context of the **Sweeney** case.
Tuesday, 13 June	The sentence handed down to Craig Sweeney generates hostile media coverage. The *Sun* criticises 'the arrogance of judges in their mink-lined ivory towers who leave the rest of us to cope with the real crisis of soaring crime' and adds that 'judges are a law unto themselves'. The *Daily Express* brands the judiciary as 'deluded, out-of-touch and frankly deranged' and 'combining arrogance with downright wickedness', suggesting that 'our legal system has not only lost touch with public opinion but with natural justice itself . . . [sentencing] now bears no relation at all to the seriousness of the crime'.

→

	The Prime Minister's spokesman defends John Reid, suggesting that it was right 'to articulate the concern the public has'. Jack Straw MP, Leader of the House of Commons, agrees that it was 'perfectly appropriate' for John Reid to have intervened. Lord Morris of Aberavon, the former Attorney-General, states that 'our courts are not run by Government ministers . . . As far as sentencing is concerned, they [judges] are independent. If he [John Reid] has a concern . . . he can amend the acts of Parliament'. Alun Michael, a Cardiff MP, calls on judges to 'wake up and smell the coffee' and suggests that 'some judges simply aren't getting it'.
Thursday, 15 June	The Lord Chancellor appears on the BBC's 'Question Time'. He says 'we need to be extremely careful that we don't attack the judges on these issues where it is the system' and 'the whipping boys for this have become the judges and that is completely wrong . . . If we attack the judges, we attack an incredibly important part of the system when it is not their fault . . . it wasn't the judge's fault'. But he also defends John Reid and claims that he 'did not attack the judge'.
Friday, 16 June	Vera Baird QC, Parliamentary Under-Secretary of State at the DCA, appears on the BBC's 'Any Questions?' She says, 'it seems to me that this judge has just got this formula wrong, so I'm critical of the judge for three reasons – one, starting too low; two, deducting too much for the guilty plea; and three, getting the formula wrong'.
Sunday, 18 June	Judge Keith Cutler, Secretary of the Council of HM Circuit Judges, appears on the BBC's 'Broadcasting House'. He says that his colleagues are feeling 'pretty low' about the **Sweeney** case and adds, 'some of the judges felt that there was quite a silence, and there was no-one actually speaking on behalf of the judges'. He concludes, 'we are thinking that we must perhaps change that'.
Monday, 19 June	Vera Baird is forced to apologise for her comments on 'Any Questions?' The Lord Chancellor accepts her apology.
Tuesday, 4 July	The Lord Chancellor gives evidence to the House of Commons Constitutional Affairs Committee. He accepts that the **Sweeney** case 'has had an impact on undermining confidence in the judiciary'.
Monday, 10 July	The Attorney-General decides not to challenge the sentence imposed by the trial judge, concluding that it was *not* 'unduly lenient'.
Tuesday, 18 July	The Lord Chief Justice, speaking at the Lord Mayor of London's annual judges' dinner, labels the recent attacks on judges as 'intemperate, offensive and unfair'.

CHAPTER 5 CONCLUSIONS AND RECOMMENDATIONS

Executive and judiciary

Managing the tensions

172 The **Sweeney** case was the first big test of whether the new relationship between the Lord Chancellor and the judiciary was working properly, and it is clear that there was a

systemic failure. Ensuring that ministers do not impugn individual judges, and restraining and reprimanding those who do, is one of the most important duties of the Lord Chancellor. In this case, Lord Falconer did not fulfil this duty in a satisfactory manner. The senior judiciary could also have acted more quickly to head off the inflammatory and unfair press coverage which followed the sentencing decision.

173 The key to harmonious relations between the judiciary and the executive is ensuring that ministers do not violate the independence of the judiciary in the first place. To this end, we recommend that when the Ministerial Code is next revised the Prime Minister should insert strongly worded guidelines setting out the principles governing public comment by ministers on individual judges.

Constitutional change

174 We agree that the advent of the Ministry of Justice, whilst obviously a machinery of government change, has significant constitutional implications.

175 We are disappointed that the Government seem to have learnt little or nothing from the debacle surrounding the constitutional reforms initiated in 2003. The creation of the Ministry of Justice clearly has important implications for the judiciary. The new dispensation created by the Constitutional Reform Act and the Concordat requires the Government to treat the judiciary as partners, not merely as subjects of change. By omitting to consult the judiciary at a sufficiently early stage, by drawing the parameters of the negotiations too tightly and by proceeding with the creation of the new Ministry before important aspects had been resolved, the Government failed to do this. Furthermore, the subsequent request made by the judiciary for a fundamental review of the position in the light of the creation of the Ministry of Justice was in our view a reasonable one to which the Government should have acceded in a spirit of partnership.

176 We believe that the role of Lord Chancellor is of central importance to the maintenance of judicial independence and the rule of law. Prime Ministers must therefore ensure that they continue to appoint to the post candidates of sufficient status and seniority.

177 We sincerely hope that constitutional affairs remain central to the Ministry of Justice's responsibilities and are not downgraded in importance compared to the other duties of the Ministry.

178 The integrity of the legal system depends on it being properly funded. We consider it one of the vital tasks of the Lord Chancellor to ensure that the Courts Service and Legal Aid budgets uphold that integrity. Whilst it is not for us to suggest how the courts budget should be agreed in future, we do urge the Lord Chancellor to ensure that it receives maximum protection from short-term budgetary pressures upon and within the new Ministry. Moreover, the budget-setting process must be transparent and the judiciary must be fully involved, both in determining the process and in its implementation.

179 We are not convinced by the judiciary's claims that the creation of the Ministry of Justice lends any additional urgency to their desire for an autonomous court administration. However, the status of Her Majesty's Courts Service is of central importance to the administration of justice, and we urge the Government to engage meaningfully with the judiciary on this issue in order to find a mutually acceptable way forward.

Human Rights Act

Ministerial compatibility statements and parliamentary scrutiny
180 Where a department has any doubt about compatibility of a bill with Convention rights, ministers should seek the involvement of the Law Officers at a formative stage of policy-making and legislative drafting.

Greater guidance to the executive from the courts?
181 Whilst we have sympathy with the difficulties outlined by Charles Clarke in relation to the Human Rights Act, his call for meetings between the Law Lords and the Home Secretary risks an unacceptable breach of the principle of judicial independence. It is essential that the Law Lords, as the court of last resort, should not even be perceived to have prejudged an issue as a result of communications with the executive.

Should there be a system of abstract review?
182 Whilst a system of 'abstract review' of legislation might seem attractive in some respects, we believe that it could compromise the impartiality of the senior judiciary and that it would not in any case prevent successful challenges under the Human Rights Act to ministerial exercise of statutory powers.

Review of Bills by a committee of distinguished lawyers
183 We do not believe that a committee of distinguished lawyers tasked with scrutinising legislation for compatibility with Convention rights is desirable at this time. If, however, at some future time the composition of the House of Lords changes, this is an idea that may well merit further consideration.

Advisory declarations
184 We recommend that the Government and the judiciary give further consideration to how advisory declarations might be used to provide guidance on questions relating to Convention rights.

Parliament and judiciary

Laying written representations before Parliament
185 We recommend that any written representations received from the Lord Chief Justice under section 5 of the Constitutional Reform Act 2005 should be published in *Hansard*; that the business managers should find time for the issue to be debated in the House at the earliest possible opportunity; and that the Government should respond to such representations in good time before either House has finished considering the bill or initiative in question. Further, this Committee will endeavour to scrutinise any such representations in time to inform deliberations in the House.

The question of accountability

The role of select committees
186 We believe that select committees can play a central part in enabling the role and proper concerns of the judiciary to be better understood by the public at large, and

in helping the judiciary to remain accountable to the people via their representatives in Parliament. Not only should senior judges be questioned on the administration of the justice system, they might also be encouraged to discuss their views on key legal issues in the cause of transparency and better understanding of such issues amongst both parliamentarians and the public. However, under no circumstances must committees ask judges to comment on the pros and cons of individual judgments.

A parliamentary committee on the judiciary

187 We are not currently convinced of the need for a joint committee on the judiciary, but we shall keep the situation under review, not least in evaluating our Committee's effectiveness in providing the necessary oversight and contact. The Constitutional Affairs Select Committee in the House of Commons also has an important role to play.

Post-legislative scrutiny

188 We repeat our earlier conclusion that post-legislative scrutiny is highly desirable and should be undertaken far more generally. This would boost the level of constructive dialogue between Parliament and the courts.

Confirmation hearings

189 We urge the Government to clarify their position on the introduction of appointment hearings for judges at the earliest opportunity, since this would be an innovation with very profound implications for the independence of the judiciary and the new judicial appointments system.

An annual report on the judiciary

190 We welcome the Judicial Executive Board's decision that the Lord Chief Justice should lay an annual report before Parliament, an innovation which this Committee had discussed with the Lord Chief Justice and other senior judges in the course of our deliberations. We suggest that the annual report should be formally laid under section 5 of the Constitutional Reform Act. We further suggest that the report might encompass administrative issues and – where appropriate – areas of concern about the justice system, provided that there is no discussion of individual cases. We believe that the report will provide a useful opportunity for both Houses of Parliament to debate these matters on an annual basis, and for the Lord Chief Justice to engage effectively with parliamentarians and the public.

Judiciary, media and public

Public perceptions

191 We believe that the media, especially the popular tabloid press, all too often indulge in distorted and irresponsible coverage of the judiciary, treating judges as 'fair game'. A responsible press should show greater restraint and desist from blaming judges for their interpretation of legislation which has been promulgated by politicians. If the media object to a judgment or sentencing decision, we suggest they focus their efforts on persuading the Government to rectify the legal and policy framework. In order to ensure more responsible reporting, we recommend that the Editors' Code of Practice, which is enforced by the Press Complaints Commission, be regularly updated to reflect these principles.

The role of individual judges

192 Whilst judges should never be asked to justify their decisions outside the courtroom, it is desirable for them to communicate with the public and the media on appropriate issues. We therefore strongly encourage the occasional use of media releases alongside judgments, as for example in the **Charlotte Wyatt** case. Further, we cannot see any reason why judges should not co-operate with the media on features about their activities outside the courtroom, if they so wish. However, we are strongly of the opinion that whatever the media pressure, judges should not give off-the-record briefings.

The role of the Lord Chief Justice

193 It is wholly within the discretion of the Lord Chief Justice to determine how he can most effectively communicate with the media and the public. However, we suggest that he may from time to time need to re-appraise his strategy in light of the new constitutional relationship between the judiciary, the executive and Parliament. We believe that, in these days of greater separation of powers, it is highly desirable for him to ensure that the views of the judiciary are effectively conveyed to the public.

The role of the Judicial Communications Office

194 We conclude that the judges should consider making the Judicial Communications Office more active and assertive in its dealings with the media in order to represent the judiciary effectively. We suggest that consideration be given to appointing one or more spokesmen with appropriate qualifications and legal experience who would be permitted to speak to the media with the aim of securing coverage which accurately reflects the judgment or sentencing decision. However, under no circumstances should such spokesmen seek to justify decisions as opposed to explaining them.

 The full report of the House of Lords Select Committee on the Constitution, 'Relations between the Executive, the Judiciary and Parliament' (2007) is available on the internet at:
www.parliament.the-stationery-office.co.uk/pa/ld200607/ldselect/ldconst/151/151.pdf

Background of the judges

Historically judges have been predominantly white, male and from an upper middle-class background. This picture is gradually changing. The Ministry of Justice gathers and publishes statistics regarding the background of the judges. The first table reproduced below shows quite poignantly that while black people are increasingly represented among the lower rungs of the judicial profession, none has yet been appointed to sit in the senior courts. The second table shows that there is also a problem of women being underrepresented in the judiciary.

Ethnic minorities in the judiciary
as at 1 September 2005

Post	Sex	Mixed	Asian or Asian British	Black or Black British	Chinese (inc. other)	Other ethnic group	Total ethnic minority	Total in post	% Ethnic minority
Lord of Appeal in Ordinary	Men	0	0	0	0	0	0	11	0
	Women	0	0	0	0	0	0	1	0
	Total	0	0	0	0	0	0	12	0
Heads of Division (Lord Chancellor, Lord Chief Justice, Master of the Rolls, President of Family Division, Vice-Chancellor)	Men	0	0	0	0	0	0	5	0
	Women	0	0	0	0	0	0	0	0
	Total	0	0	0	0	0	0	5	0
Lord Justice of Appeal	Men	0	0	0	0	0	0	35	0
	Women	0	0	0	0	0	0	2	0
	Total	0	0	0	0	0	0	37	0
High Court Judge	Men	0	0	0	0	0	0	97	0
	Women	1	0	0	0	0	1	10	10
	Total	1	0	0	0	0	1	107	0.93
Circuit Judge (including judges of the Court of Technology and Construction)	Men	2	2	2	0	0	6	559	1.07
	Women	0	0	0	0	0	0	67	0
	Total	2	2	2	0	0	6	626	0.96
Recorder	Men	11	22	13	1	0	47	1217	3.86
	Women	3	4	6	0	0	13	197	6.6
	Total	14	26	19	1	0	60	1414	4.24
Recorder in training	Men	0	0	0	0	0	0	37	0
	Women	0	1	0	0	0	1	13	7.69
	Total	0	1	0	0	0	1	50	2

→

Post	Sex	Mixed	Asian or Asian British	Black or Black British	Chinese (inc. other)	Other ethnic group	Total ethnic minority	Total in post	% Ethnic minority
District Judge (including Family Division)	Men	3	4	0	0	0	7	348	2.01
	Women	1	1	0	0	0	2	85	2.35
	Total	4	5	0	0	0	9	433	2.08
Deputy District Judge (including Family Division)	Men	3	4	8	0	0	15	602	2.49
	Women	4	5	6	0	0	15	195	7.69
	Total	7	9	14	0	0	30	797	3.76
District Judge (Magistrates' Courts) As at 31-08-00 all Stipendiary Magistrates became District Judges (Magistrates' Courts)	Men	1	2	0	0	0	3	102	2.94
	Women	0	1	0	0	0	1	27	3.7
	Total	1	3	0	0	0	4	129	3.1
Deputy District Judge (Magistrates' Court) As at 31-08-00 all Stipendiary Magistrates became District Judges (Magistrates' Courts)	Men	1	6	1	0	0	8	131	6.11
	Women	0	0	2	1	0	3	38	7.89
	Total	1	6	3	1	0	11	169	6.51

 The statistics on ethnic minorities in the judiciary are published on the internet at: www.dca.gov.uk/judicial/ethmin.htm

Women in the judiciary
as at 1 October 2005

Post	Sex	Former barristers	Former solicitors	Total
Lord of Appeal in Ordinary	**Women**	1	0	1
	Men	10	0	10
	Total	11	0	11
	% Women	9.09	0	9.09
Heads of Division (Lord Chancellor, Lord Chief Justice Master of the Rolls, President of Family Division, Vice-Chancellor)	**Women**	0	0	0
	Men	4	0	4
	Total	4	0	4
	% Women	0	0	0
Lord Justice of Appeal	**Women**	2	0	2
	Men	31	0	31
	Total	33	0	33
	% Women	6.06	0	6.06

Post	Sex	Former barristers	Former solicitors	Total
High Court Judge	Women	10	0	10
	Men	94	2	96
	Total	104	2	106
	% Women	9.62	0	9.43
Circuit Judge (including judges of the Court of Technology and Construction)	Women	56	11	67
	Men	481	76	557
	Total	537	87	624
	% Women	10.43	12.64	10.74
Recorder	Women	172	27	199
	Men	1117	101	1218
	Total	1289	128	1417
	% Women	13.34	21.09	14.04
Recorder in training	Women	9	2	11
	Men	23	1	28
	Total	32	3	39
	% Women	28.13	66.67	28.21
District Judge (including Family Division)	Women	11	76	87
	Men	18	329	347
	Total	29	405	434
	% Women	37.93	18.77	20.05
Deputy Judge (including Family Division)	Women	49	146	195
	Men	77	523	601
	Total	126	669	796
	% Women	38.89	21.82	24.5
District Judge (Magistrates' Courts) As at 31-08-00 all Stipendiary Magistrates became District Judges (Magistrates' Courts)	Women	10	17	27
	Men	33	69	102
	Total	43	86	129
	% Women	23.26	19.77	20.93
Deputy District Judge (Magistrates' Court) As at 31-08-00 all Stipendiary Magistrates became District Judges (Magistrates' Courts)	Women	15	23	38
	Men	46	83	129
	Total	61	106	167
	% Women	24.59	21.7	22.75

The statistics on women in the judiciary are published on the Department for Constitutional Affairs' website at:

www.dca.gov.uk/judicial/womjudfr.htm

Criticism of the judicial appointments process

There has been considerable criticism of the judicial appointments process in the past. The Judicial Appointments Commission (JAC) has been responsible for auditing the judicial appointments process and its annual reports have been highly critical of the appointment process then being practised. An example of such criticism is provided below which subsequently led to some interesting correspondence between the Lord Chancellor and the Commission.

The Commission for Judicial Appointments Annual Report 2005

Diversity issues

2.63 In the Recorder (Midland Circuit) competition our analysis of the competition outcomes suggested that candidates who were male, Oxbridge-educated or barristers fared disproportionately well. We also noted that the Lord Chancellor's involvement at the end of the process increased the proportion of Oxbridge-educated candidates who were appointed, over and above those recommended by officials.

2.64 We were pleased that the proportion of candidates who classified themselves as being from an ethnic minority had increased from the previous competition and that the overall success rates of white and ethnic minority candidates were broadly similar. We are concerned that ethnic minority candidates fared disproportionately badly at interview, but we do not have enough information to try and assess why this might be.

2.65 We were disappointed not only that female candidates performed disproportionately badly in this competition, but also that the proportion of female candidates was lower than the proportion of the legal profession who could reasonably be expected to be 'in the field' for appointment. We noted that women who did apply tended to be more experienced than men. This would confirm research suggesting that women may be less confident about applying for judicial office than men and may do so at a later point in their career.

2.66 We hope that a move to competency-based competitions in which candidates attend assessment centres will lead to a fairer process. This is not, however, guaranteed. Further work may be required to ensure that this is the case. For example, the DCA [Department for Constitutional Affairs] are concerned that ethnic minorities may have fared disproportionately badly in the 2004/05 Deputy District Judge (Magistrates' Courts) competition, which was competency-based and involved the use of an assessment centre. The review we are currently conducting of that competition is therefore seeking to establish if that was the case and, if so, whether there were any particular aspects of the selection process that unjustifiably discriminated against particular groups of candidates.

2.67 We have in any case recommended that the DCA, and in due course the JAC, should carefully consider all aspects of assessment processes with a view to identifying any factors that discriminate against particular groups of candidates, and removing any that cannot be justified. In doing this, we suggest they should take account of our findings in the Recorder (Midland Circuit) competition review and of the outcome of our current detailed research into the 2004/05 Deputy District Judge (Magistrates' Courts) competition. We shall report on this research in our final annual report.

 The Judicial Appointments Commission Annual Report for 2005 is available on its website at:
www.cja.gov.uk/reports.htm

Letter from the Lord Chancellor to Sir Colin Campbell at the Commission for Judicial Appointments

19 October 2005

Dear Colin,

COMMISSION FOR JUDICIAL APPOINTMENTS ANNUAL REPORT

I understand that you are due to publish both your Annual Report and your Review of the Recorder 2004/05 Competition (Midland Circuit) today. I will obviously need to study these reports in considerable detail.

However, in advance of that, it has been brought to my attention that both these reports contain statements about me which are inaccurate.

Both the Annual Report and the Recorder Competition Review contain a number of statements in relation to the Government's declared policy to increase judicial diversity – a policy I know the Commission supports.

Page 12, paragraph 3.34 of Review of the Recorder Competition states that 'in some of the marginal cases, the Lord Chancellor substituted his own assessment, based on less evidence and possibly irrelevant factors, for that of his officials.' The footnote says that 'the competition report provided details of candidates' educational background including (for Oxbridge educated candidates) details of which college the attended and if they achieved a First Class degree.' The plain implication is that I was influenced by details of which Oxbridge college they attended, and whether they obtained First Class Degrees. This is wrong. The candidates' educational background played no part in the process. This is supported by the reference in the report on page 89, paragraph 29.

I changed the recommendations for appointment on the basis that the successful candidates had all achieved a higher ranking in the assessment process. This is confirmed at page 64, paragraph 14 of the Recorder Competition Review, where the Review notes that 'the Lord Chancellor . . . indicated his view that three of the candidates rolled over from the SE Circuit with a middle B ranking [candidates 9, 15, and 16] were stronger than [candidates 12 and 13], ranked as lower B in the Midland Circuit competition.' I made the appointments based entirely on the merit of the individuals concerned. Paragraph 3.34 on page 12 of the Recorder Competition Review also makes it clear that there was no evidence for the implication you have made.

→

You have further reflected your comments on the Recorder Competition in the judicial diversity section of your Annual Report (page 20, paragraph 2.63). I comprehensively reject any implication that I was influenced by the fact of the candidates' educational background, or any implication that my intention was to increase the proportion of Oxbridge candidates who were appointed. This is simply wrong. It is wrong in fact, wrong in implication, and wrong in conclusion.

As you should know, the principle for making judicial appointments is entirely based on merit. As I said at a hearing of the House of Commons Constitutional Affairs Select Committee (CASC) yesterday, we have worked hard to appoint a judiciary which is more reflective of society as a whole, with a better gender and racial balance. We are working to increase the pool from which judges are selected. But this does not mean that we should, or would, undermine our commitment to appointment on merit. This is the case for all appointments I have made, including those for the Midland Circuit Recorder competition. I would hope that the Commission share this commitment.

It is therefore both inappropriate for the Commission to continue to make statements which imply a bias on my part against the principles of diversity and merit. It is damaging and offensive to the candidates who have been successful in the competitions. I regret your decision to do so.

As I said yesterday at CASC in relation to your comments about the Specialist Circuit Judge Competition, your analysis and conclusions are unfair and wrong. You have not analysed the material properly, and have produced inaccurate and damaging reports.

Your letter of 12 September to me promised to publish comments made by the Department on your reports. I would be grateful if this letter was therefore placed on your website alongside those reports.

Lord Falconer of Thoroton

Letter from Sir Colin Campbell at the Commission for Judicial Appointments to the Lord Chancellor

21 October 2005

Dear Lord Falconer,

COMMISSION FOR JUDICIAL APPOINTMENTS ANNUAL REPORT

Thank you for your letter of 19 October.

The Commissioners' report of their review of the Recorder 2004/05 (Midland Circuit) Competition, which was submitted to you on 12 September, stated correctly on pages 88 and 89 that Oxbridge educated candidates fared disproportionately better than those educated elsewhere. This is a proven statistical fact. It also correctly recorded that your decisions, in the two instances where you disagreed with your officials' advice about who should be appointed, had the effect of increasing the proportion of Oxbridge educated candidates who were appointed. This is also a proven fact.

Paragraph 3.34 of the Report, which you mention, records our concern that you substituted your own assessment, based on less evidence and possibly irrelevant factors, for that of your officials. The process of 'distilling' information, in order to present recommendations to you in the form of the competition report, must inevitably mean that some of the evidence available to panel members and the Competition Manager will not be provided to you. In other words your assessment is based on less evidence. As far as irrelevant factors are concerned, the footnote (to paragraph 3.34) gives educational background as an example of irrelevant material included in the competition report.

Neither in the Recorder audit report nor in the Annual Report, which also mentions these points, do we infer from these facts that you were biased in favour of Oxbridge educated candidates. Indeed we point out, as you rightly mention, at paragraph 29 on page 89 of the Recorder audit report, that we have seen no evidence to suggest that candidates' educational background directly influenced any part of the appointment process. The implication of bias, which you so vehemently reject, is in fact one that you yourself and only you have drawn.

We agree that one of the key factors facing those with responsibility for the judicial appointment process is how to increase the diversity of judicial office whilst maintaining the principle of selection on merit. Our report welcomed your commitment to increasing judicial diversity and we congratulate you on the positive steps you have already taken towards achieving this. The relationship between merit and diversity is a key feature of our Annual Report.

One of the biggest challenges in this area is to ensure that the selection process is no longer susceptible to perceptions that people fitting a certain stereotype, or 'mould', are more suitable for judicial office and to demonstrate that this is the case. Providing information to you in competition reports about the educational background of candidates creates the perception that there is a possibility that this could influence outcomes. It could reinforce the views of those who believe that the judicial appointment process is dominated by a 'mould' (especially where one outcome of the final stage of the decision making process is actually to increase the number of Oxbridge-educated candidates appointed). This is primarily a criticism of the process. We had hoped that the Department would respond on this point by not including this information in future.

You say that you changed recommendations for appointment 'on the basis that the successful candidates had all achieved a higher ranking in the assessment process.' We acknowledged that those candidates, whom you appointed against your officials' recommendations, were ranked higher than those who were suggested by your officials, but whom you decided not to appoint. We also note, however, that you appointed some Midland Circuit candidates ranked as lower B, rather than some middle B ranked candidates 'rolled over' from the South Eastern Circuit. Furthermore, there is nothing in the record of your decision to indicate that ranking order played any role in your decisions, let alone the predominant role suggested in your letter.

Your letter also mentions our report about a Specialist Circuit Judge competition. I have not yet seen a transcript of your evidence to the Constitutional Affairs Select Committee. We are not, however, aware that any aspect of that report is factually inaccurate (your Department was given the opportunity to check the accuracy of the facts contained in it and did not raise any concerns with us). We have seen nothing to suggest that our analysis or conclusions were flawed.

I see that you have now placed your letter and your Press Release on the DCA website. Accordingly I am arranging for this letter to be placed on the CJA web-site, together with the Recorder (Midland Circuit) audit report, alongside our Annual Report. I am very pleased that you will be attending the International Summit on Judicial Diversity, which we are holding on 2 November. I look forward to seeing you again then.

Yours sincerely,

Sir Colin Campbell

Reform of the judicial appointments process

The judicial appointments process has been the subject of major reforms in recent years. The Constitutional Reform Act 2005 established a Judicial Appointments Commission, which came into operation in 2006. The weaker Commission for Judicial Appointments which existed briefly prior to this reform issued a report in 2004 containing a strong critique of the relevant provisions in the Constitutional Reform Bill which were subsequently enacted despite this criticism.

Judicial Appointments Annual Report 2003–2004
October 2004

Deficiencies in the Constitutional Reform Bill

We have five main outstanding concerns with the current policy set out in the Bill. These are:

Audit

First the Bill makes no provision for any proactive audit of judicial appointment competitions to complement the reactive role of the proposed Ombudsman in dealing with complaints. We believe this would be a significant loss. The audits we have carried out since

2002 have been key to highlighting some of the worst previous appointment practices and helping the Government to drive them out . . .

Lay majority on the JAC

Secondly we believe there should be a lay majority on the JAC to ensure the introduction of modern, accountable, fair and transparent selection processes. The Lord Chancellor has told us he wants the lay element to bring to the JAC top quality HR and recruitment expertise of its own, which 'has simply not been available to the Department', so that the JAC can produce an appointment system that is modern, transparent and open.

The major tasks facing the JAC will therefore be organisational – developing operational policies, systems and processes for appointments. It will need to design the systems to ensure that an appropriate high quality search and selection process is applied proportionately to all the 2,000 plus judicial vacancies that need to be filled each year. (Even this high figure excludes the appointment of the – far more numerous – lay magistrates, which it is envisaged the JAC will in due course take on.)

These are not the areas where judicial expertise needs to be focused or which judges are best fitted to deliver. Judges do not need to be heavily involved in the organisation of the systems and processes required. Indeed that would probably be a waste of the expertise they offer. We believe there may be some misunderstanding among the judiciary about the work that the JAC itself will actually do.

Senior judicial expertise should rather be focused on the point of selection in each and every judicial appointment competition. This is where the application of scarce judicial resource will add most value. It is in the individual selection panels where judicial expertise should be applied. Indeed one of the early tasks of the JAC is bound to be to draw up a panel of senior judges who can be assigned to carry out this role across the various competitions . . .

A hybrid commission

Thirdly our continuing preference is for a hybrid Commission, which would have the final say in selections for the 2,000 or so appointments each year at Circuit Judge level and below (excluding, as set out above, JPs). We accept there is an argument for the Secretary of State to have the discretion to reject candidates for the small annual number of senior appointments at High Court level and above. But below this level such a review process, even if it were operated properly, would require wasteful bureaucratic double checking of large numbers of recommendations just to have them pointlessly rubber-stamped.

There would also be a serious possibility that this review process could result in the JAC's recommendations being called into question on the basis of less or inferior evidence to that which was available to the JAC. The Lord Chancellor has given us the following as one example of where the Secretary of State could ask the JAC to reconsider. This is that the recommended candidate 'was someone whom the Lord Chief Justice or the judge involved in the selection process had, on consultation, opposed for selection on the basis that they were unsuitable and the Secretary of State agreed with their view'. Such an approach could lead to a more obscure process and reintroduce the likelihood that changes in the JAC's recommendations would be seen as the result of patronage by powerful political or judicial figures rather than of better evidence of merit. This could in turn discourage the likelihood of applications from a more diverse field of candidates, to whom it might appear that there was little point in applying.

UK Supreme Court selection commissions

Fourthly we believe that similar concerns apply to the Bill's provisions for the UK Supreme Court Selection Commissions, as for the England and Wales JAC. In particular, there should be a lay majority in order to give the public confidence in the appointment process, just as there should be for the JAC.

The Concordat

Our last major concern is that, whatever the merits of what the Concordat [between the judges and the Government] proposed, these (and all other) matters should remain fully open to challenge and amendment, where that is justified, through the normal processes of Parliamentary debate, as the Constitutional Reform Bill proceeds through its various Parliamentary stages. It is for Parliament to settle these constitutional proposals.

We are concerned that the existence of the Concordat appears to have been regarded by some members of the Select Committee as pre-empting open Parliamentary discussion of the proposals the Bill contains. It is essential that the Bill's provisions should be settled in Parliament on their merits, not by reference to whether they accord with the terms of a Concordat between the Lord Chancellor and the Lord Chief Justice.

Overall risks of the current proposals

In our view these deficiencies make the current proposals significantly less likely than they would otherwise be to achieve the objective of commanding the confidence of all interested stakeholders, whether judges, practising lawyers or the general public. Ensuring the appointments system has a higher standing in the eyes of the public should lead to greater public confidence in the quality of the appointments the JAC makes or recommends and thereby to greater public confidence in the quality of the administration of justice as a whole.

It has been put to us that there is a real risk that the present proposals will deliver only the present system of selection, but dressed in different clothes, since the JAC cannot start from a clean sheet, but must necessarily take over the present deeply flawed arrangements. It will, for example, be essential to bring in new expertise, especially at senior levels, if this is to be avoided.

The present proposals include that there will be no preponderance of expertise on modern recruitment practice on the JAC and no external assessment of what the JAC is doing from an independent audit function. We can therefore understand the fear that it will thus be only too easy for the JAC, perhaps not immediately but nevertheless pretty quickly, to settle back into the traditional and familiar ways of doing things.

The Lord Chancellor himself said, in his foreword to last year's (2002–03) Judicial Appointments Annual Report: 'We are committed not only to opening up the system of appointments to a wider range of suitably qualified candidates from different social backgrounds and a wider range of legal practice, but also to actively promoting participation. The fundamental principle in appointing judges must continue to be selection on merit. To achieve this, we must embrace best practice in recruitment and selection procedures. But confidence, transparency and a belief in their freedom from political interference and bias are also critical. It is for these reasons that I have announced our intention to establish an independent Judicial Appointments Commission to recommend candidates for appointment to judicial office.'

Without the changes we have outlined above, we do not think the public can be sure the proposed new arrangements will deliver the improvements the Lord Chancellor set out as essential.

The 2004 annual report of the Commission for Judicial Appointments is available at: **www.dca.gov.uk/judicial/ja-arep2004/partone.htm**

Planned reforms to the judicial appointment process

The reforms that have been introduced over the last decade to the judicial appointment process have undoubtedly improved the transparency and fairness of the process. However, the government has acknowledged that further improvements could still be made and some of these are considered in its White Paper entitled 'The Governance of Britain – Constitutional Reform' (2008).

The Governance of Britain – Constitutional Renewal (2008)

The way forward

113 As set out in *The Governance of Britain* Green Paper, the Government believes that the role of the executive in the appointment of judges should be reduced, that the existing arrangements for these appointments should be streamlined and that those who exercise power should be made more accountable. The Government therefore proposes to make changes to the role of the executive in the appointment of judges. These changes are set out below.

114 Remove the Lord Chancellor from the selection process for judicial appointments below the High Court – The Government proposes the removal of the Lord Chancellor's discretion to reject, or power to ask the JAC to reconsider, a JAC selection for appointment to a judicial office below the High Court. The Lord Chancellor will retain his current discretion to reject a candidate on medical grounds, and his discretion to withdraw entirely (after consulting the Lord Chief Justice), a request to fill a vacancy, if he considers the selection process was unsatisfactory – for example, where there may have been a procedural error or systemic flaw in the appointments process.

115 Remove the Prime Minister entirely from making judicial appointments – The most senior judges (the Law Lords, Lord Chief Justice, Heads of Division, and Court of Appeal judges) are appointed by Her Majesty The Queen on the advice of the Prime Minister. In practice the Prime Minister advises Her Majesty The Queen on a recommendation from the Lord Chancellor, and the Prime Minister's role is essentially a formality.

116 Set out key principles in legislation – The Government proposes the inclusion in legislation of a series of key principles, which represent best practice in making judicial appointments. These principles would help to guide all the bodies involved in the appointment process. They would also provide a basis on which to hold them more accountable.

. . .

118 The Lord Chief Justice should no longer be required to consult the Lord Chancellor, or to obtain his concurrence, before deploying, authorising, nominating, or extending the service of judicial office holders – The Lord Chief Justice is currently required to consult the Lord Chancellor, or in some instances, to obtain his concurrence, in relation to a wide range of deployments, authorisations and nominations of individual judicial office holders to particular roles or offices. In addition, he is required to obtain the Lord Chancellor's concurrence in relation to the extension of service of judicial office holders.

119 In the interests of streamlining the process, we asked in the consultation whether this requirement should continue, other than in circumstances where there were financial implications. There was general agreement that it should be removed. Given the responses to consultation, the Government proposes to remove the requirement on the Lord Chief Justice to consult the Lord Chancellor, (or in some cases to obtain his concurrence), when he is exercising specified functions relating to the authorisation, nomination and extension of service of judicial office-holders, other than those where there are financial implications.

New considerations

122 A number of further issues have emerged during the consultation period, on which the Government invites comment. These are set out below.

123 Providing additional accountability mechanisms – The Government is concerned to avoid any *accountability gap* in the event that the Lord Chancellor is removed from the selection of some judicial appointments. The Lord Chancellor already has a number of powers in relation to the JAC and the appointments process which are set out explicitly in the CRA. Other powers are implicit, or implied. Currently, the Lord Chancellor's explicit, statutory powers in relation to the JAC are:

- a power to require information in certain circumstances;
- a power to require the JAC to cover certain matters in its annual report;
- a power to issue guidance (exercisable following an affirmative order); and
- a power to remove the Chair and commissioners of the JAC (exercisable by Her Majesty The Queen on the recommendation of the Lord Chancellor).

124 The Lord Chancellor is the Minister responsible for the maintenance of the justice system, and, importantly, for maintaining confidence in it. If he is to satisfy himself fully that he is discharging his duties in ensuring the business need is met, he needs to ensure that the overall appointments process is sufficiently robust and that the JAC will operate efficiently and effectively. In addition, if he is to be held accountable for any failure of the JAC, he arguably needs to have the means at his disposal to intervene in the process in order to reduce the risk of failure. He cannot, therefore, be removed entirely from the judicial appointments system, and he needs to retain the usual powers exercisable by a Minister in respect of a non-departmental public body.

125 The possibility of additional powers for the Lord Chancellor, and in particular a power to set performance targets and to direct the JAC in certain matters was not raised in our consultation document or in formal responses. However, such powers would be consistent with the Cabinet Office's guidance on non-departmental public bodies.

126 These additional powers could provide the Lord Chancellor with a better ability to satisfy himself about how efficiently and effectively the JAC worked. For example, performance targets for operational issues (as opposed to individual selection) could be used to ensure that the JAC made selections within a specified time period, and within an allocated budget. They could also be used to set targets for increasing the proportion of applications for appointment from certain groups such as solicitors, women, or BME applicants. Powers of direction (again applied in respect of the operation of the JAC as opposed to any individual selections) could be used in situations where a disagreement has arisen (such as in relation to eligibility criteria) where, in the interests of ensuring the continued effectiveness of the justice system, the Lord Chancellor decides he must take the final decision, and consequently directs the JAC accordingly.

127 Even though these are powers to ensure that the system works well, the Government recognises that they may be seen as giving the Lord Chancellor the ability to influence, or to determine who is appointed, and thereby undesirably extending the executive's influence over the JAC's operations. One way to reduce such concerns might be for the powers to be exercisable only following consultation or concurrence with the Lord Chief Justice, or for them to be clearly expressed as limited to the JAC's processes as opposed to individual selections. If Parliament were to grant such powers, they would enable the Lord Chancellor to ensure that the appointments process is compatible with the key principles, with his own duty to ensure there is an efficient and effective system to support the carrying on of the business of the courts and, with other Ministers of the Crown, for upholding the continued independence of the judiciary.

128 While in their consultation response the JAC suggested that the Lord Chancellor's existing power to issue guidance should be removed given that the power had not been exercised. Most respondents recognised the important role which the Lord Chancellor performs in ensuring the effectiveness of the appointments system and accounting to Parliament for that. While there is a good case to support their introduction, the Government recognises that the taking of powers for the Lord Chancellor to set performance targets for, and to direct, the JAC raises complex issues.

129 Rather than seek to introduce any change now, the Government raises the question of whether such additional powers would be appropriate and would like to consider the issue further in the light of any views from respondents and from the Joint Committee which will be established to consider the draft Constitutional Renewal Bill.

130 There are two other areas where the Government considers that some clarification in the draft Bill would enable the Lord Chancellor more effectively to discharge his duties in respect of the maintenance of the justice system. Firstly, by clarifying the circumstances in which he may specify any additional requirements for a particular post. And secondly, by clarifying the circumstances in which he may require information to be provided to him by the JAC.
. . .

132 A role for Parliament – On 23 January 2008 the Prime Minister announced that the Government had written to and would welcome views from the House of Commons Liaison Committee on a list of public appointments that it proposed should be subject to pre-appointment scrutiny by their relevant select committee. Along with a number of other public office holders, this list included any future Chair of the JAC.

133 Respondents to the consultation generally acknowledged the useful role played by the legislature in scrutiny of the overall process. However, a substantial majority opposed any role for the legislature in the selection or making of judicial appointments, and in particular to confirmation hearings for individual appointments to judicial posts. While the Government welcomes the continued and valuable scrutiny performed by the various parliamentary select committees, there could be merit in a meeting of the House of Commons Justice Affairs Committee and the House of Lords Constitution Committee to hold the system to account on an annual basis.

> The White Paper, 'The Governance of Britain – Constitutional Renewal' (2008) is published on the website of the Ministry of Justice at: **www.justice.gov.uk/docs/constitutional-renewal-white-paper.pdf**

Judicial career guide

The government has issued a brochure encouraging a wide range of people to apply for the post of judge. Below is an extract from this guide.

Step Up to a Judicial Career: A Guide to Career Opportunities as a Judge

Introduction

As a legal professional contemplating the next stage of your career, you may be asking yourself if you have the experience and qualities needed to be a judge. And would life on the Bench suit you?

This booklet sets out the wide range of judicial career opportunities that is now available for lawyers from all backgrounds and different career paths. It explains the work of a judge, eligibility requirements and the appointments procedure. The booklet also aims to dispel some of the misconceptions about who can become a judge in order to encourage more applications from candidates from diverse backgrounds.

Working towards a diverse judiciary

Significant efforts have been made over the past decade by the Department for Constitutional Affairs (DCA), the judiciary, the Bar Council, the Law Society and minority lawyers' groups to encourage greater diversity in the appointment of judges. However, misconceptions persist that judicial appointment is open only to people from a narrow social, educational and professional background.

Such misconceptions have serious consequences, not least because they tend to dent the general public's confidence in the judicial system and deter eligible, first-rate candidates from putting themselves forward. As of October 2004 15.8% of judges in courts (as opposed to tribunals) were women and 3.4% were from minority ethnic backgrounds. In the High Court and above only 8% of posts were occupied by women and only one person was from a minority background. Figures are not currently available for the number of judges with disabilities.

Modernising the judicial system

The judicial appointments system is undergoing major changes with the aim of:

- making the appointments process more transparent and clearly separate from Parliament and Government;
- encouraging more applications from under-represented groups, including female, minority ethnic and disabled candidates, to provide a judiciary which better reflects the society it serves;
- increasing public confidence in the judiciary.

Despite the reforms that have already taken place to attract people from more diverse backgrounds, they remain seriously under-represented on the Bench. There are a number of reasons why this is so. It has taken longer than expected to see evidence of the 'trickle up' effect anticipated from the increase in the number of women and people from minority ethnic backgrounds joining the legal profession. Many potential applicants fail to apply because they think that their personal circumstances – family commitments, a disability, a lack of opportunity to build a professional reputation – make them ineligible or otherwise unsuitable for a judicial position. They are often unaware that requirements and procedures are now applied much more flexibly.

. . .

Case study 1
Katharine Marshall, District Judge (Magistrates' Courts), London

There aren't many judges who have come from the ranks of employed lawyers. I started my career in independent practice at the Bar. After a two-year break to look after my three very young children in the early 80s I returned to law as a legal adviser in the Magistrates' Courts Service, a job which gave me routine, set hours and financial security. It never occurred to me that I could be a judge until a female magistrate on the Bench I was advising took me aside and asked when I was going to apply. Only then did I think that it was within my capabilities and that I had the qualities to be a judge.

My experience in the courtroom and of training and advising magistrates stood me in good stead and gave me an insight into the difficulties of decision making. It was the ultimate work-shadowing experience, and when I was appointed a judge I felt I had a real advantage in knowing how things worked. My present jurisdiction as a District Judge (Magistrates' Courts) covers crime, youth and family cases. As a female judge you can have a different interaction with defendants, particularly in the youth court.

Being a judge is a job where you really feel you can make a difference in peoples' lives; to the community in general by dealing appropriately with people who pose a threat, or by giving individuals the opportunity to make reparation or turn their lives around.

. . .

Non-traditional career backgrounds
Applications from people with non-traditional backgrounds are encouraged. There is a recognition of factors that might have led to a lack of opportunity to build a professional reputation.

Nationality requirements
Judicial appointments are only open to citizens of the United Kingdom, the Republic of Ireland or a Commonwealth country. Holders of dual nationality that includes one of the above may also apply.

Age limits
There is no upper or lower age limit for candidates for judicial appointments apart from the statutory retirement age of 70 for all judges and a retirement age of 65 for Recorders and Deputy District Judges. However, the minimum age for appointment will be determined in part by the requirement to have been qualified as a barrister or solicitor for a set number of years. Similarly the age at which someone is appointed must allow for a reasonable length of service to justify the costs of appointment and initial training.

Merit
Judicial appointments are made strictly on merit regardless of age, gender, ethnic origin, marital status, sexual orientation, political affiliation, religion or belief, disability or other irrelevant factor.

The competency framework
In addition to the statutory qualifications and requirements for each judicial office, candidates are also assessed against the following competencies:

Judgment
- Investigating and analysing
- Resolving and deciding

Professionalism
- Demonstrating technical knowledge and expertise
- Demonstrating integrity and independence
- Showing authority
- Developing knowledge
- Managing workload

People skills
- Communicating
- Building positive relationships.

In the High Court slightly different competencies apply.

. . .

Case study 5
Alison Raeside, District Judge, London and South East

I enjoyed my practice at the Bar but when I had my first baby I realised I didn't want to work full time any more. When I had my second child I gave up the Bar completely and undertook research and law reporting to keep my hand in. By pure chance I bumped into someone who asked me if I was sitting on the Bench, and it seemed such a good idea – I always wanted to work in a court setting.

For a number of years I sat as a Deputy District Judge for two days a week during term time, which suited me very well when the children were very young. I now sit 200 days a year as a part-time salaried District Judge at Guildford County Court and take 15 days' unpaid leave each year so that I can take August off to be with my three children.

I love the broad range of civil and family work that I do and being able to make decisions that matter. Working as a District Judge also enables me to spend a decent time with my children and as such is very family friendly. My job is under control: I know where I'm working, my hours are roughly 9–5 and I can book my leave in advance. It's so much better for organising childcare, school holidays and all my other commitments.

When I first applied to be a judge it took perseverance to be appointed and one was expected to be in full-time practice, which I no longer was, but that's now changed. I have recently been helping to develop the policy introduced by the DCA to allow for part-time working, which I hope will make it easier for people in a situation similar to mine to apply to become judges.

 The publication 'Step Up to a Judicial Career: A Guide to Career Opportunities as a Judge' is available on the internet at:
www.dca.gov.uk/judicial/diversity/bb_judge.pdf

Court clothes

The government is anxious that judges should appear to the public to be in touch with society. One of the ways this can be achieved is through their personal presentation. Court clothes, therefore, are currently under the spotlight. In 2004, the government commissioned some research into what the public think of the clothes worn by the judges and other people working in the courts. Following this consultation process, it decided to abolish wigs for civil-court judges and to simplify the gowns that the judges wear.

Public Perceptions of Working Court Dress in England and Wales

Executive summary and conclusions

In advance of publishing a consultation paper, the Lord Chancellor's Department commissioned a national public opinion survey in England and Wales. The subject of the survey was the working dress of judges, advocates, clerks and ushers in courts in England and

Wales. The survey involved in-street interviews with 1,500 members of the general public and 500 court users [court users were defined as people who had attended one of the relevant courts in the capacity of claimant, defendant, juror, witness or victim within the last two years]. Individuals were presented with sets of photographs depicting three options for working court dress for each official (Option A consistently being current dress). Respondents were asked to select their preferred dress option, together with their reasons, for each court official.

. . .

Conclusions

In conclusion, support for reform of court dress varied between different types of court officials. Some 15% of respondents wanted to retain current dress for court clerks, and around one-third were in favour of retaining current dress for court ushers (31%), civil judges (31%) and advocates (34%). Support for change was somewhat less strong for criminal judges, where 42% of respondents opted to retain the current wig and robe.

There was some disparity in the views of court users and general public. Court users were more in favour of retaining current dress for criminal judges and court ushers.

Wigs emerged as a key and highly symbolic feature of current court dress, and central to any debate about change. Views on the 'appropriateness' of a wig were key in determining respondents' preferred dress options. This was informed by relative assessment of the status of the official within what was perceived as a hierarchy of court officials – with judges and advocates considered more important (and therefore more worthy of a wig) than ushers and clerks. As such, support for retention of a wig differed according to the type of court official:

- two-thirds wanted to retain the wig for criminal judges;
- one-third wanted to retain the wig for civil judges and advocates; and
- 15% wanted to retain the wig for court clerks.

A further consideration when assessing the appropriateness of a wig for judges was whether they were civil or criminal. The strength of symbolism meant that respondents felt the wig served to make the atmosphere intimidating, which was considered befitting for a criminal trial yet not for civil proceedings. This was endorsed by court users, who described feelings of trepidation and intimidation when facing a judge wearing a wig. Whilst on balance there was consistent support to change court dress, there was no clear majority view in terms of preferred dress options for most officials. The exceptions were advocates and clerks, where Option C (business dress) was preferred.

 The report 'Public Perceptions of Working Court Dress in England and Wales' is available on the internet at:
www.dca.gov.uk/consult/courtdress/orcreport.pdf

11 The legal professions

Introduction

This chapter looks at:

- moves towards changing the way students qualify as solicitors;
- the Bar Council's ideas for reforming the qualification process for barristers;
- problems with the way complaints against solicitors are handled;
- Sir David Clementi's Report of 2004 looking at ways to reform the legal professions;
- the resulting Legal Services Act 2007; and
- the Compensation Act 2006, seeking to regulate claims management companies which pass work to solicitors at a fee.

Qualifying as a solicitor

The Solicitors Regulation Authority is considering reforming the qualification process to become a solicitor. It issued a consultation paper entitled 'A New Framework for Work Based Learning' (2007). This was followed by a public statement on the progress of changes to the final stage of solicitor training which is reproduced in full below.

Moving Forward with a New Framework for Work Based Learning (2007)

The Solicitors Regulation Authority (SRA) recently issued a second consultation on a new framework for work based learning. The consultation built on proposals to replace the training contract with an assessed period of work based learning based on a set of clearly defined competence standards. The feedback we received from the second consultation was extremely valuable and has helped us to chart a clear way forward.

Our original proposals suggested two clearly defined routes to qualification: one for trainees in an accredited training firm and one for trainees who were not in an accredited training firm but who were gaining appropriate legal experience which could count towards qualification. We planned to develop a method for assessing the competence of trainees on both routes through an online portfolio. We also proposed that trainees, who were not employed in an accredited training firm, should have the opportunity to be assessed by the SRA prior to qualification.

We received 60 responses to the consultation, mainly from larger firms and organisations, and were encouraged that the majority of respondents continued to support the key objectives of the proposals: the introduction of an assessed period of work based learning based on a clearly defined set of competence standards and the opportunity for LPC graduates with relevant, practical, legal experience to seek qualification without the need for a training contract. We had hoped to receive more responses from smaller firms and individuals involved in the training process, and we will continue to seek feedback from these groups through the pilot development phase.

Our proposed standards for the period of work based learning incorporated contributions from a range of stakeholders. We are pleased that consultation responses indicated broad assent that these standards reflect the level of competence which should be achieved by trainee solicitors during the period of work based learning. A key concern, however, was how it might be possible to assess trainees against the standards. It was suggested that we should undertake further work to develop clear guidance on how the standards might be applied and demonstrated in practice.

Other concerns raised through the consultation included the following:

● Many respondents were unconvinced that a standard portfolio tool would be desirable or that a portfolio was the only, or indeed an effective, method of assessing trainees against the standards.

● Respondents reiterated the concerns already expressed in the first consultation that two separate routes to qualification could result in a 'two tier' qualification.

● Firms, in particular, were concerned that too much prescription by the SRA about the learning and assessment to be undertaken by trainees during the period of work based learning would result in an inflexible and overly bureaucratic system which did not recognise the fact that the majority of training establishments have in place well established training programmes and are training their trainees to a high standard.

The SRA Board has considered all of the feedback received through the consultation exercises and shares, in particular, the concerns about creating a two tier profession and the need to avoid overly bureaucratic and inflexible requirements for firms responsible for training solicitors. The SRA Board remains committed to the requirement that all trainees should complete a period of assessed, practical, legal experience prior to qualification. This will ensure that anyone qualifying as a solicitor will:

- have opportunities to practice legal and professional skills in a working environment;
- have opportunities to develop and demonstrate the necessary practical and legal skills required to qualify as a solicitor;
- be exposed to practical solutions and problems in a supported environment;
- have reached a required standard of competence;
- have developed an understanding of ethical principles and issues in practice in a supported environment;
- have developed their knowledge and skills in a range of areas including contentious and non contentious work;
- have opportunities to reflect on and improve their performance in the work place prior to qualification.

We will achieve this through transparent, proportionate and consistent regulatory requirements and the avoidance of unnecessary prescription. The SRA's role in the new framework for work based learning is to set and enforce standards, rather than to prescribe or provide assessment tools and methodologies.

The Board has agreed to continue to move towards the launch of a pilot scheme but will not develop a standard portfolio or assessment tool, and will not seek to provide assessments itself. The new scheme will focus on one set of common standards to be achieved by all trainees prior to qualification rather than on the way or the route by which these standards are achieved. This 'outcomes' based approach is at the heart of the SRA's education and training strategy and will provide flexibility to accredited employers of trainees to continue to develop and design their own training programmes for trainees. In addition to their training programmes, firms will need to demonstrate that they have assessed their trainees against the work based learning standards, but the method and means of assessment will be up to the individual firm – provided it meets the standards set by the SRA.

Where firms do not wish to develop an in house accredited learning and assessment process in-house but are happy to support their employees through to qualification as a solicitor, we plan to offer one or more accredited professional learning and assessment organisations to provide the framework for the learning and assessment – again to standards set by the SRA.

This does not mean that individuals will be able to work towards qualification without the knowledge or support of their employer or that the employer will not have a role to play in the process. Employers will still need to support trainees through qualification and verify their performance along the way. It will, however, mean that individuals who are not in a training contract (but who are working in an appropriate legal environment, supervised by a qualified solicitor, and with the support of their employer) can seek to qualify as a solicitor, with the framework for their learning, additional support and the overall assessment provided by an external organisation. This approach should encourage firms who wish to support their employees through to qualification but who do not have the time or resources or inclination to develop structured training programmes or undertake assessments, to work with external assessment organisations who will be able to provide this on their behalf. The use of professional learning and assessment organisations, who will be required to assess trainees against the same standards as the firms assessing trainees in-house, should allay fears about a reduction of standards and a two tier profession.

This outcomes-based approach means that the content of learning and assessment programmes may vary considerably, as it does now, depending on the environment in which the trainee is employed – but the SRA will play a key role in ensuring that the outcomes achieved reach the required standard and are being consistently applied. This will be achieved through a robust approval and inspection regime for anyone seeking to train and assess trainee solicitors.

Our pilot scheme for the outcomes-based approach will be based on the following key principles:

- There will be **one route to qualification and one common standard** for the period of work based learning – anyone wishing to qualify as a solicitor will be assessed against this standard;
- The new framework will offer **flexibility to solicitors' firms/organisations** to develop and implement their own learning and assessment strategies if they wish to;
- The new framework will offer the **opportunity to trainee solicitors to contract, if they wish, with an external provider** (with the support of their employer) to provide the learning and assessment framework;
- The SRA will be **non-prescriptive about the content and format of learning and assessment tools**;
- The SRA will **set the principles and standards for learning and assessment strategies** but will not provide assessments itself;
- The SRA will **validate and inspect** solicitors' firms/organisations and external assessment organisations to develop and deliver learning and assessment strategies;
- Through the validation and monitoring system, the SRA will **ensure standards, fairness and consistency of the learning and assessment process**.

We have already started to talk to stakeholders about moving forward on the basis of these principles – initial reactions have been favourable. We are confident that we now have a sound basis for developing a pilot scheme which addresses the concerns raised during the consultation process and enables us to achieve our desired objectives.

 The consultation paper issued by the Solicitors Regulation Authority entitled 'A New Framework for Work Based Learning' (© The Law Society) is available on its website at:
www.sra.org.uk/securedownload/file/276

Qualifying as a barrister

The barrister profession is also considering what reforms would be desirable to its qualification process. The Bar Council set up an internal working party to consider this issue, which has now published its final report.

Entry to the Bar Working Party Final Report (2007)

Chairman's foreword

The Bar can only flourish and retain public confidence if it is a diverse and inclusive profession. Diversity and inclusivity extend not only to gender, ethnic origin, physical ability, religious belief, and sexual orientation, but every bit as much to social, economic, and educational circumstances and background, and to age. Diversity and inclusivity are essential if a modern profession is to maximise its credibility and to contribute towards a fairer and more effective society. Moreover, they are not inconsistent with selection on the grounds of ability and potential, which are both vital criteria for practice at the Bar. On the contrary, there is a perception that the Bar is only open to the more privileged, and, like many perceptions, this has a strong element of self-fulfilment. Many from less fortunate backgrounds are thereby put off even considering a career at the Bar; and there are aspects of the entry procedures and training, particularly the cost and the risk, which exacerbate the problem. It is only right to acknowledge the positive steps that the Bar Council, the four Inns of Court, and many sets of Chambers have already taken over recent years, with a view to improving access and training. It is equally true, however, that more can and should be done.

. . .

Our aims in summary terms

19 As already stated, it is essential that, as far as possible, the Bar is, and is seen to be, equally open to everyone with the requisite ability and ambition, irrespective of irrelevant personal characteristics or background. Inextricably connected with this is another aim namely, to ensure that all practising barristers (whether employed or self-employed) are as well trained as possible for their professional responsibilities.

20 It can fairly be said that these aims are applicable to any profession, and indeed to every type of job, but they are perhaps of particular importance to the Bar. Barristers are in one of the most high profile of the professions and should lead the way, and be seen to be leading the way, in promoting equality of opportunity and professionalism. Further, as much as any other profession, it is ability which attracts success at the Bar. Additionally, members of the Bar advise and represent all members of all categories of society, often in relation to a crucially important issue in their lives. Finally, and uniquely, it is from the ranks of barristers that the majority of Judges are selected, and, to maintain a high level of public confidence, the pool from which such selection is made (and indeed the judiciary itself) must be as diverse and inclusive as possible.

21 We referred to the fact that ability is a pre-requisite for success at the Bar. The word 'ability', at least without amplification, begs many questions. The representations made

by Middle Temple suggested that we 'should attempt a general statement of the qualities required of a successful practitioner'. We agree: although some qualities can be developed, it is sensible for anyone thinking of becoming a barrister to assess whether he or she may be well suited for that demanding career before spending the cost, time and effort on training for the Bar.

22 We would suggest that the qualities needed for a career at the Bar are a mixture of attributes of temperament and of talents. As to temperament, what is required is a combination of honesty, courage, commitment, common sense, and perseverance. As to talents, we would list analytical skills, intellect, persuasiveness, organisational skills, good judgment, and fluency. That is not to say that a person could not succeed unless he or she has all these qualities, or that reasonable adjustments may not be required as appropriate, but, on any view, honesty is essential.

23 It is not only unfair if access to the Bar is much more difficult for someone with these attributes wanting to become a barrister, if he or she comes from a disadvantaged group. It is also damaging to our society and our culture. That is partly because any palpable unfairnesses or inequalities would undermine respect for, and confidence in, the Bar. It is also because, if the pool from which candidates are selected is small, then many of the most able people will be prevented from being barristers which results in a less effective Bar as a whole. Of course, the inherently unequal nature of many aspects of our society, notably in education, financial means and social background, may well mean that it is impossible to ensure a completely even playing field for everybody. However, that is no excuse for not seeking to improve the present situation as much as is possible. Indeed, it underlines the need to do so. And that is what we are aiming to achieve.

. . .

36 It is also right to make it clear that the Working Party accepts that the Bar is a high profile, competitive profession, which does, will inevitably, and should, attract significantly more entrants than can succeed. None of the measures we recommend will, or should, change these realities. Indeed, the profession's very competitiveness is what makes it so attractive to many, and most of the people who find a barrister's career attractive expect, and thrive on, competition and challenge. Thus, whatever the Bar Council and the Inns of Court do, many entrants will not become established in self-employed or employed practice. Only the very best should succeed. That is the nature of the profession, and it is its excellence that ensures its survival. None of this is to be deprecated. On the contrary, it is in the public interest.

37 Nonetheless, this does highlight another tension that we recognise. On the one hand, it is very important to improve access to the Bar for those members of society from less privileged backgrounds. On the other hand there is a strong perception that there are already too many people on the BVC: annually there are approximately four times as many BVC graduates as there are available pupillages. These two factors might appear to pull in opposite directions, but at least if we are careful, they should not do so.

38 Another point arises from the perception in some quarters that the numbers of self-employed barristers will decline, referred to in paragraph 9 above. If the size of the self-employed Bar does decrease, then many of the problems considered in this Report are likely to be exacerbated, not least as it would be almost inevitable that the number of pupillages

in Chambers, already the 'pinch point' in terms of entry into practice, will decline further. In this connection, it is appropriate to emphasise that improving access to the Bar is not at all necessarily the same thing as increasing the number of entrants.

39 In formulating our proposals, realism, as well as desirability and practicality, has a vital part to play. It is therefore right to bear in mind the question of resources, which we consider in Chapter 9. Almost all recommendations which can be put forward for improving access to the Bar have financial implications. The Bar is a relatively small profession (with approximately 15,000 members), and the Bar Council, with its many responsibilities, is almost entirely dependent on their subscriptions. While the Inns have substantial available income, it is effectively fully devoted to scholarships, training, library and other professional needs.

This report
40 The Working Party's objectives, then, are:

(a) To ensure that, as far as possible, the Bar selects and is seen to select, the best entrants from all backgrounds regardless of social background, economic circumstances, educational advantages, ethnicity, gender, disability status, sexual orientation, age, religion or belief;

(b) To ensure that the education and training for barristers is, and is seen to be, as of high a quality as possible.

If these objectives are not achieved, we believe that the existence of the profession will be threatened. It is this that makes the work of the Working Party so crucial.

41 This Report considers each stage of a potential barrister's career in successive chapters. The Schools section emphasises the need to bring the possibility and attractions of a career at the Bar to as many people as possible at an early stage. This should enable many children, who would not otherwise do so, to consider such a career before they make irrevocable choices about examinations and courses. In Chapter 4, the University stage, we state that the Bar should think, and act, more equitably as between the various universities.

42 The BVC raises a number of issues, at the entry, course, and exit stages. As to funding for the BVC and pupillage, we have a number of suggestions, including the new idea of a funding pool, and proposals to ease bank loans. In relation to pupillage, we discuss a number of issues on which we have some significant suggestions, in particular to increase numbers by a mixture of new ideas (including a clearing house) and extending present arrangements (such as having more employed pupils), and some recommendations with regard to selection. We go on to consider the selection of tenants by Chambers, and career patterns and retention thereafter. Finally, we discuss the implementation of our recommendations.

 The report 'Entry to the Bar Working Party Final Report' (2007) is available on the Bar Council's website at:
www.barcouncil.org.uk/news/TheEntrytotheBarWorkingPartyFinalReport/

Complaints against solicitors

There have been ongoing concerns about the way in which complaints against solicitors are handled. This problem was highlighted in the context of complaints against solicitors who had carried out work on the Coal Health Compensation Scheme, a scheme set up by the government to compensate minors who had suffered ill health due to their work underground in British Coal mines. The Legal Services Complaints Commissioner, who oversees the handling of complaints against solicitors, published a special report in 2008 into the handling of these complaints.

Legal Services Complaints Commissioner Special Report (2008)

Investigation into the Handling of Coal Health Compensation Scheme complaints by the Legal Complaints Service and the Solicitors Regulation Authority

Background to the Coal Health Compensation Schemes

Coal Health Compensation Schemes are the biggest personal injury schemes in British legal history. They were negotiated to compensate miners and their families for two mining-related health problems, caused by working underground in British Coal mines. The two conditions are:

● Chronic Obstructive Pulmonary Disease (COPD) – respiratory disease (chronic bronchitis and emphysema) resulting from the dusty conditions; and
● Vibration White Finger (VWF) – a disease caused by using vibrating tools.

British Coal was found guilty of negligence in two group actions in 1997 in relation to VWF and in 1998 in relation to lung diseases.

In January 1998 the Department of Trade and Industry (DTI), took over responsibility for the accumulated personal injury liabilities of the British Coal Corporation.

DTI, in negotiation with the Claimants Solicitors' Groups and subject to the approval of the High Court, introduced two compensation schemes for former miners, one for COPD and one for VWF. Potential claimants could make applications for compensation via their legal representative. The Government met the cost of the claimant's legal representation, where these claims were successful.

The schemes have now been closed to new entrants. As at 7 October 2007, a total of 762,000 claims had been made, 634,000 settled and total compensation of £3.6 billion had been paid to individuals under the schemes. It is expected that by the time they close, the Government will have spent around £7 billion in total on the schemes.

Solicitors' involvement in the Coal Health Compensation schemes and deductions from miners' compensation payments

The Claims Handling Agreements negotiated between the DTI and the Claimant Solicitors' Groups provided very detailed procedures that had to be followed when dealing with claims arising out of these specific industrial injuries. They also set out how much solicitors would be paid for each successful case.

There was widespread publicity for the compensation schemes, particularly in mining areas. Many claimants were referred to solicitors by trade unions, whilst others were referred by claims handling intermediaries. Some claimants approached solicitors directly, often in response to local marketing activity.

Some solicitors made deductions of success fees from miners' compensation awards, in addition to the costs they would receive from the DTI, in order to compensate for the fact that they would not be paid in unsuccessful cases. However, this often meant that the solicitor was being paid twice for the same piece of work. The deduction of success fees was commonplace until 1999 when most, though not all, solicitors stopped the practice after the introduction of claims-handling agreements.

Where claims-handling agents or trade unions were involved in referring miners to a solicitor, claimants were often asked to sign agreements authorising the solicitor to deduct a fee out of any compensation received, in the event that their claims were successful.

However, because the compensation schemes were set up to ensure that all costs incurred on behalf of claimants were recoverable from public funds, miners and their families were able to pursue their claims at no cost to themselves. Their solicitor should have advised them on this.

Complaints about solicitors

If a consumer has a complaint about the way their solicitor has handled their case, and is unable to resolve that complaint directly with the solicitor concerned, they can complain to the complaints handling arm of the solicitor's professional body – the Law Society.

In January 2006, the Law Society formally announced its re-organisation into 3 distinct bodies. These are: the Legal Complaints Service (LCS) which deals with complaints by consumers who are complaining about the service received from their solicitor; the Solicitors Regulation Authority (SRA) which regulates solicitors and deals with some consumer complaints where misconduct is alleged; and the Law Society which represents solicitors and promotes their work.

On receipt of a complaint, the LCS caseworker in the first instance will investigate it and attempt to reach an agreement on how it will be resolved between the consumer and the solicitor through an informal process called conciliation. If the LCS caseworker has been unable to resolve the matter informally, they can further investigate and prepare a report for an LCS adjudicator who will investigate and then make a decision.

Amongst other functions, SRA is responsible for regulatory and disciplinary matters; setting and maintaining standards and handling complaints that allege misconduct against solicitors. SRA caseworkers will investigate the complaint about the solicitor's conduct and if misconduct is identified, it can also refer the solicitor to the Solicitors Disciplinary Tribunal (SDT).

SRA conduct investigations can result in a range of outcomes. Where no misconduct is found, the file will be closed. For minor or technical breaches a letter of advice can be issued to the solicitor. If the case is referred for adjudication and misconduct is found but the breach is less serious then a finding can be made and a warning issued by SRA.

For more serious breaches, adjudicators can issue a reprimand or severe reprimand.

It has recently been reported that the SRA will be able (from January 2008) to handle serious disciplinary cases and award compensation up to a maximum of £2,000.

The most serious cases can be referred to the SDT. These would include for example cases where there is suspected dishonesty, a serious criminal conviction or a major breach of the accounting rules.

At the SDT a solicitor can be:

- Reprimanded
- Fined
- Suspended from practice
- Struck off the Roll.

It is also proposed that from January 2008, the SDT will be able to administer unlimited fines for the most serious cases, when currently fines are limited to £5,000.

If a complaint has both service and conduct elements, the service element will generally be investigated first by LCS and then passed to SRA to investigate conduct issues.

LCS responsibilities

Since 2003, and up to the point of the latest OLSCC investigation, LCS had received 1,792 complaints from miners and their families.

Our audits have found the main reasons for miners to complain to LCS are:

- Deductions from compensation awards of miners by solicitors to cover solicitors' fees;
- Other deductions made from compensation awards of miners for example union fees or in lieu of union fees; and
- Other aspects of poor service on the part of the solicitor such as failure to explain fully the costs of the claim.

There is a small and dedicated team within the LCS that deals specifically with individual enquiries and complaints from miners in relation to the Coal Health Compensation schemes. This dedicated unit sits within the LCS Parliamentary Casework Team, which, as of October 2007, comprised a total of 27 staff. Caseworkers are supported and led by a Team Manager and also have access to specialist assistance and advice from Casework Advisers as well as a Coach who has previous casework experience within the team.

The caseworkers' remit includes investigating whether solicitors have provided an Inadequate Professional Service (IPS) to the miners. In terms of assessing whether the service was inadequate, LCS can consider whether the solicitors correctly advised the miner in relation to any deduction by explaining that the Government was paying of the solicitor's legal fees or that other solicitors were offering the same service and not making similar deduction from the compensation award. LCS can also consider, whether a claims handling agreement was signed by a miner with a trade union or with a referral agency, whether the solicitor adequately advised the miner on the implications of that agreement.

The majority of complaints from miners relate to the assertion that solicitors have made a deduction in some form from miners' compensation awards. Following the publication and findings of the Legal Services Ombudsman's Special Report, LCS adjudicators have determined that the deductions taken from miners' compensation awards are a direct financial consequence of the poor service provided by the solicitor and are recoverable by the miner. In addition to this, adjudicators have awarded an additional amount in recognition of the distress and inconvenience experienced by the miner in brining the complaint, if the case is referred to them. The audit identified that 83 cases had been adjudicated out of the total (1792) of miners complaints received at the point of the audit, this amounts to 4.6%.

Where no deductions have been made, LCS policy still requires caseworkers in eligible cases to discuss and clarify, with the miner or their representative, whether there are any issues of IPS by the solicitor that could result in a payment of compensation for associated distress and inconvenience, and whether the miner wishes to pursue these issues.

 The special report of the Legal Services Complaints Commissioner entitled 'Investigation into the Handling of Coal Health Compensation Scheme Complaints by The Legal Complaints Service and The Solicitors Regulation Authority' (2008) is published on the website of the Office of the Legal Services Complaints Commissioner at:
www.olscc.gov.uk/docs/miners_special_report.pdf

Reform of the legal professions

The legal professions have been the subject of a number of critical reports which are likely to result in major reforms being introduced in the near future. The most influential of these reports is that of Sir David Clementi, which was published in 2004.

Report of the Review of the Regulatory Framework for Legal Services in England and Wales

Foreword

To the Secretary of State for Constitutional Affairs

1 I have pleasure in submitting my Review of the Regulatory Framework for Legal Services in England and Wales.

2 I was appointed on 24th July 2003 and the Terms of Reference for the Review are:

> To consider what regulatory framework would best promote competition, innovation and the public and consumer interest in an efficient, effective and independent legal sector.
> To recommend a framework which will be independent in representing the public and consumer interest, comprehensive, accountable, consistent, flexible, transparent, and no more restrictive or burdensome than is clearly justified.
> To make recommendations by 31 December 2004.

. . .

5 The Terms of Reference include the word 'independent' twice. I infer that the first reference calls for independence of the legal profession from outside influences, particularly from Government; and that the second reference calls for a regulatory framework which is independent in representing the public and consumer interest of those being regulated. Replies to the Consultation Paper from representatives of the legal profession have drawn my attention most often to the first reference. I judge that both are important.

6 In line with the Terms of Reference the Review seeks a regulatory approach to encourage competition. The grain of Government legislation over the years has been in the direction of encouraging greater competition between different types of lawyer. The Administration of Justice Act 1985 permitted licensed conveyancers to compete with solicitors in the conveyancing market. The Courts and Legal Services Act 1990 enabled solicitors to acquire rights of audience in higher courts, previously the preserve of members of the Bar; and since then two other professional bodies have been allowed to grant limited rights of audience to their members. Today there are around 2,000 solicitors with higher court rights; and a significant amount of advocacy, primarily in the lower courts but increasingly in the higher courts, is done by solicitors. At the same time there are a large number of barristers, such as those who advise on tax or conveyancing issues, whose job is similar to many solicitors. The cultures of the Bar Council and Law Society are markedly different; but whilst they may remain separate professional bodies they cannot be regarded as separate professions.

7 Against this background, a number of observers have wondered whether I might recommend that there should be fusion between the Bar Council and the Law Society. There would be advantage in such a move in areas such as education, and it would ease some of the existing regulatory and competition issues. But I do not make such a recommendation in this Review, because I regard issues of mergers between overlapping professional bodies, or for that matter de-mergers within existing professional bodies, as ones for the bodies themselves and their members. The regulatory framework needs to be able to accommodate either merger or de-merger. It needs to recognise too that, whilst the Bar Council and Law Society account for a significant part of the legal services industry, there are other bodies that the system needs to accommodate, in particular the Institute of Legal Executives, the Office of the Immigration Services Commissioner, the Council for Licensed Conveyancers, the Chartered Institute of Patent Agents, the Institute of Trade Mark Attorneys and the Faculty Office. I note that the Chartered Institute of Patent Agents and the Institute of Trade Mark Attorneys co-operate on a variety of issues; they submitted a joint response to the Consultation Paper and it cannot be ruled out that at some point they might choose to merge their organisations.

8 If this Review favours greater competition between lawyers, it also seeks to permit competition between different types of economic units: for example, between sole practitioners, lawyers working in chambers, unlimited partnerships, limited liability partnerships and companies. There are advantages and disadvantages in each type of economic unit. I do not believe that the public and consumer interest are always better served by one type of economic unit as against another. The Review favours a regulatory framework which permits a high degree of choice: choice both for the consumer in where he goes for legal services, and for the lawyer in the type of economic unit he works for.

9 In this debate it is important to distinguish between facilitative and mandatory proposals. The key recommendations in this Review in the area of business structures are intended to be facilitative. Whilst I accept that sole practitioner status, when combined with the chambers system, has merit as a way to provide advocacy services, and I accept also that the partnership model adopted by many solicitors has significant strengths, I do not accept that other structures for the provision of legal services should not be permitted.

10 Whilst it is plain that there is competition between lawyers within the current system, and the proposals in this Review are intended to increase this, I have learnt that certain lawyers dislike being described as part of an industry. They see a conflict between lawyers as professionals and lawyers as business people. The idea that there is a major conflict is in my view misplaced. Access to justice requires not only that the legal advice given is sound, but also the presence of the business skills necessary to provide a cost-effective

service in a consumer-friendly way. In the Consumers' Association's summary of a survey of those dissatisfied with legal services it comments: '*The biggest cause of dissatisfaction was delay. According to one respondent "it would have been quicker to do a course in conveyancing". Cost also ranked highly: "We feel that we were misled as to costs from the very start."*' Research shows that complaints arise as much from poor business service as from poor legal advice. If certain lawyers continue to reject the notion that they are in business, such complaints will continue until they are indeed out of business.

11 The issue of costs is an important one: high quality legal services are important to society, but of limited value if available only to the very rich or those paid for by the State. In developing business systems to minimise costs whilst maintaining high standards, there is no reason why lawyers should not work alongside those with other skills, for example in finance or IT; and the Review makes recommendations designed to facilitate this. In proposing reforms designed to encourage cost-effective practices, there is no suggestion of diminution in standards, either in the quality of legal advice provided or in the ethical standards of practitioners.

12 The current regulatory regime incorporates some strands of regulation which are based around professional bodies, and some which are based around particular services. Whilst it would be intellectually tidy to move strongly towards either a professionally based regulatory system, or one which is service based, it would come at a price and some degree of hybridity is likely to remain. The change in regulatory emphasis which is proposed in this Review is a shift in emphasis towards regulation of the economic unit and away from regulation of individual lawyers. This is particularly relevant for the regulation of new business practices which bring together lawyers from different backgrounds; but it also has relevance for some existing legal practices, where regulatory emphasis needs to be on practice management and systems as much as on individuals.

. . .

14 The issues which this Review has inquired into are raised using the same chapter headings from *A* to *F* as in the Consultation Paper.

15 *Chapter A* proposes that the first step in defining the regulatory regime should be to make clear what the objectives of the regime are. The Chapter proposes six primary objectives for the regime. These would be the objectives against which the Regulator must determine the appropriate regulatory action; and against which it would be held accountable. The Chapter also looks at legal precepts or principles, such as a lawyer's duty to the client, which should be incorporated within the regulatory arrangements.

16 *Chapter B* addresses the key architectural issues around the design of a regulatory system which meets the Terms of Reference; and it looks at the arguments around the different models set out in the Consultation Paper. It also looks at the costs of different models. The Chapter concludes that regulatory functions are best dealt with by a model based on what the Consultation Paper referred to as Model B+. This model provides for the setting up of an oversight regulator, the Legal Services Board (LSB), vested with regulatory powers which it would delegate to recognised frontline bodies, where it was satisfied as to their competence and that appropriate arrangements, in connection with governance issues and the split between regulatory and representative functions, had been made. The Chapter discusses the current governance arrangements of the Law Society and the Bar Council and concludes that they are inappropriate for the regulatory tasks they face.

17 *Chapter C* concentrates on complaints mechanisms. It examines the problems which exist with the current system and possible solutions. The Chapter concludes that for reasons of independence, simplicity, consistency and flexibility a single independent complaints body for all consumer complaints should be adopted. The Office for Legal Complaints (OLC) would be independent in dealing with individual complaints but would need to work closely with the LSB to ensure that regulatory oversight served to minimise complaints at source. The OLC would be part of a single regulatory framework, with the LSB at its head.

18 Issues about professional conduct, including disciplinary action, would be handed down to the front-line bodies. The Chapter's overall conclusion is that the disciplinary systems of the front-line regulators work reasonably well and could be left, subject to a small number of changes, broadly as they are.

19 *Chapter D* focuses on the governance and accountability issues around the LSB. It proposes a Board of between 12 and 16 members with both Chairman and Chief Executive being non-lawyers. It makes proposals for how such appointments should be made. It sets out arrangements for consultation with relevant parties and explains how the LSB might be accountable to Parliament, to Ministers, to the public and to practitioners. It comments on the process for appeal from decisions of the Regulator; and it looks at how the regulatory system might be funded.

20 *Chapter E* raises issues of definition and regulatory gaps. The Chapter includes a broad definition of the 'outer circle' of legal services; and then sets out a definition of the 'inner circle' of reserved legal services which may be carried out only by those authorised to do so. It discusses the asymmetry which arises in respect of outer circle services, which come within the regulated net if provided by practitioners such as solicitors, but are unregulated if provided by practitioners outside a front-line body. It proposes that the determination of how widely the regulatory net should be cast should rest with Government, and suggests criteria which would be employed in the relevant cost/benefit analysis accompanying any change.

21 *Chapter F* looks at issues around the permission of alternative business practices. Legal Disciplinary Practices (LDPs) are law practices which bring together lawyers from different bodies to provide legal services to third parties. The Chapter proposes that non-lawyers should be permitted to become principals or 'Managers' of such practices, subject to the principle that lawyers should be in a majority by number in the management group. It also proposes that outside ownership should be permitted, subject to a 'fit to own' test and also to a number of safeguards built around the identity of those who manage the practice and the management systems they employ. Within England and Wales outside ownership is already permitted in respect of legal practices which provide licensed conveyancing services; it is proposed that it should, subject to safeguards, now be permitted in other areas of the legal services market.

22 In the regulation of LDPs, Chapter F proposes that the focus of the regulatory system should be upon the economic unit, rather than the individual lawyer. Recognised front-line regulatory bodies would apply to the LSB for authorisation to regulate designated types of LDPs; and the LSB would determine each application against the recognised body's competence in particular legal service areas and the governance and administrative arrangements that the recognised body had in place.

23 Chapter F also looks at Multi-Disciplinary Practices (MDPs). These are practices which bring together lawyers and other professionals to provide legal and other services to third parties. There are considerable issues in connection with such practices, in particular that of regulatory reach since the LSB would have no jurisdiction beyond the legal sector. The setting up of a regulatory system for LDPs would represent a major step towards MDPs, if at some subsequent moment it were determined that there were appropriate safeguards to permit such practices.

24 Taken together the proposals set out in Chapters A to F form my recommendations for a new framework. I believe this framework would represent a considerable advance on the '*outdated, inflexible, over-complex and insufficiently accountable or transparent*' regime which currently exists. The establishment of the LSB as a single oversight regulatory body, separate from Government Departments where many of the oversight functions currently sit, and the split in front-line bodies between their regulatory and representative functions, should provide a framework independent of Government in which to promote competition and innovation, including in the area of alternative business structures. By giving the LSB clear regulatory objectives, by requiring it to consult in respect of any major decision and by insisting that it reports to, among others, Parliament, it should be a transparent and accountable Regulator. By giving the LSB powers over all existing front-line bodies and powers to recognise new bodies, the system should be able to be consistent, comprehensive and flexible. In a number of ways, in particular through the LSB as a regulator which counts consumer protection among its statutory objectives and through the OLC as a single complaints body independent of the existing professional bodies, the new system should better serve both the public and the consumer interest. The analysis of costs suggests that the OLC, as a single complaints body, might yield some savings compared with the current system with its many complaints handling and oversight bodies. Taken together the LSB and OLC should not impose on the system any materially greater burden of cost than the current arrangements.

. . .

What happens next?

32 What happens next is a matter for Ministers. Whilst some lawyers will continue to argue that the current system 'ain't broke', I believe there is strong evidence of the need for major reform: (i) to the regulatory framework which, as described in the Government's own Scoping Study, is flawed; (ii) to the complaints system which needs change to benefit the consumer; and (iii) to the types of business structures permitted to provide legal services to the consumer, which have changed little over a significant period. It is for Ministers to determine whether they wish to press ahead with reform.

33 Reform will not be easy. Whilst there is pressure for change, from consumer groups and also from many lawyers, reform will be resisted by other lawyers who are comfortable with the system as it is. Lawyers who are opposed to the reforms in this Review will either argue that I am mistaken and have failed to understand the special characteristics that set the law apart, or call for further research and consultation, kicking reform into the long grass. Changes will require significant political commitment, partly to meet the expected criticism from some lawyers and partly because reform will need primary legislation, which requires scarce Parliamentary time.

34 I hope that Ministers, and subsequently Parliament, will conclude that reform is necessary. In my view it is long overdue.

Sir David Clementi
December 2004

 Sir David Clementi's Report is available at:
www.legal-services-review.org.uk/content/report/foreword.htm

Legal Services Act 2007 – implementing recommendations

The Legal Services Act 2007 contains the legislative provisions necessary for the implementation of many of Sir David Clementi's recommendations. The key provisions of this piece of legislation are reproduced below, along with the accompanying explanatory notes.

Legal Services Act 2007

PART 1
THE REGULATORY OBJECTIVES

1 The regulatory objectives

(1) In this Act a reference to 'the regulatory objectives' is a reference to the objectives of—

(a) protecting and promoting the public interest;
(b) supporting the constitutional principle of the rule of law;
(c) improving access to justice;
(d) protecting and promoting the interests of consumers;
(e) promoting competition in the provision of services within subsection (2);
(f) encouraging an independent, strong, diverse and effective legal profession;
(g) increasing public understanding of the citizen's legal rights and duties;
(h) promoting and maintaining adherence to the professional principles.

(2) The services within this subsection are services such as are provided by authorised persons (including services which do not involve the carrying on of activities which are reserved legal activities).

(3) The 'professional principles' are—

(a) that authorised persons should act with independence and integrity,
(b) that authorised persons should maintain proper standards of work,
(c) that authorised persons should act in the best interests of their clients,
(d) that persons who exercise before any court a right of audience, or conduct litigation in relation to proceedings in any court, by virtue of being authorised

persons should comply with their duty to the court to act with independence in the interests of justice, and

(e) that the affairs of clients should be kept confidential.

(4) In this section 'authorised persons' means authorised persons in relation to activities which are reserved legal activities.

PART 2

THE LEGAL SERVICES BOARD

Constitution

2 The Legal Services Board

(1) There is to be a body corporate called the Legal Services Board ('the Board').

(2) Schedule 1 is about the Board.

General functions

3 The Board's duty to promote the regulatory objectives etc.

(1) In discharging its functions the Board must comply with the requirements of this section.

(2) The Board must, so far as is reasonably practicable, act in a way—
(a) which is compatible with the regulatory objectives, and
(b) which the Board considers most appropriate for the purpose of meeting those objectives.

(3) The Board must have regard to—
(a) the principles under which regulatory activities should be transparent, accountable, proportionate, consistent and targeted only at cases in which action is needed, and
(b) any other principle appearing to it to represent the best regulatory practice.

. . .

PART 4

REGULATION OF APPROVED REGULATORS

Introductory

27 Regulatory and representative functions of approved regulators

(1) In this Act references to the 'regulatory functions' of an approved regulator are to any functions the approved regulator has—
(a) under or in relation to its regulatory arrangements, or
(b) in connection with the making or alteration of those arrangements.

(2) In this Act references to the 'representative functions' of an approved regulator are to any functions the approved regulator has in connection with the representation, or promotion, of the interests of persons regulated by it.

→

General duties of approved regulators

28 Approved regulator's duty to promote the regulatory objectives, etc.

(1) In discharging its regulatory functions (whether in connection with a reserved legal activity or otherwise) an approved regulator must comply with the requirements of this section.

(2) The approved regulator must, so far as is reasonably practicable, act in a way—
(a) which is compatible with the regulatory objectives, and
(b) which the approved regulator considers most appropriate for the purpose of meeting those objectives.

(3) The approved regulator must have regard to—
(a) the principles under which regulatory activities should be transparent, accountable, proportionate, consistent and targeted only at cases in which action is needed, and
(b) any other principle appearing to it to represent the best regulatory practice.

Separation of regulatory and representative functions

29 Prohibition on the Board interfering with representative functions

(1) Nothing in this Act authorises the Board to exercise its functions in relation to any representative function of an approved regulator.

(2) But subsection (1) does not prevent the Board exercising its functions for the purpose of ensuring—
(a) that the exercise of an approved regulator's regulatory functions is not prejudiced by its representative functions, or
(b) that decisions relating to the exercise of an approved regulator's regulatory functions are, so far as reasonably practicable, taken independently from decisions relating to the exercise of its representative functions.

. . .

PART 5

ALTERNATIVE BUSINESS STRUCTURES

Introductory

71 Carrying on of activities by licensed bodies

(1) The provisions of this Part have effect for the purpose of regulating the carrying on of reserved legal activities and other activities by licensed bodies.

(2) In this Act 'licensed body' means a body which holds a licence in force under this Part.

72 'Licensable body'

(1) A body ('B') is a licensable body if a non-authorised person—
(a) is a manager of B, or
(b) has an interest in B.

(2) A body ('B') is also a licensable body if—
(a) another body ('A') is a manager of B, or has an interest in B, and
(b) non-authorised persons are entitled to exercise, or control the exercise of, at least 10% of the voting rights in A.

(3) For the purposes of this Act, a person has an interest in a body if—
(a) the person holds shares in the body, or
(b) the person is entitled to exercise, or control the exercise of, voting rights in the body.

(4) A body may be licensable by virtue of both subsection (1) and subsection (2).

(5) For the purposes of this Act, a non-authorised person has an indirect interest in a licensable body if the body is licensable by virtue of subsection (2) and the non-authorised person is entitled to exercise, or control the exercise of, voting rights in A.

. . .

PART 6
LEGAL COMPLAINTS

Complaints procedures of authorised persons

112 Complaints procedures of authorised persons

(1) The regulatory arrangements of an approved regulator must make provision requiring each relevant authorised person—
(a) to establish and maintain procedures for the resolution of relevant complaints, or
(b) to participate in, or make arrangements to be subject to, such procedures established and maintained by another person, and provision for the enforcement of that requirement.

(2) The provision made for the purposes of subsection (1) must satisfy such requirements as the Board may, from time to time, specify for the purposes of that subsection.

(3) In this section—
'relevant authorised person', in relation to an approved regulator, means a person in relation to whom the approved regulator is a relevant approved regulator;
'relevant complaint', in relation to a relevant authorised person, means a complaint which—
(a) relates to an act or omission of that person, and
(b) may be made under the scheme provided for by this Part.

. . .

Overview of the scheme

113 Overview of the scheme

(1) This Part provides for a scheme under which complaints which—
(a) relate to an act or omission of a person ('the respondent') in carrying on an activity, and
(b) are within the jurisdiction of the scheme (see section 125), may be resolved quickly and with minimum formality by an independent person.

→

(2) Under the scheme—
(a) redress may be provided to the complainant, but
(b) no disciplinary action may be taken against the respondent.

(3) Section 157 prevents provision relating to redress being included in the regulatory arrangements of an approved regulator, or licensing rules made by the Board in its capacity as a licensing authority.

(4) But neither the scheme nor any provision made by this Part affects any power of an approved regulator, or the Board in its capacity as a licensing authority, to take disciplinary action.

(5) 'Disciplinary action' means the imposition of sanctions, in respect of a breach of conduct rules or discipline rules, on a person who is an authorised person in relation to an activity which is a reserved legal activity.

The Office for Legal Complaints

114 The Office for Legal Complaints

(1) There is to be a body corporate called the Office for Legal Complaints (in this Act referred to as 'the OLC').

(2) Schedule 15 is about the OLC.

115 The ombudsman scheme

(1) The scheme provided for by this Part is to be administered by the OLC in accordance with this Part and with scheme rules made under this Part.

(2) In this Part 'scheme rules' means rules made by the OLC.

(3) The scheme is to be operated under a name (which must include the word 'ombudsman') chosen by the OLC, and is referred to in this Act as 'the ombudsman scheme'.

116 General obligations

(1) In discharging its functions the OLC must comply with the requirements of this section.

(2) The OLC must, so far as is reasonably practicable, act in a way—
(a) which is compatible with the regulatory objectives, and
(b) which it considers most appropriate for the purpose of meeting those objectives.

(3) The OLC must have regard to any principles appearing to it to represent the best practice of those who administer ombudsman schemes.

 The Legal Services Act 2007 is available on the website of the Office for Public Sector Information at:
www.opsi.gov.uk/acts/acts2007/ukpga_20070029_en_1

Legal Services Act 2007 Explanatory Notes

Summary

7 Part 1: The Regulatory Objectives sets out the eight regulatory objectives, which guide the Legal Services Board (the Board), the approved regulators, and the Office for Legal Complaints (OLC) in exercising their functions.

8 Part 2: The Legal Services Board sets out the structure and functions of the Board, including its duty to act compatibly with the regulatory objectives, to assist in the maintenance and development of standards in regulation, education and training and to establish a Consumer Panel. It also sets out the requirements for both appointment to, and membership of, the Board and the powers that the Lord Chancellor has in relation to these processes.

9 Part 3: Reserved Legal Activities lists and defines the reserved legal activities. It explains who is entitled to carry out these activities, and the penalties for those who carry out, or pretend to be entitled to carry out, these activities where they are not entitled. It provides for transitional arrangements for those currently allowed to carry on reserved legal activities. It also explains the process for altering the scope of the reserved legal activities. Approved regulators are the bodies that authorise and regulate persons to carry on reserved legal activities. This Part of the Act explains what an approved regulator is, lists those bodies designated by the Act as approved regulators, and explains how other bodies can become an approved regulator in the future.

10 Part 4: Regulation of Approved Regulators prescribes the general duties of approved regulators, and the powers that the Board has to ensure that these are being properly carried out. It details how the Board can intervene when there is a problem, the procedures that it must follow, and the persons that it must consult. The Board's powers include targetsetting, censure, financial penalties, direct intervention in the approved regulator's regulation of its members, and, ultimately, the power to recommend to the Lord Chancellor that an order be made cancelling the approved regulator's designation.

11 Part 5: Alternative Business Structures (ABS) makes provision for the licensing of new business structures in legal services. These will allow lawyers and non-lawyers to work together to deliver legal and other services. This Part of the Act sets out the arrangements for authorisation, by the Board, of licensing authorities and how, in the absence of an appropriate licensing authority, the Board can license ABS firms directly. It makes provision for the regulation of ABS.

12 Part 6: Legal Complaints establishes an independent OLC, which is responsible for administering an ombudsman scheme, under which all complaints will be dealt with by a Chief Ombudsman, assistant ombudsmen, and staff appointed by the OLC. Part 6 removes the ability of approved regulators to provide redress to complainants, and grants this power to the ombudsman scheme. The OLC will draw up scheme rules setting out the detail of the ombudsman scheme. This Part makes provision for the appointment process and terms of office for members of the OLC Board and the Chief Ombudsman and the assistant ombudsmen. It also makes provision for the accountability of the OLC to the Board, the framework of rules by which the OLC will establish its operating procedures, and changes to the regulatory arrangements of approved regulators.

13 Part 7: Further Provisions Relating to the Board and the OLC makes provision as to the guidance that the Board may give. It also requires the Board to make rules providing for the payment by approved regulators of a levy, to recoup the expenditure of the Board and OLC. The rules may include provision as to the rate and times at which the levy is payable, and circumstances in which the levy may be waived. This section also makes provision for the Board to enter into voluntary arrangements with any person, for example to promote best regulatory practice.

14 Part 8: Miscellaneous Provisions about Lawyers makes provision for the following matters:

- the requirement for alteration of the rules of the Solicitors Disciplinary Tribunal to be approved by the Board, and empowering the Board to give a limited range of directions to the Tribunal;
- the maintenance of the register of trade mark attorneys and the register of patent attorneys;
- the application of legal professional privilege in relation to authorised persons who are not barristers or solicitors;
- amendment of the Immigration and Asylum Act 1999 (which regulates the provision of immigration advice services) and the Compensation Act 2006 (which makes provision in relation to claims management services), in consequence of the new regime established by the Act;
- the making of costs orders in relation to *pro bono* legal representation; and
- conferring competence on the Scottish Legal Complaints Commission in respect of certain reserved matters.

15 Part 9: General makes provision regarding offences committed by bodies corporate and unincorporated bodies. It provides that certain functions conferred on the Lord Chancellor by the Act may not be transferred to another Minister by a transfer of functions order. It states how notices issued pursuant to provision made in the Act are to be given and makes provision governing the procedure for making orders and regulations under powers in the Act. It allows for minor and consequential amendments to be made by order, and makes provision regarding the extent, commencement and short title of the Act.

16 The Legal Services Act establishes a new framework for the regulation of legal services in England and Wales.

17 The Act makes provision for:

- **A new regulatory framework** that replaces the existing framework which comprises a number of oversight regulators with overlapping responsibilities.
- **The establishment of the Legal Services Board**: a single oversight body, independent both from Government and from the 'front-line' approved regulators such as the Law Society and Bar Council. The Board has a duty to promote the regulatory objectives set out in Part 1.
- **The establishment of an independent Office for Legal Complaints**: a body with statutory power to establish a scheme for handling complaints about service provided by persons subject to oversight regulation by the Board, and to award redress in appropriate circumstances.
- **Alternative Business Structures** to enable lawyers and non-lawyers to work together to deliver legal and other services. New business structures are expected to give legal providers greater flexibility to respond to market demands, within the UK and overseas. Licences will be conferred by licensing authorities, with various safeguards in place.
- It is for the Board to advise the Government on any areas where it identifies problems within the legal services market, or 'regulatory gaps'.

Background

18 In 2001 the Office of Fair Trading (OFT) published a report recommending that rules governing the legal professions should be subject to competition law and that unjustified restrictions on competition be removed. Following this, the Government carried out a consultation, and published a report into competition and regulation in the legal services market.

19 In 2003 Sir David Clementi was appointed by the Government to conduct an independent review of the regulation of legal services. He found that many areas were in need of restructuring and development, and agreed with the Government's earlier conclusion that the current regulatory framework was 'inflexible, outdated and over-complex'. Sir David highlighted concerns about the current:

● regulatory framework,
● complaints handling systems, and
● restrictive nature of business structures.

20 In October 2005 the Government published a White Paper, *The Future of Legal Services: Putting Consumers First*. The White Paper set an agenda for reforming the delivery of legal services. It proposed a new regulatory framework that would direct regulation to those areas where it is needed:

> We will create a Legal Services Board, an Office for Legal Complaints and we will take steps to enable firms to provide services under alternative business structures to those presently available.

21 The draft Legal Services Bill was published in May 2006 and was subject to pre-legislative scrutiny by a Joint Committee of both Houses of Parliament. The Joint Committee reported in July 2006, and the Government published its response to this in September of the same year.

The legal services sector prior to the Act

22 Six pre-existing forms of legal service or activity are covered by the Act. These are:

● the right of audience in the courts;
● the right to conduct litigation;
● reserved instrument activities;
● probate activities;
● notarial activities;
● the administration of oaths.

23 Prior to the commencement of this Act, these services were regulated by legal professional bodies such as the Law Society or the Bar Council, as well as – to varying degrees – higher level regulators such as the Secretary of State, the Master of the Rolls and the OFT. In addition to these different regulators, there were also a range of major purchasers in the market who acted as quasi-regulators, by setting their own contract terms and prices – for example, the Legal Services Commission, and commercial organisations who operate 'panel' systems. This Act does not directly affect these quasi-regulators.

24 Prior to commencement, there were a number of restrictions on the type of business structures through which legal services could be provided, mainly in regulators' professional rules. Some existing regulators prohibited lawyers from entering into partnership with non-lawyers. They also placed restrictions on unregulated persons being formally involved in the management of these businesses, and unregulated persons having any stake in the ownership of such businesses. In many cases, these restrictions were at least partly due to the fact that legal regulators did not have the powers they needed to effectively regulate practices in which non-lawyers exercised some form of control. This generally meant that lawyers were limited in the extent to which they could form businesses with non-lawyers or with different types of lawyer. The Act seeks to facilitate a regulatory framework in which different types of lawyer and non-lawyer are able to form businesses together, and in which regulators can be given effective powers to regulate such businesses.

25 Previously, if consumers wished to complain about any of the legal services listed above, they needed to take that complaint up, in the first instance, with the person they were complaining about. If the complaint was not resolved in-house, consumers could then make a complaint to the regulatory body responsible for regulating the person providing the service (for example, the Law Society, the Bar Council). In the event that a complainant was not satisfied with the way in which a complaint has been handled by a regulatory body, the complainant was then able to refer the complaint to the Legal Services Ombudsman. The Ombudsman investigated the way in which the complaint was handled and the response from the professional body. If the Ombudsman believed that a complaint had not been investigated properly, they could require that the professional body look at the matter again. The Ombudsman also had powers to investigate individual complaints. In 2004, the Ombudsman exercised this power in less than 1% of cases.

The Explanatory Notes to the Legal Services Act 2007 are available on the website of the Office for Public Sector Information at:
www.opsi.gov.uk/acts/acts2007/en/ukpgaen_20070029_en.pdf

Compensation Act 2006 – an attempt at regulation

Claims management companies attract clients for legal services through major marketing exercises, such as television adverts. They then charge solicitors a fee to refer cases to them. The government has been concerned at the unscrupulous behaviour of some claims management companies, for example television adverts which encourage people to make a legal claim where they do not have realistic grounds for a claim. Parliament has now passed the Compensation Act 2006 which contains provisions to regulate the activities of claims management companies.

Compensation Act 2006

PART 2
CLAIMS MANAGEMENT SERVICES

4 Provision of regulated claims management services

(1) A person may not provide regulated claims management services unless—

(a) he is an authorised person,

(b) he is an exempt person,

(c) the requirement for authorisation has been waived in relation to him in accordance with regulations under section 9, or

(d) he is an individual acting otherwise than in the course of a business.

(2) In this Part—

(a) 'authorised person' means a person authorised by the Regulator under section 5(1)(a),

(b) 'claims management services' means advice or other services in relation to the making of a claim,

(c) 'claim' means a claim for compensation, restitution, repayment or any other remedy or relief in respect of loss or damage or in respect of an obligation, whether the claim is made or could be made—
(i) by way of legal proceedings,
(ii) in accordance with a scheme of regulation (whether voluntary or compulsory), or
(iii) in pursuance of a voluntary undertaking,

(d) 'exempt person' has the meaning given by section 6(5), and

(e) services are regulated if they are—
(i) of a kind prescribed by order of the Secretary of State, or
(ii) provided in cases or circumstances of a kind prescribed by order of the Secretary of State.

(3) For the purposes of this section—

(a) a reference to the provision of services includes, in particular, a reference to—
(i) the provision of financial services or assistance,
(ii) the provision of services by way of or in relation to legal representation,
(iii) referring or introducing one person to another, and
(iv) making inquiries, and

(b) a person does not provide claims management services by reason only of giving, or preparing to give, evidence (whether or not expert evidence).

(4) For the purposes of subsection (1)(d) an individual acts in the course of a business if, in particular—

(a) he acts in the course of an employment, or

(b) he otherwise receives or hopes to receive money or money's worth as a result of his action.

. . .

5 The Regulator

(1) The Secretary of State may by order designate a person ('the Regulator')—

(a) to authorise persons to provide regulated claims management services,

(b) to regulate the conduct of authorised persons, and

(c) to exercise such other functions as are conferred on the Regulator by or under this Part.

→

(2) The Secretary of State may designate a person only if satisfied that the person—

(a) is competent to perform the functions of the Regulator,

(b) will make arrangements to avoid any conflict of interest between the person's functions as Regulator and any other functions, and

(c) will promote the interests of persons using regulated claims management services (including, in particular, by—

(i) setting and monitoring standards of competence and professional conduct for persons providing regulated claims management services,

(ii) promoting good practice by persons providing regulated claims management services, in particular in relation to the provision of information about charges and other matters to persons using or considering using the services,

(iii) promoting practices likely to facilitate competition between different providers of regulated claims management services, and

(iv) ensuring that arrangements are made for the protection of persons using regulated claims management services (including arrangements for the handling of complaints about the conduct of authorised persons)).

(3) If the Secretary of State thinks that no existing person (whether an individual or a body corporate or unincorporate) is suitable for designation under subsection (1), he may by order establish a person for the purpose of being designated.

(4) The Regulator shall—

(a) comply with any directions given to him by the Secretary of State;

(b) have regard to any guidance given to him by the Secretary of State;

(c) have regard to any code of practice issued to him by the Secretary of State;

(d) try to meet any targets set for him by the Secretary of State;

(e) provide the Secretary of State with any report or information requested (but this paragraph does not require or permit disclosure of information in contravention of any other enactment).

(5) The Secretary of State shall lay before Parliament any code of practice issued by him to the Regulator.

(6) The Secretary of State may pay grants to the Regulator (which may be on terms or conditions, including terms and conditions as to repayment with or without interest).

 The Compensation Act 2006 is available on the website of the Office for Public Sector Information at:
www.opsi.gov.uk/acts/acts2006/pdf/ukpga_20060029_en.pdf

Compensation Act 2006 Explanatory Notes

PART 2: CLAIMS MANAGEMENT SERVICES

Summary

27 Part 2 of the Act sets out the framework for the regulation of claims management services.

Background

28 The Better Regulation Task Force (BRTF) report: *Better Routes to Redress* published in May 2004 found that the 'compensation culture' is a myth but that it is a damaging myth that needs to be tackled. The BRTF identified the activities of claims intermediaries as contributing to a 'have a go culture' and recommended that claims intermediaries should be subject to statutory regulation, if self-regulation did not work.

29 One of the concerns identified by the BRTF was that while there were established complaints mechanisms and bodies to help people who are unhappy with the way they have been treated by solicitors or insurers, there has been no clear-cut equivalent in the case of claims intermediaries. It has been suggested that as a result, more claims for redress have been brought against solicitors and insurers because there has been no regulatory way to proceed against anyone else.

30 The Government published a consultation and responses paper on the simplification of conditional fee agreements (CFAs) in June 2004 *Making Simple CFAs a Reality* which included a discussion of the widespread concern over claims intermediaries' activities and work underway to try to produce a self-regulatory solution. The Government responded to the BRTF's report in November 2004 accepting the recommendation that regulation of claims intermediaries should be considered if self-regulation failed.

31 The legislative framework is flexible and allows the Secretary of State to designate a body to regulate claims management services, to establish a body to regulate (where he thinks that no existing body is suitable for designation) or to regulate himself. The Act provides the outline regulatory framework to authorise providers who would be required to comply with rules and codes of practice. The Act also includes power for the Regulator to investigate unauthorised activities and to prosecute those who try to evade regulation.

32 If the Secretary of State designates a body to regulate claims management services he will retain oversight responsibility for the body. He will have the power to issue directions, provide guidance, require the body to try to meet regulatory targets and to provide information on its regulatory responsibility. It is anticipated that the regulation of claims management services will in due course be integrated into the proposed new regulatory framework for legal services set out in the Draft Legal Services Bill (Cm 6839).

Commentary on sections: Part 2

Section 4: Provision of regulated claims management services

33 This section prohibits the provision of regulated claims management services by those who are not authorised, exempted from authorisation or subject to a waiver, or an individual acting otherwise than in the course of a business. *Subsection 1(d)* makes it clear that the prohibition does not apply to individuals who offer claims management services on a voluntary basis (for example a friend offering advice on a claim for compensation). It

would, however, apply to voluntary or not-for-profit organisations (although not to individual volunteers providing their services through such an organisation).

34 *Subsection 2* defines 'authorised person' as a person authorised by the Regulator. This would also allow the Regulator to authorise claims management companies (as 'person' also applies to a body corporate or unincorporate (Schedule 1 to the Interpretation Act 1978)). Thus employees or members of a company or other organisation would be covered by the authorisation granted to the 'parent' company or organisation for which they are providing claims management services, avoiding the need for specific authorisation of each individual (natural) person. This subsection also defines claims management services as 'advice or other services in relation to the making of a claim'. The claim may be for compensation, restitution, repayment or other remedy or relief in respect of loss or damage, or in respect of an obligation – whether pursued through the courts or by other means (for example the Employment Tribunals, Criminal Injuries Compensation Scheme or complaints to insurers or the Financial Ombudsman, about the mis-selling of financial products such as endowment policies). Only those claims management services that the Secretary of State prescribes by order under section 4(2)(e) will be subject to regulation. The Secretary of State can therefore target regulation in areas where he considers there to be a particularly high risk to consumers.

35 *Subsection 3* gives examples of activities which constitute the provision of services (where they are connected with a claim). The list, which is not exhaustive, includes financial services (for example assisting with the purchase of insurance or loans); legal representation (for example acting on a claimants behalf in pursuing a claim); referring or introducing one person to another (for example referring a claim to a solicitor); and making inquiries (for example contacting witnesses in the course of investigating a claim). The provision of advice does not extend to the preparation or giving of evidence. For example, if a person were asked to give evidence in a personal injury claim (whether or not expert evidence) this would not amount to providing claims management services.

36 *Subsection 4* sets out the circumstances in which, for the purposes of sub-section 1(d), an individual acts in the course of a business. Individuals acting in the course of employment or who otherwise receive or hope to receive reward (directly or indirectly) as a result of the provision of services will need to apply for authorisation unless they are exempt or subject to a waiver. Individuals who are not acting in the course of a business will fall within subsection 1(d) and will not need to be authorised.

37 *Subsection 5* provides that the Secretary of State may by order provide that a claim for a specified benefit shall be treated as a claim for the purposes of this Part. Such an order would allow claims management services provided in relation to specified benefits to be regulated in an order under subsection 2(e).

38 *Subsection 6* requires that the Secretary of State only specify a benefit under subsection 5 if it appears to him to be a United Kingdom social security benefit designed to provide compensation for industrial injury.

The Explanatory Notes to the Compensation Act 2006 are available on the website of the Office for Public Sector Information at:
www.opsi.gov.uk/acts/acts2006/en/ukpgaen_20060029_en.pdf

12

The jury system

Introduction

This chapter looks at:

- the House of Lords' judgment of **R** v **Abdroikof** considering when people employed in the criminal justice system can sit as jurors;

- research examining the jurors' perceptions, understanding, confidence and satisfaction in the jury system;

- judicial attempts to control the length of criminal trials;

- government efforts to abolish jury trials in serious fraud cases; and

- research into the judges' own attitudes towards jury trials in serious fraud cases.

Membership of the jury

Following the Criminal Justice Act 2003, a wider range of people are potentially allowed to sit as jurors. The aim, following Sir Robin Auld's recommendations on the subject, was to make juries more representative of the public. But these reforms have themselves thrown up new problems about when lawyers, the police and others employed in the criminal justice system, should be allowed to sit as jurors. This issue was considered by the House of Lords in **R v Abdroikof** (2007).

R v Abdroikof (2007), House of Lords

Lord Bingham of Cornhill

My Lords,

1 These three appellants were tried on indictment in different courts on unrelated charges and were convicted. In the first two cases the trial jury included among its members a serving police officer, and in the third case it included a solicitor employed by the Crown Prosecuting Service. The common question raised by these three conjoined appeals is whether a fair-minded and informed observer, on the facts of the three cases, would conclude that there was a real possibility that the trial jury was biased.

2 The Court of Appeal (Lord Woolf CJ, Richards and Henriques JJ) which also heard the appeals together, held that the observer would not so conclude: [2005] EWCA Crim 1986, [2005] 1 WLR 3538. The appellants challenge that ruling.

3 The first appellant, Nurlon Abdroikof, faced counts of theft (to which he pleaded guilty) and attempted murder (to which he pleaded not guilty, but of which he was convicted). The trial last for six days in August 2004 before the Common Serjeant of London at the Central Criminal Court. There was a minor issue concerning one aspect of the evidence of a police witness. On Friday 27 August, when the jury were in retirement considering their verdicts, the foreman of the jury sent a note to the judge revealing that he was a serving police officer. He was concerned that if required to report for duty at the Notting Hill Carnival on the following Bank Holiday Monday, when the court was not sitting, he might meet one or more police officers who had been called to give evidence at the trial. With the acquiescence of defending counsel, who had not previously known of the foreman's occupation, the juror was directed not to report for duty on the Monday.

4 The second appellant, Richard John Green, was stopped by police officers on 18 March 2004. He was searched by one of the officers, Sergeant Burgess, and in the course of the search the sergeant put his hand into the appellant's pocket and pricked his finger on a used syringe. The appellant was charged with offences of assault occasioning actual bodily harm and having a bladed or pointed article. He pleaded not guilty and was tried before His Honour Judge Statman and a jury at Woolwich Crown Court. There was a dispute on the evidence between him and the police sergeant concerning the manner in which he was searched and what he and the sergeant respectively said. The appellant was convicted and sentenced. Some time after the trial, by chance, the appellant's solicitor discovered that a police officer, PC Mason, had been a member of the trial jury, a fact not known to the appellant at the time. PC Mason was at the time posted to Eltham Police Station, within an Operational Command Unit which committed its work to Woolwich Crown Court. PC Mason and Sergeant Burgess were both serving in the same borough at the time of the incident and had once served in the same police station at the same time, but the two officers were not known to one another.

5 The third appellant, Kenneth Joseph Williamson, was charged with two very serious offences of rape, of which he was convicted on 3 February 2005 after a trial before His Honour Judge Hale and a jury in the Crown Court at Warrington. The jury included among its members Mr McKay-Smith. Before the trial began he wrote to the court to say he had been summoned to serve as a member of the jury at Warrington. He recorded that he worked for the Crown Prosecution Service and had done so since its inception in 1986. He had previously worked for the Greater Manchester Council as a prosecuting solicitor, having been in private practice for five years before that. He was a Higher Court Advocate and had practised as such in many local courts including that at Warrington on behalf of the Crown, although he had not conducted a trial in the Crown Court. His current job was to advise the police on charging out of hours. He said that as a matter of policy the CPS had asked those summoned to ensure that the judge had all the necessary information to hand in order to exercise discretion as to the feasibility of an individual CPS employee serving. This letter was passed to defending counsel, who sought to challenge Mr McKay-Smith, contending that the court should not only do what is right but should be seen to have done what is right. He complained of potential bias and relied on the appellant's fair trial right under article 6 of the European Convention on Human Rights. The judge ruled that he had to operate within the law passed by Parliament and he could see no objection to this juror sitting in the light of the current legislation. Mr McKay-Smith duly sat, and became the foreman of the jury.

. . .

The criminal trial jury in England and Wales
8 The present questions arise as a result of changes made in the Criminal Justice Act 2003 to the rules formerly governing the qualification and disqualification of jurors.

. . .

Conclusion
23 It must in my view be accepted that most adult human beings, as a result of their background, education and experience, harbour certain prejudices and predilections of which they may be conscious or unconscious. I would also, for my part, accept that the safeguards established to protect the impartiality of the jury, when properly operated, do all that can reasonably be done to neutralise the ordinary prejudices and predilections to which we are all prone. But this does not meet the central thrust of the case made by Mr Richard Carey-Hughes QC for the appellants: that these cases do not involve the ordinary prejudices and predilections to which we are all prone but the possibility of bias (possibly unconscious) which, as he submits, inevitably flows from the presence on a jury of persons professionally committed to one side only of an adversarial trial process, not merely (as the Court of Appeal put it) 'involved in some capacity or other in the administration of justice'. Lord Justice Auld's expectation that each doubtful case would be resolved by the judge on a case by case basis is not, he pointed out, met if neither the judge nor counsel know of the identity of a police officer or the juror, as appears to be the present practice.

24 This is not an argument I feel able, in principle, to dismiss. It is not a criticism of the police service, but a tribute to its greatest strength, that officers belong to a disciplined force, bound to each other by strong bonds of loyalty, mutual support, shared danger and responsibility, culture and tradition. The Morris Committee thought it self-evident that officers could not be, or be seen to be, impartial participants in the prosecution process, a disqualification which in the judgment of ACPO (accepted by the committee) extended to civilian employees of the police. The facts revealed in the recent case of **R** *v* **Pintori** ([2007] EWCA Crim 1700, 13 July 2007, unreported) perhaps suggest that this is not an out-dated perception. Serving police officers remain ineligible for jury service in Scotland, Northern Ireland, Australia, New Zealand, Canada, Hong Kong, Gibraltar and a number of states in the United States, the remainder of the states providing a procedure to question jurors on their occupations and allegiances. But Parliament has declared that in England and Wales police officers are eligible to sit, perhaps envisaging that their identity would be known and any objection would be the subject of judicial decision.

25 In the case of the first appellant, it was unfortunate that the identity of the officer became known at such a late stage in the trial, and on very short notice to the judge and defence counsel. But had the matter been ventilated at the outset of the trial, it is difficult to see what argument defence counsel could have urged other than the general undesirability of police officers serving on juries, a difficult argument to advance in face of the parliamentary enactment. It was not a case which turned on a contest between the evidence of the police and that of the appellant, and it would have been hard to suggest that the case was one in which unconscious prejudice, even if present, would have been likely to operate to the disadvantage of the appellant, and it makes no difference that the officer was the foreman of the jury. In the event, confronted with this question at very short notice, defence counsel raised no objection. I conclude, not without unease, that having regard to the parliamentary enactment the Court of Appeal reached the right conclusion in this case, and I would dismiss the appeal.

26 The second appellant's case is different. Here, there was a crucial dispute on the evidence between the appellant and the police sergeant, and the sergeant and the juror, although not personally known to each other, shared the same local service background. In this context the instinct (however unconscious) of a police officer on the jury to prefer the evidence of a brother officer to that of a drug-addicted defendant would be judged by the fair-minded and informed observer to be a real and possible source of unfairness, beyond the reach of standard judicial warnings and directions. The second appellant was not tried by a tribunal which was and appeared to be impartial. It cannot be supposed that Parliament intended to infringe the rule in the **Sussex Justices** case, still less to do so without express language. I would allow this appeal, and quash the second appellant's conviction.

27 In the case of the third appellant, no possible criticism is to be made of Mr McKay-Smith, who acted in strict compliance with the guidance given to him and left the matter to the judge. But the judge gave no serious consideration to the objection of defence counsel, who himself had little opportunity to review the law on this subject. It must, perhaps, be doubted whether Lord Justice Auld or Parliament contemplated that employed Crown prosecutors would sit as jurors in prosecutions brought by their own authority. It is in my opinion clear that justice is not seen to be done if one discharging the very important neutral role of juror is a full-time, salaried, long-serving employee of the prosecutor. This is a much stronger case than **Pullar** (see para 17 above): it is as if, on the facts of that case, F had been employed in the department of the procurator fiscal. Had that been so, one may be sure the court would have agreed with the commission. The third appellant was entitled to be tried by a tribunal that was and appeared to be impartial, and in my opinion he was not. The consequence is that his convictions must be quashed. This is a most unfortunate outcome, since the third appellant was accused of very grave crimes, of which he may have been guilty. But even a guilty defendant is entitled to be tried by an impartial tribunal and the consequence is inescapable. I would allow the appeal and remit the case to the Court of Appeal with an invitation to quash the convictions and rule on any application which may be made for a retrial.

The House of Lords' decision of **R** v **Abdroikof** (2007) is available on Parliament's website at:

www.publications.parliament.uk/pa/ld200607/ldjudgmt/jd071017/abdro-1.htm

---

Jury experience

The Home Office commissioned research into the experience of being a juror which was published in 2004. Below is a summary of the research findings, which was published by the Home Office at the same time as publishing the full report.

Jurors' Perceptions, Understanding, Confidence and Satisfaction in the Jury System: A Study in Six Courts

Roger Matthews, Lynn Hancock and Daniel Briggs

The research . . . was based on interviews . . . with 361 jurors who had recently completed jury service at six Crown Court centres . . . The research examined jurors' experiences of their role within the criminal justice system, whilst being careful not to contravene Section 8 of the Contempt of Court Act (1981), which prohibits discussion or investigation into jurors' deliberations about individual cases. More specifically, the study looked at:

– their perceptions and attitudes towards jury service
– their understanding of the information and the evidence they received
– jurors' confidence as a result of their contact with the court system
– their satisfaction with the process in general.

. . .

Jurors' perceptions

Half of those included in the survey claimed to be 'enthusiastic' or 'very enthusiastic' following receipt of their summons, while just under a third of respondents claimed to be 'reluctant' or 'very reluctant' (Table 1). Where reluctance was expressed this was often due to work or domestic pressures, whilst enthusiasm stemmed from believing that it would be an interesting or valuable experience or that it was a moral duty that had to be undertaken.

The inconvenience of undertaking jury service at the allocated time prompted just over a third (36%) to apply for deferral, excusal or exemption. This finding is in line with previous research (Airs and Shaw, 1999). Many jurors had previous court experience as:

- witnesses (13%);
- defendants (8%);
- victims (4%);
- jurors on a previous occasion (19%).

The majority (65%) of respondents felt confident about taking on their role as a juror.

While over half of the jurors interviewed said that the media had been influential in shaping their perceptions of the jury system, most jurors expressed a healthy scepticism toward the media.

Just under two-thirds of those engaging in jury service had a more positive view of the jury trial system after completing their service than they did before. The main factors associated with this positive change were the professionalism of the judge and court staff and how jurors were treated. Indeed, jurors greatly appreciated the work of the court personnel in general and of judges in particular. Negative views of respondents usually centred on the court system rather than the jury system. In particular, critical responses were largely shaped by delays, the trivial nature of some cases that jurors heard, the way in which some cases were presented and the standard of some court facilities. Some jurors were not impressed by the court rituals, dress and procedures and some were critical of other jurors who were not seen to take their duties seriously.

Jurors' understanding

In general, many jurors felt that engaging in jury service had been a good learning experience that had taught them about the operation of the criminal court system.

The vast majority of jurors found the summons and the leaflet *You and Your Jury Service*, as well as the induction video, to be straightforward and informative. (*You and Your Jury Service* is a 14-page leaflet given to jurors on confirmation of their attendance containing information on rules, roles and procedures.) The main impediment to understanding proceedings was the use of legal terminology. Some jurors expressed confusion in relation to discussion of 'points of law' and the requirement for the jury to leave the courtroom while these were discussed. Other confusions centred around whether or not they should take notes during a trial or whether it was appropriate to ask questions.

Jurors felt that evidence was not always presented in the clearest ways and that maps, diagrams, photographs and other visual aids were under-used in courts. Problems also stemmed from jurors not being able to hear evidence or understand the evidence of witnesses or victims.

Table 1 Reaction to receiving the jury summons

Reaction	No. of jurors	%
Very enthusiastic	30	8
Enthusiastic	152	42
Indifferent	67	19
Reluctant	75	21
Very reluctant	37	10
Total	361	100

Factors affecting confidence

Previous research on confidence in the criminal justice system has identified a number of factors which contributed in various ways to public confidence. These include the perceived 'fairness' of the process, the adherence to due process and the efficiency and professionalism of the court staff (Mirrlees-Black, 2001; Southgate and Grosvenor, 2000). Many of these views were reflected in the current study when jurors were asked to say what factors most influenced their confidence.

Positive factors affecting confidence

Diversity
The most important reported factor that had a positive influence on juror confidence in this study was the perceived benefits of having a diverse group of people from different social and economic backgrounds with different viewpoints and experiences. Diversity was seen as an essential component in deciding guilt and innocence in all trials ranging from the minor cases to the most serious.

Fairness of the trial process
The second most important factor positively influencing confidence was the perceived fairness of the trial process. Great significance was attached to the ways in which defendants were treated, their rights respected and the way evidence was presented.

Professionalism and staff competence
The professionalism and competence of the court staff was considered to be an important part of providing a fair and efficient trial. The commitment of the staff and fellow jurors influenced levels of confidence, and jurors who were seen not to be taking their responsibilities seriously were generally frowned upon.

Negative factors affecting confidence
The most important factors or conditions that had a negative influence on juror confidence were poor preparation of cases or poor quality of evidence and the inclusion of what were considered trivial or minor cases. It should be noted, however, that some jurors felt that allowing such cases to be heard in the Crown Court was an important democratic right and that their very inclusion increased the jurors' overall confidence in the trial process and the criminal justice system.

Amongst those who had not performed jury service in the past, over two-fifths (43%) left jury service with a higher level of confidence in the court system than before their service. One-fifth left with a lower level of confidence. Those who had visited a court in the past, either as victims or witnesses, were more likely to leave with a higher level of confidence following their service.

Juror satisfaction
The most positive aspects of engaging in jury service were:

- having a greater understanding of the criminal court trial;
- a feeling of having performed an important civic duty;
- meeting new people/finding it personally fulfilling (Table 2).

Table 2 Positive aspects of jury service

Positive aspect	Number of jurors	%
Have a greater understanding of the criminal trial/positive learning experience	207	57
A feeling that my 'civic duty' had been done	146	40
I met new people	144	40
It was personally fulfilling	79	22
The experience enhanced my confidence in the criminal justice system	62	17
The experience enhanced my self-confidence	30	8
Good facilities	13	4

Over half (55%) said that they would be happy to do jury service again, while 19% said they 'wouldn't mind' doing it again. Only 15% said that they definitely would not want to do it again. The great majority of minority ethnic and mixed race jurors interviewed said that they would be happy to undertake jury service again.

Table 3 The significance of juries to our system of justice

Significance of jurors	Number	%
Very important, essential, integral or necessary	224	62
Quite important	120	33
Not important	15	4
No response	2	1
Total	361	100

The vast majority of respondents (95%) considered juries 'very important', 'essential', 'necessary' or 'quite important' in our system of justice (Table 3). Participating in jury service appeared to produce a remarkable level of social solidarity amongst jurors while enhancing their sense of citizenship.

Reported negative aspects included complaints about the heating, air conditioning and the comfort of seating for jurors. In terms of the court's general amenities and facilities, the main complaints were about:

– the service and quality of food available in the canteen (33%);
– the lack of facilities to alleviate boredom (14%);
– the general accommodation (14%);
– the lack of separate areas for smokers and nonsmokers (14%);
– parking facilities (3%).

Just over one-third of jurors (36%) reported that they felt intimidated or very uncomfortable in the courtroom, often at the prospect of meeting the defendant or his or her family on the street or coming out of court. Female jurors were more likely to express these feelings.

Some jurors experienced stress as a consequence of doing their service, associated with worry about reaching the 'wrong' verdict (19%), or feeling under pressure to reach a verdict

(5%) as well as work-related and domestic responsibilities. Nearly one-fifth of all jurors and nearly half of women reported being greatly inconvenienced because of their jury service.

One in five jurors felt that delays, waiting around, cases being dismissed or their being involved in what they considered to be minor or trivial cases was a waste of public money. Among these jurors, the emphasis was on making the trial process more efficient and improving co-ordination.

Conclusion

For the majority of jurors covered by this research, engaging in jury service was a unique experience, which increased their sense of social solidarity and citizenship, while enhancing their confidence in the jury system. Clearly, for the vast majority of respondents here, juries are seen as an essential component of providing a fair and just trial process, and the diversity of the jury is seen as the best way of avoiding bias and arriving at a sound verdict. Although jurors expressed views which embodied tensions and ambiguities, their general experience of the jury system was extremely positive.

The report 'Jurors' Perceptions, Understanding, Confidence and Satisfaction in the Jury System: A Study in Six Courts' (No. 05/04) by Roger Matthews, Lynn Hancock and Daniel Briggs (2004) is available on the Home Office website: **www.homeoffice.gov.uk/rds/pdfs2/r227.pdf**

Controlling the length of criminal trials

Following the collapse of the Jubilee extension fraud trial, which had lasted over two years and cost the taxpayer £60 million, the Lord Chief Justice issued a protocol to try to avoid such a disaster occurring again. The protocol gives the courts instructions on how to control and manage heavy fraud and complex criminal cases.

Control and Management of Heavy Fraud and Other Complex Criminal Cases

A Protocol Issued by The Lord Chief Justice of England and Wales – 22 March 2005

Introduction

There is a broad consensus that the length of fraud and trials of other complex crimes must be controlled within proper bounds in order:

(i) To enable the jury to retain and assess the evidence which they have heard. If the trial is so long that the jury cannot do this, then the trial is not fair either to the prosecution or the defence.

(ii) To make proper use of limited public resources: see *Jisl* [2004] EWCA Crim 696 at [113]–[121].

There is also a consensus that no trial should be permitted to exceed a given period, save in exceptional circumstances; some favour 3 months, others an outer limit of 6 months.

Whatever view is taken, it is essential that the current length of trials is brought back to an acceptable and proper duration.

This Protocol supplements the Criminal Procedure Rules and summarises good practice which experience has shown may assist in bringing about some reduction in the length of trials of fraud and other crimes that result in complex trials. Flexibility of application of this Protocol according to the needs of each case is essential; it is designed to inform but not to prescribe.

This Protocol is primarily directed towards cases which are likely to last eight weeks or longer. It should also be followed, however, in all cases estimated to last more than four weeks. This Protocol applies to trials by jury, but many of the principles will be applicable if trials without a jury are permitted under section 43 of the Criminal Justice Act 2003.

The best handling technique for a long case is continuous management by an experienced Judge nominated for the purpose.

It is intended that this Protocol be kept up to date; any further practices or techniques found to be successful in the management of complex cases should be notified to the office of the Lord Chief Justice.

1 The investigation

(i) The role of the prosecuting authority and the judge

(a) Unlike other European countries, a judge in England and Wales does not directly control the investigative process; that is the responsibility of the Investigating Authority, and in turn the Prosecuting Authority and the prosecution advocate. Experience has shown that a prosecution lawyer (who must be of sufficient experience and who will be a member of the team at trial) and the prosecution advocate, if different, should be involved in the investigation as soon as it appears that a heavy fraud trial or other complex criminal trial is likely to ensue. The costs that this early preparation will incur will be saved many times over in the long run.

(b) The judge can and should exert a substantial and beneficial influence by making it clear that, generally speaking, trials should be kept within manageable limits. In most cases 3 months should be the target outer limit, but there will be cases where a duration of 6 months, or in exceptional circumstances, even longer may be inevitable.

(ii) Interviews

(a) At present many interviews are too long and too unstructured. This has a knock-on effect on the length of trials. Interviews should provide an opportunity for suspects to respond to the allegations against them. They should not be an occasion to discuss every document in the case. It should become clear from judicial rulings that interviews of this kind are a waste of resources.

(b) The suspect must be given sufficient information before or at the interview to enable them to meet the questions fairly and answer them honestly; the information is not provided to give the suspect the opportunity to manufacture a false story which fits undisputable facts.

(c) It is often helpful if the principal documents are provided either in advance of the interview or shown as the interview progresses; asking detailed questions about events a considerable period in the past without reference to the documents is often not very helpful.

. . .

(iv) Initial consideration of the length of a case

If the prosecutor in charge of the case from the Prosecuting Authority or the lead advocate for the prosecution consider that the case as formulated is likely to last more than 8 weeks, the case should be referred in accordance with arrangements made by the Prosecuting Authority to a more senior prosecutor. The senior prosecutor will consider whether it is desirable for the case to be prosecuted in that way or whether some steps might be taken to reduce its likely length, whilst at the same time ensuring that the public interest is served.

Any case likely to last 6 months or more must be referred to the Director of the Prosecuting Authority so that similar considerations can take place.

(v) Notification of cases likely to last more than 8 weeks

Special arrangements will be put in place for the early notification by the CPS and other Prosecuting Authorities, to the LSC and to a single designated officer of the Court in each Region (Circuit) of any case which the CPS or other Prosecuting Authority consider likely to last over 8 weeks.

(vi) Venue

The court will allocate such cases and other complex cases likely to last 4 weeks or more to a specific venue suitable for the trial in question, taking into account the convenience to witnesses, the parties, the availability of time at that location, and all other relevant considerations.

2 Designation of the trial judge

(i) The assignment of a judge

(a) In any complex case which is expected to last more than four weeks, the trial judge will be assigned under the direction of the Presiding Judges at the earliest possible moment.

(b) Thereafter the assigned judge should manage that case 'from cradle to grave'; it is essential that the same judge manages the case from the time of his assignment and that arrangements are made for him to be able to do so. It is recognised that in certain court centres with a large turnover of heavy cases (e.g. Southwark) this objective is more difficult to achieve. But in those court centres there are teams of specialist judges, who are more readily able to handle cases which the assigned judge cannot continue with because of unexpected events; even at such courts, there must be no exception to the principle that one judge must handle all the pretrial hearings until the case is assigned to another judge.

3 Case management

(i) Objectives

(a) The number, length and organisation of case management hearings will, of course, depend critically on the circumstances and complexity of the individual case. However, thorough, well-prepared and extended case management hearings will save court time and costs overall.

(b) Effective case management of heavy fraud and other complex criminal cases requires the judge to have a much more detailed grasp of the case than may be necessary for many other Plea and Case Management Hearings (PCMHs). Though it is for the judge in each case to decide how much pre-reading time he needs so that the judge is on top of the case, it is not always a sensible use of judicial time to allocate a series of reading days, during which the judge sits alone in his room, working through numerous boxes of ring binders.

See paragraph 3 (iv) (e) below.

(ii) Fixing the trial date

Although it is important that the trial date should be fixed as early as possible, this may not always be the right course. There are two principal alternatives:

(a) The trial date should be fixed at the first opportunity – i.e. at the first (and usually short) directions hearing referred to in subparagraph (iii). From then on everyone must work to that date. All orders and pre-trial steps should be timetabled to fit in with that date. All advocates and the judge should take note of this date, in the expectation that the trial will proceed on the date determined.

(b) The trial date should not be fixed until the issues have been explored at a full case management hearing (referred to in subparagraph (iv)), after the advocates on both sides have done some serious work on the case. Only then can the length of the trial be estimated.

Which is apposite must depend on the circumstances of each case, but the earlier it is possible to fix a trial date, by reference to a proper estimate and a timetable set by reference to the trial date, the better.

It is generally to be expected that once a trial is fixed on the basis of the estimate provided, that it will be **increased** if, and only if, the party seeking to extend the time justifies why the original estimate is no longer appropriate.

(iii) The first hearing for the giving of initial directions

At the first opportunity the assigned judge should hold a short hearing to give initial directions. The directions on this occasion might well include:

(a) That there should be a full case management hearing on, or commencing on, a specified future date by which time the parties will be properly prepared for a meaningful hearing and the defence will have full instructions.

(b) That the prosecution should provide an outline written statement of the prosecution case at least one week in advance of that case management hearing, outlining in simple terms:

(i)   The key facts on which it relies.
(ii) The key evidence by which the prosecution seeks to prove the facts.

The statement must be sufficient to permit the judge to understand the case and for the defence to appreciate the basic elements of its case against each defendant. The prosecution may be invited to highlight the key points of the case orally at the case management hearing by way of a short mini-opening. The outline statement should not be considered binding, but it will serve the essential purpose in telling the judge, and everyone else, what the case is really about and identifying the key issues.

(c) That a core reading list and core bundle for the case management hearing should be delivered at least one week in advance.

(d) Preliminary directions about disclosure: see paragraph 4.

(iv) The first case management hearing

(a) At the first case management hearing:

(i)   The prosecution advocate should be given the opportunity to highlight any points from the prosecution outline statement of case (which will have been delivered at least a week in advance).

(ii) Each defence advocate should be asked to outline the defence.

If the defence advocate is not in a position to say what is in issue and what is not in issue, then the case management hearing can be adjourned for a short and limited time and to a fixed date to enable the advocate to take instructions; such an adjournment should only be necessary in exceptional circumstances, as the defence advocate should be properly instructed by the time of the first case management hearing and in any event is under an obligation to take sufficient instructions to fulfil the obligations contained in sections 33–39 of Criminal Justice Act 2003.

(b) There should then be a real dialogue between the judge and all advocates for the purpose of identifying:

(i)   The focus of the prosecution case.

(ii) The common ground.

(iii) The real issues in the case. (Rule 3.2 of the Criminal Procedure Rules.)

(c) The judge will try to generate a spirit of co-operation between the court and the advocates on all sides. The expeditious conduct of the trial and a focussing on the real issues must be in the interests of **all** parties. It cannot be in the interests of any defendant for his good points to become lost in a welter of uncontroversial or irrelevant evidence.

(d) In many fraud cases the primary facts are not seriously disputed. The real issue is what each defendant knew and whether that defendant was dishonest. Once the judge has identified what is in dispute and what is not in dispute, the judge can then discuss with the advocate how the trial should be structured, what can be dealt with by admissions or agreed facts, what uncontroversial matters should be proved by concise oral evidence, what timetabling can be required under Rule 3.10 Criminal Procedure Rules, and other directions.

(e) In particularly heavy fraud or complex cases the judge may possibly consider it necessary to allocate a whole week for a case management hearing. If that week is used wisely, many further weeks of trial time can be saved. In the gaps which will inevitably arise during that week (for example while the advocates are exploring matters raised by the judge) the judge can do a substantial amount of informed reading. The case has come 'alive' at this stage. Indeed, in a really heavy fraud case, if the judge fixes one or more case management hearings on this scale, there will be need for fewer formal reading days. Moreover, a huge amount can be achieved in the pre-trial stage, if all trial advocates are gathered in the same place, focussing on the case **at the same time**, for several days consecutively.

(f) Requiring the defence to serve proper case statements may enable the court to identify:

(i)   what is common ground; and

(ii) the real issues.

It is therefore important that proper defence case statements be provided as required by the Criminal Procedure Rules; Judges will use the powers contained in sections 28–34 of the Criminal Proceedings and Evidence Act 1996 (and the corresponding provisions of the CJA 1987, sections 33 and following of the Criminal Justice Act 2003) and the Criminal Procedure Rules to ensure that realistic defence case statements are provided.

(g) Likewise this objective may be achieved by requiring the prosecution to serve draft admissions by a specified date and by requiring the defence to respond within a specified number of weeks.

(v) Further case management hearings

(a) The date of the next case management hearing should be fixed at the conclusion of the hearing so that there is no delay in having to fix the date through listing offices, clerks and others.

(b) If one is looking at a trial which threatens to run for months, pre-trial case management on an intensive scale is essential.

(vi) Consideration of the length of the trial

(a) Case management on the above lines, the procedure set out in paragraph 1 (iv), may still be insufficient to reduce the trial to a manageable length; generally a trial of 3 months should be the target, but there will be cases where a duration of 6 months or, in exceptional circumstances, even longer may be inevitable.

(b) If the trial is not estimated to be within a manageable length, it will be necessary for the judge to consider what steps should be taken to reduce the length of the trial, whilst still ensuring that the prosecution has the opportunity of placing the full criminality before the court.

(c) To assist the judge in this task,

(i) The lead advocate for the prosecution should be asked to explain why the prosecution have rejected a shorter way of proceeding; they may also be asked to divide the case into sections of evidence and explain the scope of each section and the need for each section.

(ii) The lead advocates for the prosecution and for the defence should be prepared to put forward in writing, if requested, ways in which a case estimated to last more than three months can be shortened, including possible severance of counts or defendants, exclusions of sections of the case or of evidence or areas of the case where admissions can be made.

(d) One course the judge may consider is pruning the indictment by omitting certain charges and/or by omitting certain defendants. The judge must not usurp the function of the prosecution in this regard, and he must bear in mind that he will, at the outset, know less about the case than the advocates. The aim is to achieve fairness to all parties.

(e) Nevertheless, the judge does have two methods of pruning available for use in appropriate circumstances:

(i) Persuading the prosecution that it is not worthwhile pursuing certain charges and/or certain defendants.

(ii) Severing the indictment. Severance for reasons of case management alone is perfectly proper, although judges should have regard to any representations made by the prosecution that severance would weaken their case. Indeed the judge's hand will be strengthened in this regard by Rule 1.1(2)g of the Criminal Procedure Rules. However, before using what may be seen as a blunt instrument, the judge should insist on seeing full defence statements of all affected defendants. Severance may be unfair to the prosecution if, for example, there is a cut-throat defence in prospect. For example, the defence of the principal defendant may be that the defendant relied on the advice of his accountant or solicitor that what was happening was acceptable. The defence of the professional may be that he gave no such advice. Against that background, it might be unfair to the prosecution to order separate trials of the two defendants.

. . .

6 The trial

(i) The particular hazard of heavy fraud trials

A heavy fraud or other complex trial has the potential to lose direction and focus. This is a disaster for three reasons:

(a) The jury will lose track of the evidence, thereby prejudicing both prosecution and defence.

(b) The burden on the defendants, the judge and indeed all involved will become intolerable.

(c) Scarce public resources are wasted. Other prosecutions are delayed or – worse – may never happen. Fraud which is detected but not prosecuted (for resource reasons) undermines confidence.

(ii) Judicial mastery of the case

(a) It is necessary for the judge to exercise firm control over the conduct of the trial at all stages.

(b) In order to do this the judge must read the witness statements and the documents, so that the judge can discuss case management issues with the advocates on – almost – an equal footing.

(c) To this end, the judge should not set aside weeks or even days for pre-reading (see paragraph 3(i)(b) above). Hopefully the judge will have gained a good grasp of the evidence during the case management hearings. Nevertheless, realistic reading time must be provided for the judge in advance of trial.

(d) The role of the judge in a heavy fraud or other complex criminal trial is different from his/her role in a 'conventional' criminal trial. So far as possible, the judge should be freed from other duties and burdens, so that he/she can give the high degree of commitment which a heavy fraud trial requires. This will pay dividends in terms of saving weeks or months of court time.

. . .

(iii) Assistance to the judge

Experience has shown that in some very heavy cases, the judge's burden can be substantially offset with the provision of a Judicial Assistant or other support and assistance.

The protocol 'Control and Management of Heavy Fraud and Other Complex Criminal Cases' is available on the internet at:
www.dca.gov.uk/criminal/procrules_fin/contents/pd_protocol/pd_protocol.htm

Moves to abolish the jury in serious fraud cases: a case study

Sir Robin Auld's recommendations on juries

Consecutive governments have been interested in reducing the role of juries in the criminal justice system, primarily because they can be slow and expensive. It now looks increasingly likely that the jury trial will be abolished for serious fraud cases. In 1999, the government asked Sir Robin Auld to carry out a review into the working of the criminal courts. In his final report, published in 2001, one of his recommendations was that jury trials for serious fraud cases should be abolished.

Review of the Criminal Courts of England and Wales

Sir Robin Auld

Fraud and other complex cases

The issues and the options

173 There has long been concern about the special problems posed for trial by jury in cases of serious and complex fraud. In recent years the increasing sophistication and complications of commercial and international fraud have added to that concern. There are well-founded anxieties about possible injustice in the difficulties they pose for juries in understanding them and the enormous financial and other demands that jury trial imposes on the system and on all involved in it. This is not just a matter of expense and toil flowing from the use of procedures peculiar to jury trial in such difficult cases. The remorseless increase in the length of such trials over recent years has become a severe intrusion on jurors' working and private lives. It cannot be good for them or for justice.

174 At present the problem is compounded by the unrepresentative nature of juries, particularly in serious fraud and other complex cases. Judges are reluctant to require busy working people to prejudice their livelihoods or their employers' businesses by taking them from their work, frequently for months at a time. The Bar Council, while opposing any move away from jury trial in such cases, has acknowledged in its submission in the Review that it is difficult to find juries for them which are a true cross-section of society. If, as I have recommended, steps are taken to ensure that juries generally are more representative of the broad range of skills and experience of the community, the hardships that such cases impose on many jurors would be greater.

175 Long serious fraud and other complex cases, or their prospect, are also often too much for defendants. As the Serious Fraud Office has commented in a paper submitted in the Review, ill health, or claimed ill health, is a particularly troublesome cause of substantial delay and, often severance. Such delay, when added to the already long incubation periods for these cases can then lead to applications to stay the proceedings for abuse of process.

176 In 1983 Lord Roskill was appointed to chair a Fraud Trials Committee to consider how more justly, expeditiously and economically these cases could be conducted. In 1986 the Committee reported, recommending a number of procedural changes in the trial of serious and complex fraud, many of which were implemented the following year in the Criminal Justice Act 1987. These included the establishment of the Serious Fraud Office and procedural and evidential reforms. In addition, a new regulatory framework, including the introduction of the Financial Services Tribunal, was introduced by the Financial Services Act 1986.

177 The majority of the Roskill Committee also recommended the replacement of juries for trials of serious and complex fraud by a Fraud Trials Tribunal consisting of a judge and a small number of specially qualified lay members. It was the most widely supported proposal of those who gave evidence to the Committee, the other three being special juries, trial by judge alone and trial by a panel of judges. One of its members, Walter Merricks, in a powerfully reasoned dissenting note, argued that there was no firm basis for removing the established right to jury trial in such cases. He said that, in the absence of general research into the workings of juries, the way forward was to simplify and otherwise improve trial procedures.

178 Mr Merricks' dissent on this point was strongly taken up by the Criminal Bar, and the Government of the day put to one side the majority's proposal. It did so in part to see how far the recommended procedural changes would go in remedying the problems of handling these cases. But a number of ensuing high profile trials drew attention to continuing problems of manageability caused by their complexity and length. In more than one case that reached the Court of Appeal, the Court commented that such problems put at risk the fairness of trial, imposed great personal burdens on all those involved and made great demands on limited and expensive resources.

179 In 1993 the Runciman Royal Commission, whilst implicitly acknowledging the continuing problems, felt unable to make recommendations on the matter without the benefit of jury research which, it considered, was barred by section 8 of the Contempt of Court Act 1981.

180 Since then, the debate has rumbled on, prompting the Home Office, in February 1998, to issue a consultation document setting out four possible alternatives to jury trial in serious and complex fraud cases. These were special juries, a judge or judges alone or sitting with expert assessors, a 'Roskill' style tribunal and a single judge sitting with a jury on key issues for decision.

181 The arguments for and against the present form of jury trial in cases of serious and complex fraud have been canvassed many times. Arguments for, include:

- jury trial is a hallowed democratic institution and a citizen's right in all serious cases which necessarily include serious and complex frauds;
- the random nature of selection of juries ensures their fairness and independence;
- mostly the question is one of dishonesty, which is essentially a matter for a jury who, by reason of their number and mix, are as well as, or better equipped than, a smaller tribunal, however professional, to assess the reliability and credibility of witnesses;
- there is no evidence, for example in the form of jury research, that juries cannot cope with long and complex cases or that their decisions in them are contrary to the evidence; on the contrary, most judges and legal practitioners' assessment, based on their trial experience, is that their verdicts are in the main 'correct'; and

- there is an openness and public intelligibility in the parties having to accommodate the jury's newness to the subject matter by presenting their respective cases in a simple and easily digestible form, and that there is scope for improvements in such presentation.

Arguments against, include:

- if jurors are truly to be regarded as the defendant's peers, they should be experienced in the professional or commercial discipline in which the alleged offence occurred;
- although the issue of dishonesty is essentially a matter for a jury, the volume and complexities of the issues and the evidence, especially in specialist market frauds, may be too difficult for them to understand or analyse so as to enable them to determine whether there has been dishonesty;
- the length of such trials, sometimes of several months, is an unreasonable intrusion on jurors' personal and, where they are in employment, working lives, going way beyond the conventional requirement for such duty of about two weeks' service;
- that has the effect of making juries even less representative of the community than they are already, since the court excuses many who would otherwise be able and willing to make short-term arrangements to do their civic duty;
- such long trials are also a great personal strain and burden on everyone else involved, not least the defendant, the victim and witnesses;
- judges, with their legal and forensic experience, and/or specialist assessors would be better equipped to deal justly and more expeditiously with such cases;
- that would also have the benefit of greater openness, since there would then be a publicly reasoned and appealable decision instead of the present inscrutable and largely unappealable verdict of the jury; and
- the length of jury trials in fraud cases is very costly to the public and also, because of limited judicial and court resources, unduly delays the efficient disposal of other cases waiting for trial.

182 I have considered these conflicting arguments with care. Like the Roskill Committee, I have concluded that those for replacing trial by judge and jury with some other form of tribunal in serious and complex fraud cases are the more persuasive. Indeed, they have become more pressing since the Committee reported, given the ever lengthening and complexity of fraud trials and their increasingly specialised nature and international ramifications. Moreover, the main basis for not implementing the Roskill Committee's recommendation for a Fraud Trials Tribunal, the hope that the procedural and evidential reforms in the 1987 Act would significantly reduce the problems of jury trial, has not been realised.

183 If I had to pick two of the most compelling factors in favour of reform, I would settle on the burdensome length and increasing speciality and complexity of these cases, with which jurors, largely or wholly strangers to the subject matter, are expected to cope. Both put justice at risk. The Director of the Serious Fraud Office has recently said that the average length of a serious fraud prosecuted by it is six months, which would come largely before a jury of 'the unemployed or unemployable'. I have considered the thoughtful submissions of the Criminal Bar Association, the Law Society, the Fraud Advisory Panel and some others that further improvements in the conduct and presentation of the issues and evidence in fraud trials could ease those difficulties. But, as the Criminal Bar Association has acknowledged in putting them forward, they are 'no more than scratching the surface' on the general issue of the use of juries in such trials. The fact is that many fraud and other cases, by reason of their length, complexity and speciality, now demand much more of the traditional English jury than it is equipped to provide. The point that juries have not kept pace with modern requirements of the criminal justice system in this respect has been made in a number of recent writings and submissions to the Review.

184 I am firmly of the view that we should wait no longer before introducing a more just and efficient form of trial in serious and complex fraud cases. The main candidates are those considered by the Roskill Committee, namely: special juries, trial by judge alone, trial by a panel of judges and trial by a tribunal of a judge and lay members.

. . .

Judge and lay members

190 The Roskill Committee favoured this model of a judge sitting with lay members drawn from a panel of persons experienced in the world of business and finance. As I have said, it was the option most widely supported by those who gave evidence to the Committee. It envisaged that the judge would, in the main, sit and rule on his own on matters of law, procedure and the admissibility of evidence. On matters of fact he and each of the lay members would have the same vote; their decision could be by a majority, but the judge would give a single reasoned judgment of the tribunal.

191 In my view, there is much to be said for a proposal of this sort. However, I share the ambivalence of many contributors to the Review who have looked for an alternative to jury trial, as to whether it should be trial by judge alone or sitting with lay members drawn from a panel of persons with financial expertise. The Serious Fraud Office, the Crown Prosecution Service, the police, including the Association of Chief Police Officers, and a number of departmental investigation and prosecution bodies favoured some sort of combined tribunal. The Serious Fraud Office has cautioned, however, that lay members selected for any particular trial should be drawn from a different discipline from that in issue, otherwise they might assume the role of untested expert witnesses. This caution seems to run counter to the Roskill Committee's intention that lay members should be selected for their specialist knowledge of the business or financial activity the subject matter of the case, not simply for their general business and financial experience. In my view, the caution is well-founded. There could be difficulties where lay members' views are possibly conditioned by their own out of date or narrow experience, or by a 'bee in their bonnet' about the norms of professional conduct in the area of speciality in issue. In such circumstances, it is doubtful what proper role they could perform in assisting a judge to assess conflicting expert evidence in the case. That is not to say that specialists in the particular discipline or market concerned should never be part of the tribunal, simply to note the need to avoid too close a connection where working practices and norms are likely to be an issue as distinct from an understanding of the system and mechanics of the alleged fraud.

192 My first instinct had been to recommend that the court could direct trial by judge and jury or by judge and lay members or by judge alone, as he considered appropriate. However, after considerable thought, I consider that the need for reform would be best met by a combination of enabling the court to direct trial by judge and jury or by judge and lay members. It seems to me that if a defendant in such cases is deprived against his wish of trial by jury, he should be entitled, if he wishes, to trial by a tribunal comprising in part persons with appropriate business and financial experience. However, it should also be open for a defendant to opt, with the court's consent, to trial by judge alone under the general provisions for doing so that I have recommended.

193 The first step would be to allocate the case to a judge, whether a High Court Judge or Circuit Judge, with experience of trying serious and complex fraud. He should decide, after hearing representations from both sides, whether it should be heard with a jury or by himself and lay members or, if the defendant has opted for trial by judge alone, by himself. If he decides on trial with lay members, he should determine, again after hearing representations from both sides, from what, if any, speciality(ies) they should be drawn. Consistently with my recommendations on mode of trial decisions in either-way and jury 'waiver' cases, I do not suggest that an agreement of the parties as to any of these modes of trial should bind the judge, but such agreement would no doubt be an important factor for him in reaching his decision.

194 Where the judge has a choice between directing trial by himself and lay members or, at the defendant's option, of trial by himself alone, one factor that may influence the decision is the extent to which the case requires some knowledge of a specialist market or other commercial discipline. Another may be whether the issue is likely to turn on a factual understanding and analysis of the evidence or on conflicting contentions on professional or commercial norms and, if so, whether expert evidence is to be called. There may be other considerations depending on the individual circumstances of the case. All these mode of trial decisions should, in my view, be subject to a right of speedy appeal by either side to the Court of Appeal (Criminal Division).

195 The lynch-pin of all three potential forms of trial in serious and complex frauds is the judge. It is vital that he or she is of a high level of judicial competence with a good knowledge and experience of commercial and financial matters. At present there are 51 Circuit Judges nominated to try cases that meet current criteria for 'serious frauds'. Those criteria are broadly those which meet the Serious Fraud Office's definition of seriousness and complexity for it to undertake the prosecution, to which I refer in more detail below. In addition, particularly 'heavy' cases of serious and complex fraud with a high degree of public interest, are tried by High Court Judges, usually drawn from the Commercial Court and nominated on a case by case basis by the Lord Chief Justice.

196 As to procedure at the trial, I envisage something similar to that of the District Court Division of the new unified Criminal Court that I recommend in Chapter 7. I would expect the judge normally to sit on his own in pre-trial hearings and when ruling on law and such matters as the admissibility of evidence. However, as the Roskill Committee noted, the lay members could be of assistance in discussions as to the manner in which certain evidence could most helpfully be presented. I also agree with the Roskill Committee that the judge and lay members should retire to consider their decision without any prior public direction from the judge on the law, and that, once they have reached their decision, he should express it in a publicly and fully reasoned judgment of the court. The judge should be the sole judge of law, but on matters of fact, each would have an equal vote, and, as the Roskill Committee recommended, a majority of any two could suffice for conviction. As to sentence, this should be left entirely to the judge, since the lay members are not selected for any expertise in that field. Appeal should lie to the Court of Appeal (Criminal Division), against conviction and/or sentence on the same basis as appeals after conviction by a jury.

197 I have given anxious consideration to a number of other practical considerations that should be borne in mind by those responsible for deciding whether and how to undertake such a radical reform.

. . .

I recommend that:

- as an alternative to trial by judge and jury in serious and complex fraud cases, the nominated trial judge should be empowered to direct trial by himself sitting with lay members or, where the defendant has opted for trial by judge alone, by himself alone;
- the category of cases to which such a direction might apply should, in the first instance, be frauds of seriousness or complexity within sections 4 and 7 of the Criminal Justice Act 1987;
- the overriding criterion for directing trial without jury should be the interests of justice;
- either party should have a right of appeal against such decision to the Court of Appeal, (Criminal Division);
- judges trying such cases, by whatever form of procedure, should be specially nominated for the purpose as now, and provided with a thorough, structured and continuing training for it;
- there should be a panel of experts, established and maintained by the Lord Chancellor in consultation with professional and other bodies, from which lay members may be selected for trials;
- the nominated trial judge should select the lay members after affording the parties an opportunity to make written representations as to their suitability;
- lay members should be paid appropriately for their service;
- in a court consisting of a judge and lay members, the judge should be the sole judge of law, procedure, admissibility of evidence and as to sentence; as to conviction, all three should be the judges of fact;
- the decision of a court so constituted should wherever possible be unanimous, but a majority of any two could suffice for a conviction; and
- the judge should give the court's decision by a public and fully reasoned judgment.

The 'Review of the Criminal Courts of England and Wales' by Sir Robin Auld is available at:

www.criminal-courts-review.org.uk/

Criminal Justice Act 2003 – removal of juries from trials for serious fraud

Following Sir Robin Auld's report, the Criminal Justice Act 2003 was passed, which contained provisions for the removal of juries from serious fraud cases. The provisions restricting the use of juries faced considerable opposition in the House of Lords and, as a result, a compromise was reached that they could only be brought into force following a further vote in both Houses and the provisions have not been brought into force.

Criminal Justice Act 2003

PART 7

TRIALS ON INDICTMENT WITHOUT A JURY

43 Applications by prosecution for certain fraud cases to be conducted without a jury

(1) This section applies where—

(a) one or more defendants are to be tried on indictment for one or more offences, and

(b) notice has been given under section 51B of the Crime and Disorder Act 1998 (c. 37) (notices in serious or complex fraud cases) in respect of that offence or those offences.

(2) The prosecution may apply to a judge of the Crown Court for the trial to be conducted without a jury.

(3) If an application under subsection (2) is made and the judge is satisfied that the condition in subsection (5) is fulfilled, he may make an order that the trial is to be conducted without a jury; but if he is not so satisfied he must refuse the application.

(4) The judge may not make such an order without the approval of the Lord Chief Justice or a judge nominated by him.

(5) The condition is that the complexity of the trial or the length of the trial (or both) is likely to make the trial so burdensome to the members of a jury hearing the trial that the interests of justice require that serious consideration should be given to the question of whether the trial should be conducted without a jury.

(6) In deciding whether or not he is satisfied that that condition is fulfilled, the judge must have regard to any steps which might reasonably be taken to reduce the complexity or length of the trial.

(7) But a step is not to be regarded as reasonable if it would significantly disadvantage the prosecution.

 All recent Acts of Parliament are available on the website of the Office of Public Sector Information at:
www.opsi.gov.uk/acts.htm

Judges' views on jury trials for serious fraud cases

The government has made several unsuccessful attempts to abolish juries for serious fraud trials, amid strong opposition. Robert Julian has written an interesting article which was published in the *Criminal Law Review* in 2007 in which he discusses his research into the judges' views on juries sitting in serious fraud trials.

Judicial Perspectives on the Conduct of Serious Fraud Trials (2007)

Robert Julian

Introduction

Detailed interviews were conducted with nine sitting judges who both hold serious fraud tickets and have actual serious fraud litigation experience both as a barrister and as a judge. All nine judges expressed strong support for juries, voicing both a high level of agreement with jury verdicts, and a firm belief that juries have the capacity to understand properly litigated complex fraud cases. Each judge interviewed also voiced his principled belief that trial by jury should continue in all serious fraud cases. Many of the judges expressed significant concerns about the actual and perceived fairness of judge only trials.

. . .

Judicial agreement with the jury in serious fraud cases

The interviews were conducted in the shadow of the 2007 parliamentary debate about trial without jury in serious fraud cases. Permeating every interview was the strong belief expressed by each of the judges that trial by jury was entirely appropriate in serious fraud cases and that trial by judge should not replace trial by jury. The judges unanimously voiced their faith in, and commitment to, the jury system. The common rationale of the judges interviewed was that juries were usually able to understand a complex fraud case upon the completion of the trial, explaining that usually the complexity of a serious fraud case gradually evaporates as the trial progresses when the proof is competently and carefully presented. They further suggest that a longer trial can sometimes give jurors a greater understanding of the facts. Finally each judge expressed a very high rate of agreement with jury verdicts in the cases they have presided over.

Judge no. 1:

I have a great faith in the jury system generally, occasionally something can go wrong but until somebody has a better idea and nobody has to date, I would use the jury in all cases except in the most complex fraud case.

I agree with the decisions of most juries. I have been surprised less often by the jury's verdict in long cases than perhaps in shorter cases. I agree with the jury 70% of the time or even more in complex cases.

There are very few fraud cases that are so complex that he or she (jurors) cannot understand it . . . There's going to be one or two, but even then I think we will still need a jury.

Judge no. 2:

I have agreed with juries in all of my serious frauds trials.

In longer trials the verdict is more accurate.

I am far more likely to agree with juries in complex fraud cases than I am in sex cases.

In fraud trials the verdicts are frequently a mixed bag, the jury finding on some indictments and not on others. I am a strong supporter of juries in complex fraud cases.

Generally I agree with juries in other cases. Over the years (12 years experience on the bench) I can count on one hand the number of cases in which I think the jury got it wrong.

In serious fraud cases jurors are able to handle the concepts.

I am aware of the notion that these cases are far too complex for a jury to understand. If the case has been properly managed from the outset and the result is that a relatively clear and simple trial is going to take place at the end of the day when all of the elements have been heard, the issue to be heard is no more complex than your rather average case wherein the jurors are making judgments about people's intentions, states of mind, and whether what they are doing by standard of ordinary people are acts that are honest or dishonest. I always say to a jury don't be overwhelmed by it, . . . it may seem daunting by the sheer volume of material but by the end of the trial it will be fairly clear to you what you have to decide, and at the end of it when you are to consider your verdict, you will not be in any doubt as to what the question is . . .

Judge no. 3:

I agree with jury in the great majority of cases and when I don't agree, I usually understand their verdict. I might not, where there are a number of defendants, agree with a complete verdict.

Judge no. 4:

I am a traditionalist and I don't want to lose the trial by jury system.

I have seen both at the bar and as a judge, cases in which the jury has trouble grasping (the facts) and it has been difficult for the advocates and the judge to communicate those issues to them clearly.

Juries can find it difficult to focus on the issues in a frauds trial and understand if it is a heavy documents or an accounting case . . .

It's hard over months to retain the knowledge and focus on the issues.

Some of these cases can fail because the jury cannot understand the issues.

On the whole we can trust them to do what we ask them to do.

Most of them work on cases conscientiously.

My overall impression is that juries want to do the right thing . . .

I think on balance I favour retaining the jury system across the board.

I trust the jury system. I agree with jury verdicts most of the time, but there are surprises.

. . .

Judicial opinions about jury comprehension

Not only is there a substantial agreement with the jury in serious fraud cases, there is also a strong judicial consensus that juries have a reasonable comprehension of these cases. The judges interviewed believe that juries engage in informed and relatively sophisticated decision making, acquitting certain defendants and convicting others. Individual judges stated that while they might dispute certain of the individual acquittals, the acquittals were understandable based on the proof in the case. One judge opined that in certain of the acquittals he felt the jury was expressing its independence and collective individuality.

Many of the judges offered objective bases for their favourable opinions about jury understanding, distinct from the observation by the judge of jury reactions during the trial. For example, regarding questions sent to the judge by the jury during deliberations, it was observed that juror analysis can be favourably inferred when compared to the proof and the ultimate verdict:

> You can tell from the questions how they are approaching it. You can sometimes tell from the questions which order of the count they are going through thematically.

Several of the judges indicated that the specifics of the verdict could also be suggestive of jury comprehension:

> The propensity of many juries in multiple defendant cases is to convict some defendants and acquit others, thereby suggesting a discerning reasoning process by the jury that is generally understandable to the trial judge who heard the same facts. It does suggest some sort of analysis . . .

> You can tell from the questions (the extent of) their understanding – the verdicts also reveal it.

An analysis of the annual reports of the Serious Fraud Office offers support for the judges' opinions in that of 19 trials to a verdict with more than one defendant from 2003 to 2006, there were eight mixed verdicts in which there were both convictions and acquittals of certain defendants in the same case. While it is possible that the Serious Fraud Office has overcharged certain defendants, it remains a positive for juries that they are able to discern such a flaw in the indictments and distinguish between indictments. The analysis also assumes that there is no higher rate of cut-throat defences (defendants blaming each other) in serious fraud trials as compared to other crimes. (This is an area that will require further research.) That the jury would by verdict find some co-defendants guilty and acquit others objectively addresses the concerns of the former Master of the Rolls, Lord Donaldson of Lymington, who argued during the 2003 House of Lords debate on the Criminal Justice Act 2003 that the 86% conviction rate reported in fraud trials could be an indication that juries are so confused that they are blindly convicting in serious fraud trials:

> It is said that juries are wholly suitable for such trials because the conviction rate is 86%. That figure frightens me . . . I wonder . . . whether the jury simply does not understand and comes to the conclusion in some cases that people would not have been charged if they had not been guilty.

Lord Donaldson's concern that jury confusion weighs toward verdicts in favour of the prosecution was likewise not confirmed by post-trial interviews with the **Jubilee Line** case jurors which demonstrated sound jury comprehension. The **Jubilee Line** jurors 'were adamant that the jury had a very good understanding of the evidence, some commenting that it was not all that difficult' and the post trial interviews conducted six months after the trial's collapse were reported as demonstrating that a number of the jurors had a solid understanding of the facts.

There is other objective support for the judges' opinions. The most persuasive is a trial simulation study utilising mock jurors which evaluated jury comprehension and competence in a complex trial which concluded as follows about jury compliance:

> We estimate that a majority of the participants in our studies – around four out of five – may be regarded as sufficiently competent to serve on a major fraud trial.

. . .

Judge-only trials are not favoured

In stark contrast to favouring the use of juries in serious fraud cases, the judicial interviews yielded no support for judge – only trials as a replacement for juries. The judges' views were similar to those expressed by the **Jubilee Line** jurors, favouring the preservation of the jury system, and disfavouring judge only trials as a substitute.

> It seems to me that it is far better to be judged by twelve of your peers than one judge. That is a right I believe we should maintain.

The opinions of the judges ranged from the notion that judges are simply unable to fairly engage in bench trials (no. 3); to the belief that judges are capable of fairly serving as the trier of fact, but the jury should not be supplanted (no. 5); to the opinion that the jury should decide guilt or innocence and the judge should determine the extent of the fraud (no. 1).

> I would be wary of trying a fraud case on my own (without a jury).

> I would be concerned in judge only trials that judges would become hardened by their experience generally.

> I sit uneasily with the idea that I am the sole judge of fact in these circumstances (serious fraud cases).

> It is a prevailing view that the very nature of a judge-alone trial creates an unsatisfactory pre-trial and courtroom environment and that the perceived primary advantages of a judge-only trial, which are a more brief trial duration and an avoidance of indictment pruning, are unlikely to happen in reality.

13

Magistrates

Introduction

This chapter looks at:

- the requirement under the judicial oath for magistrates to decide cases according to the law and not according to their own personal beliefs; and
- the future for lay magistrates in the criminal justice system.

Magistrates and the judicial oath

A Christian magistrate argued that he had been subjected to discrimination when he had refused to hear adoption cases involving single-sex partners, because such adoptions ran counter his religious beliefs. His appeal was rejected by the Employment Appeal Tribunal, which pointed out that he was required to decide cases according to the law and should for these purposes put aside his personal beliefs.

McClintock v Department of Constitutional Affairs [2008]

The Honourable Mr Justice Elias (President)

1 The appellant is a married man with a family, and a practising Christian. He has served as a Justice of the Peace in Sheffield since 1988, and still holds that office. He states that he cannot in conscience, and compatibly with his philosophical and religious beliefs, agree to place children with same-sex couples. By section 79 of the Civil Partnerships Act, which amends the Adoption Act 2002, civil partners and same-sex partners living in a same-sex relationship were added to those couples who may in some way (such as by adoption, fostering or care) look after children. (In fact there was no barrier to individuals in same-sex relationships from looking after children even before the amendment, but apparently the appellant was not aware of this.)

2 The possibility that he may have to place children in that way arose from the fact that he was a member of the Family Panel. He sought to be relieved from the duty to officiate in such cases by an administrative arrangement. When it was indicated to him that an exception would not be made in his case, he resigned from that Panel, although he continues to serve as a Justice of the Peace on the Adult Panel, dealing with criminal and motoring matters.

3 He brought proceedings alleging that he had been forced to resign from membership of the Family Panel by the refusal by the Department to accommodate his beliefs. He asserted that this constituted discrimination contrary to the Employment Equality (Religion or Belief) Regulations 2003 which gives effect to Council Directive 2000/78/EC which imposes a general framework for equal treatment in employment and occupation. He claimed that he had been discriminated against directly, contrary to regulation 3(1)(a); indirectly, contrary to regulation 3(1)(b), and had been subject to harassment contrary to regulation 5(1)(a). He also alleged that his human rights had been infringed, and in particular his rights under Article 9 of the ECHR which protects freedom of conscience, religion and belief. However, it was recognised that there is no right to enforce free standing human rights in the employment tribunals, as Mummery LJ recognised in **Copsey** v **WWB Devon Clays Ltd** (2005) para 8, because tribunals only have the power to hear cases allocated to them by statute. (It was not argued that the Directive might confer directly enforceable rights.) However, it was common ground that Article 9 was material to the extent that the Regulations should be read, if possible, so as to be compatible with the rights therein provided: see section 3 of the Human Rights Act.

. . .

The tribunal's conclusions

24 The Tribunal rejected the direct discrimination claim, finding that it failed 'at the first hurdle'. They accepted Mr Lynch's submission that the basis on which the appellant had sought to refuse to carry out his duties on the Family Panel was that he thought that children were being treated as guinea pigs in what was part of an unacceptable social experiment. He required more information. He had never made it plain that his objection was underscored by any conscientious or religious convictions. The Tribunal summarised this conclusion as follows (para 45):

. . .

29 In any event, even if there had been a prima facie case of indirect discrimination, the Tribunal concluded that this was manifestly a situation where the defence of justification applied. They said this:

> . . . To have allowed the Appellant, or anyone else for that matter, to opt out of cases where they disapproved or were less than enamoured with the law because of their views on a particular matter or because their conscience would not allow them to consider doing something, would have been abdication of the responsibilities of those whose task it is to uphold the administration of justice in this country. Even if a Judge personally has particular views on any subject, he or she must put those views to the back of his or her mind when applying the law of the land impartially as their judicial oaths of office require them to do. It is the only way the public can place any trust in the law. To allow Judges with a particular point of view the ability to avoid cases which come before them because they feel it will likely cause them embarrassment or difficulty could, apart from anything else, impose greater burdens on others or lead to a situation whereby another pool of Judges with views in another direction might have to sit and adjudicate on such cases. The Respondent's stance was therefore wholly proportionate and wholly justified and, in our view, wholly necessary. In a country where there is such a diverse range of opinions and beliefs held and expounded by people from many religions and walks of life, it would be invidious were judges to pick and choose which cases they were prepared to sit on. It would undermine the basis of our judicial system, one that 'warts and all' has served people well for a very long time.

30 Finally, with respect to the Human Rights argument, the Tribunal found no conflict between Article 9 and the Regulations, and they found no breach of the former in any event. Mr McClintock had chosen to resign from the Family Panel and remained entitled to hold his religious or philosophical views, and to espouse those views, at all times.

. . .

Two other objections

48 But even assuming that it could be said that Mr McClintock's objection constituted a religious or similar philosophical belief, and that the requirement to abide by the oath disadvantaged him and others sharing that belief, the claim for indirect discrimination must still have failed for two further reasons, which were only obliquely challenged in the grounds of appeal.

49 The first ground is, as we have seen, that the Tribunal found that any prima facie discrimination was justified i.e. it was in order to achieve a legitimate objective and was proportionate to that end. Mr Diamond raised a number of issues which appear to have been directed to the question of proportionality.

50 The first was that it is desirable that JPs are recruited from a wide cross section of society and that it will undermine that objective if they have to apply laws which they cannot in conscience accept. The second was that there have been occasions in the past when the DCA or its predecessors have reacted sensitively and been willing to take administrative action to prevent such conflicts arising. The third was that the Tribunal had failed to have regard to the extensive evidence adduced before them which suggested that same-sex parenting was not in the best interests of the child. This third point was linked to a submission that the Tribunal had misstated the argument when they suggested that Mr McClintock was seeking to opt out of his obligation to obey the will of Parliament; on the contrary, he was seeking to give effect to the obligation to advance the best interests of the child. Indeed, in somewhat flowery terms Mr Diamond suggested that Mr McClintock was upholding judicial independence against oppressive interference from the Executive.

51 We do not accept that any of these grounds constitutes a reason for concluding that the Tribunal has erred in law in its approach to justification. No doubt it is desirable that JPs should be widely recruited. But there is no evidence that requiring adherence to the judicial oath prevents this, and in any event it is a matter for the Department what weight it gives to that factor. As the Tribunal pointed out, the issue is whether a judge should be allowed a blanket objection not to have to hear cases which involve a consideration of laws to which they have a principled or conscientious objection. It does not of course mean that he or she will have to hear particular cases where, because of their activities or public pronouncements, their hearing the case might give the appearance of bias.

52 As to the second issue, the Tribunal considered this but did not think that they were truly analogous, save perhaps for the situation of Judge Christmas Humphreys. In his case he had effectively negotiated an exception before he took office. In any event, even if it were the case that administrative exceptions have been made in the past with respect to particular cases, this would not in our view begin to demonstrate that there was a legal obligation to make an exception in all cases to cater for religious or other philosophical beliefs. No doubt in this case an administrative exception could have been made, but it does not follow that there was a duty to make it.

53 Mr Diamond made the perfectly cogent point that it seems to be something of a paradox if a magistrate can properly recuse himself from a particular case on the grounds that his public actions or words have created the appearance of bias (as was the basis for Lord Scott's proposed recusal with respect to any Hunting Act appeals) and yet will not be permitted to do so where the objection to the law may be for entirely the same reasons but have been only privately expressed. We recognise the force of that. However, the apparent paradox dissolves once the purpose of the rules is appreciated. Recusal for apparent bias occurs where the parties have a reasonable suspicion arising from some particular factor, such as the fact that the judge has a financial interest, or exceptionally because he or she has expressed strong views on an issue, that the judge may not be able to conduct the trial fairly and impartially. This is different from a situation where the judge is refusing to apply the law because he has moral objections to it, or thinks that it has been introduced prematurely or has been insufficiently considered. He is then expected to put his personal views to one side – which judges frequently have to do – and there is no reason why the parties should not trust him to be able to do that.

54 Mr Diamond placed significant emphasis on the third feature, namely that Mr McClintock had adopted a rational position, supported by a host of experts, (although in fact the

Tribunal found that expert opinion was divided.) He complained that the Tribunal had not paid proper regard to this fact. In our judgment this submission is misconceived. It was not for the Tribunal to question the wisdom of Parliament, which must be taken to have assumed that there was no inherent conflict in the legal position which it had created. It could not conceivably be the function of an employment tribunal to express a view that JPs could or should ignore a law passed by Parliament on the grounds that it was apparently inconsistent with other statutory provisions.

55 In any event, the issue was not whether Mr McClintock could provide a rational basis for adopting the stance he did; no doubt the wisdom of many laws can be questioned on perfectly rational grounds. Indeed, if his objection was religious or philosophical, it could in principle be relied upon whether it was rational or irrational, sensible or misguided. Furthermore, in the context of proportionality, the issue was whether the Department was entitled to take the view that they could require those who had taken the judicial oath to honour it and subordinate their own particular personal views about the merits of the law. The rationality of those objections may be relevant to the desirability of passing the law in the first place, but it is quite irrelevant to the issue of justification.

56 Nor do we accept that Mr McClintock can properly contend that he is willing to obey the law and is unable to perform his legal duties. Mr Diamond accepted in the course of argument that on a true analysis Mr McClintock was not willing to apply the law involving placing children with same-sex parents unless and until satisfied that the duties which he perceived to be conflicting could be reconciled. It is also fanciful and wrong to describe this case as an example of the Executive interfering with the independence of the judiciary. It was the legislature – Parliament – which passed the Civil Partnership Act, not the Executive, and Mr McClintock's duty, as reflected in the judicial oath, is to give effect to the laws which Parliament enacts. The principle of the independence of the judiciary does not mean that they have the right to pick and choose which laws they will apply.

57 Accordingly, in our view none of these issues undermines in any way the Tribunal's clear conclusion with respect to the issue of proportionality.

58 The further hurdle facing a successful challenge to the finding on indirect discrimination is this. Although the Tribunal did not in its conclusions return specifically to consider regulation 10, they did state that the appellant had resigned voluntarily and without pressure once it was explained to him that the DCA did not consider it appropriate to adopt an administrative filter to create an exception in his case. That is a finding of fact wholly sustainable on the evidence. The Tribunal was entitled to conclude that this neither constituted a detriment nor a dismissal from office.

59 True it is that matters might have been brought to a head later in circumstances involving his removal. However, the possibility that such action might have been taken at a later stage, if Mr McClintock had chosen to remain on the Panel and refused to hear these cases, is not enough to bring him within the scope of Article 10 so as to found a cause of action.
. . .

Conclusions

62 The Tribunal acknowledged, as do we, that Mr McClintock demonstrated candour and integrity in his handling of what for him was a sensitive issue. However, he expressed his objections on grounds which the Tribunal was entitled to find did not engage the terms of

the Religion and Belief Regulations. Even had they done so, the Tribunal found that the Department was fully justified in insisting that magistrates must apply the law of the land as their oath requires, and cannot opt out of cases on the grounds that they may have to apply or give effect to laws to which they have a moral or other principled objection. The Tribunal was manifestly entitled to reach that view, and in our judgment they acted in accordance with the Regulations, which were themselves compatible with Article 9. It follows that the appeal fails.

The future for lay magistrates

During the early years of the present Labour government there was concern that it favoured professional judges over lay judges. However, it is now becoming clear that lay judges will continue to play an important role in the criminal justice system. The government's current priority appears to be to strengthen the role of lay magistrates, rather than abolish them. In 2004, it carried out a consultation exercise in which magistrates were asked what changes they would like to see introduced. The then Lord Chancellor subsequently gave a speech at a conference for magistrates in which he told them, in the light of the consultation process, what his vision was for their future.

Magistrates' Courts and Local Justice – Connected, Respected, Effective

Speech of Lord Falconer, 14 March 2005

In October I announced a new programme of work – Supporting Magistrates to Provide Justice. Not a Whitehall review, not a consultation without consequence, not a paper exercise. Instead, this programme marks a significant shift in the relationship between Government and the magistracy. Less about us telling you what to do. Much more about you telling us how you want to do things differently and more efficiently. What I want to do today is report back to you what you have told us to do. For the first time, setting out what you want. Your ideas. Your suggestions. Your proposals. All designed to make the magistracy work better – for us all.

But, first, the context. Let me begin by setting out my vision for the magistracy – a vision that sees Magistrates' Courts at the very centre of our response to crime and anti-social behaviour . . .

My vision for the magistracy can be captured in the title of the conference and in three words: connected, respected, effective. There is much meaning contained in these simple words.

I want a magistracy which is connected to the communities it serves – and seen to be connected. Where local magistrates understand the issues specific to their neighbourhoods. The importance of the local aspect of justice is vital. Where the decisions of the magistrates' court make a real difference – reducing anti-social behaviour and reducing crime. Where people understand the local justice system, understand how and why you, as magistrates, come to your decisions. And where they know what the other local agencies do – and work with them. And the magistracy should be respected. You are the judges who, crucially, will determine whether the community have faith in the court system. For the magistracy to be respected, it must be representative. We need magistrates drawn from across the community, from different age groups, from all ethnic and social backgrounds. But we will not dilute the current high quality of magistrates to achieve this. And, crucially, the magistracy should be effective. Court orders obeyed. Sentences served. Trials happening on time. Victims and witnesses supported. I know that this vision is one that very many of you share – I hear the same desires when I talk to magistrates across the country.

Much has happened which will help us achieve this vision. But I wanted to know how we could do more to remove the barriers that prevent you from doing the job as well as you want. So we asked every single magistrate and District Judge in the country for their ideas, their suggestions, their views. I also asked court staff and other groups working in the criminal justice system.

We got more than 2,000 responses – the breadth and depth of the responses was fantastic. My principal job here today is to set out the initial responses and findings. To play back to you for the first time what you are telling us.

Some of the ideas can be implemented quickly and easily, some we need to look at more closely. I can't say yet that we will be able to agree to everything you're proposing. But I can say that there are real possibilities and real prospects for real change and real improvement on which I'm confident we can work together. There is a real agenda here for the future. We will publish a full account of the responses we have received as soon as possible.

Before any of these three themes however, is the question of recruitment and retention. A vital task if we are to support the magistracy and allow you to be as effective, connected and respected as you can be, is to ensure that we recruit diverse and high calibre magistrates and do all we can to keep magistrates when they have been recruited. We have the highest possible calibre at the moment. I repeat, I will do nothing to lower the current standards. But how do we make it easier to recruit a more diverse bench, and then retain it?

It is vital that the magistracy is reflective of the community it serves. This idea is the historic lynchpin of the magistracy – local justice delivered by local people. We must ensure that this idea is not lost, and indeed, that it is promoted. And that every part of the community feel they are represented. And we must do all this without diluting the quality of the magistracy. You're telling us in the survey that the sitting burden for all magistrates must be manageable. We must reverse the trend of sitting in panels of two rather than three. We must ensure that benches can accommodate those magistrates – typically younger magistrates in employment – who cannot commit to more than the minimum number of sittings.

You're telling us that you want employers to be supportive and to release you for your magisterial duties. You want flexibility in your terms and conditions. You want us to look at the recognition, rewards and allowances you receive. You want us to use modern recruiting practices to encourage more applications to become a magistrate. I support your aims – I agree with that feedback. We do need to attract more younger people, more people with disabilities, more people from ethnic minorities, particularly where the composition of the bench does not reflect the local community, and more people in full-time work. So, we will work closely with Advisory Committees to improve our recruitment efforts, target recruitment at communities under-represented on the bench and raise awareness of the crucial role magistrates have in the criminal justice system. We will also encourage employers to release staff to sit as magistrates. We know many of you face tensions in that area. We will try and ease them. We will take steps, including facing up to the public sector at middle management level and we must do more.

We are working closely with the Magistrates Association and the Senior District Judge to develop good practice guidance on court cancellations. You take great effort to allow you to attend courts throughout the year. When courts need to be cancelled because of unavoidable circumstances you have a right to early advice and the administration has a responsibility to understand and take account of the impact changes to the programme have for you. And you should, where appropriate, get credit for cancelled sittings.

We will have in place local systems for developing flexible and effective rosters. And I am pleased to report that following consultation with the Magistrates Association and senior Judiciary an agreed protocol will ensure that HMCS will give the most careful consideration to the creation of any new District Judge (Magistrates' Courts) post. Such an exercise will need to be underpinned by a business case to ensure there is appropriate work for both magistrates and a District Judge and that local Benches and MA branches for the areas concerned, are informed of the intention to prepare such a business case. The protocol also provides that if a case for a new post is approved any consequential appointment will be commenced taking into account the importance of avoiding changes to rotas for magistrates. Or if changes are unavoidable, ensure the appointment takes effect where the maximum possible notice of changes to rotas can be given . . .

A diverse magistracy is important. So too is a diverse judiciary. I want to open up the pathways to becoming a judge. The robust test of merit will in no way be diluted – it will be just as hard to pass the test. But I will be looking closely at how we could make a broader range of people, with appropriate and measured experience, eligible for judicial appointment in the higher judiciary. Who am I thinking of? I am thinking of ILEX-qualified legal executives. I am thinking of legal academics. I am thinking perhaps of patent and trademark attorneys. But I am thinking also of magistrates with an appropriate legal qualification. These are examples and we need to look at the detail. And there may well be other ways in which the knowledge and experience of magistrates might be taken into account on the route towards judicial appointment. For example, it might be possible to allow barristers and solicitors who are Justices of the Peace to apply for salaried judicial appointment, with their sittings as lay magistrates counting in lieu of service in fee-paid judicial office. Or we might be able to say that a barrister or a solicitor who is a magistrate will become eligible for appointment to fee-paid judicial appointment after a reduced period of call or admission. On current timescales, that might be after five years' call or admission, as compared to the required seven or ten.

We need to capitalise on magistrates' experience and the skills they offer. Before arriving at a decision, we will need to be satisfied that we have the right selection processes in place, both for fee-paid and salaried appointments. We must also have a robust system for appraising fee-paid office-holders. There is plenty for us all to do, but looking at it now will mean that we can be ready when an appropriate legislative opportunity arises.

 The response paper 'Supporting Magistrates to Provide Justice' is available at: **www.dca.gov.uk/magist/support/response.pdf**

14

The administration of justice

Introduction

This chapter looks at:

- the role of the Ministry of Justice;
- the Attorney-General's legal advice on the legality of the war against Iraq; and
- planned reforms to the Attorney-General's involvement in prosecution decisions.

The Ministry of Justice

The Ministry of Justice was created in 2007 with responsibility for the court service, the penal system and legal aid. Its website explains the strategy and goals of this important Ministry.

Our strategy

Our work is focused around four strategic objectives:

Departmental strategic objectives

1 Strengthen democracy, rights and responsibilities
2 Deliver fair and simple routes to civil and family justice
3 Protect the public and reduce reoffending
4 Ensure a more effective, transparent and responsive criminal justice system for victims and the public.

1 We lead the government's constitutional, rights and legal reform programmes, which include work on institutional reform, data protection and sharing, electoral modernisation, human rights, devolution and encouraging people to take an active part in the democratic process.

2 We want to give people access to an efficient and effective civil and family justice system and try to help them avoid disputes that end up in court.

3 Protecting the public and reducing reoffending is central to our whole purpose. We are increasing prison capacity and an independent working group will be reporting on better ways to align supply and demand through the sentencing framework. We are committed to offender management reforms and delivering more effective community penalties that reflect the needs of local people. We are also working more collaboratively across government to protect the public and reduce reoffending.

4 We lead the new cross-government Justice for All public service agreement to deliver a more effective, transparent and responsive criminal justice system for victims and the public. We are taking a problem-solving approach to improving the criminal justice system which fully reflects the priorities of local communities as well as victims and the public.

Public service agreement

The Public Service Agreement sets out the key priority outcomes the government wants to achieve in the next spending period (2008–2011). The Ministry of Justice contributes to the following PSA targets:

● ensure controlled, fair migration that protects the public and contributes to economic growth;
● improve the safety of children and young people;
● increase the number of children and young people on the path to success;
● address the disadvantage that individuals experience because of their gender, race, disability, age, sexual orientation, religion or belief;

- increase the proportion of socially excluded adults in settled accommodation and employment, education or training;
- build more cohesive, empowered and active communities;
- make communities safer;
- deliver a more effective, transparent and responsive criminal justice system for victims and the public (Ministry of Justice lead department);
- reduce the harm caused by alcohol and drugs;
- reduce the risk to the UK and its interests overseas from international terrorism.

 The website of the Ministry of Justice is available at:
www.justice.gov.uk/about/about.htm

The Attorney-General and legal advice

The Attorney-General is the government's legal adviser. His most controversial legal advice in recent years concerned whether or not it was lawful to go to war with Iraq. Initially, the government refused to publish this advice on the basis that it was confidential, but following a number of leaks to the press and growing pressure from the media and politicians, the advice was published shortly before the May 2005 elections.

Blair Publishes Iraq War Advice
Times Online, 28 April 2005

The Prime Minister, supported by Gordon Brown at a lengthy press conference dominated by the Iraq issue, said that he was ordering the publication of the 13-page memo from Lord Goldsmith, the Attorney-General, to show that he had nothing to hide from voters. 'The so-called smoking gun has turned out to be a damp squib', he declared. But, with only a week to go until polling day, opposition parties refused to let sleeping dogs lie. Michael Howard abandoned a Conservative education manifesto launch to focus entirely on whether Mr Blair had lied to the country over the legality of the Iraq war.

He said: 'There is no more serious or grave decision than for a Prime Minister to take the country to war. You have to be straight with the people, you have to tell the truth. I don't believe Mr Blair did so.'

After Channel 4 News yesterday published the six key paragraphs of Lord Goldsmith's advice, Mr Blair ordered that the whole memo be posted on the official Downing Street website. The Government had until now always refused to release the advice, claiming that it was covered by lawyer-client confidentiality.

The memo was sent to Mr Blair on March 7, 2003, as Jack Straw, the Foreign Secretary, was arguing for a UN Security Council resolution giving explicit approval to a US-led invasion. That plan was scuppered a few days later when France, a permanent member of the council, threatened to veto it.

The memo showed that Lord Goldsmith had major doubts about the legality of an invasion, but an argument could be made that it was legal. But he warned that failure to push a resolution through the Security Council would make that argument difficult to sustain.

He also warned that the Government would not necessarily be able to defeat any legal challenge to the war. 'There are a number of ways in which the opponents of military action might seek to bring a legal case, internationally or domestically, against the UK, members of the Government, or UK military personnel,' he wrote. 'We cannot be certain that they would not succeed.'

There has been no explanation, however, as to why the Attorney-General had changed his mind quite so drastically when he told Cabinet ten days later – on the eve of a crucial vote in Parliament – that the war would be legal because of an accumulation of previous Security Council resolutions demanding that Iraq disarm or face the consequences.

 The Attorney-General's advice to the Prime Minister has now been published on the Prime Minister's website at:
www.number-10.gov.uk/output/Page7445.asp

The Attorney-General and prosecutions

The powers of the Attorney-General have become increasingly controversial and one area that the government is considering reforming is the Attorney-General's powers in relation to the bringing of criminal prosecutions. These are considered in the White Paper entitled 'The Governance of Britain – Constitutional Renewal' (2008).

The Governance of Britain – Constitutional Renewal (2008)

Attorney-General

Functions in relation to the prosecuting authorities

70 A small minority of respondents considered that the Government should have no (or only a very limited) role in relation to the prosecuting authorities. On this approach, no Minister would superintend the prosecuting authorities.

71 The Government is committed to decisions in relation to individual cases being taken by the independent prosecuting authorities themselves. But the prosecuting authorities exercise functions which have a very significant impact on members of the public, including whether a person should be prosecuted for a criminal offence and the level of sentence which should be sought when a person is convicted. The Government considers that Ministers have a legitimate interest in the overall objectives and priorities applied by the prosecuting authorities in taking these decisions. For example, the Government has a legitimate interest in ensuring that the overall approach taken, and priority given, to the prosecution of given categories of offence such as terrorism, rape, fraud and knife crime, reflects the public interest and accords with the rule of law. The Government also has a role in supervising how the prosecuting authorities deploy their resources.

72 The Government also considers that ending the superintendence relationship between the Attorney-General and the main prosecuting authorities would expose the Directors of the prosecuting authorities to the risk that they would be drawn into the political area. This could, perversely, expose them to more political pressure, rather than less. This approach would also weaken accountability to Parliament for the operation of the prosecuting authorities.

73 The Constitutional Affairs Select Committee (now the Justice Committee) suggested that the Attorney-General's functions in relation to the prosecuting authorities could be transferred to another Minister, possibly in the Ministry of Justice. This option was rejected by the overwhelming majority of respondents who expressed a view on it.

74 The Government has rejected this option. Transferring responsibility for the prosecuting authorities to a mainstream policy department would risk exacerbating any perceived risk of political influence over those authorities and their decisions, and give rise to new risks of conflicts of interests. It would also risk diluting the position of the prosecutors within wider departmental interests. The Government also notes that there was strong resistance to this option from the majority of respondents who expressed a view on this matter.

75 The Government considers that it is right that the prosecuting authorities continue to be superintended by a Minister and that that Minister be the Attorney-General. The Attorney-General's role as an independent lawyer and guardian of the public interest, with professional and ethical duties and a constitutional role in upholding the rule of law, means that the Attorney is the Minister who is in the best position to ensure that prosecution decisions are fully informed by relevant considerations without being subject to improper pressures.

76 However, the Government is proposing significant changes to the Attorney-General's role in relation to the prosecuting authorities.

77 Successive Attorney-Generals have exercised their superintendence functions on the basis that they could, if appropriate, give the prosecuting authorities a direction as to how to handle a particular case. However, no recent Attorney has in fact sought to give a direction in relation to an individual case. And in practice, the Attorney-General has no role in the vast majority of criminal prosecutions (the CPS alone deals with 1.5 million cases each year).

78 The Government has, however, listened carefully to the large number of respondents who expressed concerns about the extent of the Attorney's role in relation to individual criminal prosecutions. The Government also notes the unease expressed about the lack of clarity as to the relationship between the Attorney and the prosecuting authorities. A relationship which relies on implied checks and balances is inevitably less transparent.

79 For these reasons, the Government proposes to legislate to provide that the Attorney-General's function of superintending the prosecuting authorities does not entail an ability to give a direction in relation to a particular case. Thus it will not be open to the Attorney, as superintending Minister, to direct a prosecuting authority to prosecute a particular case or not to prosecute a particular case.

80 The Government proposes to legislate in broad terms on this point; the legislation will prevent the Attorney giving a direction 'in relation to an individual case'. This will ensure that the Attorney has, in general, no power to direct in relation to a particular criminal prosecution or any other matter being handled by the prosecuting authorities (for example, civil proceedings under proceeds of crime legislation).

81 In addition, the Government proposes to require the Attorney-General to set out more fully how the relationship between the main prosecuting authorities and the Attorney is to operate, by means of a protocol. The protocol will be prepared by the Attorney-General in consultation with the main prosecuting authorities and will be laid before Parliament. The protocol will have statutory force, in that both the Attorney and the Directors of the prosecuting authorities will be obliged to have regard to it.

82 The Government also proposes to enhance further the independent status of the prosecuting authorities by legislating to provide for fixed term appointments for the Director of Public Prosecutions, the Director of the Serious Fraud Office and the Director of Revenue and Customs Prosecutions. The legislation will also provide that a Director may only be removed from office by the Attorney-General on certain limited grounds. (This was not an option outlined in the consultation document but was proposed by a small number of respondents. At present the term of appointment and grounds for dismissal are determined by the Attorney-General.)

83 Under these proposals, the Law Officers would continue to have a say in setting overall prosecution policy and strategy, and the way in which this is delivered by the prosecuting authorities. The expectation is that such issues would be settled through consultation between the Attorney and the individual Directors (as happens now). The proposed protocol will provide the opportunity to clarify how the superintendence relationship is to operate.

Attorney's functions in relation to other prosecuting authorities

84 In addition to superintending the main prosecuting authorities (the CPS, SFO and RCPO), the Attorney-General also exercises *non-statutory oversight over the casework of the military prosecuting authorities and the other Government prosecutors (such as BERR, DWP and DEFRA)*. That relationship enables the Attorney, for example, to issue guidelines to prosecutors on common issues such as disclosure. Those authorities generally value the relationship with the Attorney. No change to these arrangements is proposed.

Cases which give rise to issues of national security

85 For the reasons given above, the Government does not consider that the Attorney-General should generally have a role in individual cases. However, the Government, in line with the majority of respondents, considers that special provision is needed for an exceptional category of case, namely those which have implications for national security. This is an issue on which Ministers (but not necessarily the prosecuting authorities) have significant expertise. And it is Ministers (rather than the prosecuting authorities) who are ultimately responsible for protecting the security of the nation.

86 The Government has given significant thought to form this provision should take, noting that respondents expressed a number of different views on this point.

87 The Government has concluded that the Attorney-General should have the power, in exceptional cases, to give a direction to stop a prosecution where this is necessary to safeguard national security. The power would also extend to investigations being conducted by the Serious Fraud Office. There would be a requirement for the Attorney-General to give a report to Parliament about each occasion when such a power was exercised (without disclosing details which would be damaging to the public interest). In considering whether to exercise this power, the Attorney-General would be able to consult Ministerial colleagues about the public interest implications in appropriate cases through a 'Shawcross exercise'.

88 This approach will make it clear who has taken the decision to halt a prosecution in these exceptional cases and so make it clear who should be held to account for that decision.

89 The Government expects the number of cases in which such a direction would be given to be very small. Even in cases which give rise to considerations of national security the Attorney-General may consider that it is unnecessary to do more than to discuss the matter with the relevant prosecuting authority.

Functions of the Attorney-General in relation to prosecutions

90 The Government has approached the issue of the Attorney-General's powers to consent to prosecutions in line with the principles outlined above. It has also taken on board the views of respondents, the majority of whom thought most consent powers should be transferred to the prosecuting authorities, and considered the recommendations of the Law Commission in this area.

91 In light of this, the Government proposes the following reforms in relation to the consent regime:

- in relation to offences where there is no pressing need for there to be a requirement to obtain consent (of the Attorney or another person), the requirement to obtain consent should be abolished;
- in relation to a very small range of offences which are particularly likely to give rise to consideration of public policy or public interest (such as most Official Secrets Act offences and war crimes), the obligation to obtain the consent of the Attorney-General should be retained; and
- in relation to other offences, the power to consent should be transferred to the Director of Public Prosecutions or other appropriate Director.

92 The draft Bill contains a number of amendments to prosecution consent functions on a provisional basis. However, further work is needed to determine into which of the categories specified above each of the Attorney's current prosecution consent functions falls into.

93 The Government, in line with the approach being taken in relation to the extent of the powers of the Attorney-General in relation to individual cases, considers that the Attorney-General should cease to have the power to enter a *nolle prosequi* (to stop a trial on indictment).

94 The Government does not propose to transfer the power to enter a *nolle prosequi* to the prosecuting authorities. But consideration will be given as to whether other measures are needed as a consequence of abolishing the power of the Attorney to enter a *nolle prosequi*. Such measures might include expanding the current powers of the prosecuting authorities to discontinue a prosecution.

95 The Government is not proposing any change to the Attorney-General's power to *refer unduly lenient sentences to the Court of Appeal*. This function was viewed by some respondents as a form of prosecution appeal which could be exercised by the prosecuting authorities themselves. However, the Government, and a number of respondents, consider that the function should be viewed as one which should be exercised independently of the prosecution, in the public interest.

Attorney's role in relation to formulation of criminal justice policy

96 The Government recognises the importance of the prosecutors having a 'voice' in the formulation and implementation of criminal justice policy, and in ensuring that policy decisions and legislation in that area are operationally workable. The Government also agrees with the majority of respondents that that 'voice', to be effective, needs to be a Ministerial one. The Government considers that it would be artificial to divorce Ministerial responsibility for the superintendence of the prosecuting authorities from Ministerial responsibility for ensuring the 'front-line' experience of the prosecutors informs the development of criminal justice policy.

97 For this reason, the Government does not propose any change to the Attorney-General's role, in conjunction with the Home Secretary and Justice Secretary, in relation to the formulation of criminal justice policy.

98 Clauses to reflect these proposals can be found in the draft Constitutional Renewal Bill (CM 7342–2).

 The White Paper, 'The Governance of Britain – Constitutional Renewal' (2008) is available on the website of the Ministry of Justice at:
www.justice.gov.uk/docs/constitutional-renewal-white-paper.pdf

HUMAN RIGHTS

15   Introduction to human rights

Introduction

This chapter looks at:

- the Human Rights Act 1998;
- case law illustrating the judicial approach to the protection of human rights;
- the shift in the government's approach to human rights after the July 2005 terrorist attacks in London;
- the courts' approach to control orders which can present a significant challenge to an individual's personal rights and freedoms; and
- the European Charter of Fundamental Rights.

Human Rights Act 1998 – protection under domestic law

A turning point for the protection of human rights in the UK was the passing of the Human Rights Act 1998, which incorporated into domestic law the European Convention on Human Rights.

Human Rights Act 1998

The
Convention
Rights.

Introduction

1.—(1) In this Act 'the Convention rights' means the rights and fundamental freedoms set out in—

(a) Articles 2 to 12 and 14 of the Convention,

(b) Articles 1 to 3 of the First Protocol, and

(c) Articles 1 and 2 of the Sixth Protocol,

as read with Articles 16 to 18 of the Convention.

(2) Those Articles are to have effect for the purposes of this Act subject to any designated derogation or reservation (as to which see sections 14 and 15).

(3) The Articles are set out in Schedule 1.

(4) The Secretary of State may by order make such amendments to this Act as he considers appropriate to reflect the effect, in relation to the United Kingdom, of a protocol.

(5) In subsection (4) 'protocol' means a protocol to the Convention—

(a) which the United Kingdom has ratified; or

(b) which the United Kingdom has signed with a view to ratification.

(6) No amendment may be made by an order under subsection (4) so as to come into force before the protocol concerned is in force in relation to the United Kingdom.

Interpretation
of
Convention
rights.

2.—(1) A court or tribunal determining a question which has arisen in connection with a Convention right must take into account any—

(a) judgment, decision, declaration or advisory opinion of the European Court of Human Rights,

(b) opinion of the Commission given in a report adopted under Article 31 of the Convention,

(c) decision of the Commission in connection with Article 26 or 27(2) of the Convention, or

(d) decision of the Committee of Ministers taken under Article 46 of the Convention,

whenever made or given, so far as, in the opinion of the court or tribunal, it is relevant to the proceedings in which that question has arisen.

(2) Evidence of any judgment, decision, declaration or opinion of which account may have to be taken under this section is to be given in proceedings before any court or tribunal in such manner as may be provided by rules.

(3) In this section 'rules' means rules of court or, in the case of proceedings before a tribunal, rules made for the purposes of this section—

(a) by the Lord Chancellor or the Secretary of State, in relation to any proceedings outside Scotland;

(b) by the Secretary of State, in relation to proceedings in Scotland; or

(c) by a Northern Ireland department, in relation to proceedings before a tribunal in Northern Ireland—

(i) which deals with transferred matters; and

(ii) for which no rules made under paragraph (a) are in force.

Legislation

Interpretation of legislation.   **3.**—(1) So far as it is possible to do so, primary legislation and subordinate legislation must be read and given effect in a way which is compatible with the Convention rights.

(2) This section—

(a) applies to primary legislation and subordinate legislation whenever enacted;

(b) does not affect the validity, continuing operation or enforcement of any incompatible primary legislation; and

(c) does not affect the validity, continuing operation or enforcement of any incompatible subordinate legislation if (disregarding any possibility of revocation) primary legislation prevents removal of the incompatibility.

Declaration of incompatibility.   **4.**—(1) Subsection (2) applies in any proceedings in which a court determines whether a provision of primary legislation is compatible with a Convention right.

(2) If the court is satisfied that the provision is incompatible with a Convention right, it may make a declaration of that incompatibility.

(3) Subsection (4) applies in any proceedings in which a court determines whether a provision of subordinate legislation, made in the exercise of a power conferred by primary legislation, is compatible with a Convention right.

(4) If the court is satisfied—

(a) that the provision is incompatible with a Convention right, and

(b) that (disregarding any possibility of revocation) the primary legislation concerned prevents removal of the incompatibility,

it may make a declaration of that incompatibility.

➜

(5) In this section 'court' means—
(a) the House of Lords;
(b) the Judicial Committee of the Privy Council;
(c) the Courts-Martial Appeal Court;
(d) in Scotland, the High Court of Justiciary sitting otherwise than as a trial court or the Court of Session;
(e) in England and Wales or Northern Ireland, the High Court or the Court of Appeal.

(6) A declaration under this section ('a declaration of incompatibility')—
(a) does not affect the validity, continuing operation or enforcement of the provision in respect of which it is given; and
(b) is not binding on the parties to the proceedings in which it is made.

Right of Crown to intervene

5.—(1) Where a court is considering whether to make a declaration of incompatibility, the Crown is entitled to notice in accordance with rules of court.

(2) In any case to which subsection (1) applies—
(a) a Minister of the Crown (or a person nominated by him),
(b) a member of the Scottish Executive,
(c) a Northern Ireland Minister,
(d) a Northern Ireland department,
is entitled, on giving notice in accordance with rules of court, to be joined as a party to the proceedings.

(3) Notice under subsection (2) may be given at any time during the proceedings.

(4) A person who has been made a party to criminal proceedings (other than in Scotland) as the result of a notice under subsection (2) may, with leave, appeal to the House of Lords against any declaration of incompatibility made in the proceedings.

(5) In subsection (4)—'criminal proceedings' includes all proceedings before the Courts-Martial Appeal Court; and 'leave' means leave granted by the court making the declaration of incompatibility or by the House of Lords.

Public authorities

Acts of public authorities.

6.—(1) It is unlawful for a public authority to act in a way which is incompatible with a Convention right.

(2) Subsection (1) does not apply to an act if—
(a) as the result of one or more provisions of primary legislation, the authority could not have acted differently; or
(b) in the case of one or more provisions of, or made under, primary legislation which cannot be read or given effect in a way which is

compatible with the Convention rights, the authority was acting so as to give effect to or enforce those provisions.

(3) In this section 'public authority' includes—
(a) a court or tribunal, and
(b) any person certain of whose functions are functions of a public nature,

but does not include either House of Parliament or a person exercising functions in connection with proceedings in Parliament.

(4) In subsection (3) 'Parliament' does not include the House of Lords in its judicial capacity.

(5) In relation to a particular act, a person is not a public authority by virtue only of subsection (3)(b) if the nature of the act is private.

(6) 'An act' includes a failure to act but does not include a failure to—
(a) introduce in, or lay before, Parliament a proposal for legislation; or
(b) make any primary legislation or remedial order.

Proceedings.   7.—(1) A person who claims that a public authority has acted (or proposes to act) in a way which is made unlawful by section 6(1) may—
(a) bring proceedings against the authority under this Act in the appropriate court or tribunal, or
(b) rely on the Convention right or rights concerned in any legal proceedings,
but only if he is (or would be) a victim of the unlawful act.

(2) In subsection (1)(a) 'appropriate court or tribunal' means such court or tribunal as may be determined in accordance with rules; and proceedings against an authority include a counterclaim or similar proceeding.

(3) If the proceedings are brought on an application for judicial review, the applicant is to be taken to have a sufficient interest in relation to the unlawful act only if he is, or would be, a victim of that act.

(4) If the proceedings are made by way of a petition for judicial review in Scotland, the applicant shall be taken to have title and interest to sue in relation to the unlawful act only if he is, or would be, a victim of that act.

(5) Proceedings under subsection (1)(a) must be brought before the end of—
(a) the period of one year beginning with the date on which the act complained of took place; or
(b) such longer period as the court or tribunal considers equitable having regard to all the circumstances,
but that is subject to any rule imposing a stricter time limit in relation to the procedure in question.

→

(6) In subsection (1)(b) 'legal proceedings' includes—
  (a) proceedings brought by or at the instigation of a public authority; and
  (b) an appeal against the decision of a court or tribunal.

(7) For the purposes of this section, a person is a victim of an unlawful act only if he would be a victim for the purposes of Article 34 of the Convention if proceedings were brought in the European Court of Human Rights in respect of that act.

Judicial remedies.   **8.**—(1) In relation to any act (or proposed act) of a public authority which the court finds is (or would be) unlawful, it may grant such relief or remedy, or make such order, within its powers as it considers just and appropriate.

(2) But damages may be awarded only by a court which has power to award damages, or to order the payment of compensation, in civil proceedings.

(3) No award of damages is to be made unless, taking account of all the circumstances of the case, including—
  (a) any other relief or remedy granted, or order made, in relation to the act in question (by that or any other court), and
  (b) the consequences of any decision (of that or any other court) in respect of that act,
the court is satisfied that the award is necessary to afford just satisfaction to the person in whose favour it is made.

(4) In determining—
  (a) whether to award damages, or
  (b) the amount of an award,
the court must take into account the principles applied by the European Court of Human Rights in relation to the award of compensation under Article 41 of the Convention.

(5) A public authority against which damages are awarded is to be treated—
  (a) in Scotland, for the purposes of section 3 of the Law Reform (Miscellaneous Provisions) (Scotland) Act 1940 as if the award were made in an action of damages in which the authority has been found liable in respect of loss or damage to the person to whom the award is made;
  (b) for the purposes of the Civil Liability (Contribution) Act 1978 as liable in respect of damage suffered by the person to whom the award is made.

(6) In this section—
  'court' includes a tribunal;
  'damages' means damages for an unlawful act of a public authority; and
  (b) an appeal against the decision of a court or tribunal.
    . . .

Remedial action

Power to take remedial action.

10.—(1) This section applies if—

(a) a provision of legislation has been declared under section 4 to be incompatible with a Convention right and, if an appeal lies—

(i) all persons who may appeal have stated in writing that they do not intend to do so;

(ii) the time for bringing an appeal has expired and no appeal has been brought within that time; or

(iii) an appeal brought within that time has been determined or abandoned; or

(b) it appears to a Minister of the Crown or Her Majesty in Council that, having regard to a finding of the European Court of Human Rights made after the coming into force of this section in proceedings against the United Kingdom, a provision of legislation is incompatible with an obligation of the United Kingdom arising from the Convention.

(2) If a Minister of the Crown considers that there are compelling reasons for proceeding under this section, he may by order make such amendments to the legislation as he considers necessary to remove the incompatibility.

(3) If, in the case of subordinate legislation, a Minister of the Crown considers—

(a) that it is necessary to amend the primary legislation under which the subordinate legislation in question was made, in order to enable the incompatibility to be removed, and

(b) that there are compelling reasons for proceeding under this section,

he may by order make such amendments to the primary legislation as he considers necessary.

(4) This section also applies where the provision in question is in subordinate legislation and has been quashed, or declared invalid, by reason of incompatibility with a Convention right and the Minister proposes to proceed under paragraph 2(b) of Schedule 2.

(5) If the legislation is an Order in Council, the power conferred by subsection (2) or (3) is exercisable by Her Majesty in Council.

 The Human Rights Act 1998 is available on the website of the Office of Public Sector Information at:
www.opsi.gov.uk/acts/acts1998/19980042.htm

Judges protecting human rights

A controversial judicial decision which highlights the tension between the roles of the judges, Parliament and the executive is **A and Z and Others v Secretary of State for the Home Department** (2004). Following fear over the increased risks of terrorism, Parliament had passed the Anti-Terrorism, Crime and Security Act 2001. This allowed the government to detain in prison suspected terrorists without trial. The subsequent detention of nine foreign nationals was challenged through the courts and the House of Lords ruled that their detention was unlawful because it violated the Human Rights Act. As a result, the legislation was repealed and replaced by the Prevention of Terrorism Act 2005. This established control orders, which can potentially amount to house arrest – the first time we have seen this measure in the UK. Lord Hoffmann gave one of the judgments in favour of releasing the detainees.

A and Z and Others v Secretary of State for the Home Department (2004)

Lord Hoffmann

My Lords,

86 . . . This is one of the most important cases which the House has had to decide in recent years. It calls into question the very existence of an ancient liberty of which this country has until now been very proud: freedom from arbitrary arrest and detention. The power which the Home Secretary seeks to uphold is a power to detain people indefinitely without charge or trial. Nothing could be more antithetical to the instincts and traditions of the people of the United Kingdom.

87 At present, the power cannot be exercised against citizens of this country. First, it applies only to foreigners whom the Home Secretary would otherwise be able to deport. But the power to deport foreigners is extremely wide. Secondly, it requires that the Home Secretary should reasonably suspect the foreigners of a variety of activities or attitudes in connection with terrorism, including supporting a group influenced from abroad whom the Home Secretary suspects of being concerned in terrorism. If the finger of suspicion has pointed and the suspect is detained, his detention must be reviewed by the Special Immigration Appeals Commission. They can decide that there were no reasonable grounds for the Home Secretary's suspicion. But the suspect is not entitled to be told the grounds upon which he has been suspected. So he may not find it easy to explain that the suspicion is groundless. In any case, suspicion of being a supporter is one thing and proof of wrongdoing is another. Someone who has never committed any offence and has no intention of doing anything wrong may be reasonably suspected of being a supporter on the basis of some heated remarks overheard in a pub. The question in this case is whether the United Kingdom should be a country in which the police can come to such a person's house and take him away to be detained indefinitely without trial.

88 The technical issue in this appeal is whether such a power can be justified on the ground that there exists a 'war or other public emergency threatening the life of the nation' within the meaning of Article 15 of the European Convention on Human Rights. But I would not like anyone to think that we are concerned with some special doctrine of European law. Freedom from arbitrary arrest and detention is a quintessentially British liberty, enjoyed by the inhabitants of this country when most of the population of Europe could be thrown into prison at the whim of their rulers. It was incorporated into the European Convention in order to entrench the same liberty in countries which had recently been under Nazi occupation. The United Kingdom subscribed to the Convention because it set out the rights which British subjects enjoyed under the common law.

89 The exceptional power to derogate from those rights also reflected British constitutional history. There have been times of great national emergency in which habeas corpus has been suspended and powers to detain on suspicion conferred on the government. It happened during the Napoleonic Wars and during both World Wars in the 20th century. These powers were conferred with great misgiving and, in the sober light of retrospect after the emergency had passed, were often found to have been cruelly and unnecessarily exercised. But the necessity of draconian powers in moments of national crisis is recognised in our constitutional history. Article 15 of the Convention, when it speaks of 'war or other public emergency threatening the life of the nation', accurately states the conditions in which such legislation has previously been thought necessary.

90 Until the Human Rights Act 1998, the question of whether the threat to the nation was sufficient to justify suspension of habeas corpus or the introduction of powers of detention could not have been the subject of judicial decision. There could be no basis for questioning an Act of Parliament by court proceedings. Under the 1998 Act, the courts still cannot say that an Act of Parliament is invalid. But they can declare that it is incompatible with the human rights of persons in this country. Parliament may then choose whether to maintain the law or not. The declaration of the court enables Parliament to choose with full knowledge that the law does not accord with our constitutional traditions.

91 What is meant by 'threatening the life of the nation'? The 'nation' is a social organism, living in its territory (in this case, the United Kingdom) under its own form of government and subject to a system of laws which expresses its own political and moral values. When one speaks of a threat to the 'life' of the nation, the word life is being used in a metaphorical sense. The life of the nation is not coterminous with the lives of its people. The nation, its institutions and values, endure through generations. In many important respects, England is the same nation as it was at the time of the first Elizabeth or the Glorious Revolution. The Armada threatened to destroy the life of the nation, not by loss of life in battle, but by subjecting English institutions to the rule of Spain and the Inquisition. The same was true of the threat posed to the United Kingdom by Nazi Germany in the Second World War. This country, more than any other in the world, has an unbroken history of living for centuries under institutions and in accordance with values which show a recognisable continuity.

92 This, I think, is the idea which the European Court of Human Rights was attempting to convey when it said (in **Lawless** v **Ireland (No. 3)** (A/3) (1979–80) 1 EHRR 15) that it must be a 'threat to the organised life of the community of which the State is composed', although I find this a rather dessicated description. Nor do I find the European cases particularly helpful. All that can be taken from them is that the Strasbourg court allows a wide 'margin of appreciation' to the national authorities in deciding 'both on the presence of such an emergency and on the nature and scope of derogations necessary to avert it':

Ireland *v* **United Kingdom** (1978) 2 EHRR 25, at para 207. What this means is that we, as a United Kingdom court, have to decide the matter for ourselves.

93 Perhaps it is wise for the Strasbourg court to distance itself from these matters. The institutions of some countries are less firmly based than those of others. Their communities are not equally united in their loyalty to their values and system of government. I think that it was reasonable to say that terrorism in Northern Ireland threatened the life of that part of the nation and the territorial integrity of the United Kingdom as a whole. In a community riven by sectarian passions, such a campaign of violence threatened the fabric of organised society. The question is whether the threat of terrorism from Muslim extremists similarly threatens the life of the British nation.

94 The Home Secretary has adduced evidence, both open and secret, to show the existence of a threat of serious terrorist outrages. The Attorney-General did not invite us to examine the secret evidence, but despite the widespread scepticism which has attached to intelligence assessments since the fiasco over Iraqi weapons of mass destruction, I am willing to accept that credible evidence of such plots exist. The events of 11 September 2001 in New York and Washington and 11 March 2003 in Madrid make it entirely likely that the threat of similar atrocities in the United Kingdom is a real one.

95 But the question is whether such a threat is a threat to the life of the nation. The Attorney-General's submissions and the judgment of the Special Immigration Appeals Commission treated a threat of serious physical damage and loss of life as necessarily involving a threat to the life of the nation. But in my opinion this shows a misunderstanding of what is meant by 'threatening the life of the nation'. Of course, the government has a duty to protect the lives and property of its citizens. But that is a duty which it owes all the time and which it must discharge without destroying our constitutional freedoms. There may be some nations too fragile or fissiparous to withstand a serious act of violence. But that is not the case in the United Kingdom. When Milton urged the government of his day not to censor the press even in time of civil war, he said:

> Lords and Commons of England, consider what nation it is whereof ye are, and whereof ye are the governours.

96 This is a nation which has been tested in adversity, which has survived physical destruction and catastrophic loss of life. I do not underestimate the ability of fanatical groups of terrorists to kill and destroy, but they do not threaten the life of the nation. Whether we would survive Hitler hung in the balance, but there is no doubt that we shall survive Al-Qaeda. The Spanish people have not said that what happened in Madrid, hideous crime as it was, threatened the life of their nation. Their legendary pride would not allow it. Terrorist violence, serious as it is, does not threaten our institutions of government or our existence as a civil community.

97 For these reasons I think that the Special Immigration Appeals Commission made an error of law and that the appeal ought to be allowed. Others of your Lordships who are also in favour of allowing the appeal would do so, not because there is no emergency threatening the life of the nation, but on the ground that a power of detention confined to foreigners is irrational and discriminatory. I would prefer not to express a view on this point. I said that the power of detention is at present confined to foreigners and I would not like to give the impression that all that was necessary was to extend the power to United

Kingdom citizens as well. In my opinion, such a power in any form is not compatible with our constitution. The real threat to the life of the nation, in the sense of a people living in accordance with its traditional laws and political values, comes not from terrorism but from laws such as these. That is the true measure of what terrorism may achieve. It is for Parliament to decide whether to give the terrorists such a victory.

The House of Lords' judgment **A and Z and Others v Secretary of State for the Home Department** (2004) is available on the House of Lords' judicial business website at:

www.publications.parliament.uk/pa/ld200405/ldjudgmt/jd041216/ a&oth-1.htm

Human rights following the July 2005 terrorist attacks

Following the terrorist attacks on the London underground system in July 2005, there was concern that the law needed to get the right balance between human rights and preventing human atrocities by terrorists. The Prime Minister made a statement at a press conference at Number 10 Downing Street where he stated that 'the rules of the game are changing'.

Prime Minister's Press Conference (5 August 2005)

Prime Minister

Since the 7th of July the response of the British people has been unified and dignified and remarkable. Of course there is anxiety and worry, but the country knows the purpose of terrorism is to intimidate, and it's not inclined to be intimidated. Of course too, there have been isolated and unacceptable acts of racial or religious hatred. But they have been isolated, by and large Britain knows it is a tolerant and good natured nation, it's rather proud of it, and it's responded to this terrorism with tolerance and good nature in a way that's won the admiration of people and nations the world over. However, I'm acutely aware that alongside these feelings is also a determination that this very tolerance and good nature should not be abused by a small but fanatical minority, and an anger that it has been.

Time and again over the past few weeks I've been asked to deal firmly with those prepared to engage in such extremism, and most particularly with those who incite it or proselytise for it. The Muslim community, I should emphasise, have been and are our partners in this endeavour. Much of the insistence on strong action to weed out extremism is coming most vigorously from Muslims themselves, deeply concerned lest the activities of the fanatical fringe contaminate the good reputation of the mainstream Muslim community in this country. The action I am talking about has in the past been controversial, each tightening of the law has met fierce opposition, regularly we have a defeat in parliament or in the courts. The anti-terrorism legislation of course passed in 2002 after September 11th was declared partially invalid, the successor legislation hotly contested. But for obvious reasons, the mood now is different, people do not talk of scare-mongering, and to be fair the Conservative leadership has responded with a genuine desire to work together for the good of the country, as have the Liberal Democrats.

Over the past two weeks there have been intensive meetings and discussions across government to set a comprehensive framework for action in dealing with the terrorist threat in Britain, and today I want to give our preliminary assessment of the measures we need urgently to examine. In the meantime, in so far as administrative measures not requiring legislation can be taken, we will act with immediate effect.

In looking both at the law and administrative measures we have surveyed extensively practice in other countries, including in particular other European countries, and to assist this process there will be a series of consultation papers over the coming weeks starting with a research paper that will detail experience in other countries. There will also be a cross government unit staffed by senior hand-picked officials to drive this forward under the guidance of Bill Jeffrey the Intelligence and Security Co-ordinator, and the Cabinet Committee on Counter Terrorism, which I chair. The Home Secretary, with whom I've been talking closely in the past week will have the Cabinet responsibility for co-ordinating this.

Here are the measures either being taken now, immediately, or under urgent examination.

First, the Home Secretary today publishes new grounds for deportation and exclusion. Deportation is a decision taken by the Home Secretary under statute. The new grounds will include fostering hatred, advocating violence to further a person's beliefs, or justifying or validating such violence. These grounds will be subject to a short consultation period which will finish this month. Even under existing grounds, however, we are today signalling a new approach to deportation orders. Let no-one be in any doubt, the rules of the game are changing. These issues will of course be tested in the courts, up to now the concern has been that orders for deportation will be struck down as contrary to Article 3 of the European Convention on Human Rights as interpreted by the European Court in the **Chahal** case in 1996, and indeed we have had such cases struck down.

However, the circumstances of our national security have self evidently changed, and we believe we can get the necessary assurances from the countries to which we will return the deportees, against their being subject to torture or ill treatment contrary to Article 3. We have now concluded a Memorandum of Understanding with Jordan, and we are close to getting necessary assurances from other relevant countries. For example, just yesterday I had very constructive conversations with the leaders of Algeria and Lebanon. There are around 10 such countries with whom we are seeking such assurances. France and Spain, to name just two other European countries, do deport by administrative decision. The effect is often immediate and in some cases the appeal is non-suspensive, in other words it takes place outside of their country. The assurances given by the receiving nation are adequate for their courts, and these countries are also of course subject to the European Convention on Human Rights and apply it directly in their own law. So it is important to test this anew now in view of the changed conditions in Britain. Should legal obstacles arise, we will legislate further including, if necessary, amending the Human Rights Act in respect of the interpretation of the European Convention on Human Rights. In any event we will consult on legislating specifically for a non-suspensive appeal process in respect of deportations. One other point on deportations, once the new grounds take effect, there will be a list drawn up of specific extremist websites, bookshops, networks, centres and particular organisations of concern. Active engagement with any of these will be a trigger for the Home Secretary to consider the deportation of any foreign national.

Secondly, as has already been stated, there will be new anti-terrorism legislation in the Autumn. This will include an offence of condoning or glorifying terrorism. The sort of remarks made in recent days should be covered by such laws. But this will also be applied to justifying or glorifying terrorism anywhere, not just in the United Kingdom.

Thirdly, anyone who has participated in terrorism, or has anything to do with it anywhere will be automatically refused asylum in our country.

Fourth, we already have powers to strip citizenship from those individuals with British or dual nationality who act in a way that is contrary to the interests of this country. We will now consult on extending these powers, applying them to naturalised citizens engaged in extremism, and making the procedures simpler and more effective.

Fifth, cases such as Rashid Ramda, wanted for the Paris Metro bombings ten years ago, and who is still in the UK whilst France seeks extradition are completely unacceptable. We will begin consultation on setting a maximum time limit for all future extradition cases involving terrorism.

Sixth, we are already examining a new court procedure which would allow a pretrial process. We will also examine whether the necessary procedure can be brought about to give us a way of meeting the police and security service request that detention, pre-charge of terrorist suspects, be significantly extended.

Seventh, for those who are British nationals and cannot be deported, we will extend the use of control orders, any breach of which can mean imprisonment.

Eighth, to expand the court capacity necessary to deal with this and other related issues. The Lord Chancellor will increase the number of special judges hearing such cases.

Ninth, we will proscribe Hizb-ut-Tahira and the successor organisation of Al Mujahiroun. We will also examine the grounds for proscription to widen them and put forward proposals in the new legislation.

Tenth, it is now necessary in order to acquire British citizenship that people attend a citizenship ceremony, swear allegiance to this country, and have a rudimentary grasp of the English language. We will review the threshold for this to make sure it is adequate, and we will establish with the Muslim community a commission to advise on how, consistent with peoples complete freedom to worship in the way they want and to follow their own religion and culture, there is better integration of those parts of the community presently inadequately integrated. I have asked Hazel Blears to make this part of the work she is currently undertaking.

Eleventh, we will consult on a new power to order closure of a place of worship which is used as a centre for fomenting extremism, and will consult with Muslim leaders in respect of those clerics who are not British citizens to draw up a list of those not suitable to preach and who will be excluded from our country in future.

Twelfth, we will bring forward the proposed measures on the security of our borders with a series of countries specifically designated for biometric visas over the next year. Meanwhile the Home Office and the Foreign & Commonwealth Office are compiling an international database of those individuals whose activities or views pose a threat to Britain's security. Anyone on the database will be excluded from entry with any appeal only taking place outside the country.

We will consult widely on these measures, including with the other political parties of course. It is evidently a heavy agenda to take forward, but it's necessary, and let me also again repeat and make it clear, if legislation can be made ready in time, and the right consensus is achieved, we are ready to recall parliament in September, at least to begin the debate over these measures.

I want to make it clear yet again that this is not in any way whatever aimed at the decent law-abiding Muslim community of Great Britain. We know that this fringe of extremism does not truly represent Islam. We know British Muslims, in general, abhor the actions of the extremists. We acknowledge once again Muslim contribution to our country and welcome it. We welcome those who visit our country from abroad in peace, welcome those who know that in this country the respect and tolerance towards others which we believe in, is the surest guarantee of freedom and progress for people of all religious faiths.

But coming to Britain is not a right, and even when people have come here, staying here carries with it a duty. That duty is to share and support the values that sustain the British way of life. Those that break that duty and try to incite hatred or engage in violence against our country and its people have no place here. Over the coming months in the courts, in Parliament, in debate and engagement with all parts of our communities, we will work to turn these sentiments into reality, and that is my duty as Prime Minister.

 The full press conference given by the Prime Minister on 5 August 2005 is available on the Prime Minister's website at:
www.number-10.gov.uk/output/Page8041.asp

Control orders

The Prevention of Terrorism Act 2005 established control orders, under which major restrictions can be imposed on people who are considered to be a potential terrorist threat, but who have not been convicted of any crime. The legality of the procedures by which the imposition of a control order can be challenged were considered by the House of Lords in **Secretary of State for the Home Department v MB** (2007). The House of Lords concluded that there was no breach of the right to a fair hearing under article 6 of the European Convention on Human Rights provided strenuous efforts were made by all the parties involved to achieve a fair hearing. The House referred MB back to the first instance judge for these 'strenuous efforts' to be made.

Secretary of State for the Home Department v MB (2007), House of Lords

Lord Bingham

My Lords,

1 By his appeal to the House, MB seeks to challenge a non-derogating control order made by the Secretary of State on 5 September 2005 under sections 2 and 3(1)(a) of the Prevention of Terrorism Act 2005. That order was maintained in force by Sullivan J in a decision of 12 April 2006 ([2006] EWHC 1000 (Admin), [2006] HRLR 878, but he declared section 3 of the Act to be incompatible with MB's rights to a fair hearing under Article 6(1) of the European Convention on Human Rights. On 1 August 2006 the Court of Appeal (Lord Phillips of Worth Matravers CJ, Sir Anthony Clarke MR and Sir Igor Judge P) allowed an appeal against the judge's decision and set aside his declaration of incompatibility: [2006] EWCA Civ 1140, [2007] QB 415.

. . .

3 In granting this certificate, Ouseley J identified four questions, which it is convenient to label issues (1) to (4):

Issue (1). Whether the cumulative impact of the obligations imposed on AF by the control order dated 11 September 2006 and pursuant to the 2005 Act amounted to a deprivation of liberty within the meaning of Article 5(1) of the European Convention.

Issue (2). If the answer to issue (1) is in the affirmative, in circumstances where the court is satisfied that the Secretary of State was entitled to conclude that there is a reasonable suspicion that AF is or has been involved in terrorist-related activity and that it was necessary to make a control order imposing obligations on AF for purposes connected with protecting members of the public from a risk of terrorism, whether it is a proper exercise of the discretion under section 3(12) of the 2005 Act or generally to order that a control order should be quashed as a whole and *ab initio* rather than to quash individual obligations and/or direct the Secretary of State to modify individual obligations.

Issue (3). Whether a non-derogating control order imposed under the 2005 Act constitutes a criminal charge for the purposes of Article 6 of the European Convention.

Issue (4). Whether the procedures provided for by section 3 of the 2005 Act and the Rules of Court are compatible with Article 6 of the Convention in circumstances where they have resulted in the case made against AF being in its essence entirely undisclosed to him and in no specific allegation of terrorism-related activity being contained in open material.

. . .

37 MB is a 24 year-old student, born in Kuwait. He is a British citizen, naturalised as such in January 1998 after his mother was granted indefinite leave to remain. On 1 March 2005 he was seeking to fly to Syria from Manchester Airport when he was stopped and questioned by police officers and officers of the Security Service. On the following day he was at Heathrow, this time seeking to fly to Yemen, when he was again stopped and questioned by the police. His passport was seized and he was released. The content of these interviews is disputed. The Secretary of State asserts that on each occasion MB intended to travel on to Iraq to fight against coalition forces, which MB denies.

38 On 1 September 2005 the Secretary of State applied to the court under section 3(1)(a) of the 2005 Act for permission to make a non-derogating control order. The application was supported by a witness statement and an open statement with supporting documents. The open statement said, so far as material:

3 MB is an Islamist extremist who, as recently as March 2005, attempted to travel to Syria and then Yemen. The Security Service assessment is that MB was intending to travel onwards to Iraq . . .

8 The Security Service is confident that prior to the authorities preventing his travel, MB intended to go to Iraq to fight against coalition forces. Despite having been stopped from travelling once, MB showed no inclination to cancel his plans. The police prevented his travel on a second occasion, and seized his passport . . .

The Secretary of State's application was also supported by a closed statement and further documents and an application to withhold the closed material. Permission was granted, subject to minor amendments, under section 3(2)(b) of the Act, and the order was made on 5 September 2005. The obligations imposed on MB by this order, plainly directed to preventing him leaving the country, were very much less stringent than in the cases of **JJ and Others, E and AF**. Thus he was obliged to live at a specified address, to report to his local police station daily and to surrender his passport, and was forbidden to leave the UK or enter any airport or sea port, but he was otherwise subject to no geographical restriction, was subject to no curfew and was subject to no restriction on his social contacts. MB served a witness statement and the Secretary of State served a second open statement, which added little, and a second closed statement. The special advocate appointed to represent MB's interests did not challenge the Secretary of State's application to withhold the closed material, and accepted that it would not be possible to serve a summary which would not contain information or material the disclosure of which would be contrary to the public interest. The hearing under section 3(10) of the Act took place between 4–7 April 2006 before Sullivan J, who gave judgment on 12 April.

39 In his judgment (para 66) the judge recorded the description by counsel for the Secretary of State of his open case as 'relatively thin' and referred to part of the passage quoted in the last paragraph above. He observed (para 67):

> The basis for the Security Service's confidence is wholly contained within the closed material. Without access to that material it is difficult to see how, in reality [MB] could make any effective challenge to what is, on the open case before him, no more than a bare assertion.

Taking account also of other aspects of the hearing, on some of which he misdirected himself, the judge concluded that MB had not had a fair hearing (para 103).

40 The Court of Appeal thought it plain (para 27 of its judgment) that the justification for the obligations imposed on MB lay in the closed material, and it was the impact, on the facts of the case, of the provisions in the 2005 Act for the use of closed material that caused the court most concern (para 70). But having reviewed some of the authorities, it concluded (para 86):

> If one accepts, as we do, that reliance on closed material is permissible, this can only be on terms that appropriate safeguards against the prejudice that this may cause to the controlled person are in place. We consider that the provisions of the [2005 Act] for the use of a special advocate, and of the rules of court made pursuant to paragraph 4 of the Schedule to the [Act], constitute appropriate safeguards, and no suggestion has been made to the contrary.

41 The Council of Europe Commissioner for Human Rights, in paragraph 21 of his report referred to above (para 16), and the Joint Committee on Human Rights, in paragraph 76 of its report referred to above (para 16), had difficulty in accepting that a hearing could be fair if an adverse decision could be based on material that the controlled person has no effective opportunity to challenge or rebut. This is not a case (like E) in which the order can be justified on the strength of the open material alone. Nor is it a case in which the thrust of the case against the controlled person has been effectively conveyed to him by way of summary, redacted documents or anonymised statements. It is a case in which, on the judge's assessment which the Court of Appeal did not displace, MB was confronted by a bare, unsubstantiated assertion which he could do no more than deny. I have difficulty in accepting that MB has enjoyed a substantial measure of procedural justice, or that the very essence of the right to a fair hearing has not been impaired.

42 Ouseley J observed (in para 11 of his judgment) that the open case for a control order against AF was very short. AF came to the attention of the Security Service before his arrest in May 2006. It was alleged that he had links with Islamist extremists in Manchester, some of whom were affiliated to the Libyan Islamic Fighting Group. The LIFG became a proscribed organisation on 14 October 2005. The judge found (para 61) it to be clear that the essence of the Secretary of State's case against AF was in the closed material, and AF did not know what the case against him was. The open material disclosed to AF did not give grounds for reasonable suspicion (para 131), and it was not contended that it did. There were no more than links to extremists, who also had innocent links to him. The judge thought it clear (para 131) that more than reasonable grounds for suspicion existed, but only on the closed material. The judge was similarly satisfied that a control order was necessary (para 133) but that conclusion depended on the closed evidence. The judge accepted (para 146), without qualification, submissions by counsel for AF that no, or at least no clear or significant, allegations of involvement in terrorist-related activity were disclosed by the open material, that no such allegations had been gisted, that the case made by the Secretary of State against AF was in its essence entirely undisclosed to him and that no allegations of wrongdoing had been put to him by the police in interview after his arrest, affording him an idea by that side wind of what the case against him might be. Having noted the decision of the Court of Appeal in **MB** and the decision of the House in **Roberts**, above, the judge concluded (para 166) that there was no clear basis for a finding of incompatibility.

43 This would seem to me an even stronger case than **MB**'s. If, as I understand the House to have accepted in **Roberts**, above, the concept of fairness imports a core, irreducible minimum of procedural protection, I have difficulty, on the judge's findings, in concluding that such protection has been afforded to AF. The right to a fair hearing is fundamental. In the absence of a derogation (where that is permissible) it must be protected. In this case, as in **MB**'s, it seems to me that it was not.

 The House of Lords' judgment **Secretary of State for the Home Department v MB** is available on the internet at:
www.publications.parliament.uk/pa/ld200607/ldjudgmt/jd071031/home-1.htm

The European Union and human rights

The European Union looks set to become more involved in the protection of human rights within Europe. Article 6 of the Reform Treaty (signed in Lisbon in 2007 and due to come into force in 2009) recognises the rights and freedoms set out in the European Charter of Fundamental Rights. This Charter lays down more extensive rights than those contained in the European Convention on Human Rights because, as well as containing civil and political rights, it lays down social and economic rights, such as freedom of information, freedom of the arts and sciences and rights for children and the elderly. The Charter also extends some of the existing Convention rights to a more modern context. Thus it includes the established right to life and prohibition of torture, but also prohibits more modern problems of human trafficking, forced labour, human cloning and the sale of body parts. An extract from the Charter of Fundamental Rights is reproduced below.

Charter of Fundamental Rights

CHAPTER I
DIGNITY

Article 1
Human dignity

Human dignity is inviolable. It must be respected and protected.

Article 2
Right to life

1. Everyone has the right to life.
2. No one shall be condemned to the death penalty, or executed.

Article 3
Right to the integrity of the person

1. Everyone has the right to respect for his or her physical and mental integrity.
2. In the fields of medicine and biology, the following must be respected in particular:
   - the free and informed consent of the person concerned, according to the procedures laid down by law,
   - the prohibition of eugenic practices, in particular those aiming at the selection of persons,
   - the prohibition on making the human body and its parts as such a source of financial gain,
   - the prohibition of the reproductive cloning of human beings.

Article 4
Prohibition of torture and inhuman or degrading treatment or punishment

No one shall be subjected to torture or to inhuman or degrading treatment or punishment.

Article 5
Prohibition of slavery and forced labour

1. No one shall be held in slavery or servitude.

2. No one shall be required to perform forced or compulsory labour.

3. Trafficking in human beings is prohibited.

CHAPTER II
FREEDOMS

Article 6
Right to liberty and security

Everyone has the right to liberty and security of person.

Article 7
Respect for private and family life

Everyone has the right to respect for his or her private and family life, home and communications.

Article 8
Protection of personal data

1. Everyone has the right to the protection of personal data concerning him or her.

2. Such data must be processed fairly for specified purposes and on the basis of the consent of the person concerned or some other legitimate basis laid down by law. Everyone has the right of access to data which has been collected concerning him or her, and the right to have it rectified.

3. Compliance with these rules shall be subject to control by an independent authority.

Article 9
Right to marry right to found a family

The right to marry and the right to found a family shall be guaranteed in accordance with the national laws governing the exercise of these rights.

Article 10
Freedom of thought, conscience and religion

1. Everyone has the right to freedom of thought, conscience and religion. This right includes freedom to change religion or belief and freedom, either alone or in community with others and in public or in private, to manifest religion or belief, in worship, teaching, practice and observance.

→

2. The right to conscientious objection is recognised, in accordance with the national laws governing the exercise of this right.

Article 11
Freedom of expression and information

1. Everyone has the right to freedom of expression. This right shall include freedom to hold opinions and to receive and impart information and ideas without interference by public authority and regardless of frontiers.

2. The freedom and pluralism of the media shall be respected.

Article 12
Freedom of assembly and of association

1. Everyone has the right to freedom of peaceful assembly and to freedom of association at all levels, in particular in political, trade union and civic matters, which implies the right of everyone to form and to join trade unions for the protection of his or her interests.

2. Political parties at Union level contribute to expressing the political will of the citizens of the Union.

Article 13
Freedom of the arts and sciences

The arts and scientific research shall be free of constraint. Academic freedom shall be respected.

Article 14
Right to education

1. Everyone has the right to education and to have access to vocational and continuing training.

2. This right includes the possibility to receive free compulsory education.

3. The freedom to found educational establishments with due respect for democratic principles and the right of parents to ensure the education and teaching of their children in conformity with their religious, philosophical and pedagogical convictions shall be respected, in accordance with the national laws governing the exercise of such freedom and right.

Article 15
Freedom to choose an occupation and right to engage in work

1. Everyone has the right to engage in work and to pursue a freely chosen or accepted occupation.

2. Every citizen of the Union has the freedom to seek employment, to work, to exercise the right of establishment and to provide services in any Member State.

3. Nationals of third countries who are authorised to work in the territories of the Member States are entitled to working conditions equivalent to those of citizens of the Union.

Article 16
Freedom to conduct a business

The freedom to conduct a business in accordance with Community law and national laws and practices is recognised.

Article 17
Right to property

1. Everyone has the right to own, use, dispose of and bequeath his or her lawfully acquired possessions. No one may be deprived of his or her possessions, except in the public interest and in the cases and under the conditions provided for by law, subject to fair compensation being paid in good time for their loss. The use of property may be regulated by law in so far as is necessary for the general interest.

2. Intellectual property shall be protected.

Article 18
Right to asylum

The right to asylum shall be guaranteed with due respect for the rules of the Geneva Convention of 28 July 1951 and the Protocol of 31 January 1967 relating to the status of refugees and in accordance with the Treaty establishing the European Community.

Article 19
Protection in the event of removal, expulsion or extradition

1. Collective expulsions are prohibited.

2. No one may be removed, expelled or extradited to a State where there is a serious risk that he or she would be subjected to the death penalty, torture or other inhuman or degrading treatment or punishment.

. . .

CHAPTER IV
SOLIDARITY

Article 27
Workers' right to information and consultation within the undertaking

Workers or their representatives must, at the appropriate levels, be guaranteed information and consultation in good time in the cases and under the conditions provided for by Community law and national laws and practices.

Article 28
Right of collective bargaining and action

Workers and employers, or their respective organisations, have, in accordance with Community law and national laws and practices, the right to negotiate and conclude collective agreements at the appropriate levels and, in cases of conflicts of interest, to take collective action to defend their interests, including strike action.

→

Article 29
Right of access to placement services

Everyone has the right of access to a free placement service.

Article 30
Protection in the event of unjustified dismissal

Every worker has the right to protection against unjustified dismissal, in accordance with Community law and national laws and practices.

Article 31
Fair and just working conditions

1. Every worker has the right to working conditions which respect his or her health, safety and dignity.

2. Every worker has the right to limitation of maximum working hours, to daily and weekly rest periods and to an annual period of paid leave.

Article 32
Prohibition of child labour and protection of young people at work

The employment of children is prohibited. The minimum age of admission to employment may not be lower than the minimum school-leaving age, without prejudice to such rules as may be more favourable to young people and except for limited derogations.

Young people admitted to work must have working conditions appropriate to their age and be protected against economic exploitation and any work likely to harm their safety, health or physical, mental, moral or social development or to interfere with their education.

Article 33
Family and professional life

1. The family shall enjoy legal, economic and social protection.

2. To reconcile family and professional life, everyone shall have the right to protection from dismissal for a reason connected with maternity and the right to paid maternity leave and to parental leave following the birth or adoption of a child.

Article 34
Social security and social assistance

1. The Union recognises and respects the entitlement to social security benefits and social services providing protection in cases such as maternity, illness, industrial accidents, dependency or old age, and in the case of loss of employment, in accordance with the rules laid down by Community law and national laws and practices.

2. Everyone residing and moving legally within the European Union is entitled to social security benefits and social advantages in accordance with Community law and national laws and practices.

3. In order to combat social exclusion and poverty, the Union recognises and respects the right to social and housing assistance so as to ensure a decent existence for all those who lack sufficient resources, in accordance with the rules laid down by Community law and national laws and practices.

Article 35
Health care

Everyone has the right of access to preventive health care and the right to benefit from medical treatment under the conditions established by national laws and practices. A high level of human health protection shall be ensured in the definition and implementation of all Union policies and activities.

Article 36
Access to services of general economic interest

The Union recognises and respects access to services of general economic interest as provided for in national laws and practices, in accordance with the Treaty establishing the European Community, in order to promote the social and territorial cohesion of the Union.

Article 37
Environmental protection

A high level of environmental protection and the improvement of the quality of the environment must be integrated into the policies of the Union and ensured in accordance with the principle of sustainable development.

Article 38
Consumer protection

Union policies shall ensure a high level of consumer protection.

 The European Charter of Fundamental Rights is available on the website for the European Parliament at:
www.europarl.europa.eu/charter/pdf/text_en.pdf

16 Remedies for infringement of human rights

Introduction

This chapter looks at:

- reforms made to the police misconduct procedures;

- the Independent Police Complaints Commission in the light of the investigation into the shooting by the police of Jean Charles de Menezes; and

- criticisms made by the Legal Action pressure group of the Independent Police Complaints Commission.

Reform of police misconduct procedures

Significant reforms were introduced in 1999 to the state's response to police misconduct. The Home Office has carried out research looking at how effective these reforms have been in tackling this problem.

An Evaluation of the New Police Misconduct Procedures
Home Office Online Report 10/03

Paul Quinton

Reform of the police disciplinary process

Following concerns raised by the Home Affairs Committee, significant changes were made to the existing system for dealing with police misconduct. The reforms were embodied in the new misconduct procedures which were introduced in April 1999 (to replace the old discipline procedures). The procedural reforms were based around:

- a reduction in the standard of proof at disciplinary hearings from 'beyond reasonable doubt' to the 'balance of probabilities';
- the introduction of tribunal panels to preside over hearings;
- new fast-track procedures for cases with clear evidence of serious misconduct;
- a Code of Conduct setting out standards of behaviour expected from police officers;
- written warnings for dealing with less serious incidents of police misconduct; and
- separate procedures for dealing with poor performance outside the disciplinary process.

The primary aim of procedural changes was to improve the effectiveness of the disciplinary process. The procedures also aimed to improve police standards and secure confidence in the process without adversely affecting operational police practice and officer morale.

The research
The aim of the study is to evaluate the impact of the changes to the police disciplinary process, particularly in terms of the effectiveness of the new misconduct procedures, their use, and effect on operational police officers. The evaluation draws on a sample of eight police forces from across England and Wales. The data sources used in the evaluation consisted of:

- force monitoring statistics;
- disciplinary case files;
- 29 in-depth interviews with Complaints and Discipline department staff; and
- individual and group interviews with operational police officers (106 officers in total).

As such, the report is specifically intended for policy makers and those working in the sphere of police discipline in the police service and partner agencies.

Impact on the disciplinary process

Overall, there was no evidence to suggest that the reforms had prompted any significant changes:

- **Perceived effectiveness**. There was a widespread view that the new misconduct procedures had little impact in practical terms and that, despite being effective, were no more so than the old discipline procedures. Although implementation was reported to be relatively smooth, concerns were raised about the 'lead-in' time for the reforms and the level of training provided to officers.
- **Investigations**. The number of investigations did not increase significantly in the sample forces after the reforms; investigations decreased and increased in metropolitan and non-metropolitan forces respectively, in line with longer-term trends. The prevailing view amongst those interviewed was that cases had remained at a 'broadly similar' level.
- **Charges**. Provisional analysis of case files indicated that, perhaps contrary to expectations, the average number of charges per officer in each case had declined slightly (1.7 charges under the new misconduct procedures compared to 2.1 charges under the old discipline procedures). About one-third of those interviewed reported no change in the number of charges brought.
- **Outcome of cases**. Provisional evidence suggested that hearings had not increased as might be expected. Indeed, the number carried out after the reforms was not as high as in previous years (but this may change in the longer-term). Early evidence also indicated that the outcome of cases had not changed significantly, although it is too early to say for certain because of the number of pending cases.

There was evidence that the reforms had prompted some positive changes, particularly in terms of the use of written warnings. The number of warnings issued increased substantially in the sample forces, increasing from 174 to 254 after their introduction. Warnings were seen by Complaints and Discipline department staff as one of the most significant reforms with about two-thirds viewing them in positive terms. Concerns were raised, however, that their use at a local level was patchy and inconsistent. Provisional analysis of the disciplinary case files also showed a reduction in the time taken for cases to be concluded. However, Complaints and Discipline department staff were negative about the impact of the new misconduct procedures on reducing delays in the system. There is also a question about whether the size of the broad statistical change would have an impact on individual cases at a more local level.

Impact on complaints and discipline departments

The research looked at the impact of the new misconduct procedures on the process of disciplining officers from the perspective of Complaints and Discipline department staff:

- **Investigation process**. A majority of those interviewed reported that the new misconduct procedures had not greatly changed the investigation process. The lower standard of proof was not seen to have had much impact; the same level and type of evidence would be gathered. However, a small number questioned whether it had been implemented fully.
- **The code of conduct**. Views amongst Complaints and Discipline department staff about the new Code of Conduct were mixed. It was clear from those interviewed that charging officers had become a more involved and detailed process following its introduction. A significant proportion felt that it was more difficult to charge officers; the principles set out in the code were described as being imprecise and open to interpretation. The Code of Conduct was, however, not always seen as a major change and its introduction was viewed positively by some.

- **Disciplinary hearing**. There was no prevailing view about how the 'balance of probabilities' had affected hearings; whereas a significant proportion reported that it was being used along a sliding scale, a small number reported that it had no impact. Tribunal panels were viewed positively by Complaints and Discipline department staff. Panels were generally seen to be effective and fair, and were able to draw on more 'grounded' experiences of policing. They were also seen to encourage leadership amongst panel members at a local level.

Impact on operational officers

To assess the wider impact of the reforms (particularly on police practice and officer morale), the research examined the perceptions and experiences of operational police officers:

- **Officer knowledge**. There was an overall awareness amongst operational officers that new procedures had been introduced, although knowledge of specific changes was limited to the change in the standard of proof. Training was generally seen to be limited.
- **Views on the disciplinary process**. The officers generally viewed the new misconduct procedures in negative terms. For example:
  - the procedures were seen as a mechanism for dismissing officers, rather than a tool for reducing misconduct;
  - officers were also insecure about, and distrustful of, the investigation process;
  - the use of the 'balance of probabilities' was seen to be unfair and that they were vulnerable as a result of the reforms; and
  - the length of time and the perceived lack of communication during the disciplinary process were highlighted as key concerns and the cause of much resentment.
- **Defining police misconduct**. There was uncertainty amongst officers about how misconduct was defined under the new Code of Conduct; a significant proportion commented that the old Discipline Code was much clearer and more specific. Given the apparent gap between the Code of Conduct and the need for a clear framework, operational officers seemed to have developed their own working definitions of misconduct. Rather than being fixed and precise, these tended to consist of examples of behaviour considered by officers to be unacceptable.
- **Officer practice and morale**. There was no evidence from the interviews to suggest that the new police misconduct procedures had affected the perceived risks associated with policing (e.g. in terms of receiving a complaint). The reforms were not in the forefront of officers' minds and not reported to have adversely affected their decision-making or practices. Officers did report, however, being more cautious in their use of language and in public encounters. This was reported to have been prompted by broad, longer-term factors (e.g. changes in police culture, integrity tests, negative public and media attitudes) rather than the procedural reforms.

There was no evidence that morale had been affected by the new misconduct procedures. Again, officer morale was linked more to other factors (e.g. staffing and the views of the public and media). It should also be noted that the effect of these other factors was seen to be cumulative.

Discussion, conclusions and recommendations

Overall, the research shows that, during the first two years of implementation, the new misconduct procedures have had a relatively limited impact. However, although the report has focused on the impact of procedural reforms, it should be recognised that a range of different methods exist for addressing misconduct and promoting integrity. These include, for example, leadership, proactive investigation, training, and organisational learning. Progress in tackling misconduct might be made in using disciplinary procedures alongside more proactivity and targeted methods, in an holistic approach to the problem. The interventions put in place in Merseyside Police provide a promising example of an holistic approach to misconduct. Based primarily on the analysis of complaints data, an officer referral scheme and communication strategy, the approach has led to a significant reduction in the number of recorded complaints.

The research points to a range of targeted recommendations.

The Home Office (in partnership) should:

- review and clarify the guidance to improve the practicality of the procedures;
- attempt to resolve some of the practical problems with the Code of Conduct (e.g. using examples and 'operating guidelines' to help illustrate and support the existing principles);
- extend the current mechanisms for communication to encourage the sharing of best practice and consistency between forces;
- monitor the use and impact of the new misconduct procedures on an ongoing basis;
- identify good practice and ways of improving efficiency and effectiveness of the current procedural framework; and
- be sensitive to the needs of forces and partner agencies in future policy changes, and provide extensive implementation support to assist the delivery of reforms.

Police Complaints and Discipline departments should:

- use the procedures within a broader, holistic approach to misconduct based on proactivity and problem-solving – these should be monitored and evaluated;
- ensure that poor performance is not processed under the new misconduct procedures – such issues need to be addressed by the appropriate department;
- monitor decisions at the investigation and hearing stages, and the use of written warnings, to ensure consistency;
- develop, with training departments, communication strategies to educate officers about ethical standards in an operational context and how to minimise the risks of misconduct;
- encourage active supervision at a local level in order to identify, monitor and challenge problems of officer conduct;
- strengthen the existing mechanisms for reporting misconduct; and
- take forward ways of helping to secure confidence in the disciplinary process (e.g. reducing delays, demonstrating openness and fairness, improving communication with complainants and officers).

 The full report 'An Evaluation of the New Police Misconduct Procedures', Home Office Online Report 10/03, by Paul Quinton, is available on the Home Office website at:
www.homeoffice.gov.uk/rds/pdfs2/rdsolr1003.pdf

The shooting of Jean Charles de Menezes

Jean Charles de Menezes was tragically shot by police at Stockwell tube station when he was mistaken for a potential suicide bomber. His killing has been investigated by the Independent Police Complaints Commission and it has passed its report into the case to the Crown Prosecution Service. At the inquest of Jean Charles's death, the coroner gave a direction to the jury that it could not return a verdict of unlawful killing, because he considered there to be insufficient evidence to support this verdict. Such a verdict could have paved the way for a criminal prosecution for murder or manslaughter against members of the police force. Ultimately, the jury at the inquest returned an open verdict having been dissatisfied by some of the evidence given by the police.

De Menezes Jury Rejects Police Account

13 December 2008, *Financial Times*

Megan Murphy

London's police force was plunged deeper into turmoil on Friday night after the inquest jury examining the shooting of an innocent Brazilian man mistaken for a suicide bomber determined that a catalogue of police failings contributed to his death.

The open verdict returned by the jury was the most damning available to it after the coroner had earlier ruled out a finding that Jean Charles de Menezes was unlawfully killed by police in July 2005 – two weeks after a series of deadly suicide bomb attacks ripped through the capital.

A lawyer representing de Menezes's family called on Friday for a separate perjury investigation after the jury's rejection of several aspects of police officers' sworn account of the shooting.

The 27-year-old electrician's family has vowed to press forward with a legal challenge to the coroner's controversial decision to ban an unlawful killing verdict.

The dramatic outcome of the inquest, which ran for 12 weeks and is estimated to have cost £6 m, is another blow to London's Metropolitan Police force severely tested in recent months by the departure of Sir Ian Blair as commissioner and a race discrimination case with a senior Asian officer.

Sir Paul Stephenson, the acting Met commissioner, apologised on Friday for de Menezes's death and said his force must accept 'full responsibility'.

'In the face of enormous challenges faced by officers on that day, we made the most terrible mistake', Sir Paul said. 'I am sorry.'

De Menezes was shot seven times in the head at point-blank range by specialist firearms officers on an underground train at Stockwell station in south London on 22 July 2005 after being mistaken for one of the men who launched failed suicide bomb attacks in the capital the day before.

Asked to respond to questions about the incident as part of their deliberations, members of the inquest jury decided they did not believe officers had shouted 'armed police' before opening fire on the unarmed Brazilian.

They also answered 'No' when asked if de Menezes had moved towards the officers before he was shot.

'The jury's verdict is a damning indictment of the multiple failures of the police and the lies they told', said Patricia Armani da Silva, de Menezes's cousin.

'It is clear from the verdict today that the jury could have gone further had they not been gagged by the coroner.'

Sir Michael Wright QC, the coroner who presided over the inquest, said he would be passing his own report on police practices to the acting commissioner, the Metropolitan Police Authority and the Home Secretary.

The Crown Prosecution Service, which decided in 2006 that no police officers should face criminal prosecution over the killing, said it would 'consider the verdicts and any fresh evidence very carefully and decide whether we need to review our decision'.

Criticism of the Independent Police Complaints Commission

The pressure group, Legal Action, has questioned the effectiveness of the Independent Police Complaints Commission to identify and respond to abuses of power by the police. In its monthly magazine in 2008, it published an article highlighting problems with the way the Commission worked in practice.

A Watchdog without Bite
Legal Action (2008)

Jon Robins

One Saturday morning in November 2005, Nicola Dennis, a 27-year-old single mother, was in her groundfloor maisonette in Woolwich, south east London, with a friend, Gemma, showing her the Christmas presents she had bought for her three children when the door-bell rang. Nicola Dennis opened the door but no one was there. She tried to close the door; the lock did not catch, and so she opened it again. Pandemonium broke out: armed police officers ordered both Nicola Dennis and her friend to put their hands in the air. 'Officers grabbed hold of me like a piece of meat whilst one of them walked Gemma over to the left of the house. They dragged me a distance from the house and threw me to the floor, kicked my legs open and started shouting. It was completely terrifying', recalls Nicola Dennis.

This incident happened a few months after the killing of Jean Charles de Menezes, who was shot dead by Metropolitan police officers at Stockwell tube station, south west London in July 2005. 'I thought I was going to die', recalls Nicola Dennis. 'I could not think of anything worse than having a policeman holding a gun to your head. They act on impulse, and if they think they are in danger they pull the trigger.' Nicola Dennis was on the pavement, face down, with her hands taped with plastic strips behind her back. She was detained for 40 minutes. She was innocently caught up in the search for the killers of PC Sharon Beshenivsky, who was shot dead as she responded to an alarm at a travel agent's shop in Bradford, West Yorkshire.

There are situations when a simple 'sorry' is not enough and, two-and-a-half years later, Nicola Dennis has yet to receive a proper explanation from the police, let alone an apology. Instead, she has been stuck in the police complaints process.

The IPCC was set up in April 2004 under the Police Reform Act (PRA) 2002 to replace a discredited Police Complaints Authority (PCA). The watchdog has been under fire since the killing of Jean Charles de Menezes. That criticism intensified this year when more than 100 members of the Police Action Lawyers' Group (PALG) withdrew their backing for the IPCC and Tony Murphy and Raju Bhatt, of Bhatt Murphy solicitors, resigned from the commission's advisory board as representatives of PALG.

An officer did come around that evening to visit Nicola Dennis, not to apologise but, as she recalled later in a statement to her solicitors, to explain that she happened to be 'in the wrong place at the wrong time'. The woman officer also told her that when the police investigate [the death of] one of their own they 'go in harder'. Nicola Dennis complained to the Metropolitan Police and they carried out a supervised investigation. That investigation came back in April 2007 with the sole finding that a stop and search form had not been completed.

The following month, Nicola Dennis appealed to the IPCC. Its response, in July 2007, was 'confusing and confused', reckons Marian Ellingworth of Tuckers solicitors. The watchdog conceded that the officer's actions were 'overzealous' and said that he deserved 'words of advice'. 'My client suffered a terrifying and wholly unnecessary ordeal. There was no justification for suspecting Nicola or using such a high level of force and no explanation as to why she was treated so differently from Gemma. The death of PC Beshenivsky was clearly a terrible tragedy but it does not give licence to officers to behave in this way', says Marian Ellingworth. 'Nicola's detention was either lawful or it was not. The IPCC seems to acknowledge that it was wrong in fact but, as a result of weak analysis, it failed to reach the only proper conclusion that it was wrong in law.' Nicola Dennis has applied for permission to proceed with judicial review of the IPCC's decision. 'We are defending our position', says an IPCC spokesperson.

Crisis in confidence

The failure to deal adequately with concerns about the actions of the police were themes running through both Lord Scarman's inquiry into the Brixton riots of the early 1980s and the Macpherson inquiry into the 1993 killing of Stephen Lawrence. 'Investigation of police officers by their own or another Police Service is widely regarded as unjust, and does not inspire public confidence', Sir William Macpherson wrote in his report (Chapter 47).

The IPCC is run by a chairperson, a deputy chairperson and 13 commissioners who, under the PRA, must not have served in the police force. Its investigators must handle the most serious complaints autonomously and have the same powers as police to make arrests and seize documents. Not only was the IPCC conceived as constitutionally independent but it would be run by independently-minded people such as Nick Hardwick, former chief executive of the Refugee Council, as its chairperson, and John Wadham, a former director of Liberty (now legal director at the Equality and Human Rights Commission), as its deputy chairperson.

Tony Murphy points out rightly that proper investigation of complaints against the police has 'long been held as essential for our democracy'. He says the leadership is 'failing to fulfil its responsibilities in relation to that vital task. Urgent action is needed if the IPCC is not to become another obstacle on the road to police accountability'.

In January 2008, Tony Murphy and Raju Bhatt wrote to Nick Hardwick pointing out that they had participated in its advisory board because they felt it could be 'an important means for the IPCC to take account of the interest of complainants and other stakeholders'. 'Almost four years on, it is a source of deep disappointment to find that our involvement has reaped little benefit for the complainants represented by members. Indeed, it has had a negative effect insofar as it has taken us away from our clients for nil return', they wrote.

Nick Hardwick denies that the IPCC is facing 'a crisis of confidence'. Instead, he insists it is business as usual and that the commission continues to deal with PALG members 'on a day-to-day basis without any problems. Sometimes we agree, sometimes we do not', he says.

PALG members are keen to say that the views expressed by Tony Murphy and Raju Bhatt are endorsed throughout the group. 'The IPCC should be playing an important constitutional role in holding the police to account when officers abuse their powers', says Jules Carey, head of the police action team at Tuckers. The IPCC is 'failing dismally' at this, he adds.

'Right from the start, when the IPCC took over the legacy cases from the PCA, our experience was that decision-making was poor and taken by people that were inexperienced or, to take a more cynical point of view, had a tendency to believe the police', reckons Stefano Ruis of south London firm Fisher Meredith. He cites the example of one client, Carole Tibbitts, who was arrested in May 2002 during a demonstration over a proposed development in Titnore Woods, Worthing. His client was prosecuted for assaulting a police officer but video evidence played in court told another story. 'The video shows the officer assaulting Carole, not the other way round', the solicitor says. Carole Tibbitts was acquitted.

The complaint was investigated by the local police before transferring to the IPCC. Stefano Ruis says: 'Despite the clear evidence of perjury, the IPCC agreed with the finding that the officer had "not deliberately lied" and that the officer received informal words of advice in light of the "very poor evidence given in court" and that a detailed assessment of his training needs was to be carried out.' He complained to the IPCC that the decision was 'not sustainable in law' but the commission upheld it. The solicitor then wrote a letter before claim before judicially reviewing the IPCC. John Wadham, the then deputy chairperson, looked at the case and referred it to a disciplinary panel which, according to the IPCC spokesman, 'ruled the case not proven'. Carole Tibbitts is pursuing a civil action against the police. What is Stefano Ruis's view of the IPCC? 'I have sympathy with many of my clients who have decided it is very much a waste of time', he replies. 'The only realistic way for my clients to seek redress and accountability is to resort to legal action in the courts.'

The families' experience

This is far from a local argument between the legal profession and the IPCC. Helen Shaw of Inquest, who is also on the IPCC's advisory board, shares the 'frustrations in trying to get the IPCC to listen to concerns from bereaved families over the quality of investigations and the way that the IPCC has approached families'. 'Our experience has been until very recently that the IPCC has paid lip-service to what we have been saying', she adds.

The first test case for the new watchdog came with the killing of Jean Charles de Menezes. The decision by the IPCC, which was announced on 21 December 2007, not to recommend disciplinary action against four senior officers as a result of the fatal shooting was described by Vivian Figuierdo, cousin of Jean Charles de Menezes, as 'a scandal'. 'Sadly, we have come to expect this from the IPCC – they had done nothing to hold the police to account for the killing of an innocent man', she said.

So what, in the de Menezes family's view, did the IPCC do wrong? Yasmin Khan, a spokesperson for the family, starts with its 'reluctance or inability to stand up' to Sir Ian Blair, the Metropolitan Police Commissioner and the Home Office after it was 'locked out' of the investigation in the immediate aftermath of the shooting. 'We already know CCTV footage from the platform went missing during this time, what other evidence could have been removed or tampered with?' she asks.

Then Yasmin Khan raises 'the failure to correct misinformation' in the press. 'The family was insisting to the world's press that their loved one did not have a bulky jacket or a bag or did not run and yet the IPCC said nothing.' It led to a leak of investigation papers by IPCC staff in August 2005. Yasmin Khan says: 'Had that leak not been made public, we would presumably not have known until over two years after the shooting that Jean did nothing wrong . . . It seems that the IPCC is just as capable of carrying out a whitewash as the discredited [PCA] it replaced.'

These are views echoed by the family of another high-profile police killing. In 1999, Roger Sylvester died after being restrained by six police officers who detained him under the Mental Health Act. 'We feel the IPCC has not changed much from the days of the PCA', says his cousin, Justin Waldron. In August 2007, the IPCC announced that no officers were going to be disciplined despite an inquest verdict of unlawful killing in 2003. 'We did not think it was a thorough investigation', Justin Waldron says. 'It means the police are allowed to avoid scrutiny and accountability by the IPCC washing its hands of a case.'

The perception of the IPCC as a toothless watchdog is apparently contributing to a loss of confidence in the community. Stafford Scott, who is an independent adviser to the Metropolitan police Trident Operational Command Unit (that investigates gun crime in the black community) and chairperson of the black independent advisory group to the police in Haringey, north London, believes that the body has 'no credibility'. 'The confidence of complainants in the group provides a barometer to public confidence', he says. 'We sue the police – that is what we do now. We do not go through the IPCC. We go through the civil courts.'

DISPUTE RESOLUTION

17 Paying for legal services

Introduction

This chapter looks at:

- the government's five-year plan for legal aid;
- the risks for the public of conditional fee agreements;
- the recognition in the case known as the 'McLibel Two' that access to a lawyer can be necessary in order for a person to have a fair trial under Article 6 of the European Convention on Human Rights;
- research into the impact of the employment of public defenders; and
- moves towards the introduction of new procurement methods for criminal defence services, known as 'best value tendering'.

Five-year plan for legal aid

The Community Legal Service was established in 2001 to distribute state funding for legal services. It has set out its five-year plan in a consultation paper, 'Making Legal Rights a Reality' (2005).

Making Legal Rights a Reality: A Summary

Community Legal Service

Community legal services and the Legal Services Commission

The Community Legal Service (CLS) was established by the Access to Justice Act 1999, which describes the CLS not as a single body or organisation but in terms of its purpose: principally to promote the availability of legal services – information, advice and representation – in civil law. The Legal Services Commission (LSC) has the duty of developing and maintaining the CLS. However, the CLS potentially includes all those who fund, provide or facilitate civil legal and advice services. Key stakeholders in the CLS therefore include local authorities and central government departments, the solicitor and advice sectors, as well as, of course, clients – those who actually receive the services. It is a central theme of this strategy that all of these stakeholders working together can achieve better results than working in isolation.

The core objective in promoting the availability of legal and advice services through the Community Legal Service (CLS), and in the LSC directly funding such help, is to protect and promote people's rights. In particular:

- to enable individuals to protect their fundamental rights in the face of action by public authorities and to receive a fair hearing in, for example, mental health and public law children cases;
- to help them resolve private law disputes such as private law family and clinical negligence cases, through negotiation and non-court based solutions where possible, and through access to the courts where this is the only, or most appropriate route; and
- to address problems, such as those relating to debt, welfare benefits, and housing, which contribute to social exclusion, and thereby helping to combat it.

Many of the people that the CLS helps are poor (and so unable to pay privately for access to legal services), socially excluded and dependent on help provided by other government and local authority agencies. Research also shows that where people have one problem capable of legal resolution they are likely to have others.

These client groups and areas of law have been our greatest focus in our wider role of establishing, developing and maintaining the CLS, and therefore form the primary focus of our work with other CLS stakeholders.

Our vision for the Community Legal Service

Our vision is for a Community Legal Service that places the client at its heart and focuses on the rights of individuals. We will develop legal and advice services to uphold these rights, targeted at people for whom, without its support, access to justice might not be possible. We also have a clear view that the CLS should have at its core a commitment to use the law to achieve positive change: in individual lives, in communities that share a common problem and across groups facing particular issues. It is also a vision which recognises that people need access to an integrated and seamless service, and do not face 'legal problems' but problems to which the law may offer a solution.

All of this fits within a context of acknowledging the contribution of many other services which work to address the same problems for clients. From health and education services to social care and family support services, it is clear that the CLS is but one of a package of tools to help individuals address the problems that they may face.

We want to develop the Community Legal Service so that it is:

- client-focused and accessible;
- independent;
- cost-effective and co-ordinated; and
- quality-assured.

The need for change

We consider that there are five key points arising from the evidence and analysis summarised in Volume Two of our consultation paper:

- There is a need for the LSC to provide clear leadership of the CLS including providing strategic direction and working with others to address the causes of problems;
- Not all Community Legal Service Partnerships (CLSPs) have delivered the evidence to allow for a more focused commissioning of legal and advice services to meet priority needs;
- There is a need for improved access to early legal advice for both existing clients and those who do not get advice about the problems that they face;
- Social welfare legal and advice services need to be provided in an integrated and seamless manner to have the most impact for the most deprived clients; and
- Currently services are not necessarily in the right places to meet identified priorities in a strategic manner. In future services should be commissioned against agreed targets on access as well as on the range of services delivered.

We wish to consult widely, with all CLS stakeholders, about the proposals and develop them further in partnership. However, we are clear that change is essential if we are to fully realise the potential benefits of the CLS for its clients and meet the key challenges that we have set out above.

The consultation paper of the Legal Services Commission 'Making Legal Rights a Reality' (2005) is available on the Legal Services Commission website: **www.legalservices.gov.uk/docs/civil_consultations/cls_strategy_vol1_english.pdf**

Conditional fee agreements (CFAs)

In 1990 the Courts and Legal Services Act made provision for the funding of litigation through the use of conditional fee agreements, more commonly known as 'no win, no fee' agreements. Such agreements have become increasingly common, but the Citizens Advice Bureau has carried out research in 2004 highlighting the dangers to the public of such financial arrangements.

No Win, No Fee, No Chance (December 2004)

James Sandbach, Citizens Advice Bureau

Summary and introduction

The challenge of access to compensation

1 Around 2.5 million people in the UK sustain accidental injuries every year. As a result, they may lose income or independence, and face lifestyle changes. Fault may rest with the driver of another car, a public authority such as a local authority or hospital, an employer or another individual whose action or inaction was the cause of the accident and the injury sustained. Under UK law, the liable party must compensate the injured person for any loss (i.e. the polluter pays).

2 Far from there having been a recent boom in consumers claiming compensation for injuries, only 31% of accident victims actually claim compensation using legal processes. Indeed, the actual number of claims for injuries following accidents has reduced since the new method of funding legal actions in personal injury cases, the 'conditional fee agreement', was rolled out, as the table in Appendix 1 shows. Since the abolition of legal aid for personal injury cases in 2000, CABx have handled over 130,000 enquiries relating to personal injury claims.

3 Seeking compensation for injuries and harm is not a social problem or the sign of the emergence of a 'compensation culture', but simply realising a civil and legal right. Where an individual has suffered injuries, a compensation award can help them to afford help and services to enable them to adjust and fully recover or make up for financial loss. People who have been injured may have lost pay, or even their jobs, as a result of being unwell. They may have experienced a dramatic change in lifestyle where social opportunities were closed off to them, they may have incurred costs to adapt their life and their homes to deal with the injury, whether during a period of recovery or permanently. They may also have experienced stress, depression and anxiety. Failure to address these problems can contribute to social exclusion.

4 A financial award of compensation (damages) from the person or body responsible can help to reduce public costs of services and benefits to the individual affected. Also, lessons learnt from claims ought to benefit others and the public at large by putting right the problems that caused the injury in the first place. Whether as employers, service providers or citizens, we all have obligations to avoid causing harm to others, and to take all reasonable steps to prevent such harm arising.

5 The effectiveness of any system for compensation is whether the system:

● ensures access to all who need to use the process;
● is effective at providing fair compensation and redress to individuals;

- is transparent;
- involves proportionate processes which do not involve excessive costs or procedures for either side;
- ensures quality of advice and representation for those people who need it;
- provides redress when legal advice is inadequate or things go wrong; and
- results in problems that caused the accident being solved.

Personal injury compensation is failing consumers

6 Citizens Advice's evidence is that these criteria are not currently being met by the system. For many thousands of people who have experienced accident or injuries through no fault of their own, often suffering disabling effects, the system is failing. It is extremely complex for an unrepresented individual to pursue a claim for compensation. They will need legal advice on their likely prospects of success and help collecting their evidence and putting their case, which may need to go to court. So pursuing a claim efficiently and effectively is likely to involve using legal services and incurring court costs at some stage.

7 Legal aid for these costs was withdrawn in 2000 and a new system of conditional fee agreements, colloquially known as 'no win no fee', was extended. In the new system, the legal and other costs of taking the case are covered by the 'losing' side. The consumer takes out insurance to cover themselves against the risk of having to meet both sides' costs if they lose.

8 The complex financial and legal processes involved are often misunderstood by consumers, and consumers' needs can be misunderstood by the service providers. There is widespread mis-selling of legal and insurance products, and consumers are often induced into signing conditional fee agreements (CFAs) inappropriately. On this basis alone policy makers should be wary of extending conditional fee funding to other areas of civil law. CAB evidence is that the withdrawal of legal aid and the advent of conditional fees ('no win, no fee') has contributed to a system which involves relatively high legal costs and delays.

9 Problems with the present system include:

- Consumers are subjected to **high-pressure sales tactics** by unqualified intermediaries introducing them to a legal process. **Inappropriate marketing and sales practices** are used – for example, with salesmen approaching accident victims in hospital.
- Few consumers seem to understand the **risks and liabilities** they are exposing themselves to as the risks of conditional fee agreements have not been clearly explained to them at the outset by salesmen. Consumers are misled into thinking the system will be genuinely 'no win no fee' but can often find that costs are hidden and unpredictable.
- Loan financed insurance premiums, in addition to other legal costs, can often erode the value of claimants' compensation. In some cases consumers even owe money at the end of the process. This turns the whole claims process into a **zero-sum gain** for consumers and denies effective access to compensation.
- The system does not deliver anything effective to consumers on **rehabilitation**. International comparisons show that the UK trails behind other countries in getting injury victims back to work. The arduous legal processes and money only results of our current system of compensation often means that victims are not being sufficiently helped to resume a normal life in both society and the workplace. Over time this failure increases the overall cost both to society and the public purse and needs to be addressed.
- Conditional fee agreements create perverse incentives for the legal profession and provide the conditions for **cherry-picking** of high-value cases with high chances of success. This

results in lawyers refusing to take on good small claims which may nevertheless be of enormous financial and personal significance to the client, thus denying access to justice.
- There is no effective joined-up **system for regulating** conditional fee arrangements to ensure consumers are protected on both quality of advice and costs. In particular, the activities of claims management companies seem to fall largely outside the system of regulation yet they are increasingly the primary introducer of the consumer to the claims process as well as a complex package of financial services – consequently the information and advice they give is of critical significance to the consumer. A voluntary code is still in its infancy.

10 This report looks at the experience of CAB clients who have pursued personal injury compensation through CFAs. Typically the consumers we help are on low incomes and may often be vulnerable because they have suffered some level of personal physical injury for which compensation could be available if elements of fault liability and causation can be established.

11 The report proceeds to examine the evidence, the policy options for reform and alternative methods of redress in personal injury cases. Although the former system of funding personal injury claims only represented a net cost to the public of 4% of legal aid annual expenditure, **we do not advocate a simple return to public funding for personal injury cases based on current legal aid eligibility criteria**. Legal aid is very restricted and means tested, and by definition was not actually of assistance to many consumers.

12 However, there are significant problems in this market which need remedying so as to provide better protection and service to individual consumers, improve access to justice and outcomes and give the public a better system for dealing with personal injury compensation. Citizens Advice is also concerned about the emerging policy direction to extend the use of conditional fee agreements as a method of funding legal cases in other areas of law, for example with public law cases.

13 Key messages for reform of funding for personal injury cases include:

- Claims managers, intermediaries and organisations introducing consumers to legal processes should be subject to independent regulation. Regulation should cover competence, quality and costs and secure a proper focus on protecting the consumer, who is after all funding the system.
- The Financial Services Authority and the Office of Fair Trading should produce a joint policy on how they will regulate sales of linked insurance and credit products designed to fund legal actions.
- The Financial Ombudsman Service and the Legal Services Ombudsman should co-ordinate complaints procedures about conditional fee agreements so that there is a 'one stop shop' for any consumer complaints.
- There should be statutory regulation of the form and content of CFAs.
- The Office of Fair Trading should undertake a market study into the market for conditional fee agreements, to establish whether this market works effectively for consumers.
- The Department for Constitutional Affairs should undertake a feasibility study into whether a contingency legal aid fund could be a viable alternative for funding personal injury cases.
- The Department for Constitutional Affairs should review the legal costs system for personal injury in civil courts to examine whether there are any alternatives to frontloading most of the costs.

- The government should establish a task force on compensation to look at the viability of introducing ADR or no fault based systems to deal with personal injury cases, and review how to achieve fair rehabilitative compensation and proportionality between costs and damages.
- The Department for Constitutional Affairs should evaluate the impact of the introduction of conditional fee agreements on personal injury claims before proceeding to replace legal aid with CFA-funding for other types of cases.

The report 'No Win, No Fee, No Chance' (2004) is available on the website of the Citizens Advice Bureau:

www.citizensadvice.org.uk/index/campaigns/social_policy/evidence_reports/ er_legalaffairs/no_win_no_fee_no_chance

The 'Mclibel Two'

In certain situations the government is obliged by the European Convention on Human Rights to award parties involved in litigation state funding. This right was highlighted by the case of **Steel and Morris** v **UK** (2005), which has come to be known as the 'McLibel Two' case. The defendants were two environmental campaigners who had distributed leaflets outside McDonald's restaurants. These leaflets criticised the nutritional content of the restaurants' food. McDonald's sued the two defendants for defamation. The defendants were refused legal aid because it is not generally available for defamation cases. They therefore represented themselves throughout the proceedings, with only limited help from some sympathetic lawyers who provided a small amount of assistance for free. McDonald's was represented by a team of specialist lawyers. The libel trial lasted for 313 days and was the longest civil action in English legal history. The defendants lost the case and were ordered to pay £60,000 in damages (later reduced to £40,000 on appeal). They challenged the fairness of the UK proceedings in the European Court of Human Rights. That challenge was successful. The European Court held that the 'McLibel Two' had not had a fair trial in breach of Article 6 of the European Convention on Human Rights.

Steel and Morris v UK (2005), European Court of Human Rights

The Court's assessment

59 The Court recalls that the Convention is intended to guarantee practical and effective rights. This is particularly so of the right of access to court in view of the prominent place held in a democratic society by the right to a fair trial (see the **Airey** v **Ireland** judgment of 9 October 1979, Series A no. 32, § 24). It is central to the concept of a fair trial, in civil as in criminal proceedings, that a litigant is not denied the opportunity to present his or her case effectively before the court (ibid.) and that he or she is able to enjoy equality of arms with the opposing side (see, among many other examples, **De Haes** v **Belgium**, judgment of 24 February 1997, *Reports* 1997-I, § 53).

60 Article 6 § 1 leaves to the State a free choice of the means to be used in guaranteeing litigants the above rights. The institution of a legal aid scheme constitutes one of those means but there are others, such as for example simplifying the applicable procedure . . .

61 The question whether the provision of legal aid is necessary for a fair hearing must be determined on the basis of the particular facts and circumstances of each case and will depend *inter alia* upon the importance of what is at stake for the applicant in the proceedings, the complexity of the relevant law and procedure and the applicant's capacity to represent him or herself effectively . . .

62 The right of access to a court is not, however, absolute and may be subject to restrictions, provided that these pursue a legitimate aim and are proportionate (see **Ashingdane v United Kingdom**, judgment of 28 May 1985, Series A no. 93, pp 24–25, § 57). It may therefore be acceptable to impose conditions on the grant of legal aid based, *inter alia*, on the financial situation of the litigant or his or her prospects of success in the proceedings (see **Munro**, above). Moreover, it is not incumbent on the State to seek through the use of public funds to ensure total equality of arms between the assisted person and the opposing party, as long as each side is afforded a reasonable opportunity to present his or her case under conditions that do not place him or her at a substantial disadvantage *vis-à-vis* the adversary . . .

63 The Court must examine the facts of the present case with reference to the above criteria. First, as regards what was at stake for the applicants, it is true that, in contrast to certain earlier cases where the Court has found legal assistance to have been necessary for a fair trial (for example, **Airey** and **P, C and S**, both cited above), the proceedings at issue here were not determinative of important family rights and relationships. The Convention organs have observed in the past that the general nature of a defamation action, brought to protect an individual's reputation, is to be distinguished, for example, from an application for judicial separation, which regulates the legal relationship between two individuals and may have serious consequences for any children of the family (see **McVicar**, § 61 and **Munro**, both cited above).

However, it must be recalled that the applicants did not choose to commence defamation proceedings, but acted as defendants to protect their right to freedom of expression, a right accorded considerable importance under the Convention (see paragraph 87 below). Moreover, the financial consequences for the applicants of failing to verify each defamatory statement complained of were significant. McDonald's claimed damages up to GBP 100,000 and the awards actually made, even after reduction by the Court of Appeal, were high when compared to the applicants' low incomes: GBP 36,000 for the first applicant, who was, at the time of the trial, a bar-worker earning approximately GBP 60 a week, and GBP 40,000 for the second applicant, an unwaged single parent . . . McDonald's have not, to date, attempted to enforce payment of the awards, but this was not an outcome which the applicants could have foreseen or relied upon.

64 As for the complexity of the proceedings, the Court recalls its finding in the **McVicar** judgment . . . that the English law of defamation and rules of civil procedure applicable in that case were not sufficiently complex as to necessitate the grant of legal aid. The proceedings defended by Mr McVicar required him to prove the truth of a single, principal allegation, on the basis of witness and expert evidence, some of which was excluded as a result of his failure to comply with the rules of court. He had also to scrutinise evidence submitted on behalf of the plaintiff and to cross-examine the plaintiff's witnesses and experts, in the course of a trial which lasted just over two weeks.

65 The proceedings defended by the present applicants were of a quite different scale. The trial at first instance lasted 313 court days, preceded by 28 interlocutory applications. The appeal hearing lasted 23 days. The factual case which the applicants had to prove was highly complex, involving 40,000 pages of documentary evidence and 130 oral witnesses, including a number of experts dealing with a range of scientific questions, such as nutrition, diet, degenerative disease and food safety. Certain of the issues were held by the domestic courts to be too complicated for a jury properly to understand and assess. The detailed nature and complexity of the factual issues are further illustrated by the length of the judgments of the trial court and the Court of Appeal, which ran in total to over 1,100 pages . . .

66 Nor was the case straightforward legally. Extensive legal and procedural issues had to be resolved before the trial judge was in a position to decide the main issue, including the meanings to be attributed to the words of the leaflet, the question whether the applicants were responsible for its publication, the distinction between fact and comment, the admissibility of evidence and the amendment of the Statement of Claim. Overall, some 100 days were devoted to legal argument, resulting in 38 separate written judgments (ibid.).

67 Against this background, the Court must assess the extent to which the applicants were able to bring an effective defence despite the absence of legal aid. In the above-mentioned **McVicar** case (§§ 53 and 60), it placed weight on the facts that Mr McVicar was a well-educated and experienced journalist, and that he was represented during the pre-trial and appeal stages by a solicitor specialising in defamation law, from whom he could have sought advice on any aspects of the law or procedure of which he was unsure.

68 The present applicants appear to have been articulate and resourceful; in the words of the Court of Appeal, they conducted their case 'forcefully and with persistence' (see paragraph 33 above), and they succeeded in proving the truth of a number of the statements complained of. It is not in dispute that they could not afford to pay for legal representation themselves, and that they would have fulfilled the financial criteria for the grant of legal aid. They received some help on the legal and procedural aspects of the case from barristers and solicitors acting *pro bono*: their initial pleadings were drafted by lawyers, they were given some advice on an *ad hoc* basis, and they were represented during five of the pre-trial hearings and on three occasions during the trial, including the appeal to the Court of Appeal against the trial judge's grant of leave to McDonald's to amend the Statement of Claim (see paragraph 16 above). In addition, they were able to raise a certain amount of money by donation, which enabled them, for example, to buy transcripts of each day's evidence 25 days later (ibid.). For the bulk of the proceedings, however, including all the hearings to determine the truth of the statements in the leaflet, they acted alone.

69 The Government have laid emphasis on the considerable latitude afforded to the applicants by the judges of the domestic courts, both at first instance and on appeal, in recognition of the handicaps under which the applicants laboured. However, the Court considers that, in an action of this complexity, neither the sporadic help given by the volunteer lawyers nor the extensive judicial assistance and latitude granted to the applicants as litigants in person, was any substitute for competent and sustained representation by an experienced lawyer familiar with the case and with the law of libel . . . The very length of the proceedings is, to a certain extent, a testament to the applicants' lack of skill and experience. It is, moreover, possible that had the applicants been represented they would have been successful in one or more of the interlocutory matters of which they specifically complain, such as the admission in evidence of the Haringey affidavit (see paragraph 21 above). Finally, the disparity between the respective levels of legal assistance enjoyed by the applicants and McDonald's (see paragraph 16 above) was of such a degree that it could not have failed, in this exceptionally demanding case, to have given rise to unfairness, despite the best efforts of the judges at first instance and on appeal.

70 It is true that the Commission declared inadmissible an earlier application under, *inter alia*, Article 6 § 1 by these same applicants (**HS and DM** *v* **the United Kingdom**, no. 21325/93, Commission decision of 5 May 1993, unreported), observing that 'they seem to be making a tenacious defence against McDonald's, despite the absence of legal aid . . .'. That decision was, however, adopted over a year before the start of the trial, at a time when the length, scale and complexity of the proceedings could not reasonably have been anticipated.

71 The Government argued that, even if legal aid had been in principle available for the defence of defamation actions, it might well not have been granted in a case of this kind, or the amount awarded might have been capped or the award made subject to other conditions. The Court is not, however, persuaded by this argument. It is, in the first place, a matter of pure speculation whether, if legal aid had been available, it would have been granted in the applicants' case. More importantly, if legal aid had been refused or made subject to stringent financial or other conditions, substantially the same Convention issue would have confronted the Court, namely whether the refusal of legal aid or the conditions attached to its grant were such as to impose an unfair restriction on the applicants' ability to present an effective defence.

72 In conclusion, therefore, the Court finds that the denial of legal aid to the applicants deprived them of the opportunity to present their case effectively before the court and contributed to an unacceptable inequality of arms with McDonald's. There has, therefore, been a violation of Article 6 § 1.

The judgment **Steel and Morris** *v* **United Kingdom** (2005), application number 6841/01, is available on the website for the European Court of Human Rights at: **http://cmiskp.echr.coe.int/tkp197/view.asp?item=3&portal=hbkm&action=html &highlight=Steel%20%7C%20v%20%7C%20Morris&sessionid=5865189&skin= hudoc-en**

Public defenders

A controversial innovation of the present Labour government has been to introduce public defenders. These are state employees who are employed to represent defendants in criminal trials. Critics have expressed concern that these lawyers will not be sufficiently independent of the state, which is responsible for bringing the prosecution. Research has been carried out by Cyrus Tata and others evaluating the success of the Public Defence Solicitors in Scotland.

Note: in the extract, the abbreviation 'FN' in square brackets refers to a footnote reproduced at the end of the text.

Does Mode of Delivery Make a Difference to Criminal Case Outcomes and Clients' Satisfaction?
The Public Defence Solicitor Experiment

Cyrus Tata and others

Few subjects give vent to as much passion among criminal lawyers in the United Kingdom as the introduction of 'staff' or 'salaried' lawyers to run alongside delivery by 'private' lawyers. Vociferous debate about independence, quality, cost and client satisfaction accompanied the introduction of a three-year pilot scheme to test a new Public Defence Solicitors' Office in Scotland. Its introduction was accompanied by acrimony at both ground and senior level, with for example, the Edinburgh Bar Association excluding the PDSO from membership.

In 1998, the Public Defence Solicitors' Office ('PDSO') was established in Edinburgh. As part of a 'mixed economy', the PDSO was intended as a pilot scheme to test and evaluate the provision of criminal assistance through solicitors employed directly by the Scottish Legal Aid Board. In its enabling legislation [FN 15] the Government was forced to make important concessions. The legislation gave the Board authority to set up a single office, employing no more than six solicitors, for an experimental period of five years. The Act also required that the experiment be independently monitored and a report had to be laid before the Scottish Parliament within three years of the start of the Office, setting out the results of the study.

In January 1999, following an exploratory methodological study, [FN 16] the authors were commissioned to carry out an independent evaluation of the PDSO. We were asked to compare the delivery of legally-aided criminal legal assistance through the PDSO with delivery through private practitioners in Edinburgh, paid on a case-by-case basis under the legal aid scheme. The comparison was according to four criteria:

- the quality of services provided (especially case outcomes);
- cost effectiveness;
- client satisfaction; and
- the contribution of each delivery method to the efficiency of the criminal justice system, including the impact on the courts, the procurator fiscal service, [FN 17] the police and the judiciary.

Due to space constraints, this article will be restricted to reporting on the results in relation to 'quality': specifically case outcomes (limited here to conviction/acquittal and sentence);

and secondly to client satisfaction. Findings on cost effectiveness and contribution to the efficiency of the criminal justice system are available in the full report. [FN 18]

. . .

The imposition of 'direction': official expectation and practice

To help the PDSO rapidly build up its volume of casework, the government decided that the Scottish Legal Aid Board ('SLAB') should 'direct' a random sample of accused people to use the PDSO. The sample was based on birth month. From October 1, 1998 to July 1, 2000, all January or February born people prosecuted under summary jurisdiction before Edinburgh District or Sheriff Court lost their normal entitlement to summary legal aid through a private solicitor. Instead, they were 'directed' to use the PDSO.

. . .

Comparison of process and case outcomes achieved by public and private defence solicitors

A major element of the evaluation was to look at the outcome of cases. We compared how public defenders and private legal aid solicitors processed cases through the courts and what impact this had on the result, both in terms of conviction and sentence.

Outcomes have been the focus of several Canadian studies comparing staff lawyers with their private legal aid counterparts. Reviewing research in Canada, the Canadian Department of Justice has stated that staff lawyers: spend less time per case than private lawyers; tend to plead clients guilty earlier and more often, but nonetheless achieve similar outcomes in terms of conviction and sentence. [FN 26]

Case trajectory: influences on solicitors

A common criticism made of Scottish summary procedure is that guilty pleas occur too late. From 1990 to 1995, the Scottish Office sponsored a research programme into summary legal aid. One of the central questions addressed by the research was how far the legal aid provisions influenced case progression. Did the differential payments between advice and assistance and summary legal aid encourage solicitors to advise an initial plea of not guilty, only to advise a change of plea before trial? Elaine Samuel argued strongly that most late pleas were driven by system factors rather than simply by solicitors' attempts to maximise their income through 'supplier-induced demand'. [FN 27]

The introduction of the PDSO allowed this vexed question to be revisited, affording greater methodological control than had been possible under a judicare only system of payment. Comparing caseloads as a whole, would PDSO clients be more likely to plead guilty earlier than the clients of private solicitors?

Like other studies of the lower courts around the world, most people going through the Edinburgh summary courts plead guilty eventually. Among non-directed clients using the normal legal aid scheme, 76% pled guilty, either in whole or in part; 11% were abandoned by the prosecution and only 13% went to trial. The plea rate for PDSO clients was slightly higher (at 78%). However, this was not the main difference between the public and private solicitor client groups.

The main difference was that PDSO clients pleaded guilty earlier. PDSO cases were more likely to be resolved at the pleading diet or intermediate diet, and less likely to be resolved on the day of the trial, either before or after evidence was led. This finding was robust. In the court samples, 59% of private non-directed cases were resolved at the pleading or intermediate diet, compared with 65% of PDSO cases. When we used multiple regression analysis to control for known variations in cases, the difference widened. The analysis suggested that, had the PDSO dealt with similar cases to those handled by private solicitors, over 70% would have been resolved at pleading or intermediate diet (a difference that is highly statistically significant at the 99% level).

Advice on pleading

It has been suggested that public defenders might pressurise clients to plead guilty – a criticism that emerged from both the Canadian literature and from private practice solicitors in Edinburgh. In interviews PDSO solicitors described similar factors to other private solicitors: bail, the identity of the sheriff and the fraught nature of the court. They were at pains to point out that they would never pressurise a client to plead guilty against their will. However, they were also aware that they did not operate under the same financial incentives as private practice. One PDSO solicitor described a scenario in which a client offered to plead to two out of four charges:

> If I was a private practitioner, if I plead not guilty for him and he gets bail and I go along the next day to sort it out with the Fiscal's Office having got legal aid, I get paid £500. If I sort it out there and then at the custody court I might not get paid anything or I'll probably get paid £25 for filling in a pink form. So I've got a choice – I can get paid £25 or £500. The case will take a couple more days to sort out, the client will be just as happy. (PDSO solicitor interview)

Interviews with private and PDSO solicitors revealed differences in tone and emphasis. Decisions over plea are complex and driven by a range of factors. Technically, the decision rests with the accused, but is influenced by advice from the defence solicitor who in turn is influenced by the actual or expected actions of the prosecution and the expected reaction of the sheriff. PDSO solicitors felt that they were now more focused on getting on with the case. On the other hand, we found no evidence to suggest that PDSO solicitors put explicit pressure on clients to plead guilty. None of our client interview respondents complained about being 'pressured' to plead guilty. The only criticism made of the PDSO was that they were too neutral and too willing to go along with whatever the client decided. This view is consistent with the PSDO's insistence that:

> the one overriding principle is that we would never make someone plead guilty that wanted to plead not guilty. If at the end of the day the client wants to plead not guilty and wants to go to trial, that's his decision. (PDSO solicitor interview 2000)

If the PDSO did influence their clients to plead guilty more often or to plead guilty earlier, it was through the lack of positive support to maintain a not guilty plea rather than through any direct pressure to plead guilty.

We asked clients whether their solicitor had advised them on how to plead: almost three-quarters (74%) said that they had, a figure that was identical for both PDSO and private clients. There was, however, a sizeable and statistically significant difference [FN 28] between directed and volunteer PDSO clients: only 67% of directed clients reported being advised about how to plead, compared with 82% of volunteers. In our interviews, some directed clients complained that their solicitor had been too neutral: 'I got the feeling that he was pleading not guilty solely on my behalf without any input at all.' This also links in with solicitors' perceptions that the direction system meant that they were 'living in a goldfish bowl' and had to be 'very, very, careful in everything' that they said (PDSO solicitor interview).

So far the results are consistent with those reported by Canadian studies. 'Staff' (public) lawyers tended to resolve cases at an earlier stage of the process than their private counterparts, usually through a guilty plea. The change in economic incentives involved in receiving a salary rather than a legal aid payment appeared to produce a change in behaviour, which, although difficult to detect in a single individual case, was measurable over comparable caseloads as a whole.

Do PDSO and private solicitors achieve different conviction outcomes?

What effect (if any) do earlier pleas have on the overall conviction rate? The Canadian studies found that although the clients of staff lawyers pled guilty more often, this had no effect on the conviction rate. [FN 29] It would appear that staff lawyers correctly predicted the outcome of cases, and only advised guilty pleas in cases that would have ended in a conviction in any event.

In Edinburgh the conviction rate was high for both samples. Most accused proceeded against summarily in the sheriff or district courts are convicted of at least something. We compared cases handled by the PDSO with those handled by private solicitors for non-directed cases. Given that the PDSO handled slightly different types of case, it was necessary to control for variations in case (including client) characteristics. Multiple regression analyses were conducted to identify what features led to no conviction as opposed to a conviction of some sort (whether as libelled or partial). [FN 30] Controlling for these intrinsic case factors, we found that PDSO cases were more likely to result in conviction. This contrasts with the Canadian studies (which did not control for intrinsic case factors or to a more limited extent). Controlling for intrinsic case features through modelling techniques, the odds of a PDSO client being convicted were 52% higher than similar cases handled by private solicitors, a finding that was statistically significant at the 95% level. In practical terms, such a difference means that, according to the model controlling for case variables, PDSO representation appears to have increased the chances of a client being convicted (of at least one charge even if reduced), from around 83% to 88%. [FN 31]

In general, there was a marked attrition effect. The longer an accused persisted with a plea of not guilty, the greater their chances of not being convicted. The chances that the prosecution would be abandoned were almost negligible at the pleading diet (at 2%). They rose slightly at the intermediate diet (to 4–6%), and became appreciably greater just before the trial started, when the prosecution discovered whether the witnesses had appeared. Among private, nondirected cases reaching the day of trial, 16% of cases were abandoned. The chances of no conviction were highest after evidence had been led (at 38–44%). PDSO clients who pled guilty at the pleading diet or intermediate diet exchanged the small but measurable chance of a later acquittal or the case being dropped for the certainty of immediate conviction for something, at least. [FN 32]

The quantitative data suggested that PDSO solicitors were more likely to conclude a case with a mixed plea: 55% of all PDSO guilty pleas were mixed, compared to 50% of all private, non-directed cases. However, when one controlled for case characteristics, the finding was only significant at the 90% level. [FN 33]

Three-quarters of all pleas made just before trial were mixed, a rate that was similar for both PDSO and private solicitor cases. Thus, it seems that the PDSO was more proactive in agreeing pleas earlier in the process. The effect this had on the total number of negotiated pleas was partially offset by the greater tendency of private solicitor cases to hold out until the day of the trial.

There was no great difference in the proportion of clients convicted at each stage of the process. Instead, the higher conviction rate was linked to the apparent PDSO tendency to facilitate earlier pleas of guilty. During interviews, both private solicitors and fiscals suggested that if one pushed a case to trial, there was a good chance that the prosecution would collapse. The main reason for waiting until the trial diet was that 'you get a better deal just before trial'. A fiscal put this point clearly:

> A case goes through three stages: when you mark it [i.e. at the time of the complaint], you think, well, that'll prove. When you look at it later and cite the witnesses etc you think, it might prove. And when you read it through at trial you think it will never prove. So it's always easier to [negotiate at the trial diet] and I think most defence agents will tell you that. The time for [the defence agent] to put the screws on to get a good plea is probably . . . on the morning of the trial. (Fiscal interview)

The interviewee was correct. Most defence agents did tell us that busy fiscals, faced with more trials than they could possibly handle, were particularly amenable to lesser pleas immediately before trial.

There was, however, a downside to pleading guilty immediately before trial when all the prosecution witnesses had been forced to appear. Such strategies may irritate sheriffs. Several solicitors noted that sheriffs did occasionally object to such late changes of plea: 'the sheriff might ask the witnesses into court and go through the lawyer like a dose of salts'. Most felt, however, that this rarely trumped the benefits of a late plea. In the view of one solicitor, this sometimes amounted to 'a bit of footstamping that isn't necessarily convincing'. Another solicitor agreed:

> The sheriff still has to look over his back and think, well, I've got to sentence this person on what he did, and justify that to the Court of Appeal – and not lose my rag and say this is ridiculous. (Private solicitor interview)

Furthermore, solicitors could use a last minute plea bargain to divert the attention of an otherwise irate sheriff. On the day of trial, fiscals were often desperate to reduce the number of trials. As a fiscal put it: 'we go to trial court with more cases than we can hope to prosecute, so we rely on some dropping out'. Thus it was usually possible for a defence agent to secure some reduction in the complaint, even if it was only in deletions of minor words in the charges. This would be enough to show that the client was not pleading guilty as libelled. As one solicitor put it: 'it gives you something to say' so that 'you feel you don't have to explain why you didn't plead guilty until the trial diet'.

. . .

Clients' evaluations of public defence solicitors

Can criminal clients make valid judgments of their solicitors?

Whether or not it is in a client's best interests to 'hold out' as long as possible, (possibly while remanded in custody), and endure the accompanying anxiety, or, plead guilty early to at least a reduced charge is highly debatable, but lawyers play a pivotal role in shaping that decision. Across the English-speaking world most of the literature on the relationship between defence lawyers and their clients has highlighted the passivity of clients whose wishes and expectations are managed by their defence lawyers. [FN 42] Studies of civil work also stress the importance lawyers place on managing their image with the client.

It may be therefore that clients tend to be in a poor position to judge their solicitors. However, there has been less work investigating what clients themselves thought. One of the largest qualitative studies of clients was carried out by Ericson and Barenek in an anonymous Canadian city. They described defendants as 'dependants' in the criminal process, whose main characteristics were low expectations, forced trust and an inability to judge the service they receive. Failing any other means to judge the service, clients fell back on outcome as the main evaluative criterion. Where negative feelings were expressed, it was frequently because the outcome did not match their expectations. [FN 43] At the start of the PDSO study many solicitors dismissed the idea that their clients were capable of judging the performance of their defence lawyer; a point which sits uneasily with the great importance the same solicitors attached to client choice in selecting or returning to a defence solicitor.

However, the idea that clients judge mainly on outcome has been disputed. Large-scale quantitative work suggests that process – that is, the way that clients are treated by the system – is very important to clients. For example, Casper, Tyler and Fisher analysed data from those convicted of felonies in three US cities. They concluded that clients' evaluations of their treatment by the criminal justice process did not depend entirely on the sentence received: 'rather their sense of fairness – in terms of both procedural and distributive justice . . .'. [FN 44]

In their study of legal aid clients in England and Wales, Somerland and Wall found that clients judged solicitors on a variety of interpersonal as well as technical criteria. Interpersonal criteria were judged highly important, [FN 45] a point which was strongly highlighted in the PDSO client interviews. Support, honesty and communication were all seen as crucial. Their study echoes research with matrimonial clients [FN 46] in suggesting that, unless solicitors established good rapport with clients, they would fail to elicit enough information to perform a technically competent service.

Our interviews with clients confirmed the important finding of earlier work that criminal accused are normally passive spectators in the criminal process. Clients described how stressful the experience was and how little they understood of it. They played only a small part in the process outside the court and were largely silent within it. Clients readily said that they could not judge the technical aspects of what lawyers did. Indeed, clients' judgements about their solicitors were not primarily made on the basis of outcomes but on assessments of how good their solicitors were at: listening to them; believing them; being able to explain the process; being accessible; 'standing up for' them, etc.

Reflections on the evaluation of case outcomes and client satisfaction

In terms of case outcomes, the data presented here summarise four key findings from the comparison of PDSO and private solicitor performance. These are:

(1) The PDSO was more likely than private solicitors acting for non-directed clients to resolve the case at the pleading diet or intermediate diet, and less likely to go to a trial diet.

(2) PDSO cases were more likely to end in a conviction for something than cases handled by private solicitors for non-directed clients.

(3) Even though PDSO cases were slightly (but statistically significantly) more likely to plead guilty and do so earlier than private solicitors, there was no difference for otherwise similar cases in the rate of custodial sentences imposed on PDSO clients compared with non-directed clients.

(4) After the end of direction PDSO clients and private solicitor clients expressed broadly similar levels of satisfaction, although clients tended to complain that their PDSO solicitor was 'too businesslike'.

From a managerial perspective, the fact that public defenders resolved cases at an earlier stage has advantages. It has the potential to save legal aid costs and also reduced court and prosecution costs, inconveniencing fewer witnesses. Clients were spared the wait and worry of repeated court diets and were less likely to be held in detention pending the resolution of their case. On the other hand, earlier resolution also led to a slight (but statistically robust) higher rate in convictions. By pleading guilty at the pleading diet or intermediate diet, rather than holding out until the day of the trial, clients substituted the certainty of conviction for the possibility that the prosecution case would collapse. A crucial mediating factor is the client's level of anxiety and attitude to risk.

What is particularly significant from the Edinburgh study is that it would appear that clients may not have benefited (in terms of sentence passed) from pleading guilty and doing so earlier than holding out to the trial. It would be useful to pursue this question further to see whether this apparent lack of overall sentence 'discounting' masks specific types of cases where there may indeed be sentence 'discounting'.

This study also highlights that the decision about how to plead is not a simple matter of fact under the overall control of the accused/defendant. [FN 50] Despite the vociferous public denials by their leaders, in having to make ethically indeterminate judgements, solicitors appear to have been routinely influenced in significant part (albeit not exclusively) by the incentives under which they operate.

Footnotes

. . .

FN 15. Now Legal Aid (Scotland) Act 1986, section 28A, sections inserted by the Crime and Punishment (Scotland) Act 1997, section 50.

FN 16. T. Goriely, C. Tata, P. Duff, A. Henry, S. Anderson, E. Samuel, A. Sherr, R. Moorhead (1998) 'Evaluation of the Pilot Public Defence Solicitor Project: Report of Feasibility Study', presented to the Scottish Office.

FN 17. Scotland has a distinct prosecution service. Summary cases are prosecuted by procurators fiscal and their deputies – colloquially known as 'fiscals'.

FN 18. T. Goriely, P. McCrone, P. Duff, M. Knapp, A. Henry, C. Tata, B. Lancaster, 'The Public Defence Solicitors' Office in Edinburgh: Independent Evaluation', p 271, presented to the Scottish Parliament.

. . .

FN 26. Canadian Department of Justice (1994). See also P. Brantingham, 'The Burnaby, British Columbia Experimental Public Defender Project: An Evaluation' (Department of Justice Canada, 1981).

FN 27. E. Samuel 'Criminal Legal Aid Expenditure: Supplier or System Driven? The case of Scotland', in R. Young and D. Wall (eds) *Access to Criminal Justice: Legal Aid, Lawyers and the Defence of Liberty* (Blackstone Press, 1996). On supplier-induced demand, see A. Gray, P. Fenn, N. Rickman (1996) 'Controlling Lawyers' Costs through Standard Fees: An Economic Analysis', in R. Young and D. Wall (eds) *Access to Criminal Justice: Legal Aid, Lawyers and the Defence of Liberty* (Blackstone Press, London, 1996); see also G. Bevan, T. Holland, M. Partington, 'Organising Cost Effective Access to Justice', Social Market Foundation Memorandum, July 1994.

FN 28. P.0.031.

FN 29. The Manitoba evaluation, for example, found that, after controlling for prior record and type of case, 72.0% of staff cases ended with a conviction of some sort, compared to 71% of private clients (R. Sloan, 'Legal Aid in Manitoba' (Department of Justice Canada, 1987)). Similarly, in the Burnaby experiment, 60% of clients of both the staff office and the local bar were convicted (Brantingham, 1981), op. cit.

FN 30. Two features in particular that were significantly more likely to be associated with a conviction were prosecution in the sheriff court (as opposed to the district court) and multiple charges. Compared to road traffic cases, offences of violence were significantly less likely to lead to conviction. Cases with multiple accused were also less likely to result in a conviction. However, most offender characteristics (such as age or sex) did not affect the chances of conviction.

FN 31. If, as discussed earlier, there were a bias against guilty pleas in cases reaching the PDSO, the effect would be even stronger.

FN 32. One possible hypothesis, which the research south of the border is investigating, is that the difference in conviction rate could be explained by the relative criminal defence background of individual PDSO solicitors. For example, the conviction rates could vary between public defence solicitors who had well established private criminal defence businesses before entering the service and those who previously had to rely mainly on duty solicitor work. However, given the small numbers of PDSO solicitors (as specified in the legislation) it is not possible to make a meaningful comparison of this kind.

FN 33. It was significant only at the 90% level, which means that there was a one in ten likelihood that the difference had occurred by chance.

. . .

FN 42. A. Blumberg, *Criminal Justice* (Quadrangle Books, 1967); A. Bottoms and J. Maclean, *Defendants in the Criminal Process* (Routledge, 1976); P. Carlen, *Magistrates Justice* (Martin Robertson, 1976); R. Ericson and P. Baranek, *The Ordering of Justice* (University of Chicago Press, 1982); McConville *et al.*, *Standing Accused* (Clarendon, 1992); D. Rosenthal, *Lawyers and Clients* (Russell Sage Foundation, 1974); A. Sarat and W. Felstiner, *Divorce Lawyers and their Clients* (Oxford University Press, 1995).

FN 43. Ericson and Baranek (1982) p 89.

FN 44. J. Casper, T. Tyler and B. Fisher 'Procedural Justice in Felony Cases' (1988) 3 *Law & Society Review*, p 483 at p 503.

FN 45. H. Somerland and D. Wall, 'Legally Aided Clients and their Solicitors: Qualitative Perspectives on Quality and Legal Aid' (Law Society Research Study No.34, London, 1999).

FN 46. G. Davis, *Partisans and Mediators: The Resolution of Divorce Disputes* (Clarendon Press, Oxford, 1988).

. . .

FN 50. M. McConville 'Plea Bargaining: Ethics and Politics' (1998) 25 *Journal of Law and Society*, 562–87.

> The article 'Does Mode of Delivery Make a Difference to Criminal Case Outcomes and Clients' Satisfaction? The Public Defence Solicitor Experiment' by Cyrus Tata and others was published in the *Criminal Law Review* in 2004 at p 120, and is also available from the Westlaw on-line subscription database.

Best value tendering (BVT)

In 2005, the Lord Chancellor asked Lord Carter to carry out a review of the legal aid system. Major reforms to the system were recommended by Lord Carter in his report, 'Legal Aid: a Market-Based Approach to Reform' (2006). In the light of this report, the Legal Services Commission issued a consultation paper entitled 'Best Value Tendering for Criminal Defence Services' (2007). It considers Lord Carter's recommendation for the introduction of a new procurement process for state funded legal aid, known as best value tendering. This would involve asking legal service providers to make bids for contracts to deliver categories of state funded legal services in a particular geographical area. The reforms are likely to be introduced for criminal defence work in 2010. The aim is to control the cost and quality of legal aid and to promote efficiency of service in the public interest.

Best Value Tendering of Criminal Defence Services: A Consultation Paper (2007)

1 Introduction

Background to this consultation

1.1 In his final report in July 2006 (www.legalaidprocurementreview.gov.uk) Lord Carter of Coles recommended moving towards a market-based approach to legal aid procurement, which would allow for the delivery of quality services at the best value for money.

1.2 Following the consultation on Lord Carter's proposals the Government published its response *Legal Aid Reform: the Way Ahead* in November 2006. This paper concluded that 'it is essential to move towards a competitive market as soon as practicable, so that the market can determine the best price for providing the service'.

1.3 There have been a number of consultation papers and responses since Lord Carter's original proposals were published that have described the detail and impact of the reform programme to date. Respondents may find it useful to review these papers for background purposes and in advance of submitting their views. They can be found on the LSC's website (www.legalservices.gov.uk/criminal.asp).

1.4 This consultation paper is also accompanied by a stand-alone *Cumulative Impact Assessment: Legal Aid Reform Programme (Phase 1)* that models the combined effect of these changes against claims for 2005/6. Although it is not a statement of actual impact, the assessment shows the regions where the reform programme have the greatest impact.

. . .

2 The case for best value tendering (BVT)

2.1 The Carter review of legal aid procurement set out three principles to guide the procurement of legal services. These were that:

- clients have access to good quality legal services;
- a good quality, efficient supplier base thrives and remains sustainable;
- the taxpayer and government receive value for money.

2.2 The Commission agrees that BVT offers the best mechanism to fulfil these objectives. This chapter is intended to illustrate the case for BVT against other options set out in *Legal Aid Reform: the Way Ahead*.

2.3 We invite providers to consider which, if any, of the options set out below they believe is the most desirable for the future direction of legal aid reform and whether there are any other practical options that have not so far been considered by the Commission.

Option 1: continue the current practice of setting fees administratively

2.4 The Commission believes that its current and developing practice of administratively setting fixed and graduated fees does not fully adhere to the three principles set out by Lord Carter, even though they offer some advantages.

2.5 Under this system, we use historic data on fee payments and other costs for each area of the country to administratively set a local market rate of fixed and graduated fees.

2.6 Administratively setting fees gives the Commission the advantage of being able to predict budgets and work within them. As hourly rates do not provide the right incentives to increase efficiency we have already introduced, or are introducing, fixed fees (e.g. in the police station) as these offer providers an incentive to work efficiently and to make changes to the way they organise their work.

2.7 These changes are fundamental to our new approach and there is no intention of returning to a system that relies exclusively on hourly rates. We see fixed and graduated fees as a key component of any new developments. Full details can be found on our website at www.legalservices.gov.uk. Follow the links to >transforming legal aid >legal aid reform and you are likely to wish to take these developments into account in your response to this consultation.

2.8 However, it is difficult to assess whether administratively set fees offer a 'fair' price, if not a competitive one. To do so would require the Commission to collect a mass of information about the local conditions that feed into the historic costs – for example, the cost of living, the distance travelled to courts, and other local factors like the way the court system operates. Furthermore, these factors are constantly changing. Supplying such levels of data would increase the non-productive workload burden on providers.

2.9 The best comparison that can be made currently is between the administratively set fees in different areas of the country. Here there are such big variations, for example, between metropolitan areas and rural regions, that it is difficult to assess 'fairness'.

2.10 However, most fundamentally, the current system provides no mechanism to demonstrate objectively that the Commission is paying sufficient amounts to ensure a sustainable and quality service, but no more than is necessary to ensure best value for the taxpayer.

Option 2: national roll-out of the Public Defender Service

2.11 Another alternative would be to roll-out the Public Defender Service to make it a fully national scheme and the only provider of legal aid funded criminal defence services. This model potentially provides the Commission with maximum control. But it would require major disruption and may be difficult to build such a service as many practitioners who own their businesses may be unwilling to become public sector employees.

2.12 However, an alternative to a full national roll-out of the Public Defender Service could be to steadily expand the role of the Public Defender Service giving the Commission more direct control over the level of expenditure.

Option 3: best value tendering (BVT)

2.13 A system of best value tendering would create a process by which:

● services are purchased from quality providers;
● market prices for categories of legal aid services are determined;
● competition is introduced in a managed way;
● the benefits of competition including innovations and selection of the most efficient providers are expected to occur.

2.14 The Commission sees BVT as offering the best potential for securing value for money, as well as:

● enabling legal aid providers to bid, taking account of the market conditions and the cost of delivering those services in their local area;
● enabling the Commission to allocate work to those providers who offer the best value for money while safeguarding quality and allowing such providers to benefit from their efficiency by taking on more work where it is available, at more competitive prices.

2.15 An aim of any tender process is to establish an economically meaningful price for the service being tendered that would allow competition among quality providers. The supplier will bid at the price at which they can profitably deliver the service and the purchaser will receive the most efficient price set by the market.

2.16 BVT is not a simple price competition – as well as producing price efficiency, best value tendering must be capable of maintaining the quality and integrity of the criminal legal aid service. The issue of quality and its relationship to BVT is crucial to any discussion on reform. Peer Review and other quality control mechanisms designed to reduce the impact of price competition on quality are considered in more detail in Chapter 3.

2.17 The Commission believes that prices resulting from best value tendering may differ from current levels, potentially rising or falling dependent on the nature of each individual market. However, we expect that overall the current cost of criminal legal aid will not rise as a result of BVT. It may well fall helping us to rebalance the legal aid budget in the first instance and enabling us to help more people within our budgetary limits.

2.18 If, however, the evidence of the first phase is that prices overall are rising, the Commission would address with the Government how best to deal with this. In this instance we would consider the current scope of Legal Aid as a whole in order that we can keep within our budget.

2.19 In the first instance we anticipate that the introduction of BVT could include one or more of the following:

- introduced on a national basis with prices allowed to rise and fall, within reason, as dictated by the market;
- a phased approach to implementation;
- the first phase could be relatively small and include a rural/urban area mix;
- the first phase could include Police Station and Magistrates' Court work but exclude Crown Court work;
- a set of entry requirements for firms wishing to tender for legal aid work before price is considered, including a quality threshold of Peer Review rating of three.

2.20 We acknowledge that the impact of BVT on providers is difficult to assess without knowing the detail of any scheme. However, we believe that your early feedback at this stage will help to minimise any adverse impact of a move to BVT and creates a real opportunity for providers to mould the detail of the system we develop over the coming months.

2.21 This will also help to inform our understanding of the impacts of BVT.

Civil providers

2.22 We are conscious of the need to ensure that we have an understanding of the impact, if any, upon civil legal aid provision as a result of any tender outcome for those firms who provide both criminal and civil legal aid services. For this reason, the Commission will be carrying out a full risk analysis to ensure that any risks are recognised and appropriately addressed.

 The report 'Best Value Tendering of Criminal Defence Services: A Consultation Paper' (2007) is available on the website of the Legal Services Commission at: **https://consult.legalservices.gov.uk/inovem/consult.ti/bestvaluetendering/ listdocuments**

Pushing forward with best value tendering

The government's plans to introduce best value tendering for state-funded legal services have been the subject of considerable criticism from legal-aid lawyers. Lord Carter's strategy has been dismissed by critics as 'pile them high, sell them cheap'. Black and minority ethnic solicitors frequently work as sole practitioners or in small, legal-aid firms, and this has led to concern that such firms may suffer if these reforms are introduced. Such concerns were submitted to the government as part of the consultation process but in its published response the Legal Services Commission stated it would nevertheless push ahead with the reforms.

Best Value Tendering of Criminal Defence Services: A Response to Consultation (2008)

Foreword

I am very grateful to all those, including the representative bodies, who gave their time both in drafting responses to the best value tendering consultation and attending our events around the country.

We have listened with great interest to the views expressed, and have reflected those views in this response. We appreciate the position expressed by those respondents who commented that it is not possible to provide a final view on best value tendering (BVT) until a fully developed model for BVT is available for consideration. This exercise has, however, been extremely useful in bringing to the fore some of the key issues about BVT.

We have carefully considered providers' views alongside the Legal Services Commission's statutory responsibilities to ensure that access to assistance and representation is secured for individuals involved in criminal investigations or proceedings, and to aim to obtain the best possible value for money. These responsibilities mean that the Legal Services Commission (LSC) must have regard to a range of stakeholders in the criminal legal aid system, including clients and taxpayers as well as providers. The LSC must also have regard to UK and EU laws on the procurement of public services. We share providers' desire for a longer-term approach to procurement of their services, one that offers them greater certainty and greater stability with an opportunity to plan their businesses.

This consultation has highlighted the wide range of concerns providers have about the impact competition could have on the criminal legal aid market. Those views from providers are understandable, particularly in the absence of a completed model of BVT that sets out exactly how such a system could work. It remains our view, however, that with careful planning and attention to detail we can create a competitive system that overcomes providers' concerns and ours, and that is sustainable in the long term. Whilst we believe we should continue to follow the blueprint set out by Lord Carter and further explore how competition could work in detail, we recognise the need to allow more time to work with providers and representative bodies on our proposals.

Competition remains our preferred option, although we will make no final decision on moving ahead until you have had further opportunity to consider and comment on the detailed proposals that we intend to present for consultation at the end of this year.

In light of the strength of concern expressed during consultation we have also decided that, rather than a 'phased implementation' approach to competition, that BVT should be piloted in the first instance. The detail and timetable of how such a pilot may work in practice will be included in our second consultation. It is likely that this will need to be piloted in a large enough area or areas to enable us to effectively assess the real impact of competition. However, before we make any final decision on a phased national implementation, we would propose a full assessment of the impact of the pilot to be published within six months to one year of the first BVT contracts being let. The criteria for success of any BVT pilot will also be included in our consultation at the end of this year.

I will explain briefly why a move to competition remains our preferred option.

Administratively set fees are our current system and some respondents favoured maintaining this status quo, commenting that the introduction of fixed and graduated fees had been less problematic than expected. Many respondents felt that the fee rates should be increased and a large proportion, including representative bodies argued the case for an independent panel recommending rates.

An independent panel would have no more information than the LSC on which to base rates. Our statutory obligation to obtain value for money would remain in place and the panel would be required to operate within this framework. Such a system would require significant administrative complexity, as it is accepted by the majority of providers that rates need to be sensitive to local conditions, which would also need to be factored into an independent panel's assessments of how rates should be set. It must be noted that the continuation of administratively set rates will not afford those firms that can deliver services at the right quality and the most efficient price the opportunity to access optimum volumes of work. Many feel this essential for sustainability. Finally, any independent panel would still be constrained by the fact that the legal aid budget as a whole is limited and would have to take its decisions in light of this fact.

Our view is that the current rates, based on historic billing on a local basis, are proving to be sustainable at the present time. There continues to be full national coverage following the recent re-tender of the criminal contract, and in many areas providers have indicated a desire to expand the volume of work they undertake. The current system does not offer this opportunity. In some areas more providers have been awarded a contract than were previously contracted. Whilst this gives reassurance that criminal legal aid remains attractive and viable for businesses, it further limits the ability of suppliers to access optimum volumes.

We believe that further exploration of a system where rates are set by providers on a competitive basis, rather than administratively set fees, will help to address this continuing trend.

We acknowledge that in some areas there is a case for rates falling and in other areas there is a case for rates rising. Competition that includes an element of price offers the prospect of this happening, based on the local market, at a level which providers themselves have set through the process. This would meet our statutory requirement to secure the best possible value for money, whilst ensuring that the most efficient firms were being paid the correct price for the volume they could deliver, creating a sustainable provider base for the 21st century.

We are very aware of the strong and understandable concerns put forward by providers about BVT. We recognise that the design of the BVT model will need to take into account many of these concerns; these are concerns for the LSC also. Section 2 of this response details our current thinking on how the next stage of development will seek to address the issues raised.

It is important to make clear that the LSC can never give a guarantee that all providers will stay in business under competition. At the same time we are committed to ensuring that whatever changes we make are done so in an orderly manner, with the impact properly assessed. We have a duty to ensure that our processes are transparent and reasonable; that firms have sufficient time to prepare for change; that our processes do not unlawfully discriminate; and that there are effective mechanisms to assure quality. We also believe that risks, such as changes in the wider criminal justice system (CJS), should be shared on a proper basis between the LSC and providers.

The aim of any competitive process, therefore, would be to ensure the sustainability of quality services for clients and best value for the taxpayer. We intend now to work up a concrete and detailed scheme for BVT to cover the initial areas, to be published for further consultation towards the end of this year. Our plans will aim as far as possible to meet providers' concerns, and we will engage closely over the coming months with the representative bodies in particular to help us with this. Our final decision on whether to introduce competition will depend on whether the scheme creates an appropriate balance between the need for value for money, the interests of clients and the need for a sustainable service. This will be informed by the further consultation.

Sir Michael Bichard
Chair of the Legal Services Commission

Executive summary

This is the response to the LSC's consultation Best Value Tendering of Criminal Defence Services, published in December 2007. A total of 202 formal responses were received and over 1,000 providers attended a national programme of BVT consultation events.

The consultation focused on the principle of best value tendering (BVT) and some broad design issues rather than on a detailed model for a possible BVT system; it asked respondents to give their views on a number of issues. These ranged from the question of how government should procure criminal defence services in the future, to policy questions concerning the operation of BVT contracts were that option to be pursued.

Future method of procurement

Following consultation, the LSC has decided:

- to undertake further work on the design of a pilot for a competitive system and consult on this towards the end of the year, to be published alongside an updated impact assessment;
- to maintain the present system of administratively set fees while work is undertaken on designing and, if introduced, assessing an effective competitive process;
- to carry out no further work at present on the option of an expanded Public Defender Service (PDS).

These decisions have been made in light of the LSC's statutory duties; its obligations to clients to continue to provide full coverage of a criminal defence service (CDS) and taxpayers and government to ensure that value for money is achieved. To ensure long-term sustainability of the CDS, providers must be able to work within an environment where remuneration reflects the costs of work undertaken locally and efficiently, together with a profit margin. Section 2 contains a full appraisal of the options.

Competition based on price and quality therefore remains the LSC's preferred way forward in light of our statutory responsibilities. A number of respondents to the first consultation suggested that in order to comment fully, they would need to understand more clearly the operation of any tender and firm proposals on the market rules that would govern delivery under any BVT system. The second consultation will give this opportunity.

Broad design issues for a BVT system

The LSC recognises the concerns raised by providers in response to the first consultation. The LSC believes that to a considerable extent those concerns can be addressed within the design of the system and by taking a pilot approach. Any future system should be based on the principles of revealing the true price of work, transparency and appropriate risk sharing.

Following consultation, the LSC has decided that the design of the model will be based on the following approach:

- a transparent tendering system will be developed for piloting that has been subject to full public consultation and testing before any final decision is taken to implement;
- tendering gives providers more than one opportunity to secure work and ensures that we minimise the risk of accepting unsustainably low bids;
- any system will continue with an element of client choice; clients will be able to choose from the successful bidders and not directed to a particular individual provider;
- Crown Court work will not be tendered as part of the pilot, any proposals for competing for this work will be subject to a full separate consultation if this is deemed a viable option going forward;
- Prison Law and Criminal Complaints Review Commission work will be excluded from the model we are developing;
- our current assumption is that a Peer Review three rating will be the standard for the initial areas, and that the LSC will continue to examine ways to raise standards of quality as any system develops.

 The report 'Best Value Tendering of Criminal Defence Services: A Response to Consultation' (2008) is available on the website of the Legal Services Commission at:
https://consult.legalservices.gov.uk/inovem/gf2.ti/f/59106/1978245.1/pdf/ -/BVT_consultation_response_no_cover_16070

18 The police

Introduction

This chapter looks at:

- government plans to modernise police powers;
- the introduction of community support officers to assist the police;
- the inquiry into the unsuccessful police investigation of the murder of the black teenager, Stephen Lawrence;
- Home Office research into the impact of the Stephen Lawrence inquiry; and
- research on the exercise of police powers to stop and search.

Modernising police powers

In 2007, the Home Office issued a consultation paper in which it considered some possible reforms to police powers. The purported aim of the Home Office was to re-focus police investigation and evidence-gathering processes on serving the needs of victims and witnesses, and helping raise the efficiency and effectiveness of the police service.

Modernising Police Powers – Review of the Police and Criminal Evidence Act (PACE) 1984, Consultation Paper (2007)

At the police station

PACE Part IV and Code C

3.11 PACE quite rightly makes the police station a place in which significant safeguards and rights must be made available to the detained person. Ensuring the detainee has access to these rights is important for the protection of the individual but, equally, it also provides a high degree of integrity and evidential status in respect of the investigative and interviewing processes.

3.12 But, as the Minister indicates in his Foreword, it is the procedural formalities which we need to examine. We know that computerised custody records and other electronic processes help raise the levels and quality of reporting, monitoring and accountability. We need to examine whether there are elements around detention and the custodial process which hinder or present barriers to achieving successful outcomes to investigations.

3.13 Recording what happens to a person at the police station enables effective monitoring and accountability. But there may be scope to look at existing processes. Particularly welcome are suggestions which help reduce bureaucracy and enable arresting officers in particular to spend less time at the police station.

3.14 The PACE 'detention clock' and the review process have been subject to relatively little change since its introduction in the 1984 Act. There has been some change around superintendent's authorisation and remote reviewing of detention. We are keen to examine if there are ways in which we can effect further change which results in reducing the burden on officer time, improving recording of reviews and, importantly, which can result in the detained person spending less time in police detention.

3.15 The person's period in detention can result in him or her being seen by several representatives – solicitor, healthcare professional, interpreter, appropriate adult and independent custody visitor. Whilst it is unlikely that every detainee will experience the full range, access to and waiting time for their attendance can have an impact on the handling of the investigation and the level of officer and staff time. It can also have a more serious impact on the nature and mood of the detained person. Suggestions are welcome from all stakeholders around more integrated working and ability to better plan investigations in consultation with each of the agencies and collectively.

3.16 Healthcare provision – both mental and physical – is an area of growing interest and attention for the police service. The professional intervention of a healthcare professional and at what stage can be a crucial factor affecting the welfare of the detainee and the interests of the criminal justice system. We are working with health and other stakeholders to identify how best professional healthcare can be delivered for those who come into police contact. However, as part of this Review, we would like to examine the existing PACE provisions. In particular, whether the current legislative arrangements are best suited to enabling custody officers to make decisions based on the best information; whether healthcare professionals are able to intervene at the most appropriate stages at the police station; and any competing demands between the investigative processes and the care and welfare of the detainee.

Bail (street bail and police bail)

3.17 The presumption at the police station is for bail to be granted. From a policing perspective, bail is a key part of planning the investigation and making best use of the detention time allowed under PACE and best use of officer time. It also enables best use to be made of custody accommodation.

3.18 Street bail (bail elsewhere than at a police station) was introduced under the Criminal Justice Act 2003. Again, the key focus of its introduction was to enable officers to better plan their investigation, to spend more time on operational activity on the streets and to place less pressure on the use of the custody suite.

3.19 We know that street bail has limited take up by forces. We also know that where it is in place that it is working and is effective. But we would welcome views on how we can encourage more officers to make use of street bail. As with a fair proportion of street activity, concern lies around identification of the person; being satisfied that they will turn up at the requested place; confident that they will not commit further crime or return to the scene of the offence or the vicinity of victims or witnesses.

3.20 Possible options may revolve around being able to take biometric information at the scene and the ability to raise confidence in the use of street bail. We would welcome views on the benefits of these and other approaches and views of what safeguards should be in place and, in the event of a breach, what action should be possible.

3.21 Bail at the police station already has much of these elements in place. However, it is an area which may benefit from clarification. There are also concerns around the power to enter premises to enforce bail, how to deal with an anticipated breach of bail and detention clock issues around failure to answer bail at a specified police station.

3.22 There is the ability to provide consistency on how we approach street and 'station' bail and we are looking for proposals on how best this can be achieved.

Use of non-designated police stations/other accommodation

3.23 PACE places considerable emphasis on the use of designated police stations for the detention and questioning of persons suspected of involvement in an offence. Non-designated police stations are not required to have appointed custody officers to oversee the person's detention. The functions of the custody officer at these stations must be performed by an officer (of any rank) who is not involved in the investigation, but if no such officer is available, the role may be carried out by the arresting officer on the condition that he/she informs an inspector at a designated police station of the situation as soon as practicable.

3.24 Section 45A of PACE was introduced to utilise technology and raise oversight by a custody officer at non-designated police stations by enabling a custody officer in a designated police station to use video-conferencing facilities to carry out the functions in relation to a person detained at a non-designated police station.

3.25 Section 45A remains subject to enabling regulations. We are aware of the advances in technology which help promote the case to commence these provisions. The option provides distinct benefits for minimising risks associated with the transportation of suspects, the needs of the investigation and the ability for front-line officers to remain in their operational area rather than travelling substantial distances to the nearest designated police station.

3.26 We would welcome as part of this consultation that respondees help identify the criteria that should accompany potential roll-out of this provision. We would also welcome views on the appropriateness of rolling out this provision.

Short-term holding facility

3.27 The vast majority of people arrested spend less than 24 hours in police detention. In fact, the average time spent is normally between 2–4 hours. Part of the necessity criteria for arrest under section 24 of PACE is that a person fails or refuses to give a satisfactory name or address.

3.28 The absence on the street of giving identity or providing satisfactory evidence of identity often means that people are taken to the police station, go through the custody process and take up both accommodation and officer and staff time to be charged or issued with a penalty notice when their identity is confirmed. Importantly, it takes police officers off the street and away from front-line duties.

3.29 The problem is particularly acute in busy urban areas. The volume of suspected offenders means that the efficiency of custody throughput is severely impacted, often with people suspected of low level but still important offences such as shoplifting. A potential solution in dealing with high volume offending is to enable the police to make use of short term holding facilities (STHF) located in shopping centres or town centres. The STHF would be under the supervision of a custody officer and would consist of a number of secure holding areas within the accommodation. These would provide secure accommodation but would not equate to the standard cell design.

3.30 The function of the STHF would be to confirm the identity of the suspect and process the person by reporting for summons/charging by post, a penalty notice or other disposal. Persons detained would be subject to detention up to a maximum period of 4 hours to enable fingerprinting, photographing and DNA sampling. The STHF would not be used in cases where the arresting officer considers that an investigation was required and authority to transfer a person from a STHF to a designated police station would require the authority of an Inspector. The aim would be to locate STHFs in busy areas to allow quick access and processing of suspects to enable the officer to resume operational duties as quickly as possible.

 The Consultation Paper, 'Modernising Police Powers – Review of the Police and Criminal Evidence Act 1984' (2007) is available on the website of the Home Office at: **www.homeoffice.gov.uk/documents/PACE-cover/cons-2007-pace-review?view=Binary**

Modernising police powers after the consultation process

Once interested organisations and members of the public had taken the opportunity to respond to the government's consultation process on modernising police powers, the government issued a document containing its response to the views expressed and its conclusions on how police powers should be modernised.

Review of the Police and Criminal Evidence Act (PACE 1984) Summary of Responses (2007) Home Office

3 Arrest powers

3.1 Section 24 of PACE, as amended by The Serious Organised Crime and Police Act (SOCAP) 2005, provides a power of arrest for a constable for any offence subject to the test of necessity.

3.2 A consequence of that important rationalisation of police powers was that a number of summary offences previously deemed arrestable prior to the amendment to PACE no longer attracted the so-called 'trigger powers' of entry and search associated with the power of arrest. Respondents have requested that these powers are re-instated for those summary offences previously deemed by Parliament as requiring these additional powers to ensure effective investigation and enforcement of those offences. There are 17 such offences in total previously listed under section 24 of PACE prior to the SOCAP amendment.

3.3 On a wider issue, the introduction of the single power of arrest based on the necessity criteria has been widely welcomed. The consultation exercise highlighted two areas of concern over the application of the necessity criteria set out in PACE Code G. The first related to the application of the criteria in relation to the granting of bail elsewhere other than at a police station (street bail). The street bail provisions require that a person must be arrested before street bail can be granted. The power of arrest is required in order to detain the person for the purposes of granting the bail. As one respondent indicated, this is confusing and appears at odds with the necessity criteria itself.

3.4 A more fundamental issue has been raised about the current list of circumstances which form the criteria. One respondent suggested that the current criteria lacks sufficient clarity and needs to be more expansive.

3.5 Although not raised within the consultation exercise itself, we aware from enquiries raised directly with us that there is a need for clarity on the role of the custody officer in determining whether the necessity criteria has been met when considering if there are sufficient grounds to authorise detention following arrest.

3.6 A further area raised in the consultation exercise relates to when known offenders are committing an offence but refuse to stop and police are unable to stop a 'continuation' of the offence. This relates to public order offences and clarity is sought on the ability of an officer to use the power of arrest after a warning has been given.

3.7 Two other areas were raised. First, that the power of arrest by someone other than a constable (citizen's power of arrest) should be able to be exercised in relation to any offence rather than the current threshold of an indictable offence; and second, that the granting of the power of arrest for a Police Community Support Officers (PCSOs) should be considered. A PCSO has the power to detain for 30 minutes to await the arrival of a constable and the ability to use reasonable force to enforce this. It is argued that this is a *de facto* arrest and that PCSOs powers should be reviewed to remove uncertainty.

4 Bail

4.1 Respondents' clear concern was that pre-charge bail provisions had become complex and confusing. The need to refer to PACE in sections 34, 37 and 47 whilst at the same time consulting the Bail Act reflected the benefits of consolidating the provisions. Pete Hutin, Sussex Police Bail suggested that there should be two forms of bail – one with conditions and one without conditions governed by one section of PACE.

4.2 A number of respondents provided suggestions in specific areas to improve the bail management process which would benefit operational effectiveness and the handling of the process from the bailee's perspective. There was a particular focus on dealing with breaches of bail and sanctions.

4.3 A number of respondents considered that sanctions should be the same for breaching any condition of bail. Any breaches should be recorded on the PNC for a national accurate record of bail compliance. On pre-charge bail in particular, it was suggested that sanctions for a breach of conditions should become an offence for which the penalty is detention until charge advice or court appearance. Such breaches should become a recordable offence which the court can take into consideration when reviewing an individual's bail status.

4.4 It was suggested that the requirement for a suspect to return to the station from where they were originally given bail should be removed. Instead they should be able to be taken to the nearest designated police station. This would enable the arresting officer to return to frontline duties sooner and reduce the amount of time that a suspect would spend in custody with the potential of earlier court appearance.

4.5 Clarification was sought on the status of extending bail by post and how to improve bail management processes. On the latter, it was suggested that it should be a requirement in the PACE Codes for forces to run an effective bail management system. It was considered that this would ensure the more effective management of suspects; and place a statutory requirement on forces to have an effective monitoring system in place which would enable them to anticipate demand on custody suite resources.

4.6 Street bail was recognised as potentially a very useful tool in managing investigations and custody resources and reducing the amount of time a person spent in custody. However, it was not used to the extent it could be due to the absence of suitable training and guidance.
. . .

8 Questioning after charge

8.1 The consultation process outlined the potential for considering questioning after charge and questioning following a decision to refer a case to the prosecutor for a charging decision.

8.2 The majority of respondents on this issue recognised that there should be the ability to question after charge based on the needs of the investigations rather within the existing parameters allowed under PACE, Code C.

8.3 Chief Superintendent Derek Barnett, Police Superintendents' Association for England and Wales said '[The Association] recognises that a significant amount of additional material is likely to be gained in some cases after a decision to charge has been made. The ability to ask questions at the earliest and most appropriate stage can result in both the effective delivery of justice and more effective in latter stages of the CJS process. However, we do not believe that such questioning should be a matter of routine and should be the subject of a test by senior police or judicial staff.'

8.3 Following on from the level of authorisation, it was suggested that any period of detention for the purposes of questioning after charge or after referral to a prosecutor for a charging decision should be subject to a Superintendent or Magistrate's authority.

8.4 Of the opinions against extending the current provisions enabling questioning after charge, concern was raised by Dr Michael Stockdale and Natalie Wortley, Northumbria University 'that it could result in the creation of a more inquisitorial system with issues being raised during a succession of interviews rather than in the adversarial context of a trial. The point of charge may become less important.'

8.5 Concern was also raised that removing the existing framework would result in dilution of the safeguards for the suspects and that evidence would need to show why such an ability was required.

. . .

10 Short-term holding facilities/non-designated police stations

10.1 Responses on this area clearly identified the importance attached by stakeholders and practitioners to the safeguards and protections afforded at a designated police station. Moving away from the standard that a designated station provides should only be considered with significant caution and any departure would need to ensure its own high level of protections.

10.2 Significant concerns were raised on the use of short-term holding facilities (STHFs). Whilst it was recognised that STHFs would provide operational benefits and may result in a person spending significantly less time in detention, there was doubt that such a facility would provide the suspect with the same level of protections and that it may be used simply as an alternative to designated police stations when their custody areas were full. There was also the need to set specific criteria on the types of offenders and types of offences which could be dealt with in STHFs.

10.3 From an operational perspective, benefits were seen in enabling custody facilities to be located in areas of high offending and for access to those facilities during periods of high demand. Sergeant David Warren, Kent Police said 'The . . . concept of STHF is exactly what forces such as Kent needs. STHF should not be restricted to shopping centres, but should be an option that the police should use other facilities such as smaller police stations, sporting or entertainment centres, hospital sites or local authority sites. Prisoner processing-STHF could be processed by "remote workers". STHF should be available for processing defendants who have not been arrested, therefore not detained under PACE, but perhaps under obligation to attend the STHF to provide fingerprints, DNA, etc., or to be issued with a caution, reprimand, etc.'

10.4 The use of non-designated stations by way of video link to a custody officer at a designated station was considered a huge responsibility on custody officers, particularly if the non-designated station was holding detainees with particular risks or vulnerabilities. However, non-designated police stations could be used, if suitably staffed, to carry out enquiry checks, etc.

The Home Office report 'Review of the Police and Criminal Evidence Act 1984: Summary of Responses' (2007) is published on the website of the Home Office at: **www.homeoffice.gov.uk/documents/PACE-cover/PACE-ResponseSummary?view=Binary**

Community support officers

The Police Reform Act 2002 created community support officers. These are civilians who are allowed to exercise some police powers. They are a new and very visible presence patrolling our streets and public spaces. Their creation has been quite controversial. The Police Federation, which represents all police officers, is opposed to their creation. It has published its views on its website and these are reproduced below.

Community Support Officers

Community Support Officers (CSO's) are designed to act as the eyes and ears of the police force but have been the subject of much debate over issues that include accountability, role definition, powers and responsibility.

The Federation feel that CSO's should not be judged purely upon the visible presence they provide. It has not been proven that CSO's have a tangible impact upon crime. It would be imprudent to increase CSO numbers until robust analysis of their performance and cost-effectiveness has taken place. Although we await the results of the research into the use of powers by Metropolitan CSO's with interest, we are disappointed that more widespread research has not been conducted.

The Police Federation has always opposed the creation and presence of an ill-equipped and ill-trained second layer of law enforcers. Does it not cause members of the public more confusion as to who has what power, in what circumstances, and for how long when a better alternative is that offered by a fully trained auxiliary police force who receive the same basic training and are able to fully support the regular police.

Questions over the sustainability of CSO funding also remain unanswered despite the Federation's repeated call for clarification. It is essential that the government establishes a clear and unambiguous definition of the demarcation of powers between police and non-police personnel and how CSO's will be financed in the future.

The views of the Police Federation on the establishment of community support officers are published on its website at:
www.polfed.org/we_stand_D93FA810488D48608FDD6B7826A70F20.asp

The Stephen Lawrence Inquiry – institutional racism

Stephen Lawrence was a young black A-level student who was murdered in London by a group of racist youths in 1993. Nobody has been successfully prosecuted for his murder. Following concern at the police handling of the criminal investigation, a judicial inquiry headed by a former High Court judge, Sir William Macpherson, was set up by the government in 1997 and its report was published in February 1999. It found that the Metropolitan Police Service suffered from institutional racism.

The Stephen Lawrence Inquiry

Report of an inquiry by Sir William Macpherson

Conclusion and summary

46.1 The conclusions to be drawn from all the evidence in connection with the investigation of Stephen Lawrence's racist murder are clear. There is no doubt but that there were fundamental errors. The investigation was marred by a combination of professional incompetence, institutional racism and a failure of leadership by senior officers. A flawed Metropolitan Police Service review failed to expose these inadequacies. The second investigation could not salvage the faults of the first investigation.

46.2 At least now many of the failures and flaws are accepted. For too long the family and the public were led to think that the investigation had been satisfactorily carried out. The belated apologies offered at this Inquiry acknowledge the truth, but there is no remedy for the grief which the unsuccessful investigation piled upon the grief caused by the murder itself.

46.3 We were not presented with evidence to persuade us that collusion and corruption infected the investigation of the murder.

46.4 There are dangers in summarising, but it is necessary to set out here the main thrust of our criticisms. Only a reading of the Report will fully convey its message. The impact of the evidence itself is hard to convey. Those who heard all the evidence found the experience depressing. The following paragraphs simply attempt to refer to the heart of the deficiencies which marred the investigation.

First Aid
46.5 No police officer did anything by way of First Aid, apart from the small amount of testing to see whether Stephen Lawrence was still breathing and whether his pulse was beating. We strongly criticise the training and retraining of police officers in First Aid. A senior officer (Inspector Groves) signally failed properly to assess the situation and to ensure that proper steps were being taken to recognise and deal with Stephen Lawrence's gross injuries.

Initial response
46.6 We were astonished at the lack of direction and organisation during the vital first hours after the murder. Almost total lack of proper documentation makes reconstruction of what happened during those hours difficult. But lack of imagination and properly co-ordinated action and planning which might have led to the discovery and arrest of suspects

was conspicuous by its absence. No officers early on the scene took any proper steps at once to pursue the suspects. There were large numbers of police officers available, but inadequate measures were taken to use them actively and properly. This was due to failure of direction by senior officers, many of whom attended the scene, who seem simply to have accepted that everything was being done satisfactorily by somebody else.

Family liaison and victim support

46.7 From the first contact with police officers at the hospital, and thereafter, Mr and Mrs Lawrence were treated with insensitivity and lack of sympathy. One of the saddest and most deplorable aspects of the case concerns the failure of the family liaison. Mr and Mrs Lawrence were not dealt with or treated as they should have been. They were patronised. They were never given information about the investigation to which they were entitled. Family liaison failed, despite the good intentions of the officers allocated to this task. Senior officers never intervened to rectify the failure. Both Mr and Mrs Lawrence as the murder victim's parents, and Duwayne Brooks who was himself a victim of the attack, were inadequately, inappropriately and unprofessionally treated and were not treated according to their needs.

The senior investigating officers

46.8 Detective Superintendent CRAMPTON – Mr Crampton was SIO [Senior Investigating Officer] until Monday 26 April. Revealing and detailed information reached the investigating team from 23 April onwards. There was no wall of silence. A vital and fundamental mistake was made in failing to arrest the suspects named in that information by the morning of 26 April. Enough information was available to make the arrests by the evening of 24 April, at about the time when Mr Crampton says that he made a *'strategical'* decision not to arrest. This decision is nowhere recorded. By Monday 26 April evidence, in a statement signed by Stacey Benefield, reinforced the information available about two of the suspects. That evidence would in itself have justified the arrest of David Norris and Neil Acourt and would have entitled the team to search their premises in connection with the murder of Stephen Lawrence. This flawed decision as to arrest is fundamental. Its consequences are plain to see.

46.9 Detective Superintendent WEEDEN – When the investigation was handed over to Mr Weeden he perpetuated the wrong decisions made in the vital early days. He did not exercise his own critical faculties in order to test whether the right decisions had been made. He was confused as to his power of arrest. His fundamental misjudgment delayed arrests until 7 May, at which time the arrests were made because of outside pressures. His decisions and actions show lack of imagination and a tendency simply to allow things to drift. He failed to address with sensitivity the problems of family liaison.

46.10 Detective Inspector BULLOCK – As Deputy Investigating Officer Mr Bullock must be associated with the decisions and actions of the SIOs. He failed to process properly vital information given to the team by James Grant. He was often passive, and not up to his job. The major responsibility for the team's failures lie with those who supervised Mr Bullock, but as DIO he bears his share of responsibility for the team's failures.

46.11 Detective Chief Superintendent ILSLEY – Mr Ilsley allowed himself to go along with the weak and unenterprising decisions made by his SIOs, in which he had been himself directly involved. He tended to disconnect from responsibility for the investigation when faced with justifiable criticisms. He failed to supervise and to manage effectively this highly sensitive murder investigation. He acted insensitively and unwisely when arranging to take over the family liaison on 6 May 1993.

Failure to arrest Clifford Norris

46.12 The failure of the team to do all that was possible to arrest Clifford Norris and to remove him from the scene is unexplained and incomprehensible, particularly in the light of the Stacey Benefield case and the belief that Clifford Norris' influence was inhibiting young potential witnesses.

Surveillance

46.13 The surveillance operation was ill-planned, badly carried out, and inadequately documented. If this surveillance was part of the SIOs' strategy in substitution for arrests the decision-making in this regard was flawed and incompetent. The indications are that the team was simply going through the motions in order to establish association. There was inadequate direction and lack of urgency in this operation.

The incident room

46.14 The HOLMES system was inadequately staffed. The Incident Room was not supervised by responsible and trained officers. This may account for many delays apparent in the processing of information reaching the investigation team.

The red Astra and elimination of suspects

46.15 It is a cause of concern and criticism that there was serious delay and failure to take necessary action in connection with the occupants of the red Astra car seen twice on the night of the murder. Furthermore there were serious omissions and failures in the steps taken properly to investigate and eliminate from the investigation associates of the five suspects who were reported also to be suspected of involvement in the murder.

Identity parades

46.16 The identification parades were poorly planned. There were clear breaches of the Codes of Practice governing identity parades. In particular, witnesses were allowed to be together before parades took place. Witnesses were not properly supervised. Successful identification might well have been compromised by these breaches.

The fair-haired attacker

46.17 Witnesses, including Duwayne Brooks, indicated that one of the offenders was fair haired. Further information supported this evidence. We agree with Kent's conclusion that the failure to deal logically and thoroughly with this line of inquiry is a clear source of criticism of the first investigation.

Searches

46.18 When the arrests were made on 7 May it is plain that the searches of all the suspects' premises were inadequate. Information expressly suggested that knives might be concealed under floorboards. There is no evidence that a single floorboard was removed during any of the searches.

'James Grant'

46.19 The handling of James Grant by Detective Sergeant Davidson and Detective Constable Budgen, and the failure to register him as an informant is the subject of criticism. Senior officers failed to ensure that this man, and other hesitant witnesses, were properly followed up and sensitively handled.

Policy and records

46.20 Policy decisions were ill considered and unrecorded. Records and notes were not made or retained.

The Barker Review

46.21 Detective Chief Superintendent BARKER – The Review was factually incorrect, and inadequate. Mr Barker allowed himself to impose shackles upon his consideration of the investigation which resulted in the production of a flawed and indefensible report. There is concern about the reception of the Barker Review by all senior officers. That part of his Review which dealt with Mr and Mrs Lawrence is inaccurate, insensitive and thoughtless.

46.22 Deputy Assistant Commissioner OSLAND – Mr Osland accepted that he was responsible for all operational and administrative activities [in the relevant area]. Yet the evidence shows that he was much too ready to accept that things were going satisfactorily during the course of the investigation. Having established the Barker Review, he uncritically accepted what had been reported, and allowed the Review to go to senior officers including the Commissioner without critical appraisal. No senior officer at any level tested or analysed the Review. Mr Osland's attitude to Mr and Mrs Lawrence and their solicitor is reprehensible.

46.23 There can be no excuses for such a series of errors, failures, and lack of direction and control. Each failure was compounded. Failure to acknowledge and to detect errors resulted in them being effectively concealed. Only now at this Inquiry have they been laid bare.

The second investigation

46.24 The second investigation attempted to salvage the situation. Forthright steps were taken. Clifford Norris was arrested. Sophisticated surveillance of the suspects took place. By 1994, however, the case was becoming stale. No satisfactory fresh witnesses have ever come forward. We have no criticism of this investigation by Mr Mellish. Indeed, it was managed with imagination and skill. The trust of Mr and Mrs Lawrence was regained by the sensitive approach of Mr Nove.

Racism

46.25 We do not attempt to summarise Chapter 6 which deals with this central and vital issue. Save to repeat two of its paragraphs, which we apply to the evidence and facts of the Stephen Lawrence case:

> **6.4** 'Racism' in general terms consists of conduct or words or practices which advantage or disadvantage people because of their colour, culture or ethnic origin. In its more subtle form it is as damaging as in its overt form.

> **6.34** 'Institutional Racism' consists of the collective failure of an organisation to provide an appropriate and professional service to people because of their colour, culture or ethnic origin. It can be seen or detected in processes, attitudes and behaviour which amount to

discrimination through unwitting prejudice, ignorance, thoughtlessness, and racist stereotyping which disadvantage minority ethnic people.

46.26 At its most stark, the case against the police was that racism infected the Metropolitan Police Service and that the catalogue of errors could only be accounted for by something more than incompetence. If corruption and collusion did not play its part then, say the critics, the case must have been thrown or at least slowed down because officers approached the murder of a black man less energetically than if the victim had been white and the murderers black. An example of this approach was that posed by Mr Panton, the barrister acting for Greenwich Council, who argued that if the colour of the victim and the attackers was reversed the police would have acted differently:

> In my submission, history suggests that the police would have probably swamped the estate that night and they would remain there, probably for the next however long it took, to ensure that if the culprits were on that estate something would be done about the situation.

46.27 We understand why this view is held. We have examined with anxiety and care all the evidence and have heeded all the arguments both ways. We do believe, (paragraph 6.48) that institutional racism is apparent in those areas described. But we do not accept that it was universally the cause of the failure of this investigation, any more than we accept that a finding of institutional racism within the police service means that all officers are racist. We all agree that institutional racism affects the METROPOLITAN POLICE SERVICE, and Police Services elsewhere. Furthermore, our conclusions as to Police Services should not lead to complacency in other institutions and organisations. Collective failure is apparent in many of them, including the Criminal Justice system. It is incumbent upon every institution to examine their policies and the outcome of their policies and practices to guard against disadvantaging any section of our communities.

46.28 Next we identify those areas which were affected by racism remembering always that that emotive word covers the whole range of such conduct. In this case we do not believe that discrimination or disadvantage was overt. There was unwitting racism in the following fields:

(i) Inspector Groves' insensitive and racist stereotypical behaviour at the scene. He assumed that there had been a fight. He wholly failed to assess Duwayne Brooks as a primary victim. He failed thus to take advantage of the help which Mr Brooks could have given. His conduct in going to the Welcome Inn and failing to direct proper searches was conditioned by his wrong and insensitive appreciation and conclusions.

(ii) Family Liaison. Inspector Little's conduct at the hospital, and the whole history of later liaison was marred by the patronising and thoughtless approach of the officers involved. The treatment of Mr and Mrs Lawrence was collective, in the sense that officers from the team and those controlling or supervising them together failed to ensure that Mr and Mrs Lawrence were dealt with and looked after according to their needs. The officers detailed to be family liaison officers, Detective Sergeant Bevan and Detective Constable Holden, had (as Mrs Lawrence accepted) good intentions, yet they offended Mr and Mrs Lawrence by questioning those present in their house as to their identity, and by failing to realise how their approach to Mr and Mrs Lawrence might be both upsetting and thoughtless.

(iii) This sad failure was never appreciated and corrected by senior officers, in particular Mr Weeden, who in his turn tended to blame Mr and Mrs Lawrence and their solicitor for the failure of family liaison. The failure was compounded by Mr Barker in his Review.

(iv) Mr Brooks was by some officers side-lined and ignored, because of racist stereotyping particularly at the scene and the hospital. He was never properly treated as a victim.

(v) At least five officers, DS Davidson, DC Budgen, DC Chase, DS Bevan and DC Holden simply refused to accept that this was purely a racist murder. This (as we point out in the text) must have skewed their approach to their work.

(vi) DS Flook allowed untrue statements about Mr and Mrs Lawrence and Mr Khan to appear in his statement to Kent. Such hostility resulted from unquestioning acceptance and repetition of negative views as to demands for information which Mr and Mrs Lawrence were fully entitled to make. DS Flook's attitude influenced the work which he did.

(vii) The use of inappropriate and offensive language. Racism awareness training was almost non-existent at every level.

Community concerns

46.29 Wider issues than those closely connected to the investigation of the murder of Stephen Lawrence dominated Part Two of our Inquiry. It may be thought that in this respect we have strayed outside our terms of reference. We are convinced that the atmosphere in which racist crime is investigated is bound to influence the outcome of such investigation. We believe that Mr and Mrs Lawrence and all who have been involved in this Inquiry would agree that this is so.

46.30 First and foremost amongst our conclusions flowing from Part 2 is that there is a striking and inescapable need to demonstrate fairness, not just by Police Services, but across the criminal justice system as a whole, in order to generate trust and confidence within minority ethnic communities, who undoubtedly perceive themselves to be discriminated against by *'the system'*. Just as justice needs to be *'seen to be done'* so fairness must be *'seen to be demonstrated'* in order to generate trust. An essential first step in creating that trust is to ensure that it is a priority for all Police Services. The existing system of Ministerial Priority is the obvious route by which this may be achieved (Recommendation 1).

46.31 The need to re-establish trust between minority ethnic communities and the police is paramount. Such distrust and loss of confidence is particularly evident in the widely held view that junior officers discriminate in practice at operational level, and that they support each other in such discrimination. We have referred to the primary problem of 'stop and search', including those stops which are unrecorded within the present statistics. The minority communities' views and perceptions are formed by their experience of all 'stops' by the police. They do not perceive any difference between a 'stop' under the Police and Criminal Evidence Act from one under the Road Traffic Act whilst driving a vehicle. It is essential to obtain a true picture of the interactions between the police and minority ethnic communities in this context. All 'stops' need to be recorded, and related self-defined 'ethnic data' compiled. We have considered whether such a requirement would create too great a bureaucracy for operational officers, and we are persuaded that this is not the case. The great weight of extra recording would undoubtedly relate to 'traffic stops' many of which are already recorded via the HORTI (production of driving documents) procedure. In this context we have also specifically considered whether police powers to 'stop and search' should be removed or further limited. We specifically reject this option. We fully accept the need for such powers to continue, and their genuine usefulness in the prevention and detection of crime (Recommendations 60–63).

46.32 Seeking to achieve trust and confidence through the demonstration of fairness will not in itself be sufficient. It must be accompanied by a vigorous pursuit of openness and accountability across Police Services. Essentially we consider that the principle which should govern the Police Services, and indeed the criminal justice system, is that they should be accountable under all relevant legislative provisions unless a clear and specific case can be demonstrated that such accountability would be harmful to the public interest. In this context we see no justification for exemption of the Police Service from the full provisions of the Race Relations Act. Chief Officers should be vicariously liable for the actions of their officers. Similarly we consider it an important matter of principle that the Police Services should be open to the full provisions of a Freedom of Information Act. We see no logical grounds for a class exemption for the police in any area (Recommendations 9–11).

46.33 The depth of the failure of the investigation into the murder of Stephen Lawrence is such that there is a particular need for the Metropolitan Police Service to be given a current *'clean bill of health'* by a process of vigorous independent inspection. The Metropolitan Police Service must also be shown to be as open and accountable as possible by ensuring that the levels of their accountability mirror those of other services. We therefore welcome the forthcoming introduction of a Police Authority for London. However, we see neither logic nor justification for limiting its powers in comparison with those existing in other Police Services in England and Wales. In particular, we suggest that openness and accountability require that all the Metropolitan Police Service Chief Officers should be appointed by the Police Authority and be fully accountable to them (Recommendations 3, 4 and 6).

46.34 If racism is to be eliminated from our society, there must be a co-ordinated effort to prevent its growth. This need goes well beyond the Police Services. The need for training of police officers in addressing racism and valuing cultural diversity is plain. Improved understanding and attitudes will certainly help to prevent racism in the future, as will improved procedures in terms of recording and investigating racist incidents. Just as important, and perhaps more so, will be similar efforts needed from other agencies, particularly in the field of education. As we have indicated, the issue of education may not at first sight sit clearly within our terms of reference. Yet we cannot but conclude that to seek to address the well founded concerns of minority communities simply by addressing the racism current and visible in the Police Services without addressing the educational system would be futile. The evidence we heard and read forces us to the conclusion that our education system must face up to the problems, real and potential, which exist. We therefore make a number of Recommendations aimed at encouraging schools to address the identified problems (Recommendations 67–69).

. . .

Chapter forty-seven

Recommendations
We recommend:

Openness, accountability and the restoration of confidence
1 That a Ministerial Priority be established for all Police Services:

   To increase trust and confidence in policing amongst minority ethnic communities.

2 The process of implementing, monitoring and assessing the Ministerial Priority should include Performance Indicators in relation to:

(i) the existence and application of strategies for the prevention, recording, investigation and prosecution of racist incidents;

(ii) measures to encourage reporting of racist incidents;

(iii) the number of recorded racist incidents and related detection levels;

(iv) the degree of multi-agency cooperation and information exchange;

(v) achieving equal satisfaction levels across all ethnic groups in public satisfaction surveys;

(vi) the adequacy of provision and training of family and witness/victim liaison officers;

(vii) the nature, extent and achievement of racism awareness training;

(viii) the policy directives governing stop and search procedures and their outcomes;

(ix) levels of recruitment, retention and progression of minority ethnic recruits; and

(x) levels of complaint of racist behaviour or attitude and their outcomes.

The overall aim being the elimination of racist prejudice and disadvantage and the demonstration of fairness in all aspects of policing.

3 That Her Majesty's Inspectors of Constabulary (HMIC) be granted full and unfettered powers and duties to inspect all parts of Police Services including the Metropolitan Police Service.

4 That in order to restore public confidence an inspection by HMIC of the Metropolitan Police Service be conducted forthwith. The inspection to include examination of current undetected HOLMES based murders and Reviews into such cases.

5 That principles and standards similar to those of the Office for Standards in Education (OFSTED) be applied to inspections of Police Services, in order to improve standards of achievement and quality of policing through regular inspection, public reporting, and informed independent advice.

6 That proposals as to the formation of the Metropolitan Police Authority be reconsidered, with a view to bringing its functions and powers fully into line with those which apply to other Police Services, including the power to appoint all Chief Officers of the Metropolitan Police Service.

7 That the Home Secretary and Police Authorities should seek to ensure that the membership of police authorities reflects so far as possible the cultural and ethnic mix of the communities which those authorities serve.

8 That HMIC shall be empowered to recruit and to use lay inspectors in order to conduct examination and inspection of Police Services particularly in connection with performance in the area of investigation of racist crime.

9 That a Freedom of Information Act should apply to all areas of policing, both operational and administrative, subject only to the 'substantial harm' test for withholding disclosure.

10 That Investigating Officers' reports resulting from public complaints should not attract Public Interest Immunity as a class. They should be disclosed to complainants, subject only to the 'substantial harm' test for withholding disclosure.

11 That the full force of the Race Relations legislation should apply to all police officers, and that Chief Officers of Police should be made vicariously liable for the acts and omissions of their officers relevant to that legislation.

Definition of racist incident
12 That the definition should be:

> A racist incident is any incident which is perceived to be racist by the victim
> or any other person.

13 That the term 'racist incident' must be understood to include crimes and non-crimes in policing terms. Both must be reported, recorded and investigated with equal commitment.

14 That this definition should be universally adopted by the Police, local Government and other relevant agencies.

Reporting and recording of racist incidents and crimes
15 That Codes of Practice be established by the Home Office, in consultation with Police Services, local Government and relevant agencies, to create a comprehensive system of reporting and recording of all racist incidents and crimes.

16 That all possible steps should be taken by Police Services at local level in consultation with local Government and other agencies and local communities to encourage the reporting of racist incidents and crimes. This should include:

– the ability to report at locations other than police stations; and
– the ability to report 24 hours a day.

17 That there should be close cooperation between Police Services and local Government and other agencies, including in particular Housing and Education Departments, to ensure that all information as to racist incidents and crimes is shared and is readily available to all agencies.

Police practice and the investigation of racist crime
18 That ACPO [the Association of Chief Police Officers], in consultation with local Government and other relevant agencies, should review its *Good Practice Guide for Police Response to Racial Incidents* in the light of this Report and our Recommendations. Consideration should be given to the production by ACPO of a manual or model for such investigation, to complement their current *Manual of Murder Investigation*.

19 That ACPO devise Codes of Practice to govern Reviews of investigations of crime, in order to ensure that such Reviews are open and thorough. Such codes should be consistently used by all Police Services. Consideration should be given to such practice providing for Reviews to be carried out by an external Police Service.

20 That Metropolitan Police Service procedures at the scene of incidents be reviewed in order to ensure co-ordination between uniformed and CID officers and to ensure that senior officers are aware of and fulfil the command responsibilities which their role demands.

21 That the Metropolitan Police Service review their procedures for the recording and retention of information in relation to incidents and crimes, to ensure that adequate records are made by individual officers and specialist units in relation to their functions, and that strict rules require the retention of all such records as long as an investigation remains open.

22 That the Metropolitan Police Service review their internal inspection and accountability processes to ensure that policy directives are observed.

Family liaison

23 That Police Services should ensure that at local level there are readily available designated and trained Family Liaison Officers.

24 That training of Family Liaison Officers must include training in racism awareness and cultural diversity, so that families are treated appropriately, professionally, with respect and according to their needs.

25 That Family Liaison Officers shall, where appointed, be dedicated primarily if not exclusively to that task.

26 That Senior Investigating Officers and Family Liaison Officers be made aware that good practice and their positive duty shall be the satisfactory management of family liaison, together with the provision to a victim's family of all possible information about the crime and its investigation.

27 That good practice shall provide that any request made by the family of a victim which is not acceded to, and any complaint by any member of the family, shall be formally recorded by the SIO and shall be reported to the immediate superior officer.

28 That Police Services and Victim Support Services ensure that their systems provide for the proactive use of local contacts within minority ethnic communities to assist with family liaison where appropriate.

Victims and witnesses

29 That Police Services should together with the Home Office develop guidelines as to the handling of victims and witnesses, particularly in the field of racist incidents and crimes. The Victim's Charter to be reviewed in this context.

30 That Police Services and Victim Support Services ensure that their systems provide for the proactive use of local contacts within minority ethnic communities to assist with victim support and with the handling and interviewing of sensitive witnesses.

31 That Police Services ensure the provision of training and the availability of victim/ witness liaison officers, and ensure their use in appropriate areas particularly in the field of racist incidents and crimes, where the need for a sensitive approach to young and vulnerable victims and witnesses is paramount.

Prosecution of racist crimes

32 That the standard of proof of such crimes should remain unchanged.

33 That the CPS [Crown Prosecution Service] should consider that, in deciding whether a criminal prosecution should proceed, once the CPS evidential test is satisfied there should be a rebuttable presumption that the public interest test should be in favour of prosecution.

34 That Police Services and the CPS should ensure that particular care is taken at all stages of prosecution to recognise and to include reference to any evidence of racist motivation. In particular it should be the duty of the CPS to ensure that such evidence is referred to both at trial and in the sentencing process (including Newton hearings). The CPS and Counsel to ensure that no 'plea bargaining' should ever be allowed to exclude such evidence.

35 That the CPS ensure that a victim or victim's family shall be consulted and kept informed as to any proposal to discontinue proceedings.

36 That the CPS should have the positive duty always to notify a victim and victim's family personally of a decision to discontinue, particularly in cases of racist crime, with speed and sensitivity.

37 That the CPS ensure that all decisions to discontinue any prosecution should be carefully and fully recorded in writing, and that save in exceptional circumstances, such written decisions should be disclosable to a victim or a victim's family.

38 That consideration should be given to the Court of Appeal being given power to permit prosecution after acquittal where fresh and viable evidence is presented.

39 That consideration should be given to amendment of the law to allow prosecution of offences involving racist language or behaviour, and of offences involving the possession of offensive weapons, where such conduct can be proved to have taken place otherwise than in a public place.

40 That the ability to initiate a private prosecution should remain unchanged.

41 That consideration should be given to the proposition that victims or victims' families should be allowed to become 'civil parties' to criminal proceedings, to facilitate and to ensure the provision of all relevant information to victims or their families.

42 That there should be advance disclosure of evidence and documents as of right to parties who have leave from a Coroner to appear at an Inquest.

43 That consideration be given to the provision of Legal Aid to victims or the families of victims to cover representation at an Inquest in appropriate cases.

44 That Police Services and the Courts seek to prevent the intimidation of victims and witnesses by imposing appropriate bail conditions.

Training: First Aid
45 That First Aid training for all 'public contact' police officers (including senior officers) should at once be reviewed and revised to ensure that they have basic skills to apply First Aid. Officers must be taught to 'think first aid', and first and foremost 'A (Airways), B (Breathing) and C (Circulation)'.

46 That training in First Aid including refresher training should include testing to recognised and published standards in every Police Service.

47 That Police Services should annually review First Aid training, and ensure that 'public contact' officers are trained and tested to recognised and published standards.

Training: racism awareness and valuing cultural diversity
48 That there should be an immediate review and revision of racism awareness training within Police Services to ensure:

(a) that there exists a consistent strategy to deliver appropriate training within all Police Services, based upon the value of our cultural diversity;

(b) that training courses are designed and delivered in order to develop the full understanding that good community relations are essential to good policing and that a racist officer is an incompetent officer.

49 That all police officers, including CID and civilian staff, should be trained in racism awareness and valuing cultural diversity.

50 That police training and practical experience in the field of racism awareness and valuing cultural diversity should regularly be conducted at local level. And that it should be recognised that local minority ethnic communities should be involved in such training and experience.

51 That consideration be given by Police Services to promoting joint training with members of other organisations or professions otherwise than on police premises.

52 That the Home Office together with Police Services should publish recognised standards of training aims and objectives in the field of racism awareness and valuing cultural diversity.

53 That there should be independent and regular monitoring of training within all Police Services to test both implementation and achievement of such training.

54 That consideration be given to a review of the provision of training in racism awareness and valuing cultural diversity in local Government and other agencies including other sections of the Criminal Justice system.

Employment, discipline and complaints
55 That the changes to Police Disciplinary and Complaints procedures proposed by the Home Secretary should be fully implemented and closely and publicly monitored as to their effectiveness.

56 That in order to eliminate the present provision which prevents disciplinary action after retirement, disciplinary action should be available for at least five years after an officer's retirement.

57 That the Police Services should through the implementation of a Code of Conduct or otherwise ensure that racist words or acts proved to have been spoken or done by police officers should lead to disciplinary proceedings, and that it should be understood that such conduct should usually merit dismissal.

58 That the Home Secretary, taking into account the strong expression of public perception in this regard, consider what steps can and should be taken to ensure that serious complaints against police officers are independently investigated. Investigation of police officers by their own or another Police Service is widely regarded as unjust, and does not inspire public confidence.

59 That the Home Office review and monitor the system and standards of Police Services applied to the selection and promotion of officers of the rank of Inspector and above. Such procedures for selection and promotion to be monitored and assessed regularly.

Stop and search
60 That the powers of the police under current legislation are required for the prevention and detection of crime and should remain unchanged.

61 That the Home Secretary, in consultation with Police Services, should ensure that a record is made by police officers of all 'stops' and 'stops and searches' made under any legislative provision (not just the Police and Criminal Evidence Act). Non-statutory or so called 'voluntary' stops must also be recorded. The record to include the reason for the stop, the outcome, and the self-defined ethnic identity of the person stopped. A copy of the record shall be given to the person stopped.

62 That these records should be monitored and analysed by Police Services and Police Authorities, and reviewed by HMIC on inspections. The information and analysis should be published.

63 That Police Authorities be given the duty to undertake publicity campaigns to ensure that the public is aware of 'stop and search' provisions and the right to receive a record in all circumstances.

Recruitment and retention
64 That the Home Secretary and Police Authorities' policing plans should include targets for recruitment, progression and retention of minority ethnic staff. Police Authorities to report progress to the Home Secretary annually. Such reports to be published.

65 That the Home Office and Police Services should facilitate the development of initiatives to increase the number of qualified minority ethnic recruits.

66 That HMIC include in any regular inspection or in a thematic inspection a report on the progress made by Police Services in recruitment, progression and retention of minority ethnic staff.

Prevention and the role of education
67 That consideration be given to amendment of the National Curriculum aimed at valuing cultural diversity and preventing racism, in order better to reflect the needs of a diverse society.

68 That Local Education Authorities and school Governors have the duty to create and implement strategies in their schools to prevent and address racism. Such strategies to include:

● that schools record all racist incidents;
● that all recorded incidents are reported to the pupils' parents/guardians, school Governors and LEAs;
● that the numbers of racist incidents are published annually, on a school by school basis; and
● that the numbers and self defined ethnic identity of 'excluded' pupils are published annually on a school by school basis.

69 That OFSTED inspections include examination of the implementation of such strategies.

70 That in creating strategies under the provisions of the Crime & Disorder Act or otherwise Police Services, local Government and relevant agencies should specifically consider implementing community and local initiatives aimed at promoting cultural diversity and addressing racism and the need for focused, consistent support for such initiatives.

 The report of the Stephen Lawrence Inquiry by Sir William Macpherson is available at:
www.archive.official-documents.co.uk/document/cm42/4262/4262.htm

The Impact of the Stephen Lawrence Inquiry

The Home Office has carried out research into the impact of the Stephen Lawrence Inquiry on policing. The conclusions of this research were fairly positive, though it notes that further progress is needed.

Assessing the Impact of the Stephen Lawrence Inquiry
Home Office Research Study 294 (2005)

Janet Foster, Tim Newburn and Anna Souhami

Foreword

The Inquiry into the failed police investigation of Stephen Lawrence's murder and broader issues of minority ethnic communities' trust in policing, led by Sir William Macpherson, was one of the defining moments in the recent history of the police service in England and Wales. The Inquiry Report pointed to fundamental flaws in the investigation that were attributed to professional incompetence, institutional racism and a failure of leadership. To combat these individual and organisational problems, the Inquiry urged the police service to examine how its policies and practices had allowed these flaws to exist, and set out a wide range of recommendations for improvement which have been described as the most extensive reform programme there has ever been on police–community relations.

The Home Secretary published an action plan for implementing the recommendations of the Inquiry in 1999. The Lawrence Steering Group (LSG), consisting of independent members, the police and other agencies, was also set up to support the delivery of the action plan and to oversee its implementation. The LSG became increasingly interested in assessing the impact of the Inquiry on the police service and its relationship with minority ethnic communities. The need to look at the outcomes arising from the implementation of the recommendations was also underlined by the Home Secretary in a recent meeting of the LSG. Researchers from the Home Office's Research, Development and Statistics (RDS) were therefore, commissioned by the LSG to carry out an evaluation of the changes prompted by the Inquiry in the police service.

The resulting research, carried out by the Mannheim Centre for Criminology at the London School of Economics, was one of the most extensive and detailed to have been conducted on police-community relations in England and Wales. It drew on a large national survey of police officers and approximately 2,000 hours of observations. The research report highlights the progress that has been made in policing since the Inquiry's publication, and points to a number of areas where the Inquiry has been an important lever for change. It also suggests the areas where further work is required to deal with the more challenging, systemic issues. The research's comprehensive and nuanced analysis illustrates how these issues manifest themselves in day-to-day policing and, as a result, identifies where further reform is required.

Many of the issues identified in this study point to the need for a greater appreciation of the needs of different communities by the police service. The proposals put forward in the recent Government White Paper *Building Communities, Beating Crime* (2004) can be seen as an attempt to address this. The White Paper sets out ways to strengthen the processes for the recruitment, retention, progression and support of minority ethnic and female staff in the police service. A strategy aimed at using learning and development to improve police performance on race and diversity, to be published in the next five years, reinforces the Government's workplace proposals. Importantly, the strategy will focus on improving and assessing individual officer, team and force performance in the critical area of race and diversity. The broader police reform agenda outlined in the White Paper also directly deals with the issue of cultural changes in the police. In promoting citizen focused policing, it seeks to engender a more responsive and customer-focused culture in the service and underlines how important front-line staff are in maintaining the reputation of the police and the broader criminal justice system. Communities need to be at the centre of policing, through neighbourhood policing teams, public engagement, and new accountability structures. Moreover, greater emphasis will be placed on public satisfaction and community confidence through their incorporation into the police performance framework.

Carole F. Willis
Assistant Director, Research Development and Statistics
Crime Reduction and Community Safety Group

. . .

Executive summary

Introduction

This report outlines the findings from a large study designed to assess the impact of the Stephen Lawrence Inquiry on policing. The Inquiry's terms of reference were 'to identify the lessons to be learned for the investigation and prosecution of racially motivated crimes' through a detailed analysis of the events surrounding the murder of Stephen Lawrence and the police response to it.

The primary aim of the study was:

> to evaluate the overall impact of the Stephen Lawrence Inquiry on the police in England and Wales examining changes prompted by the Inquiry in, and relationships between, police policy, operational practice, and the confidence of minority ethnic communities in the police, both at a national and at individual force level.

Methodology

The information and data for the study were collected between 2002 and 2004, and the research was divided into three key phases:

- **Initial phase** – qualitative research in four sites (two in London, and two in small/medium county forces) to establish officers' perceptions of the Lawrence Inquiry and 'scoping' interviews with some key stakeholders.
- **Three national surveys** – to gauge opinion about the Lawrence Inquiry and to establish a picture of its impact at a national level. The surveys involved:
  - 1,267 face-to-face interviews with officers of all ranks except those in the Association of Chief Police Officers (ACPO);
  - a postal survey of ACPO officers and staff; and
  - a postal survey of police authority members and staff.
- **In-depth qualitative research** – over 18 months of fieldwork that included:
  - a detailed examination of operational policing in four forces;
  - a case study of murder investigation in London; and
  - research with minority ethnic communities exploring their experiences of policing.

Attempting to establish the impact of the Lawrence Inquiry on policing was a complex task as there were no easy means by which practices and behaviour at the time of Stephen Lawrence's murder and the publication of the Inquiry Report could be compared with those at the time of the research.

It was possible to draw on earlier studies of policing for comparison. Some changes, particularly those involving structural developments, such as the introduction of new procedures or processes, do not require baseline data. However, where there were no appropriate baseline data available, the normative framework employed by the Lawrence Inquiry was used as the benchmark against which police practices and behaviour might be assessed. In the absence of benchmarking data, the study focused on officers' *perceptions* of changes since the Lawrence Inquiry, as well as the attitudes and experiences of minority ethnic communities.

Summary of findings

The Lawrence Inquiry appears to have been an important lever for change in the police service and there have been some substantial and positive changes in policing in the past five years. There have been significant improvements in:

- the recording, monitoring and responses to hate crime;
- the organisation, structure and management of murder investigation;
- liaison with families of victims of murder;
- consultation with local communities; and
- the general excision of racist language from the police service.
  However, there remain a number of important caveats to this picture.
- The positive developments noted here were not uniformly visible across police forces.
- Forces – perhaps understandably – tended to focus attention on those changes that were most obviously identifiable and achievable.
- The greatest continuing difficulty is understanding the nature of, and designing responses to, the problem of 'institutional racism' within policing. As a result, despite the intentions of police forces and their staff, certain groups still receive an inappropriate or inadequate service because of their culture or ethnic origin.

Understanding and responding to the Lawrence Inquiry

- The Lawrence Inquiry was perceived as an important moment in policing by officers in all force sites, and its overall impact to have been broadly positive.
- However, there was also considerable anger about the Inquiry in all sites, with officers feeling it unfair. The reaction was particularly powerful in London where the Inquiry and its immediate aftermath was described in strongly emotional terms. In sites outside London, the Inquiry appeared to have less resonance, as officers felt the failings it identified were indicative of an incompetent Metropolitan Police Service (MPS) rather than reflecting general practices in the police service more broadly.
- Staff both inside and outside the MPS thought the failings of the Lawrence investigation were rooted in incompetence rather than in racist practices.
- MPS officers consistently perceived the Inquiry to have been less fair – to their force, to senior officers in the MPS, and to detectives involved in the case – compared with officers serving elsewhere. Interestingly, Black and Minority Ethnic (BME) officers generally felt the Inquiry was fairer than their White colleagues did.

Institutional racism

- Much of the anger officers felt about the Lawrence Inquiry stemmed from use of the term 'institutional racism'. This was the single most powerful message that police officers received from the Inquiry.
- However, both survey data and observational fieldwork suggested that the term 'institutional racism' is not widely understood in the police service. Almost all front-line officers and some senior officers in the fieldwork sites thought that institutional racism signified a widespread problem of racist behaviour and attitudes among police staff. This misunderstanding was reflected in media coverage of the Inquiry and in broader public reactions. It is, therefore, not surprising that the term created widespread resentment and anger.
- The confusion was most likely exacerbated by the definition of institutional racism used by the Lawrence Inquiry and the use of the word 'racism' in the term itself.

Impact

- Officers of all ranks overwhelmingly believed that the services provided by the police had improved in the years since the Lawrence Inquiry. Just under three-quarters (72%) of officers felt the overall impact of the Stephen Lawrence Inquiry had been positive.
- One of the most significant impacts of the Inquiry was that police officers felt under greater and more intense scrutiny. In all sites, officers reported their heightened sensitivity and anxiety in dealing with BME communities after the Inquiry. Some officers feared that public awareness of the Inquiry made it more likely they would be accused of racism.
- The officer survey indicated that greatest anxiety existed in relation to stop and search – with officer confidence having notably declined since the Lawrence Inquiry. In all sites officers reported a climate in the aftermath of the Inquiry in which 'people were too afraid' to stop and search for fear of being accused of racism.
- The Inquiry also appeared to have brought into focus officers' uncertainty and confusion about the use of their powers. Officers, with their perception of increased scrutiny, thought that it was more difficult for them to break the rules around stop and search.
- These anxieties suggested that the Lawrence Inquiry had alerted officers to the possibility that their behaviour might be perceived and, crucially, successfully defined in a way that was at odds with their own intention and perception.

The changing climate of policing

- Although institutional racism was the central focus of the Lawrence Inquiry, one of the primary responses of the police service focused on eliminating racist language among police staff.
- The qualitative research undertaken showed that explicit racist language has been almost entirely excised from the police service and is no longer tolerated in all force sites. This is an important and marked change to the climate as little as ten years ago. The Lawrence Inquiry appeared to be an important catalyst in this change.
- The change in language appeared to be strongly related to a climate of increased scrutiny, and a heightened awareness of potential disciplinary responses.
- However, some BME [Black and Minority Ethnic] staff felt the absence of racist language was largely cosmetic and did not represent a genuine change in the culture of the force. BME officers were also more likely than their White counterparts to believe that minority officers faced discrimination in their work.

- Further, the urgency in tackling racist language was not mirrored in the response to other forms of discriminatory language and behaviour. In all sites, a greater tolerance of sexist and homophobic language was apparent and sexist language and behaviour was widespread in all sites.
- The experiences of women and minority staff suggest that the excision of explicitly racist language in the service had not led to broader changes in the internal culture of the police organisation. Women, gay and lesbian officers, in all sites, reported feeling excluded by a predominantly male, heterosexist culture. Women officers frequently felt undermined and undervalued. Strong feelings of exclusion and discrimination described by women and minority staff went largely unrecognised and unaddressed in all forces. Across all research sites there was little organisational understanding or support of the differential needs of minority ethnic staff, for example in relation to the racist abuse they received from the public.

Relationships with minority communities

- There have been significant improvements in the structures for consulting with local communities, and in understanding the need to consider community impact more broadly. In all research sites, local citizens felt the police had made such advances in the way they consulted with communities that they were now equal or better than other agencies.
- The introduction of independent advice has been an important development: over four-fifths of forces had established a force-wide Independent Advisory Groups (IAGs), seven in ten at a divisional (Basic Command Unit) level; and two-thirds for specific campaigns or operations.
- In all research sites, senior staff recognised the need for liaising with communities in response to events that had the potential for 'critical' impact on local communities (although understanding of what constituted a 'critical' incident varied).
- However, while the principle of consultation between the police and local citizens appeared to be well-established, its precise purpose was often unclear and oriented to police-led agendas rather than community needs and concerns. Forces varied in the extent to which they actively involved communities in strategy and practice, and in the extent to which they attempted to address difficult problems of representation in consultation forums.
- The development of posts dedicated to liaison with local minority communities has been a consistent and important development. These staff were responsible for much of the progressive work in developing relationships with minority and other communities and were valued by community workers in all research sites.
- In all sites there were other officers without a specific community portfolio who made considerable efforts to develop relationships with local minority communities. In particular, officers who had more contact with local communities, such as beat officers, had a better understanding of local needs and concerns and were able to foster better relationships.
- However, the roles of liaison and beat officers were generally not integrated into mainstream policing. As a result, officers in these roles often felt marginalised and were subject to other pressures (such as frequent abstraction) which undermined their ability to sustain community contacts.

Local service delivery

- In response to the Lawrence Inquiry, all forces had instituted diversity or Community Race Relations (CRR) training as a means of sensitising staff to the diverse cultures and experiences of minority groups. In the officer survey, the majority of staff found the training worthwhile and described the impact of CRR training primarily in terms of an increased awareness of some differences in cultural protocols.

- Difficulties with language were a relatively common problem in interactions with some BME groups. Officers were often unsure how to access interpreters, or when it was appropriate to do so. Moreover, it was not often feasible for interpreters to be available for help at the point of immediate need.
- There are continuing problems connected with routine working practice and service delivery which had negative consequences for relationships with some local communities. These largely stemmed from a failure to recognise differences in the ways policing was perceived in different communities. This issue is of crucial importance to the police service and goes to the heart of the central notion of institutional racism identified in the Lawrence Inquiry.
- In all sites, BME research participants described mistrust of the police and an expectation of discrimination. This widespread expectation of discrimination within BME communities was a key lens through which the actions of individual police officers were understood. Within such a context, inappropriate or simply poor service by individual officers was often perceived as racist.
- Police tactics that focused activity on BME communities, particularly minority youth, were frequently experienced as provocative and discriminatory. Appreciation within police forces that routine policing might be experienced in such a manner varied considerably. The absence of such appreciation was, without doubt, a barrier to increasing trust in local communities.

Murder investigation

- The MPS introduced a number of important changes to the structure and organisation of murder investigation as a result of the Lawrence case and the Inquiry's findings. These have resulted in significant improvements both to the overall quality of murder investigation and the treatment of victim's families. These included the introduction of new standards and procedures for the management of murder scenes; a requirement to record investigative decisions and their rationale; and trained and dedicated Family Liaison Officers.
- Other changes to murder investigation also occurred between Stephen Lawrence's death and the Lawrence Inquiry that were linked (though not exclusively) with the Lawrence case. These involved the introduction of: dedicated Murder Investigation Teams to concentrate skills and improve the quality of investigations; a Homicide Assessment Team who attended and advised at life threatening assault, unexplained death and murder scenes; more oversight of Senior Investigating Officers and their investigations; critical incident training; and formal reviews of murder investigations. These changes led to an improved initial response at murder scenes and increased scrutiny of investigations.
- However, these developments were oriented around pragmatic and tangible measures that favoured procedural changes in investigative practice. This left the broader issues raised by the Lawrence Inquiry and its findings, particularly in relation to institutional racism, relatively unaddressed within murder investigation.

Responding to hate crime

- The police service has made significant strides in dealing with and responding to hate crimes and the Lawrence Inquiry seems to have been an important catalyst in this regard.

Services generally, and the recording and monitoring of racist incidents in particular, had improved in all research sites. Officers in all but one site appeared to understand the definition and nature of 'racist incidents' as defined by the Lawrence Inquiry.

● The greatest changes, especially structurally, had been made in the MPS sites with the introduction of dedicated Community Safety Units. Outside London the story was mixed. In particular, there was one site that appeared to be lagging significantly behind all others.

● The greatest continuing concern arises from the low status of such work. Even within the MPS it was commonly felt such work was not perceived to be 'real police work'.

Levers for change

● While the changes stimulated, in part, by the Lawrence Inquiry were evident in all research sites, there were some notable differences among forces in the extent to which these changes occurred.

● The context in which forces operated appeared to be an important factor in the extent to which the Lawrence Inquiry and its recommendations were seen to be relevant to the force area, and consequently in the immediacy with which they were tackled. These included the demographic profile of the force (the size of BME population); the perceived levels of racist incidents; the perceived relevance of the Lawrence Inquiry to the force; and local issues, such as episodes of racist disorder.

. . .

Racism and institutional racism

It was the application of the term *institutional racism* to the MPS in particular, and the police service more generally, that generated the most debate following the publication of the Lawrence Inquiry Report. The Inquiry took evidence from several experts on the importance of distinguishing the discriminatory practices of organisations from the actions of individuals. It considered the deliberations of the Scarman Inquiry and was critical of its arguments for acknowledging the existence of 'unwitting' or 'unconscious' racism yet confining the idea of 'institutional racism' to overtly racist policies and practices consciously pursued by an institution. By contrast, the Lawrence Inquiry took the view that institutional racism consists of:

> The collective failure of an organisation to provide an appropriate and professional service to people because of their colour, culture, or ethnic origin. It can be seen or detected in processes, attitudes and behaviour which amount to discrimination through unwitting prejudice, ignorance, thoughtlessness and racist stereotyping which disadvantage minority ethnic people. (Para 6.34)

The Inquiry concluded that 'institutional racism . . . exists both in the Metropolitan Police Service and in other Police Services and other institutions countrywide' (para 6.39). Consequently, the research reported here examines policing in England and Wales generally and not solely in the MPS.

The use of the term institutional racism in this way was not unproblematic. In particular, it led both to considerable misunderstanding and resentment within the police service. Indeed, despite the intention that it should draw attention to problems at the level of organisational policies and practices, 'institutional racism' was interpreted as indicating a widespread problem of individual racism. Media coverage of the Lawrence Inquiry, together with the reaction of some key stakeholders, were important factors in this (mis)reading of the Inquiry's intent. However, aspects of the Inquiry Report itself may have contributed to such misunderstanding.

The Lawrence Inquiry sought to draw attention to embedded organisational practices and policies that result in a failure to provide an appropriate service to minority ethnic communities. However, the definition used by the Inquiry included terms such as 'unwitting prejudice' and 'racist stereotyping' more suggestive of individual, not institutional racism. Further, the Lawrence Inquiry shifted its attention between the actions of individuals and organisations. The Inquiry was understandably concerned both with investigating and understanding the actions of particular police officers at the scene of the murder and during the subsequent investigation, as well as examining the broader practices and policies of the MPS. However, in doing so it drew attention to not one but three processes: unwitting (individual) discriminatory behaviour; conscious racism; and, collective or systemic discrimination. The difficulty is that the three processes were not clearly separated within the Inquiry's definition of institutional racism, leading to the potential for confusion among those receiving and reading the Report.

 The Home Office Research Study 294 (2005), 'Assessing the Impact of the Stephen Lawrence Inquiry', by Janet Foster, Tim Newburn and Anna Souhami is available on the Home Office website at:
www.homeoffice.gov.uk/rds/pdfs05/hors294.pdf

Complaints about stop and search

One of the most sensitive areas of policing involves the power to stop and search members of the public. There has been concern that this power has been misused on occasion. Research has been carried out into complaints made against the police following a stop and search.

Stop and Search Complaints (2000–2001)
A Police Complaints Authority Study

Summary of main findings

The main study examined 100 complaints made against police in relation to stop and search incidents between April 2000 and March 2001. Ninety-eight members of the public raised a total of 298 separate complaint matters involving 231 police officers. Typically, the complainants were males, in their early 30s and were mainly of white (49.9%) or black (40.0%) ethnic origin. In only 11% of cases was more than one incident involved in the complaint.

The stops and/or searches complained about were equally likely to be conducted on pedestrians or vehicle occupants, with the initial stops justified as based on 'intelligence led policing' in just over one-third of cases, on 'behavioural cues' in one quarter and on traffic violations in a further quarter. In nearly 40% of incidents the stop alone resulted in arrest whilst a further third were escalated to a search. Of those searched, 'no offences' were detected in three quarters of cases, while ten individuals were arrested for drug related offences, weapons offences or public order offences. The majority of complainants were dissatisfied with the way in which officers conducted the stop and/or search and around a third alleged that the officers were uncivil or behaved in an oppressive manner. Almost half of all complainants alleged that officers assaulted them during the stop and search incident. The justification for the stop provoked dissatisfaction in a number of cases and around 20% of complaints involved allegations of racially discriminatory behaviour. The PCA [Police Complaints Authority] supervised 16 of the investigations, granting dispensations in a further 26 cases. Of the 74 fully investigated files, 31 were referred to the CPS [Crown Prosecution Service] but in only one case was an officer charged with a criminal offence. Of the 231 officers complained about, only ten received disciplinary outcomes – six received 'advice', a reprimand was issued to two officers, and one officer received a caution.

Comparison between our data and total complaint populations

The data presented in the main study represents just over 1% of the 8,880 complaint files handled by the PCA between April 1st 2000 and March 31st 2001, and so extrapolations must be made with caution particularly as the number of cases is also relatively small. Nonetheless, comparisons with the overall complaint population from the same period are illuminating. Stop and search complainants are broadly similar to the general complaint population in terms of age, although complaints relating to stop and search were slightly less likely to be made by females than other types of complaints against police (stop and search – 15%; all complaints 23%). However, the most dramatic difference between the study complainants and the general complaint population relates to ethnicity. In the total complaint population, complainants of black origin made up 10% of all complaints, as against 40% of the stop and search complaints in the current study. The elevated rate of complaints about stop and search by black complainants is also evidenced in the pilot study where 29% of the complaints were from black complainants compared with 13% of the overall complaint population. As has been reported in a number of previous studies on stop and search (e.g. Stone and Pettigrew, 2002), members of the black community often feel targeted by stop and search activities because of their skin colour and negative stereotypes of ethnic minority communities that are still widespread in the police service. This concern may be reflected in a complaint rate reported in both pilot and main studies that is considerably in excess of the Home Office research data (Home Office, 2002) indicating that, of 686,114 stops and searches in 2000–2001, 10% were carried out on people of black origin, 5% Asian, and 1% were of 'other' ethnic minorities.

It is also reflected in complaints reported to and overseen by the PCA. Complaint allegations of racially motivated discriminatory behaviour were made against officers 647 times during 2000–2001. These allegations represented 3.6% of all complaint matters recorded during this period, compared with 19.0% in the main study, almost two-thirds of these made by complainants of black ethnicity. This would clearly suggest that stop and search is a police power that provokes a particular kind of dissatisfaction in the black community, as indicated by Miller and colleagues (2000), in research undertaken by the Home Office.

However, these findings can be interpreted a number of ways. They may suggest that black people are treated particularly badly during such encounters, that they are particularly sensitised to the adverse effects of being stopped and searched or that they are more likely to complain about being stopped and searched. The main PCA research study reported above does suggest that the nature of the complaints are different for black people – while it is not surprising that black complainants are more likely to allege discriminatory behaviour, it is worthy of note that black complainants were more likely to complain about the justification for the initial stop, a finding perhaps explained by the fact that black complainants were significantly less likely than their white equivalents to be arrested on the basis of the stop alone. In contrast, black complainants were more likely to have the stop escalated to a search.

One interpretation of this may be that the evidential threshold for stopping white complainants was significantly higher than for stopping black complainants. Concerns about racial bias in the criminal justice [system] are unlikely to be allayed by the finding that white complainants were significantly more likely to have their complaints referred to the CPS (in just under half of the cases compared with 15% for black complainants).

Additionally, a white complainant brought the only complaint that led to criminal charges. While this would seem to provide a partial support for Bowling and Philips (2002) argument [that] the perceived ineffectiveness of the complaints procedure has led those dissatisfied with stop and search encounters increasingly to forgo the complaints procedure and take civil action instead, the finding that stop and search related complaints by black complainants occur with much greater frequency than general complaints against police by the same group does not provide obvious support for this claim.

. . .

Finally, it is important to discuss the location effects identified in the study. The Metropolitan Police Service is the largest force in England and Wales and our analysis revealed a number of differences between complaints against Metropolitan Police Service officers and those from the other forces. These differences are worthy of inclusion and comment. Stop and search complaints from the Metropolitan Police Service area attracted more complaints matters per incident than the rest of the country, and incidents within the Metropolitan Police Service were more likely to involve stops on groups of young people in public places, leading to allegations of oppressive conduct, incivility and racial discrimination. Complaints from the Metropolitan Police Service were dispensed with at twice the rate of elsewhere in the country, and had a significantly lower substantiation rate than in other forces (10.8% compared to 2.9%). Any attempts at explaining these variations would be speculative but future research is essential to assess whether these are robust effects and, if so, to attempt to offer some explanation for them.

Recommendations

Although there are limitations to the study particularly in terms of sample size, there are a number of important lessons that can be learned from the two pieces of research outlined above:

(1) It is essential that the IPCC [Independent Police Complaints Commission] ensure that all complaints resulting from stop and search incidents are investigated thoroughly and consistently and that the information presented enables adequate monitoring, evaluation and research of this highly contentious police power.

(2) We echo recommendation 61 of the Macpherson report in relation to stop and search recording. It is essential that all police managers ensure that all police stops are recorded regardless of whether or not the stop is then escalated to a search and that a record of the incident is made available to the individual stopped, preferably at the time of the incident. Failure to do so should be regarded as a disciplinary [offence].

(3) Police managers should be proactive in their oversight of the use of these powers to ensure that they are used fairly and proportionately, and in a way that is sensitive to the perceptions of the local community.

(4) When complaints do arise, it is imperative that alternatives to the formal complaints procedure are available, in particular local resolution to ensure that mutually acceptable longterm solutions can be found based on sensitive and effective policing and community awareness of police policies and practices with regard to stop and search.

(5) The Independent Police Complaints Commission and the Home Office should invest in a programme of research to assess two of the main group differences identified in the current research, comparing force variations in complaint profiles and outcomes in the Metropolitan Police Service and elsewhere in the country, and assessing the differences in complaint profile and outcome as a function of the ethnicity of the complainant.

(6) Police forces should review their policy for forwarding stop and search files to the CPS to ensure that there are no racially discriminatory practices underpinning this decision process.

 The full report of this research, 'Stop and Search Complaints (2000–2001)' is published on the website of the Independent Police Complaints Commission at: **www.ipcc.gov.uk/stopandsearchfullreport.pdf**

19

The criminal trial process

Introduction

This chapter looks at:

- the Code for Crown Prosecutors laying down guidance about when prosecutions should be brought;

- the involvement of judges in the plea bargaining process;

- the Code of Practice for Victims of Crime; and

- whether television cameras should be allowed into court rooms.

Crown Prosecution Service

The Crown Prosecution Service is responsible for bringing prosecutions on behalf of the state. Its employees base their decisions on whether to prosecute on guidance in the 'Code for Crown Prosecutors'. In the Stephen Lawrence case (discussed on p 270), the decision of the Crown Prosecution Service not to prosecute led to an unsuccessful private prosecution being brought.

Code for Crown Prosecutors

1 Introduction

1.1 The decision to prosecute an individual is a serious step. Fair and effective prosecution is essential to the maintenance of law and order. Even in a small case a prosecution has serious implications for all involved – victims, witnesses and defendants. The Crown Prosecution Service applies the Code for Crown Prosecutors so that it can make fair and consistent decisions about prosecutions.

1.2 The Code helps the Crown Prosecution Service to play its part in making sure that justice is done. It contains information that is important to police officers and others who work in the criminal justice system and to the general public. Police officers should apply the provisions of this Code whenever they are responsible for deciding whether to charge a person with an offence.

1.3 The Code is also designed to make sure that everyone knows the principles that the Crown Prosecution Service applies when carrying out its work. By applying the same principles, everyone involved in the system is helping to treat victims, witnesses and defendants fairly, while prosecuting cases effectively.

2 General principles

2.1 Each case is unique and must be considered on its own facts and merits. However, there are general principles that apply to the way in which Crown Prosecutors must approach every case.

2.2 Crown Prosecutors must be fair, independent and objective. They must not let any personal views about ethnic or national origin, disability, sex, religious beliefs, political views or the sexual orientation of the suspect, victim or witness influence their decisions. They must not be affected by improper or undue pressure from any source.

2.3 It is the duty of Crown Prosecutors to make sure that the right person is prosecuted for the right offence. In doing so, Crown Prosecutors must always act in the interests of justice and not solely for the purpose of obtaining a conviction.

2.4 Crown Prosecutors should provide guidance and advice to investigators throughout the investigative and prosecuting process. This may include lines of inquiry, evidential requirements and assistance in any pre-charge procedures. Crown Prosecutors will be proactive in identifying and, where possible, rectifying evidential deficiencies and in bringing to an early conclusion those cases that cannot be strengthened by further investigation.

2.5 It is the duty of Crown Prosecutors to review, advise on and prosecute cases, ensuring that the law is properly applied, that all relevant evidence is put before the court and that obligations of disclosure are complied with, in accordance with the principles set out in this Code.

2.6 The Crown Prosecution Service is a public authority for the purposes of the Human Rights Act 1998. Crown Prosecutors must apply the principles of the European Convention on Human Rights in accordance with the Act.

3 The decision to prosecute

3.1 In most cases, Crown Prosecutors are responsible for deciding whether a person should be charged with a criminal offence, and if so, what that offence should be. Crown Prosecutors make these decisions in accordance with this Code and the Director's Guidance on Charging. In those cases where the police determine the charge, which are usually more minor and routine cases, they apply the same provisions.

3.2 Crown Prosecutors make charging decisions in accordance with the Full Code Test (see section 5 below), other than in those limited circumstances where the Threshold Test applies (see section 6 below).

3.3 The Threshold Test applies where the case is one in which it is proposed to keep the suspect in custody after charge, but the evidence required to apply the Full Code Test is not yet available.

3.4 Where a Crown Prosecutor makes a charging decision in accordance with the Threshold Test, the case must be reviewed in accordance with the Full Code Test as soon as reasonably practicable, taking into account the progress of the investigation.

4 Review

4.1 Each case the Crown Prosecution Service receives from the police is reviewed to make sure that it is right to proceed with a prosecution. Unless the Threshold Test applies, the Crown Prosecution Service will only start or continue with a prosecution when the case has passed both stages of the Full Code Test.

4.2 Review is a continuing process and Crown Prosecutors must take account of any change in circumstances. Wherever possible, they should talk to the police first if they are thinking about changing the charges or stopping the case. Crown Prosecutors should also tell the police if they believe that some additional evidence may strengthen the case. This gives the police the chance to provide more information that may affect the decision.

4.3 The Crown Prosecution Service and the police work closely together, but the final responsibility for the decision whether or not a charge or a case should go ahead rests with the Crown Prosecution Service.

5 The full code test

5.1 The Full Code Test has two stages. The first stage is consideration of the evidence. If the case does not pass the evidential stage it must not go ahead no matter how important or serious it may be. If the case does pass the evidential stage, Crown Prosecutors must proceed to the second stage and decide if a prosecution is needed in the public interest. The evidential and public interest stages are explained below.

The evidential stage

5.2 Crown Prosecutors must be satisfied that there is enough evidence to provide a 'realistic prospect of conviction' against each defendant on each charge. They must consider what the defence case may be, and how that is likely to affect the prosecution case.

5.3 A realistic prospect of conviction is an objective test. It means that a jury or bench of magistrates or judge hearing a case alone, properly directed in accordance with the law, is more likely than not to convict the defendant of the charge alleged. This is a separate test from the one that the criminal courts themselves must apply. A court should only convict if satisfied so that it is sure of a defendant's guilt.

5.4 When deciding whether there is enough evidence to prosecute, Crown Prosecutors must consider whether the evidence can be used and is reliable. There will be many cases in which the evidence does not give any cause for concern. But there will also be cases in which the evidence may not be as strong as it first appears. Crown Prosecutors must ask themselves the following questions:

Can the evidence be used in court?

Is the evidence reliable?

(a) Is it likely that the evidence will be excluded by the court? There are certain legal rules which might mean that evidence which seems relevant cannot be given at a trial. For example, is it likely that the evidence will be excluded because of the way in which it was gathered? If so, is there enough other evidence for a realistic prospect of conviction?

(b) Is there evidence which might support or detract from the reliability of a confession? Is the reliability affected by factors such as the defendant's age, intelligence or level of understanding?

(c) What explanation has the defendant given? Is a court likely to find it credible in the light of the evidence as a whole? Does it support an innocent explanation?

(d) If the identity of the defendant is likely to be questioned, is the evidence about this strong enough?

(e) Is the witness's background likely to weaken the prosecution case? For example, does the witness have any motive that may affect his or her attitude to the case, or a relevant previous conviction?

(f) Are there concerns over the accuracy or credibility of a witness? Are these concerns based on evidence or simply information with nothing to support it? Is there further evidence which the police should be asked to seek out which may support or detract from the account of the witness?

5.5 Crown Prosecutors should not ignore evidence because they are not sure that it can be used or is reliable. But they should look closely at it when deciding if there is a realistic prospect of conviction.

The public interest stage

5.6 In 1951, Lord Shawcross, who was Attorney-General, made the classic statement on public interest, which has been supported by Attorneys-General ever since: 'It has never been the rule in this country – I hope it never will be – that suspected criminal offences must automatically be the subject of prosecution'. (House of Commons Debates, volume 483, column 681, 29 January 1951)

5.7 The public interest must be considered in each case where there is enough evidence to provide a realistic prospect of conviction. Although there may be public interest factors against prosecution in a particular case, often the prosecution should go ahead and those factors should be put to the court for consideration when sentence is being passed. A prosecution will usually take place unless there are public interest factors tending against prosecution which clearly outweigh those tending in favour, or it appears more appropriate in all the circumstances of the case to divert the person from prosecution (see section 8 below).

5.8 Crown Prosecutors must balance factors for and against prosecution carefully and fairly. Public interest factors that can affect the decision to prosecute usually depend on the seriousness of the offence or the circumstances of the suspect. Some factors may increase the need to prosecute but others may suggest that another course of action would be better.

The following lists of some common public interest factors, both for and against prosecution, are not exhaustive. The factors that apply will depend on the facts in each case.

Some common public interest factors in favour of prosecution

5.9 The more serious the offence, the more likely it is that a prosecution will be needed in the public interest. A prosecution is likely to be needed if:

(a) a conviction is likely to result in a significant sentence;

(b) a conviction is likely to result in a confiscation or any other order;

(c) a weapon was used or violence was threatened during the commission of the offence;

(d) the offence was committed against a person serving the public (for example, a police or prison officer, or a nurse);

(e) the defendant was in a position of authority or trust;

(f) the evidence shows that the defendant was a ringleader or an organiser of the offence;

(g) there is evidence that the offence was premeditated;

(h) there is evidence that the offence was carried out by a group;

(i) the victim of the offence was vulnerable, has been put in considerable fear, or suffered personal attack, damage or disturbance;

(j) the offence was committed in the presence of, or in close proximity to, a child;

(k) the offence was motivated by any form of discrimination against the victim's ethnic or national origin, disability, sex, religious beliefs, political views or sexual orientation, or the suspect demonstrated hostility towards the victim based on any of those characteristics;

(l) there is a marked difference between the actual or mental ages of the defendant and the victim, or if there is any element of corruption;

(m) the defendant's previous convictions or cautions are relevant to the present offence;

(n) the defendant is alleged to have committed the offence while under an order of the court;

(o) there are grounds for believing that the offence is likely to be continued or repeated, for example, by a history of recurring conduct;

(p) the offence, although not serious in itself, is widespread in the area where it was committed; or

(q) a prosecution would have a significant positive impact on maintaining community confidence.

Some common public interest factors against prosecution

5.10 A prosecution is less likely to be needed if:

(a) the court is likely to impose a nominal penalty;

(b) the defendant has already been made the subject of a sentence and any further conviction would be unlikely to result in the imposition of an additional sentence or order, unless the nature of the particular offence requires a prosecution or the defendant withdraws consent to have an offence taken into consideration during sentencing;

(c) the offence was committed as a result of a genuine mistake or misunderstanding (these factors must be balanced against the seriousness of the offence);

(d) the loss or harm can be described as minor and was the result of a single incident, particularly if it was caused by a misjudgment;

(e) there has been a long delay between the offence taking place and the date of the trial, unless:

- the offence is serious;
- the delay has been caused in part by the defendant;
- the offence has only recently come to light; or
- the complexity of the offence has meant that there has been a long investigation;

(f) a prosecution is likely to have a bad effect on the victim's physical or mental health, always bearing in mind the seriousness of the offence;

(g) the defendant is elderly or is, or was at the time of the offence, suffering from significant mental or physical ill health, unless the offence is serious or there is real possibility that it may be repeated. The Crown Prosecution Service, where necessary, applies Home Office guidelines about how to deal with mentally disordered off-enders. Crown Prosecutors must balance the desirability of diverting a defendant who is suffering from significant mental or physical ill health with the need to safeguard the general public;

(h) the defendant has put right the loss or harm that was caused (but defendants must not avoid prosecution or diversion solely because they pay compensation); or

(i) details may be made public that could harm sources of information, international relations or national security.

5.11 Deciding on the public interest is not simply a matter of adding up the number of factors on each side. Crown Prosecutors must decide how important each factor is in the circumstances of each case and go on to make an overall assessment.

The relationship between the victim and the public interest

5.12 The Crown Prosecution Service does not act for victims or the families of victims in the same way as solicitors act for their clients. Crown Prosecutors act on behalf of the public and not just in the interests of any particular individual. However, when considering the public interest, Crown Prosecutors should always take into account the consequences for the victim of whether or not to prosecute, and any views expressed by the victim or the victim's family.

5.13 It is important that a victim is told about a decision which makes a significant difference to the case in which they are involved. Crown Prosecutors should ensure that they follow any agreed procedures.

6 The threshold test

6.1 The Threshold Test requires Crown Prosecutors to decide whether there is at least a reasonable suspicion that the suspect has committed an offence, and if there is, whether it is in the public interest to charge that suspect.

6.2 The Threshold Test is applied to those cases in which it would not be appropriate to release a suspect on bail after charge, but the evidence to apply the Full Code Test is not yet available.

6.3 There are statutory limits that restrict the time a suspect may remain in police custody before a decision has to be made whether to charge or release the suspect. There will be cases where the suspect in custody presents a substantial bail risk if released, but much of the evidence may not be available at the time the charging decision has to be made. Crown Prosecutors will apply the Threshold Test to such cases for a limited period.

6.4 The evidential decision in each case will require consideration of a number of factors including:

- the evidence available at the time;
- the likelihood and nature of further evidence being obtained;
- the reasonableness for believing that evidence will become available;
- the time it will take to gather that evidence and the steps being taken to do so;
- the impact the expected evidence will have on the case;
- the charges that the evidence will support.

6.5 The public interest means the same as under the Full Code Test, but will be based on the information available at the time of charge which will often be limited.

6.6 A decision to charge and withhold bail must be kept under review. The evidence gathered must be regularly assessed to ensure the charge is still appropriate and that continued objection to bail is justified. The Full Code Test must be applied as soon as reasonably practicable.

 The Code for Crown Prosecutors is available on the Crown Prosecution Service website:
www.cps.gov.uk/victims_witnesses/code.html

Plea bargaining

Plea bargaining is the process of negotiations between the prosecution and defence lawyers over the outcome of a case. Effective plea bargaining requires the cooperation of the judge. In **R** v **Turner** (1970) the Court of Appeal had opposed such involvement but it made a U-turn in **R** v **Goodyear** (2005).

R v Goodyear (2005)

Lord Woolf CJ

Advance indication of sentence

29 In the light of the issues raised in this appeal, we have re-examined the principles which govern an indication of sentence given by the trial judge to a defendant.

30 The starting point is fundamental. The defendant is personally and exclusively responsible for his plea. When he enters it, it must be entered voluntarily, without improper pressure. There is to be no bargaining with or by the judge. These principles are derived from **R** v **Turner** [1970] 2 QB 321 itself.

31 Prior to **R** v **Turner**, it was not unusual for counsel to be seen (often separately from their solicitors) by the trial judge in his chambers, and for the judge to tell counsel his view of the sentence which would follow an immediate guilty plea. Archbold's Criminal Pleading, Evidence and Practice, 37th edn (1969) says nothing at all, and certainly nothing critical about this practice. It was **R** v **Turner** that brought the 'vexed question of so-called "plea-bargaining"' into the open [1970] 2 QB 321, 326. We must briefly summarise the facts.

32 The defendant, a man with many previous convictions, pleaded not guilty to theft. During an adjournment in the trial, counsel indicated that he wished to have a discussion with the judge, and went and did so. After he had spoken to the judge, and following that discussion, he advised Turner that in his (counsel's) opinion, if he pleaded guilty, the outcome might well be a non-custodial sentence, but that if the case proceeded and he was convicted by the jury, he ran the risk of going to prison.

33 The defendant received the impression that the views expressed to him by counsel represented the views the judge had communicated to counsel. This court decided that this represented improper pressure on the defendant to plead guilty, and that in the circumstances, the appropriate course would be to treat the guilty plea as a nullity.

34 It was immediately acknowledged that it was counsel's duty to give the accused the best advice he could, and 'if need be advice in strong terms': p 326. This advice would normally convey the potential value as a mitigating factor of a guilty plea. We pause to note that, inevitably, robust advice from counsel creates a degree of pressure on his client, and, what is more, the situation in which the defendant is placed itself constitutes a further source of pressure. Neither of these is improper. **R** v **Turner** emphasised that as far as possible justice should be administered in open court. Nevertheless for a variety of reasons, freedom of access between counsel and the judge was not prohibited. The problem arose from any discussion between them about sentence. This created the danger of pressure, or the appearance of pressure on the defendant to plead guilty. Such pressure, coming from the court, was unacceptable.

35 In essence, **R v Turner** decided that whereas counsel may give advice, which includes advice about the likely sentence on a guilty plea, such information coming from the court itself was impermissible:

> The judge should, subject to the one exception referred to hereafter, never indicate the sentence which he is minded to impose. A statement that on a plea of guilty he would impose one sentence but that on a conviction following a plea of not guilty he would impose a severer sentence is one which should never be made. This could be taken to be undue pressure on the accused, thus depriving him of that complete freedom of choice which is essential. (p 327)

The court referred to occasions when the judge would tell counsel that on the basis of the information before him, the sentence which would follow a guilty plea would be non-custodial, without saying anything about what would happen if the case proceeded to trial and conviction.

> Even so, the accused may well get the impression that the judge is intimating that in that event a severer sentence, maybe a custodial sentence would result, so that again he may feel under pressure. This accordingly must also not be done.

The only exception to the rule that an indication of sentence should not be given is:

> that it should be permissible for a judge to say, if it be the case, that whatever happens, whether the accused pleads guilty or not guilty, the sentence will or will not take a particular form, e.g. a probation order or a fine, or a custodial sentence. (p 327)

36 The principles in **R v Turner** have been consistently applied. The authorities are summarised in *Archbold's Criminal Pleading, Evidence and Practice*, 2005 edn, paras 4-78–4-81 and in *Blackstone's Criminal Practice 2005*, paras D11.53–D11.54. The principles were consolidated in the Practice Direction (Criminal Proceedings: Consolidation) [2002] 1 WLR 2870, Pt IV, para 45 and the Attorney-General issued guidance to counsel for the prosecution on the acceptance of pleas, with observations about the duty of the advocate for the Crown when discussions leading to a sentence indication arose: Attorney-General's Guidelines on the Acceptance of Pleas [2001] 1 Cr App R 28. We have considered all this material.

37 There have been earlier suggestions that the principle in **R v Turner** [1970] 2 QB 321, at any rate in its full ambit, merits re-examination. In the Report of the Royal Commission on Criminal Justice (July 1993) (Cm 2263), chairman Viscount Runciman of Doxford, ch 7, para 48, it was noted that:

> a significant number of those who now plead guilty at the last minute would be more ready to declare their hand at an earlier stage if they were given a reliable early indication of the maximum sentence that they would face if found guilty.

38 The report analysed the implications of the judgment in **R v Turner**, noting that the Crown Court study conducted for the commission showed overwhelming support among both judges and barristers for a change. It recommended, at paras 50–51, that:

> **50** . . . at the request of defence counsel on instructions from the defendant, judges should be able to indicate the highest sentence that they would impose at that point on the basis of the facts as put to them . . .

> **51** We envisage that the procedure which we recommend would be initiated solely by, and for the benefit of, defendants who wish to exercise a right to be told the consequence of a decision which is theirs alone.

The commission implied that the single question which the judge would have a discretion to answer would be: 'What would be the maximum sentence if my client were to plead guilty at this stage?'

39 The report then addressed the management and structure of the process, if the constraints in **R** *v* **Turner** were to be relaxed.

40 In Sir Robin Auld's Review of the Criminal Courts of England and Wales (October 2001), the advance indication of sentence was discussed at pp 434–444.

41 After examining the evidence, Sir Robin concluded, at p 443, that, subject to a number of specified safeguards:

on the request of a defendant, through his advocate, the judge should be entitled, formally to indicate the maximum sentence in the event of a plea of guilty at that stage and the possible sentence on conviction following a trial . . .

42 He believed that the ability of the judge to give an indication to a defendant who wished to know the maximum sentence he would receive in the event of a plea of guilty would 'enable the guilty defendant and those advising him to evaluate the judge's indication and assess the advantage or otherwise of proceeding with a plea': p 442. He believed that a comparison between the sentence on a plea of guilty and a possible sentence on conviction was justified, explaining, at p 442:

That comparison is precisely what a defendant considering admitting his guilt wants to know. He knows and will, in any event, be advised by his lawyer that a plea of guilty can attract a lesser sentence and broadly what the possible outcomes are, depending on his plea. So what possible additional pressure, unacceptable or otherwise, can there be in the judge, whom he has requested to tell him where he stands, indicating more precisely the alternatives?

43 Like the Royal Commission, Sir Robin then explained his views about the structure and management of any post-**Turner** procedure.

44 In the White Paper entitled *Justice for All* (2002) (Cm 5563), prepared after and in response to Sir Robin's review, there appeared to be a general welcome to a system for an advance indication of sentence made in response to a formal request initiated by the defendant: paras 4.42 and 4.43.

45 Some departure from the principles in **R** *v* **Turner** is now permitted by statute. In Schedule 3 to the Criminal Justice Act 2003, dealing with the allocation of cases triable either way, and sending cases to the Crown Court, paragraph 6, substituting section 20 of the Magistrates' Courts Act 1980, addresses the procedure where summary trial appears more suitable. The accused is entitled to request an indication of sentence, whether 'a custodial sentence or non-custodial sentence would be more likely to be imposed if he were to be tried summarily . . . and to plead guilty'. The court is entitled, but not obliged, to respond to such a request. In short, there is no longer any absolute prohibition against an advance indication of sentence.

46 With effect from 4 April this year the Criminal Procedure Rules 2005 (SI 2005/384) and, by amendment to Practice Direction (Criminal Proceedings: Consolidation) [2002] 1 WLR 2870, Practice Direction (Criminal Proceedings: Case Management) [2005] 1 WLR 1491 came into force. The plea and case management hearing in the Crown Court now

specifically requires the judge to seek and be given information on the following matters. First, following the guidance published by the Sentencing Guidelines Council in December 2004 on 'Reduction in Sentence for a Guilty Plea', whether the defendant has in fact been advised about the credit to be obtained for a guilty plea, and second, what steps had been taken to see whether the case might be resolved without a trial.

47 These matters sufficiently demonstrate a very different culture to that which obtained when **R v Turner** was decided. In all these circumstances the time has therefore come for this court to reconsider it.

48 R v Turner emphasised that the defendant was entitled to receive advice from his counsel about the sentence possibilities, so as properly to inform himself whether to plead guilty or not. That was deemed not to involve the risk of pressure on him. However **R v Turner** did not directly address the situation which would apply if the defendant personally was seeking an indication of sentence from the judge. After **R v Turner**, it became the practice to assume that he was not entitled to do so. Therefore, a somewhat strange situation developed that although the defendant's decision about his plea could properly be informed by the views of counsel about the sentence the judge would be likely to pass (provided always that he, counsel, had not participated in any discussions with the judge) it had simultaneously to be made ignorant of the judge's own views, even if the defendant wanted to know them. That position requires examination. In any event, the further question remains whether it continues to be appropriate to proceed on the basis that clear, and if necessary strong, but inevitably incompletely informed advice from counsel, about the advantages which would accrue from and the consequences which would follow an early guilty plea is permissible, while an intimation of these matters initiated by the judge should always, without more, be deemed to constitute improper pressure on the defendant, and therefore prohibited.

49 In our judgment, there is a significant distinction between a sentence indication given to a defendant who has deliberately chosen to seek it from the judge, and an unsolicited indication directed at him from the judge, and conveyed to him by his counsel. We do not see why a judicial response to a request for information from the defendant should automatically be deemed to constitute improper pressure on him. The judge is simply acceding to the defendant's wish to be fully informed before making his own decision whether to plead guilty or not guilty, by having the judge's views about sentence available to him rather than the advice counsel may give him about what counsel believes the judge's views would be likely to be.

50 We cannot, and do not seek to water down the essential principle that the defendant's plea must always be made voluntarily and free from any improper pressure. On closer analysis, however, we cannot discern any clash between this principle, and a process by which the defendant personally may instruct his counsel to seek an indication from the judge of his current view of the maximum sentence which would be imposed on the defendant. In effect, this simply substitutes the defendant's legitimate reliance on counsel's assessment of the likely sentence with the more accurate indication provided by the judge himself. In such circumstances, the prohibition against the judge giving an unsolicited sentence indication would not be contravened, and any subsequent plea, whether guilty or not guilty, would be voluntary. Accordingly it would not constitute inappropriate judicial pressure on the defendant for the judge to respond to such a request if one were made.

51 We have further reflected whether there should continue to be an absolute prohibition against the judge making any observations at all which may trigger this process. The judge is expected to check whether the defendant has been advised about the advantages which would follow an early guilty plea. Equally he is required to ascertain whether appropriate steps have been taken by both sides to enable the case to be disposed of without a trial. Following this present judgment he will know that counsel is entitled to advise the defendant that an advance indication of sentence may be sought from him. In these circumstances, we do not believe that it would be logical, and it would run contrary to the modern views of the judge's obligation to manage the case from the outset, to maintain as a matter of absolute prohibition that the judge is always and invariably precluded from reminding counsel in open court, in the presence of the defendant, of the defendant's entitlement to seek an advance indication of sentence. The judge would no doubt approach any observations to this effect with caution, first, to avoid creating pressure or the perception of pressure on the defendant to plead guilty and, second, bearing in mind the risk of conveying to the defendant that he has already made up his own mind on the issue of guilt, or indeed that for some reason he does not wish to try the case. If notwithstanding any observations by the judge, the defendant does not seek an indication of sentence, then, at any rate for the time being, it would not be appropriate for the judge to give or insist on giving an indication of sentence, unless in any event he would be prepared to give the indication permitted by **R v Turner** (see para 35 above) that the sentence will or will not take a particular form.

52 To that extent therefore, and subject to the guidance which follows, the practice in **Turner** and the subsequent authorities which applied it, need no longer be followed.

Guidelines

53 The objective of these guidelines is to ensure common process and continuing safeguards against the creation or appearance of judicial pressure on the defendant. The potential advantages include, first and foremost, that the defendant himself would make a better informed decision whether to plead, or not. Experience tends to suggest that this would result in an increased number of early guilty pleas, with a consequent reduction in the number of trials, and the number of cases which are listed for trial, and then, to use current language, 'crack' at the last minute, usually at considerable inconvenience to those involved in the intended trial, and in particular, victims and witnesses. Properly applied, too, there may be a reduced number of sentences to be considered by the Attorney-General, and where appropriate, referred to this court as unduly lenient. In short, an increase in the efficient administration of justice will not impinge on the defendant's entitlement to tender a voluntary plea.

54 In our judgment, any advance indication of sentence to be given by the judge should normally be confined to the maximum sentence if a plea of guilty were tendered at the stage at which the indication is sought. In essence we accept the recommendation of the Report of the Royal Commission that the judge should treat the request for a sentence indication, in whatever form it reaches him, as if he were being asked to indicate the maximum sentence on the defendant at that stage. For the process to go further, and the judge to indicate his view of the maximum possible level of sentence following conviction by the jury, as well as its level after a plea of guilty, would have two specific disadvantages. First, by definition, the judge could not be sufficiently informed of the likely impact of the trial on him (or the trial judge) in the sentencing context. It would be unwise for him to bind himself to any indication of the sentence after a trial in advance of it, in effect on a hypothetical basis. If he were to do so, to cover all eventualities he would probably have to indicate a very substantial possible maximum sentence. This would lead to a second problem, arising from the comparison between the two alternatives available to the defendant, that is the maximum level after a trial, and the maximum level following an immediate plea. With some defendants at any rate, the very process of comparing the two alternatives would create pressure to tender a guilty plea.

Victims and the criminal trial process

Victims and other witnesses play a vital role in getting convictions and thereby achieving justice, but historically the criminal justice system has paid insufficient attention to the needs of victims and witnesses of crime, with lawyers taking the centre stage in legal proceedings instead. Organisations such as Victim Support have campaigned for many years to persuade the government to recognise that victims should have distinct rights. The government has accepted these arguments and in 2006 the Home Office published a Code of Practice for Victims of Crime. This Code sets out the services victims should expect to receive from the criminal justice system, including the right to be notified of any arrests and court hearings related to their case, the right to be told if charges are being dropped and the right to be informed about whether or not they are eligible to compensation.

The Code of Practice for Victims of Crime

Obligations of service providers

5 The police
5.1 All police forces for police areas in England and Wales, the British Transport Police and the Ministry of Defence Police (the 'police') have the following obligations.

Crime reporting, assessment and Victim Support
5.2 Following the report of a crime to which the NCRS applies (criminal conduct); if the police, using their professional judgment, decide that there will be no investigation into that crime, they will advise the victim of that fact as soon as possible and within five working days at the latest. Once this decision is made the only sections of the Code which will apply are 5.3 (in all cases) and 5.4 (subject to the exceptions in 5.5 and 5.6).

5.3 The police must ensure that victims can access information about local support services and contact details for those services as soon as possible after an allegation of criminal conduct is made and no later than five working days after an allegation is made. The police can provide this information by either giving the victim a copy of the current local 'Victims of Crime' leaflet or by ensuring that the victim can access the information in another format, such as via the internet. Subject to availability from national sources, any local 'Victims of Crime' leaflet given to a victim by the police must be provided in a language or format the victim can understand.

5.4 Subject to the exceptions in paragraphs 5.5 and 5.6 below, the police must clearly explain to the victim that their details will be passed on to Victim Support unless they ask the police not to. The police must then provide the relevant local Victim Support Group with the victim's contact details no later than two working days after the day an allegation of criminal conduct is made.

5.5 In accordance with the victim referral agreement between the police and Victim Support, the police should not routinely pass over to a relevant local Victim Support Group the details of victims of the following criminal conduct:

(a) theft of a motor vehicle;
(b) theft from a motor vehicle;
(c) minor criminal damage; and
(d) tampering with motor vehicles.

However, aggravating factors such as repeat victimisation, victim request for contact, vulnerable victims or victims of hate crime will ensure a referral to Victim Support.

5.6 The police should only pass Victim Support the details of victims of sexual offences or domestic violence or the details of the relatives of homicide victims if the victims or relatives have given their explicit consent.

Identification of vulnerable or intimidated victims
5.7 The police must take all reasonable steps to identify vulnerable or intimidated victims using the criteria given at section 4.

5.8 Where a vulnerable or intimidated victim may be called as a witness in criminal proceedings, and may be eligible for assistance by way of special measure under Chapter I of Part II of the Youth Justice and Criminal Evidence Act 1999, the police must explain to the victim the provision about special measures in that Act and record any views the victim expresses about applying for special measures.

Investigation
5.9 If no suspect is arrested, charged, cautioned, reprimanded, given a final warning or subject to other non court based disposal in respect of relevant criminal conduct, the police must notify the victim on at least a monthly basis, of progress in cases being actively investigated up until the point of closure of the investigation.

5.10 Where an investigation into a serious crime is concluded with no person having been charged with the offence, the police must advise the victim, or family if bereaved, of this fact and the reasons for it. At this time, the fact that the case will be subject to periodic review must be discussed with the victim or family representative and they must be given the opportunity to decide whether they wish to be advised of any review procedures which take place. This decision must be recorded by the senior investigating officer at the time of the discussion.

5.11 If the victim or family representative expresses a wish to be advised of any review procedures, the police must ensure that information about the review is passed on to the victim or family representative within one working day of the review procedure commencing.

5.12 The victim or family must also be given the opportunity at this stage to say whether they wish to be advised of the reopening of the investigation due to new evidence or changes in forensic procedures. This decision must be recorded by the senior investigating officer at the time of the discussion. If an enquiry is reopened, the police must consider the expressed wishes of the victim or family before making contact with them and record the reasons for any decision made in this respect.

Family Liaison Officers

5.13 Where a victim has died as a result of criminal conduct or suspected criminal conduct, the police must assign a Family Liaison Officer to any relatives which the police consider appropriate and make a record of the assignment. The police must also provide close relatives of the victim with the packs 'Advice for bereaved families and friends following murder or manslaughter', or 'Advice for bereaved families and friends following death on the road', or equivalent packs.

Arrest and bail

5.14 If a suspect is arrested on suspicion of an offence in respect of relevant criminal conduct, the police must notify the victim of this within one working day for vulnerable or intimidated victims and no later than five working days for all other victims.

5.15 If the suspect is released with no further action being taken, the police must notify the victim of this event and the relevant reasons for no further action being taken within one working day for vulnerable or intimidated victims and no later than five working days for all other victims.

5.16 If the suspect is released on police bail to return to the police station, the police must notify vulnerable or intimidated victims of this event, reasons for bail and any relevant bail conditions within one working day and notify other victims within five working days.

5.17 If police bail is altered by change of bail conditions, date of return on bail or bail is cancelled, the police must notify vulnerable or intimidated victims of these events and the reason within one working day and notify other victims within five working days.

Decisions to bring criminal proceedings

5.18 If a suspect is interviewed and/or reported for offences by a police officer in relation to relevant criminal conduct, the police must notify the victim of this fact and the fact that a file will be submitted for a decision on prosecution to be made or summons to be issued. This notification must be within three working days of the suspect being interviewed and/or reported. When a summons is issued by the court the victim must be notified of this fact and the date of the first hearing within five working days of the police being notified of the summons being issued.

5.19 It will be the duty of the police to notify victims of all decisions to bring any criminal proceedings for a relevant offence. If a decision is made not to prosecute the suspect, the victim must be notified of this fact. If the decision is made by the police, the responsibility for notification lies with the police. In this case vulnerable or intimidated victims must be notified within one working day of the person being charged. All other victims must be notified within five working days of the person being charged.

5.20 In cases where, following a discussion between the investigating officer and a Crown Prosecutor, a decision is taken that there is insufficient evidence to charge a suspect with a relevant criminal offence, or a suspect is charged with an offence, it will be the responsibility of the police to notify the victim of this fact within one working day for vulnerable or intimidated victims and within five working days for all other victims.

Bailing of persons to court

5.21 If a suspect is charged with an offence in relation to relevant criminal conduct and released on police bail to appear at a court, the police must notify the victim of this event, the date of the court hearing and any relevant bail conditions within one working day for vulnerable or intimidated victims and within five working days for other victims. Where the decision to charge a suspect with a relevant offence is made by the police in accordance with the Director's Guidance on Charging, the notification must also state that the decision is subject to review by the CPS and that if after review the CPS takes a decision to substantially alter or drop any charge, the CPS will notify the victim.

5.22 If bail conditions are amended by the police prior to the suspect appearing at court the police must notify vulnerable or intimidated victims of any relevant changes to the bail conditions within one working day and all other victims within five working days.

5.23 If a suspect is charged with an offence in relation to relevant criminal conduct and the police will be applying to the court to remand the suspect in custody, the police must notify a vulnerable or intimidated victim of this event and the date of the remand hearing within one working day.

5.24 If a suspect in respect of relevant criminal conduct is remanded in custody by the court in circumstances where the police had applied for the suspect to be remanded in custody the police must notify a vulnerable or intimidated victim within one working day and all other victims within five working days.

5.25 The police must inform all victims if a suspect in respect of relevant criminal conduct is given bail by the court in circumstances where the police made an application to remand the suspect in custody. At the same time, the police must also inform all victims of any conditions attached to the bail that relate to, involve or affect the victim, and what the victim can do if conditions are broken. This information must be provided by the police within one working day for vulnerable or intimidated victims and within five working days for all other victims.

Other disposal methods

5.26 If a suspect is cautioned (simple or conditional), reprimanded, given a final warning, issued a penalty notice for disorder, or given any other non-court disposal method, in respect of relevant criminal conduct, the police must notify the victim of this event no later than one working day after the day of the event in the case of vulnerable or intimidated victims and within five working days after the day of the event in the case of other victims.

Youth Offending Teams

5.27 In cases where the perpetrator of relevant criminal conduct is under the age of eighteen, the police must pass the victim's contact details to the Youth Offending Team (unless the victim asks the police not to) to enable victims to have access to reparation or other restorative justice type initiatives.

 The Code of Practice for Victims of Crime is published on the Home Office website at:
www.homeoffice.gov.uk/documents/victims-code-of-practice?view=Binary

Televising the courts

The government considered whether it would be appropriate to allow television cameras into courts, to make the court proceedings more accessible to the public. It issued a consultation paper on this subject, 'Broadcasting Courts' (2004), but its final conclusion was that it was not in the public's interests to allow cameras into the court room.

Broadcasting Courts
Consultation Paper (2004)

Foreword by Lord Falconer, Secretary of State for Constitutional Affairs

Justice must be done and justice must be seen to be done. That notion exactly catches the argument about television and the courts.

The justice system exists to do justice. If it does not do justice in public it risks slipping into unacceptable behaviour, and losing public confidence. With a few exceptions, our courts are open to the public, but very few people who are not involved in cases ever go near a court. Most people's knowledge and perception of what goes on in court comes from court reporting and from fictionalised accounts of trials. The medium which gives most access to most people, television, is not allowed in our courts.

Should that change? Is there a public interest in allowing people through television to see what actually happens in our courts in their name? In a modern, televised age, I think there is a case to be considered here. Your responses to the questions posed in this paper will form part of that consideration. There are many difficult questions involved and I believe they warrant a full and considered public debate. I want to ensure that we get a wide range of views from all sides of the argument before we decide whether to take action.

At present I can see no case for televising cases involving children and I think we will need to consider very carefully the question of broadcasting criminal trials. These are bound to give rise to the greatest interest, but their success rests on people giving evidence. No change to make our courts more open and more accessible should worsen or jeopardise in any way the position of witnesses and victims or make witnesses reluctant to appear. I am concerned at overseas research showing that people believe that if their evidence might be televised that would reduce the likelihood of their coming forward as witnesses.

I know these are difficult and delicate issues. I know that broadcasters, and perhaps others, will press for change. But my responsibility is to consider the issues fully and carefully, focusing on the doing of justice by the courts. I want you, as stakeholders or as members of the public, to help me do that by giving me your views.

Cameras in the courtroom would be a big step. We have to make sure that any such step would benefit justice, not burden justice. We must protect witnesses and jurors and victims. Justice being done and being seen to be done is a priority list, not two parts of equal standing. Our watchword in the debate will be clear. Justice should be seen to be done. But our priority must be that justice is done.

Lord Falconer of Thoroton

 The consultation paper 'Broadcasting Courts' (2004) is available on the internet at:
www.dca.gov.uk/consult/courts/broadcasting-cp28-04.htm

20 | Sentencing

Introduction

This chapter looks at:

- Lord Carter's report on the prison system;
- the debate as to whether a structured sentencing framework should be introduced; and
- Home Office research into whether women suffer discrimination when being sentenced.

A structured sentencing framework

The government asked Lord Carter to review the prison system because it was concerned by the growing prison population and the related problems of increased costs and over-crowding. Lord Carter wrote a report in which he recommended that large new prisons should be built and that judges should be given less sentencing discretion by establishing a structured sentencing framework. The report starts with a letter addressed to the government from Lord Carter which is reproduced below along with his key recommendation for a structured sentencing framework.

Securing the Future: Proposals for the Efficient and Sustainable Use of Custody in England and Wales (2007)

In June this year you asked me to consider options for improving the balance between the supply of prison places and demand for them and to make recommendations on how this could be achieved.

I enclose my final report with my proposals for how to resolve the current and historical pressures facing our prison system.

The increased prison population of the past decade is a result of a concerted and successful effort to catch, convict and detain for longer periods the most dangerous and serious offenders. However, the causes and symptoms of the current problems and pressures facing our prisons demonstrate to me and to those I have consulted with that we need a long term strategy to create an affordable and sustainable solution to the limitations in the way we create demands on our custodial resources and then respond to them.

The proposals that I am making to you today are intended to provide you with a long term strategy as well as suggestions for measures to manage the immediate pressures that the prison system faces.

My key recommendations are:

- a significant expansion of the current prison building programme should begin immediately so that up to 6,500 additional new places, on top of the significant expansion already planned, can be provided by the end of 2012;
- larger, state of the art prisons should be planned and developed now so that from 2012 there can be approximately 5,000 new places that will allow for a programme of closures of old, inefficient, and ineffective prisons offering better value for money and much improved chances of reducing re-offending and crime;
- that a structured sentencing framework and permanent Sentencing Commission should be developed, with judicial leadership, to improve the transparency, predictability and consistency of sentencing and the criminal justice system; and
- there are grounds for a more efficient approach to the way operations and headquarters' overheads are structured and managed.

The pressures now facing the prison system inevitably mean that I have to recommend that the current building programme has to be accelerated and expanded. In addition to the expansion of prison capacity, I believe that you should make immediate changes to existing sentencing legislation to modify the use of custody for certain types of low risk offenders and offences and encourage use of alternative remedies, in accordance with your strategy for reserving custody for the most serious and dangerous offenders.

Changes in governance and organisational arrangements are needed to aid the delivery of this large, costly and complex package. The major challenges that these changes will need to address are the management of the expanded construction programme, achieving greater financial control across the prison system and standardising the way that the services provided by public and private sector prisons are specified and monitored.

The issues I explore in my report will continue to be an important agenda for you and the public. The debate around prison must be conducted in a focussed and informed manner which is why above all other recommendations I hope government, parliament and judiciary can work together to establish rapidly a working group to look at the advantages and feasibility of a structured sentencing framework and permanent Sentencing Commission for England and Wales. I have separately written to the judiciary setting out my proposals on this significant and important issue.

. . .

Lord Carter of Coles

Developing a structured sentencing framework

22 The recommendations set out so far in this chapter are intended to mitigate a constant and steady increase in the pressures in the prison population over the next six years. The history of the prison population since 1945 and the experience of other developed countries suggest that these pressures are unlikely to abate in the foreseeable future.

23 There is therefore a need for a focussed and informed public debate about penal policy. It will be important to consider whether to continue to have one of the largest prison populations per capita in the world and to devote increasing sums of public expenditure to building and running prisons and responding to fluctuating pressures as they emerge. Not only is it costly, inefficient and a demand on scarce land, but the sporadic way in which the pressures emerge and are responded to inhibits the delivery of effective offender management and rehabilitation.

24 Two of the alternatives to continuous and expensive prison building are to overcrowd prisons to indecent and unsafe levels or implement continuous measures to release offenders from prison earlier, diminishing the authority of the court and eroding public confidence and the integrity of the criminal justice system. Neither of these alternatives is attractive, as the following examples from the US illustrate.

Record overcrowding in California with no end in sight

In the period 1990 to 2000, California's prison population increased by 60%. Part of this increase followed the adoption, in 1994, of the 'three strikes and you're out' law, which sentenced criminals found guilty of a third serious criminal offence to life imprisonment. To meet increasing demand, the state invested $817 million in prison construction, increasing the number of correctional facilities from 20 to 33. Yet despite this investment California still suffers a net deficit of prison places. In June 2007, the 33 state prisons, designed to hold 100,000, held as many as 172,000 prisoners, almost double the peak overcrowding rate in England and Wales in the 20th century. In May 2007, Governor Schwarzenegger announced a further prison expansion programme, creating some 53,000 spaces and costing $6.1bn (£2.9bn), to meet continuing increases in demand.

Attrition and meaningless sentencing in North Carolina

During 1990–1994, prisoners in North Carolina served an average of 20–30% of their maximum custodial sentence, regardless of offence type. Offenders served as little as 35% of their sentences for the most serious violent crimes, and just 19% for the least serious. At its worst, those convicted of less serious offences served 6% of their sentences. In response to these figures, judges increased sentence lengths to try to influence the parole commission, yet to keep the system within the limits of the prison cap the parole commission was forced to release more offenders, often several hundred per week. Thus, a vicious circle ensued with average sentence lengths announced by judges increasing at the same time as the average times served declining.

---

25 The only other alternative that has been put to the Review and found to have worked in practice is where a structured sentencing framework has been developed.

The current sentencing framework

26 The current sentencing framework is based on legislation, the decisions of the Court of Appeal, including guideline judgments, and sentencing guidelines issued by the Sentencing Guidelines Council. Parliament is responsible for laying down maximum and in some cases minimum sentences for offences, usually on the basis of measures introduced by the government. Court of Appeal judgments provide guidance to the courts. In addition, since 2004, the Sentencing Guidelines Council has had the responsibility for framing sentencing guidelines in respect of offences or offenders, or in respect of particular matters affecting sentencing.

27 As with most other common law systems, the sentencing framework is based upon multiple and fragmented legislation developed and added to, over many decades. In addition to the basic legislative framework, sentencing practice may also be affected by numerous and unquantifiable influencing factors including political rhetoric, government activity and media pressure as set out in chapters one and two.

28 The complexity and uncertain effect of external factors makes the sentencing framework opaque. Predicting the factors that determine and influence sentencing is therefore difficult and inhibits government decision making and planning on the use of finite penal resources.

29 A structured sentencing framework has been a clear precedent, from a number of jurisdictions, as shown in several jurisdictions to bring greater to how this can be successfully achieved through a transparency, predictability and consistency to structured sentencing framework, developed and sentencing and the criminal justice system. There is monitored by a permanent Sentencing Commission.

Pioneering structured sentencing in Minnesota

Minnesota pioneered the implementation of a structured sentencing framework, which came into effect in 1980, replacing the old indeterminate sentencing system. The value of a structured sentencing framework to the state's criminal justice system has been exemplified by its ability to project in the prison population accurately and manage capacity appropriately.

Minnesota has one of the lowest incarceration rates in the United States, but has still had a growth in its prison population from approximately 6,000 in 2000 to 9,000 in 2007. For example, since 1989 increased sentences for drug offences have caused a rise in proportion of the prison population for these offenders from 5% to 24%. Sentences for sex offenders have also increased significantly and this group is expected to have the highest growth rate over the next ten years. However this growth has been managed and responded to without eroding sentences or through chronic overcrowding.

The state is able to accurately project the prison population using its structured sentencing simulation model, which includes key assumptions about the impact of any changes in the law and the projected capacity of institutional and community programmes. In 2006, the state was able to predict the prison population to within 0.7% or just 66 offenders per month.

Responding to chronic overcrowding and eroded sentences in North Carolina

In 1994, North Carolina introduced a structured sentencing framework. Under the new system, it is possible to accurately predict the changes that will occur to the prison population; indeed, over a recent 6 month period they were able to predict their overall state prison population of 38,500, to within 11 places. The state also implemented a deliberate strategy to increase the use of community sanctions for non-violent offenders. Prisoners now serve an average of about 80% of their sentences.

The reform has attracted a broad political consensus, because the probabilities of incarceration and lengths of sentences have increased for violent offenders. North Carolina's success in managing the use of its prison resources is especially remarkable because it occurred over a period in which the United States as a whole was experiencing enormous prison growth.

The components of a structured sentencing framework

30 The main feature of a structured sentencing framework is a single comprehensive set of indicative guideline ranges. This would cover sentence lengths, types of community sentences and the level of financial penalty, for groups of all offences, ranked by seriousness and offender characteristics (e.g. criminal history and culpability).

31 One method used frequently in designing such a framework is to produce a first version derived from current sentencing practice for all offences. Subsequent versions would draw on current sentencing practice, but would be modified so far as necessary as to take account of:

● the principles of sentencing as set down in legislation (e.g. Criminal Justice Act 2003); and
● the total impact on prison places and other penal services to ensure that they would come within a published financial envelope as set out by government to Parliament.

32 Provision would be made in sentencing framework law to give effect to the final guidelines.

33 A structured sentencing framework proposal does not mean that individual sentencers have to have regard to resources at the time they sentence in individual cases. The task of ensuring that aggregate sentencing outcomes remain within the envelope of available prison places and other penal services is undertaken in the design of the structured sentencing framework.

34 Sentencers would, of course, continue to pass sentences on the evidence and aggravating and mitigating factors in each case. Sentencers must retain the independence to depart from an indicative range where they consider it appropriate (subject to the statutory maximum and any statutory minimum requirements).

35 The ranges would need to be developed in such a way that departure is kept to a minimum as the breadth of the range would be designed to account for the vast majority of usual aggravating and mitigating factors seen in current sentencing practice.

36 In exercising the discretion to depart from a presumptive sentence, the judge would explain in sufficient detail, the particular identifiable circumstances. In addition to his sentencing remarks, the judge would record the reasons for the departure so that his decision, could if necessary, be reviewed on appeal.

Developing and overseeing a structured sentencing framework

37 Most jurisdictions that have introduced successful structured sentencing frameworks have done so through the work and guidance of an independent statutory body (usually known as a Sentencing Commission). Successful Sentencing Commissions are invariably led by a member of the senior judiciary with further judicial input as well as from prosecution, defence, and victims' representatives and significant statistical, analytical and legal support.

38 The task of a Sentencing Commission is to develop a comprehensive set of indicative ranges according to the objectives set down by the legislature and in consultation with all key parties and the public. Once a table of indicative ranges is in place the Commission monitors their use and carries out a number of other reporting and advisory functions.

39 There are different mechanisms for seeking the assent, or approval, of the legislature to the set of indicative ranges produced by the Sentencing Commission. It will be necessary to develop a similar process for this jurisdiction. One possible model is:

(a) the Commission would present them to government along with the accompanying prison population and correctional resources forecast. Government would present them to Parliament for affirmative approval in a format as set out under the originating primary legislation;

(b) at the stage of seeking approval, both the Commission and the government would endorse the options that went before Parliament;

(c) the government would be prevented by statute from unilaterally altering the set of indicative ranges. If the government wished to make any amendments they would have to consult and agree them with the Commission, who would model the impact, update projections and possibly consult wider before giving agreement. The Commission should be involved throughout the parliamentary process in providing further advice as required; and

(d) in order for this process to be completed in a timely and managed way, a table of indicative ranges should, in the first instance, be completed for either-way and indictable offences.

Once completed and passed by Parliament a similar process would begin for all summary offences.

40 If such a process were to be established for England and Wales it would build on the work of the separate Sentencing Advisory Panel and the Sentencing Guidelines Council.

Bringing transparency and control to the factors that influence sentencing

41 Once a set of comprehensive indicative ranges was in place they would be overseen by the Court of Appeal. The ongoing role for a Commission would be to collect information on each of the factors that affect the prison population, including the impact of the table of indicative ranges and issues relating to remand, recall, the work of the Parole Board and the number of offences brought to justice.

42 A Commission would be responsible for advising the government on the likely effect of these factors on the prison population and assist in finding solutions to these problems, including by designing and calculating the impact of changes to the structured sentencing framework. Any substantive changes to the sentencing ranges would have to go through the same consultative and Parliamentary process as the original ranges set out above.

43 A Commission could be asked to advise on policy decisions on other drivers of the population but adoption and implementation of such solutions would continue to be the responsibility of government and Parliament.

44 A Commission could also be required under the original statute to assess all national policy proposals. This will include proposed legislation which could have an impact on each of the factors which contribute to the prison population so as to estimate report and if asked, advise on the likely impact of these proposals on prison places. A Commission could produce the official prison projections and report annually to Parliament.

45 These continuing responsibilities of a permanent Commission are necessary to ensure that the criminal justice system has the capability to predict the size of the prison population and use of other penal resources with greater accuracy than the current system. This would allow for improved planning and governance of policy decisions and the process by which decisions are made would be far more transparent than at present.

Informing the public debate and developing options

46 Further work is needed in order to focus the public debate as to whether the development and adoption of a structured sentencing framework is the course that government and Parliament wish to follow for finding a long-term solution to prison population pressures. This work should be undertaken by a group of people with the time, skills and status to acquire and assess data to produce a first set of indicative ranges based on current practice. A draft terms of reference for such a group can be found at annex G.

47 As part of the contract with the public, the government will need to ensure that the sentences passed by the Court within a possible structured sentencing framework are delivered effectively and in a way which maximises public protection and reduces re-offending. Delivery of the reforms envisaged by the government is the critical driver in this process.

48 The preliminary work may enable Parliament to decide whether to endorse the creation of a Sentencing Commission, potentially in a fourth session criminal justice bill in autumn 2008.

> **Recommendation 3: structured sentencing and an effective planning mechanism**
>
> The government should establish a working group to consider the advantages, disadvantages and feasibility of a structured sentencing framework and permanent Sentencing Commission, which will lead and inform the public debate on these issues.
>
> The working group will examine detailed proposals through consultation for a possible Sentencing Commission for England and Wales, with a view to its possible establishment in the next three years.
>
> The working group will report to the Lord Chancellor and Lord Chief Justice by summer 2008.

Lord Carter's report 'Securing the Future: Proposals for the Efficient and Sustainable Use of Custody in England and Wales' (2007) is available on the website of the Ministry of Justice at:
www.justice.gov.uk/docs/securing-future.pdf

Rejection of a structured sentencing framework

Upon Lord Carter's recommendation, the government referred the question of establishing a structured sentencing framework to a Working Party chaired by Lord Gage. Its report, entitled 'Sentencing Guidelines in England and Wales: An Evolutionary Approach' (2008) rejected this recommendation. Instead it recommended:

- the creation of an enhanced Sentencing Guidelines Council (SGC) combining the current SGC and the Sentencing Advisory Panel in one body;
- the collection of more data on sentencing practice including a national sentencing survey;
- placing a duty on the SGC to estimate the effect of its guidelines in terms of the prison population and other correctional resources; and
- obliging the government, when changing the law or policy, to invite the SGC to assess its impact on correctional resources.

Sentencing Guidelines in England and Wales: An Evolutionary Approach (2008)

Introduction

1.1 For many years the prison population has been rising. However, in recent years it has risen more rapidly. Between June 1995 and June 2007 the increase was 60% or more than 30,000 places. By November 2007 the prison population stood at a record level of 81,500. We address the causes and significance of this rise in Chapter 2. In June 2007 Lord Carter of Coles was asked by the Prime Minister, the Chancellor of the Exchequer and the Lord Chancellor and Secretary of State for Justice, to consider options for improving the balance between the supply of prison places and the demand for them. Lord Carter was asked to make recommendations on how this balance could be achieved. In his Report entitled 'Securing the Future' dated December 2007, Lord Carter proposed both a major new building programme to increase prison capacity to a net 96,000 places by 2014 and recommended that longer term measures be found to try to avoid continuous and expensive prison building, prison overcrowding and new measures to release offenders from prison early.

1.2 In his Report, Lord Carter identified as a possible approach the use of a US-style structured sentencing framework and Sentencing Commission. Lord Carter recommended that a Working Group be set up to examine the advantages, disadvantages and feasibility of a structured sentencing framework and permanent Sentencing Commission and to lead and inform debate on these issues. In accordance with this recommendation the Working Group was established in January 2008 by the Lord Chancellor and the Lord Chief Justice. Lord Justice Gage was appointed Chair of the Working Group with terms of reference and membership as set out in Annex A to this report. What follows is the report of the Working Group setting out its findings and its recommendations which we submit to the Lord Chancellor and the Lord Chief Justice.

1.3 We point out at the outset that the question of whether or not the overall sentencing framework should be tied to financial resources is a political issue. How Parliament's intentions on criminal justice policy should be kept consistent with the capacity of the prison and probation services to deal with sentenced offenders is pre-eminently a political matter. Our task has been solely to advise on the advantages, disadvantages and feasibility of mechanisms for achieving this purpose if Parliament decides it should be accomplished.

1.4 The phrase 'sentencing framework' can be used in two ways. The first sense refers to the provisions relating to sentences in statute e.g. in the sentencing provisions of the Criminal Justice Act 2003. The second sense refers to a guidelines framework, either a US-style grid system or narrative guidance to sentencers, such as issued by the Sentencing Guidelines Council (SGC). This report discusses the second sense. Our terms of reference do not embrace a review of sentencing policy, whether in order to identify a means of reducing or controlling the prison population, or to analyse costbenefit effectiveness in sentencing. Such a review may be desirable but our consideration of current sentencing policy in England and Wales has been limited to its relevance to our terms of reference. We note that in June 2001 the Halliday report, 'Making Punishments Work', travelled that ground.

. . .

Chapter 9
Findings, conclusions and recommendations

9.1 In this final chapter we summarise our main findings and conclusions and set out our recommendations.

9.2 The Working Group finds that there have been several separate causes of the increase in the prison population in recent years, some of which are not related to the sentencing process and cannot be affected in any way by sentencing guidelines.

9.3 The Working Group finds that structured sentencing frameworks on the US grid model increase consistency and predictability of sentences but at the cost of an inflexibility that makes them unsuitable and unacceptable in England and Wales. The Working Group recommends that the process of introducing guidelines through the SGC be retained and the introduction of a US-style grid be rejected.

9.4 The Working Group finds that effective planning for correctional resources requires significantly better short, medium and longer term prediction of outcomes than currently is possible in England and Wales.

9.5 The Working Group finds that current data collection in England and Wales in respect of sentencing is inadequate and that it is impossible to predict the effect of sentencing guidelines or to predict the requirement for future correctional resources. It concludes that a more comprehensive system of data collection in respect of sentencing in the Crown Court and the Magistrates' Court is required. It recommends that such a system is devised and put into effect as soon as possible. This task is urgent, considerable and needs appropriate funding. It also recommends that the SGC conducts a national survey of current sentencing practice.

9.6 The Working Group concludes that the SGC is best positioned to devise, commission and take ownership of an expert system of data collection and, by that means, to provide Government and the public with reliable assessments of the likely impact of its guidelines. It recommends that the SGC publish such assessments at regular intervals.

9.7 The Working Group concludes that the SAP and SGC would work more efficiently and speedily if the two bodies were combined whilst preserving the essence of their existing constituent representation and advisory functions. The Working Group describes this single body as an enhanced SGC. It concludes that in order properly to perform its new functions the SGC will need greater resources in staff and expertise. It recommends that such resources are provided and that it be provided with statutory authority to undertake its enhanced responsibilities.

9.8 The Working Group recommends that the Secretary of State, when introducing a Bill into Parliament and when proposing a significant policy initiative, which affects correctional resources, consults the SGC and invites it to carry out and publish its assessment of the proposals on correctional resources.

9.9 The Working Group concludes and recommends that the SGC should be provided with information by the Government in respect of factors, other than sentencing, which affect the prison population, so that it can provide at regular intervals a comprehensive overview of the effects of all factors on future correctional resources.

9.10 The Working Group concludes that the workload of the Chair of the enhanced SGC will be such as to require a substantial commitment of time. Therefore, it will not be possible for the Lord Chief Justice to remain as Chair. It concludes that in the first instance the Chair should be a member of the senior judiciary, in order to maintain the confidence of the judiciary as a whole in the guidelines. It recommends that the Chair be appointed jointly by the Lord Chief Justice and the Lord Chancellor.

9.11 The Working Group recommends that the SGC produces as soon as possible definitive guidelines for all major high-volume offences. It recommends that the SGC gives further narrative guidance on the treatment of previous convictions and aggravating and mitigating factors and gives some guidance on the totality principle.

9.12 A majority of the Working Group recommends that the test for departures from the guidelines be made more robust by providing that the court may only pass a sentence outwith the guidelines if it is of the opinion that it is in the interests of justice to do so.

A minority of the Working Group recommends that there should be no amendment to the statutory tests contained in the Criminal Justice Act 2003.

9.13 The Working Group recommends that the SGC monitor the application of the guidelines.

9.14 The Working Group, whilst concluding that the guidelines must be based on the need to do justice in individual cases, recognises that it is important for there to be better alignment of the supply of correctional services and the demand for them. It concludes that at present it is impractical to place a duty on the SGC to design guidelines to fit within current and reasonably foreseeable capacity. But, it recommends that Parliament should express its intentions with regard to correctional resources at regular intervals. It concludes that this obligation together with the SGC's publication of its assessment of the effect of guidelines on correctional resources will allow for more rational planning.

9.15 A minority of the Working Group believes that it would be advantageous for a duty to be placed on the SGC to have regard to Parliament's intentions on resources, together with other matters to which it must have regard, when formulating its guidelines. It recommends that such a statutory duty be placed on the SGC.

9.16 A majority of the Working Group is of the opinion that it would be inappropriate to place such a duty on the SGC and makes no such recommendation.

9.17 A minority of the Working Group believes that it would be advantageous for guidelines to be placed before Parliament for approval and would recommend that such a system for doing so be established.

9.18 A majority of the Working Group believes that the advantages of placing guidelines before Parliament for approval would be outweighed by the disadvantages. It therefore makes no such recommendation.

 Lord Gage's report 'Sentencing Guidelines in England and Wales: An Evolutionary Approach' (2008) is available on the website of the Ministry of Justice at: **www.justice.gov.uk/docs/sentencing-guidelines-evolutionary-approach.pdf**

Women offenders and sentencing

There has been some concern as to whether male and female offenders are treated equally when sentencing decisions are made. The Home Office has carried out research exploring this issue.

Understanding the Sentencing of Women
Home Office Research Study 170 (1997)

Summary

A superficial examination of the criminal statistics suggests that, for virtually every type of offence, women are treated more leniently than men. This report describes the results of a two-part study of the sentencing of women.

In Part I, sentencing patterns are explored in more detail using samples of men and women convicted of shoplifting, violence and drug offences in 1991. The results of this analysis, which was based on more than 13,000 cases, were then used to inform Part II of the study in which magistrates were interviewed about what they thought were the main influences on their decision-making.

Part I

Statistical tests were used, first, to examine whether an offender's sex appeared to affect the likelihood of a prison sentence once criminal and sentencing history was taken into account; and then, to model the likelihood of various other sentencing outcomes. The penalties that the model *predicted* each offender would receive were compared with the *actual* sentence men and women received.

- Women shoplifters were less likely than comparable males to receive a prison sentence. They were also more likely to be sentenced to a community penalty or to be discharged. However, the results should not be interpreted as evidence of a general policy of leniency towards women shoplifters. They suggest rather that sentencers may be reluctant to fine a woman – possibly because they may be penalising her children rather than just herself. This results in many women receiving a discharge but others receiving community penalties which are rather more severe than fines.
- Men and women stood an equal chance of going to prison for a first violent offence. However, among repeat offenders women were less likely to receive a custodial sentence.
- Women first offenders were significantly less likely than equivalent men to receive a prison sentence for a drug offence, but recidivists were equally likely to go to prison.
- Among first and repeat offenders, women convicted of violence and drug offences were always more likely to be discharged and men more likely to be fined. But again, this seems to be less a consequence of a policy of leniency than a reluctance to impose one particular sentence – the fine – on women.

Part II

Nearly 200 magistrates were interviewed individually or in groups at five courts using a semi structured questionnaire and a small sentencing exercise involving two stereotypical cases designed to bring out differences in their thinking about men and women offenders. These interviews, which were carried out between June and December 1995, took account of the findings in *Part I*.

. . .

Conclusion

What emerges from the interviews with magistrates is a complexity that goes well beyond a simple male/female offender distinction, but appears to be closely tied to it. Magistrates generally seemed to make distinctions between offenders depending on whether they could understand the offence as a matter of survival, see it as a result of provocation or coercion, or attribute it to illness rather than irresponsibility.

How magistrates perceived defendants in the court room is influenced by considerations other than the simple 'facts of the case'. Appearance and demeanour, the novice status of first-timers or 'know it all' status of experienced offenders, the 'believability' of defendants, expressions and perceptions of remorse, and the reading or misreading of cues about ethnicity and culture all seemed to play a part in shaping magistrates' perceptions of the offenders before them. Such factors cut across simple sex differences, but we can surmise that the relative inexperience of female defendants and their concomitant 'nervousness' might lead magistrates to view them as more 'believable' than others – a point which reiterates the findings of Hedderman (1990) in earlier research. Additionally, women's relative inexperience in offending might be reflected in their behaviour in court – showing deference and remorse – thus leading the magistrates to view them more sympathetically than some of the male defendants who were experienced offenders, well-rehearsed in court room procedures and thus seemingly less remorseful.

A distinction between 'troubled' and 'troublesome' offenders was, thus based on the perceived motivation for the offence and the demeanour of defendants in court. In turn, magistrates may make different decisions for bail and certainly choose different options for sentencing. They appeared to favour the use of probation orders or discharges for women – the 'troubled' offenders – as a means of assisting rather than just punishing them. Only occasionally did magistrates believe that male offenders merited assistance, and sometimes 'assistance' for men came in the form of Community Service Orders (CSO) or custody.

Even allowing for the fact that women were more likely to be first offenders or less frequent offenders than men, and were more likely to behave respectfully in court, on the basis of these interviews it would seem that magistrates are less inclined to sympathise with men and to impose a sentence intended to address their underlying problems and needs . . .

Magistrates were unanimous in arguing that, while the nature of the offence, motivation, and behaviour in court all set the parameters for their decision-making, the offender's personal circumstances could also play a part. What type of circumstances did magistrates believe were relevant to their decisions? To what extent did their expectations of what was 'normal' shape this? We asked magistrates about a range of factors including family responsibilities, family history, employment and area of residence to see what made them more or less sympathetic to offenders (what would mitigate or aggravate) and how this affected their decisions.

Family responsibilities

While defence solicitors frequently mentioned children or partners (particularly pregnant partners) in mitigation for male and female clients, magistrates gave little credence to such arguments when dealing with the majority of male defendants. Magistrates were clear that being a parent would only mitigate against a sentence for a man if he was a single parent with sole responsibility for his children.

In contrast, over 80% of the magistrates who took part in individual or group interviews said that female offenders invariably had childcare responsibilities, and that they believed that women with children should be kept out of prison. The magistrates explained that, in their experience, women who came to court tended to be single mothers. Imprisoning such women might well lead to their children going into care, penalising the family rather than the offender alone and adding childcare costs to that of providing custody. Indeed, 10 individuals and three groups of magistrates said that women with children should be kept out of custody, regardless of whether another carer was available, because children need their mothers. After mild prompting, in which the interviewer described a range of different forms of support women might have available (e.g. sister, mother, or male partner) to see where magistrates would draw the line, seven individuals and two groups said that the availability of another carer would reduce the relevance of children as a mitigation. Where the only other potential carer was a woman's male partner, however, two of these magistrates specifically commented that they would not assume that such a relationship was stable enough to entrust the man with responsibility for childcare. In this sense, therefore, mitigation because of children was on a graduated scale, with single mothers or 'unstable' partnerships having most impact on magistrates' decision-making, where magistrates were concerned that children might end up in care. It is important to note, however, that at least some of the 61% of women in prison whom a recent study showed to be primary child-carers (Caddle and Crisp, 1997) were probably sent there by magistrates – suggesting that what magistrates do, and what they think they do, may differ.

Magistrates also said that they tended to rule out Community Service Orders for most women because of their childcare responsibilities. Similarly, magistrates said that fining a woman could have implications for her children, but saw fining a man as only having consequences for him. Having dependent children did not give women a licence to commit crime, but their existence could supersede the influence of factors such as offence seriousness on the sentence for women, even though at least some magistrates recognised that they were responding to 'children' as a cultural stereotype rather than to an individual woman's childcare responsibilities:

> I've often asked myself the question, to what extent we reinforce stereotypes in the courts, because women **are** seen to be the primary carers. They're not . . . in all cases . . . the primary carers.
>
> Sometimes if they – they're working, for example, and the husband is the house-husband . . . and **he's** the primary carer . . . sometimes . . . we don't really maintain objectivity as much as . . . perhaps we should.
>
> Group 1, Milton court (female) (emphasis in original)

Interestingly, when asked specifically about the sentencing of childless women, a number of magistrates (9 individual magistrates, all men) commented that women should be kept out of custody in general – that they should treat 'the fairer sex as the fairer sex' (Mag. 4, Hallam court) – even if they had no children. They believed there was something 'wrong' about remanding or sentencing a woman to custody, so they would be more hesitant to resort to custody than they would in an equivalent case involving a man. The differential treatment of men and women was not, therefore, *solely* due to having responsibility for children, but the powerfulness of this responsibility as a mitigating factor was unmistakable. Magistrates had mixed reactions to the question of whether dependants such as elderly parents would mitigate in the same way as children would. Their initial response was usually that this almost never came up, but then they added that if it did, they would take it into consideration. While most said that other dependants would mitigate to a similar extent (a view held by 20 out of the 29 and 6 out of the 8 groups of magistrates who discussed it), the remainder were of the opinion that this would be less influential:

> . . . the poor, ageing, ailing [parents] are usually dragged out of the cupboard for convenience.
>
> Mag. 11, Hallam court (female)

Some explained that such mitigation would depend on the extent of the disability, but others commented that elderly people were more likely to have other people available to care for them. Other magistrates believed that children were a more important consideration because they were more malleable and vulnerable. They concluded that the elderly, on the other hand, had lived their lives and were not likely to be damaged in the long term from the loss of the defendant's care.

Family structure and social control

> I think that's evident, in quite a lot of cases, that usually criminality starts from a break-up in the family structure.
>
> Chairman of one of the sample courts (male)

An offender's family structure seemed to be of interest to magistrates in a variety of contexts. Children were a chief mitigating factor, as mentioned above. Although they did not mitigate to the same extent, parents and other family members also added to the 'jigsaw' – as magistrates described the process of decision-making – because it influenced their impression of whether the offender's environment placed him or her at risk of further offending. For example, three magistrates commented that in dealing with young offenders from single parent families they were conscious that this background failed to provide the atmosphere of discipline necessary to prevent further offending. Family structure seemed to feature particularly prominently when we asked about the decision to grant bail. First, extended families seemed to pose particular problems when setting conditions of residence. For example, on more than one occasion we observed cases of defendants who resided at one address during the week, then at another address (e.g. with a grandparent) at the weekend – a situation which often flummoxed the magistrates. Second, magistrates were clearly confused when they learned that someone described as the defendant's 'uncle' was not a blood relation. Third, from their comments, we judged that magistrates took being married as a sign of stability whereas cohabiting was regarded as a more transient state:

> Marriage means stability. It means commitment. And otherwise, what's to stop anybody [from] going together a few months and then disappearing, which is what they do.
>
> Mag. 3, Shelley court (male)

> One of our last stipendiaries said to me that the courts would be more useful if they were a marriage bureau or some sort . . . because people will either stop offending because they've married and got a 'good woman' quite probably, or because they've died!
>
> Group 3, Shelley court (F)

However, living with someone else was always a better state to be in than living alone, because it provided a degree of 'social control'. Single people, particularly young people, who lived on their own we re viewed as being more of a risk than others because of the perceived lack of supervision or stability in their lives:

> If they're girls, they invite the lads in to knock them [up] . . . If they're lads, they're into drugs because there's nobody to keep an eye on them.
>
> Stipe. at one of the sample courts (male)

From the interviews it became clear that magistrates tended to believe that men should live either with parents or preferably with a wife or girlfriend. Women too should live with their parents or husbands (or long-term partner), or at least have family in the area, though responsibility for children was in itself also recognised as exerting a controlling influence. In this sense, partners or family perhaps provided support for a woman with children, but social control and stability for a man.

Ten of the 19 individual magistrates who discussed it, baulked at the idea of a homosexual partnership being able to provide the same stability as a heterosexual one. (In fact, only a few of the justices had come across this situation in practice.) Magistrates gave credit to defendants who had partners or relatives (especially parents or grandparents in the case of young offenders) with them at court, which they saw as evidence of the family's concern and support for the defendant. Further, magistrates gleaned extra information from the demeanour and body language of the family and friends who came to court. People who did not have parents or partners in the gallery gave magistrates the impression that they had little social support and might therefore be a bail risk. Support from peers, however, could actually act against the defendant. A few magistrates believed that defendants who had a 'fan club' in the gallery would play up to this and behave arrogantly to impress their friends (5 individuals and 2 groups of magistrates mentioned this). This type of 'support' could even adversely affect the bail decision.

Interestingly, two magistrates commented that people from ethnic minorities (Asian males in particular) were more likely than others to have a 'fan club' present in court.

There was general agreement that *current* family circumstances were more likely to mitigate than an offender's *background*. For example, being the head of a one-parent family was more influential than coming from a one parent family, and being abused was more important than having been abused as a child. However, opinions were divided on whether background had any substantive effect:

> . . . the fact that their father abused them as a child if they are adults, it is an adult world – the world doesn't owe them anything; they have got to stand on their own two feet and accept responsibility for their actions. We all have to do it.
>
> Mag. 8, Byron court (male)

> Personally I would be more inclined to punish heavier someone who'd had every chance, coming from a home background than someone who clearly had been brought up in deprived conditions.
>
> Group 3, Byron court (male)

This division was most apparent during the magistrates' discussions of the 'Jane' case study. While some magistrates believed that information about her childhood was irrelevant, others argued that this information would mitigate, as it explained her present concerns and reaction to them.

Magistrates seemed to make little distinction between male and female offenders in terms of family history.

Employment and income

The four courts we visited were all in areas of relatively high unemployment, which meant not only that most defendants in court were unemployed – as most magistrates recognised – but also that magistrates wanted to make sure that those who had jobs could keep them. Two Justices were blunt enough to say that unemployed defendants were 'layabouts' who leeched off the state to supplement their life of crime. They excepted women caring full-time for small children from this, considering them to have no time for anything else (even Community Service).

Forms of mitigation

Being employed was viewed very positively for a number of reasons. First, it was seen as ensuring that people were occupied (and thus had less time to commit offences than they would if they were unemployed). Second, magistrates also tended to see employed offenders as hard-working, as doing something constructive for themselves, supporting their families, and putting something back into the community (unless, of course, the person had offended against an employer).

Magistrates regarded people who came to court with the *promise* of employment with scepticism. Some even joked that coming to court was one of the fastest cures for unemployment. However, even a job prospect could mitigate if a defendant brought the court proof of a job offer.

It was clear from magistrates' comments that the use of fines and compensation was directly linked to income, and thus (indirectly) to employment:

> . . . at the back of my mind often, I feel: are we guilty of punishing people for being poor?
>
> Group 3, Byron court (male)

If the offender had no (declared) income beyond State benefits, magistrates described themselves as facing a frustrating choice between resorting to other options or imposing what they saw as a 'derisory' fine. If they sentenced someone to a Community Service Order or to custody because he or she had no money to pay a fine, they felt that they were discriminating against people who had no money. On the other hand, fining an unemployed offender £50 where an employed person would have been fined a much larger sum seemed to disproportionately penalise an offender for having an income.

Six individual magistrates and three groups commented that an offender's income or family responsibilities should not justify altering the nature of a penalty from a fine to another order, but only the size of the fine (the legally correct decision). However, most magistrates seemed to think that moving between types of penalties was a practical necessity.

For unemployed male offenders at least, magistrates said they would often resort to a nominal fine, based on the offender's means, in place of the higher amount they otherwise considered appropriate to the offence.

However, when we asked why men might be given fines while women were discharged or put on probation (see Part I), a third of the individuals and the groups responded that this was because such women had no money of their own (and because they were usually responsible for dependent children).

The question of dependence on another person's income raises an important issue: to what extent should a financial penalty be based on a 'household' income rather than on the income of the offender? Twenty-four of the 30 individuals and six of the seven groups who discussed this point believed that penalties should be assessed on the basis of the household income, if that income is given in court. Most said that they based this on the assumption that, traditionally, the woman was the care-taker while the man was the wage-earner. The woman was therefore entitled to a housekeeping allowance, and was also the one to claim any Family Benefit. Such a view assumes that a reciprocal relationship exists in the household. However, this may be unrealistic, for example, where the woman is a victim of domestic violence (see, for example, Yllö, 1993). As one magistrate explained to another in one of our group discussions:

> Well, maybe in your house there **is** one pot of money, but I suspect in some households there are **two** separate pots of money, and her pot happens to be empty. And if . . . she is told to pay compensation and has no money, and her husband says, 'Well, I'm sorry, but you're not having any of mine, dear,' where is she?
>
> Group 1, Shelley court (male) (emphasis in original)

This also begs the question of whether it is appropriate to penalise the non-offending wage earner for the offences committed by his or her partner. It is perhaps helpful to draw an analogy with the Youth Court, where parents are held financially responsible for their children's behaviour; we might question whether partners should be deemed responsible for each other's behaviour in the same way, and indeed, whether the idea of a 'household income' works the same way for a man as for a woman – a point which remains for further research.

The magistrates mainly considered awarding compensation for violent offences or in cases where the cost of property damage or theft could be assessed with a reasonable degree of accuracy. For violent offences, awarding compensation was heavily influenced by the role of the victim in the offence. The decision to award compensation also took the offender's income into account, although this did not stop magistrates from imposing compensation in either case study where 'Jason' was receiving benefits, and 'Jane' was dependent on her husband's income.

We also asked magistrates if voluntary work could mitigate in the same way as paid employment. Only two interviewees claimed to have dealt with offenders in this position. Of the small number of magistrates (7) who compared them, five did not put the same weight on voluntary work as on paid employment because voluntary work could be continued relatively easily following a Community Service Order or time in custody, whereas paid employment might be lost altogether. Further, loss of voluntary work was thought to have less of an impact on a family than would a loss of income. The other two argued that voluntary work could mitigate, as it reflected positively on the character of the defendant. The magistrates made no distinction between male and female defendants in this respect.

Conclusion

The results of our discussions with magistrates about what sorts of factors might mitigate sentencing decisions for men and women suggest that female defendants were likely to find mitigation in dependants, primarily children, whereas men rarely benefitted from the fact of having dependent children.

Most magistrates had fairly firm views regarding the type of social structure which provided enough stability and discipline to influence a bail or sentencing decision in a positive way. The support of family or long-term partners, preferably in the same house, materially improved both male and female defendants' chances of avoiding custody and possibly mitigated against the eventual sentence as well. Family history too may have a bearing, but would depend more on its interaction with other features of the case.

Paid employment often mitigated in remand and sentencing decisions for those defendants fortunate enough to have it, but the lack of full-time employment seemed to be viewed less negatively for women than men because magistrates believed that most of the women they dealt with were mothers who were (and should be) occupied with childcare. On the other hand, paid employment often resulted in larger financial penalties for men. As Part I of the current study shows, however, this does not always result in women being dealt with more leniently. The locality and permanence of a defendant's address was acknowledged to play some part in bail decisions, but not on sentencing. Magistrates did not generally distinguish between male and female defendants in their comments about these factors.

While all of these factors – family circumstances and background, employment, and locality – may have a bearing on the decisions magistrates make, they will not necessarily in themselves have a material impact on a decision. For this reason, we asked magistrates whether each particular factor would push a potential penalty up or down if the case were on the borderline. Interestingly, and consistent with the results from Part I, the borderlines seemed to differ greatly for men and women. The custody threshold showed the clearest difference here, with magistrates doing everything possible to keep a woman out of custody, but sentencing men primarily in response to the seriousness of their offending. They also avoided using fines for women, but used them frequently for men. Much of this seemed to be based on the fact that magistrates considered family circumstances and responsibilities to be much more relevant when dealing with female than with male offenders. Therefore, although personal circumstances carried weight for both groups, they were given more weight with regard to female offenders.

The patterns of mitigation, particularly as they relate to men and women, clearly reflect the same divisions between 'troubled' offenders (those who deserve sympathy and assistance) and 'troublesome' offenders (those who deserve punishment). The issues are exceedingly complex, however, and reflect considerations of family responsibilities, family structure and the potential for social control through the family, the influence of family history as mitigation, employment and income and the links between these factors and the ability to pay fines and compensation. Some of these factors, but by no means all, appeared to carry differential degrees of influence depending on whether the magistrates were discussing men or women. Overall, magistrates appeared to consider family circumstances and responsibilities to be much more relevant in mitigation when dealing with female than with male defendants. This finding confirms the earlier research findings of Farrington and Morris (1983) and Eaton (1983, 1986) who describe family circumstances as a key factor in decision-making relating to women, but much less important in decision-making in relation to men.

. . .

The topic of sex discrimination is one on which people often hold such strong (and usually fixed) opinions. Up to this point, therefore, we have endeavoured to present the findings of this research quite straightforwardly and with only minimal interpretation. This conclusion, however, reflects the four authors' shared interpretations of both the statistical exercises described in Part I and the interviews carried out in Part II. We summarise what the research findings mean and how they feed into our understanding of the sentencing of women.

Few people would seriously contest the notion that the criminal justice system should dispense justice fairly, regardless of sex, race, class or any other improper influence. No one is more aware of this need than the magistracy, who already spend a proportion of their training on such (human awareness) issues. But what exactly does fairness consist of in this context?

In our view, it lies in consistency of approach rather than uniformity of outcome. In other words, it involves asking the same questions about factors such as employment status, family responsibilities and financial circumstances regardless of the offender's sex, rather than presuming that certain questions will only apply to males or females. From this perspective, to criticise sentencing practices on the grounds that the official statistics show different sentencing patterns would be unfair and, in any case, a futile exercise. These patterns may simply reflect the fact that the men and women who come to court differ across a wide range of factors which sentencers take into consideration when determining an appropriate sentence. In order to look at whether there is disparity in sentencing decisions, one needs therefore to look at the characteristics of those coming to court and at how sentencers say they weigh these and other factors in their decision-making. This research set out to do both these things.

 The report 'Understanding the Sentencing of Women' (1997), edited by Carol Hedderman and Loraine Gelsthorpe, is available on the Home Office website at: **www.homeoffice.gov.uk/rds/pdfs/hors170.pdf**

21 Young offenders

Introduction

This chapter looks at:

- the introduction of referral orders into the youth justice system;

- the success of restorative justice projects; and

- provisions in the Criminal Justice and Immigration Act 2008 for youth rehabilitation orders.

Referral orders

Referral orders were introduced by the Youth Justice and Criminal Evidence Act 1999. When young offenders plead guilty and are convicted for a first offence by the courts, they are referred to a Youth Offender Panel. The Panel agrees a contract with the offender under which the young offender must make reparation for their offence. The aim of referral orders is to move the young people away from the formality of the courts and the mainstream criminal justice system and push them to confront their offending behaviour. The Home Office has carried out research looking at how far the introduction of referral orders has been successful.

The Introduction of Referral Orders into the Youth Justice System: Final Report (2002)

Tim Newburn and others

Conclusion

Simply by the fact of being a mandatory sentence referral orders are unusual. However, it is the more particular aim of utilising some of the principles of restorative justice that distinguishes this disposal most significantly from the bulk of other sentences available to the Youth Court. The referral order presented a series of novel challenges to those tasked with its implementation. These included:

- the recruitment, training and management of large numbers of voluntary community panel members;
- the establishment and running of youth offender panels chaired not by professionals but by community panel members;
- the active involvement of parents/guardians, victims and others in the criminal justice process;
- the agreement of contracts with young offenders that both help challenge offending behaviour and allow for constructive activities including reparation.

The Youth offender teams (Yots) that piloted referral orders undertook all this within the context of a youth justice system already undergoing profound change. This report suggests that, in the main, the pilots successfully accomplished the implementation of referral orders and youth offender panels. Across the pilot areas the majority of the key aims underpinning referral orders were well realised.

The pilot areas successfully recruited and trained large numbers of community panel members and identified community-based venues for panels. This they achieved within a very tight timetable. Though, perhaps predictably, difficulties were experienced in attempting to recruit a 'representative' body of panel members, Yots have continued to recruit in sufficient numbers and are developing strategies for broadening the base from which they recruit. Once recruited and trained, the panel members have shown themselves able to meet the demands of leading and facilitating panel meetings. The community panel members appear to work well with their professional Yot colleagues and, as chairs, are shown increasingly to take a clear lead in directing and running panel meetings. Relationships between

Yot staff and community members, as they mature, are largely based on mutual respect and a recognition of the skills and attributes that each brings to the panel process. It is important to recognise therefore that the contribution of community panel members has been to bring something new – something less formal and more inclusive – to the youth justice process. In doing so, the Yots involved in the pilots have had to contend with the necessity of both specific practical changes and wider cultural adjustment.

Referral orders have quickly been accepted by the professionals working in the youth justice system and by the Youth Court. Yot staff, magistrates and justices' clerks all supported the aim of increasing the restorative element in work with young offenders. However, during the course of the pilots magistrates appeared to become more concerned about the loss of discretion brought about by the introduction of this new mandatory penalty and, in particular, to have doubts about the appropriateness of referral orders for dealing with certain minor offences.

One of the most encouraging aspects of the referral order pilots has been the experience of the youth offender panels. Within a relatively short period of time the panels have established themselves as constructive, deliberative and participatory forums in which to address young people's offending behaviour. The informal setting of youth offender panels would appear to allow young people, their parents/carers, victims (where they attend), community panel members and Yot advisers opportunities to discuss the nature and consequences of a young person's offending, as well as how to respond to this in ways which seek to repair the harm done and to address the causes of the young person's offending behaviour. This view is echoed by all participants in panels, including community panel members, offenders and their parents, victims, Yot staff and is also confirmed by the observational fieldwork undertaken as part of this study.

All the major participants affected by the introduction of referral orders appear both to support the reforms in principle and to be broadly satisfied with the way in which they have been implemented in practice. Thus, both magistrates and clerks endorsed the extension of restorative justice principles to the youth justice system. Yot staff have remained very positive about referral orders throughout the pilots and have worked well in recruiting, training, managing and working with community panel members. The community panel members confirm that they have excellent working relationships with Yot staff and the positive nature of this relationship is in part reflected in the experience that young offenders and their parents have at panels. Though initially slightly unsure of what to expect, the vast majority of offenders and their parents say that they feel they are treated with respect at youth offender panels and that the panel members treat them fairly. The panel process and outcomes are viewed as satisfying significant levels of procedural, restorative and substantive justice. Both young people and parents accord youth offender panels high levels of procedural satisfaction. This was also true of victims where they attended panel hearings.

Furthermore, the pilots succeeded in general in bringing the idea of reparation further to the fore in youth justice. In particular, reparation formed the most common compulsory element in all contracts agreed at initial panel meetings. There is a clear need for Yots to develop a broad base of programmes of activity and reparation schemes for young offenders. More particularly, if youth offender panels are to become genuinely community-based it will be necessary for them to draw more fully upon community resources than is currently the case.

The major difficulty encountered during the pilots concerned the involvement of victims. To date, the level of victim participation in panels has been very low. There appear to be a number of reasons for this. In part, it no doubt stems from a degree of unfamiliarity in some of the pilot areas with the best ways of involving victims in restorative processes. There would also seem to be some reticence about doing so, and also some concerns about the resource implications of fully involving victims. The fact that levels of victim involvement vary considerably among the pilots, together with evidence of restorative practices elsewhere, suggests that there are techniques that can be used to improve on current levels of involvement. There is a need to foster and enhance a culture within Yots and throughout their work that embraces and supports the centrality of victim input and participation within the referral order process. When arranging panel meetings, the needs of the victim(s) should be given prominent consideration at every stage, particularly when determining the location, venue and time of meetings. Victims should be given the opportunity to make well informed choices regarding the nature and extent of their involvement or input in their offender's referral order and be kept informed on the progress and outcome of the young person's activities.

The issue of victim involvement is, in essence, a problem of implementation rather than a problem of principle. Indeed, the majority of the general principles underlying referral orders appear both to be capable of being operationalised in practice and to receive high levels of approval from all the major participants. In a short period of time referral orders have gone from being an interesting set of proposals to a generally robust set of working practices that, notwithstanding some of the tensions identified in this report, look set to have a considerable impact on the youth justice system in England and Wales.

The research 'The Introduction of Referral Orders into the Youth Justice System: Final Report' (2002), Home Office Research Study 242, by Tim Newburn and others is available on the Home Office website at:
www.homeoffice.gov.uk/rds/pdfs2/hors242.pdf

Restorative justice

Restorative justice tries to confront the defendant with the harm they have caused, sometimes by arranging for the offender to meet the victim. The youth justice system pioneered the use of restorative justice. The Youth Justice Board has commissioned research into the effectiveness of restorative justice and its conclusions have been quite positive.

The National Evaluation of the Youth Justice Board's Restorative Justice Projects (2004)

Aidan Wilcox and Carolyn Hoyle

Summary

This report is based on an evaluation of 46 restorative justice projects which were funded by the Youth Justice Board (the Board). The data are based on the final reports submitted by the independent local evaluator for each project. The main areas covered in this report include a description of the projects and of the characteristics of the young people on these projects, a discussion of the implementation problems which staff in the projects have faced, and an assessment of the outcomes of the restorative interventions in terms of completion rates, reconviction and feedback from participants. The report concludes with the main lessons which have emerged for evaluation and implementation of restorative justice projects.

The national evaluation

The main role of the national evaluator has been to pull together the findings from diverse projects which had been evaluated by local evaluators using different methodologies and with varying levels of resources at their disposal. Since national evaluators were appointed after projects had been awarded funding, we were unable to control either the nature of the programmes or the methodology employed by the local evaluators.

However, in order to encourage consistency in the collection and reporting of data, we provided local evaluators with questionnaires for use with victims and offenders, an evaluation form to record the nature of the restorative intervention, and a template to structure their final reports. Despite this, the quality of data contained in local evaluators' reports was variable and many local evaluators were unable to supplement basic quantitative data with feedback from victims and offenders.

Description of projects and characteristics of young people

Restorative justice seeks to involve those affected by crime – victims, offenders and the wider community – by providing an opportunity for these parties to meet or communicate, to consider the harm caused by the offence and how it could be repaired, and to help reintegrate offenders back into their communities.

There is a wide range of practices which claim to be restorative, and the 46 projects which have been funded in this category offer the following: family group conferencing; mediation (direct and indirect); reparation (direct and to the community) and victim awareness. These are not equally restorative, and McCold and Wachtel (2000) argue that they can be ranked according to how well they facilitate dialogue between the offender, victim and community. For example, they describe family group conferencing as fully restorative and victim awareness as partly restorative. Most of the 46 projects could be described as generalist, since they offered all or most of these types of restorative intervention. Less than a fifth offered only conferencing or mediation.

The 42 projects for which data were available worked with over 6,800 young people, of whom the majority were male (76%), aged 14 to 17 (80%) and white (91%). Almost two-thirds (63%) of those starting a restorative intervention were at either Final Warning or Reparation Order stage demonstrating that such interventions were focused on those in the early stages of a criminal career. Theft was the most common offence leading to referral (30%) followed by violence (23%).

The most common form of restorative intervention was community reparation (35%) followed by victim awareness (21%). The proportion of cases involving direct meetings was 13.5%, which compares favourably with other large restorative programmes in this country. The method of delivery of the projects varied. Thirty-seven per cent of projects were 'in-house' (i.e. delivered by the Youth Offending Team [Yot]), the rest were either totally independent of the Yot or a mixture of both ('hybrid'). Local evaluators reported that in-house projects were less likely than either independent or hybrid projects to experience problems in contacting victims or in communication, and were also less likely to suffer a low level of referrals.

In order to increase the number of referrals or to improve victim contact, 83% of projects changed their referral criteria, the range of interventions offered or the location of project staff.

The total financial cost of the 46 projects was around £13.3m (over half of which was provided by the Board), which equated to over £280,000 per project. The data on costs were not sufficiently detailed to allow for a calculation of unit costs.

Implementation of the projects

Local evaluators identified the main problems which had affected the implementation of projects, and reported examples of effective practice.

Victim contact and participation

The involvement of the victim is a key element in restorative justice. The legislation governing victim contact has been ambiguous, with the result that different Yots and police forces interpreted their responsibilities in different ways. Local evaluators reported that who contacted victims and how they were contacted had a significant influence on the extent of victim participation.

In 61% of projects, the police officer in the Yot made the initial contact with victims – in the rest, this task was conducted by a dedicated restorative justice project worker. Local evaluators suggested that it was preferable for project workers to make this contact since they were specially trained and had more time than police officers to conduct this in a sensitive manner.

In a third of projects, victims were contacted by telephone in the rest either via an 'opt-in' or 'opt-out' letter. Telephone contact had the advantage of being faster than a letter, and enabled the victim's questions to be answered more easily. Telephone contact was the method favoured by the police, whereas project workers were more likely to write to victims. It was reported that the police did not always have adequate knowledge and experience of the restorative options available to explain these properly to victims. Use of an 'opt-out' letter, which required the victim to contact the project if they did not wish to be involved, was felt to be the most effective means of generating victim participation.

There were some difficulties involved in recording the level of victim contact and in defining victim participation. However, local evaluators reported that almost 80% of known victims were contacted, and of those contacted 67% agreed to some form of participation (thus 53% of all identifiable victims participate to some extent). In the minority of cases, this participation involved attendance at a meeting with the offender, but it was more likely to mean that the victim agreed to their views being made known to the offender, agreed to receive a letter of apology or made some suggestion as to the kind of reparative activity the offender could undertake.

Low level of referrals

Over half of the projects experienced lower than expected referrals and a lower than expected proportion of cases progressing to the intervention. To some degree this was a consequence of unrealistic targets in the original bids. However, other reasons included poor victim contact procedures, poor communication between Yots and projects resulting in insufficient or inappropriate referrals, and a lower than expected number of relevant court orders. Many projects were able to increase referrals, for example by making presentations to the courts and the Yot to improve communication, streamlining the victim contact and referral procedures or expanding the range of interventions offered.

Fast-tracking

The pressure to reduce delays in the criminal process ('fast-tracking') was reported to have affected adversely the quality of assessment and work with victims. In addition, the short length of the action plan and reparation orders meant it was sometimes difficult to complete the agreed number of hours of reparation or to initiate breach proceedings within the timescale. Some courts were very prescriptive in the nature of the orders they imposed, which limited the ability of project staff to incorporate the wishes of victims. In other areas, project staff developed good relationships with the courts (through joint training and updating them on the outcomes of their cases) to encourage the use of more 'flexible' orders.

Over-reliance on community reparation

Community reparation rightly has a place in the menu of restorative options, for example where victims do not wish to have any involvement in the process. In such cases, it is recommended that reparation placements be offered which: relate to the offence as far as possible; match the young person's interests and skills; and encourage the young person to consider the consequences of their actions on the victim and the community.

However, local evaluators for some projects expressed concern at what they believed was an over-reliance on community reparation, either as a result of the local courts' policy, or the project's failure to contact victims or engage them in more direct restorative interventions. Two local evaluators reported that offenders tended to view community reparation as a punishment with no direct benefit to the victim, and that the placements were not relevant to the offence.

Recruitment

Almost 60% of projects experienced problems either in recruiting or training staff. The late recruitment of key workers delayed the implementation of some projects and staff turnover affected capacity in other projects. The quality and coverage of training was variable. As staff moved on, new staff did not always receive adequate training.

Many projects made successful use of volunteers or sessional workers. This enabled projects to increase their capacity, to devote more time to individual cases and to be more flexible in terms of when interventions could be offered.

Outcomes

Eighty-three per cent of offenders successfully completed their order or Final Warning intervention. Where the views of victims and offenders were sought, the responses were encouraging. On average, over three-quarters of both victims and offenders felt well prepared by project staff, found the process fair, agreed that their participation was voluntary and believed that the intervention had helped the offender to take responsibility for the offence, and seven out of 10 thought that the offender better understood the impact of the offence on the victim.

Reconviction

The design and implementation of the projects did not permit an experimental approach to the evaluation, thus there was no control group with which to compare the reconviction rate for our sample. As yet, there is no method of calculating a predicted rate of reconviction for young offenders. The results of this study were therefore compared to a Home Office sample of young offenders sentenced in 2000.

Using data from the Police National Computer (PNC), we were able to follow up 728 offenders from 34 projects. The overall reconviction rate within 12 months was 46.6% compared to a rate of 26.4% for the Home Office sample. The two samples differed significantly, however, in terms of the number of previous appearances the offenders had – 71% of the Home Office sample had no previous appearances, compared to just 23% of the restorative justice sample. When we weighted the restorative justice sample to reflect this, we found that the reconviction rate would be 28.6%. This was slightly higher than the rate for the Home Office sample (but was not a statistically significant difference), and may be because those thought by Yot staff to have a higher risk of reoffending were more likely to receive a restorative intervention (at Final Warning stage, at least).

We compared the type of offence, seriousness and disposal at the conviction which led to referral (target conviction) with the offence at first reconviction. There was no significant difference in terms of the types of offence committed at target conviction and first reconviction. However, of those who were reconvicted, 37% were reconvicted of less serious offences (as measured by the Board gravity score) than at the target conviction, whereas just 23% were reconvicted of more serious offences. Due to the large proportion being reconvicted of offences of the same gravity, the median gravity score of both target conviction and first reconviction was three, although the distribution of scores (as described above) indicated a slight but statistically significant decline in offence seriousness. The disposal at first reconviction increased in seriousness as one would expect. The proportion of disposals involving a Final Warning or Caution fell from 29% to 5%, while there was an increase in custodial sentences and Supervision Orders. The proportion of reparation orders fell from 37% at target conviction to just 12% at first reconviction. It was suggested that this might reflect a belief among magistrates that restorative options should be used only once.

Looking at the frequency of offending as measured by conviction, we found that in the 12 months before the target conviction, 55.1% of offenders had been convicted, whereas in the 12 months after the target conviction 46.6% had been convicted. This represented a fall of around 15%, but in the absence of information about the expected rate of conviction, it is impossible to say whether this is better or worse than would have obtained if there had been no intervention.

By grouping the types of intervention into the categories described by McCold and Wachtel (*above*), it was possible to look at reconviction by type of restorative intervention. No association was found between how restorative the intervention was and the reconviction rate. For example, while offenders who had met the victim (fully restorative) were least likely to be reconvicted (41.6%), those who had had only victim awareness (least restorative) had the second lowest rate of reconviction (42.1%).

. . .

Learning points

The timescale and structure of the evaluation have not permitted an assessment of the effectiveness of individual restorative justice projects in terms of reconviction or cost effectiveness. However, several important lessons have emerged with respect to the evaluation and implementation of these projects. The national evaluation would have had more success in assessing outcomes had the following changes to timescale and structure been made:

- appointing national evaluators before local evaluators to allow evaluation tools appropriate to the projects' aims to be developed and implemented;

- allowing sufficient time to let projects overcome initial difficulties and to enable outcomes (such as reconviction) to be measured effectively;
- concentrating resources on a more in-depth evaluation of fewer projects – being more prescriptive as to what will be funded as 'restorative justice' and ensuring that practice is observed and monitored.

The main problems in implementation revolved around victim contact, lack of communication between different agencies and securing sufficient numbers of adequate referrals. Examples of solutions to these problems included:

- Local evaluators suggested that victim contact was best conducted by trained restorative justice staff rather than the police officer on the Yot, and that initial contact should be made via an 'opt-out' letter. Victim participation was also increased when restorative justice staff were given access to all referrals.
- Communication between agencies was improved by holding joint training, making presentations on the aims of the project and providing feedback on the outcomes of cases.
- For independent projects, communication was improved and referrals increased when workers were based in the Yot.
- Improving relationships with the courts led, in some cases, to more flexibility in the orders made, enabling workers to explore mediation after sentence.
- Reparation was considered to be more effective when it was clearly offence related, matched the young person's skills or interests, or developed new ones, and encouraged the young person to consider the victim's perspective.

 The report 'The National Evaluation of the Youth Justice Board's Restorative Justice Projects' (2004) by Aidan Wilcox and Carolyn Hoyle is available on the Youth Justice Board's website at:
**www.youth-justice-board.gov.uk/publications/scripts/
prod.asp?idProduct=166&eP=YJB**

Youth rehabilitation orders

In 2003, the government published a consultation paper 'Youth Justice – the Next Steps'. This paper set out possible reforms to the youth justice system. Some of these reform proposals can now be found in the Criminal Justice and Immigration Act 2008. The provisions relating to the sentencing of young offenders are expected to be brought into force in Autumn 2009. The Act provides for the creation of youth rehabilitation orders. These will combine the existing community sentences into one generic community sentence for young people. When imposing a youth rehabilitation order, a court will be able to choose from a 'menu' of requirements with which the offender must comply.

A youth rehabilitation order will be the standard community sentence for the majority of young offenders. It will be imposed if the court considers that:

- the offending was serious enough to warrant it;
- the requirements forming part of the order are the most suitable for the offender; and
- the restrictions on liberty imposed by the order are commensurate with the seriousness of the offence.

Referral orders will continue to exist. The aim of this reform is to both simplify the law and make the sentencing interventions more flexible. If the youth rehabilitation order is breached, the young person will be issued with a warning. If there is wilful and persistent non-compliance, the young person can be placed in custody.

Criminal Justice and Immigration Act 2008

PART 1
YOUTH REHABILITATION ORDERS

Youth rehabilitation orders

1 Youth rehabilitation orders

(1) Where a person aged under 18 is convicted of an offence, the court by or before which the person is convicted may in accordance with Schedule 1 make an order (in this Part referred to as a 'youth rehabilitation order') imposing on the person any one or more of the following requirements—

    (a) an activity requirement (see paragraphs 6 to 8 of Schedule 1),

    (b) a supervision requirement (see paragraph 9 of that Schedule),

    (c) in a case where the offender is aged 16 or 17 at the time of the conviction, an unpaid work requirement (see paragraph 10 of that Schedule),

    (d) a programme requirement (see paragraph 11 of that Schedule),

    (e) an attendance centre requirement (see paragraph 12 of that Schedule),

    (f) a prohibited activity requirement (see paragraph 13 of that Schedule),

    (g) a curfew requirement (see paragraph 14 of that Schedule),

    (h) an exclusion requirement (see paragraph 15 of that Schedule),

    (i) a residence requirement (see paragraph 16 of that Schedule),

    (j) a local authority residence requirement (see paragraph 17 of that Schedule),

    (k) a mental health treatment requirement (see paragraph 20 of that Schedule),

    (l) a drug treatment requirement (see paragraph 22 of that Schedule),

    (m) a drug testing requirement (see paragraph 23 of that Schedule),

    (n) an intoxicating substance treatment requirement (see paragraph 24 of that Schedule), and

    (o) an education requirement (see paragraph 25 of that Schedule).

(2) A youth rehabilitation order—

    (a) may also impose an electronic monitoring requirement (see paragraph 26 of Schedule 1), and

    (b) must do so if paragraph 2 of that Schedule so requires.

(3) A youth rehabilitation order may be—

    (a) a youth rehabilitation order with intensive supervision and surveillance (see paragraph 3 of Schedule 1), or

    (b) a youth rehabilitation order with fostering (see paragraph 4 of that Schedule).

→

(4) But a court may only make an order mentioned in subsection (3)(a) or (b) if—

(a) the court is dealing with the offender for an offence which is punishable with imprisonment,

(b) the court is of the opinion that the offence, or the combination of the offence and one or more offences associated with it, was so serious that, but for paragraph 3 or 4 of Schedule 1, a custodial sentence would be appropriate (or, if the offender was aged under 12 at the time of conviction, would be appropriate if the offender had been aged 12), and

(c) if the offender was aged under 15 at the time of conviction, the court is of the opinion that the offender is a persistent offender.

(5) Schedule 1 makes further provision about youth rehabilitation orders.

(6) This section is subject to—

(a) sections 148 and 150 of the Criminal Justice Act 2003 (c. 44) (restrictions on community sentences etc.), and

(b) the provisions of Parts 1 and 3 of Schedule 1.

PART 2
SENTENCING

General sentencing provisions

9 Purposes etc. of sentencing: offenders under 18

(1) After section 142 of the Criminal Justice Act 2003 (c. 44) insert—

'142A Purposes etc. of sentencing: offenders under 18

(1) This section applies where a court is dealing with an offender aged under 18 in respect of an offence.

(2) The court must have regard to—

(a) the principal aim of the youth justice system (which is to prevent offending (or re-offending) by persons aged under 18: see section 37(1) of the Crime and Disorder Act 1998),

(b) in accordance with section 44 of the Children and Young Persons Act 1933, the welfare of the offender, and

(c) the purposes of sentencing mentioned in subsection (3) (so far as it is not required to do so by paragraph (a)).

(3) Those purposes of sentencing are—

(a) the punishment of offenders,

(b) the reform and rehabilitation of offenders,

(c) the protection of the public, and

(d) the making of reparation by offenders to persons affected by their offences.'

The Criminal Justice and Immigration Act 2008 is available on the website for the Office of Public Sector Information at:
www.opsi.gov.uk/acts/acts2008/ukpga_20080004_en_1

22

The civil justice system

Introduction

This chapter looks at:

- Lord Woolf's report 'Access to Justice' (1996) which lead to the introduction of major reforms to the civil justice system;

- research looking at the impact of Lord Woolf's reforms;

- a planned review of civil court costs following concern that Lord Woolf's reforms might have pushed costs too heavily to the start of the litigation process;

- a government consultation paper on whether there should be a single, unified, civil court system; and

- a report of the Better Regulation Taskforce into whether the UK has developed a compensation culture.

Lord Woolf's reforms

The government commissioned a senior judge, Lord Woolf, to review the civil justice system and put forward suggestions for reform. In 1996 Lord Woolf published his final report, 'Access to Justice'. Most of his recommendations were accepted by the government and major reforms were introduced to the civil justice system in 1999.

Access to Justice: Final Report (1996)

Lord Woolf

Section I

Overview

The principles

1 In my interim report I identified a number of principles which the civil justice system should meet in order to ensure access to justice. The system should:

(a) be *just* in the results it delivers;
(b) be *fair* in the way it treats litigants;
(c) offer appropriate procedures at a reasonable *cost*;
(d) deal with cases with reasonable *speed*;
(e) be *understandable* to those who use it;
(f) be *responsive* to the needs of those who use it;
(g) provide as much *certainty* as the nature of particular cases allows; and
(h) be *effective*: adequately resourced and organised.

The problems

2 The defects I identified in our present system were that it is too expensive in that the costs often exceed the value of the claim; too slow in bringing cases to a conclusion and too unequal: there is a lack of equality between the powerful, wealthy litigant and the under resourced litigant. It is too uncertain: the difficulty of forecasting what litigation will cost and how long it will last induces the fear of the unknown; and it is incomprehensible to many litigants. Above all it is too fragmented in the way it is organised since there is no one with clear overall responsibility for the administration of civil justice; and too adversarial as cases are run by the parties, not by the courts and the rules of court, all too often, are ignored by the parties and not enforced by the court.

The basic reforms

3 The interim report set out a blueprint for reform based on a system where the courts with the assistance of litigants would be responsible for the management of cases. I recommended that the courts should have the final responsibility for determining what procedures were suitable for each case; setting realistic timetables; and ensuring that the procedures and timetables were complied with. Defended cases would be allocated to one of three tracks:

(a) an expanded small claims jurisdiction with a financial limit of £3,000;

(b) a new fast track for straightforward cases up to £10,000, with strictly limited procedures, fixed timetables (20–30 weeks to trial) and fixed costs; and

(c) a new multitrack for cases above £10,000, providing individual hands on management by judicial teams for the heaviest cases, and standard or tailor made directions where these are appropriate.

The second stage of the Inquiry

4 My general analysis of the problems in the present system, and the broad agenda for reform which I proposed in the interim report, have provided the foundation for the more detailed work I have carried out in the second stage of the Inquiry. This has concentrated on particular areas of litigation where, in my view, the civil justice system is failing most conspicuously to meet needs of litigants. These areas are medical negligence, housing and multi party litigation. I have also developed more detailed proposals on procedure and costs for the new fast track. Another focus of special attention was the Crown Office List, which has a particularly important function in enabling individual citizens to challenge decisions of public bodies including central and local government.

5 In all these areas a particular concern has been to improve access to justice for individuals and small businesses. I am also concerned about the level of public expenditure on litigation, particularly in medical negligence and housing. In both of these areas substantial amounts of public money are absorbed in legal costs which could be better spent, in the one case on improving medical care and in the other on improving standards of social housing. An efficient and cost effective justice system is also of vital importance to the commercial, financial and industrial life of this country and I was anxious to improve this, especially because of the evidence I received that there was a substantial risk of the existing system changing our competitive position in relation to other jurisdictions. Finally, I was anxious to ensure that the judiciary and the resources of the Court Service were deployed to the best effect.

6 All the work I have carried out in the second stage of the Inquiry has confirmed the conclusions I reached in the interim report about the defects in the present system. This report therefore builds on the contents and recommendations of the interim report . . .

Rules of court

7 An important part of my task in the Inquiry was to produce a single, simpler procedural code to apply to civil litigation in the High Court and county courts. This report is accompanied by a draft of the general rules which will form the core of the new code. In the second part of the Inquiry I have looked in detail at the specialist jurisdictions of the High Court with a view to accommodating them so far as possible within the general procedural framework embodied in the core rules. As a result of the work done by the Inquiry, it is apparent that a great many of the existing specialist rules are no longer required. Work is continuing on the more limited body of special rules which are still considered essential. Here I await with interest the views of those engaged in the specialist jurisdictions who could not express a formal opinion as to what extra rules are still needed until they had seen the general rules which have been prepared by the Inquiry.

The new landscape

8 If my recommendations are implemented the landscape of civil litigation will be fundamentally different from what it is now. It will be underpinned by Rule I of the new procedural code, which imposes an obligation on the courts and the parties to further the overriding objective of the rules so as to deal with cases justly. The rule provides a definition of 'dealing with a case justly', embodying the principles of equality, economy, proportionality and expedition which are fundamental to an effective contemporary system of justice. These requirements of procedural justice, operating in the traditional adversarial context, will give effect to a system which is substantively just in the results it delivers as well as in the way in which it does so.

9 The new landscape will have the following features.

Litigation will be avoided wherever possible
(a) People will be encouraged to start court proceedings to resolve disputes only as a last resort, and after using other more appropriate means when these are available.

(b) Information on sources of alternative dispute resolution (ADR) will be provided at all civil courts.

(c) Legal aid funding will be available for pre litigation resolution and ADR.

(d) Protocols in relation to medical negligence, housing and personal injury, and additional powers for the court in relation to pre litigation disclosure, will enable parties to obtain information earlier and promote settlement.

(e) Before commencing litigation both parties will be able to make offers to settle the whole or part of a dispute supported by a special regime as to costs and higher rates of interest if not accepted.

Litigation will be less adversarial and more cooperative
(a) There will be an expectation of openness and cooperation between parties from the outset, supported by pre litigation protocols on disclosure and experts. The courts will be able to give effect to their disapproval of a lack of cooperation prior to litigation.

(b) The court will encourage the use of ADR at case management conferences and pre-trial reviews, and will take into account whether the parties have unreasonably refused to try ADR or behaved unreasonably in the course of ADR.

(c) The duty of experts to the court will be emphasised. Single experts, instructed by the parties, will be used when practicable. Opposing experts will be encouraged to meet or communicate as early as possible to narrow the issues between them. The court will have a power to appoint an expert.

Litigation will be less complex
(a) There will be a single set of rules applying to the High Court and the county courts. The rules will be simpler, and special rules for specific types of litigation will be reduced to a minimum.

(b) All proceedings will be commenced in the same way by a claim.

(c) The claim and defence will not be technical documents. The claim will set out the facts alleged by the claimant, the remedy the claimant seeks, the grounds on which the remedy is sought and any relevant points of law. The defence will set out the defendant's detailed response to the claim and make clear the real issues between the parties. Both 'statements of case' will have to include certificates by the parties verifying their contents so tactical allegations will no longer be possible.

(d) During the course of proceedings the court on its own initiative, or on the application of either party, will be able to dispose of individual issues or the litigation as a whole where there is no real prospect of success.

(e) Claimants will be able to start proceedings in any court. It will be the court's responsibility to direct parties or to transfer the case, if necessary, to the appropriate part of the system.

(f) Discovery will be controlled; in a minority of cases the present scale of discovery will be possible but in the majority of cases there will be a new standard test for more restricted disclosure.

(g) There will be special procedures, involving active judicial case management, to deal with multi party actions expeditiously and fairly.

(h) Instead of an irrational kaleidoscope of different ways of appealing or applying to the High Court against the decisions of other bodies, there will be a unified code.

The timescale of litigation will be shorter and more certain
(a) All cases will progress to trial in accordance with a timetable set and monitored by the court.

(b) For fast track cases there will be fixed timetables of no more than 30 weeks.

(c) The court will apply strict sanctions to parties who do not comply with the procedures or timetables.

(d) Appeals from case management decisions will be kept to the minimum, and will be dealt with expeditiously.

(e) The court will determine the length of the trial and what is to happen at the trial.

The cost of litigation will be more affordable, more predictable, and more proportionate to the value and complexity of individual cases
(a) There will be fixed costs for cases on the fast track.

(b) Estimates of costs for multitrack cases will be published by the court or agreed by the parties and approved by the court.

(c) There will be a special 'streamlined' track for lower value or less complex multitrack cases, where the procedure will be as simple as possible with appropriate budgets for costs.

(d) For classes of litigation where the procedure is uncomplicated and predictable the court will issue guideline costs with the assistance of users.

(e) There will be a new test for the taxation of costs to further the overriding objective. It will be that there should be allowed 'such sum as is reasonable taking account of the interests of both parties to the taxation'.

. . .

Conclusion

20 In the course of the Inquiry there has been unprecedented consultation with all involved in the civil justice system. Over the last year, judges, practitioners and consumers have worked together to hammer out new ways of tackling problems and to contribute to what is proposed in this final report. I see a continuing need for such involvement in the process of implementation. Much has been done. But much more remains to be done. The continuing involvement of all those who use the civil justice system will be given coherence and leadership by the Civil Justice Council which I recommended in the interim report. Local user committees, a specialist IT sub-committee and working groups developing further detail for the new fast track would all come under its aegis. The Council would continue and develop the process of co-operation and creativity that the Inquiry has benefited from.

21 The civil justice system in this country urgently needs reform. The time is right for change. The public and businesses want change, and the majority of the legal profession agree. The judiciary has strongly supported my Inquiry. I have been given a unique opportunity to help achieve the change which is needed.

22 My recommendations, together with the new code of rules, form a comprehensive and coherent package for the reform of civil justice. Each contributes to and underpins the others. Their overall effectiveness could be seriously undermined by piecemeal implementation. Their implementation as a whole will ensure that all the supporting elements of the civil justice system are directed towards the fundamental reform that is required.

23 Nevertheless, there should be a degree of flexibility in the approach to implementation. All the recommendations I have made, both in the interim report and in this report, are designed to meet the objectives for the civil justice system which I set out at the beginning of this overview. My detailed recommendations are based on a thorough review of the present system, including the wide consultation I have mentioned, but the objectives are of primary importance. The individual proposals should not be too rigidly applied if it is found that there are better ways of achieving the objectives. My overriding concern is to ensure that we have a civil justice system which will meet the needs of the public in the twenty-first century.

 Lord Woolf's report, 'Access to Justice', is available on the website of the former Department for Constitutional Affairs:
www.dca.gov.uk/civil/final/overview.htm

Evaluation of Lord Woolf's reforms

Following the introduction of Lord Woolf's reforms to the civil justice system, the government commissioned research to look at the success of these reforms.

Further Findings
A Continuing Evaluation of the Civil Justice Reforms, August 2002

Executive summary

The aim of this paper is to present further findings on the effects of the Civil Justice Reforms which were introduced in April 1999, implementing many of the recommendations in Lord Woolf's final report on *Access to Justice*.

Early findings based upon evidence obtained over the first two years were presented in the paper *Emerging Findings* published in March 2001. This paper builds on that evidence and includes some additional information.

Key findings

In general, the findings that were included in the previous paper have been confirmed.

- Overall there has been a drop in the number of claims issued, in particular in the types of claim most affected by the new Civil Procedure Rules introduced in April 1999.

- Evidence suggests that pre-action protocols are working well to promote settlement and a culture of openness and co-operation.
- Part 36 has been welcomed by all interested groups as a means of resolving claims more quickly: claims which settle without court proceedings and those where proceedings are issued.
- There is evidence to show that settlements at the door of the court are now fewer and that settlements before the hearing day have increased.
- After a substantial rise in the first year following the introduction of the Civil Procedure Rules, there has been a levelling off in the number of cases in which Alternative Dispute Resolution is used.
- The use of single joint experts appears to have worked well. It is likely that their use has contributed to a less adversarial culture and helped achieve earlier settlements.
- Case Management Conferences are a key factor in making litigation less complex, and appear to have been a success.
- The time between issue and hearing for those cases that go to trial has fallen. The time between issue and hearing for small claims has risen since the introduction of the Civil Procedure Rules but may now be falling.
- The number of appeals in the course of proceedings appears to have fallen sharply.
- It is still too early to provide a definitive view on costs. The picture remains relatively unclear with statistics difficult to obtain and conflicting anecdotal evidence. Where there is evidence of increased costs, the causes are difficult to isolate.
- The views of litigants in person are difficult to obtain as they tend to use the system only once. Whilst research is currently being undertaken to assess their views, anecdotally it appears that courts are providing the assistance required. Court Service User surveys have returned good results.

. . .

2 Further findings – an introduction

Further findings from the civil justice reforms

2.1 In section 1.9 of *Access to Justice Final Report 1996*, Lord Woolf described the new land-scape of civil litigation as having ten features. *Emerging Findings* looked at the first six of these features and used some aspects of these as the criteria for measuring the success of the procedural reforms. In this paper we have continued with that method and have included information on some of the work that has been undertaken in the other four areas as well. The ten features are:

- Litigation will be avoided wherever possible.
- Litigation will be less adversarial and more co-operative.
- Litigation will be less complex.
- The timescale of litigation will be shorter and more certain.
- The cost of litigation will be more affordable, more predictable, and more proportionate to the value and complexity of individual cases.
- Parties of limited financial means will be able to conduct litigation on a more equal footing.
- There will be clear lines of judicial and administrative responsibility for the civil justice system.
- The structure of the courts and the deployment of judges will be designed to meet the needs of litigants.

- Judges will be deployed effectively so that they can manage litigation in accordance with the new rules and protocols.
- The civil justice system will be responsive to the needs of litigants.

2.2 The overall view reported in '*Emerging Findings*' was that, with a few exceptions, the reforms were working well. There were specific areas singled out for praise in various surveys, such as the change in culture and a reduction in litigation. Although there was criticism from some quarters about litigation becoming slower and more costly, that was a minority view. The evidence we have included in this report indicates that time from issue to trial has continued to decrease, and there is mixed evidence on costs. In general, views remain positive about the overall thrust of the reforms.

2.3 The Law Society Woolf Network was established in April 1999 when the first tranche of the Civil Procedure Rules came into force. It is made up of a group of about 130 solicitors who originally gave a commitment to answer twice yearly questionnaires on how the reforms are working in practice. This has since been reduced to once a year.

2.4 In the third survey, published in February 2001, the reforms received a very positive overall response: 80% of the respondents felt the reforms were an improvement on the previous system with comments such as: 'the reforms increased settlement and the spirit of co-operation', 'the reforms make the process quicker and less adversarial'.

2.5 In the fourth survey, published in February 2002, respondents were asked about their overall impressions of the reforms this stage: 25% said that the reforms were working well and another 69% said they were working well with some reservations. Only 6% of respondents said that the reforms were not working well. 84% of respondents thought that the new procedures were quicker and 70% felt they were more efficient, but a large majority of 81% did not agree that the new procedures were cheaper for their clients.

2.6 Commenting on the results of the fourth survey, Carolyn Kirby, then Law Society Vice-President, said:

> There is little doubt that the new Woolf reforms have improved the civil justice system already and achieved tangible successes. However for clients and court users really to feel the benefit the system must be properly resourced and we must not allow the pre-action protocols . . . to be undermined by lack of enforcement. There must also be further guidelines about the assessment of costs to ensure greater consistency.

2.7 Despite some concerns, there is a widely held view that there has been a change of culture and there remains a willingness among all those interested in civil justice to work in partnership in the continuing programme of reform. District Judge Michael Walker, Secretary of the Association of District Judges, remarked 'One of the real surprises has been the way in which the Lord Chancellor's Department, the Court Service and the Judiciary have together striven to work through problems as they have arisen, understanding the concerns of each other and seeking to find the most appropriate outcome, in a spirit of co-operation that echoes the Overriding Objective.'

 The research 'Further Findings: A Continuing Evaluation of the Civil Justice Reforms' (2002) has been published on the website of the former Department for Constitutional Affairs and can be found at:
www.dca.gov.uk/civil/reform/ffreform.htm

Review of civil court costs

In 2008 the Master of the Rolls asked the High Court judge, Lord Justice Jackson, to carry out a review of civil court costs. There is concern that Lord Woolf's reforms might have created heavy costs at the start of the litigtaion process, so that cases are expensive to settle. This review has been discussed by the journalist, Neil Rose, in an article in *The Times*.

Are High Costs Failing Those Looking for Justice?
The Times, 13 November 2008

Neil Rose

The fundamental review of costs of litigation in the civil courts set up under Lord Justice Jackson was described as the biggest thing since the Woolf report, at the Civil Justice Council's (CJC) costs forum last month – which is appropriate, given that high costs are a particular failure of the former Lord Chief Justice's reforms.

Even more to the point, Rupert Jackson, QC, as he was then, was one of Lord Woolf's five assessors. Sir Rupert will deliver his report to Sir Anthony Clarke, Master of the Rolls, who has given him the brief to make recommendations that 'promote access to justice at proportionate cost'.

The problem of how to make costs proportionate to damages has dogged the justice system over the past decade. The judge knows this all too well: last month he ruled in the construction dispute over Wembley Stadium, criticising the £20 million run up in legal costs that far exceeded the sums in dispute.

The judge, who joined the Court of Appeal only recently, will spend most of 2009 working full-time on his investigation with the support of his own panel of assessors, including Mr Justice Cranston, the former Solicitor-General who was academic consultant to the Woolf report; Michael Napier, senior partner at Irwin Mitchell; and Jeremy Morgan, QC, of 39 Essex Street, a leading costs counsel.

He will still sit as a judge, however, and this month get a first-hand taste of the continuing costs war being fought through the appeals in which liability insurers are attacking the Law Society-endorsed Accident Line after-the-event (ATE) insurance scheme.

The Ministry of Justice has politely welcomed the costs review. But the big difference with Woolf is that his inquiry was commissioned by the Government (by the Lord Chancellor in 1994). The MoJ has made clear that the judge's work will not delay its own mooted appraisal of how 'no win, no fee' cases are working. An announcement on whether to take this forward is expected soon.

On that, some wonder if the Government's mind is already made up. It is under pressure from media organisations unhappy with the costs in libel actions – see the speech by Paul Dacre, Editor of the *Daily Mail*, at the weekend – trade unions unhappy with equal pay claims solicitors are bringing in employment tribunals, and from MPs, newspapers and others unhappy with the amount that the NHS pays out to claimant lawyers acting under conditional fee agreements (CFAs).

Jack Straw told the Labour Party conference in September that 'the behaviour of some lawyers in ramping up their fees in cases is nothing short of scandalous'. He wished to address that and to consider 'capping more tightly the level of success fees the lawyers can charge'.

Could his solution be simply to reduce the 100% cap on the uplift on normal fees that solicitors acting successfully under a CFA can charge? What impact would that have on access to justice and solicitors taking on riskier cases? And what about the bargain this Government struck with the profession when it expanded CFAs, promising that success fees would compensate for the risk of losing and thus being paid nothing?

There are concerns about whether the CFA/ATE model is sustainable even though it appears robust and is finding the capacity to run big cases (*Law*, November 7). Various self-funding bolt-ons to the legal aid scheme have been mooted instead – such as the conditional legal aid fund, long championed by the Bar, and a supplementary legal aid scheme, which operates on a much smaller scale in Hong Kong – but perhaps a more realistic, if more controversial, alternative is the US-style contingency fee.

Many in the profession and public would need convincing that contingency fees are the answer – even if CFAs mean that we are already most of the way there. Research to be published soon by the CJC should help to debunk popular myths of their corrupting influence on the US legal system.

It has found no evidence that contingency fees necessarily promote frivolous claims or a litigation culture there, and should say that contingency fees could work in England and Wales – but might narrow access to justice for low-value cases.

Already on the move is third-party funding of litigation – a disinterested party taking on the risk of paying all the costs in return for a cut of any damages. While third-party funding has excited the interest of City litigators, who until now have largely ignored alternatives to clients paying by the hour, it will benefit only the relatively small number of large commercial or group actions where the potential rewards will attract funders.

This is good news for group actions that have all but stalled because of funding problems, and is why the CJC is working to ensure that third-party funding has a solid base in England and Wales.

There was a time when lawyers talking about their costs was simply not the done thing. Now, they seem to talk about little else.

A unified civil court system

In 2005, the government issued a consultation paper which considers the possibility of replacing the existing civil courts of first instance with a single civil court.

A Single Civil Court?

Consultation Paper (2005)

The proposals

1 Some now argue that unification of the civil court jurisdictions can be seen as the logical next step after the Woolf and Bowman [appeal process] reforms and the unified administration programme. And studying the reforms down the years shows the concept of unification is by no means a new one. As long ago as 1869 the Judicature Commissioners recommended a move towards a unified regime.

2 More recently, on the civil-side, the Civil Justice Review held back from recommending unification (which it saw as theoretically ideal) only because of 'practical grounds', many of which have significantly reduced in importance since the Woolf reforms changed the land-scape of civil litigation. Lord Woolf himself considered unification when writing his interim report in 1995. At that stage, he rejected the idea mainly on constitutional grounds relating to the need to maintain the separate status of the High Court judges. Any reform would need to ensure that these concerns are addressed, taking into account that the Concordat [an agreement between the senior judges and the Lord Chancellor] has set a new context in which the status and independence of the judiciary are safeguarded.

3 On the family side, as shown above, the concept of unification has been mooted since the mid-1960s. The Finer Report strongly recommended establishing a single family court. And the interdepartmental consultation paper considered the options again in 1986. The proposals received public backing.

4 Those currently advocating unification suggest that reducing or removing the present boundaries in the system would offer benefits in three main areas:

- **User benefits**. A system that is difficult for users to understand will be difficult for them to use: it may deter some people altogether and cause others to make potentially costly mistakes about where to bring their cases. Reducing the actual and apparent complex-ities of the system should enhance users' access to it. And savings from a more efficient system would be reflected in court fees paid by litigants in general.
- **Judicial benefits**. The complexities of the current system, with all its boundaries – geographical, financial and subject-specific – unnecessarily complicates the allocation of work to the most appropriate judges. Greatly simplifying these structures would foster flexibility. Procedural judges would direct cases to the most appropriate level and venue. Proponents of reform argue inflexibilities inherent in the current structure sometimes hinder the allocation of work to the lowest appropriate tier of judge and that unification would facilitate the more efficient use of judicial resources.
- **Administrative benefits**. The body responsible for administering the courts (from April 2005, Her Majesty's Courts Service) would no longer have to maintain separate systems, leading to greater efficiencies and savings on things like IT, training and forms.

5 To create a single civil court, primary legislation would be required. The simplest approach would be to abolish the county courts. This would leave the High Court and its com-prehensive national jurisdiction as the single civil court. And its powers, procedures and judiciary could be adjusted to ensure that it had all the necessary features of a court covering all that the current High Court and county courts do now. Of course, there is then the issue of what to do with the Family Proceedings Court business . . .

6 These proposals would represent a major change. It may be that the Civil Procedure Rules and other recent reforms have delivered most of the possible benefits. If so, further change could just be expensive and superficial. Or it may be that the structural demarca-tions between courts remain a barrier to achieving the full benefits of recent reforms. So this consultation paper considers what a unified court might look like and raises key questions for discussion. Responses to it will inform further analysis to test the costs and benefits of reform against the status quo. But the Government will not decide about the feasibility and worth of these structural reforms until that analysis has been carried through. The Partial Regulatory Impact Assessment (PRIA) annexed to this paper is a preliminary step to produc-ing the further analysis we need. It considers the relative merits of three broad alternatives:

- **Do nothing** – retention of the status quo.
- **Primary legislative reform** – creation of a single court by abolishing the county courts.
- **Reform by existing secondary powers** – these already provide considerable flexibility that could be used to simplify and streamline the current system further. It may be that reforms using these powers could approximate most of the main benefits of a unified jurisdiction at a lower cost than primary legislation to create a single court.

7 The rest of this paper discusses the key features of the unified court that could be created through primary legislation.

 The consultation paper 'A Single Civil Court' is available on the internet at: **www.dca.gov.uk/consult/civilcourt_cp0605.htm**

A compensation culture

There has been concern that the UK might be moving towards a 'compensation culture'. A compensation culture exists where people bring trivial and unwarranted claims to court. This issue has been considered by the Better Regulation Taskforce, which is an independent advisory group that offers advice to the government.

Better Routes to Redress

Better Regulation Taskforce (2004)

1 Foreword

It is a commonly held perception that the United Kingdom is in the grip of a 'compensation culture'. Newspapers complain that the UK is becoming like the United States with stories of people apparently suing others for large sums of money, and often for what appear to be trivial reasons. Media reports and claims management companies encourage people to 'have a go' by creating a perception, quite inaccurately, that large sums of money are easily accessible.

It is this perception that causes the real problem: the fear of litigation impacts on behaviour and imposes burdens on organisations trying to handle claims. The judicial process is very good at sorting the wheat from the chaff, but all claims must still be assessed in the early stages. Redress for a genuine claimant is hampered by the spurious claims arising from the perception of a compensation culture. The compensation culture is a myth; but the cost of this belief is very real.

It has got to be right that people who have suffered an injustice through someone else's negligence should be able to claim redress. What is not right is that some people should be led to believe that they can absolve themselves from any personal responsibility for their actions and then expect someone else to pick up the pieces when something goes wrong, regardless of whose fault it was.

Handling compensation claims can be expensive. One large council we spoke to estimated that this year it would spend over £2 million of its highways budget of nearly £22 million handling claims for compensation. Multiply that by all the local authorities and councils are spending a staggering amount of money each year dealing with compensation claims. Many claims will be genuine, and should act as an encouragement for better risk management, but many may be spurious. It is the money spent dealing with these claims which could be better spent for the benefit of local residents.

The prospect of litigation for negligence may have positive effects in making organisations manage their risks better, but an exaggerated fear of litigation, regardless of fault can be debilitating.

The fear of litigation can make organisations over cautious in their behaviour. Local communities and local authorities unnecessarily cancel events and ban activities which until recently would have been considered routine. Businesses may be in danger of becoming less innovative – and without innovation there will be no progress.

. . .

2 Introduction

Almost every day there is a report in the media – newspaper, radio or television, suggesting that the United Kingdom is in the grip of a compensation culture. Headlines shout about people trying to claim what appear to be large sums of money for what are portrayed as dubious reasons.

The culture that is crippling Britain

Daily Mail, 21 February 2004

Blame culture 'is road to suicide' Lloyd's Chairman believes Britain is following America's compensation path into an abyss for insurers

Daily Telegraph, 3 February 2004

A chef who cut his finger is suing a hotel for £25,000 compensation by claiming no-one warned him about the danger posed by an avocado

BBC News website, 6 January 2004

Postman sues customer who sent 'too many' letters

Daily Telegraph, 20 December 2003

But what is not always reported is the outcome. The reality is often very different. Litigating is not easy. Many claims never reach court. Some will, of course, be settled out-of-court; others disappear because the claim had little chance of succeeding in the first place. For a claimant to succeed they have to be able to prove that first someone else owed them a duty of care and then that the same person was negligent.

The term 'compensation culture' is not used to describe a society where people are able to seek compensation. Rather a 'compensation culture' implies that a decision to seek compensation is wrong. 'Compensation culture' is a pejorative term and suggests that those that seek to 'blame and claim' should be criticised. It suggests greed; rather than people legitimately enforcing their rights. Few would oppose the principle that if people's rights are infringed, appropriate action should be available to the injured party to gain compensation from the guilty party. So why the double standards?

This report looks at the impact of and the reality behind the 'compensation culture'. It examines how those with a genuine grievance can seek and gain appropriate redress efficiently and effectively. We look at how people enter the redress process and how the service they receive is funded; what mechanisms exist to weed out frivolous or vexatious claims; what forms of redress are available, and how they might be made more available. Central to our report is the injured party – the most important person in the process.

Developments in recent years, principally the introduction of 'no win no fee' arrangements – where the claimant only pays their lawyer's fees in the event of success – and the emergence of claims management companies have increased access to justice.

But they have also meant that more people have been encouraged to 'have a go' at claiming redress for a wrong they feel they have suffered.

We live in a much richer, but more risk averse, society than ever before. We are also much better informed about our rights, which means we are more aware when there is a case to answer. However, some people may be persuaded, by what they have read in the papers or through the contact they have had with claims management companies, to look for compensation where none is available and therefore decide to 'have a go'. This has had both positive and negative impacts. On the positive side the public sector, such as schools, rather than canceling trips and activities as the media would have us believe, have become much better at assessing and managing risks. Local authorities have put sophisticated systems in place to manage, for example, repairs to their pathways and highways.

However, on the negative side, the 'have a go' culture that encourages people to pursue misconceived or trivial claims:

- has put a drain on public sector resources;
- may make businesses and other organisations more cautious for fear of litigation;
- contributes to higher insurance premiums; and
- clogs up the system for those with indisputable claims.

Local authorities are spending a great amount of money dealing with all the claims they receive. Every claim made, however frivolous or vexatious it is eventually found to be, has to be handled. That costs money: money raised from local residents; and money which could otherwise be spent on maintaining roads and pavements. Those who make unsubstantiated claims fail to realise that they ultimately are the ones that have to pay through higher taxes. But the local authorities believe that if they do not challenge every claim, the floodgates could open.

> Responses from 212 councils in England and Wales revealed that 85% of councils agree that 'The introduction of conditional fee arrangements has increased the annual cost to my authority of handling compensation claims.'
>
> *Suing the council – helping the citizen or harming the community?*
> Zurich Municipal and Local Government Association, January 2004

Others would do well to follow their lead. Businesses should be more inclined to challenge claims rather than settling out of court. One successfully challenged case might persuade others to do the same. An apology can also go a long way. We need to move away from the situation where an apology is seen as an admittance of liability. In a survey commissioned by the Chief Medical Officer in 2002, 34% of respondents who have been affected by medical injury wanted an apology or explanation.

However, the so-called 'compensation culture' cannot be blamed for all these problems. Some have arisen from poor operational practices by companies.

We recognise that the 'compensation culture' is a very controversial issue, but it is one we feel needs to be debated. Those with grievances need a system of redress that provides them with effective remedies; whilst those without should be kept out of the system. It is important for us to realise that we have to take responsibility for our own actions – and not seek someone else to blame when things go wrong. Aside from starting a debate on 'compensation culture', this report looks at the regime of seeking and securing redress from the perspective of our five principles of good regulation – proportionality, accountability, consistency, transparency and targeting.

 The report of the Better Regulation Taskforce, 'Better Routes to Redress' (2004) is available on the Better Regulation Commission website: **www.brc.gov.uk/publications/liticompensation.asp**

23

Tribunals

Introduction

This chapter looks at:

- the report by Sir Andrew Leggatt into the tribunal system;
- the government White Paper, *Transforming Public Services: Complaints, Redress and Tribunals* (2004); and
- the Tribunals, Courts and Enforcement Act 2007.

Review of the tribunals

At the request of the Lord Chancellor, Sir Andrew Leggatt undertook a review of the tribunals, and his report was published in 2001.

Tribunals for Users: One System, One Service
Report of the Review of Tribunals (2001)

Chapter One – Introduction

1.1 The last 50 years have brought an accelerating accumulation of tribunals as bodies whose function it is to decide disputes that would otherwise have to go to the courts. Together they form the largest part of the civil justice system in England and Wales, hearing about a million cases each year. That number of cases alone makes their work of great importance to our society, since more of us bring a case before a tribunal than go to any other part of the justice system. Their collective impact is immense.

1.2 Choosing a tribunal to decide disputes should bring two distinctive advantages for users. First, tribunal decisions are often made jointly by a panel of people who pool legal and other expert knowledge, and are the better for that range of skills. Secondly, tribunals' procedures and approach to overseeing the preparation of cases and their hearing can be simpler and more informal than the courts, even after the civil justice reforms. Most users ought therefore to be capable of preparing and presenting their cases to the tribunal themselves, providing they have the right kind of help. Enabling that kind of direct participation is an important justification for establishing tribunals at all.

1.3 What we have found, however, is that the present collection of tribunals has grown up in an almost entirely haphazard way. Individual tribunals were set up, and usually administered by departments, as they developed new statutory schemes and procedures. The result is a collection of tribunals, mostly administered by departments, with wide variations of practice and approach, and almost no coherence. The current arrangements seem to us to have been developed to meet the needs and conveniences of the departments and other bodies which run tribunals, rather than the needs of the user. That levels of dissatisfaction are not higher is largely due to the commitment and resourcefulness of tribunal members, and of those who work for them; and everything which follows must be read in the light of the important public service that they render.

1.4 We do not believe that the current arrangements meet what the modern user needs and expects from an appeal system running in parallel to the courts. First, users need to be sure, as they currently cannot be, that decisions in their cases are being taken by people with no links with the body they are appealing against. Secondly, a more coherent framework for tribunals would create real opportunities for improvement in the quality of services than can be achieved by tribunals acting separately. Thirdly, that framework will enable them to develop a more coherent approach to the services which users must receive if they are to be enabled to prepare and present cases themselves. Fourthly, a user-oriented service needs to be much clearer than it is now in telling users what services they can expect, and what to do if the standards of these services are not met.

. . .

Coherence

1.15 The necessary skills for tribunal decision-makers, and the services provided by their staff, will be greatly improved if they are brought together to form a coherent system and services; and without that coherence the improvements which are necessary for tribunals to remain a distinctive and viable alternative to courts cannot be achieved. We start to explain why with a brief appraisal of tribunals as we have found them. More detailed views on individual tribunals can be found in Part II of the report.

The tribunal world today

1.16 The Appeals Service, by far the largest tribunal, deals with about one-quarter of all cases. At the other extreme, there are some tribunals which have not sat for years. The subjects tribunals deal with cover the whole range of political and social life, including social security benefits, health, education, tax, agriculture, criminal injuries compensation, immigration and asylum, rents, and parking. Against that background, no generalisation will be true of all of them or in all cases. But there are enough resemblances to make it worth trying to describe the tribunal world in broad terms. This section sets out what we have seen for ourselves, what we have learned from the responses to the consultation document we issued in June 2000 and from material given to us by the Council on Tribunals, and what emerged from the findings of the research study undertaken for us by MORI.

1.17 The first point to note is the public-spiritedness and conscientiousness of most of the chairmen, members and staff we met. Although we have criticisms of many of the tribunals, we would like to pay tribute to the individuals who work within them.

1.18 The most striking feature of tribunals is their isolation. This is a serious problem. Apart from the narrowness of outlook which it engenders, it leads to duplication of effort. Each tribunal invents its own IT, its own internal processes, and its own service standards, though not all of them do have such standards. There is under-investment in training in many tribunals. The bigger tribunals have good accommodation, frequently under-used; the smaller ones are scratching around for suitable venues for hearings. The Appeals Service has invested in relatively up-to-date IT; most other tribunals' IT is much more primitive and is years behind the systems we found in Australia. Most tribunals find it difficult to retain suitable staff, especially in London, because of the limited career prospects they can offer. In most cases, tribunals feel that they are at the back of the queue for resources.

The relationship with departments

1.19 There is also an uneasy relationship between most tribunals and the departments on whose decisions they are adjudicating. In those tribunals which are paid for by the sponsoring departments, the chairmen and members feel that they cannot be seen as independent, however impartial they are, and however scrupulous departments are. Indeed, plainly they are not independent. Even in tribunals which are no longer paid for by 'their' departments, there can be an unhealthy closeness. For example, the General Commissioners of Income Tax, although now sponsored by the Lord Chancellor's Department, are still wholly dependent on the Inland Revenue for case listing and for the flow of information to enable them to take their decisions. At the same time, paradoxically, many tribunals do not enter into the appropriate dialogue which would enable departments to learn from adverse tribunal decisions and thereby to improve their primary decision-making.

The relationship with users

1.20 Tribunals are in general careful about reaching their decisions. But there can be unacceptable delays in resolving cases. Sometimes delay may actually suit the user (some tax cases, for example, and immigration cases); more often delay is at best irritating and at worst distressing for the user. Either way it is not in the interests of justice for cases to be allowed to drift. The causes of drift include: inefficient document-handling systems which result in parties at the hearing discovering that they do not all have the same bundle of papers; poor listing practices; procedural default by the department being appealed against; over-readiness to grant adjournments, sometimes on flimsy grounds; reluctance to give a decision on the day; and post-hearing inefficiencies. For example, decisions are sometimes written in long-hand, sent in weeks after the hearing, and then sent to a remote typing service. All of these are remediable, and many tribunals are working hard to reduce the delays which are within their own control.

1.21 To the user, however, the length of time which matters is the time between receiving the original decision by the department and the final implementation of the tribunal's decision on the appeal. Much of the delay we have seen occurs between the primary decision-maker and the tribunal, and between the tribunal and the appellate body. The tribunal process needs to be viewed in that wider context. Some tribunals and departments are now conducting end-to-end reviews of the process from first decision to ultimate implementation. We commend this initiative.

1.22 During the tribunal process, the information provided to the user is patchy. Departments do not always provide reasons for their decisions, nor do they always explain how to appeal against their decisions. Tribunals' communications with users are sometimes terse and impersonal; some letters are still written in officialese; and telephone arrangements can be amateur. Users frequently feel in the dark about whether they have a good case or not, and about where their case has gone to, and why it is taking so long. Departments and tribunals are, however, increasingly aware that they should provide clear, timely information in a user-friendly way. Our recommendations in Chapter Four draw on some of the good practices we have seen and are intended to help departments and tribunals to improve further.

Procedures

1.23 At the hearings, users can experience some quite old-fashioned processes. Examples include a legal representative reading out in full a paper submission which is already in front of all the parties; witnesses being asked to read out their written statements; or witnesses being taken slowly through detailed, uncontroversial, factual material where simple confirmation that the position is as set out in the documents would suffice.

1.24 In some tribunals, proceedings are informal. In others, they are at least as formal as those of the courts. Normally, users welcome informality. They may, however, be disconcerted if the proceedings are totally unstructured, because they are then uncertain when to bring in particular points. The MORI research study found that approaches sometimes differ within the same tribunal.

1.25 However informal the atmosphere, and however sympathetic the chairmen and members are to the user, the experience of a tribunal hearing is extremely stressful for most users. They value the option of presenting their case personally, and in general they feel that they are given a fair hearing. But the issue, whether it is their tax bill or the level of their social security benefits, the schooling of their child or the level of their rent, matters personally to them, and the hearing is an important and possibly daunting occasion. Perhaps the biggest challenge for tribunals is to enable users who feel that they have been unfairly treated to come to the tribunal without undue apprehension, and to leave feeling that they have been given a fair opportunity to put their case.

 The full report of the Review of Tribunals, 'Tribunals for Users: One System, One Service' (2001), is available at:
www.tribunals-review.org.uk/leggatthtm/leg-01.htm

Tribunal reform

Following the publication of Sir Andrew Leggatt's report on tribunals, the government issued a White Paper, 'Transforming Public Services: Complaints, Redress and Tribunals' (2004). This paper accepted many of the recommendations of Sir Andrew Leggatt which were subsequently included in the Tribunals, Courts and Enforcement Act 2007.

Transforming Public Services: Complaints, Redress and Tribunals

Foreword

The Department for Constitutional Affairs was created to drive forward the reform and improvement of the justice system, to deliver better services for the public and to reform and safeguard the constitution so that it serves the public effectively. It is our task to ensure that the faith the public have in government is improved. Few things matter more to people than their ability to obtain justice in their dealings with the State and in their workplace but, as this White Paper shows, the institutions which are there to safeguard justice in administration and in the workplace lack systematic design and are poorly organised. This White Paper takes forward the proposals for the reform of Tribunals set out in Sir Andrew Leggatt's Report. Tribunals matter. More people go to tribunals than go to court and for many they may be their only contact with the justice system.

But this White Paper goes wider than this. The public do not want to go to a Tribunal, they want their complaint or dispute resolved quickly and fairly. The White Paper therefore looks at the whole issue of dispute resolution between citizen and State and in the workplace and explores how better to deliver resolution and fairness as part of our public sector reform programme.

This White Paper deliberately takes a bold approach. It explains the context in which we seek reform. It sets out what we believe we should seek to achieve. And it is an invitation to all those involved in redress – judges, officials, lawyers, advice workers – to work together to create a new organisation and a new approach which genuinely meets the community's needs.

The Right Honourable Lord Falconer of Thoroton
Secretary of State for Constitutional Affairs and Lord Chancellor

Introduction

. . .

We accept Sir Andrew Leggatt's key recommendation that tribunals provided by central government should be brought together into a unified system within what is now the Department for Constitutional Affairs. We believe that this will be more effective and efficient, and will firmly embed the principle of independence. But we see this new body as much more than a federation of existing tribunals. This is a new organisation and a new type of organisation. It will have two central pillars: administrative justice appeals, and employment cases. Its task, together with a transformed Council on Tribunals, will not be just to process cases according to law. Its mission will be to help to prevent and resolve disputes, using any appropriate method and working with its partners in and out of government, and to help to improve administrative justice and justice in the workplace, so that the need for disputes is reduced.

 The White Paper 'Transforming Public Services: Complaints, Redress and Tribunals' is available on the internet at:
www.dca.gov.uk/pubs/adminjust/transformfull.pdf

Tribunals, Courts and Enforcement Act 2007 – major reform

Following Andrew Legatt's review, and the government's consultation process, the Tribunals, Courts and Enforcement Act 2007 was passed by Parliament, which constituted a major reform of the tribunal system. These reforms are clearly explained by the explanatory notes that accompanied the Act.

Tribunals, Courts and Enforcement Act 2007, Explanatory Notes

PART 1: TRIBUNALS AND INQUIRIES

Summary

4 The policy intention underlying Part 1 of the Act is to create a new, simplified statutory framework for tribunals, bringing existing tribunal jurisdictions together and providing a structure for new jurisdictions and new appeal rights.

5 The Act provides a new unified structure by creating two new tribunals, the First-tier Tribunal and the Upper Tribunal. It gives the Lord Chancellor power to transfer the jurisdiction of existing tribunals to the two new tribunals. Further, the Lord Chancellor is empowered to transfer to himself certain statutory powers and duties in relation to the administration of tribunals. The Act places the Lord Chancellor under a general duty to provide administrative support to the new tribunals, and also to the employment tribunals, Employment Appeal Tribunal and Asylum and Immigration Tribunal (AIT).

6 The Act also creates a new judicial office, the Senior President of Tribunals, to oversee tribunal judiciary. The Senior President will be the judicial leader of the tribunals system. The Senior President of Tribunals holds a distinct statutory office and in carrying out the functions of that office is not subject to the direction of any other judicial office holder. The Act provides for the membership of the tribunals, rights of appeal from the tribunals and the making of new Tribunal Procedure Rules. The Act also gives the Upper Tribunal the power to exercise a judicial review jurisdiction in certain circumstances. Further, the Act also replaces the Council on Tribunals with the Administrative Justice and Tribunals Council, which will have a broader remit over the whole of the administrative justice system.

Background

7 Tribunals constitute a substantial part of the justice system. They deal with a wide range of disputes including those between the individual and the state (such as benefits, tax and immigration) and between private individuals (such as employment disputes).

8 Until now, most tribunals have been created by individual pieces of primary legislation, without any overarching framework. Many have been administered by the government departments responsible for the policy area in which that tribunal has jurisdiction. Those departments are sometimes responsible for the decisions which are appealable to the tribunal.

9 In the report of his Review of Tribunals, *Tribunals for Users – One System, One Service*, published in August 2001, Sir Andrew Leggatt recommended extensive reform to the tribunals system. He recommended that tribunals should be brought together in a single system and that they should become separate from their current sponsoring departments. He recommended that such a system be administered instead by a single Tribunals Service, in what was then the Lord Chancellor's Department.

10 The Government agreed and published its response to the report in the White Paper *Transforming Public Services: Complaints, Redress and Tribunals* in July 2004.

The new tribunals

11 The Government's response to Sir Andrew Leggatt's recommended single tribunal system is to create two new, generic tribunals, the First-tier Tribunal and the Upper Tribunal, into which existing tribunal jurisdictions can be transferred. The Upper Tribunal is primarily, but not exclusively, an appellate tribunal from the First-tier Tribunal.

12 The Act also provides for the establishment of 'chambers' within the two tribunals so that the many jurisdictions that will be transferred into the tribunals can be grouped together appropriately. Each chamber will be headed by a Chamber President and the tribunals' judiciary will be headed by a Senior President of Tribunals.

Membership, deployment and composition

13 A distinctive feature of tribunals in their current form is their membership. Some tribunals consist of a lawyer sitting alone. Others comprise a lawyer sitting with one or more members who may be experts in their field (such as doctors or accountants) who have experience relevant to the work of the tribunal, or have no relevant experience but have generic skills. A few tribunals have no legal members at all.

14 At present, there is no coherent system in place for deploying tribunal members. While some sit in more than one jurisdiction, this will be as a result of the member having gone through the whole appointments process for each additional jurisdiction.

15 The Act creates new offices for the First-tier and Upper Tribunal. It creates new titles (giving the legal members the title of judges) and a new system of deployment. Judges of the First-tier Tribunal or Upper Tribunal will be assigned to one or more of the chambers of that tribunal, having regard to their knowledge and experience. The fact that a member may be allocated to more than one chamber allows members to be deployed across the jurisdictions within the tribunal. It is expected that the current members of transferred tribunals, apart from the General Commissioners, will become members of the new tribunals.

Reviews and appeals and the judicial review jurisdiction of the tribunals

16 Currently there is no single mechanism for appealing against a tribunal decision. Appeal rights differ from tribunal to tribunal. In some cases there is a right of appeal to another tribunal. In other cases there is a right of appeal to the High Court. In some cases there is no right of appeal at all. The Act provides a unified appeal structure. Under the Act, in most cases, a decision of the First-tier Tribunal may be appealed to the Upper Tribunal and a decision of the Upper Tribunal may be appealed to a court. The grounds of appeal must relate to a point of law. The rights to appeal may only be exercised with permission from the tribunal being appealed from or the tribunal or court, as the case may be, being appealed to.

17 It will also be possible for the Upper Tribunal to deal with some judicial review cases which would otherwise have to be dealt with by the High Court or Court of Session. The Upper Tribunal has this jurisdiction only where a case falls within a class specified in a direction given by the Lord Chief Justice or in certain other cases transferred by the High Court or Court of Session, but it will not be possible for cases to be transferred to the Upper Tribunal if they involve immigration or nationality matters.

18 Instead of tribunal rules being made by the Lord Chancellor and other government Ministers under a multiplicity of different rule-making powers, a new Tribunal Procedure Committee will be responsible for tribunal rules. This committee has been modelled on existing rule committees which make rules of court.

Transfer of tribunal functions

19 It is intended that the new tribunals will exercise the jurisdictions currently exercised by the tribunals listed in Parts 1 to 4 of Schedule 6, which constitute most of the tribunal jurisdictions administered by central government. The Government's policy is that in the future, when a new tribunal jurisdiction is required to deal with a right of review or appeal, that right of appeal or review will be to these new tribunals.

20 Some tribunals have been excluded from the new structures because of their specialist nature. Tribunals run by local government have for now been excluded, as their funding and sponsorship arrangements are sufficiently different to merit a separate review.

21 There are also tribunals that will share a common administration, and the leadership of the Senior President of Tribunals, but whose jurisdictions will not be transferred to the new tribunals. They are the AIT, the employment tribunals and the Employment Appeal

Tribunal. The AIT has a unique single-tier structure (as prescribed by the Nationality, Immigration and Asylum Act 2002, as amended by the Asylum and Immigration (Treatment of Claimants etc.) Act 2004) which would not fit into the new structure established by the Act. The employment tribunals and the Employment Appeal Tribunal are excluded because of the nature of the cases that come before them, which involve one party against another, unlike most other tribunals which hear appeals from citizens against decisions of the State.

Administrative Support

22 In *Transforming Public Services*, the Government set out its plans to create a single Tribunals Service to provide common administrative support to the main central government tribunals. The new Service, an executive agency of what was the Department for Constitutional Affairs (DCA) and is now the Ministry of Justice (MoJ), was launched in April 2006. It provides support to a range of tribunals, including the Asylum and Immigration Tribunal, the Social Security and Child Support Tribunals, the employment tribunals and the Employment Appeal Tribunal, and the Mental Health Review Tribunals in England. Most tribunals which are the responsibility of central government are now administered by the Tribunals Service, or will join the Service over the next few years.

23 The Tribunals Service was created by machinery of government changes. Legislation was not required. The Act does not, therefore, set out a blueprint for the new agency. The Act does, however, give the Lord Chancellor the power to transfer to himself certain statutory powers and duties that primarily relate to the provision of administrative support for tribunals. It entrenches these powers and duties with the office of the Lord Chancellor so that they can be transferred to another minister only by primary legislation.

24 In developing these proposals, the intention has been to follow the principles underlying the evolving constitutional settlement between the executive and the judiciary set out in the concordat agreed between the Lord Chancellor and the Lord Chief Justice for England and Wales in January 2004, and the Constitutional Reform Act 2005 ('CRA 2005').

Oversight of tribunals and inquiries

25 The Council on Tribunals ('the Council') operates under the Tribunals and Inquiries Act 1992 ('the 1992 Act'). Its statutory purpose is to keep under review and report on the constitution and working of tribunals under its supervision. The Council has to consider and report on particular matters that may be referred to it under the 1992 Act with respect to tribunals and, where necessary, to consider and report on the administrative procedures of statutory inquiries. The Council is also under a statutory duty to make an annual report about its work, which is to be laid before Parliament. The Council seeks to ensure that tribunals and inquiries meet the needs of users through the provision of an open, fair, impartial, efficient, timely and accessible service.

26 Sir Andrew Leggatt recommended that the Council on Tribunals should play a central role in the new tribunals system (recommendations 168–182). *Transforming Public Services* built on these recommendations in the wider context of the Government's proposals for reforming the Administrative Justice System. Chapter 11 of the White Paper proposed that with the creation of the Tribunals Service in April 2006 it was also necessary for the Council to change. It proposed that the Council should take on a wider remit to become an Administrative Justice and Tribunals Council and in particular to focus on the needs of the public and users.

Administrative Justice and Tribunals Council

27 Under this Act, the Administrative Justice and Tribunals Council ('the AJTC') will adopt a role in relation to the supervision of tribunals similar to that currently exercised by the Council on Tribunals. But in addition to taking on the Council on Tribunals' current remit, the AJTC will be charged with keeping the administrative justice system as a whole under review. It is tasked with considering how to make the system more accessible, fair and efficient, and advising the Lord Chancellor, the Scottish Ministers, Welsh Ministers and the Senior President accordingly.

28 The AJTC's wider administrative justice role will be concerned with ensuring that the relationships between the courts, tribunals, ombudsmen and alternative dispute resolution routes satisfactorily reflect the needs of users.

29 The AJTC will be of a comparable size to the present Council on Tribunals, with between 10 and 15 members appointed by the Lord Chancellor, and by Ministers from the devolved administrations. One of those appointed members will be nominated by the Lord Chancellor, after consultation with the Scottish and Welsh Ministers, to chair the AJTC. Whereas the Council has just a Scottish Committee, the AJTC will have Scottish and Welsh Committees.

 The Explanatory Notes to the Tribunals, Courts and Enforcement Act 2007 are available on the website for the Office of Public Sector Information at: **www.opsi.gov.uk/acts/acts2007/en/ukpgaen_20070015_en_1**

24

Appeals and judicial review

Introduction

This chapter looks at:

- the consultation paper considering whether to abolish the House of Lords and establish a Supreme Court for the United Kingdom;

- the government's report analysing the responses to the consultation process;

- the Constitutional Reform Act 2005; and

- the Criminal Cases Review Commission.

Moves towards a Supreme Court

In July 2003 the government issued a consultation paper in which it considered the possibility of abolishing the House of Lords as the highest court in the land, and replacing it with a new, independent Supreme Court.

The questions asked in this extract are the questions that the government specifically wanted respondents to answer.

A Department for Constitutional Affairs Consultation Paper
Constitutional Reform: A Supreme Court for the United Kingdom, July 2003

1 Setting up a new Supreme Court for the United Kingdom

1 The Government announced on 12 June that it intended to consult on the establishment of a new Supreme Court for the United Kingdom. This is part of its continuing drive to modernise the constitution and public services. The intention is that the new Court will put the relationship between the executive, the legislature and the judiciary on a modern footing, which takes account of people's expectations about the independence and transparency of the judicial system. There have been a number of calls for such a change in recent years, for example by the Senior Law Lord, Lord Bingham of Cornhill, in his Constitution Unit Lecture in May 2002, in which he said 'Our object is plain enough: to ensure that our supreme court is so structured and equipped as best to fulfil its functions and to command the confidence of the country in the changed world in which we live'. The Chairman of the Bar Council, in an article in *The Times* on 2 April 2003, said 'Judges should have no part of the legislature . . . It is very difficult to understand why our Supreme Court (the Law Lords) should be a committee of the second House of Parliament'.

Why change?

2 The functions of the highest courts in the land are presently divided between two bodies. The Appellate Committee of the House of Lords receives appeals from the courts in England and Wales and Northern Ireland, and in civil cases from Scotland. The Judicial Committee of the Privy Council, in addition to its overseas and ecclesiastical jurisdiction, considers questions as to whether the devolved administrations, the Scottish Parliament, the National Assembly for Wales and the Northern Ireland Assembly are acting within their legal powers. Both sets of functions raise questions about whether there is any longer sufficient transparency of independence from the executive and the legislature to give people the assurance to which they are entitled about the independence of the judiciary. The considerable growth of judicial review in recent years has inevitably brought the judges more into the political eye. It is essential that our systems do all that they can to minimise the danger that judges' decisions could be perceived to be politically motivated. The Human Rights Act 1998, itself the product of a changing climate of opinion, has made people more sensitive to the issues and more aware of the anomaly of the position whereby the highest court of appeal is situated within one of the chambers of Parliament.

3 It is not always understood that the decisions of the 'House of Lords' are in practice decisions of the Appellate Committee and that non-judicial members of the House never take part in the judgments. Nor is the extent to which the Law Lords themselves have decided to refrain from getting involved in political issues in relation to legislation on which they might later have to adjudicate always appreciated. The fact that the Lord Chancellor, as the Head of the Judiciary, was entitled to sit in the Appellate and Judicial Committees and did so as Chairman, added to the perception that their independence might be compromised by the arrangements. The Human Rights Act, specifically in relation to Article 6 of the European Convention on Human Rights, now requires a stricter view to be taken not only of anything which might undermine the independence or impartiality of a judicial tribunal, but even of anything which might appear to do so. So the fact that the Law Lords are a Committee of the House of Lords can raise issues about the appearance of independence from the legislature. Looking at it from the other way round, the requirement for the appearance of impartiality and independence also increasingly limits the ability of the Law Lords to contribute to the work of the House of Lords, thus reducing the value to both them and the House of their membership.

4 The position of the Appellate Committee as part of the House of Lords has inevitably limited the resources that can be made available to it. Space within the Palace of Westminster is at a premium, especially at the House of Lords end of the building. Although the facilities for hearings in Committee rooms 1 and 2 are good, the Law Lords' administration works in cramped conditions: one Law Lord does not even have a room. The position in the Palace cannot be improved without asking other peers to give up their desks. A separately constituted Supreme Court suitably accommodated could ensure that these issues were properly addressed.

5 In proposing that the time has come to change these arrangements, no criticism is intended of the way in which the members of either Committee have discharged their functions. Nor have there been any accusations of actual bias in either the appointments to either body or their judgments arising from their membership of the legislature. The arrangements have served us well in the past. Nonetheless, the Government has come to the conclusion that the present position is no longer sustainable. The time has come for the UK's highest court to move out from under the shadow of the legislature.

6 The Lord Chancellor has had an important role in preserving judicial independence. The Secretary of State for Constitutional Affairs will have a continuing responsibility for this vital safeguard. He will, both within Government and publicly, be responsible for defending judicial independence from any attack. As noted in the consultation paper Constitutional Reform: A New Way of Appointing Judges, consideration should be given to whether that responsibility should be embodied in statute setting up the proposed new Judicial Appointments Commission.

7 The Government believes that the establishment of a separate Supreme Court will be an important part of a package of measures which will redraw the relationship between the Judiciary, the Government, and Parliament to preserve and increase our judges' independence.

2 The present position: the Appellate Committee and the Judicial Committee of the Privy Council

The Law Lords

8 The judicial business of the House of Lords is carried out by the Lords of Appeal in Ordinary, commonly known as the Law Lords. Their number is fixed by statute, amendable by Order, and is presently set at a maximum of 12. In addition to these 12, any holder of high judicial offices who is a member of the House under the age of 75 is also eligible to sit:

there are presently 14 members of the House so entitled (excluding Lord Falconer of Thoroton, who has said that he will not do so).

9 The 12 Law Lords have been specifically appointed under the Appellate Jurisdiction Act of 1876 to conduct the judicial business of the House. 'In Ordinary' means that the lords receive a salary for their judicial work, paid from the Consolidated Fund not the budget of the House of Lords. All Law Lords are full members of the House and are holders of life peerages. Although the Law Lords sometimes conduct judicial work sitting as the House itself, they usually hear appeals as a Committee of the House called the Appellate Committee.

. . .

The Judicial Committee of the Privy Council

15 The Judicial Committee of the Privy Council was established under the Judicial Committee Act of 1833 . . .

16 The main functions of the Judicial Committee are threefold. First, it is the final court of appeal for a number of Commonwealth jurisdictions and for the Crown Dependencies of Jersey, Guernsey and the Isle of Man. Second, it hears devolution cases which are referred to it either from the courts in Scotland, Northern Ireland or England and Wales or directly by the UK Government or one or other of the devolved administrations. Its function is to determine issues relating to the legal competence of the devolved administrations, Parliament or Assemblies having regard to the relevant devolution legislation. Its judgments in such matters are binding even on the House of Lords. Third, it has a number of more technical jurisdictions e.g. dealing with appeals against pastoral schemes in the Church of England. Most of the previous jurisdiction over appeals from the decisions of various governing bodies in the healthcare professions has, since 1 April 2003, been passed down to the High Court and the Court of Session.

. . .

3 The government's proposals for a new Supreme Court

The establishment of a new Supreme Court

18 The Government will legislate to abolish the jurisdiction of the House of Lords within the UK's judicial system. The functions currently performed by the Appellate Committee will be vested instead in a new Supreme Court, quite separate from Parliament.

Jurisdiction

19 The separation of the Supreme Court from the UK Parliament raises the question of whether to transfer to it the jurisdiction of the Judicial Committee of the Privy Council over devolution issues. The decision to refer devolution cases to the Judicial Committee was deliberately taken at the time of the devolution Acts. The present arrangements have not been in existence for very long and are working well. They have the advantage that the panel of available judges for the Judicial Committee is wider than for the Appellate Committee and therefore there are more opportunities to have Scottish and Northern Ireland judges sitting on devolution cases.

20 The argument in favour of this transfer is that there would no longer be any perceived conflict of interest in which a party with an interest in a dispute about jurisdiction – the UK Parliament – was apparently sitting in judgment over the case. The new Supreme Court represents a very material change in circumstances. It will in no way be connected to the UK Parliament. The establishment of the new Court accordingly gives us the opportunity to restore a single apex to the UK's judicial system where all the constitutional issues can be considered. It would ensure that there is no longer a danger of conflicting judgments arising, for example on human rights cases which might have come to the Judicial Committee as devolution issues and to the House of Lords as ordinary appeal cases. It should be remembered that the judgment of the Judicial Committee in these matters is binding on all courts. Arrangements can and would be made to provide for additional judges to be involved where that appeared to be appropriate, although the composition of the panel for a particular case would be a matter for the President of the Court.

21 On balance, the Government believes that it would be right to transfer the jurisdiction on devolution cases from the Judicial Committee to the new Supreme Court with arrangements which enable additional Scottish and Northern Ireland judges to sit in cases raising devolution issues where that is appropriate.

Question 1: Do you agree that the jurisdiction of the new court should include devolution cases presently heard by the Judicial Committee?
22 Apart from this, the Government does not propose any further changes in the role of the new Supreme Court.

23 A Supreme Court along the United States model, or a Constitutional Court on the lines of some other European countries would be a departure from the UK's constitutional traditions. In the United States, the Supreme Court has the power to strike down and annul congressional legislation, and to assert the primacy of the constitution. In other countries, for example Germany, there is a federal constitutional court whose function is to protect the written constitution. In our democracy, Parliament is supreme. There is no separate body of constitutional law which takes precedence over all other law. The constitution is made up of the whole body of the laws and settled practice and convention, all of which can be amended or repealed by Parliament. Neither membership of the European Union nor devolution nor the Human Rights Act has changed the fundamental position. Such amendment or repeal would certainly be very difficult in practice and Parliament and the executive regard themselves as bound by the obligations they have taken on through that legislation, but the principle remains intact.

24 Many of the same arguments apply in relation to the proposal that the UK should have a Supreme Court on the lines of the European Court of Justice – that is, one to which questions as to the meaning of the law could be referred for a definitive ruling. UK courts traditionally work by applying the law to the facts of a particular case. Any arrangement which required the new Court to consider issues in the abstract would sit very uneasily with our judicial traditions. As soon as a Court looked at an issue on the facts of a case, however, it would effectively become a court of appeal rather than of reference. The situation in the European Union, where a common meaning of EU legislation across the different member states is needed, is quite different.

25 There is therefore no need to extend the jurisdiction of the Court into areas which have not previously been covered.

26 As noted above, there are differences in the treatment of Scottish cases compared to those from England and Wales and Northern Ireland. There is no appeal from the High

Court of Justiciary in criminal cases to the House of Lords. This is for historic and practical reasons; there are considerable differences between the two systems, described by Lord Hope of Craighead as 'as distinct from each other as if they were two foreign countries'. (**R v Manchester Stipendiary Magistrate,** *ex parte* **Granada Television Ltd** [2000] 2 WLR 1, 5) There is no evidence that the Scottish criminal appeal system requires change. To the extent that a further appeal may be required after the first tier of appeal has been exhausted, there is the possibility of a reference back at any time to the court of appeal by the Scottish Criminal Cases Review Commission. Where a devolution issue may be involved, there is currently recourse to the Judicial Committee of the Privy Council and there will in future be the possibility of a reference to the new Supreme Court.

27 Scottish civil appeals can however go to the House of Lords at present. The organisation of the judicial system in Scotland is largely devolved. The Scottish Executive has indicated that it has no plans at present to alter the current arrangements and is in principle content for civil appeals to the new Court to be on the same basis as currently operates in relation to the House of Lords. There are benefits to the Scottish justice system in having important cases reviewed by judges with a different background, and indeed advantages to the larger jurisdiction also in drawing on the resources of a different legal tradition at the highest level. A particular feature of the Scottish system is that in the great majority of cases there is no requirement to seek the leave to appeal either from the Court of Session or the House of Lords. On the other hand, there is a requirement for two Counsel to certify the reasonableness of the appeal. The effect is that only a small number of cases reach the House of Lords and there is no reason to assume that this would change under the new arrangements. Paragraph 56 below looks in more detail at the question of leave arrangements, including those for Scottish civil appeals.

Non-devolution functions of the Judicial Committee

28 It has also been suggested that the Judicial Committee of the Privy Council should be merged altogether with the Appellate Committee. As noted above, the Judicial Committee also has responsibility as the final court of appeal for a number of Commonwealth and overseas territory jurisdictions, as well as for the Crown Dependencies. In that capacity, it is acting as a court of appeal for independent jurisdictions. It does not belong to the UK alone. Whatever the outcome on devolution cases, the Government proposes to keep the Judicial Committee in being to continue to provide this important function. Instead of the Lords of Appeal in Ordinary being appointed to the Judicial Committee, the members of the Supreme Court would be so appointed. The right of other senior judges who are Privy Councillors to sit on the Judicial Committee would remain untouched. The administrative and support arrangements for the Judicial Committee would therefore remain unchanged.

The membership of the new Supreme Court

29 The initial members of the new Supreme Court will be the existing Lords of Appeal in Ordinary.

30 There are presently 12 such Lords of Appeal. They do the bulk of the work of the Appellate Committee. However, it is presently open to them to call upon other members of the House of Lords qualified to sit, including retired Law Lords, if there are particular demands on their time, or a need for expertise in a particular area which one of those lords can supply.

31 The Government would welcome views on whether a fixed membership of 12 will be sufficient for the work of the Court in the future. A slightly larger number would allow for more cases to be dealt with simultaneously, or allow for the continued release of members of the Court to undertake other functions such as the chairing of public enquiries. On the other hand, the larger the number of members of the court, the greater the scope for potential problems over the selection of which judges are to sit on which cases (see paragraphs 50–53 below for further discussion on this). On balance, the Government thinks that the present number of 12 full-time members of the Court is right, but that the Court should continue to be able to supplement its full-time membership. This option will be particularly important when hearing devolution issues to reflect the particular expertise in devolution issues in the same way as now the composition of the Judicial Committee of the Privy Council may reflect the nature of the case before it. However, there may also be other circumstances where it would be appropriate to call on additional judges to sit with full-time members, where, for example, they had acknowledged expertise in a particular area of law.

32 The membership of the Appellate Committee is presently set out in statute. Apart from the Lords of Appeal in Ordinary, of whom there are now a maximum of 12 (that number can be amended by Order), other holders of high judicial office are allowed to sit (section 5 of the Appellate Jurisdiction Act). 'High judicial office' for these purpose is defined as the Lord Chancellor, or a judge of one of the 'superior courts', that is the High Court and the Court of Appeal (in both England and Wales and Northern Ireland) and the Court of Session in Scotland. The limiting factor is that they must also be members of the House of Lords. Without that limiting factor, the pool of potential additional members of the Court would be very wide unless it were defined more narrowly in some way. It might be that the qualification for sitting alongside the full-time members would, as at present with the Judicial Committee, be to have held high judicial office and be a member of the Privy Council.

Question 2: Do you agree that the number of full-time members of the court should remain at 12 but that the court should have access to a panel of additional members?

Question 3: If there were such a panel, under what circumstances could the court call on it?

. . .

Relationship with the House of Lords

34 The primary objective of the new arrangements is to establish the Court as a body separate from Parliament. However, for the time being, all the members of the Court are in a personal capacity also members of the House of Lords. There will therefore continue to be at least some potential for alleged conflicts of interest where a member of the Court has previously taken part in debates which are relevant to a case which he is hearing. That has already been recognised in practice; the current members have decided to reduce very significantly the extent to which they take part in the general proceedings of the House since the passage of the Human Rights Act. They have made a formal statement to the House confirming that

> first, the Lords of Appeal in Ordinary do not think it appropriate to engage in matters where there is a strong element of party political controversy; and secondly, the Lords of Appeal in Ordinary bear in mind that they might render themselves ineligible to sit judicially if they were to express an opinion on a matter which might later be relevant to an appeal to the House.

(House of Lords, *Hansard*, 22 June 2000, col 419)

This might point to providing that members of the Court should not be eligible to be members of the House.

35 On the other hand, it is suggested that there are benefits to the Law Lords themselves in being able to hear at first hand the deliberations in Parliament. The Law Lords also make a valuable contribution to the work of the House more generally, for example in the chairmanship of select committees. Set against this, there is a strong argument that the possibility of conflict between judge and legislator should be removed, which may be reinforced by the judges' decisions that they should now only rarely speak or vote in debate.

36 On balance, the Government believes that it would be better to sever completely any connection between the Court and the House of Lords. It therefore proposes that members of the Court should lose the right to sit and vote in the House while they are members of the Court. Any one who is a member of the House before joining the Court will retain the peerage and title, and will be free to return to the House when he or she ceases to sit on the Court. This will give the House the continued benefit, which it very much values, of the experience of the retired Law Lords. There are presently 14 such retired Law Lords in the House, so such a cohort would still be able to make a significant contribution. In time, of course, on this basis there will be no retired Law Lords in the House. Subject to any other reforms of the House of Lords that may by then be in place, should appointment of **former** members of the Supreme Court to the House become the presumption?

37 The Government would welcome views on whether the provision to exclude active members of the Supreme Court from the House should extend to the other holders of high judicial office who presently sit in the House of Lords, and to any potential members of a reserve panel for the Court, should one be set up. On the one hand, there is the logic which says that active members of the judiciary should no longer be members of the legislature. On the other hand, it is much easier for those office holders to avoid sitting on any case where there might be a perceived conflict of interest because there is a larger pool of judges to choose from in each case. In any case, the Government would want to re-examine the present presumption that the holders of certain judicial offices should be granted peerages and thus be made members of the House of Lords. It might appear anomalous to continue to award peerages to those who would then be unable to make a full contribution for a number of years.

Question 7: Should the link with the House of Lords and the Law Lords be kept by appointing retired members of the Supreme Court to the House?

Question 8: Should the bar on sitting and voting in the House of Lords be extended to all holders of high judicial office?

Question 9: Should there be an end to the presumption that holders of high judicial office receive peerages?

Selection of members in the future

38 The Government would welcome views on two broad methods of approach to selecting future members of the Court. Obviously this has to take into account the establishment of a Judicial Appointments Commission for England and Wales as well as the arrangements for appointments in Scotland and Northern Ireland. The Government does not, however, favour allowing the Appointments Commission or Board in each jurisdiction to nominate members for their own jurisdiction. The Court will sit as a single UK court and it is important that it is seen to be a collegiate body.

39 The first alternative is, as in the case of Lords of Appeal in Ordinary, to have membership of the Court as an appointment made by the Queen on the advice of her ministers. The judges are independent servants of the Crown. That should be recognised by the appointment of at least the most senior members of the profession by the Queen rather than by a panel. The constitutional convention is that the Queen acts on the advice of ministers. This would mean recommendations being put to her by the Prime Minister following consultation with the First Minister in Scotland and the First and Deputy First Ministers in Northern Ireland. It could be argued that for appointments of this seniority, there should continue to be the political accountability presented by senior ministers' involvement. That is the case for the posts of Lord President of the Court of Session, for example, and for the Lord Chief Justice of England and Wales. On that approach, as now, there would be a process of consultation with the senior members of the Judiciary also in each jurisdiction about suitable candidates. That consultation is, however, presently carried out by the Lord Chancellor. A Secretary of State would be in rather a different position. On the other hand, it is the First Minister in Scotland who recommends to the Prime Minister the appointment of the Lord President of the Court of Session. Such involvement of a non-judicial minister would not therefore be unprecedented. The alternative would have to be consultation by the Prime Minister and the First Minister in Scotland or the First and Deputy First Ministers in Northern Ireland with the heads of the Judiciary in each of the three jurisdictions.

40 Alternatively, it could be argued that the whole climate of opinion now requires that there is some transparent process which leads to the identification of names, even if the final recommendations are still made by the Prime Minister following consultation with the First Minister or First and Deputy First Ministers as appropriate. That is the whole thrust of the reforms to the judicial appointments system discussed in the paper *Constitutional Reform: A New Way of Appointing Judges* which was also published on 14 July. The question is whether such a process is suitable for appointments at this level, where intimate knowledge of performance by a defined group is the best evidence that is likely to be available.

41 Three models of Commission are discussed in *Constitutional Reform: A New Way of Appointing Judges*. These are:

- a Commission which would take over the Lord Chancellor's role in directly making appointments up to the level of Circuit Judge and in advising The Queen on appointments at that level and above; or
- a Commission which would make recommendations to a Minister as to whom he or she should appoint (or recommend that The Queen appoint).
- a Commission which combines the functions above by directly making more junior appointments (for example, part-time judicial and tribunal appointments) and by recommending more senior appointments.

Of the three models discussed above, the Government considers that the proposal for a Commission which recommended a limited number of names to the Prime Minister (ie the middle one) would be the best for appointments to the Supreme Court. Given the small number of appointments, and the likely limited field of candidates, it would be sufficient for the Commission to present the names of only one or two candidates. The Prime Minister should then consult the First Minister for Scotland and the First and Deputy First Ministers in Northern Ireland.

42 On the whole, the Government thinks that the model which would entrust selection to an independent panel directly advising The Queen is less suitable for appointments at this level.

43 Whichever model were adopted, the Commission would have to be separate from the judicial appointments commissions which will exist in the separate jurisdictions once the England and Wales body is set up. As the Court will be the Supreme Court for the whole United Kingdom, it is important that its membership is also selected by those who are representative of all three of the legal jurisdictions within the country. However, rather than set up another new body to deal especially with the very small number of appointments there will be each year, a Commission to advise on appointments to the Supreme Court could be drawn from all three commissions and boards.

Question 10: Should appointments to the new Supreme Court continue to be made on the direct advice of the Prime Minister, after consultation with the First Minister of Scotland and First and Deputy First Ministers in Northern Ireland and with the profession?

Question 11: If not, should an Appointments Commission recommend a short-list of names to the Prime Minister on which to advise The Queen following consultation with the First Minister of Scotland and First and Deputy First Ministers in Northern Ireland? Or should it be statutorily empowered to advise The Queen directly?

Question 12: If there is to be an Appointments Commission for Supreme Court appointments, how should it be constituted? Should it comprise members drawn from the existing Appointments bodies in each jurisdiction?

44 Whichever method of appointment is adopted, should this be on the basis of open applications rather than simply of consultation among the senior members of the profession? The Government is aware that there is sometimes reluctance among those who already hold very senior positions to put themselves forward through an open application process. It may be argued that the pool of candidates will be sufficiently well known for the Commission or Ministers to act without formal applications. Those who are likely to be the strongest candidates will have their performance consistently evaluated by the courts above them, including the existing members of the Supreme Court. Given the size of the pool and the specialist nature of the post, this could seem an artificial procedure whose added-value is not clear. The present members of the Court will also have views on the particular needs of the Supreme Court and whether expertise in any particular area of law is required. The Commission or Ministers would in any case be required to seek comments from a defined group of those who would be expected to be aware of the qualities of both the candidates and the requirements of the position. As against this, the Government is seeking generally to make the whole judicial appointments process open and transparent. Such a process might also contribute to enhancing the diversity of the court, while respecting the overwhelming criterion of appointment on merit. These objectives can be argued to apply equally to the most senior appointments as to the more junior.

Question 13: Should the process of identifying candidates for the new court include open applications?

45 It has been suggested that one way of enhancing the status of the members of the Court would be for them to be subject to confirmation hearings before one or other of the Houses of Parliament. This could, it is argued, help ensure that Parliament has confidence in the Judiciary. The Government sees difficulty in such a procedure. MPs and lay peers would not necessarily be competent to assess the appointees' legal or judicial skills. If the intention was to assess their more general approach to issues of public importance, this would be inconsistent with the move to take the Supreme Court out of the potential political arena. One of the main intentions of the reform is to emphasise and enhance the independence of the Judiciary from both the executive and Parliament. Giving Parliament the right to decide or have a direct influence on who should be the members of the Court would cut right across that objective.

Qualifications for membership

46 The present qualification for appointment as a Law Lord is either two years' holding of high judicial office or 15 years standing as a barrister, advocate or solicitor in England and Wales or Scotland, or as a barrister or a solicitor in Northern Ireland. The Government is not minded to change this. It has been suggested that changes should be made to make it easier for distinguished academics to be appointed, because, for example, this would make it easier to enhance the diversity of the court. In those circumstances, a more open appointment process would be desirable. It could, however, be argued that this is not the level for opening up the field in this way, and it is at lower levels of the Judiciary that the criteria might need to be re-examined. It might be felt that some experience of judicial work should be gained before joining the highest court of appeal and such aspirant members should at least sit part-time in one of the lower courts. It is likely that the 15-year qualification would make most of these technically eligible in any event. However, the Government would be interested in views on whether that is the case, or whether specific criteria for those who are not active in the courts should be drawn up.

Question 14: Should there be any change in the qualifications for appointment, for example to make it easier to appoint distinguished academics? Or should this be a change limited to appointment to lower levels of the judiciary, if it is appropriate at all?

Criteria for selection

47 The criteria for selection for members of the Court must be consistent with those for selection to the lower courts. The principles will be that selection must be made from a pool of properly qualified candidates on merit alone. The impartiality of the Judiciary must be maintained, and appointments must be free from improper influence. Merit will be judged by assessment against a number of defined qualities. For the present system, these are qualities such as legal knowledge and experience; intellectual and analytical ability; sound judgement; decisiveness; communication and listening skills; authority and case management skills; integrity and independence; fairness and impartiality; understanding of people and society; maturity and sound judgement; courtesy; and commitment, conscientiousness and diligence.

48 Because the Court will be the Supreme Court for the whole of the United Kingdom, it is important that it should include persons of knowledge and experience in the law in the different jurisdictions. There is a long-standing convention that there should be two Scottish Law Lords. In recent years there has also been a Northern Ireland Law Lord. Such arrangements should certainly continue. The Government would be interested in views on whether they should be expressed as a formal quota. If the Court is to take on responsibility for devolution issues, some regard should also be had to ensuring that the Welsh dimension of the England and Wales judicial system is respected. Ensuring adequate representation from each jurisdiction will in any case be a guideline to those responsible for selecting members. There are various ways of setting such guidelines: the Government can do so purely administratively; they can be set out in a Code of Practice which is subject to parliamentary approval; or they can be set out in the legislation.

Question 15: Should the guidelines which apply to the selection of members of the new court be set out administratively, or through a code of practice subject to parliamentary approval, or in legislation?

Question 16: What should be the arrangements for ensuring the representation of the different jurisdictions?

. . .

Question 17: What should be the statutory retirement age? 70 or 75?

Question 18: Should retired members of the court up to five years over the statutory retirement age be used as a reserve panel?

How should the court operate?

50 It might be felt that the issues in this and the next section are ones which are best left to the Court itself to determine. However, because they have implications for the overall size of the Court, and may have implications for the legislation, the Government is seeking views on them here.

51 The present Appellate Committee usually sits in a panel of five members and provides a panel for the Judicial Committee and if numbers permit a second panel for the Appellate Committee. For some very important cases, seven or even nine members sit. The statutory minimum is 3. Other comparable courts have other arrangements. For example, the United States Supreme Court always sits en banc, that is every member of the Court sits on every case unless indisposed or unavailable for some other reason. The reason for this is to prevent the possibility that the composition of the panel will affect the outcome of the case.

52 This is clearly an important consideration. However, in every other court, the selection of the judge to hear the case may at least in theory affect the outcome. It is impossible to tell after the event whether it has done so or not. It is not a unique or over-riding consideration in relation to the Supreme Court. Enabling the Court to sit in panels will enable it to deal with more cases. It will also enable panels to be constituted with regard to their expertise and background, thus getting the best qualified panel in each case. If all the members of the Supreme Court sat *en banc*, this would also mean that none would be available to sit in the Judicial Committee at the same time. In the United States, appointments to the Supreme Court are more political, and therefore there is a stronger possibility that the composition of the court might affect the outcome. This is not the case in the United Kingdom.

Question 19: Should the court continue to sit in panels, rather than every member sitting on every case?

A leave filter

53 At present, cases can reach the Appellate Committee by two routes: by leave to appeal from the lower court or by petition to the House of Lords itself. UK cases reach the Judicial Committee on devolution issues as described above.

54 The Government would welcome views on whether this system should be altered, so that the presumption was that the Court itself decided which cases it would hear.

55 The advantage of switching to a system whereby the Court itself decided which cases it should hear, subject only to the special exception of rulings on competence under the Scotland, Northern Ireland and Government of Wales Acts 1998 is that such a general rule would give the Supreme Court the control it needs over its own caseload, and would enable it to develop its own policies and approach about the categories and importance of the cases on which it should rule. It would enable it to work out where it sees its greatest added value and concentrate on developing jurisprudence in the areas which most need it. It would also bring the Court broadly into line with other English-speaking Supreme Courts. It would, however, mean a change in relation to Scottish civil appeals.

56 It could be argued in response that it is an unjustified anomaly that citizens in different parts of the Kingdom have different rights of access to its highest court. The disadvantages of changing this are threefold. First, in respect of Scotland, the arrangement whereby Scottish civil cases currently lie to the House of Lords as of right is long established; there is no evidence that change is needed; and there are strong arguments for leaving the position unchanged. The second disadvantage, in all respects, is that it would mean that more of the work of the Court would be absorbed in deciding what cases to hear, rather than hearing them. It would lead, in practice, to fewer cases being heard or to cases taking longer to come before the Court. The third disadvantage is that it would mean that all those seeking the judgment of the court would have to incur the cost of petitioning for the right to appeal.

Question 20: Should the court decide for itself all cases which it hears, rather than allowing some lower courts to give leave to appeal or allowing some appeals as of right?

Question 21: Should the present position in relation to Scottish appeals remain unchanged?

Other responsibilities of the Law Lords

57 The Law Lords presently carry out a number of functions within the House of Lords, in their capacity as members of the House. For example, the legal sub-Committee of the European Committee is traditionally chaired by one of the Law Lords. They have also chaired ad hoc select committees. That has been a valuable service to the House. However, it is not a specific professional function which cannot be fulfilled by others. There are many qualified lawyers in the House of Lords, some with judicial experience. How the House responds to the absence of the Law Lords in this context is of course a matter for it. The Government does not see any need to make special arrangements to preserve any interest of the Law Lords in this work, beyond what is discussed in paragraphs 34–37 above.

Titles

58 This paper has spoken of the creation of a new Supreme Court. The new body will indeed be the supreme court of the United Kingdom, in that it will be the highest court in all three of the jurisdictions in the realm. There is, however, already a legal entity known as the Supreme Court of England and Wales, which consists of the Court of Appeal, the High Court and the Crown Court. It is used to give jurisdiction to judges and to route work between the courts. This title is not in common usage. In Scotland, the term Supreme Court has also been used on an administrative basis to refer to the Court of Session and the High Court of Justiciary collectively. There is also a Supreme Court of Northern Ireland. However, to avoid confusion, in the future the title of Supreme Court will be reserved for the Court

to be created as a result of this consultation. The new Court cannot become part of any of the existing Supreme Courts because its jurisdiction will extend to all three jurisdictions.

59 In the absence of specific provision, members of the Court will no longer have any specific title, since they will not automatically become peers. The Government would welcome suggestions as to what to call them instead. For example, one option would be to put the letters JSC 'Justice of the Supreme Court' after their names and give them no title beforehand. As against this, however, Court of Appeal judges are already called Lord Justices of Appeal and Scottish High Court judges are called Lords. It would be misleading to leave the members of the Supreme Court with titles which appeared to accord them a lower rank. That might point to retaining the title of Lord of Appeal. At the same time, it would equally be misleading to give the judges of the Supreme Court a title that could continue to confuse the public about their relationship with the House of Lords. A further possibility might therefore be Lord Justice of the Supreme Court as a title.

Question 22: What should the existing Supreme Court be renamed?

Question 23: What should members of the new court be called?

. . .

Accommodation

67 The new Court will obviously need accommodation outside the House of Lords. The Department will consult the existing Law Lords to identify their precise accommodation needs. There are a number of options which might be suitable, and a detailed business case will need to be drawn up and costed before any firm proposals can be made. This work will be undertaken in parallel with this consultation exercise.

 The consultation paper 'Constitutional Reform: A Supreme Court for the United Kingdom' (2003) is available on the website of the former Department for Constitutional Affairs at:
www.dca.gov.uk/consult/supremecourt/index.htm

Government's response to the consultation process

Following the publication of the consultation paper, 'Constitutional Reform: A Supreme Court for the United Kingdom', the government received a wide range of responses from individuals and interested organisations. It produced a report collating these responses.

Summary of Responses to the Consultation Paper Constitutional Reform: A Supreme Court for the United Kingdom (January 2004)

Background

The Prime Minister announced on 12 June 2003 the Government's intention to create a new Supreme Court for the United Kingdom. In July Lord Falconer, Secretary of State for Constitutional Affairs and Lord Chancellor, published a consultation paper, *Constitutional*

Reform: a Supreme Court for the United Kingdom, seeking views on the form and responsibilities of the proposed new Supreme Court. The consultation paper sought views on:

- the jurisdiction of the Supreme Court;
- membership of the Supreme Court in the short and long term;
- the method and criteria for the selection of its members;
- the Court's relationship with the House of Lords;
- the Court's method of operation and its relationship with the rest of the judiciary; and
- how to secure a proper representation from the Scottish and Northern Ireland jurisdictions.

The Consultation period closed on 7 November 2003 and this report summarises the responses.

Summary of responses

A total of 174 responses to the consultation paper were received. Of these 39 were from the judges or bodies representing the judiciary, 59 from other members of the legal professions. There were also 43 responses from members of the public, academics and 13 responses from representative groups. Two Members of the House of Commons responded as did nine non-departmental public bodies, local and/or regional organisations.

While some respondents offered views on all the issues in the consultation paper, many focussed on particular questions or issues.

All the responses have been analysed and a summary for each question forms the main body of this report.

We are grateful to everyone who responded.

Question by question summaries

1 Do you agree that the jurisdiction of the new Court should include devolution cases presently heard by the Judicial Committee?

Of the 87 responses to this question 75 (86%) were in favour of the new Supreme Court taking on the devolution jurisdiction of the Judicial Committee of the Privy Council, 12 (14%) of respondents were against the proposal.

Whilst the 12 Law Lords are not in agreement on all questions posed in the consultation paper, it is clear that they are in agreement on this issue.

They state that: '*It would in our opinion be consistent with the role of a Supreme Court of the United Kingdom that it should be the final arbiter of devolution issues arising in the devolved jurisdictions*'. However, they are concerned that sufficient judicial members from the devolved jurisdictions would not be able to be drawn on unless separate rules are drawn up governing the membership of the Supreme Court when it hears devolution cases. The Law Lords are not in favour of this and so conclude that they: '*. . . with a measure of reluctance, favour preserving the status quo*'.

The response from a barristers' chambers states that: '*. . . the present system of having two top courts is confusing and gives rise to some tension. In fact the Privy Council and the House of Lords have made decisions in almost identical cases.*'

This appeared as a recurring theme throughout the positive responses.

JUSTICE argue that it is crucial that the Supreme Court take on this jurisdiction to prevent the same point being decided differently by the Judicial Committee of the Privy Council and the Supreme Court.

- The Rt Hon Lord Donaldson of Lymington argued that transferring the devolution jurisdiction: '. . . *will produce a single judicial forum for the resolution of all constitutional and other legal disputes within the United Kingdom*'.

Other respondents in favour of transferring the jurisdiction include:

- the Judges' Council;
- the Judges of the High Court and Court of Appeal in Northern Ireland;
- Charter 88;
- the Constitutional and Administrative Law Bar Association;
- the Law Society of England and Wales;
- the Law Society of Scotland; and
- the Faculty of Advocates.

Lady Justice Hale is also in favour of the proposal and argues that: '. . . *these are precisely the matters the Supreme Court of the United Kingdom should be considering*'.

There is some concern that enough Scottish Judges are able to hear such cases if the proposals are accepted, and the Rt Hon Lord Jauncey of Tullichettle states that there: '. . . *must be mechanisms in place to allow Scottish judges who are not members of the Supreme Court to sit in devolution matters*'.

The Scottish Executive are content with the proposal as long as there are appropriate arrangements to ensure that Scottish judges sit on devolution cases.

A number of respondents however are not in favour of the proposals.

The Rt Hon Lord MacKay of Clashfern and The Bar Council of Northern Ireland do not agree with the proposal.

The Rt Hon Lord Cullen of Whitekirk and the Senators of the College of Justice are concerned that the transferral of the jurisdiction in devolution cases in criminal matters would lead to the growing Anglicisation of Scottish criminal law. They would prefer it if these particular cases stayed with the Judicial Committee of the Privy Council, as it would be easier to ensure that the judges hearing the case are suitably trained and experienced in Scottish law.

2 Do you agree that the number of full-time members of the Court should remain at 12 but that the Court should have access to a panel of additional members?

There were 89 respondents to this question, 66 (74%) agreed to the proposal and 23 (26%) offered an alternative number of members.

The Law Lords agree that the permanent membership of the Supreme Court should be fixed at 12. They further consider that the number of full-time judges on the Supreme Court should not be increased without the agreement of the senior judge and the deputy of the Supreme Court. They are also generally in favour of access to a panel of additional members.

The Rt Hon Lord Nolan argues that a full-time membership of more than 12 judges increases the risk of diverging views. He further states that the reserve panel should only comprise retired members of the Supreme Court. The Rt Hon Lord Steyn agrees that any reserve panel should comprise retired members of the Supreme Court.

A number of respondents are concerned that there should be built-in flexibility. They agree with the general proposal that there should be 12 full-time members and argue that there should be a way of keeping this under review. These include:

- the Law Society of England and Wales; and
- the Rt Hon Lord MacKay of Clashfern.

Respondents in favour of 12 full-time members of the Supreme Court include:

- the Faculty of Advocates;
- the Judges' Council; and
- the Chancery Bar Association.

JUSTICE take the view that the full-time complement should be increased to 15 members, and that there should be no recourse to an additional panel of members. They are concerned that any additional members used on a part-time basis would lead to a two-tier judiciary within the Supreme Court.

Amongst those advocating an increase in the full-time membership of the Supreme Court are:

- the Law Society for Scotland;
- the Constitutional and Administrative Law Bar Association; and
- the Rt Hon Lord Cullen of Whitekirk and the Senators of the College of Justice.

3 If there were such a panel, under what circumstances should the Court call on it?

There were 77 responses to this question. The respondents gave a range of views that were not possible to quantify.

Generally, most of the respondents argue that any reserve panel should be called upon when either the court needs specialist assistance, or when the workload is too high and leads to a delay in cases being heard.

- The Judges' Council feel that the reserve panel should be used at the discretion of the Supreme Court; and
- Lady Justice Hale states that the reserve panel should be used on the basis of need.

A number of respondents believe that the reserve panel should be used to assist in devolution matters.

- JUSTICE believe that the reserve panel should only be used to help the court on devolution matters when a senior judge from Northern Ireland or Scotland should be co-opted on to the Supreme Court;
- The Scottish Executive feel that a reserve panel would be useful to assist in devolution cases;
- The Faculty of Advocates and the Law Society of Scotland feel it is important that the reserve panel for the Supreme Court is used to provide specialist expertise in devolution matters; and
- The Law Society for England and Wales take a similar view.

The Rt Hon Lord Donaldson of Lymington argues that there should be no fixed rules governing the use of a reserve panel, and it should generally be used when there is a need for greater judicial resources. He feels that the reserve panel should not be used to supplement the expertise of the Supreme Court as judges at this level should be able to grasp any arguments put to them.

The Rt Hon Lord Cullen of Whitekirk and the Senators of the College of Justice feel that any reserve panel should be used sparingly if the collegiate nature of the Supreme Court is to be maintained. Lord Cullen considers that the consistency of decision making could be affected by the use of a reserve panel.

4 Should the composition of the court continue to be regulated by statute or should it be more flexible?

Of the 87 who responded to this question, a majority of 79 (91%) feel that the composition of the Court should continue to be regulated by statute and a small number, 8 (9%), feel that it should be more flexible.

The Law Lords are united on this point and write that: *'We consider that the composition of the Court should continue to be regulated by statute. We do not consider that the composition should be flexible'*.

The Rt Hon Lord MacKay of Clashfern says: *'I do not think that the composition of the Court can be regulated otherwise than by statute'*.

Other respondents in favour of the Supreme Court being regulated by statute are:

- the Society of Legal Scholars;
- the Law Society of England and Wales;
- the Law Society of Scotland;
- the Constitutional and Administrative Law Bar Association;
- the Judges' Council; and
- the Bar Council of Northern Ireland.

A number of respondents argue that the composition of the Court should be governed by statute, but there should be provisions built in to allow flexibility.

The Rt Hon Lord Donaldson of Lymington states: *'. . . this statutory regulation, which should take great account of the President's view of the needs of the Court, should permit a degree of flexibility either pursuant to the wording of the statute or by allowing the statute to be easily amended by subordinate legislation'*.

The Rt Hon Lord Cullen of Whitekirk and the Senators of the College of Justice agree that there should be a built in degree of flexibility to ensure adequate representation of Scotland.

The Faculty of Advocates are of the opinion that as little as possible regarding the Supreme Court should be contained in statute as this would limit the potential for executive interference. However, as the Supreme Court will have to be created by statute they do: *'. . . not see any reason why the composition of the Court, both in relation to full and additional members, should both be the subject of legislation'*.

JUSTICE are of the view that the composition of the Supreme Court should be entirely regulated by the President of the Supreme Court.

. . .

7 Should the link with the House of Lords and the Law Lords be kept by appointing retired members of the Supreme Court to the House?

There were 88 responses to Question 7. The general view, 60 (68%) is that the link between the House of Lords and the Law Lords should be kept by appointing retired members of the Supreme Court to the House of Lords. The balance of the respondents 28 (32%) say there should be complete severance.

The Law Lords comment that it is difficult to answer Question 7 because the size and composition of the House of Lords has not yet been finally settled. The Law Lords suggest, *'. . . it might be appropriate to appoint former members of the Supreme Court to be members of the House of Lords provided they had either reached the age of retirement or announced that they would not in future sit judicially and provided they wished to be appointed'*.

Respondents who favour retired members of the Supreme Court having a link with the House of Lords include:

- the Faculty of Advocates;
- the Judges' Council;
- the Law Society of England and Wales;
- the Law Society of Scotland;
- His Honour Judge Michael Harris; and
- the Constitutional and Administrative Law Bar Association.

The Law Society for Scotland comments that '. . . *there could be benefit to the House in having available the experience of retired judges'*.

An alternative view is provided by Judge Harris who states, '*A retired law Lord should have no greater right to sit there than any other member of the public.'*

. . .

8 Should the bar on sitting and voting in the House of Lords be extended to all holders of high judicial office?

Out of 85 responses, 66 (78%) are in favour of a bar on sitting and voting in the House of Lords being extended to all holders of high judicial office. Nineteen (22%) respondents do not want to see a complete bar.

The Law Lords have said, with the abolition of the Lord Chancellor's judicial role, the opportunity should be taken to reflect the complete independence of the judiciary from the executive and the legislative. However, on this particular question, the Law Lords views varied.

Respondents who argue for a bar on sitting and voting in the House of Lords are split between a complete bar on one hand, and on the other allowing members to retain a practical link with the House.

The Judges' Council does not advocate a complete bar but argues that '. . . *the bar should not extend to the Lord Chief Justice of England and Wales, the President of the Supreme Court, the Lord President of the Court of Session or the Lord Chief Justice of Northern Ireland'*.

This is the same position taken by the Rt Hon Lords Nicholls, Hope, Hutton, Hobhouse, Millett, Scott, Rodger and Walker . . .

A further group of Law Lords (the Rt Hon Lords Bingham, Steyn, Hoffmann and Saville) believe that there should be complete separation of judicial and legislative work. The most senior judges, they argue, have ample opportunities to make their views known.

The Judges' Council argue that the House of Lords will have mainly appointed members. If the House was made up of elected members, then there would be no place for unelected judges. The judges will be in a position to contribute to debates in the House on matters affecting the justice system or the judiciary.

JUSTICE favours, in principle, the idea of a bar being extended to all holders of judicial office, but, '*a practical exemption should be made for holders of part-time appointments at the recorder level and below'*.

. . .

9 Should there be an end to the presumption that holders of high judicial office receive peerages?

Of the 81 respondents to this question, a majority of 50 (62%) agree that there should be an end to the presumption that holders of high judicial office should receive peerages. Thirty one (38%) of the respondents say that this should remain unchanged.

The Law Lords' views diverge in their response to this question. Eight Law Lords believe that peerages should be conferred on the holders of the offices of the President of the Supreme Court, the Lord Chief Justice of England and Wales, the Lord President of the Court of Session and the Lord Chief Justice of Northern Ireland. The Rt Hon Lords Bingham, Steyn, Hoffmann and Saville do not agree that future holders of these offices should receive peerages.

The Judges' Council takes the same view as the majority of Law Lords.

The Rt Hon Lord Mackay of Clashfern, the Chancery Bar Association and the Law Society of England and Wales are amongst respondents not in favour of ending the presumption. The Law Society says that retired members should automatically be appointed to the House of Lords and receive peerages. They stress there should be no discretion. The appointments should either be automatic or not at all. They argue that this is necessary '. . . *to avoid any public perception that a judge of the Supreme Court might be influenced by the fact that he or she have to rely on political patronage for appointment . . .*'.

A common response from respondents arguing against the presumption that holders of high judicial office should receive peerages is best described by JUSTICE. They argue that '. . . *it would be somewhat anomalous if other senior judicial posts, such as the office of Lord Chief Justice, also attracted automatic peerages*'.

The Faculty of Advocates also point out that if members of the new Court are to be barred from sitting and voting in the House of Lords, together with senior members of the lower courts, then there is no reason why they should be made members of the House of Lords. Other respondents in favour of the bar are:

- the Bar Council;
- the Law Society of Scotland; and
- Charter 88.

10 Should appointments to the new Supreme Court continue to be made on the direct advice of the Prime Minister, after consultation with the First Minister of Scotland and Deputy First Ministers in Northern Ireland and with the profession?

Of the 90 responses to Question 10, a significant majority 62 (69%) say the appointments system to the Supreme Court should not continue to be made on the direct advice of the Prime Minister. The remaining 28 (31%) respondents disagree.

The Law Lords identify a number of key principles, notably that appointments must be made by The Queen acting of the advice of her ministers, in this case the Prime Minister. This view is reiterated by a number of respondents.

The Law Lords comment that the Secretary of State should be bound to accept the Commission's recommendation, either initially or after reconsideration, and that the Prime Minister should be bound to advise The Queen in accordance with the Secretary of State's advice.

The following key stakeholders support the involvement of the Prime Minister:

- the Judges' Council;
- The Rt Hon Lord Cullen and the Senators of the College of Justice;
- the Faculty of Advocates; and
- the Law Society.

The 69% of respondents who disagree with the involvement of the Prime Minister in the appointment of members of the Supreme Court express a range of views about what might be a better system. A number propose that the Appointments Commission should be able to advise The Queen directly, arguing that the Executive, in this case the Prime Minister, should not be involved in appointments to an independent Supreme Court.

Lord Alexander of Weedon QC states that while he broadly supports the proposal for a new Supreme Court, he considers it would be a retrograde step for appointments to the Court to be made on the direct advice of the Prime Minister.

The Equal Opportunities Commission considers that appointments to the Supreme Court should not be made solely on the direct advice of the Prime Minister, saying, '. . . *such a procedure gives rise to question[s] about the degree of political influence in respect of appointment to the most powerful court. The independence, and the appearance of independence, of the judiciary from the Executive is paramount and therefore this practice cannot continue*'.

11 *If not, should an Appointments Commission recommend a short-list of names to the Prime Minister on which to advise The Queen following consultation with the First Minister of Scotland and Deputy First Ministers in Northern Ireland? Or should it be statutorily empowered to advise The Queen directly?*

Question 11 follows a question (Question 10) about the continued involvement of the Prime Minister in the appointment of judges to the Supreme Court.

There were 88 responses to Question 11. Of these:

- 25 respondents (28%) favoured an Appointments Commission recommending a short-list of names to the Prime Minister on which to advise The Queen following consultation with relevant First Ministers;
- 40 respondents (46%) favoured an Appointments Commission being statutorily empowered to advise The Queen directly; and
- 23 respondents (26%) proposed variations on the processes.

. . .

The Law Lords propose a small appointments commission to include members from all jurisdictions in the United Kingdom and some lay (non-judicial) members. The commission would recommend one name to the Secretary of State for Constitutional Affairs who would be authorised to invite the commission to reconsider its recommendations. The Secretary of State would then advise the Prime Minister of his recommendation, and the Prime Minister would advise The Queen accordingly.

The Law Lords comment that the appointments process needs to be apolitical and command public confidence.

Evident in the 46% of respondents favouring an Appointments Commission being statutorily empowered to advise The Queen directly is a theme that the executive should not be involved in appointments to the Judiciary because it would introduce political considerations into the process.

The Chancery Bar Association comments, '. . . *it is not easy to see what input the Prime Minister would have other than to exercise a political judgement about which name on the list to select*'.

. . .

12 *If there is to be an Appointments Commission for Supreme Court appointments, how should it be constituted? Should it comprise members drawn from the existing appointments bodies in each jurisdiction?*

There were 81 responses to Question 12. With few exceptions, respondents identify the need for an Appointments Commission for the Supreme Court to be representative of the three jurisdictions within the United Kingdom, and in particular for its membership to be drawn from the appointments commission in each jurisdiction. A number of respondents, for example Rights of Women, suggest that appointments made by means of an independent judicial appointments commission will provide a means to introduce greater equality into the Court.

. . .

13 Should the process of identifying candidates for the new court include open applications?

There were 83 responses to Question 13. A majority of 53 (64%) respondents are in favour of open applications, that is, advertising vacancies on the Supreme Court so that anyone may apply. The remaining 30 (36%) respondents favour approaches such as senior members of the judiciary carrying out consultation among themselves and then making a recommendation.

A diverse range of stakeholders support open applications. They include:

- the Law Society of Scotland;
- JUSTICE;
- the Committee on Standards in Public Life;
- the Rt Hon Lord Clyde;
- Lady Justice Hale;
- the Bar Council;
- the Law Society of England and Wales; and
- the Chancery Bar Association.

Lady Justice Hale suggests that there may be many very good candidates who could bring a great deal to the Supreme Court and who are excluded by the current arrangements.

Several respondents, for example JUSTICE, suggest that open competition is important in the interests of the appointments process being transparent. A contrasting view is presented by the Lawyers' Christian Fellowship, who say: '*We consider that judicial experience is necessary to be a judge in the highest court in the land. This is the only option that is consistent with the principle of the efficient administration of justice*'.

In addition to the Lawyers' Christian Fellowship a range of stakeholders were not in favour of open selection. They included:

- the Law Lords;
- the Chancery Bar Association;
- the Rt Hon Lord Cullen of Whitekirk and the Senators of the College of Justice; and
- the Judges' Council.

The Law Lords recognise that open applications ensure no eligible candidate is inadvertently overlooked and stated: '*These are valuable safeguards at the High Court level and below, where they have the additional advantage of enabling the stronger candidates to signal their willingness to accept appointment if invited*'. The Law Lords then argue that such safeguards are not of value when appointments at the highest level are under consideration. They say the outstanding candidates '. . . *are likely to be few and well-known; the problem is not to identify a candidate worthy of appointment but to choose between candidates all of whom have strong claims to be appointed. Thus there is no risk of inadvertent oversight*'.

The views of the Law Lords are echoed in the comments of The Rt Hon Lord Cullen of Whitekirk, who says, '*The field from which candidates for appointment to the Supreme Court would be selected would be a few senior judges whose qualities would be well known to those who are consulted. There will be a relatively limited number of appointments. Open application would not be appropriate'.*

14 Should there be any change in the qualifications for appointment, for example to make it easier to appoint distinguished academics? Or should this be a change limited to appointment to lower levels of the judiciary, if it is appropriate at all?

There are 89 responses to this two-part question. Responses may be broken down as follows:

- 33 respondents (37.5%) believe that there should be a change in the qualifications for appointment and that the change should apply to Supreme Court and lower level appointments;
- 23 respondents (25%) agree that there should be a change in relation to lower level appointments, but not Supreme Court appointments; and
- 33 respondents (37.5%) are of the view that there should be no change with regard to appointment qualifications for either the Supreme Court or lower courts.

The Law Lords argue that experience in practice or on the bench or both is '. . . *an all but essential qualification for trial judges'.* This view is shared by, amongst others:

- the Rt Hon Lord Donaldson of Lymington;
- the Rt Hon Lord Justice Buxton; and
- the Rt Hon Lord Cullen of Whitekirk and the Senators of the College of Justice.

The Rt Hon Lord Steyn believes that legislation should not preclude academics from being appointed to the new Court, a position also advanced by, amongst others:

- JUSTICE;
- Lady Justice Hale;
- the General Council of the Bar, which argues that appointment of eminent academics are likely to be rare but may '. . . *be an appropriate means of enhancing both the academic standing and the diversity of the court'.*

Notwithstanding their view about the crucial importance of trial experience, the Law Lords believe that merit is the overriding criterion. They '. . . *do not consider that the existing rule works adversely to the public interest'.*

The Judges' Council points out that a number of academics are qualified under the present rules and indeed some have already become judges. They also make the point that a number of practising lawyers can be described as distinguished academics, making it unnecessary to change the current rules for qualification.

15 Should the guidelines which apply to the selection of members of the new court be set out administratively, or through a code of practice subject to parliamentary approval, or in legislation?

Of the 77 responses received, 32 respondents (41.5%) favour these criteria being set out in legislation, while 19 (24.5%) are in favour of using a Code of Practice and 16 (21%) believe that administrative guidelines are preferable. The ten remaining responses do not select any one of the options proposed or else suggest an entirely different method, there being no discernible pattern in the answers.

. . .

*16 What should be the arrangements for ensuring the representation of the different
jurisdictions?*

There were a total of 81 responses to this question. Due to the range of views it is impossible
to provide any meaningful statistical analysis.

By convention, the Appellate Committee of the House of Lords consists of no fewer than
two Scottish Law Lords and, usually, a Law Lord from Northern Ireland.

The Law Lords are against a formalised quota system and argue that it is '. . . *undesirable
that an unmeritorious candidate should be appointed (in the unlikely event that no meritorious candidate were willing to serve) in order to fill a quota*'. The Law Lords consider that merit should
be the deciding factor in making appointments to the Supreme Court, and that the current
convention should be broadly followed and '. . . *would not wish to rule out the possibility of
an increase if, for a particular vacancy, the most meritorious candidate were to be found in Scotland
or Northern Ireland*'.

The Law Society of England and Wales argue that there should be guidance for the
representation of the jurisdictions, but not formal statutory quotas.

The Lord Chief Justice of Northern Ireland supports one member of the Supreme Court
being from Northern Ireland.

The Law Society of Scotland believes that a minimum representation from Scotland and
Northern Ireland should be provided for in legislation. They say that there should be at least
three Scottish Law Lords and one from Northern Ireland. The Bar Council of Northern
Ireland also favour a formal quota for representation of the different jurisdictions. They say
this will lead to further public confidence in Scotland and Northern Ireland in the judicial
system.

Other respondents who support this view include:

- the Faculty of Advocates;
- Lady Justice Hale; and
- His Honour Judge Richard Holman.

JUSTICE argues that each of the jurisdictions should have a minimum membership – two
from Scotland and one from Northern Ireland. However, they temper this approach by
saying that there should be flexibility to ensure that appointments are made on the basis of
merit, regardless of nationality. JUSTICE also consider that the nominating commission
should '. . . *pay regard to the desirability of the membership of the court reflecting judicial experience within Wales*'.

17 What should be the statutory retirement age? 70 or 75?

There are 82 responses to this question, of which 44 (53.5%) favour a retirement age of
70 years and 30 (36.5%) favour 75 years. Eight respondents (10%) proposed a third alternative. For example, the Rt Hon Lord Jauncey of Tullichettle believes that the retirement age
should be 72.

Those in favour of retirement at 70 include:

- the Law Society of England and Wales;
- the Rt Hon Lord Cullen of Whitekirk and the Senators of the College of Justice;
- the Rt Hon Lord Donaldson of Lymington, who suggests that judges whose present compulsory retirement age is 75 should be unaffected, and
- the Constitutional and Administrative Law Bar Association.

Those in favour of retirement at 75 include:

- the Rt Hon Lord Nolan;
- Lord Justice Mummery;
- the Judges' Council;
- the Law Lords; and
- the Bar Council.

18 Should retired members of the court up to five years over the statutory retirement age be used as a reserve panel?

Of the 83 responses to this question, 57 respondents (69%) favour the idea of retired members being used as reservists up to five years over statutory retirement age. Twenty-six respondents (31%) answered the question in the negative, for various reasons, the most common reason being that there should be a common retirement age for all judges, whether part-time or full-time.

. . .

19 Should the court continue to sit in panels, rather than every member sitting on every case?

A total of 83 respondents replied with 57 (69%) saying that the Court should sit in panels and 26 (31%) saying that they should sit *en banc.*

Many respondents favouring the option of panels do so because it is, they argue, the method most likely to allow the Court to maintain its work load. In addition, the Bar Council expresses the view that '. . . *individual appointments to the Court are less sensitive precisely because the impact of the appointment on the composition of individual panels hearing cases is less immediate'.*

The Law Society, like the Bar Council and other supporters of the panel option, expresses concern that speculation about how the Court 'divides' on cases (as happens in the US Supreme Court) is a danger when a court sits *en banc.* The following quote from Lord Bingham's lecture to the Constitution Unit in May 2002 is cited:

> If all the members of a Court decide all the cases, the opportunity arises for the appointing authority to seek quite deliberately to influence the course of the court's decision making in one direction or another when filling vacancies in the court.

Lady Justice Hale believes that there is always a possibility that the composition of the court will affect the outcome, whether or not the subject matter is political, but the important thing is that neither the parties nor the government should be able to '*pick or pack the court'.* She feels if the Court sits *en banc* there would in theory be a greater temptation to try and 'pack' it than if the Government has no influence on who hears which case. Lady Hale does note, however, that such an outcome is unthinkable in present times.

The Judges' Council view is that panels should be subject to a statutory quorum of three, but that the number of members in each case should be for the President and Deputy President to decide. The Law Lords are substantially in agreement with this view save that they argue for a quorum of three for petitions for leave to appeal or appeals. They envisage that (as happens now) panels of three should conduct oral hearings of petitions for leave to appeal, and panels of five the great majority of full appeals.

Whilst not wishing to rule out the possibility of all members sitting on a particular case, the Law Lords stress that this should by no means be the norm. This view accords substantially with that of JUSTICE which states that the President should have the power to require the new Court to sit *en banc*.

20 Should the Court decide for itself on all cases which it hears, rather than allowing some lower courts to give leave to appeal or allowing some appeals as of right?

A majority, 50 (64%), of the 78 respondents to this question propose that the system should remain unchanged. Twenty-eight (36%) are in opposition to this and would favour the Supreme Court deciding what cases it should hear.

The Law Lords are of the view that the present system works well and should not be changed. They argue that the lower courts rarely give leave in cases where it should not have been given.

JUSTICE is amongst those advocating no change and argues that a lower court should be able to indicate where it feels bound by precedent which should be reviewed. However, this power to refer '. . . *should be very sparingly used and the Supreme Court should have a large measure of control over its cases*'.

LIBERTY opposes the idea of removing the route of leave to appeal from lower courts: '*By limiting the avenues of appeal it will make the exhausting of domestic remedies more likely at an earlier stage. This will force applicants to petition the European Court of Human Rights in a situation where leave may otherwise have been granted. As the resolution of a case in Europe is likely to take several years we do not believe this will be in the interests of justice*'.

The Scottish Executive sees no need to change the current leave arrangements: '*There is no evidence from numbers or types of cases that the current arrangements lead to inappropriate or frivolous cases going to the House of Lords*'.

. . .

21 Should the present position in relation to Scottish appeals remain unchanged?

There are 67 responses to this question of which 35 (52%) favour retaining the present position regarding Scottish appeals. Thirty-two respondents (48%) argue that it should be altered.

The Law Lords are divided on this question. The Rt Hon Lord Nicholls says that this is a good opportunity to end the anomaly that different citizens in the UK have different rights of access to the highest court. Lady Justice Hale supports this: '*There is no justification for continuing to discriminate between the Scots and the rest. Everyone should be subject to a leave filter*'.

JUSTICE agrees arguing that '. . . *it is illogical for different jurisdictions to have different appeal rights to the same court*'.

On the other hand, the Rt Hon Lords Bingham, Hope, Saville and Rodger are reluctant '. . . *to disturb a long-standing procedure which gives rise to minimal difficulty in practice*'.

. . .

22 What should the existing Supreme Court be renamed?

Here, views are too varied to provide any meaningful statistical breakdown. A number of respondents chose to address the question of naming the new Court as part of their response to this question. Suggestions in this regard include:

● The High Court of the United Kingdom (The Rt Hon Lord Mackay of Clashfern);
● Her Majesty's Court of Final Appeal;
● The Superior Courts (Chancery Bar Association);
● Final Appeal Court of the United Kingdom (Lord Justice Mummery); and
● The Supreme Court of the United Kingdom (Judges' Council).

Some respondents (such as Lord Justice Mummery) who provide views about names for the new Court regard it unnecessary to rename the existing Supreme Court. They argue that the three courts do not need a collective title.

Many suggestions emerge for a new name for the existing Supreme Court, including:

- The Foremost Court of England and Wales;
- High Court of the Judicature (Law Society);
- The Superior Courts (Chancery Bar Association);
- Higher Courts of England and Wales (JUSTICE);
- Supreme Court of England and Wales (Lord Donaldson and others); and
- The Superior Court of England and Wales (Judge Dr Peter Jackson).

No clear body of opinion emerges from the responses and there is no discernible preference for either the renaming of the existing Supreme Court or the name to be given to the new Court.

23 What should members of the new court be called?

There were 78 responses to Question 23 and they provide a range of suggestions as to what the members of the new Supreme Court should be called. Suggestions include:

- Lord of Appeal in Ordinary;
- Lord Justice of the Supreme Court;
- Justices of the Court of the Realm;
- Justices of Appeal in Ordinary;
- Lords of Final Appeal; and
- Justices of Appeal.

The consultation paper proposed the title 'Justice of the Supreme Court' and this met with the approval of a range of respondents, including:

- JUSTICE;
- the Judges' Council;
- the Chancery Bar Association;
- Society of Legal Scholars;
- Hector MacQueen (University of Edinburgh);
- Lady Justice Hale;
- the Rt Hon Lord Hobhouse; and
- the Hon Mr Justice Buckley.

The Law Lords suggest two options. This first is to adopt the Scottish model where the term 'Lord' is used in the Court of Session. In this context it marks the dignity of the office but the holder does not become a peer.

The second option is to formally call the members of the Supreme Court 'Justices of the Supreme Court' but in ordinary speech (as in the United States) 'Justices'.

The Rt Hon Lord Hope and the Rt Hon Lord Millett support retaining the style (not as a Peer, but as a member of the Supreme Court) of 'Lord', while the Rt Hon Lords Bingham, Nicholls, Steyn, Hoffmann, Saville and Walker, favour the title 'Justice of the Supreme Court'.

The Law Society is of the view that the judicial nomenclature in general would benefit from being simplified in a dignified way and propose that members of the Court be known as 'Lord/Lady Justice (Family Name), Judge of the Supreme Court'. The same mode could be applied at all levels of Superior Courts.

Conclusion

The responses summarised here concern proposals for the creation of the Supreme Court and were offered in response to the consultation paper, *Constitutional Reform: A Supreme Court for the United Kingdom*. The Supreme Court is part of the Government's programme to modernise the constitution and these responses have informed the development of this important and wide ranging reform. In due course the Government will announce its finalised proposals, and intends to introduce to Parliament a Bill to enable the proposed changes to be made.

 The report 'Summary of Responses to the Consultation Paper "Constitutional Reform: A Supreme Court for the United Kingdom"' is available on the website of the former Department for Constitutional Affairs at:
www.dca.gov.uk/consult/supremecourt/scresp.htm

Legislation for a Supreme Court

Following the consultation process, the Constitutional Reform Act 2005 was passed. This contains provisions for the establishment of a Supreme Court which will replace the House of Lords. Unlike the former court, the new court will be clearly separated from Parliament, for example it will no longer sit in the Palace of Westminster.

Constitutional Reform Act 2005

PART 3
THE SUPREME COURT

23 The Supreme Court

(1) There is to be a Supreme Court of the United Kingdom.

(2) The Court consists of 12 judges appointed by Her Majesty by letters patent.

(3) Her Majesty may from time to time by Order in Council amend subsection (2) so as to increase or further increase the number of judges of the Court.

(4) No recommendation may be made to Her Majesty in Council to make an Order under subsection (3) unless a draft of the Order has been laid before and approved by resolution of each House of Parliament.

(5) Her Majesty may by letters patent appoint one of the judges to be President and one to be Deputy President of the Court.

(6) The judges other than the President and Deputy President are to be styled 'Justices of the Supreme Court'.

(7) The Court is to be taken to be duly constituted despite any vacancy among the judges of the Court or in the office of President or Deputy President.

→

24 First members of the Court

On the commencement of section 23—

(a) the persons who immediately before that commencement are Lords of Appeal in Ordinary become judges of the Supreme Court,

(b) the person who immediately before that commencement is the senior Lord of Appeal in Ordinary becomes the President of the Court, and

(c) the person who immediately before that commencement is the second senior Lord of Appeal in Ordinary becomes the Deputy President of the Court.

Appointment of judges

25 Qualification for appointment

(1) A person is not qualified to be appointed a judge of the Supreme Court unless he has (at any time)—

(a) held high judicial office for a period of at least 2 years, or

(b) been a qualifying practitioner for a period of at least 15 years.

(2) A person is a qualifying practitioner for the purposes of this section at any time when—

(a) he has a Senior Courts qualification, within the meaning of section 71 of the Courts and Legal Services Act 1990 (c. 41),

(b) he is an advocate in Scotland or a solicitor entitled to appear in the Court of Session and the High Court of Justiciary, or

(c) he is a member of the Bar of Northern Ireland or a solicitor of the Court of Judicature of Northern Ireland.

26 Selection of members of the Court

(1) This section applies to a recommendation for an appointment to one of the following offices—

(a) judge of the Supreme Court;

(b) President of the Court;

(c) Deputy President of the Court.

(2) A recommendation may be made only by the Prime Minister.

(3) The Prime Minister—

(a) must recommend any person whose name is notified to him under section 29;

(b) may not recommend any other person.

(4) A person who is not a judge of the Court must be recommended for appointment as a judge if his name is notified to the Prime Minister for an appointment as President or Deputy President.

(5) If there is a vacancy in one of the offices mentioned in subsection (1), or it appears to him that there will soon be such a vacancy, the Lord Chancellor must convene a selection commission for the selection of a person to be recommended.

(6) Schedule 8 is about selection commissions.

(7) Subsection (5) is subject to Part 3 of that Schedule.

(8) Sections 27 to 31 apply where a selection commission is convened under this section.

27 Selection process

(1) The commission must—
    (a) determine the selection process to be applied,
    (b) apply the selection process, and
    (c) make a selection accordingly.

(2) As part of the selection process the commission must consult each of the following—
    (a) such of the senior judges as are not members of the commission and are not willing to be considered for selection;
    (b) the Lord Chancellor;
    (c) the First Minister in Scotland;
    (d) the Assembly First Secretary in Wales;
    (e) the Secretary of State for Northern Ireland.

(3) If for any part of the United Kingdom no judge of the courts of that part is to be consulted under subsection (2)(a), the commission must consult as part of the selection process the most senior judge of the courts of that part who is not a member of the commission and is not willing to be considered for selection.

(4) Subsections (5) to (10) apply to any selection under this section or section 31.

(5) Selection must be on merit.

(6) A person may be selected only if he meets the requirements of section 25.

(7) A person may not be selected if he is a member of the commission.

(8) In making selections for the appointment of judges of the Court the commission must ensure that between them the judges will have knowledge of, and experience of practice in, the law of each part of the United Kingdom.

(9) The commission must have regard to any guidance given by the Lord Chancellor as to matters to be taken into account (subject to any other provision of this Act) in making a selection.

(10) Any selection must be of one person only.

. . .

33 Tenure
A judge of the Supreme Court holds that office during good behaviour, but may be removed from it on the address of both Houses of Parliament.

. . .

35 Resignation and retirement

(1) A judge of the Supreme Court may at any time resign that office by giving the Lord Chancellor notice in writing to that effect.

➔

(2) The President or Deputy President of the Court may at any time resign that office (whether or not he resigns his office as a judge) by giving the Lord Chancellor notice in writing to that effect.

(3) In section 26(4)(a) of and Schedule 5 to the Judicial Pensions and Retirement Act 1993 (c. 8) (retirement), for 'Lord of Appeal in Ordinary' substitute 'Judge of the Supreme Court'.

36 Medical retirement

(1) This section applies if the Lord Chancellor is satisfied by means of a medical certificate that a person holding office as a judge of the Supreme Court—
    (a) is disabled by permanent infirmity from the performance of the duties of his office, and
    (b) is for the time being incapacitated from resigning his office.

(2) The Lord Chancellor may by instrument under his hand declare the person's office to have been vacated.

(3) A declaration by instrument under subsection (2) has the same effect for all purposes as if the person had, on the date of the instrument, resigned his office.

(4) But such a declaration has no effect unless it is made—
    (a) in the case of an ordinary judge, with the agreement of the President and Deputy President of the Court;
    (b) in the case of the President, with the agreement of the Deputy President and the senior ordinary judge;
    (c) in the case of the Deputy President, with the agreement of the President and the senior ordinary judge.

. . .

Jurisdiction, relation to other courts etc.

40 Jurisdiction

(1) The Supreme Court is a superior court of record.

(2) An appeal lies to the Court from any order or judgment of the Court of Appeal in England and Wales in civil proceedings.

(3) An appeal lies to the Court from any order or judgment of a court in Scotland if an appeal lay from that court to the House of Lords at or immediately before the commencement of this section.

(4) Schedule 9—
    (a) transfers other jurisdiction from the House of Lords to the Court,
    (b) transfers devolution jurisdiction from the Judicial Committee of the Privy Council to the Court, and
    (c) makes other amendments relating to jurisdiction.

(5) The Court has power to determine any question necessary to be determined for the purposes of doing justice in an appeal to it under any enactment.

(6) An appeal under subsection (2) lies only with the permission of the Court of Appeal or the Supreme Court; but this is subject to provision under any other enactment restricting such an appeal.

41 Relation to other courts etc.

(1) Nothing in this Part is to affect the distinctions between the separate legal systems of the parts of the United Kingdom.

(2) A decision of the Supreme Court on appeal from a court of any part of the United Kingdom, other than a decision on a devolution matter, is to be regarded as the decision of a court of that part of the United Kingdom.

(3) A decision of the Supreme Court on a devolution matter—
   (a) is not binding on that Court when making such a decision;
   (b) otherwise, is binding in all legal proceedings.

(4) In this section 'devolution matter' means—
   (a) a question referred to the Supreme Court under section 33 of the Scotland Act 1998 (c. 46) or section 11 of the Northern Ireland Act 1998 (c. 47);
   (b) a devolution issue as defined in Schedule 8 to the Government of Wales Act 1998 (c. 38), Schedule 6 to the Scotland Act 1998 or Schedule 10 to the Northern Ireland Act 1998.

Composition for proceedings

42 Composition

(1) The Supreme Court is duly constituted in any proceedings only if all of the following conditions are met—
   (a) the Court consists of an uneven number of judges;
   (b) the Court consists of at least three judges;
   (c) more than half of those judges are permanent judges.

. . .

   (a) the number of officers and staff of the Court;
   (b) subject to subsection (3), the terms on which officers and staff are to be appointed.

(3) The civil service pension arrangements for the time being in force apply (with any necessary adaptations) to the chief executive of the Court, and to persons appointed under subsection (1), as they apply to other persons employed in the civil service of the State.

(4) In subsection (3) 'the civil service pension arrangements' means—
   (a) the principal civil service pension scheme (within the meaning of section 2 of the Superannuation Act 1972 (c. 11)), and
   (b) any other superannuation benefits for which provision is made under or by virtue of section 1 of that Act for or in respect of persons in employment in the civil service of the State.

. . .

→

50 Accommodation and other resources

(1) The Lord Chancellor must ensure that the Supreme Court is provided with the following—

(a) such court-houses, offices and other accommodation as the Lord Chancellor thinks are appropriate for the Court to carry on its business;

(b) such other resources as the Lord Chancellor thinks are appropriate for the Court to carry on its business.

(2) The Lord Chancellor may discharge the duty under subsection (1) by—

(a) providing accommodation or other resources, or

(b) entering into arrangements with any other person for the provision of accommodation or other resources.

(3) The powers to acquire land for the public service conferred by—

(a) section 2 of the Commissioners of Works Act 1852 (c. 28) (acquisition by agreement), and

(b) section 228(1) of the Town and Country Planning Act 1990 (c. 8) (compulsory acquisition),

are to be treated as including power to acquire land for the purpose of its provision under arrangements under subsection (2)(b).

(4) The Scottish Ministers may make payments by way of contribution to the costs incurred by the Lord Chancellor in providing the Court with resources in accordance with subsection (1)(b).

(5) In this section 'court-house' means any place where the Court sits, including the precincts of any building in which it sits.

The Constitutional Reform Act 2005 is available on the website of the Office for Public Service Information:
www.opsi.gov.uk/acts/acts2005/50004--a.htm

Explanatory notes

The government produces 'explanatory notes' which accompany each Act, to explain the impact of the new statutory provisions. Below is an extract from the explanatory notes for the Constitutional Reform Act 2005 relating to the establishment of a Supreme Court.

Explanatory Notes – Constitutional Reform Act 2005

PART 3 THE SUPREME COURT

Summary

58 Part 3 of the Act creates a Supreme Court of the United Kingdom (which is generally to be known as 'the Supreme Court' in the Act and other legislation) and makes provision for

the transfer to the Supreme Court of the appellate jurisdiction of the House of Lords and the devolution jurisdiction of the Judicial Committee of the Privy Council. The new Supreme Court will be separate from Parliament.

Background

59 At present the exercise of the highest level of jurisdiction in the United Kingdom is shared between the Appellate Committee of the House of Lords and the Judicial Committee of the Privy Council. The Appellate Committee of the House of Lords receives appeals from the courts in England and Wales and Northern Ireland, and in civil cases from Scotland. The Judicial Committee of the Privy Council, in addition to its overseas and ecclesiastical jurisdiction, considers questions as to whether the devolved administrations, the Scottish Parliament, the National Assembly for Wales and the Northern Ireland Assembly are acting within their legal powers. Support to the Appellate Committee is provided by the House's administration under the Clerk of the Parliaments. Support for the Judicial Committee is provided by staff supporting the Privy Council.

60 In addition to the Lords of Appeal in Ordinary certain other holders of high judicial office are also members of the House of Lords. A number of other members of the House of Lords hold other full-time or part-time judicial office and a number of members of the House of Commons hold part-time judicial-office.

61 The Act seeks to make a distinct constitutional separation between the legislature and the judiciary. It creates a Supreme Court of the United Kingdom giving it the appellate jurisdiction of the House of Lords and the devolution jurisdiction of the Judicial Committee of the Privy Council. It makes provision to allow for the appointment of members of the Court in a way that requires the participation of the judiciary and the devolved administrations throughout the United Kingdom. It makes provision to determine the practices and procedures of the court, to allow the Lord Chancellor to provide staff, equipment, security arrangements and accommodation for the Court. It also makes general provision for the proceedings of the Court to be broadcast in certain circumstances.

62 As a counterpart to the creation of the Supreme Court the Act restricts the right of members of the House of Lords to sit and vote for so long as they hold full time judicial office. Finally the Act makes consequential and transitional provisions to allow the transfer of functions to the Court.

Commentary on sections

Section 23: The Supreme Court

63 This section establishes the Supreme Court of the United Kingdom, and sets out the composition of the Supreme Court. It also sets out the method of appointing judges, including the President and Deputy President (the process for selection of persons to be recommended for appointment is to be found in sections 26–31). It also provides for the title of the judges of the Supreme Court other than the President and Deputy President.

64 Subsection (2) provides both for complement and method of appointment. The Court will comprise 12 judges, who are to be appointed by Her Majesty by letters patent. By virtue of subsection (5), Her Majesty may, also by letters patent, appoint one of the judges to be President and one to be Deputy President. It will be possible for a person to be appointed as President or Deputy President without having first served as a judge of the Supreme Court (see Section 26(4)).

65 Subsection (3) provides a power for Her Majesty to increase or further increase the number of judges of the Supreme Court by Order in Council. This may only be done, however, if, as set out in subsection (4), a draft of the Order has been laid before and approved by each House of Parliament (that is, by affirmative resolution procedure).

66 Subsection (6) provides that the judges of the Supreme Court other than the President of the Supreme Court and the Deputy President of the Supreme Court (who will have those titles) will be styled 'Justices of the Supreme Court'.

67 Subsection (7) provides that the Court will still be properly constituted even if there is a vacancy among the judges of the Court or in the office of President or Deputy President.

Section 24: First members of the Court

68 This Section provides for the first judges of the Supreme Court to be the Lords of Appeal in Ordinary holding office at the date of commencement. This is a one-off provision to provide for the transition of members of the Appellate Committee of the House of Lords from the Appellate Committee to the Supreme Court.

69 The effect of Section 24(a) is that on establishment of the Court (with the commencement of section 23), Lords of Appeal in Ordinary immediately before commencement will become the first Supreme Court judges.

70 Section 24(b) and (c) make provision for the first holders of the offices of President and Deputy President, providing that the senior Lord of Appeal in Ordinary prior to commencement will become the President and the second senior Lord of Appeal in Ordinary prior to commencement will become the Deputy President of the Court.

Appointment of judges

Section 25: Qualification for Appointment

71 This Section defines eligibility for appointment as a judge of the Supreme Court, which will be the same as eligibility for appointment as a Lord of Appeal in Ordinary.

72 Subsection (1) sets out the qualifying requirements for appointment as a Supreme Court judge. There are two separate possible routes to qualification. First, a person is eligible if he has held high judicial office, as defined in subsections (1) and (2) of section 54, for at least 2 years.

73 Alternatively, to qualify for appointment as a Supreme Court judge, a person would have to have been a qualifying practitioner for at least 15 years.

74 Subsection (2) defines 'qualifying practitioner' for the purposes of this section.

Section 26: Selection of members of the court

75 This section, together with sections 27, 28, 29, 30, and 31 and Schedule 8, provides for the process by which candidates for appointment to the Supreme Court are to be selected and recommended to Her Majesty for appointment.

76 Subsection (1) sets out the offices to which appointments are to be made by this process. Subsection (5) provides that the Lord Chancellor must convene a selection commission if there is a vacancy in one of those offices, or if it appears to the Lord Chancellor that there will soon be such a vacancy. Schedule 8, which is introduced by subsection (6), makes provision about the composition of selection commissions. Sections 27 to 29 set out the details of the process to be followed by a selection commission.

77 At the final stage of that selection process, once sections 27, 28 and 29 (and, if necessary, sections 30 and 31) have been followed, the Lord Chancellor notifies the Prime Minister of the identity of the person selected by the commission. Then, under subsections (2), (3) and (4) of section 26, the Prime Minister must recommend the Queen to appoint the person notified to him by the Lord Chancellor.

. . .

Section 27: Selection process

101 This section sets out the overall process which must be undertaken by the selection commission (the composition of which is provided for in Schedule 8) before it makes a selection of one name (subsection 10) and puts this to the Lord Chancellor (under section 28). Subsection (1) sets out the duties of the commission with regard to the particular selection process to be applied to each vacancy under consideration.

102 As provided for in subsections (5) and (6), selection must be made solely on merit. The task of setting out the criteria or competences against which merit will be tested lies with the commission. The commission can only recommend those who meet the eligibility requirements set out in section 25. Under subsection (7) anyone who is a member of the commission cannot be selected (hence the provisions in Schedule 8 for identifying persons who wish to be considered for a particular vacancy and disqualifying them from membership of the commission).

103 Subsection (8) provides that the commission must, when making selections for the appointment of judges, also take into account the need for the Court to have among its judges those with knowledge and experience of practice in the law in every part of the United Kingdom. This is intended to maintain the convention that currently applies to the House of Lords that there should generally be at least 2 Scottish judges and usually 1 from Northern Ireland. The Lord Chancellor, as provided for by subsection (9), may issue non-binding guidance to the commission about the vacancy that has arisen, for example on the jurisdictional requirements of the Court, which the commission must have regard to.

104 Subsections (2) and (3) list the persons the commission must consult during the selection process (although it may consult others). They are (subsection (2)): senior judges (as defined by Section 60) who are neither on the commission nor willing to be considered for selection, the Lord Chancellor, the First Minister in Scotland, the Assembly First Secretary in Wales and the Secretary of State for Northern Ireland. In addition (subsection (3)), the commission must, if all the 'senior judges' for a part of the United Kingdom are not able to be consulted (because they are candidates or members of the commission), consult the next most senior judge in that part who is able to be consulted. This ensures that there will always be some senior judicial input from every part of the United Kingdom into every selection process.

. . .

Section 33: Tenure

132 This section provides for the judges of the Supreme Court to hold office while they are of good behaviour, as is presently the case for Lords of Appeal in Ordinary. This is of course subject to the possibility of resignation, and the provision for retirement, set out in sections 35 and 36. (This provision does not apply to persons who, under section 38 of the Act, are acting judges of the Supreme Court. See section 38(5)(b).)

133 This section also provides, consistently with the position of all senior judicial office holders, that removal from office of any judge of the Supreme Court may only be effected following resolutions passed by both the House of Commons and the House of Lords.

. . .

Section 35: Resignation and retirement

138 This section makes provision for the resignation or retirement of judges of the Supreme Court.

139 Under subsection (1) any judge of the Supreme Court (including the President and Deputy President) may at any time resign from that office. Resignation is effected by giving notice in writing to the Lord Chancellor.

140 Subsection (2) makes separate provision for resignation from the office of President or Deputy President. The holder may so resign without resigning from the office of a judge of the Supreme Court. The resignation is again effected by giving notice in writing to the Lord Chancellor.

141 Subsection (3) amends section 26(4)(a) of, and Schedule 5 to, the Judicial Pensions and Retirement Act 1993 (retirement), so that references to 'Judge of the Supreme Court' will be substituted for 'Lord of Appeal in Ordinary'. The effect of this amendment is that the retirement age and associated provisions as to retirement which apply to Lords of Appeal in Ordinary will apply in the same way to judges of the Supreme Court.

Section 36: Medical retirement

142 This section makes provision analogous to that for other senior judicial office holders for vacation of the office of a judge of the Supreme Court (including the President and Deputy President) on medical grounds.

143 Subsection (1) provides for the scope of the section: it applies if the Lord Chancellor is satisfied by means of a medical certificate that the person holding office as a judge of the Supreme Court is both disabled by permanent infirmity from performing his duties and for the time being is incapacitated from resigning from his office.

144 In such circumstances, subsection (2) enables the Lord Chancellor to declare the office of the person in question to be vacated (subject to the conditions in subsection (4)). Subsection (3) provides for this declaration to have effect as though the person in question had himself or herself resigned on the date of the declaration. Subsection (4) requires the Lord Chancellor, before making a declaration, to secure the agreement of the appropriate judges of the Supreme Court (depending on the office which would be vacated). Without that agreement, the declaration will have no effect. In the case of an ordinary judge (as defined in section 60(3)(a)), the agreement required is that of the President and Deputy President of the Court; in the case of the President, the agreement required is that of the

Deputy President and the senior ordinary judge (as defined in section 60(3)(b)); and in the case of the Deputy President, the agreement required is that of the President and the senior ordinary judge.

. . .

Jurisdiction, relation to other courts etc.

Section 40: Jurisdiction

157 This section makes provision for the jurisdiction of the Supreme Court, which is in essence that of the House of Lords in appellate matters together with the jurisdiction of the Judicial Committee of the Privy Council in relation to devolution issues under the Scotland Act 1998, Government of Wales Act 1998 and Northern Ireland Act 1998.

158 Subsection (1) provides that the Supreme Court is to be, as is the House of Lords, a superior court of record, and accordingly has the inherent powers of such a court.

159 Subsections (2) and (3) reproduce the effect of section 3 of the Appellate Jurisdiction Act 1876, conferring on the Supreme Court the appellate jurisdiction exercised by virtue of that section by the House of Lords. The other appellate jurisdiction of the House of Lords, and the jurisdiction of the Judicial Committee of the Privy Council in relation to devolution issues, are transferred to the Supreme Court by virtue of subsection (4) and Schedule 9 (which is introduced by that subsection).

160 Since the provisions work by transferring the existing jurisdiction, the appeal process (except to the extent that it would be covered by Supreme Court Rules made under section 45) and the types of appeal from each jurisdiction, including leave requirements, and the routes of recourse otherwise, will remain the same as is currently the case for the House of Lords and Judicial Committee of the Privy Council.

161 Subsection (5) makes provision for the Supreme Court to have the power, as does the House of Lords, to determine any questions it deems necessary to determine, for the purposes of doing justice in an appeal to it, under this Act or any other Act.

Section 41: Relation to other courts etc.

162 This section makes provision as to the effect of decisions of the Supreme Court as judicial precedents. The essence of the provision is that a decision made by the Supreme Court under particular jurisdiction should have the same effect as a decision of the body in which the jurisdiction is currently vested (whether that is the House of Lords or the Judicial Committee of the Privy Council). So in the case of jurisdiction transferred from the House of Lords, a decision of the Supreme Court on an appeal from one jurisdiction within the United Kingdom will not have effect as a binding precedent in any other such jurisdiction, or in a subsequent appeal before the Supreme Court from another such jurisdiction. In the case of the devolution jurisdiction transferred from the Judicial Committee of the Privy Council, a decision of the Supreme Court will be binding in all legal proceedings except for subsequent proceedings before the Supreme Court itself.

163 Subsection (1) provides that nothing in the provisions of the Act about the Supreme Court is to affect the distinctions between the separate legal systems of the parts of the United Kingdom. This recognises that those legal systems are separate, and that there is a variety of distinctions between them, so that, for example, Scotland differs from Northern Ireland in some ways, and in other ways from England and Wales.

164 Subsection (2) provides that a decision of the Supreme Court on an appeal from a court in one part of the United Kingdom is to be regarded as the decision of a court of that part of the United Kingdom. So, for example, a decision on appeal from the Court of Session would be regarded as a decision of a Scottish court, and would have binding effect in Scottish courts accordingly, but would not have binding effect in English courts (although it might, like the decision of the House of Lords in **Donoghue** v **Stevenson**, be found by English courts to be so persuasive an authority as to be readily followed). Subsection (2) does not apply in relation to decisions in devolution proceedings.

165 Subsections (3) and (4) make provision to maintain the status quo in relation to the effect of decisions in devolution proceedings. The status quo is that, by virtue of section 103(1) of the Scotland Act 1998, section 82(1) of the Northern Ireland Act 1998 and paragraph 32 of Schedule 8 to the Government of Wales Act 1998, a decision of the Judicial Committee of the Privy Council in the exercise of its devolution jurisdiction is 'binding in all legal proceedings (other than proceedings before the Committee)'.

166 Subsection (3) accordingly provides that a decision of the Supreme Court on a devolution matter will not bind the Court itself when subsequently making a decision on a devolution matter, but will otherwise be 'binding in all legal proceedings', mirroring the wording of section 103(1) of the Scotland Act 1998 and its counterparts.

167 Subsection (4) defines 'devolution matter', by reference not only to those matters which are 'devolution issues' in the Scotland Act, Northern Ireland Act and Government of Wales Act, but also to the possibility of a reference to the Court, under the Scotland Act and Northern Ireland Act alone, of the question whether a Bill or part of a Bill of the Scottish Parliament or Northern Ireland Assembly is within the Parliament's or Assembly's legislative competence.

Composition for proceedings

168 The Supreme Court will, like the House of Lords, be able to sit in panels. Section 42, together with section 43, makes provision for the composition of panels. The underlying rule is that no panel should ever consist wholly or predominantly of non-permanent judges, but that otherwise, the Court should have considerable flexibility (essentially mirroring that of the Appellate Committee), including the flexibility, subject to the agreement of the parties, to commence or continue hearing proceedings notwithstanding that a judge is unable to continue.

Section 42: Composition

169 Subsections (1), (2) and (3) provide for the basic rule that an uneven number of judges equal to or greater than three must be designated to hear any proceedings – there is no flexibility to designate an even number of judges. Given that an uneven number must be designated, permanent judges have to be in the majority in order to ensure that the composition is never wholly or predominantly of non-permanent judges (subsection (1)(c)).

170 This does not mean that the actual hearing cannot commence before an even number of judges, as the judges will by definition have been designated to hear proceedings in advance of the beginning of the hearing proper, and section 42 is, as subsection (4) makes

clear, subject to section 43, which allows for additional flexibility. Subsection (5) makes it clear that the power to require more than three judges to be designated for particular proceedings or a particular class or classes of proceedings is exercisable by the President of the Court; and subsection (6) makes provision which ensures that the sections work on the basis that the Court is constituted for proceedings when the judges are designated to hear those proceedings (rather than when the hearing commences).

. . .

Section 50: Accommodation and other resources

187 Under subsection (1) the Lord Chancellor is responsible for ensuring that the Supreme Court is provided with such accommodation as he thinks appropriate for the Court to carry on its business. The Lord Chancellor is also responsible for providing such other resources as he thinks appropriate for the Court to carry on its business. This complements section 48, which sets out the duties of the Chief Executive. The Chief Executive will not be able to carry out his duties if the Lord Chancellor does not provide appropriate resources.

188 Subsection (2) provides that the Lord Chancellor can discharge his general duty under subsection (1) by directly providing accommodation or other resources or by entering into arrangements with third parties for their provision; and subsection (3) makes available for this purpose certain powers to acquire land for public service.

189 This section additionally, under subsection (4), enables the Scottish Ministers to make a contribution towards the resource running costs of the Court. This contribution (which will be related to the proportion of the costs of civil business attributable to appeals from Scotland) will be made by a transfer of resources from an appropriate budget.

 The Explanatory Notes to the Constitutional Reform Act 2005 are available on the website of the Office for Public Sector Information at: www.opsi.gov.uk/acts/en2005/2005en04.htm

Criminal Cases Review Commission

The Criminal Cases Review Commission was established in 1997. It considers applications from defendants (or their representatives) who no longer have a right of appeal to a court, but who claim that they have been the victim of a miscarriage of justice.

Criminal Cases Review Commission Annual Report 2004–2005

Chairman's foreword

To: The Rt Hon Charles Clarke MP
Secretary of State for the Home Department
This was a difficult year for us. The limits on our budget necessitated a temporary moratorium on appointments. This made it impossible to build up the number of Case Review Managers to 50 – the number we estimated would be necessary to clear our backlog – or

even to replace all those who had left. As a result, fewer cases have been closed and back-logs and waiting lists have risen.

A later addition to the grant came too late to resume recruitment during the year. Some new appointments are now possible in the light of the following year's budget, but the indicative budgets thereafter pose severe problems and will make it difficult to make progress towards our goals and the expectations of our stakeholders.

These pressures have, however, stimulated an intensive internal review. We made and continue to make strenuous efforts to improve our caseworking efficiency and find ways of working more quickly and cheaply, but we cannot compromise on the quality of the work we do. Even if we did, it would not survive legal challenges, which are themselves costly.

The very essence of our role involves reviewing the work of the police, prosecuting authorities, defence and prosecution lawyers, trial courts and even the Court of Appeal: to suggest that somehow we could perform that task more crudely or less meticulously is not tenable. We continue, however, to seek further ways in which we can streamline our processes . . .

While a number of individual cases attracted media attention and newspaper headlines, the subject that dominated public interest was the Attorney-General's review of infant homicides following the Court of Appeal's judgment in **Cannings**. There was not the deluge of cases that some had anticipated and the Court has now helpfully refined the **Cannings** judgment in two subsequent cases. We have taken steps internally to ensure that such cases are dealt with expeditiously and consistently. This work illustrates graphically our role not only in facilitating the correction of individual miscarriages of justice but also in restoring public confidence in the criminal justice system when it has been com-promised. It is disappointing that no progress has been made with our requests for legis-lative amendment in areas affecting our work. These are set out later in this report and we hope that opportunities will present themselves before much longer.

The Commission's record on judicial review challenges is impressive. This is a tribute both to the quality of our work, in terms of legality, and to our readiness to admit mistakes or failings when they are demonstrated and take steps to put them right. However, the burden of fending off unmeritorious applications is now very considerable. It consumes valuable resource that would otherwise be devoted to reviewing cases. There may be no easy answer to this problem, which is doubtless experienced by other public bodies, and it could be said to be a small price to pay to promote legality in public administration generally. There may, however, be steps that could be taken by the Legal Services Commission in those manifestly unmeritorious cases which are publicly funded. It is our practice in other cases to seek to recover our costs.

The Commission's new senior management team set about the task of building a fresh and constructive relationship with your officials, some of whom also were new to their roles. We recognise that a fruitful relationship with our Sponsor Unit, with the Permanent Secretary and with Ministers is of great importance. It should not be forgotten that our work is critical to confidence in the criminal justice system, which is a prominent aim of the Government's criminal justice policy: the public want to be assured that, when things have gone wrong, there is a mechanism which can ensure they are put right and they also want assurance, which we can give, that the majority of criminal prosecutions appear to result in a satisfactory outcome . . .

I have the honour to present the Commission's eighth Annual Report.
Graham Zellick

Decisions of the appeal courts in 2004–05

The appeal courts decided 40 cases referred by the Commission. 37 were heard in the Court of Appeal in England; two in the Court of Appeal in Northern Ireland (a single case relating to two individuals); and one in the Crown Court. 14 of the cases related to murder, attempted murder or manslaughter; six involved drugs; five sexual offences; three convictions for non-fatal violence; two robbery; and one receiving stolen goods. The remaining nine cases had been referred for appeals against sentence only and one of these was a summary matter relating to a dangerous dog. Most of the judgments mentioned below can be read in full on the Commission's website.

Themes

In 2004–05, the appeal courts decided that 23 of the 31 convictions referred by the Commission were unsafe (74%). Of the nine sentences referred, seven were reduced (78%). All but one of the murder convictions referred by the Commission were quashed. As in previous years, in several cases the Court was being asked by the appellant to substitute a conviction for manslaughter on the basis of diminished responsibility or provocation. Two of these, **Reynolds** [2004] EWCA Crim 1834 and **Friend** [2004] EWCA Crim 2661, related respectively to the conditions known as Asperger's Syndrome and Activity Deficit Hyperactivity Disorder, which do not appear to have been previously considered by the Court of Appeal in this context. A prominent exception to the references concerning partial defences to murder was the case of Sion Jenkins, whose murder appeal, which eventually hinged on forensic pathology evidence, attracted a great deal of media coverage. The only referral to the Northern Ireland Court of Appeal was also a murder case, stemming from a sectarian killing in 1976. Poor disclosure was a less frequent factor in the appeals heard during 2004–05 compared to previous years. Cases which did turn on non-disclosure were **Broughton** [2004] EWCA Crim 2119, **Kassar** [2004] EWCA Crim 1812 and notably **Warren** [2005] EWCA Crim 659, in which the problem arose when the doubts of one police force about the reliability of a witness were not passed on to officers in another force investigating a similar complaint by the same witness. Lord Justice Keene commented:

> This case demonstrates two matters, it seems to us: first of all, once again the valuable work being done by the Criminal Cases Review Commission, and secondly, the importance of prosecuting authorities adhering fully to the obligations on them, so far as disclosure of relevant material to the defence is concerned.

Police misconduct, a significant feature in previous years, formed the main ground for only two reference appeals: **Deans** [2004] EWCA Crim 2123 (West Midlands Police Central Drugs Squad in 1988) and **Murphy and Pope** [2004] EWCA Crim 2787 (South East Regional Crime Squad in 1990). Upholding the conviction in **Deans**, the Court commented:

> We make no criticism of the Criminal Cases Review Commission for referring this appeal. It merited the consideration of this Court. Having given it that consideration, we are satisfied that the convictions are safe and we dismiss the appeal.

In **Murphy and Pope**, the Crown no longer relied on police witnesses who had themselves been convicted of corrupt practices. The Court concluded that it would not be safe to rely on the evidence of officers, not themselves tainted, who had worked closely with the corrupt officers, so the appeals succeeded. One of the shortest judgments the Court has had to deliver in a Commission case was **Bacchus** [2004] EWCA Crim 1756, which concerned a 'facial mapping' expert whose evidence was no longer relied on by the Crown. The Commission is considering a number of other applications in which the science underlying this technique is being questioned.

In November 2004, the Court of Appeal determined a reference concerning an area of law which is frequently raised in applications to the Commission: adverse inference from silence. **Beckles** [2004] EWCA Crim 2766, [2005] 1 All ER 705 makes an important contribution towards resolving some of the issues in this contentious field.

The oldest conviction overturned during the year was in **Quinn** [2004] EWCA Crim 3026, where fresh evidence raised doubts about a conviction for receiving stolen scrap metal in 1957. Lord Justice Clarke said that while the Court did not encourage the referral of historic cases, this was a case where 'there are strong reasons for thinking that the appellant was not guilty'.

Several referrals elicited particular comments from the Court about the work of the Commission. In the sentencing case of **Nicholson** [2004] EWCA Crim 2840 and the conviction in **Burt** [2005] EWCA Crim 315 (after the Court of Appeal itself had suggested that the defendant should apply to the Commission), Lord Justice Judge, the Deputy Chief Justice, commended the Commission's 'rapid' handling of both cases.

A few judgments included some criticism of the Commission by the Court. One was a 1970 conviction previously referred to the Court by the Home Secretary before the Commission came into existence (**Stock** [2004] EWCA Crim 2238). Lord Justice May questioned the value of the 'enormously detailed re-examination of existing material' in an old case with 'no new material' and a previously failed appeal 'for which all the material had been available'. There was some implied criticism in **Benn and Benn** [2004] EWCA Crim 2100, because it concerned a scientific dispute that the Court had already resolved in December 2002, although the Court may not have realised that the Commission's decision to refer that case had been made in August 2002. Finally, in the rape case of **P.O.** [2004] EWCA Crim 2336, the Court underlined the importance of the Commission's consulting counsel in relation to disclosure, where that issue was the only ground of referral, to avoid potential waste of public funds.

Among the reduced sentences cases, three concerned credit for time spent on remand prior to sentence in those rare circumstances when no automatic credit can be given by the prison authorities when calculating release. This issue has caused difficulties for judges and counsel involved in the sentencing process, especially where discretionary life sentences are imposed. This may not be surprising given that the section governing credit for time on remand (section 67 of the Criminal Justice Act 1967) has been amended by 19 different statutes, prospectively repealed by a provision which was never brought into force (section 56 of the Crime (Sentencing) Act 1997), then replaced by another provision (section 87 of the Powers of Criminal Courts (Sentencing) Act 2000) which was itself repealed before it came into effect (by section 303 of the Criminal Justice Act 2003), leaving the original 1967 provision still in force, at least until section 240 of the Criminal Justice Act 2003 is implemented. The field is further complicated if a defendant has at some stage been recalled on licence. The Court of Appeal acknowledged the risk of error. Lord Justice Hooper described one of the references (**Keogh** [2004] EWCA Crim 1406) as 'a cautionary tale for the authorities responsible for advising courts about the effect of previously imposed sentences'. The Commission continues to receive applications based on errors caused by the lack of clarity in this area.

Another of the sentencing cases (**Smith** [2005] EWCA Crim 530) was used by the Court of Appeal as a suitable vehicle for a detailed review of the law relating to sentencing offenders on counts which are said to represent multiple offending. The Lord Chief Justice gave a judgment likely to be of assistance to prosecutors when drafting indictments in the future.

Finally, mention should be made of **Lamont**, the Commission's sole reference of a summary conviction in the magistrates' court, dealt with at Northampton Crown Court on 15 October 2004. Although the case was portrayed by commentators as an appeal by Dino the German Shepherd dog against a death sentence, it was his owner who was appealing against one element of his sentence (an order for the destruction of his property, the dog). Several years had passed since the original order was made and the dog had not been put down. Once the Commission concluded that there was a real possibility – the statutory test – that the order would not be upheld on appeal, we felt it right to make the reference. There was no basis for exercising our discretion not to refer. It is for Parliament to decide whether to remove such cases from our jurisdiction.

 The Annual Report for 2004–2005 of the Criminal Cases Review Commission is available on its website at:
www.ccrc.gov.uk/CCRC_Uploads/420165_CCRC_AR_V9lo.pdf

25

Alternative methods of dispute resolution

Introduction

This chapter looks at:

- research into how alternative dispute resolution (ADR) is working in practice;

- government use of ADR; and

- Hazel Genn's research into non-family, court-based ADR.

ADR in practice

The government has been keen to promote alternative methods of dispute resolution and the current civil procedure rules place considerable emphasis on their use to avoid court litigation. However, research carried out for the Department of Trade and Industry and the National Consumer Council suggests that frequently these services are not available or underused.

Seeking Resolution: The Availability and Usage of Consumer-to-Business Alternative Dispute Resolution in the United Kingdom (2004)

Margaret Doyle, Katrina Ritters and Steve Brooker

Summary

This report describes the findings of a month-long study into the provision and usage of independent alternative dispute resolution (ADR) for specific sectors of consumer disputes. Its focus is on the use of arbitration, mediation, and ombudsmen services.

Potential of ADR

ADR for consumer disputes is a welcome development. It can save the consumer time and money, offer a range of remedies and is perceived as less daunting than the court system. In addition, ADR can help to drive up business standards. It is timely to reflect on the progress ADR for consumer disputes has made so far – what exists, what works well and what future directions ADR should go in next.

Lottery of ADR provision

Our research revealed that provision of ADR for consumer problems is ad hoc and presents a lottery for the consumer. The nature of the lottery depends either on the type of problem faced or where the problem arises, and sometimes on the ability of the consumer to afford the fees. Aside from a few active schemes, consumers with an unresolved complaint over goods and services face very little in the way of a choice between using ADR and going to court.

This multi-level lottery also means there is a major gap between government policy of promoting ADR and the on-the-ground reality of access to effective, affordable ADR for consumers.

Of the thirteen sectors of consumer detriment we identified (using the Office of Fair Trading system), the sectors or parts of sectors well served by ADR – in the sense that there is an existing ADR scheme with adequate coverage – include travel agents/holidays, upholstered furniture, glass and glazing, floor coverings and telecommunications. Other sectors have limited coverage, for example estate agents, funerals, consumer credit, internet issues and direct selling. However, some problematic sectors, for example home maintenance and repairs (excluding the Department of Trade and Industry Quality Mark Scheme), electrical appliances and second-hand cars, have little or no ADR provision at all.

Low usage

Although a number of free or low-cost sector-specific ADR schemes exist, our research found a very low level of usage of ADR for consumer problems even where the service is offered free. Consumer disputes vary sector by sector, but for each sector the number of cases going to an existing relevant ADR service is a microscopically small fraction of the total number of complaints. While recorded complaint levels are in the thousands, use of ADR schemes is in the double digits only for most ADR schemes, and lower for many others. For good or bad, by far the majority of consumer complaints that go via a trade association are concluded through the association's internal complaints-handling process, which can range from very informal shuttle work to a more structured 'assisted negotiation'. Generally very few of these cases overall are proceeding to arbitration. The Association of British Travel Agents (ABTA) is an example: it receives 17,500 complaints every year, and 1400 (fewer than 10%) go to arbitration.

This role of 'gatekeeper' can be helpful or harmful depending on how sound the trade association's procedures are. Trade associations potentially offer advantages to the consumer, for example provision of advice and technical expertise, speed and low cost. Also, by dealing with complaints themselves in the first instance, trade associations learn of any problems or areas of bad practice, allowing them to police the relevant code of practice covering their members. However, there are possible disadvantages too: the procedures are rarely independent and lack transparency. The extent to which schemes meet recognised quality criteria for ADR or other standards also varies. There may be implications for the effectiveness of the Office of Fair Trading Code of Practice scheme if code sponsors are concluding the majority of complaints at a stage before the independent redress stage, without adequate independent scrutiny.

Barriers to overcome

Despite its potential, our research identified hurdles for ADR to overcome.

Awareness and understanding

Awareness among advisers about ADR schemes is low. Consumers require advice from someone with knowledge of their rights and of the various ADR options. Both advisers and the business community also displayed confusion about what ADR is. For example, is the complaints-handling or informal conciliation role played by many trade associations ADR or not? Is the work on assisted negotiation done by many Trading Standards departments actually mediation? More work needs to be done on communicating with these audiences what is and what is not an independent dispute resolution scheme.

Status of decisions/enforceability

Very few schemes are non-binding on the consumer but legally binding on the trader, which is one of the Office of Fair Trading criteria. There were concerns among advisers we spoke to about traders leaving their trade association to avoid complying with an award. Should the consumer have to enforce an award through a court, this can be expensive as there are additional fees to pay and expenses such as lost wages and legal representation costs are non-recoverable.

Quality assurance

There is currently no single quality assurance mechanism for ADR provision. Consumers have no way of knowing whether the ADR scheme they choose offers an effective and fair consideration of their dispute and adequate means of redress. The European Extra Judicial Network (EEJ-Net) – the system of clearing houses set up by the European Commission (EC) and run in the UK by Citizens Advice Specialist Support Unit – plays an important role in helping consumers obtain redress when things go wrong with a purchase made from a supplier in another European Union country. It provides consumers with information on available ADR schemes and legal advice and practical help on pursuing a complaint by this means. However, BEUC – the European consumers' organisation – has raised the concern that not all the ADR schemes listed on the EEJ-Net databases appear to meet the EC's seven principles for out-of-court dispute resolution. This is a concern if it raises expectations in advisers and consumers about the quality of schemes to which they might be referred.

Funding

Funding is one of the key issues for ADR provision in the consumer field. Our research found a huge range of costs to access the ADR schemes, from no fee to fees of several hundred pounds. Most consumer disputes are of relatively low value, and the cost of trying to resolve them privately is often disproportionate to the value of the claim. Even using the small claims procedure can entail costly risks, such as the cost of expert reports. For claims above the small claims limit, however, there is no protection against heavy costs in court. If industry is expected to pay for ADR provision of consumer disputes, there are questions as to whether the independence of the service is at risk and whether consumers have direct and unlimited access to it. We found that interesting ADR schemes are being developed locally, offering services free to the consumer, usually linked to a source of consumer advice. Generally, however, funding from local and central government of ADR appears to be patchy, often local, and usually short term. Some schemes are relying on the ADR providers offering their services pro bono, which also is likely to be a short-term solution.

Many consumer disputes have a 'why bother' factor that may not be the case for other types of disputes, such as those relating to housing, education, or health care. As a result consumers will be less likely to pursue a resolution of the dispute if it is costly, inconvenient, time consuming or difficult to access. We also identified several areas where we believe further research would be valuable. Because this has been essentially a fact-finding study, we have not been able to examine these areas in-depth . . .

Looking to the future

Our research uncovered a variety of models of ADR provision, and it is clear that there is no 'one size fits all' in terms of ADR for consumer disputes. Some types of disputes may be more suited to local provision of arbitration or mediation – for example, problems with local traders. Others may be best dealt with by a national scheme – for example, problems with large national chains.

Each of the ADR processes used by the schemes responding to our questionnaire – mediation, arbitration, and ombudsmen – offers very different levels of service and types of process. Some ADR schemes appear to be providing a valuable service to consumers; they publicise their schemes, enjoy good coverage of a sector, have few eligibility limits and make information on cases available in an anonymised format. In order to measure properly the effectiveness of schemes, however, more information is needed on processes and outcomes. In addition, more needs to be known about consumers' aspirations and expectations as well as their experiences of actual ADR processes.

In thinking about how to best develop and promote ADR in the UK, a number of areas emerged that merit further research. In addition to consumer surveys and evaluation of existing schemes, we could learn much from other countries' experiences of ADR. The role of trade association conciliation and complaints handling – which for good or bad acts as a gatekeeper to independent ADR services – is a critical area to unveil. There is also an opportunity to consider how to link ADR with recent developments in advice provision, including at local level. Devising ways of enabling access to ADR by disadvantaged consumers, who are often at the highest risk of detriment, is also imperative.

ADR has tremendous potential, alongside other means of resolving disputes, to provide consumers with redress when things go wrong. This research project has shed some light on the current state of ADR provision for consumer disputes in the UK, which we found to be ad hoc and patchy. It has also identified areas where further research is needed in order to provide a sound knowledge base from which to plan where and how consumer ADR should develop in future.

 The report 'Seeking Resolution: The Availability and Usage of Consumer-to-Business Alternative Dispute Resolution in the United Kingdom' is available on the Civil Justice Council's website at:
www.adr.civiljusticecouncil.gov.uk/Category.go?category_id=7

Government use of ADR

In 2001 the government pledged to use ADR in all suitable cases wherever the other party accepts it. Cases which may not be suitable for settlement through ADR include those involving intentional wrongdoing, abuse of power, public law, Human Rights and vexatious litigants. The government issues an annual report monitoring its use of ADR.

Monitoring the Effectiveness of the Government's Commitment to Using Alternative Dispute Resolution
Report for the period 2003/04

Activity under the pledge

Departments, their Agencies and the National Health Service Litigation Authority monitor their use of ADR, sending statistical information to the Department for Constitutional Affairs to collate, for this report. This shows that over the period 2003/04, ADR has been used in 229 cases, with 181 leading to settlement, which represents a success rate of 79%.

Compared to the previous year, the numbers are broadly comparable: the number of cases has slightly increased, while the settlement rate is slightly lower. This information provides evidence of a continued commitment to the use of ADR activity in Government Departments, demonstrating the Government's growing commitment to a culture of settlement rather than a culture of litigation.

While the level of ADR use is broadly comparable, savings attributable to Department's use of ADR over the period of the report, although impossible to quantify in every instance, are estimated at £14.6 m – an increase of £8 m over the previous year.

The total savings attributed to Government's use of ADR since the Pledge was announced in March 2001, are estimated at £23 m.

In line with the Pledge and with guidance issued by the Office of Government Commerce, Departments have continued to include ADR clauses in standard procurement contracts. The combined effect of the Civil Procedure Rules and the emphasis on Alternative Dispute Resolution is undoubtedly encouraging lawyers and clients to seek constructive ways of settling disputes, in many cases at an early stage. Often this does not require the assistance (and additional cost) of a mediator or other independent third party.

The headline figures do not reflect, therefore, the very substantial number of disputes, which are resolved outside formal ADR process and without recourse to litigation.

Illustrative cases

During the period of the Report, Government Departments have used and continue to use ADR methods to settle a wide range of cases. The following examples of the use of ADR give only a flavour of the actual experience, because agreements reached through an ADR process are generally subject to confidentiality agreements restricting the information which can be released.

. . .

Treasury Solicitor's Department

A major commercial arbitration concerning a procurement dispute involving the Ministry of Defence was mediated for two days in October 2003. Although settlement was not achieved at the mediation itself, the gap between the parties was closed sufficiently to enable the parties to continue direct negotiation and reach a settlement. Had it not been for the mediation, it is unlikely that settlement would have been achieved. It is estimated that the saving in respect of the claim was in the region of £4 m to £7 m, with a cost saving of £1.5 to £2 m as a result of avoiding an 8 week arbitration hearing and the attendant preparatory costs.

A claim by 30 army officers for damage to personal possessions arising from a fire in the sovereign base area in Cyprus in 1998 which destroyed 14 married quarters and damaged 16 others. The mediation was very complex because of the number of parties involved, but a settlement was reached and a good result was achieved on the issue of liability. The estimated savings as a result of settlement at mediation were £250,000 in damages and £150,000 in legal costs.

A common law claim for stress at work. Liability was admitted and the matter was set down for a damages only hearing. The claim was settled 2 weeks before the hearing, through mediation. It is estimated that savings through mediation were £150,000 with a cost saving of £15,000 in avoiding a 6-day hearing.

A case involving the Chief Land Registrar. Proceedings were brought against a Council and a Housing Association seeking rectification of the Land Register and a declaration of the court that the claimants were entitled to an indemnity in respect of erroneous registration of land which resulted in them suffering loss. The Chief Land Registrar conceded in principle that there was an error in the register and thus entitlement to the indemnity claimed, with costs following the event. The only issue was quantum. The case was settled following a mediation meeting with estimated costs savings of the matter proceeding to trial being in the region of £20,000.

→

A common law claim against a Government Department and 8 other defendants for alleged nuisance, and negligence in carrying out major road works close to a Public House which allegedly caused such severe damage that the premises had to be demolished. The claim was settled through mediation. The costs savings are difficult to estimate, given the large number of defendants involved. However, a guestimate would be around £20,000.

A Disability Discrimination Act case involving the Department for Trade and Industry was settled by mediation, leading to an estimated saving of £50,000 in compensation and £20,000 to £30,000 in legal costs. The settlement incorporated creative solutions such as using the DTI's own experts for career counselling.

Judicial review proceedings in which all three parties were public bodies were settled by mediation. Bringing together the key decision makers in an environment where they were able to speak frankly led to a settlement including an agreed statement. The costs saved as a result of the mediation are estimated to be in the region of £30,000.

 The full report 'Monitoring the Effectiveness of the Government's Commitment to Using Alternative Dispute Resolution: Report for the Period 2003/04' is available on the internet at:
www.dca.gov.uk/civil/adr/adrrep_0405.pdf

Court-based ADR

A senior academic, Hazel Genn, has carried out research looking into the effectiveness of ADR where it is directly promoted by the courts.

Court-based ADR Initiatives for Non-Family Civil Disputes: The Commercial Court and the Court of Appeal (2002)

Professor Hazel Genn

Executive summary

This report presents an evaluation of the Commercial Court's practice of issuing ADR Orders in selected commercial disputes (Chapters 2 to 4) and a review of the Court of Appeal's mediation scheme established in 1996 (Chapter 5). The broad findings of these evaluations are combined in the final Chapter of the report with the results of an earlier evaluation of the Central London County Court mediation scheme to draw conclusions about court-based ADR initiatives that might be helpful in guiding future policy development on ADR.

ADR Orders in the Commercial Court
Since 1993 the Commercial Court has been identifying cases regarded as appropriate for ADR. In such cases Judges may suggest the use of ADR, or make an Order directing the parties to

attempt ADR. If, following an ADR Order, the parties fail to settle their case they must inform the Court of the steps taken towards ADR and why they failed. Thus although the Court's practice is non-mandatory, ADR Orders impose substantial pressure on parties.

This study assessed the impact of ADR Orders on the progress and outcome of cases and explored reactions of practitioners to ADR Orders. The results are based on information collected from court files and interviews with solicitors relating to 233 ADR Orders made between July 1996 and June 2000.

During the first three years reviewed in the study, the annual number of ADR Orders issued was about 30. There was a substantial increase toward the end of the period, with some 68 Orders being issued in the final six months. This was the result of one or two judges significantly increasing the number of Orders issued.

ADR was undertaken in a little over *half* of the cases in which an ADR Order had been issued. However, the figures suggest *increasing* use of ADR towards the end of the review period, supporting evidence from elsewhere of a developing interest in the use of ADR among commercial litigants.

Of the cases in which ADR was attempted, 52% settled through ADR, 5% proceeded to trial following unsuccessful ADR, 20% settled some time after the conclusion of the ADR procedure, and the case was still live or the outcome unknown in 23% of cases.

Among cases in which ADR was *not* attempted following an ADR Order, about 63% eventually settled. About one fifth of these said that the settlement had been as a result of the ADR Order being made. However, the rate of trials among the group of cases *not* attempting ADR following an ADR Order was 15%. This compares unfavourably with the five percent of cases proceeding to trial following unsuccessful ADR.

The most common reasons given for not trying ADR following an ADR Order were:

- the case was not appropriate for ADR;
- the parties did not want to try ADR;
- the timing of the Order was wrong (too early or too late);
- no faith in ADR as a process in general.

ADR Orders were generally thought to have had a positive or neutral impact on settlement. A small minority believed that the Order had hindered settlement. Orders can have a positive effect in opening up communication between the parties, and may avoid the fear of one side showing weakness by being the first to suggest settlement.

Experience of *successful* ADR following an ADR Order was overwhelmingly positive. The factors most valued were the skill of the mediator, the ability of ADR to get past logjams in negotiation, the opportunity to focus on the strengths and weaknesses of cases, and client satisfaction. There was also a perception that successful mediation avoids trial costs, leading to substantial savings for clients.

When ADR was *unsuccessfully* attempted in compliance with an ADR Order there was a lower level of satisfaction. Concerns centred on the shortcomings of neutrals, the intransigence of opponents, and the problems caused by pressuring unwilling opponents through an ADR Order to come to the negotiating table. However, some solicitors felt that even in the absence of achieving a settlement, the ADR process had been constructive.

ADR Orders issued by the Commercial Court are said to have had a significant impact on commercial practice and the advice given by the profession to clients about commercial dispute resolution.

ADR in the Court of Appeal

The Court of Appeal ADR scheme, established in 1996, is a voluntary scheme in which the court invites parties to participate. Cases are not individually selected, but, with the exception of certain categories of case, a standard letter of invitation is sent to parties involved in appeals. Since 1999 parties refusing to mediate have been asked to give their reasons for refusal. If both parties agree to mediate, the Court of Appeal arranges mediations and mediators provide their services without charge.

Between November 1997 and April 2000 some 38 appeal cases were mediated following agreement by both sides. In an additional 99 cases *one party* was willing to mediate. When the scheme had the benefit of a full-time manager, there was a significant increase in the proportion of cases in which *both sides* agreed to mediate.

The most common reasons given for refusal to mediate were that:

● a judgment was required for policy reasons;
● the appeal turned on a point of law;
● the past history or behaviour of the opponent.

About half of the mediated appeal cases settled either at the mediation appointment or shortly afterwards. Among those cases in which the mediation did *not* achieve a settlement, a high proportion (62%) went on to trial. This suggests that there are special characteristics of appeal cases that need to be considered in selecting cases for mediation. Blanket invitations to mediate, particularly with an implicit threat of penalties for refusal, may not be the most effective approach to the encouragement of ADR at appellate level.

Solicitors' experiences of *successful* mediations in appeal cases were largely positive. However, there were expressions of concern, even among cases that were successfully mediated, about clients' perceptions of being pushed into mediation and sometimes being pressured to settle.

Solicitors involved in *unsuccessful* mediations occasionally complained about having felt compelled to mediate, even though there had been little scope for compromise. There was evidence of an occasional mismatch between the mediator's approach to the mediation and the expectations of the parties and their advisers.

Although solicitors generally approved of the Court of Appeal taking the initiative in encouraging the use of ADR in appropriate cases, it was felt that there was a need for the adoption of a more selective approach, such as that being used in the Commercial Court.

Conclusions

Bringing together the results of research on ADR Orders in the Commercial Court, the Court of Appeal ADR scheme, and the Central London County Court mediation scheme, the following conclusions can be drawn:

● Voluntary take-up of invitations to enter ADR schemes remains at a modest level, even when the mediator's services are provided free or at a nominal cost.
● Outside of commercial practice, the profession remains very cautious about the use of ADR. Positive experience of ADR does not appear to be producing armies of converts. Explanations may lie in the amount of work involved in preparing for mediation, the incentives and economics of mediation in low value cases, and the impact of the Woolf reforms. More pre-issue settlements and swifter post-issue settlements may diminish the perceived need for ADR in run-of-the mill civil cases.

- An individualised approach to the direction of cases toward ADR is likely to be more effective than general invitations at an early stage in the litigation process. This would require the development of clearly articulated selection principles.
- The timing of invitations or directions to mediate is crucial. The early stages of proceedings may not be the best time, and should not be the only opportunity, to consider using ADR.
- Subjective perceptions of the profession support the view that *successful* ADR saves the likely cost of proceeding to trial and may save expenditure by promoting earlier settlement that might otherwise have occurred. *Unsuccessful* ADR can increase the costs for parties.
- ADR generally results in a high level of customer satisfaction. Mediators with excellent skills and familiarity with the subject-area of the dispute produce the highest levels of satisfaction. The approach of mediators needs to be matched with the expectations of parties and their solicitors.
- In order to maximise take-up of court-administered schemes there is a need for dedicated administrative support.

Hazel Genn's research 'Court-based ADR Initiatives for Non-Family Civil Disputes: The Commercial Court and the Court of Appeal' (2002) has been published on the Civil Justice Council's website at:
www.adr.civiljusticecouncil.gov.uk/Category.go?category_id=7

Index